The Earth in Transition

The Earth in Transition
Patterns and Processes of Biotic Impoverishment

Based on Contributions to a Conference
Arranged by the Woods Hole Research Center
Massachusetts, October, 1986

Edited by

George M. Woodwell
Woods Hole Research Center

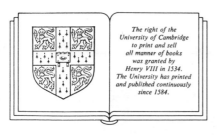

The right of the
University of Cambridge
to print and sell
all manner of books
was granted by
Henry VIII in 1534.
The University has printed
and published continuously
since 1584.

CAMBRIDGE UNIVERSITY PRESS
Cambridge
New York   Port Chester   Melbourne   Sydney

Published by the Press Syndicate of the University of Cambridge
The Pitt Building, Trumpington Street, Cambridge CB2 1RP
40 West 20th Street, New York, NY 10011, USA
10 Stamford Road, Oakleigh, Melbourne 3166, Australia

Cambridge University Press 1990

© First published 1990

Printed in the United States of America

Library of Congress Cataloging-in-Publication Data

The Earth in transition : patterns and processes of biotic
impoverishment / George M. Woodwell, editor.

    p. cm.

Based on papers presented at a symposium, held in Woods Hole in
Oct. 1986.

ISBN 0–521–39137–7. – ISBN 0–521–39818–5 (pbk.)

1. Human ecology – Congresses.   2. Biotic communities – Congresses.
I. Woodwell, G. M.
GF3.E17   1990
304.2–dc20   90–1471
                                             CIP

British Library Cataloguing in Publication Data

The Earth in transition: patterns and processes of biotic
impoverishment.
1. Ecosystems. Influence of man
I. Woodwell, George M.

ISBN 0–521–39137–7 hardback
ISBN 0–521–39818–5 paperback

Contents

v

vi   *Contents*

Part III. Chronic Disturbance and Natural Ecosystems: Woodlands, Grasslands, and Tundra

Part IV. Chronic Disturbance and Natural Ecosystems: Aquatic and Emergent Ecosystems

A. Marine Systems

Contents   vii

Preface

I recall speculating years ago with the distinguished Russian scholar, Victor Kovda, at dinner in his Moscow apartment, about the productivity of the currently impoverished vegetation surrounding the modern city of Tblisi in Soviet Georgia. I had seen in a museum in Tblisi an ancient oaken cart with wheels fashioned of single disks of oak cut from the end of a log fully 4 feet in diameter. Large oak trees or forests of any description do not exist in the region now. Kovda guessed that the current productivity of the region, measured as ecologists would measure it as "primary production," is 1% of what it once was. The cause was deforestation followed by the grazing of goats, sheep, cattle, and, later, over much of the land, by tillage, all of which contributed to the erosion of a thin soil.

Tblisi, a landscape that has sustained human occupation from time immemorial, is but one example of the cumulative effects of long-term human activities on the capacity of the landscape for sustaining life. The conference that was the basis for this book emerged from many years of puzzlement over how ecologists address the human-caused transitions that now dominate plant and animal communities globally. For many ecologists, perhaps most, the answer seems to be to focus on some of the more fascinating aspects of the evolution and extinction of species. But human effects and disturbance reach much farther than to extinction alone.

The current tragedy of the tropics is not simply the loss of species, but the transformation of a highly productive, self-maintaining landscape of great versatility and considerable resilience into a barren landscape of limited potential for support of life, including people. The tragedy is compounded by the widespread assumption that human interests are advanced by the transformation.

The earth's complement of living systems is being reduced now more rapidly than at any time previously by the spread of human influences. The changes are global; no part of the earth is unaffected,

ix

no natural or human-dominated community immune. The capacity of forests, savannas, steppes, tundras, and the planktonic communities of oceans, lakes, and streams for sustaining a habitat on earth suitable for humans is in question. The causes are many and are known: mechanical disturbance such as the destruction of forest to make way for agriculture or pasture; chemical disturbance through the release of toxins that acidify rain or poison air and soils; biotic plagues induced by carelessness in managing natural communities of plants and animals. But what are the changes? Are they systematic, cumulative, predictable? At what point in their progress do they become identifiable? To what extent are they reversible? On these points we are weak in detail, fumbling and general in our scholarship. We rely on the extremes of impoverishment to show the effects because the extremes are clearer and less equivocal.

Interpretation of the importance of changes that we have called here impoverishment hinges heavily on assumptions about how the world works. Ecologists see the world as a biotic system, dependent on natural communities such as forests for the normal supply of the goods and services that maintain environment and make civilization possible. Economists and politicians tend to see business and commerce as essential; agriculturalists see different requirements and point to the potential flexibility of agriculture in the face of changing climates. The authors of this book share the view that the world is a biotic system first, and that the human habitat is the product of a series of continuous interactions between the biota and its environment. Consideration of the climatic changes now threatening us only confirms that most fundamental relationship: the human habitat, despite the spread of human influences, remains dominated by natural communities. Although these communities may not be the richest source of succor for the current human enterprise, they have the advantage that they develop and maintain themselves indefinitely without human effort. In most instances they can be shown to supply a diversity of goods and services to people on a renewable basis.

The purpose of this symposium was the definition of the major types of changes in the structure and function of natural communities exposed to chronic disturbance. The purpose was not a cataloguing of disaster or mismanagement, despite the sorry history of carelessness revealed here, but an objective appraisal of the patterns and processes, including the causes, of biotic impoverishment wherever it occurs. The emphasis was on forests because they appear to be the great biotic flywheel that keeps the biosphere operating as a place suitable for life, but all such communities are being affected. The oceans, too, are changing in response to human activities and the changes are probably irreversible insofar as they involve changes in the chemistry of water, whether the changes are shifts in the ratios of nutrient elements or additions of exogenous toxins with which the biota has had no evolutionary experience.

We were pleased to be able to draw the attention and support of several foundations, listed in the Acknowledgments, to this problem. More than seventy scholars from around the world met in Woods Hole in October 1986 to discuss details of their experience and their perspectives on the biotic transitions that are generally seen now as impoverishment. Each carried his or her own model of what those changes might mean and what, if anything, might be done to deflect the changes. But the most important purpose was recognition that the transitions are under way, that they can be recognized, even measured, and that causes and effects and implications for the human future can be defined. Papers published here were prepared subsequent to the conference. Most have been revised for this, long-delayed, publication.

We have organized the book in much the same way that the symposium was organized, with the more general statements first, followed by what might be described as case history studies. We are soft on politics and economics and government, whose failures in controlling greed are primary causes of the failures of management outlined here. We bow to economics through Robert Repetto's splendid analysis of the causes of deforestation in the Brazilian Amazon and leave that as exemplary of current weaknesses in management.

The conference and the book will have served their purpose if they contribute to an effort to define the details of the impoverishment of the human habitat and start the process of bringing governmental interest and control to the stabilization of the biosphere. We have outlined the broad patterns of the transitions under way; we have not defined in detail a diagnostic procedure for reading the landscape. Such a procedure is nonetheless possible. It will come from future refinements in recognition and use of the patterns summarized here.

G. M. Woodwell
Woods Hole, Massachusetts
March 1989

Acknowledgments

The symposium on which this book was based was held in Woods Hole in October, 1986, and was arranged under the auspices of the Woods Hole Research Center, the World Resources Institute, the American Institute of Biological Sciences, and the U.S. Environmental Protection Agency.

Financial support for the conference and for publication has been provided by:

C. S. Fund
W. Alton Jones Foundation
World Resources Institute
Rockefeller Brothers Fund
World Wildlife Fund
U.S. Environmental Protection Agency
U.S. Department of the Interior
and
The Woods Hole Research Center

Publication of this volume has consumed much more time and effort than anyone envisioned and has required the patience and abiding assistance of various institutions, colleagues, and friends in addition to the unflagging interest and assistance of the contributors. Special thanks are due to Nancy Jack Todd for her careful copyediting, to my daughters Caroline and Jane Woodwell for diverse assistance, and to my wife, Katharine, whose incisive reviews brought continuous improvements throughout the entire procedure.

Elizabeth Bunch joined the staff of the center in 1987 and, with grace and charm and extraordinary talents, has seen this book through all the final details of publication.

To all I extend my thanks and those of the authors.

GMW
Woods Hole, Massachusetts
March, 1989

Contributors

W. D. Billings
Department of Botany
Duke University
Durham, North Carolina

James A. Blake
Battelle Ocean Sciences
Duxbury, Massachusetts

L. C. Bliss
Department of Botany
University of Washington
Seattle, Washington

F. Herbert Bormann
School of Forestry and Environmental
    Studies
Yale University
New Haven, Connecticut

John Cairns, Jr.
University Center for Environmental
    Studies and Department of Biology
Virginia Polytechnic Institute and State
    University
Blacksburg, Virginia

Margaret Bryan Davis
Department of Ecology and Behavioral
    Biology
University of Minnesota
Minneapolis, Minnesota

Philip M. Fearnside
Department of Ecology
National Institute for Amazon Research
Manaus, Brazil

Eville Gorham
Department of Ecology and Behavioral
    Biology
University of Minnesota
Minneapolis, Minnesota

J. Frederick Grassle
Institute of Marine and Coastal Science
Cook College
Rutgers University
New Brunswick, New Jersey

D. L. Hawksworth
CAB International Mycological Institute
Surrey, United Kingdom

Richard A. Houghton
Woods Hole Research Center
Woods Hole, Massachusetts

Pua Kutiel
Lowdermilk Faculty of Agricultural
    Engineering
Technion, Israel Institute of Technology

Y. Loya
Department of Zoology
Tel-Aviv University, Israel

John A. McGowan
Scripps Institute of Oceanography
La Jolla, California

Nancy J. Maciolek
Battelle Ocean Sciences
Duxbury, Massachusetts

G. D. McSweeney
Royal Forest and Bird Protection Society
Wellington, New Zealand

A. F. Mark
Department of Botany
University of Otago
Dunedin, New Zealand

Donella H. Meadows
Syndicated Journalist
Plainfield, New Hampshire

xiii

Dieter Mueller-Dombois
Department of Botany
University of Hawaii

Zev Naveh
Lowdermilk Faculty of Agricultural
  Engineering
Technion, Israel Institute of Technology

William A. Niering
Department of Botany
Connecticut College
New London, Connecticut

Michael Oppenheimer
Environmental Defense Fund
New York, New York

James R. Pratt
School of Forest Resources
College of Agriculture
The Pennsylvania State University
University Park, Pennsylvania

Robert Repetto
World Resources Institute
Washington, D.C.

David W. Schindler
Department of Zoology
University of Alberta
Edmonton, Alberta, Canada

R. L. Specht
Botany Department
University of Queensland
St. Lucia, Australia

J. Gustave Speth
World Resources Institute
Washington, D.C.

P. M. Welbourn
Institute for Environmental Studies
University of Toronto
Toronto, Ontario, Canada

Walter E. Westman
Environmental Policy Analysis Unit
University of California at Berkeley

David B. Wingate
Department of Agriculture and Fisheries
Flatts, Bermuda

George M. Woodwell
Woods Hole Research Center
Woods Hole, Massachusetts

N. D. Yan
Dorset Research Center
Ontario Ministry of the Environment
Dorset, Ontario

Part I

Global Change and the Patterns of
Impoverishment

1   The Earth under Stress: A Transition to Climatic Instability Raises Questions about Patterns of Impoverishment

GEORGE M. WOODWELL

Life occurs, as far as we know, only as part of the earthly biosphere. There is no life elsewhere in the solar system, and if there is life beyond it on one of the tens of billions of planets of the universe, it is not likely to be of more than momentary academic interest in a world preoccupied with human crises.

Life exists at once as diverse entities, individuals, populations, and species, apparently independent, yet dependent for survival itself on a web of inter-connections with other species immediately available – a community. And, in a context only slightly larger, dependent for place and time and habitat on the totality of other life that sustains the biosphere. Could we imagine a forest without decay? Or a ruminant without its cellulose-digesting flora?

The annual fluctuation in the carbon dioxide concentration in the atmo-sphere offers one of the most impressive bits of evidence of the importance of the biota in maintaining a habitat suitable for humans. Each year during the spring and summer the carbon dioxide concentration of the air of the northern hemisphere is reduced by several parts per million as forests of the temperate zone store carbon compounds through photosynthesis. Each year the carbon dioxide content rises through the fall and winter as respiration of forests and soils exceeds photosynthesis. The magnitude of the oscillation is impressive: it amounts to 1–2 percent of the carbon dioxide content of the atmosphere at Mauna Loa in the Hawaiian Islands and more than 5 percent at higher latitudes. The strength of these seasonal changes confirms the power of forests for affecting the composition of the atmosphere and climate globally.

Forests are large in proportion to the atmosphere's content of carbon as carbon dioxide. Globally they contain with their soils about three times as much carbon as the current atmosphere. The destruction of forests releases this carbon into the atmosphere as carbon dioxide; the reestablishment of forests stores carbon from the atmosphere on land. Current estimates suggest that deforestation is releasing 1–3 billion tons of carbon as carbon dioxide

3

annually. Combustion of fossil fuels releases more than 5 billion tons. These and other sources have contributed through the 1980s to an annual net accumulation of carbon in the atmosphere of 1.5 ppm or about 3 billion tons, a measure of the extent to which the effects of chronic disturbances are accumulating as global changes.

The cause of the disruption is a single species, *Homo sapiens*, which has escaped the normal limitations that keep the numbers of individuals of each species in check and has swarmed over the earth as no species has ever done previously. *Homo* has also succeeded in developing the capacity to turn other species and countless things into resources that favor the further expansion of the populations of *Homo*. The effect is a series of drastic changes in the biosphere that threaten all life.

The earth is warming. Powerful evidence suggests that the accumulation of greenhouse gasses in the atmosphere is the cause (Bolin et al. 1983; WMO/UNEP 1985, 1988; Hansen and Lebedeff 1988; Woodwell 1988). The principal gas is carbon dioxide from the combustion of fossil fuels, from the destruction of forests, and from the acceleration of respiration due to the warming of organic matter in forests and soils (Woodwell 1983, 1988). There are additional trace gasses, especially methane, whose concentrations are rising as well. Methane's presence in the atmosphere causes a disproportionate warming because it absorbs infra-red energy in a segment of the spectrum different from that of water and carbon dioxide. The concentration of methane is rising at about 1 percent annually.

Present indications are that the warming will continue as long as the greenhouse gas content of the atmosphere continues to increase. There is the possibility, now being examined in detail, that the warming will stimulate decay and the further release of carbon as carbon dioxide and methane from forests and tundra, especially from soils (Woodwell 1983, 1988). This release could be large. While there may be at least a temporary compensatory stimulation of carbon storage in certain forests such as the Boreal Forest and certain montane forests where low temperatures limit primary production, evidence is lacking for a stimulation of the storage of carbon at rates similar to the rates of release through increased respiration as the warming proceeds.

The warming is accelerating. The aggregate change over the last century appears to be between 0.5° and 0.7°C, but the rate of increase has been substantially higher in the last decade than in any previous time. The year 1988 was the warmest year on record and the decade of the 1980s has had the five warmest years in history (Hansen and Lebedeff 1988; Wigley, personal communication).

The average warming for the earth as a whole is expected to lie in the range of 0.2–1.0°/decade for the next several decades. The warming in the middle and higher latitudes will be greater. It may exceed 1.5°/decade in certain places, if the highest rates envisioned are realized. Such high rates of climatic change are well beyond adaptive capacities of forests and other types of vegetation, which will suffer severe stress, including mortality of trees, along their warmer and drier limits of distribution. Although climatic change may favor the development of forests in places now incapable of supporting forests, forests require decades to centuries to develop, not years to decades. The net effect of such changes will be a reduction in the area of forests globally over the next years and throughout any period of rapid warming. For that reason the Villach–Bellagio conferences of 1987 adopted as an immediate objective the stabilization of the composition of the atmosphere and the reduction in the rate of warming to less than 0.1°/decade (WMO/ UNEP 1988). A continuous warming will cause extraordinary disruption of the human enterprise. There is no easy alternative to a rigorously pursued commitment to maintaining the physical, chemical, and biotic integrity of the earth. That objective will require the most stringent efforts to avoid any climatic change, most of all a continuous, open-ended change such as what is under way now.

The global transition in climate is a transition to progressive instability, chronic warming. The speed of the warming may be determined less by human activities, unless rapid steps are taken to stop it, than by the warming itself, the climatically caused destruction of forests, and the oxidation of organic matter in soils and bogs. As the warming progresses and trees die at the warmer and drier margins of their distributions, organic matter from plants and soils will be released as carbon into the atmosphere, speeding the warming.

The climatic changes expected over the next years, if unchecked, will not only change the distribution of plant and animal communities but will also change their structure, function, and potential for response to disturbance. Species and ecotypes will be lost as habitats change. There will be changes in the amount and form of primary production, in the energy fixed and made available for storage and for the support of decay organisms and other consumers, including people. Although these changes seem remote and likely to be slow by comparison with the ravages of acid rain, the immediate and observable effects of toxins, and of the current destruction of forests by whatever cause, they are now entrained, under way, certain to accelerate, and hold the potential for changes in the earth's ecosystems greater than any change since humans evolved. These changes will dominate considerations of environment and resources over the next decades, perhaps longer, if steps to control the warming are not effective.

When a community such as a forest is replaced under such circumstances, what replaces it? Does shrubland replace forest, or does a grassland develop immediately? Or is forest replaced by heath? Are there stages in the replacement? How long does the transition take? Is there a basis for expecting hysteresis, a systematic lag in the transition after conditions that would normally support one community evolve into conditions suitable for another?

The answers, of course, are several and complex. They depend on place and time and season and the character of disturbance and history and other factors. Nonetheless, broad patterns exist, are predictable, and are becoming more conspicuous.

Under chronic disturbance large-bodied, long-lived organisms with low rates of reproduction are at a disadvantage; smallbodied, rapid reproducers are favored. Disturbance, carried to an extreme on land, would cause forests to disappear. Forests would be replaced by the low-growing woody and herbaceous plants now common on impoverished, chronically disturbed sites. W. D. Billings offers a classic case history: *Bromus tectorum*, a single species of exotic annual grass, incidentally introduced, has so changed the plant communities of the Great Basin as to eliminate forest and bring other profound changes to the natural vegetation of vast areas of arid land.

In a world in which energy for support of the human enterprise is already inequitably available and likely to become progressively limited as the human population moves from its present 5 billion toward 10 billion sometime early in the next century, such a fundamental and probably irreversible change in resources has profound implications, far beyond what seems to be implied by impoverishment of the biota. There is no compensating change in the human condition capable of replacing these resources, including the wildest dreams of biotechnologists.

Could an impoverished world support people? The speculation is not constructive. No one would want to live in such a world, I think, but the world would go on, life would exist, and people would survive, albeit in smaller numbers and with far fewer opportunities. The essential cycles of the major elements for life, carbon, nitrogen, phosphorus, sulphur, oxygen, would continue, driven as they are by microbial processes that are probably sufficiently resilient in the face of chronic disturbance to survive. But the loss of forests would be but the prelude to the loss of higher plants, the impoverishment of agriculture, and the further impoverishment of the earth's residual populations of higher animals.

Such an earth might support people, but it would not support civilization and the density of human population now present. Nor would it be a pleasant life by most standards.

Our purpose, if larger purpose be required, is to avoid such a cataclysm; to recognize the trends and their causes early and deflect them. Experience exists from around the world. It reaches from land to sea, from lakes to coastal waters, from air pollution to tankers leaking oil. The evidence is fragmentary and specific and seems in each case unique, but when surveyed as in the following pages from Australia to the Great Basin desert, from the lakes of Manitoba to the Great Pacific Gyre, from the effects of ionizing radiation to the depredations and recovery from the Bermudan plague of cedar scale, it is a compelling story, summarized most movingly by Donella Meadows. The transitions threaten the human enterprise fundamentally by changing the human habitat out from under the most complicated and intricate civilization ever built, one that is global and, despite its lip service to individual independence, almost totally interdependent and vulnerable.

The vulnerability appears in strange ways. The unusually warm, dry summer of 1988 in North America, widely considered an example of more to come as the earth warms, reduced the Mississippi to a trickle, grounded barges, dried out municipalities, and limited the output of power plants because they could not dump the normal amount of waste heat into water bodies. While power plants struggled to remain operating, demand for energy for cooling and air conditioning rose; barges of coal stuck in river mud could not reach the plants and added to the chaos. But, even more threateningly, a 20–30 percent reduction in grain yields in North America left the world surprised and concerned that another such year would eliminate reserves, even threaten starvation. Fossil fuels and deforestation carry some surprising burdens for the world. The indications are that there will be many more such surprises spawned by continuous climatic change and the progressive biotic impoverishment that is certain to accompany it.

References

Bolin, B., and R. B. Cook (Eds.), 1983. *The Major Biogeochemical Cycles and Their Interactions. SCOPE 21.* John Wiley and Sons, New York.

Hansen, J., and S. Lebedeff, 1988. Global surface air temperatures: update through 1987. *Geophysical Research Letters*, 15(4):323–326.

WMO/UNEP, 1985. Conference Statement: International Assessment of the Role of Carbon Dioxide and of Other Greenhouse Gases in Climate Variations and Associated Impacts, Villach, Austria, October 5.

WMO/UNEP, 1988. Developing Policies for Responding to Future Climatic Change. Report of the Villach–Bellagio Conferences, September–November, 1987.

Woodwell, G. M., 1983. Biotic effects on the concentration of atmospheric carbon dioxide: a review and projection. In *Changing Climate*. NAS Press, Washington D.C.

Woodwell, G. M., 1988. The warming of the industrialized middle latitudes 1985–2050: causes and consequences. Prepared for the Symposium Developing Policies for Responding to Future Climatic Change, Villach, Austria, September, 1987.

2 The Experimental Impoverishment of Natural Communities: Effects of Ionizing Radiation on Plant Communities, 1961–1976

GEORGE M. WOODWELL AND
RICHARD A. HOUGHTON

Editor's Note: Evolution has been for nearly a century and a half the intellectual core of biology. More recently evolution has been recognized as having shaped and stabilized the surface of the earth as the only habitat for life. The concept is attractive: evolution is building an open-ended, developmental system, self-guided, self-repairing, capable of accommodating all travails in due course, even to the point of building into the biosphere more room for life, more diversity, and greater stability of habitat. Surely, according to this concept, biotic resilience is sufficient to accommodate the activities of *Homo sapiens*, one species of the several million now on earth, all the product of this magnificently versatile and effective process.

But the timing is off. In the long term of thousands of millennia the glorious vision of a benign and effective evolutionary resilience may be appropriate. In the time of our lives it is the principles of succession and impoverishment that apply.

Succession enjoys all the optimism of any developmental progression, no matter how mean the origins: a bank account, growing with the accrual of interest. Growth is salutary, almost by definition. The pine forest that replaces the hardy herbaceous weeds of the abandoned garden over much of North America and elsewhere promises still more to come, a crop of lumber, pulp, new habitats for birds and other animals, large changes in the soil and in the moisture for plants and animals, stabilized temperatures at the soil surface and improvements in the amount and quality and availability of water in streams and in the water table. Succession is popular and is often confused with evolution.

Impoverishment, on the other hand, walks hand-in-glove with human disruption and the cumulative burdens we make for ourselves. It carries with it none of the popular promises of growth, healing, and the anticipation of effortless accumulation of vigor, even wealth. It has had little attention until recently when we began to realize that, despite the power of succession, land described as "impoverished" is the fastest growing class of land-use globally. One-third of all the land in India, more than 100 million hectares, is now recognized as impoverished to the point of uselessness in agriculture.

If evolution and succession are governed by principles sufficient to build scholarly inquiry and support prediction, what about impoverishment? Does it not offer parallel potential? What are the principles? Can we anticipate impoverishment and deflect it?

The topic has seemed at once clear and yet confounded. It is clear that toxins from smelters destroy forests and may virtually sterilize the landscape. Yet it is not clear

9

that the same process applies when effects accumulate more slowly and are not easily traced to a single source: the cumulative effects on land and water of the acidification of rain, of repeated exposures to ozone, of toxins in air. The experiments with ionizing radiation, described here by G. M. Woodwell and R. A. Houghton, are unique in that they revealed for the first time that the effects of chronic disturbance of natural communities follow patterns that are as well defined and predictable as those of evolution and succession. The principles are clear enough, reiterated and illustrated in various ways throughout this book.

The overriding principle is that chronic disturbance favors populations of small-bodied, rapid reproducers that have broad tolerance of habitats.

The implications of this observation are profound, for it is from such populations that we recognize the host of organisms that compete with various interests of people: these are the weeds of the garden, the pestiferous insects and rodents, the organisms of disease. An impoverished world abounds in problems from such populations. We usually respond by trying to make their realm more toxic. So doing, we make the problem worse.

All other principles of impoverishment are subsidiary, secondary, derivative. They emerge from the principles of ecology, from knowledge of the structure and function of ecosystems, from a strict application of evolution, from specific experience with plant and animal communities. But the experience with ionizing radiation, described here in outline, made it clear that the patterns of change are common: larger-bodied plants are more vulnerable; the smaller, hardier plants of the roadside, of impoverished soils, of disturbed sites are more resistant to chronic ionizing radiation and to disturbance in general. The experience also made it clear that secondary disturbances are common and sometimes mask the primary cause. Trees weakened by exposure to ionizing radiation may succumb unexpectedly to the ravages of the pine bark beetle or other less conspicuous disease. So, too, with other chronic disruptions. And the symptoms may be similar on the organisms, the community, and the ecosystem. It is the impoverishment of the ecosystem that counts, and the experiments with ionizing radiation lay out the details of the transitions with uncommon clarity.

Introduction

Opportunities to measure the responses of natural communities as large and complex as forests to gradients of chronic disturbance are rare, despite the spread of human influences. Between 1961 and 1976 a series of experiments was carried out at various sites in the United States in which measurements were made of the effects of exposure of natural communities to gradients of ionizing radiation administered chronically. The longest period of study was provided at Brookhaven National Laboratory in central Long Island, New York. The experiments were unique in the use of ionizing radiation over a long period, in the possibility of correlating cause and effect over years, and in the opportunity to examine effects on natural ecosystems.

The experiments were supported by the Atomic Energy Commission at the urging of Dr. John N. Wolfe of the Commission's staff. Dr. Wolfe saw a need for groups of ecologists within each region who were not only familiar with the natural communities of the region but also familiar with the hazards of the nuclear age. He believed that it was important to accumulate information about both the movement of radionuclides in, and the effects of ionizing radiation on, major types of vegetation. The objective was pragmatic: the possibility of a large release of ionizing radiation from a reactor accident or from bombs seemed real enough then and even more so now. What would be the effects of large releases of radiation on natural ecosystems, such as forests, that are the normal vegetation of a large fraction of the habitable portion of the earth? How might these effects be measured and predicted?

Wolfe sought to establish programs similar to the one at Brookhaven in other major types of vegetation, including a tropical forest stand in Puerto Rico (Odum and Pigeon 1970), a segment of the shortgrass plains in Colorado (Fraley 1971), and a boreal forest stand in Wisconsin (Rudolph 1974; Zavitkovski 1977). Of these other studies only the experiment in the shortgrass plains operated for a period long enough for the exposure to be considered chronic. The entire effort was ended during the mid-1970s as the Atomic Energy Commission evolved into the Department of Energy and interest in the ecological effects of ionizing radiation yielded, almost unopposed, to a wave of parsimony. No similar opportunity has been generated since, despite numerous efforts.

The studies were surprisingly rich, both in details of the effects of ionizing radiation and in observations on the structure and function of ecosystems. Not only did it appear that responses to ionizing radiation occurred at lower exposures than anticipated, but also the responses defined patterns in the structure and function of natural communities that had not been recognized previously. The experience with radiation drew these patterns clearly to the fore and gave them new meaning in interpreting the effects of disturbances of all types, including pollution (Woodwell 1970).

The Brookhaven Irradiated Forest Experiment was the longest running and the most definitive of the studies. An additional, shorter-term study was carried out at Brookhaven, a study of the early stages of succession in a segment of a cultivated field (Woodwell and Oosting 1965). Both forest and field were exposed chronically to a gradient of gamma radiation from single, stationary sources, centrally located and remotely controlled. These two experiments alone showed that the responses of natural communities to such disturbances follow patterns that are fully as predictable as the patterns of plant and animal succession. They also showed that the forest was very much more sensitive to disturbance than the old-field community. The overall program not only advanced definition of the effects of ionizing radiation on natural ecosystems but also offered an unusual opportunity to define the

Figure 2.1. The irradiated forest at Brookhaven National Laboratory as it appeared in September, 1976, after 15 years' exposure to chronic irradiation. The source of the radiation was 9,500 Curies of Cs^{137} exposed at the top of a 15-ft tower in the center of the circle of damage. The radiation field ranged from several thousand R/day within a few meters of the source to about 1.5 R/day at the building shown, approximately 125 m from the source.

various stages of biotic impoverishment of natural ecosystems that follow both acute and chronic disturbance.

Our purpose is to define further the normal patterns of impoverishment that can be recognized in natural ecosystems by using experience from Brookhaven and elsewhere.

The Experiments

The Irradiation of Forests

Details varied among the several experiments but the Irradiated Forest at Brookhaven is an example (Figure 2.1). That experiment was established during the spring and summer of 1961 when a 9,500-Curie Cs^{137} source of gamma radiation was established in the center of a carefully selected, nearly uniform stand of oak–pine forest on the Brookhaven Laboratory Site

(Woodwell and Hammond 1962; Woodwell 1963). Chronic irradiation consisted of continuous exposure for 20 hours daily. Access to the forest was allowed on alternate mornings and afternoons during the 4 hours that the source was shielded. The stand selected was late successional oak–pine (*Quercus alba, Q. coccinea,* and *Pinus rigida*). The source of radiation was a specially constructed array of small cylinders containing cesium-137, a gamma emitter, arranged in a cylindrical rack that was suspended in such a way that the entire assembly could be exposed at the top of a tower 15 feet tall or lowered into a large lead cask that shielded it completely. A hand-operated winch raised and lowered the source. The winch was 125 m away, where the exposure from the 9500-C source was less than 1.5 R/day. The source was not replenished; it was allowed to decay throughout the entire period of the experiment.

A similar source of radiation using Co^{60} had been used for several years previously for experimental exposures of plants under cultivation. It was this second source that was used at Brookhaven for later experiments with the early stages of plant succession (Woodwell and Oosting 1965).

Chronic versus Acute Exposures

The most convenient approach to examination of the effects of any type of insult on a living system is usually through a short-term or "acute" exposure. Effects become apparent subsequently, but with increasing time beyond some point they diminish as repair progresses. It is common in toxicology, for example, to narrow the measure to a particular characteristic and apply it at a time when the effect is clearly defined. The effect of a toxin on rats may be standarized to a measure of survival and expressed as LD_{50} at 30 days, the exposure that produces 50 percent mortality after 30 days. This approach ignores a diversity of other effects, including later mortality.

Such simplifications in treating effects of disturbance on natural communities were not considered useful. There are, moreover, many examples of responses of natural communities to acute disturbances of various types. Succession has been well defined in most types of vegetation, but responses to long-term changes in the environment have not been. The problem is the more complicated in that the effects of acute exposures of plant and animal communities may be delayed by dormancy and other factors and masked by succession and other mechanisms of recovery. Without many opportunities to experiment with acute exposures under various conditions the information gleaned from a single exposure is limited and diminishes rapidly with time. Such was the experience in Puerto Rico with the exposure of a stand of the Luquillo Forest to gamma radiation (Odum and Pigeon 1970).

The decision at Brookhaven was to use a long-term chronic exposure. The initial stages of such an experiment, of course, approach the conditions normally considered as acute. Responses are delayed and the continuation of the exposure raises a question as to the total exposure that caused the effect. In time, however, the relationship between cause and effect approaches stability and the most straightforward basis for expressing the relationship is on the basis of rate of exposure, not the total exposure, which continues to accumulate. The decision to proceed with an experiment based on a chronic exposure proved especially important. It had the advantage of offering special insights into the behavior of terrestrial ecosystems under chronic disturbance of varying intensities. It had the disadvantage of providing data that are difficult to apply to accidents that come closer to producing acute exposures than chronic exposures. These latter difficulties seemed small by comparison with the advantages in working over years with a gradient of chronic exposures.

The Effects of Chronic Exposure to Ionizing Radiation

Effects on Forests

The results were rich with surprises. The effects of irradiation were masked during the first winter and became apparent only during the spring as the weather warmed (Woodwell 1962). Trees and other plants close to the source suddenly turned brown. The circle of damage expanded during the spring and expanded further during the ensuing years to define a pattern of change in the vegetation that is now recognized as characteristic of progressive impoverishment. Drastic effects on the forest had been anticipated and specific effects on trees had been specifically predicted (Woodwell and Sparrow 1963), but the systematic zonation of the forest, which appeared almost immediately and became accentuated throughout the 15 years of the experiment, went far beyond any prediction. The quantitative relationship to exposure was, of course, of interest, but the qualitative relationships, the spectacular and systematic changes in the structure and species composition of the forest community seemed to have far greater importance because it defined in small compass specific steps in the impoverishment of natural communities.

The zonation was the product of the sorting of the indigenous species of the forest as damage accumulated. It became further accentuated with time as species not normally a part of the forest arrived, became established, and expanded their populations.

The circle of damage around the radiation source appeared in 1975, as shown in Figure 2.1. The zones were:

1   *Barren Zone:* No higher plants or conspicuous cryptogams; organic matter lost rapidly through decay.

2   *Cryptophyte Zone:* Lichens and mosses covered a conspicuous fraction of the ground. In the Irradiated Forest *Cladonia cristatella*, occasionally present in the undisturbed forest, covered more than 50 percent of the area.

3   *Herb Zone:* A continuous ground cover of hardy annual herbs, grasses, and sedges. In the Irradiated Forest *Carex pensylvanica* formed a nearly continuous cover. In the undisturbed forest *Carex* appears as scattered, small clumps and individual plants.

4   *Low-Shrub Zone:* Ground-hugging shrubs such as *Vaccinium angustifolium* formed a continuous cover.

5   *High-Shrub Zone:* High shrubs and small-statured hardy trees such as *Quercus ilicifolia* formed a well-defined stratum that shaded persistent lower strata of low shrubs, herbs, and cryptophytes.

6   *Oak Forest Zone:* The forested zone from which the pine had been eliminated. This zone seems, even to an experienced observer, to lie within the normal range of variability of the oak—pine forest in that patches of this forest often occur devoid of pine or other normal components of the forest.

7   *Oak—pine Forest:* The species composition seemed normal, but at the margin of this zone effects of radiation exposure on both pine and oak were easily measured. In this segment of the forest, however, effects accumulated and the pine and weaker oaks became vulnerable to disease or drought or other common stress over time; the margin retreated toward the less vulnerable and more nearly intact forest.

8   *Intact Forest.*

The First Sorting

These zones were the primary effect, the product of what we recognize now as the first of two sortings that marked the changes in vegetation along the gradient of exposure. The first sorting was the winnowing of the species of the original forest by chronic exposure to ionizing radiation. The effects were not simply direct effects of irradiation on the species of the forest as predicated by Sparrow and Woodwell (1962), who used a correlation that had been established previously between the cytological characteristics of plants and sensitivity to ionizing radiation to predict the effects of the irradiation; the effects were the combination of direct effects on species and the effects of the changes in the structure of the forest brought by those direct effects. The combination produced the patterns outlined.

The Second Sorting

The patterns were enhanced over time as primary effects accumulated. But they were also enhanced by the slow accumulation of hardy invaders that became established in each zone. Identifying these species as exotics to the forest is sometimes equivocal. Erechtites and other composites, for instance, occasionally occur within the oak—pine forest on wind-throw mounds and elsewhere. There is a more or less continuous rain of wind-blown seeds in the forest, presumably the product of proximity to sources of such seeds (Wagner 1966). Composites became a conspicuous part of the herb zone. *Comptonia peregrina*, a hardy shrub, is widely distributed on impoverished soils and occurs occasionally within the more impoverished segments of otherwise intact oak–pine forest. It became an important component of the low-shrub zone and produced a nearly continuous ground cover in places. *Rubus* spp. also were conspicuous and persistent invaders. We recognize this later, slower transition as the second sorting.

The successional transition implied by the second sorting continued well into the second decade of the experiment and would probably have continued into the third, except that the experiment was discontinued. These two sortings marked the major transitions, one based on the elimination of species indigenous to the forest; the second based on the arrival and success of a selection of successional species.

The second sorting was compounded by a series of changes in the areas of undisturbed forest used for control. The experiment offered two sets of data from areas free of irradiation: the data taken from the forest prior to the establishment of the experiment, and data taken during the irradiation from areas far enough away from the source of radiation to be considered "unaffected." These latter data provided a view of the changes that occur in forests over time, a series of changes not normally measured.

All the data on plant populations were taken according to the rigorous plan designed in 1961 by Woodwell and Hammond (1962). Successive samplings were made in 1961, 1966, 1971, and 1976. They showed a decline within the control forests in the number of stems of large trees (>3.0 m tall), a similar decline in the number of stems of intermediate size (1.0–3.0 m), and an increase in the number of smaller stems. The increase in the number of smaller stems occurred in each of the five major species of trees and was not the result of sprouting, but of an increase in the survival of seedlings. The decline in large trees was due largely to the changes in populations of oaks, especially *Quercus alba*, whose density of stems was reduced to less than ½ the original over the 15-year period. There was little change in the density of pines while the density of other oaks also declined.

In the intermediate-size category the white oak density also declined, pitch pine density increased slightly, and scarlet oak density doubled.

The cause of these changes is not known. The large trees were less than 50 years of age and would normally be expected to live for more than a century. Their mortality may have been caused by a set of novel conditions, including air pollution, the acidification of rain, the spread of disease, or other factors, including low-level exposure to ionizing radiation. The areas in which the data were taken received exposures at rates of less than 2.0 R/day. Most of the data came from areas exposed at 0.1–1.0 R/day, an exposure level now recognized as having effects on sensitive plants that are measurable (Sparrow and Woodwell 1962). Whatever the cause, the effect is a simpler forest canopy in which scarlet oak and pitch pine are becoming increasingly abundant. This trend is counter to the normal successional tendencies within the oak–hickory and chestnut phases of the eastern deciduous forest (Braun 1950), in which the importance of pine usually diminishes with time. The changes observed may reflect the cumulative effects of chronic pollution on forests in the metropolitan region of the northeastern United States. Such changes are not normally expected, nor are they measured in forests, but they must be assumed to provide a sensitive measure of trends in the structure of the forest in response to unusual changes in environment. The data are analogous to the data of epidemiology or social medicine that have so often shown effects of toxins at much lower exposures than more conventional studies. Data accumulated over 40 years from the Japanese populations exposed at Hiroshima and Nagasaki, for example, have been the basis recently for recognizing that the hazards of ionizing radiation are greater than recognized previously (Tatabe 1987).

Three indices designed to measure changes in the structure of the communities were applied to the gradients of ionizing radiation:

Diversity. The most direct measurement of diversity is the number of species per unit land area. The index is sensitive to the total area sampled: a sample from a large area has a better chance of including more species than a sample from a small area. In an experiment where diversity is used as an index of change, area must be constant. The sampling unit used in this work was a 2×2 m plot. In the "control" area of the Brookhaven Forest there were 50 such samples. They had an average diversity of about 7.5 species of higher plants per plot. The half-value of diversity occurred after 15 years (Figure 2.2) at 20 m or 110–120 R/day. The chronic exposure at which the half-value occurred had not changed from previous surveys (Woodwell and Rebuck 1967), but the diversity curve had been affected by both the first and second sortings. Diversity alone was an inadequate criterion for expressing the extent of disturbance.

Coefficient of Community. Another criterion of change along such a gradient is offered by a comparison of the species present in each of two sets of plots, one affected by the treatment, the other unaffected. Coefficient of community is the number of species shared by two communities expressed as a percentage of the total number of species in both. The coefficient is

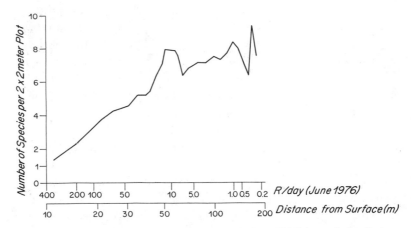

Figure 2.2. Diversity of higher plants along the gradient of ionizing radiation in the Brookhaven irradiated forest, June, 1976, 15 years after the start of the chronic irradiation. Diversity is expressed here as the number of species per 2 × 2-m plot. The curve reflects the product of the second sorting: the accumulation of invaders along the gradient as species indigenous to the forest were eliminated.

$$\frac{C}{A + B - C}$$

where C equals the number of species shared by two communities one of which has A species, and the other, B. The comparison was made separately for control plots at 150–160 m and 170–180 m (Figure 2.3) without any appreciable change in result. The half-value for coefficient of community was about 50 m or 22 R/day. The half-value in earlier surveys had occurred at nearly 120 R/day in 1963 and 80 R/day in 1964 (Woodwell and Rebuck 1967).

Percentage Similarity. Coefficient of community is based on a comparison of the species present. It takes no account of the densities or other measurements of abundance. Percentage similarity combines the presence of a species with a weighting factor based on its minimum abundance in two communities. It is calculated as:

PS = Σ lesser (a, b)

where a and b equal the density or other measure of abundance of a species in communities a and b. (The lower value of the two densities is used in the summation over all species.) Among the control communities percentage similarity was about 70 percent to a distance of 70 m from the source (Figure

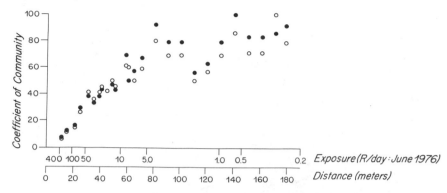

Figure 2.3. Coefficient of community for plant communities along the radiation gradient in 1976. Open circles (O) are values obtained from comparisons with the plant community at 170–178 m (0–.3 R/day); closed circles (●) are from comparisons with the 150–160-m community (0.4 – 0.5 R/day).

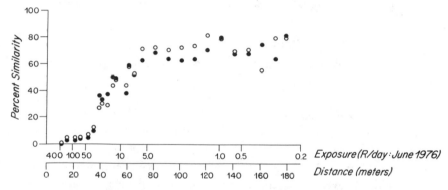

Figure 2.4. Percentage similarity for plant communities along the radiation gradient in 1976. Open circles (O) and closed circles (●) are for comparisons with the 170–178-m community (0.3 R/day) and the 150–160-m community (0.4–0.5 R/day), respectively.

2.4). It reached 35 percent, the half-value, at about 45 m (16 R/day), approximately the same as other criteria of change, and at an exposure rate much less than in previous years.

These three criteria reflect the first and second sortings defined above. Diversity alone reflects only the number of species, not the changes in the character of the community. Diversity may increase in response to disturbance during the second sorting as successional species become established. Coefficient of community and percentage similarity emphasize the changes in the character of the community along the gradient and offer a standard for comparison with other communities.

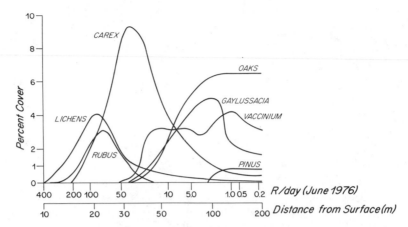

Figure 2.5. Abundance, measured as percentage of cover, for the most abundant species along the gradient of exposure to ionizing radiation in the irradiated forest, Brookhaven National Laboratory, 15 years after the start of the experiment.

The gradient of effects after 15 years' exposure is shown graphically in Figure 2.5. The pattern remains a standard for defining the extremes of impoverishment in forests.

Effects on Early Successional Communities

A similar experiment was established to examine effects on the earliest stages of terrestrial succession (Woodwell and Oosting 1965). A sector of the ploughed field around the 10,000-Curie Co^{60} source of gamma irradiation was abandoned early in the spring and allowed to develop whatever plant populations appeared. The response was similar to that of the forest in that a series of zones was established, including an inner zone where no higher plants survived. The difference was that the entire range of effects occurred at exposures that were appreciably higher than those that produced the primary sorting in the forest. A 50 percent reduction in the coefficient of community, for example, occurred at exposures of about 120 and 80 R/day in the forest after 2 and 3 years' exposure (Woodwell and Rebuck 1967) and at greater than 200 R/day after 2 years' exposure in the old field (Woodwell and Oosting 1965). After 15 years' exposure the coefficient of community in the forest was reduced by 50 percent by an exposure of 30–40 R/day after the second sorting.

The most surprising observation was that in both instances, the primary sorting of the forest and the first year of the old field, the populations of plants that survived the highest exposures were species widely recognized as common in places subject to severe disturbances, including chronic mechanical disruptions and chemical and other stress (Woodwell 1970). Advantage appeared to accrue to species that normally grow close to the surface of the ground. The observation held for higher plants (Woodwell 1967, 1970) and for cryptogams (Gochenaur and Woodwell 1974), including lichens (Woodwell and Gannutz 1967). Among the lichens, for example, the most resistant groups were crustose forms. Among the soil fungi resistance was higher among the simpler, vegetatively reproducing forms that are common in the early stages of succession and on disturbed sites (Gochenauer and Woodwell 1974).

The explanation for the closeness of the parallels between the response to ionizing radiation and other forms of disturbance is neither simple nor clear. One possibility is that the selective pressures that exist at the surface, certainly the most harsh segment of the normal terrestrial environment, induce resistance to radiation as well. Woodwell (1967) has advanced that hypothesis, pointing out that ionizing radiation has its effects primarily through mutagenesis. Resistance to mutation is probably produced by selective pressures due to many aspects of environment, including toxins, heat–cold shock, and intense ultraviolet radiation. Plant and animal communities adapted to such habitats are more resistant to ionizing radiation than communities not so adapted.

Discussion: Patterns of Disturbance and Impoverishment

Had the forest reached stability under chronic irradiation after 15 years? The primary sorting appeared to be continuing as the zones of damage expanded slowly. Older trees, especially pines at the edge of the forest, were continuing to die. Mortality was sudden, often occurred in midsummer, and affected trees that appeared vigorous except for the reduction in growth and the fasciation attributed to the reduction in elongation of stems and branches. Sprouting of trees and shrubs whose shoots were damaged by irradiation continued. The effect of the continued irradiation of the zones established in the primary sorting was a continuous, if slow, expansion of the zones. Ultimately, one would expect the forest to come into equilibrium with the source; the repair mechanisms would balance the effects of the exposure. That point had not been reached after 15 years although the rate at which further primary effects were accumulating was low by comparison with the first 10 years of the experiment.

The second sorting was also continuous well into the middle of the second decade. A few species that are rare in the undisturbed forest were continuing to accumulate in the inner, heavily impoverished zones, and were becoming a part of the new communities there. These included composites with windborne seeds such as fireweed (Erechtites) (Wagner 1966) and other species common on disturbed sites such as the pokeberry (Phytolacca) and the hardy shrub, *Myrica pennsylvanica*. A hybrid poplar (*Populus* sp.) became established in the low-shrub zone and sprouted vigorously year by year, although the sprouts died during the winter. This secondary sorting would be expected to continue, probably adding species from time to time as additional seeds or other propagules of hardy species arrived in the simplified communities of the inner zones. The process meant that the character of these zones continued to change abruptly as dominance shifted with new arrivals. The rate of change, however, was low, at least as measured by the attention span of scientists, and the experiment was stopped well before a detailed appraisal on the probable future trends of the second sorting could be defined.

Whatever the cause, the fact remains that the patterns of changes in the structure of the forest and the old-field communities induced by chronic exposure to ionizing radiation are (a) systematic and predictable, (b) common in nature, (c) cumulative and progressive through some indefinite period measured in decades, (d) measurable in stages, and (e) best characterized as "impoverishment."

The only other experiment to run long enough to provide comparable data was the experiment established in the shortgrass plains outside Fort Collins, Colorado (Fraley 1971), where similar patterns were observed in response to chronic exposure to ionizing radiation under substantially the same circumstances. Other experiments involved shorter-term exposures that gave results that were intermediate between what might be expected from an acute exposure and those observed in these chronic experiments. Some of these were sufficiently comprehensive to offer additional insights useful in interpreting both details of the effects of ionizing radiation and the patterns of impoverishment caused by chronic disturbance (McCormick 1963; Platt 1963).

These transitions are common in nature. Bormann has made the point in this volume (Chapter 3) that it is appropriate to recognize stages in the transitions in the structure of natural communities affected by chronic pollution. The destruction of forests in Europe and North America by the acidification of rain is the equivalent of the changes recognized in the experiments with ionizing radiation as the first sorting, the elimination of the normally dominant species of the forest. The second sorting, the advent of species new to the communities and the establishment of successional communities of species resistant to the disturbance, proceeds more slowly. The second sorting is especially slow when the area affected is large and species must migrate large distances as is true in forests affected by air pollution or climatic change.

Simple criteria such as diversity are not adequate. Diversity may in fact increase under disturbance as the integrity of a mature community is fractured and opportunites are produced for agressive, rapidly reproducing species to enter the community. As the disturbance continues and effects accumulate, diversity normally declines.

Other changes accompany the impoverishment. These include changes, usually reductions, in primary productivity, nutrient inventory, and evapo-transpiration. These changes are real enough but usually difficult to measure. In the Irradiated Forest at Brookhaven they appeared as changes in the structure and stature of the forest and as increases in the availability of moisture in soils as the forest was reduced (Reiners and Woodwell 1966).

Summary

The exposure of natural communities such as forests, grasslands, and old fields to gradients of intensity of ionizing radiation produces an immediate first sorting of the community in which smaller-statured, ground-hugging species are favored over larger-bodied species such as trees. With time, species that are uncommon or exotic to the forest invade and strengthen or replace the residual communities of the first sorting with new communities drawn from hardy species common in the earlier stages of succession. This second sorting follows the same patterns, with small-bodied species commonly more resistant to disturbance than larger-bodied species with longer life cycles. Clear stages are recognizable in this work. The stages are distinguished by species and stature, with cryptogam communities dominating the most disturbed sites. These patterns appear to hold, whatever the cause of the disturbance.

References

Braun, E. L., 1950. *Deciduous Forests of Eastern North America*. Blahiston, Philadelphia.
Fraley, L., Jr., 1971. The Response of Shortgrass Plains Vegetation to Chronic and Seasonally Administered Gamma Radiation. Ph.D. dissertation. Department of Radiology and Radiation Biology, Colorado State University, Fort Collins, Colo.
Gochenaur, T. P., and G. M. Woodwell, 1974. The soil microfungi of a chronically irradiated oak–pine forest. *Ecology* 55:1004–1016.
McCormick, F., 1963. Changes in a herbaceous plant community during a three-year

period following exposure to ionizing radiation gradients. In V. Schultz and A. W. Klement, Jr. (Eds.), *Radioecology*, pp. 271–276. Reinhold, New York.

Odum, H. T., and R. F. Pigeon (Eds.), 1970. *A Tropical Rain Forest. A Study of Irradiation and Ecology at El Verde, Puerto Rico.* U.S.A.E.C., Division of Technical Information, Springfield, Va.

Platt, R. B., 1963. Ecological effects of ionizing radiation on organisms, communities, and ecosystems. In V. Schultz and A. W. Klement, Jr. (Eds.), *Radioecology*. Reinhold, New York.

Reiners, W. A., and G. M. Woodwell, 1966. Water budget of a forest damaged by ionizing radiation. *Ecology* 47(2):303–306.

Rudolph, T. D., 1974. *The Enterprise, Wisconsin, Radiation Forest: Preirradiation Ecological Studies.* U.S.A.E.C., Technical Information Center, Springfield, Va.

Sparrow, A. H., and G. M. Woodwell, 1962. Prediction of the sensitivity of plants to chronic gamma irradiation. *Radiation Botany* 2:9–26.

Tatabe, N., 1987. A new estimate of gamma ray risk for A-bomb survivors based on the latest epidemiological data and revised dose. *International Perspectives in Public Health* 3:9–13.

Wagner, R. H., 1966. Herbaceous recolonization of the Brookhaven irradiated forest: the first three years. *Radiation Botany* 6:561–565.

Woodwell, G. M., 1962. Effects of ionizing radiation on terrestrial ecosystems. *Science* 138:572–577.

Woodwell, G. M., 1963. Design of the Brookhaven Experiment on the effects of ionizing radiation on a terrestrial ecosystem. *Radiation Botany* 3:125–133.

Woodwell, G. M., 1967. Radiation and the patterns of nature. *Science* 156:461–470.

Woodwell, G. M., and E. C. Hammond, 1962. *A descriptive technique for study of the effects of chronic ionizing radiation on a forest ecological system.* BNL 715(T251) Brookhaven National Laboratory, Upton, NY.

Woodwell, G. M., and A. H. Sparrow, 1963. Predicted and observed effects of chronic gamma irradiation on a near-climax forest ecosystem. *Radiation Botany* 3:231–237.

Woodwell, G. M., and J. K. Ocsting, 1965. Effects of chronic gamma irradiation on the development of old field plant communities. *Radiation Botany* 5:205–222.

Woodwell, G. M., and T. P. Gannutz, 1967. Effects of chronic gamma radiation on lichen communities of a forest. *American Journal of Botany* 54:1210–1215.

Woodwell, G. M., and A. L. Rebuck, 1967. Effects of chronic gamma irradiation on the structure and diversity of an oak–pine forest. *Ecological Monographs* 37:53–69.

Woodwell, G. M., 1970. Effects of pollution on the structure and physiology of ecosystems. *Science* 168:429–433.

Zavitkovski, J. (Ed.), 1977. *The Enterprise, Wisconsin, Radiation Forest: Radioecological Studies.* Technical Information Center, U.S. Energy and Development Administration, Springfield, Va.

3   Air Pollution and Temperate Forests: Creeping Degradation

F. HERBERT BORMANN

Editor's Note: Much of the New England landscape of today would be foreign to the New Englander of the nineteenth century, immersed as it was in 1850 in an intensive subsistence agriculture that reached to virtually every corner of the land. The nineteenth-century farm preserved access to springs, divided pastures and hayland among heirs to assure survival, and saw wildlife principally as a threat, competitors and predators in a lifelong struggle to make the farm support an expanding family. The land was heavily used, too often abused, impoverished, eroded. *Juniperus communis* var. *depressa* spread over pastures, devouring space that might otherwise have supported herdsgrass and marking at once the impoverishment of pasture, farm, and family. Swamps were drained, ploughed, and planted. Species were lost. In the 1980s much of this land, once farmed, all pastured, has returned to forest. The forest and the land are threatened now with a different set of insults: division into houselots, highways, paved commercial sites, small holdings of various types, none of them dependent on energy from the land. The land is now considered mere place, space, access to people, water, view. And its biotic resources, already impoverished through 200 years of intensive use of the land, are threatened again by an equally pervasive, less obvious assault: air and water pollution from afar.

F. H. Bormann has summarized his perspective of this latter problem with special emphasis on air pollutants common today over large areas of the globe. The threat may seem remote, the more so that the value of the land is seen to lie not in the life that it supports or in the energy that it could produce, but in mere space.

The pendulum will swing again. Fossil energy is finite; its use is changing climates globally. A shift to enduring sources of energy is desirable now. Such a shift will affect the cost of travel, the value of land, the value of forests, and the importance of natural communities in the global economy. F. H. Bormann has taken an important step in this paper in moving toward a systematic recognition of the losses incurred as toxins and toxic effects accumulate in nature.

Introduction

Forests can undergo "creeping degradation" or a slow cumulative decline, under chronic stress. Under some circumstances, the forest ecosystem may so successfully buffer stress that for long periods changes are not easily detected and biotic regulation is hardly affected. Even though the ecosystem looks

25

Table 3.1. *Some types of stress to which forest ecosystems may be subjected*

Wind	Extraction of fuelwood
Forest grazing	Fire
Insect outbreaks	Forest cutting
Air pollution	Shortened cutting rotations
Conversion to agriculture	Disease epidemics
Drought	Pesticides
Stress from normal ecosystem development	Recreational activities
Urbanization	Introduced species

healthy and unchanged, symptoms of damage may be masked by ecosystem complexity and an imperceptible loss of buffering capacity or redundancy. As redundancy is used up, the ecosystem moves nearer to the limits of its resilience and a potential collapse to a state of lower productivity and markedly less biotic regulation of energy flow and biogeochemical cycles. The response of north temperate zone forests to air pollution is explored as an example of creeping degradation. The forests of the world are currently subject to increasing levels of stress from many sources. They are shrinking in area, many are declining in diversity and stature, and are losing their capacity to carry out natural functions beneficial to people (Bormann, 1985).

Although stress is a normal part of the existence of the forest, it is being intensified globally by a range of human activities (Table 3.1). In general, anthropogenic stress results from the pressures of expanding human populations, rising economic expectations, increasing demands for renewable natural resources, and growing industrialization. Many aspects of stress are discussed in this volume. I shall focus on slow cumulative stress that not only damages the forest ecosystem but gradually wears away the buffering capacity of forests. Such stress might ultimately result in marked changes in forest landscapes and in a major reduction of the goods and services that forests yield. Such reductions can be direct, through diminished productivity; they can be indirect, through lowered species diversity, lowered amenity values, or reduced biotic regulation of local, regional, and global climate and biogeochemical cycles. I call this slow cumulative process *creeping degradation*. The effect of air pollution on forests of the north temperate zone is an example of the process.

Before presenting details of my thesis, I wish to review some of the major energy and biogeochemical functions of forest ecosystems (Figure 3.1). Forests, through the processes of photosynthesis, transpiration, reflection, and reradiation, use and affect the flow of vast amounts of solar energy. Through the direct and indirect use of energy, forest ecosystems carry out processes that determine the form of energy redispersed to the environment;

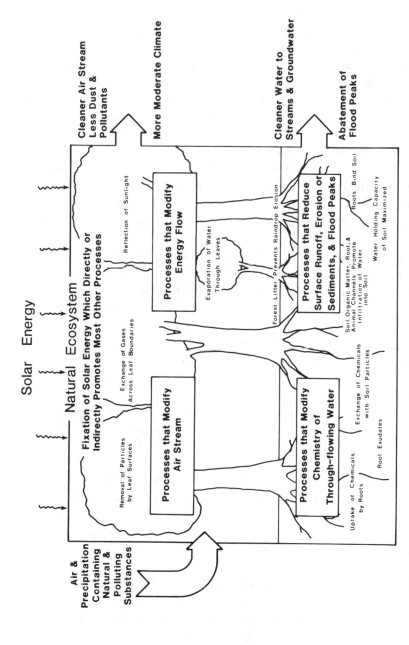

Figure 3.1.   Some direct and indirect uses of solar energy by the forest ecosystem in regulating biogeochemical cycles.

change the form, amount, and chemistry of through-flowing air and water; and determine the amount and kinds of sediments released from the ecosystem to water and air. Together these processes control the amount and kinds of outputs from the ecosystem. We call this phenomenon *biotic regulation of output* (Bormann and Likens 1979). By monitoring outputs, we can monitor the health of ecosystems with a kind of ecological blood test. For example, a statistically significant increase in dissolved nitrogen or an upsurge in sediments in drainage water can indicate that biotic regulation has been weakened by internal damage to the ecosystem.

Biotic regulation determines how an ecosystem will participate in the larger hydrologic and biogeochemical cycles of the earth and in its energy relationships. It determines the role of terrestrial ecosystems in the linkage between air–land–water ecosystems. Through biotic regulation the forest ecosystem governs, in some degree, the behavior of interconnected stream, river, and lake ecosystems, and of local, regional, and global climate. When a forest is subjected to stress and is damaged it can, through its outputs, transmit stress to interconnected systems or contribute to climate change. Human activity can affect biotic regulation not only directly through changes within the ecosystem, such as cutting, overgrazing, and fuelwood collection, but also indirectly through changes induced in the atmosphere such as air pollution or climatic changes. It is important to realize that biotic regulation can be altered by naturally occurring stress as well as anthropogenic stress. This can seriously confuse attempts to sort out the effects of stress from air pollution from other anthropogenic and naturally occurring stress.

Ecosystems are not generally so precariously balanced that one tiny push will send them into a state of collapse. They contain a capacity to buffer stress. In the historical development of forest ecosystems, they repeatedly faced a large variety of natural disturbances. Most forests have a capacity to buffer the effects of stress and, through growth and development, to repair themselves. An important aspect of the effects of stress is the degree to which effects persist once the stress has been removed. In some instances, the cumulative effect of stress may be so great that an ecosystem is driven over its boundary of resilience and loses the capacity to recover to its original state (Bormann and Likens 1979). Effects on capacity to recover are important in any analysis of the impact of stress on forest ecosystems.

I call the buffering property of ecosystems *redundancy* based on the dictionary definition of redundant as "in excess of requirements." Redundancy is founded on the ability of an ecosystem to perform functions beyond immediate needs as well as the ability of its biotic or abiotic components to adjust and respond to new circumstances created by stress. In general, redundancy in forests maintains biotic regulation at prevailing levels in the face of stress and maintains the overall integrity of the ecosystem.

Table 3.2. *Some examples of redundancy that may come into operation in forest ecosystems under air-pollution stress*[a]

Genetic response:
Phenotypic – adjustment of form and function to stress
Genotypic – shifts in gene pool in species under stress that adapt the species to stress

Population response:
Species substitution – tolerant species take over the function of sensitive species

Structural response:
Layer substitution – lower layers take over function of damaged upper layers

Excess capacity:
Infiltration and percolation capacity of water greatly exceeds current needs and can handle
    extra liquid water generated by loss of transpiration
Resistance to erosion may last for several years despite forest cutting and marked reduction in
    productivity.

Some other negative feedback loops triggered by disturbance:
Sprouting of damaged individuals
Germination of buried seeds
Release of advanced regeneration
Expansion of microbial populations with temporary uptake and net storage of nutrients that
    might otherwise leave the system (nutrient shunt)
Phenological response – extension of leaf display period, through ontogenetic, physiological, and
    genetic mechanisms, in response to a temporary rise in resource availability

---

[a] These responses are not necessarily mutually exclusive.

Redundancy is an extremely complex topic and one that has received little systematic attention from ecologists (Table 3.2). Redundancy involves such processes as: shifts in a gene pool under chronic stress to allow species to adapt, species substitutions in which tolerant species take over the role of intolerant species, and layer substitution in which lower layers of a forest take over the function of damaged upper layers. Redundancy also includes forms of excess capacity such as the ability of the ecosystem to support such functions as infiltration and percolation of water beyond immediate needs, thus buffering the effects of disturbance causing reduced evapotranspiration, and a number of other possible negative feedback loops. In terms of processes, redundancy is based on the ability of the ecosystem to carry out such vital processes as photosynthesis, decomposition, nutrient uptake, nutrient storage, and water routing in more than one way. Thus, if one pathway is impaired by stress, another pathway may take over, resulting in little long-term change in the ability of the ecosystem to fix energy or to carry out biotic regulation.

Redundancy complicates the interpretation of the effects of stress. Forests may buffer chronic stress so successfully that, for long periods of time, changes in the ecosystem are not easily detected and biotic regulation is hardly affected. However, even though it may look healthy and unchanged, redundancy is being consumed and the ecosystem is progressively moved nearer the limits of resilience and toward a collapse to a state of lower productivity and markedly less biotic regulation of energy flow and biogeochemical cycles (Bormann and Likens 1979).

How does a forest respond to increasingly severe air pollution stress? There has been considerable pioneer work by Gordon and Gorham (1963), G. M. Woodwell (1970), and others on the response of the forest ecosystem in areas around point sources of disturbance, including pollution and ionizing radiation. There has also been voluminous laboratory and field work on the responses of plants and animals to gaseous and non-gaseous pollutants. This has made it possible to propose a model of forest ecosystem decline in the face of increasingly severe air pollution, in which the level of severity may be due to greater

Table 3.3. *Model of forest ecosystem decline under air-pollution stress*

Stage	Level of anthropogenic pollution	Severity of impact on ecosystem	Effect on biotic regulation
0	Insignificant	Insignificant	None
I	Low level	Relatively unaffected, may serve as sink	None
IIA	Levels inimical to sensitive organisms	Changes in competitive ability of sensitive species; selection of resistant genotypes	Little
IIB	Increased pollution stress	Resistant species substitute for sensitive ones, some niches opened for lack of substitutes	May be disrupted, but return as the ecosystem is populated by resistant species.
IIIA	Severe levels of pollution	Large plants, trees, shrubs of all species die off; ecosystem converted to open, small-shrub, weedy herb system	Severely diminished; increased runoff, erosion, and nutrient loss
IIIB	Continued severe pollution	Ecosystem collapse. Completely degraded ecosystem.	Ecosystem seeks lower level of stability with less control over energy flow and little biotic regulation.

Source: Reprinted from Bormann 1985, with permission from *BioScience* 35:434–435. Copyright 1985 by The American Institute of Biological Sciences.

levels of pollution or to longer exposure at the same level (Table 3.3). Details of the model are discussed in Bormann (1985). It is important to note that as we proceed through the stages IIA and IIB (Table 3.3), even though interference with biotic regulation may be minimal, redundancy is being consumed.

The pattern of decline shown in the model (Table 3.3) seems repeatable and may apply to stresses other than air pollution. In testing the applicability of the model to north temperate zone forests three important questions arise:

1   What kinds of and how much pollution are reaching and have reached the forests of the north temperate zone?
2   What evidence is there that regional forests are affected and declining in accordance with the proposed model?
3   How closely can we link, quantitatively, regional forest ecosystem damage to air pollution input or to emissions at points distant from the ecosystem?

This discussion is concerned primarily with regional forest ecosystems distant from intense local point sources of pollutants. These areas constitute the great bulk of north temperate zone forest ecosystems.

What Kinds of and How Much Pollution Are Reaching and Have Reached the North Temperate Zone Forest?

Between the mid-fifties and mid-seventies the deposition of hydrogen ions in bulk precipitation became more intense over the eastern United States (Figure 3.2; Likens and Bormann 1974). Increases in hydrogen ions were accompanied by increases in other pollutants such as sulfate, nitrate, trace metals, and organics. I shall call this collection of pollutants with elevated hydrogen ion contents *acid rain*. The phenomenon illustrated by Likens and Butler (1981) is not unique to the eastern United States. A similar increase in time and scale has been documented in central and northern Europe (Likens et al. 1979). Recently, acid rain has been shown to be a widespread problem in the western United States (Lewis and Grant 1980; Roth et al. 1985; Voigt, personal communication) and an increasing threat in southeastern states (Likens et al. 1979). In 1986, Zhao and Bozen reported acid rain to be common in southern China.

Acid rain data cited above are based primarily on measurements in bulk precipitation and do not take into account deposition in cloud moisture or dry deposition. Recent studies indicate that when these two components are added to bulk precipitation, the acid rain problem is significantly greater. Dry deposition is an important but varying component of acid rain. It may be the major component in deposition in the southeastern (Lindberg et al. 1986) and western United States (Roth et al. 1985).

Several years ago, Gene Likens and I, with a number of colleagues, established the North American Cloud Water Project. Stations were set up in

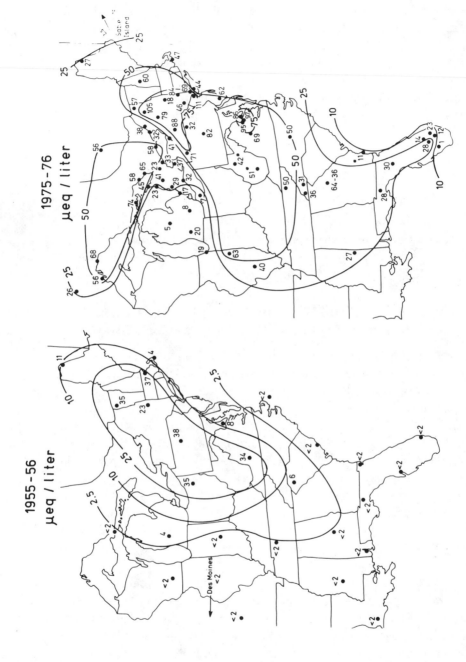

Figure 3.2. The distribution of acid rain in the eastern United States in 1955–1956 and 1975–1976. (Reprinted from Likens and Butler 1981, with permission.) Numbers are microequivalents of hydrogen ions per liter, μeq.

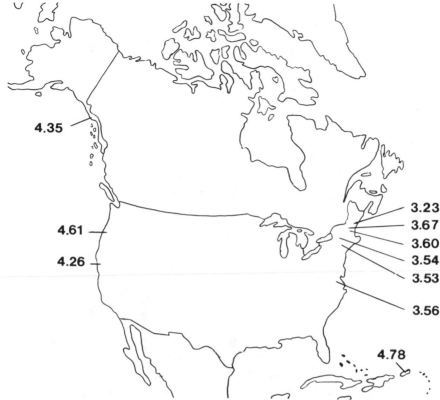

Figure 3.3. Mean annual cloudwater pH measured at various sites of the North American Cloud Water Project. (Reprinted after Weathers et al. 1988, with permission of Weathers and *Environmental Science and Technology*. Copyright 1988, American Chemical Society.)

coastal southeastern Alaska, Oregon, northern California, and Maine, and on mountains in Puerto Rico, Virginia, New York, and New Hampshire. Our goal was to gain an initial synoptic view of the chemistry of cloud water being deposited on trees. In general, we found that cloud water was about one-half a pH unit more acid than bulk precipitation falling in the same location and, further, that cloud water was significantly more contaminated at eastern stations than at western stations (Weathers et al. 1988). Mean cloud water pH in the Northeast varied from 3.25 to 3.67 (Figure 3.3) while the low pH ranged from 2.42 to 3.17. Other data (Bicknell, personal communication; Roth et al. 1985) indicate that cloud water deposited in central and southern California and northwest Washington state (Basabe, personal communication) may be as contaminated as in the eastern states. Cloud water measurements have yet to be made in the Rocky Mountain area. Deposition of heavily contaminated cloud water has also been reported in

34 F. H. Bormann

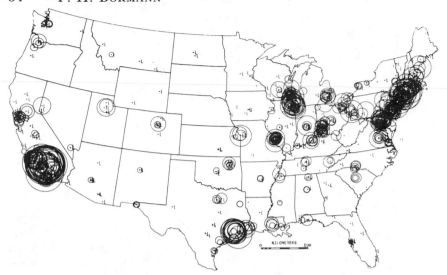

L = STATION WITH >7000 HOURS WITH VALUES LESS THAN THE STANDARD

Figure 3.4. Areas where it is 95% probable that the NAAQs for ozone (0.12 ppm) was exceeded during 1977 and 1978. (Reprinted from Ludwig and Shelar 1980, with permission of Ludwig and *Journal of the Air Pollution Control Association*.)

Europe (Furher 1985) and Japan (Weathers, personal communication). Measurements in other regions, like the Great Valley of Mexico, may well reveal serious cloud water contamination there (Bauer and Hernandez 1986).

Photochemical oxidants represent a major class of air pollutants. The only oxidant for which there is extensive geographic data is ozone. Ludwig and Shelar (1980; Figure 3.4) estimated the areas of the United States where ground-level concentrations exceeded 0.12 ppm in 1977 and 1978. Serious plant damage is known to occur at these concentrations. In general, photochemical oxidant deposition is poorly documented in the United States because of the scarcity of monitors in rural areas.

MacDonald (1985; Figure 3.5) has recently reported that high ozone deposition may overlap with areas of high hydrogen ion deposition. We also found this to occur. Between August 7 and 13, 1984, our project detected very acid cloud water containing heavy concentrations of sulphate and nitrate deposited on vegetation from Maine to Virginia (Weathers et al. 1986; Table 3.4). Hydrogen ion concentrations ranged from pH 2.80 to 3.08, and sulphate and nitrate concentrations were 7 to 43 times greater than those of the mean volume-weighted bulk precipitation. On the coast of Maine the deposition of very acid cloud water was accompanied by 6 hours of high ozone concentrations. Vegetation there was simultaneously exposed to two different extreme stresses.

These deposition data allow several important conclusions about the air pollutants reaching forest ecosystems.

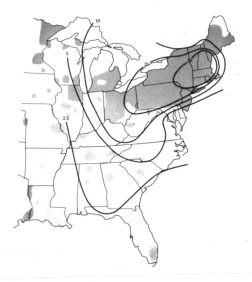

Figure 3.5. Shaded areas show counties where oxidant concentrations exceeded 0.08 ppm during 1978. H^+ concentration is in $\mu eq/l$ for 1965–1966 indicated by contours. (Reprinted from MacDonald 1985, with permission and after Chamberlain et al. 1982.)

1   Although very incomplete, monitoring data indicate that regional air pollution is a significant phenomenon in the north temperate forest zone.
2   Deposited air pollutants are often a variable mix of acid rain, photochemical oxidants, trace metals, and other pollutants in gasses, airborne particles, rain, fog, and clouds.
3   Contaminated fog and cloud water are not simply high elevation phenomena, but occur at sea level as well.
4   Regional air pollution effects are not simply mass effects (damage slowly accumulated by chronic exposure over time); depositional concentrations of ozone and cloud water suggest the occurrence of episodic effects as well.
5   The cloud water event of August 1984 indicates that episodic events of high concentrations of acidity with associated chemicals and ozone may occur simultaneously, and suggests that the pollutants may cause episodic damage either singly or interactively.
6   Finally, it seems clear that large regions of north temperate forest have received and are receiving significant amounts of a variety of air pollutants.

What Evidence Is There That These Regional Forests Are Affected and Declining in Accordance with the Proposed Model?

The best known example of regional forest damage thought to be associated with air pollution comes from West Germany, where carefully gathered

Table 3.4. *Location and elevation of cloud-water collection sites: date and pH of acidic cloud/fog event*

Site	Date	Cloud/fog field pH
Bar Harbor, Maine (10 m)[a]	7–8 August 1984	2.90
Bar Harbor, Maine (10 m)	8–9 August 1984	3.00
Bar Harbor, Maine (10 m)	9 August 1984	2.95
Mt. Washington, New Hampshire (1,524 m)	10 August 1984	2.97
Mt. Lafayette, New Hampshire (1,220 m)	10 August 1984	2.97
Mohonk Mountain, New York (467 m)	11 August 1984	2.80
Hubbard Brook, New Hampshire (765 m)	12 August 1984	2.97
Loft Mountain, Virginia (990 m)	13 August 1984	3.09

[a] Six continuous hours of ambient ozone concentrations ≥ 9 ppm.

Source: Reprinted with modifications from Weathers et al. 1986, with permission of Weathers and *Nature* Vol. 319: 658. Copyright 1986, Macmillan Magazines, Ltd.

statistical data indicates the widespread and continuing decline and death of *Picea abies* and *Abies alba* (Bormann 1985). Based on a literature survey, Postel (1986) has estimated that more than 10 million hectares or 8 percent of European forests exhibit symptoms of damage that might be attributed to air pollution (Table 3.5). In the northeastern United States, the crash of *Picea rubens* has been documented (Johnson and Siccama 1983) and spruce decline has been reported in higher elevation forests in the southern Appalachians (Mielke et al. 1986). Because decline involves both the death of sensitive trees and the occurrence of symptoms on trees over widespread areas of Europe and North America, these forests might be considered to be in stages IIA or IIB (Table 3.3), according to the model of ecosystem decline. The phenomenon of the decline of spruce and other species has received considerable study by scientists. Many, if not most, reason that the damage is directly or indirectly related to air pollution. They have produced a bewildering array of hypotheses, most of which focus on various aspects of air pollution that seem to be interacting with such naturally occurring stresses as drought, insects, and disease (Postel 1986). So far, explicit connection of decline with air pollution has yet to be established.

The qualitative connection between photochemical oxidants and forest damage is better established. It is based primarily on symptomology or the occurrence in the field of symptoms of ozone damage which have often been defined under rigorous laboratory conditions. Symptoms of ozone damage have been recorded on plants in more than half of the states of the United States (Figure 3.6) and in the Netherlands, Great Britain, Germany, Japan,

Table 3.5. *Estimated forest damage in Europe, 1985*

Country	Total forest area (thousands of hectares)	Portion of total area damaged %
Austria	3,754	24
Belgium	616	18
Czechoslovakia	4,600	27
East Germany	2,900	12
France	15,075	—
Hungary	1,600	11
Italy	6,363	6
Luxembourg	82	51
Netherlands	309	45
Norway	8,330	5
Poland	8,677	7
Sweden	26,500	4
Switzerland	1,200	34
West Germany	7,371	52
Yugoslavia	9,500	11
Other	39,087	—
TOTAL	135,964	8

Area damaged: 10.6×10^6 ha.

Source: Reprinted with modifications from Postel 1986, with permission.

Israel, and Australia (U.S. EPA 1986), and have been reported on trees in California, the southeastern United States, the Midwest, the Northeast (Bormann 1985), and in Mexico (Bauer and Hernandez 1986). Tree-ring analyses in fairly remote places in California and Virginia suggest declines in productivity associated with symptoms of photochemical oxidant damage (Bormann 1985).

Open-top chamber experiments provide the best direct quantitative evidence of air pollution damage to vegetation under field conditions (Figure 3.7). In these experiments, plants growing in chambers under field conditions (that is, in soil, under ambient rain, temperature, and light) receive ambient air or air filtered through charcoal. In a most comprehensive study, the National Crop Loss Assessment Network (NCLAN) study estimated regional productivity losses by crop plants. Test plots in North Carolina, New York, Illinois, and California detected yield losses of from 15 percent to greater than 50 percent on crops common to each region (Heck 1982). With these results it seems reasonable to ask: If crops are so damaged, what is the condition of the surrounding forest vegetation?

Wang, Karnosky, and I (Wang et al. 1986a, b) evaluated the response of *Populus tremuloides, Populus deltoides,* and hybrid popular using saplings and open-top chamber technology. Under ambient ozone conditions in rural New

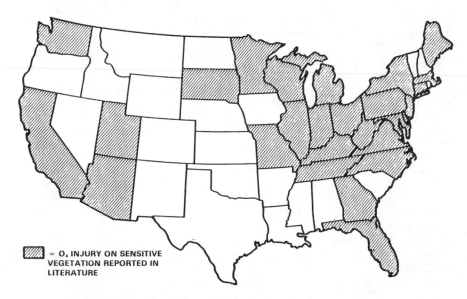

Figure 3.6. States in which some injury to vegetation has occurred as reported in the published literature (U.S. EPA 1986).

York, which is probably typical of large areas of the United States, we found reductions in productivity of 15 to 20 percent in these species (Table 3.6). Because photosynthetic fixation of solar energy is the cornerstone of all ecosystem activity, chronic depression of photosynthesis, as detected in these experiments, raises critical questions about indirect effects of air pollution on ecosystem function. What would happen, for example, if net productivity in natural ecosystems were reduced 10 percent because of chronic photochemical oxidant air pollution? Would reduced net carbon fixation over wide geographical areas contribute significantly to atmospheric carbon dioxide concentration? Would more runoff and a greater loss of nutrients in drainage water result? Would the rate of erosion subtly increase as productivity declined? Or, would resistant species replace sensitive ones with a loss in redundancy but little loss in biotic regulation?

One of the most interesting aspects of our open-top studies is that reductions in productivity or in energy flow occurred without visible symptoms of ozone damage. Other studies have noted this phenomenon (Reich and Amundson 1985). The implications of this are vast, for most of our knowledge about the geographic occurrence of ozone damage is based on the occurrence of symptoms. This finding raises the possibility that extensive hidden damage has occurred and will continue.

The data on widespread ozone symptoms, open-top chamber results, potential for hidden damage, as well as ozone-monitoring data suggest that

Figure 3.7. Open-top chambers used for the study of the effect of ambient ozone on tree saplings. Chambers are 8 feet high and 9 feet across.

Table 3.6. *Tree growth, filtered versus non-filtered chambers*

Species	Mean dry weight (grams)		% Change
	Charcoal-filtered	Non-filtered	
Aspen shoot (1982)	55.2	45.5	−18[a]
Aspen shoot (1983)	113.0	90.0	−20[a]
Aspen shoot (1984)	82.4	74.1	−10
Hybrid poplar stem (1984)	78.6	63.2	−19[b]
Cottonwood stem (1984)	88.5	76.7	−13
Black locust stem (1984)	91.5	76.2	−17

[a] Significant at 0.05
[b] Significant at 0.01

Source: Reprinted with modification from Wang et al. 1986a and 1986b, with permission of Wang and *Canadian Journal of Forest Research.*

large areas of United States forests are in stage IIA of ecosystem decline under photochemical oxidant stress. In California, extensive damage and death of *Pinus ponderosa* and *P. Jeffreyi* throughout the length of the state are thought to be due to ozone (Bormann 1985). Such areas would have advanced to the IIB stage.

The data indicate widespread photochemical oxidant damage to forests as well as deterioration thought to be directly or indirectly associated with acid rain and that the two stresses may overlap and interact. Episodic as well as chronic stress may be taking place in spite of the fact that observations of vegetation from many localities where air pollution stress may be occurring are non-existent. The evidence is mounting that air pollution is creating a severe stress on the forests of the north temperate zone.

How Closely Can We Quantitatively Link Regional Forest Ecosystem Damage to Air-Pollution Input or to Emissions at Points Distant from the Ecosystem?

My contention is that the probability of establishing reliable quantitative linkage is extremely small, or, from a practical point of view, non-existent. To establish quantitative linkage, several criteria must be met. For the basic unit of study, the stand or forest ecosystem, it is necessary to know the kinds and amounts of air pollutants that are entering or have entered the ecosystem, the changes in ecosystem structure and function that occurred over the chosen period of study, and the statistical significance of any correlation between air pollution input and changes in structure and function.

Knowledge of air pollution input to specific forest stands at points distant from emission sources is, at best, fragmentary. Not only is regional air pollution a variable mixture of acids, photochemical oxidants, trace metals, synthetic organics, and gasses, but local deposition may depart significantly from deposition estimates based on regional means. Some local sites may receive much more or less deposition because of orographic rain, wind exposure, vegetation type, topography, and local meteorology (Bormann 1983). Local variation in the deposition of pollutants has received little systematic study.

To detect trends of change in the populations, vegetational structure, or biotic regulation in a forest ecosystem that might be due to changes in air quality, we must have long-term data (Likens 1983). Such data are rare both because funding for longterm research is scarce, and because the research is difficult. When we do detect identifiable trends, through tree-ring analysis for example, relating these trends to air pollution is hampered not only by uncertainty about the air pollution input but by the background noise present in almost any ecosystem. Background variation may be caused by fluctuations in the variables controlling growth and productivity, such as precipitation, temperature, frosts, drought, and length of growing season; by developmental processes like succession; and by stochastic events such as insect outbreaks, disease epidemics, fire, cutting, or windstorm (Bormann 1983, 1985; Burgess 1984).

To assign a causation value for any identified trend, the investigator must be able to partition causation among many perturbing variables. The data needed for this are rarely available in the field studies of the forests subject to regional air pollution. Both our inability to estimate pollution deposition accurately and the complexity of ecosystem responses make it extremely difficult or virtually impossible to estimate air pollution stress effects on forest ecosystems at points distant from air pollution sources quantitatively. It is comparably difficult to link emissions with regional air pollution damage quantitatively.

The inability of ecologists to make a quantitative linkage between regional forest damage and air pollution emissions is used by some economists, politicians, and industrialists as a reason for delaying or refusing to consider more stringent air pollution emission controls. They question what billions of dollars spent in emission controls will achieve in terms of the economic benefits derived from restoring natural ecosystems and what the cost/benefit ratio in dollars will be. The difficulty ecologists have in producing reliable quantitative, dollar-oriented answers to these essentially unanswerable questions is then used to reach the conclusion that more research is needed before more stringent emission controls are considered.

Despite the fact that reliable quantitative estimates of forest damage caused by air pollution are unlikely to be produced, there is growing evidence of pollution deposition and of forest decline in Europe and North America. Further, the observational and experimental field evidence of photochemical oxidant damage to crops and trees, and the many air pollution experiments on plants under controlled conditions suggest that large areas of north temperate zone forests are in stages IIA and IIB of ecosystem decline due at least in part to air pollution stress. It is reasonable to think that north temperate zone forests are undergoing a slow but progressive decline that has remained largely masked by the complexity of the forest ecosystem and the gradual exhaustion of redundancy: in sum, creeping degradation.

A final but basic consideration affecting our view of forest health is that air pollution effects cannot be considered in isolation from other impacts on the forest. This is seen dramatically in a view of the lights of the eastern United States taken from 560 miles in space (Figure 3.8). Not only is each patch of light a center of fossil and nuclear energy consumption and a source of local air pollutants which have not been considered in this regional assay – it is, as well, a center of radiating urban influences that extend well into forest lands. These influences include the need for space for housing, roads, landfills,

42   F. H. Bormann

Figure 3.8. A satellite photomosaic of the eastern United States and a small portion
of southeastern Canada, roughly bounded by 25°–42°N latitude and the eastern
seaboard to about 97°W longitude. This photograph was taken at night from an
elevation of 540 nautical miles. The white areas are the lights of urban areas, centers
of energy consumption. The area lies within the boundaries of the temperate eastern
deciduous forest. Note that no part of this forest is very far removed from an
urban–industrial center. (Reprinted from Bormann 1976, with permission from
BioScience 26: 438. Copyright 1976 [1985] by The American Institute of Biological
Sciences.)

industrial sites, mining sites, shopping centers, new sources of water, new
campgrounds, ski areas, and such other aspects of development as increasing
populations of off-road vehicles, increased hunting and fishing pressure, and
greater risk of fire. To all of this is combined more intensive forest-harvesting
techniques, increased use of pesticides and fertilizers in forest management,
and a projected massive extension of forest road systems. It is against this
background of many forms of creeping degradation that the effects of current
and future levels of air pollution stress must be weighed.

A world view, shared by many scientists, projects that stress, including
that of air pollution, will markedly increase in the coming decades in

response to rising world populations and expanding industrialization. To accommodate future stress, forest ecosystems will need all the redundancy they can muster to maintain as much as a modified equilibrium. Ecosystem redundancy should be reserved to buffer stresses we cannot control. In a few decades, we may have to accept a lowered species diversity and less biotic regulation of energy flow and biogeochemical cycles. It seems injudicious and shortsighted to sacrifice ecosystem redundancy in order to achieve short-term financial and economic objectives.

Acknowledgments

This is a publication of the Hubbard Brook Ecosystem Study, supported by the National Science Foundation and the Andrew W. Mellon Foundation. This work was done through the cooperation of the Northeastern Forest Experiment Station, Forest Service, USDA, Broomall, Pennsylvania. This chapter was adapted from a paper by the author published in *Bioscience* 35, 1985.

References

Bauer, L. I. de, and T. Hernandez, 1986. Assessing effects of deposition in forests in Mexico. Program of the Fourth International Congress of Ecology, p. 87. State University of New York at Syracuse.

Bormann, F. H., 1976. An inseparable linkage: conservation of natural ecosystems and the conservation of fossil energy. *BioScience* 26:754–760.

Bormann, F. H., 1983. Factors confounding evaluation of air pollution stress on forests: pollution input and ecosystem complexity. In H. Ott and H. Stangl (Eds.), *Proceedings of the Karlsruhe Symposium on Acid Deposition: A Challenge for Europe*, pp. 147–166. (Preliminary Edition) XII/ENV/45/83. Commission of the European Communities, Brussels, Belgium.

Bormann, F. H., 1985. Air pollution and forests: an ecosystem perspective. *BioScience* 35:434–441.

Bormann, F. H., and G. E. Likens, 1979. *Pattern and Process in a Forested Ecosystem.* Springer-Verlag, New York.

Burgess, R. L. (Ed.), 1984. *Effects of Acidic Deposition on Forest Ecosystems in the Northeastern United States: An Evaluation of Current Evidence.* State University of New York, College of Environmental Science and Forestry, Institute of Environmental Program Affairs, Syracuse, New York.

Chamberlain, J., H. Foley, G. MacDonald, and M. Ruderman, 1982. Climatic effects of minor atmospheric constituents. In W. Clark (Ed.), *Carbon Dioxide Review*, pp. 255–277. Oxford University Press, New York.

Environmental Protection Agency (EPA). August, 1986. Air quality criteria for ozone and other photochemical oxidants, Vol. III. EPA–600/8–84–020cF, Environmental Criteria & Assessment Office, Research Triangle Park, N.C.

Fuhrer, J., 1985. Formation of secondary air pollutants and their occurrence in Europe. *Experientia* 41:286–301.

Gordon, A. G., and E. Gorham, 1963. Ecological aspects of air pollution from an iron-sinstering plant at Wawa, Ontario. *Can. J. of Botany* 41:1063–1078.

Heck, W. W., O. C. Taylor, R. Adams, G. Bingham, J. Miller, E. Preston, and L.

Weinstein, 1982. Assessment of crop loss from ozone. *J. of the Air Pol. Control Assoc.* 32(4):353–361.

Johnson, A. H., and T. G. Siccama, 1983. Acid deposition and forest decline. *Environ. Sci. & Tech.* 17:294A–305A.

Lewis, M., and M. C. Grant, 1980. Acid precipitation in the western United States. *Science* 207:176–177.

Likens, G. E., 1983. A priority for ecological research. *Bull. Ecol. Soc. Am.* 64:234–243.

Likens, G. E., and F. H. Bormann, 1974. Acid rain: a serious regional environmental problem. *Science* 184(4142):1176–1179.

Likens, G. E., and T. J. Butler, 1981. Recent acidification of precipitation in North America. *Atmos. Environ.* 15:1103–1109.

Likens, G. E., R. F. Wright, J. N. Galloway, and T. J. Butler, 1979. Acid rain. *Scientific American* 241(4):43–51.

Lindberg, S. E., G. M. Lovett, D. D. Richter, and D. W. Johnson, 1986. Atmospheric deposition and canopy interactions of major ions in a forest. *Science* 231:141–145.

Ludwig, F. L., and E. Shelar, Jr., 1980. Empirical relationships between observed ozone concentrations and geographical areas with concentrations likely to be above 120 ppb. *J. of the Air Poll. Control Assoc.* 30:894–897.

MacDonald, G. J., 1985. *Climate Change and Acid Rain.* The Mitre Corporation, McLean, Va.

Mielke, M. E., D. G. Soctomah, M. A. Marsden, and W. M. Ciesla, 1986. Decline and mortality of red spruce in West Virginia. Report No. 86–4, U.S. Dept. Agriculture, Forest Service, Forest Pest Management, Methods Application Group, Ft. Collins, Colo.

Postel, S., 1986. Altering the Earth's chemistry: assessing the risks. *Worldwatch Paper No. 71*, Worldwatch Inst. Washington, D.C.

Reich, P. B., and R. G. Amundson, 1985. Ambient levels of ozone reduce net photosynthesis in tree and crop species. *Science* 230:566–570.

Roth, P., C. Blanchard, J. Harte, H. Michels, and M. El-Ashry, 1985. The American West's acid rain tests. World Resources Institute, Washington, D.C. Research Report No. 1.

Wang, D., D. F. Karnosky, F. H. Bormann, 1986a. Effects of ambient ozone on the productivity of *Populus tremuloides* Michx. grown under field conditions. *Can J. For. Res.* 16:47–55.

Wang, D., F. H. Bormann, and D. F. Karnosky, 1986b. Regional tree growth reductions due to ambient ozone: evidence from field experiments. *Environ. Sci. & Tech.* 20:1122–1125.

Weathers, K. C., G. E. Likens, F. H. Bormann, J. S. Eaton, W. B. Bowden, J. L. Anderson, D. A. Crest, J. N. Galloway, W. C. Keene, K. D. Kimball, P. Huth, and D. Smiley, 1986. A regional acidic cloud/fog water event in the eastern United States. *Nature* 319:657–658.

Weathers, K. C., G. E. Likens, F. H. Bormann, S. Bicknell, B. T. Bormann, B. C. Daube, Jr., J. S. Eaton, J. N. Galloway, J. A. Kadlecek, W. D. Keene, K. D. Kimball, A. Lugo, W. H. McDowell, T. G. Siccama, D. Smiley, and R. Tarrant, 1988. Chemical composition of cloud water from ten sites in North America. *Environ. Sci. Tech.* 22:1018–1026.

Woodwell, G. M., 1970. Effects of pollution on the structure and physiology of ecosystems. *Science* 168:429–433.

Zhao, D., and S. Bozen, 1986. Air pollution and acid. *Ambio.* 15(1):2–5.

4   The Long-Term Effects of Air Pollutants on Lichen Communities in Europe and North America

D. L. HAWKSWORTH

Editor's Note: Lichens, many of them, are surface dwellers. They have evolved to occupy, among other places, the surface of rocks, the surface of the soil, the bark of trees. These surfaces offer some of the most difficult habitats for life, habitats marked by extremes. The surface of a rock, for example, may bake in the sun during the day and rise in temperature to 70° Celsius or more, dropping at night to freezing or below. Similar extremes in water availability accompany such changes. Yet such habitats may support communities of lichens that garner water and nutrients directly through the surfaces of their thalli. Despite the apparent hardiness of lichens, their populations have long been considered sensitive indicators of air pollution: certain lichens appear to be particularly vulnerable to air pollution and their vigor appears to offer potential as an early index of impoverishment.

The difficulty is that under disturbance the populations are ephemeral: they often disappear quickly and the index becomes neither morbidity nor other active change, but mere absence. Professor Hawksworth warns, to add to the difficulty, that it is not always appropriate to transfer experience with lichen communities from one place to another. Nonetheless, he provides compelling documentation of the sensitivity of lichen populations to airborne pollutants. The effects are unquestionably impoverishment, a reduction in diversity that is virtually universal and that applies in particular to fruticose and foliose, less to crustose, lichens. The same pattern was recognized in response to ionizing radiation, a relationship that reinforces the generality of the patterns of impoverishment. Although the generality is persuasive and useful, the effect is difficult to turn into an index of impoverishment. It is not possible to prove on the basis of the absence, or even the disappearance, of a lichen that a specific pollutant is involved.

Lichens, however, because they derive their water and nutrients in large degree from the air, can be used as highly developed filters that monitor air and rain and can be used occasionally as a sampling system. The effectiveness of this system has been demonstrated through earlier studies of the accumulation and transfer of radioactivity, especially Cs^{137} and Sr^{90} in the lichen−caribou−wolf or human food chain.

Hawksworth provides a sensitive and comprehensive review of the current perspective of one of the world's most experienced lichenologists on this complex and promising realm.

Introduction

Lichens are composite structures, comprising a fungal and one or more photosynthetic partners. They behave for all practical ecological purposes as single entities. In many of the more conspicuous species reproduction is by the dispersal of propagules containing both the fungal and photosynthetic partners. The fungal partner (mycobiont) is most commonly an ascomycete, while the photosynthetic partner (photobiont) may be a green alga or a cyanobacterium. The fungi are mainly exclusively lichen-forming but are taxonomically diverse. Many belong to orders that also contain non-lichen-forming species. In contrast, with a few notable exceptions, the photosynthetic partners belong to genera which also occur independently in nature. The nature of lichen associations has been reviewed in Hawksworth and Hill (1984) and Hawksworth (1988).

The dual organism is autotrophic and a delicate physiological balance is established between the bionts and their microenvironments. Growth is slow but individuals can continue to develop for centuries so they are continuously in equilibrium with their surroundings. There are around 13,500 lichenized species, adapted to a wide variety of microecological niches, each with particular environmental parameters. Changes in the microenvironment, for example a tree's falling or a tombstone's inclining with age, can disturb this balance and lead to death. It is the delicate nature of the balance, the complexities of which are only gradually being unravelled (Brown 1985; Kershaw 1985), that renders lichen populations especially vulnerable to environmental change and at the same time endows them with value as environmental monitors.

Disturbance affects not only the presence or absence of species but can also involve reductions in frequency, luxuriance, fertility, and the ability to establish new colonies (Hawksworth, Rose, and Coppins 1973). Such changes are part of the process of biotic impoverishment involving lichens, which occurs in a wide variety of biomes from hot arid deserts through tropical rainforests to mountains and tundra.

This paper draws attention to impoverishment in lichen communities arising from the effects of air pollution. The implications of the loss of lichens for other organisms and the ecology of the site are also highlighted.

Air pollution was known to lead to impoverishment in lichen communities by some of the earliest botanists to take an interest in the group. Darwin (1790) observed deterioration around copper mines in Anglesey, and in about 1812 Turner and Borrer (1839) noted that scarcely any lichens could exist where the air was impure. Nylander (1866) suggested that they might be used as a guide to air quality; but it was not until the work of Skye (1958) in Sweden that the tolerance limits of particular species started to be documented. The United Kingdom has a particularly widespread system of volumetric recording gauges which has made possible the devising of more sophisticated zone schemes correlating species assemblages with ambient mean sulphur dioxide levels (Gilbert 1970; Hawksworth and Rose 1970). Various indices have been proposed and subjected to theoretical scrutiny (Herben and Liška 1986). Laboratory-based physiological studies have followed in the wake of the field ecologists; a statistical comparison between a variety of experimental observations and field data demonstrates that the correlation is significant, and also that short-term fumigations might be of especial significance (Nash 1988).[1]

Extent of Impoverishment

To assess the extent of any impoverishment with confidence, data on species distributions and frequency are prerequisites. This level of information is available for only a minority of regions, mainly in Europe, and comprises published accounts and reference specimens preserved in herbaria. The richest period for such data is the late nineteenth century and the first decades of the present century. These can be compared with modern surveys. Comparisons of such data from well-studied areas in the British Isles show some drastic declines (Table 4.1), ranging from over 80% in areas where air pollution is the dominant factor to under 15% where it is insignificant. The difference between these figures gives some approximate indication of the extent of lichen impoverishment to be expected due to air pollution compared with other factors, (i.e., up to 65% of the species).

These figures of decline are mirrored in studies elsewhere in Europe: 150 species lost from s'-Hertogenbosch in the Netherlands (van Dobben 1983), 160 species lost from Kassel (Follmann 1973), and 273 (91%) from Region Untermaine (Kirschbaum 1972). Where zones with different air-pollution-related communities have been mapped, in and around urban areas at intervals over long periods, particularly drastic changes have been recorded. These include a ninefold increase of the zone without macrolichens in Zürich since 1936 (Züst 1977), a fivefold extension in this area of Salzburg since 1948–1949 (Türk 1975), and an increase in the area of the lichen desert in Caracas, Venezuela from 13% in 1953 to 89% in 1973 (Vareschi and Moreno 1973).

The depletion extends over considerable areas of Europe. Zone maps of various types indicating this impoverishment have been produced for England and Wales (Hawksworth and Rose 1970, 1976) and the Netherlands

Table 4.1. *Extent of impoverishment of the lichen flora in selected well-studied regions and sites in the British Isles due to air pollution and (or) other factors.*

	Species recorded[a]	Species lost[a]	Percentage	Source
Air pollution significant				
Bookham Common (Surrey)	54	18	33	Laundon (1973)
Edinburgh	172	82	37	Coppins (1978)
Epping Forest (Essex)	118	90	76	Hawksworth, Rose, & Coppins (1973)
Gopsall Park (Leicestershire)	106	94	89	Sowter & Hawksworth (1970)
Leicestershire	329	154	47	Hawksworth (1975)
Lickey Hills (Birmingham)	45	33	73	Lindsay (1978)
London	165	94	57	Laundon (1970)
Mendlesham (Suffolk)	161	62	39	Coppins & Lambley (1974)
Warwickshire	223	72	32	Lindsay (1980)
West Yorkshire	307	164	58	Seaward (1975)
Air pollution insignificant				
Devon	710	104	15	Hawksworth (1975)
Dorset	497	47	9	Bowen (1976)
Ilsham (Devon)	207	18	9	Hawksworth & Skinner (1974)
Isle of Wight	382	60	15	Pope (1985)
New Forest	294	35	12	Rose & James (1974)
Northumberland	589	22	4	Gilbert (1980)
Slapton (Devon)	288	26	9	Hawksworth (1986)

[a] In some cases only species on bark and wood are included; see sources for further explanation.

(de Wit 1976), and for large areas of Belgium (Barkman 1963; DeSloover and Lambinon 1965), France (Gehu, Bon, Delzenne, and Rose 1973; Bon 1974; Déruelle 1977; Lerond 1981) and Germany (Domrös 1966).

In North America, declines have long been known to be taking place (Andrews 1928) but few comparative studies have been made with the exception of Boston (Kneiper and Sherwood-Pike 1985); southern California, where 50% of the species had been lost (Sigal and Nash 1983); and New York, where 47 species were not found (Brodo 1968). Zone development has, however, been documented for Montreal in detail (LeBlanc and DeSloover 1970) and impoverishment is reported around industrial plants and urban areas in many states and provinces (Table 4.2). Factors other than air pollution may sometimes be involved, however (Stringer and Stringer 1974). In particular, in arid situations where crustose lichens predominate, as in

Table 4.2. *Selected North American studies in which air pollution has been considered as the main or only cause of lichen impoverishment.*

Canada			
Alberta	Case (1980)	Ontario	Barclay-Estrup & Sims
	Lee & Vitt (1973)		(1979)
	Maynard, Addison, &		LeBlanc & DeSloover (1970)
	Kennedy (1983)		LeBlanc & Rao (1975)
	Skorepa & Vitt (1976)		Stephenson & Merriam
			(1975)
Newfoundland	Roberts & Thompson (1980)	Quebec	Le Blanc, Rao, & Commeau
			(1972)
Nova Scotia	Brawn & Ogden (1977)		
USA			
California	Sigal & Nash (1983)	New York	Brodo (1968)
Colorado	Bennett (1983)	Ohio	Mickle (1977)
Idaho	Hoffman (1974)		Showman (1975, 1981)
Indiana	Andrews (1928)	Oregon	Denison & Carpenter (1973)
Massachusetts	Kneiper & Sherwood-	Pennsylvania	Nash (1975)
	Pike (1985)	Tennessee	Mathis & Tomlinson (1972)
	Godfrey, Mulcahy, & Searay	Washington	Johnson (1979)
	(1985)		Taylor (1978)
Michigan	Brown (1974)	Wisconsin	Newberry (1975)
Montana	Eversman (1978)		Will-Wolfe (1980)
	Sheridan, Sanderson, & Kerr		
	(1976)		

New Mexico, effects are minimal (Marsh and Nash 1979). Studies in Europe have also shown that, in drier regions, sensitivities are reduced in comparison with those with a higher precipitation (Hawksworth 1973).

Declines comparable to those seen in Europe undoubtedly occur in many other regions of the world, except the most arid. There are reports from Australia (Rogers 1977), Brazil (Troppmair 1977; Zanette et al. 1981), Hong Kong (Thrower 1980), Jamaica (Dixon and Kelly 1979), Japan (e.g., Sugiyama, Kurokawa, and Okeda 1976; Taoda 1980), New Zealand (Daly 1970), and Venezuela (Vareschi and Moreno, 1973).

Community structure itself can change. Species characteristic of low-pH barks, particularly, may increase in frequency if the bark pH falls as a result of the effects of air pollution (Hawksworth et al. 1973; Pišút and Liška 1985; Wirth 1985), so that communities normally associated with moderate pH bark give way to those demanding a lower pH. Species can also switch substrata as a result of interactions between the substrate and pollutants (Seaward 1975; Skorepa, Norden, and Windler 1979).

Causes of Impoverishment

The evidence that sulphur dioxide is the major air pollutant responsible for impoverishment of lichen communities over wide areas of Europe is now overwhelming (Burton 1986; Nash 1988). The sensitivity of different species varies considerably and this renders them especially valuable as biological monitors of ambient levels of this pollutant. Some of the most sensitive species, such as *Usnea articulata*, occur only where mean sulphur dioxide levels are below 30 µg/m^3. In contrast the most tolerant, for example, *Lecanora conizaeoides* and *Scoliciosporum chlorococcum* can survive up to about 170 µg/m^3 (Hawksworth and Rose 1970). Tolerance limits and relative sensitivities worked out in the British Isles have been found to be applicable in adjacent parts of Europe (Johnsen and Søchting 1973; Jürging 1975; Déruelle 1977) and confirmed in laboratory studies (Hill 1971; Türk, Wirth, and Lange 1974; Marti 1985).

Sulphur dioxide is not necessarily always the cause of impoverishment. Other factors acting independently or synergistically can be significant in particular locations. The temptation to apply conclusions derived in one climatic region to another must be avoided unless preliminary studies have suggested this transfer can be justified.

Fluorides are especially toxic, and relative species sensitivities do not always correspond to their tolerance to sulphur dioxide (Gilbert 1973). As a consequence of their high reactivity, fluoride effects are generally local but occur at levels from about 20–80 µg F/g tissue (Nash 1988). Of more potential concern in areas such as the southern United States is the effect of photochemical smog. Ozone and peroxy-acetyl-nitrate (PAN) formed by photochemical reactions between nitrogen oxides and hydrocarbons are only now being examined in detail with regard to their effects on lichens in field situations. In the Los Angeles area, Sigal and Nash (1983) demonstrated that impoverishment of lichen communities was directly related to higher oxidant-dose estimates. This relationship does not appear to be important in central Europe (Steubing 1981), however, where the climate is wetter. Experimental work on this topic is remarkably meager (Nash 1976; Nash and Sigal 1979; Sigal and Taylor 1979; Ross and Nash 1983) and in need of extension.

Sulphur dioxide and nitrogen oxides can be dissolved in water and deposited in precipitation as "acid rain." The relationship between the effects of acid rain and gaseous pollutants on lichens is obscure, especially as the latter have to dissolve in surface films of water before they can be absorbed. However, the levels of acidity in acid rain can be as high as pH 2.1–3 in the British Isles and have been a cause for concern for some years.

Robitaille, LeBlanc, and Rao (1977) found acidity of rain to contribute to the scarcity of cryptogams around a copper smelter in the Gaspé of Quebec. Through effects on nitrogen fixation it has been considered to limit the distribution of *Lobaria pulmonaria* in Washington (Denison et al. 1976) and to be responsible for the decline of populations of *L. pulmonaria* and *Sticta limbata* in parts of England where gaseous sulphur dioxide levels have not increased (Gilbert 1986). In the laboratory it has been found to severely reduce nitrogen fixation in *Peltigera* species (Fritz-Sheridan 1985).

Lichens can accumulate heavy metals to remarkable concentrations, but these eliminate species only in the most extreme situations. Analyses of lichens can enable deposition patterns to be determined. This practical application has led to considerable research (Nieboer et al. 1978; Puckett and Burton 1981). Studies on metal contents in specimens collected over a period of years can also indicate whether concentrations have increased. On Plummers Island, Maryland, under the Washington Beltway, lead in *Parmelia baltimorensis* rose from 82.3 µg/g in 1907 to 1,893.5 µg/g in 1978 (Lawrey and Hale 1981). Radionuclides are accrued in a parallel manner, and while the lichens appear unharmed, the accumulation is of especial concern where species are components of the lichen–caribou/reindeer–human foodchain (James 1973; Hanson 1980, 1982).

Particulate soot does not seem to be important (Hawksworth 1973; Steubing 1981), although calcareous dust can lead to local enrichments of the lichen communities by increasing bark pH and nutrient levels (Gilbert 1976).

Automobile exhausts are reported to have some physiological effects (Déruelle and Petit 1983), but, in Nova Scotia, Brawn and Ogden (1977) found no correlation between traffic volume and the abundance of common macrolichens. There were indications that diesel buses might limit the occurrence of certain species. Any such effects are essentially local and do not lead to general impoverishment.

Monitoring Impoverishment

Intensive field work is essential to produce baseline data against which changes can be compared. The value of this approach is seen in the case of Epping Forest, northeast London, which has been restudied at five periods since 1784 (Hawksworth, Rose, and Coppins 1973) and in changing zone limits in urban areas (see above) (Kandler and Poelt 1984). Examples such as those compiled in Table 4.1 would not be available in the absence of such recording.

The vital nature of such studies is increasingly appreciated. Baseline surveys have been conducted in various parts of North America in sites where air pollution has been expected to increase (Nash 1974; Hoffman and Boe 1977; Will-Wolfe 1980; Wetmore 1981; Eversman 1982). A series of networks has been established in Alberta (Case 1984).

National distribution maps of individual species are an especially valuable means of assessing the status of lichens where these are categorized by date. This approach provided data essential to the understanding of changes in distribution of species in the British Isles (Hawksworth et al. 1973; Hawksworth, Coppins, and Rose 1974; Coppins 1976); maps of 174 species based on a 10-km grid were published by Seaward and Hitch (1982). Similar collaborative schemes are being established elsewhere in Europe (e.g., Türk and Wittmann 1984) or have been conducted as a part of air pollution investigations using selected species (de Wit 1976). Critical distribution maps of lichens have appeared in ecological and systematic papers since the 1930s in Scandinavia (e.g., Degelius 1935). This is also true for North America (e.g., Thomson 1972; Brodo and Hawksworth 1977). Even where date categories are not differentiated they can be valuable for comparisons at later dates (Löfgren and Moberg 1984).

Prospects for Improvement

Falling sulphur dioxide levels were an almost unknown phenomenon in the early 1970s. However, legislation for pollution controls were gradually implemented and, in lowland Britain particularly, improvements in the lichen vegetation of urban areas started to become apparent. These have been most striking in London (Rose and Hawksworth 1981)[1] but are noted elsewhere (Gilbert 1980; Seaward 1980; Lindsay 1982; Brightman and Seaward 1983; Seaward and Henderson 1984). Parallel improvements have been noted in towns in France (Lerond 1980, 1985) and Germany (Kandler and Poelt 1984; Rabe and Wiegel 1985). It should be stressed that improvement in urban areas does not necessarily imply that this situation applies in rural situations. In the case of the British Isles, a policy of tall stacks for power station emissions has meant that 40–50 percent of the total United Kingdom's 6 m tons of sulphur dioxide emissions each year is released at a high level and is spread over wide areas. As a result, in many rural areas ambient levels are constant or increasing, with consequent continued impoverishment.

Where isolated sources in otherwise little-polluted regions cease operations, the lichen vegetation can improve (Westman 1975; Showman 1981). In one case in Austria, 25 species returned within 8 years (Hafellner and Grill 1981). Responses to ameliorating air pollution levels are not immediate, and where the chemical nature or acidity of the substratum has been substantially modified by the pollutant, responses may take many years. In such cases considerable care has to be exercised in using lichen-based scales for the estimation of ambient pollutant levels (Henderson-Sellers and Seaward 1979). If species have been totally eliminated from a wide area, chance importation of propagules may be a limiting factor to improvement.

Some of the lichens more sensitive to air pollutants are especially vulnerable to other human activities. This is particularly true for species restricted to ancient forests and woodlands which require an ecological continuity of mature trees to persist (Rose 1976). The reason for this restriction is presumed to be limited powers of dispersal. Once eliminated from a locality, species in this category are never likely to return (unless transplanted) even though the same trees on which they formerly grew are still present. Forest disturbance, destruction, and air pollution combine to make this the most endangered element in our lichen flora. For example, *Usnea longissima* requires mesic spruce forests with a continuity of ancient trees not disturbed by fire. It has been lost from 68–77 percent of the sites in central Sweden known in the 1920s and 1930s (Esseen, Ericson, Lindström, and Zackrisson 1981). Dispersal is mainly by thallus fragments which are found only rarely more than 2 m from trees on which the lichen occurs. The creation of nature reserves has been recommended for its survival, but this will be of little avail should air-pollution levels ever threaten the remaining eleven sites in the region.

Air pollution is perhaps the most insidious effect of human activities on natural communities. It is spread huge distances from its source by the wind, and is still harmful at concentrations well below those at which they are visible or detectable by their odor. Although the technology to reduce sulphur dioxide air pollution in particular exists, the costs are prohibitive and action is unlikely to be taken unless there is considerable international political pressure to adopt such a strategy. The prospects of major improvements in most regions of the world are therefore bleak in the foreseeable future.

Consequences of Lichen Impoverishment

The disappearance of lichens is not merely a cause for concern amongst lichen conservationists. It has implications both for other organisms and for the ecology of affected sites. Many of these ramifications are as yet inadequately studied, but it is pertinent to draw attention to them here so that the possible long-term consequences of lichen impoverishment through air pollution damage are appreciated.

A surprising range of organisms is reliant on lichens for food or camouflage.

Amongst the invertebrates, moths are of special note with about 30 lichen-related species in Europe alone (Richardson 1975); examples also occur in North America (Sigal 1984). Other invertebrates dependent on lichens include species of psocids, rotifers, collembolans, springtails, tardigrades, mites, weevils, and nematodes (Gerson and Seaward 1977). On bark, diminution of microarthropod diversity and equilibrium as a result of the effects of air pollution on the lichens has been described from the British Isles (Gilbert 1971) and France (André 1979) and is certainly general. It should also be remembered that it has been estimated that there are as many as 300 genera and 1,000 species of microscopic fungi which are obligately lichen-dwelling (Hawksworth 1982).

Richardson and Young (1977) found that, amongst the vertebrates, camou-flage against lichen backgrounds is seen in chameleons, geckos, tree frogs, and lizards in the tropics; 45 American birds make their nests mainly or partly of lichens; and lichens in the tundra are eaten by voles and other small mammals. Of most concern are the long-term effects on lichens, both those from trees and on the ground, which are used as forage during the winter months by reindeer and caribou. There are around 3.1 million domesticated reindeer ranging over an area of 3.6 million km^2 (Richardson and Young 1977). Experimental studies have shown that ground dwelling *Cladonia* species of lichen are susceptible to damage by sulphur dioxide (Moser et al. 1980; Lechowicz 1982; Moser, Nash, and Olafsen 1983). Around a brass-mill complex in Sweden the moss and lichen ground cover was reduced from 25–90 percent to under 1 percent, and the number of *Cladonia* species fell from 10–12 to zero (Folkesson 1984). Schofield and Hamilton (1970) first warned of this danger, which has global as well as local effects (Schofield 1975) and has implications for the survival of the reindeer herds and the livelihood of those dependent on them. The export of *C. stellaris* for use in modeling, decorations, and wreaths (Kauppi 1979), which was worth over £2.25 million in 1971 to Fennoscandia, would also be threatened.

Other species growing on the ground in Alaska are inhibited by sulphur dioxide and crude oil (Atlas and Schofield 1976). The long-term prospects of large-scale loss of lichens in the tundra, leading to soil instability and erosion, cannot be ignored. Once eliminated after burning, for example, some *Cladonia* species may require over 100 years to regain their former dominance (Scotter 1964). Any large-scale destruction of mosses and lichens would evidently also have far-reaching consequences for regional water budgets in the Canadian Middle North in view of their considerable water-holding capacity (Vowinckel and Orvig 1976).

Erosion is a threat in hot desert areas where lichens have a key role in maintaining a continuous surface, but here crustose and squamulose species more resistant to air pollution are generally involved and the calcareous substrata will tend to moderate any effects.

The role of lichens in mineral cycling is poorly documented but is certainly important and should not be overlooked. They provide a point of entry for minerals into the ecosystem by nitrogen fixation and aerosol interception (Pike 1978) and contribute to the litter fall (Esseen 1985). Lichen biomass is rarely studied; reports are in the range 2–3 tons/ha for epiphytic species and 5–8 tons/ha for terrestrial ones (Pike 1981). This is probably of particular importance in tropical forests; lichens living on perennial leaves in Amazonia, for example, may have a significant role in nutrient conservation (Jordan et al. 1980). Foliicolous species would be expected to be especially vulnerable to acid rain as it would affect the pH of leaf surfaces, but so far this has not been investigated. In the fir forests of western Oregon and Washington, *Lobaria* species containing cyanobacteria, which are particularly sulphur-dioxide sensitive, also have an important ecological role in fixing atmospheric nitrogen (Denison 1973).

In summary, the implications of lichen loss may be considerable for other organisms and for certain environments, but the extents cannot be estimated with any confidence because of a lack of baseline surveys and ecological research. Lichens merit increased attention from environmentalists because of their value as continuous biological monitors of the state of the air that all aerobic life, including humanity, shares. Deteriorating lichen communities provide an early indication that environmental parameters are changing. The causes of such changes should be investigated, and where possible rectified, before gross damage, such as the death of forests, is manifest.

Acknowledgments

I am indebted to Dr. T. H. Nash III for allowing me to see a copy of the manuscript of Nash (1987), to Ms. M. S. Rainbow for help in preparing the manuscript, and to Dr. G. M. Woodwell for enabling me to participate in the Woods Hole Research Center's symposium.

Notes

1. The literature on this topic now includes at least 1,500 papers. The topic has also been the subject of several symposia and multiauthored books; source works to be consulted for more detailed information include: Hawksworth (1971); Ferry, Baddeley, and Hawksworth (1973); Hawksworth and Rose (1976); Kärenlampi (1976); LeBlanc and Rao (1976); Skye (1979); Jürging and Burkhardt (1979–1980); Richardson and Nieber (1979); Déruelle and Lallemant (1983); Burton (1986); and Nash and Wirth (1988). Since 1974 recent literature has been abstracted regularly in *The Lichenologist*.

2. Since this paper was prepared even more dramatic improvements in London have been documented. Twenty-four species not seen during this century have re-appeared, of which eight had not been seen for 200 years. Leafy, and shrubby lichens can now be found in the central parks. This improvement coincides with a dramatic fall in mean sulphur dioxide levels, and in particular with the closure of a power station in 1983 (Hawksworth and McManus 1989a, b).

References

André, H., 1979. Introduction à l'étude ecologique des communautés de microarthropodes corticoles soumises à la pollution atmosphérique. II. Recherche de bioindicateurs et d'indices biologiques de pollution. *Annls Soc. r. zool. Belg.* 106:211–224.

Andrews, F. M., 1928. A study of lichens. *Proc. Indiana Acad. Sci.* 37:329–330.

Atlas, R. M., and E. Schofield, 1976. Responses of the lichens *Peltigera aphthosa* and *Cetraria nivalis* and the alga *Nostoc commune* to sulfur dioxide, natural gas, and crude oil in arctic Alaska. *Astarte* 8:53–60.

Barclay-Estrup, P., and R. A. Sims, 1979. Epiphytes on white elm, *Ulmus americana*, near Thunder Bay, Ontario. *Can. Fld. Nat.* 93:139–143.

Barkman, J. J., 1963. De epifyten-flora en-vegetatie van MiddenLimburg (België). *Ver. K. ned. Akad. Wet. II*, 54 (4):1–46.

Bennett, J. P., 1983. Air pollution studies on lichens in Denver, Colorado. *Am. J. Bot.* 70 (Suppl.), 4.

Bon, M., 1974. *Lichens et Pollution Atmosphérique en Picardie Occidentale.* Société Linnéenne du Nord de la France, Amiens.

Bowen, H. J. M., 1976. The lichen flora of Dorset. *Lichenologist* 8:1–33.

Brawn, K., and J. G. Ogden III, 1977. Lichen diversity and abundance as affected by traffic volume in an urban environment. *Urban Ecol.* 2:235–244.

Brightman, F. H., and M. R. D. Seaward, 1983. Notes on the bryophytes and lichens, Ruxley gravel pit. *Trans. Kent Fld. Club* 9:101–102.

Brodo, I. M., 1968. The lichens of Long Island, New York: a vegetational and floristic analysis. *Bull. N.Y. St. Mus.* 410:i–x, 1–330.

Brodo, I. M., and D. L. Hawksworth, 1977. *Alectoria* and allied genera in North America. *Opera Bot.* 42:1–164.

Brown, D. H. (Ed.), 1985. *Lichen Physiology and Cell Biology.* Plenum, New York.

Brown, R. T., 1974. Furnace-fuel, air pollution accumulated in snow and lichen growth on trees. *Michigan Academician* 7:149–156.

Burton, M. A. S., 1986. *Biological Monitoring of Environmental Contaminants (Plants).* King's College Monitoring and Assessment Research Centre, London.

Case, J. W., 1980. The influence of three sour gas processing plants on the ecological distribution of epiphytic lichens in the vicinity of Fox Creek and Whitecourt, Alberta, Canada. *Water, Air, Soil Pollut.* 14:45–68.

Case, J. W., 1984. Lichen biomonitoring networks in Alberta. *Environ. Monit. Assess.* 4:303–313.

Coppins, B. J., 1976. Distribution patterns shown by epiphytic lichens in the British Isles. In D. H. Brown, D. L. Hawksworth, and R. H. Bailey (Eds.), *Lichenology: Progress and Problems*, pp. 249–278. Academic Press, London.

Coppins, B. J., 1979. A glimpse of the past and present lichen flora of Edinburgh. *Trans. Proc. Bot. Soc. Edinb.* 42 (Suppl.):19–35.

Coppins, B. J., and P. W. Lambley, 1974. Changes in the lichen flora of the parish of Mendlesham, Suffolk, during the last fifty years. *Suffolk Nat. Hist.* 16:319–335.

Daly, G. T., 1970. Bryophyte and lichen indicators of air pollution in Christchurch, New Zealand. *Proc. N.Z. Ecol. Soc.* 17:70–79.

Darwin, E. 1790. *The Botanic Garden, a Poem in Two Parts: Part I.* Litchfield, England.

Degelius, G., 1935. Das ozeanische Element der Strauch-und Laubflechtenflora von Skandinavien. *Acta phytogeogr. suec.* 7:i–xii, 1–411.

Denison, R., B. Caldwell, B. Bormann, L. Eldred, C. Swanberg, and S. Anderson, 1976. The effects of acid rain on nitrogen fixation in Western Washington coniferous forests. *USDA Forest Serv. Gen. Techn. Rep.* NE–23, 933–949.

Denison, W. C., 1973. Life in tall trees. *Scient. Am.* 228:74–80.

Denison, W. C., and S. M. Carpenter, 1973. *A Guide to Air Quality Monitoring with Lichens.* Lichen Technology, Corvallis.

Déruelle, S., 1977. Influence de la pollution atmosphérique sur la végétation lichénique des arbres isolés dans la région de Mantes (Yvelines). *Revue bryol. lichén.* 43:137–158.

Déruelle, S., and P. J. K. Petit, 1983. Preliminary studies on the net photosynthesis and respiration responses of some lichens to automobile pollution. *Cryptogamie, bryol. lichén.* 4:269–278.

DeSloover, J., and J. Lambinon, 1965. Contribution à l'étude des lichens corticoles du bassin de la Dendre. *Bull. Soc. r. Bot. Belg.* 98:229–273.

Dixon, J., and D. Kelly, 1979. A study of Jamaican lichens. In C. Davis (Ed.), *Proceedings of a Symposium on Environmental Studies in Jamaica, 25–26 May 1979*, pp. 193–200. University of the West Indies, Mona.

van Dobben, H. F., 1983. Changes in the epiphytic lichen flora and vegetation in the surroundings of s'-Hertogenbosch (The Netherlands) since 1900. *Nova Hedwigia* 37:691–719.

Domrös, M., 1966. Luftverunreinigung und Stadtklima im Rheinisch Westfälischen Industriegebiet und ihre Auswirkung auf den Flechtenbewuchs der Bäume. *Arb. rhein. Landesk.* 23:1–132.

Esseen, P. A., 1985. Litter fall of epiphytic macrolichens in two old *Picea abies* forests in Sweden. *Can. J. Bot.* 63:980–987.

Esseen, P. A., L. Ericson, H. Lindström, and O. Zackrisson, 1981. Occurrence and ecology of *Usnea longissima* in central Sweden. *Lichenologist* 13:177–190.

Eversman, S., 1978. Soil and epiphytic lichen communities of the Colstrip, Montana, area. In E. M. Preston and R. A. Lewis (Eds.), *The Bioenvironmental Impact of a Coal-fired Power Plant, Third Interim Report*, pp. 50–64. United States Environmental Protection Agency, Washington, D.C.

Eversman, S., 1982. Epiphytic lichens of a ponderosa pine forest in southeastern Montana. *Bryologist* 85:204–213.

Ferry, B. W., S. M. Baddeley, and D. L. Hawksworth (Eds.), 1973. *Air Pollution and Lichens.* University of London, Athlone Press, London.

Folkesson, L., 1984. Deterioration of the moss and lichen cover in a forest polluted by heavy metals. *Ambio* 13:37–40.

Follmann, G., 1973. Über den Rückgang den Flechtenflora in Stadtgebiet von Kassel (Nordhessen, Bundesrepublik Deutschland). *Philippia* 1:241–257.

Fritz-Sheridan, R. P., 1985. Impact of simulated acid rains on nitrogenase activity in *Peltigera aphthosa* and *P. polydactyla*. *Lichenologist* 17:27–31.

Gehu, J. M., M. Bon, C. Delzenne, and F. Rose, 1973. Essai de cartographie de la pollution atmosphérique dans le Nord de France en relation avec la toxisensibilité des lichens epiphytes. *C. R. Séanc. Acad. Sci.* 276:729–732.

Gerson, U., and M. R. D. Seaward, 1977. Lichen–invertebrate associations. In M. R. D. Seaward (Ed.), *Lichen Ecology*, pp. 69–119. Academic Press, London.

Gilbert, O. L., 1970. A biological scale for the estimation of sulphur dioxide pollution. *New Phytol.* 69:629–634.

Gilbert, O. L., 1971. Some indirect effects of air pollution on bark-living invertebrates. *J. Appl. Ecol.* 8:77–84.

Gilbert, O. L., 1973. The effect of airborne flourides. In B. W. Ferry, M. S. Baddeley and D. L. Hawksworth (Eds.), *Air Pollution and Lichens*, pp. 176–191. University of London, Athlone Press, London.

Gilbert, O. L., 1976. A new alkaline dust effect on epiphytic lichens. *Lichenologist* 8:173–178.

Gilbert, O. L., 1980. A lichen flora of Northumberland. *Lichenologist* 12:325–395.

Gilbert, O. L., 1986. Field evidence for an acid rain effect on lichens. *Environ. Poll.* A, 40:227–231.

Godfrey, P. J., D. L. Mulcahy, and K. Searay, 1985. Air pollution and lichens. *Univ. Mass. Pl. Ecol. Lab.* 421:62–75.

Hafellner, J., and D. Grill, 1981. Der Einfluss der Stillegung einer Zellstoffabrik auf die vegetation der Umgebung. *Phyton, Horn* 21:25–38.

Hanson, W. C., 1980. Transuranic elements in arctic tundra ecosystems. In W. C. Hanson (Ed.), *Transuranic Elements in the Environment*, pp. 441–458. National Technical Information Service, Springfield, Va.

Hanson, W. C., 1982. Cs^{137} concentrations in northern Alaska eskimos, 1962–79: effects of ecological, cultural, and political factors. *Hlth. Physics* 42:433–447.

Hawksworth, D. L., 1971. Lichens as litmus for air pollution: a historical review. *Int. J. Environ. Studies* 1:281–296.

Hawksworth, D. L., 1973. Mapping studies. In B. W. Ferry, M. S. Baddeley, and D. L. Hawksworth (Eds.), *Air Pollution and Lichens*, pp. 38–76. University of London, Athlone Press, London.

Hawksworth, D. L., 1975. The changing lichen flora of Leicestershire. *Trans Leicester. Lit. Phil. Soc.* 68:32–56.

Hawksworth, D. L., 1982. Secondary fungi in lichen symbioses: parasites, saprophytes, and parasymbionts. *J. Hattori bot. Lab.* 52:357–366.

Hawksworth, D. L., 1986. The natural history of Slapton Ley Nature Reserve XVII. Additions to and changes in the fungi (including lichens). *Fld Stud.* 6:365–382.

Hawksworth, D. L., 1988. The variety of fungal–algal symbiosis, their evolutionary significance, and the nature of lichens. *Bot. J. Linn. Soc.* 96:3–20.

Hawksworth, D. L., B. J. Coppins, and F. Rose, 1974. Changes in the British lichen flora. In D. L. Hawksworth (Ed.), *The Changing Flora and Fauna of Britain*, pp. 47–78. Academic Press, London.

Hawksworth, D. L., and D. J. Hill, 1984. *The Lichen-Forming Fungi*. Blackie and Son, Glasgow.

Hawksworth, D. L., and P. M. McManus, 1989a. Lichen recolonization in London under conditions of rapidly falling sulphur dioxide levels, and the concept of zone skipping. *Bot. J. Linn. Soc.* 100:99–109.

Hawksworth, D. L., and P. M. McManus, 1989b. Lichens that tell a tale. *Country Life* 183(44):144–145.

Hawksworth, D. L., and F. Rose, 1970. Qualitative scale for estimating sulphur dioxide air pollution in England and Wales using epiphytic lichens. *Nature, Lond.* 227:145–148.

Hawksworth, D. L., and F. Rose, 1976. *Lichens as Pollution Monitors.* Edward Arnold, London.

Hawksworth, D. L., F. Rose, and B. J. Coppins, 1973. Changes in the lichen flora of England and Wales attributable to pollution of the air by sulphur dioxide. In B. W. Ferry, M. S. Baddeley, and D. L. Hawksworth (Eds.), *Air Pollution and Lichens*, pp. 330-367. University of London, Athlone Press, London.

Hawksworth, D. L., and J. F. Skinner, 1974. The lichen flora and vegetation of Black Head, Ilsham, Torquay. *Trans. Torquay Nat. Hist. Soc.* 16:121–136.

Henderson-Sellers, A., and M. R. D. Seaward, 1979. Monitoring lichen reinvasion of ameliorating environments. *Environ. Pollut.* 19:207–213.

Herben, T., and J. Liška, 1986. A simulation study of the effect of flora composition, study design and index choice on the predictive power of lichen bioindication. *Lichenologist* 18:349–362.

Hill, D. J., 1971. Experimental study of the effect of sulphite on lichens with reference to atmospheric pollution. *New Phytol.* 70:831–836.

Hoffman, G. F., and A. A. Boe, 1977. Ecological study of epiphytic cryptogams on *Populus deltoides* in southeastern South Dakota and adjacent Minnesota. *Bryologist* 80:32–47.

Hoffman, G. R., 1974. The influence of a paper pulp mill on the ecological distribution of epiphytic cryptogams in the vicinity of Lewiston, Idaho, and Clarkston, Washington. *Environ. Pollut.* 7:283–301.

James, P. W., 1973. The effects of air pollutants other than hydrogen flouride and sulphur dioxide on lichens. In B. W. Ferry, M. S. Baddeley, and D. L. Hawksworth (Eds.), *Air Pollution and Lichens*, pp. 143–175. University of London, Athlone Press, London.

Johnsen, I., and U. Søchting, 1973. Air pollution influence upon the epiphytic lichen vegetation and bark properties of deciduous trees in the Copenhagen area. *Oikos* 24:344–351.

Johnson, D. W., 1979. Air pollution and the distribution of corticolous lichens in Seattle, Washington, USA. *NW Sci.* 53:257–263.

Jordan, C., F. Golley, J. Hall, and J. Hall, 1980. Nutrient scavenging of rainfall by the canopy of an Amazonian rain forest. *Biotropica* 12:61–66.

Jürging, P., 1975. Epiphytische Flechten als Bioindikatoren der Luftverunreinigung-dargestellt an Untersuchunger und Beobachtung in Bayern. *Bibliotheca Lich., Lehre* 4:1–164.

Jürging, P., and I. Burkhardt, 1979–80. *Bibliographie: Flechten und Luftverunreinigung.* 2 vols. Landschatsokölogie, Weihnstephan.

Kandler, O., and J. Poelt, 1984. Wiederbesiedlung der Innenstadt von München durch Flechten. *Naturwiss. Rundsch.* 37:90–95.

Kärenlampi, L. (Ed.), 1976. *Proceedings of the Kuopio meeting on Plant Damages caused by Air Pollution.* University of Kuopio and Kuopio Naturalists' Society, Kuopio.

Kauppi, M., 1979. The exploitation of *Cladonia stellaris* in Finland. *Lichenologist* 11:85–89.

Kershaw, K. A., 1985. *Physiological Ecology of Lichens.* Cambridge University Press.

60 D. L. HAWKSWORTH

Kirschbaum, U., 1972. Flechtenkartierungen in der Region Untermain zur Erfassung von Immissionsbelastungen. In L. Staubing, C. Kunze, and J. Jäger (Eds.), *Belastung und Belastbarkeit von Ökosystemem, Gesellschaft für ökologie, Giessen 1972*, pp. 133–170. Gesellschaft für Okologie, Giessen.

Kneiper, E. J., and M. A. Sherwood-Pike, 1985. The former and present lichen flora of the Boston metropolitan area. *Am. J. Bot.* 72:794.

Lawrey, J. D., and M. E. Hale, 1981. Retrospective study of lichen lead accumulation in the northeastern United States. *Bryologist* 84:449–456.

Laundon, J. R., 1970. London's lichens. *London Nat.* 49:20–69.

Laundon, J. R., 1973. Changes in the lichen flora of Bookham Commons with increased air pollution and other factors. *London Nat.* 52:82–92.

LeBlanc, F., and D. N. Rao, 1976. ["1975"] Effects of air pollutants on lichens and bryophytes. In J. B. Mudd and T. T. Kozlowski (Eds.), *Responses of Plants to Air Pollution*, pp. 237–272. Academic Press, New York.

LeBlanc, F., and J. DeSloover, 1970. Relation between industrialization and the distribution and growth of epiphytic lichens and mosses in Montreal. *Can. J. Bot.* 48:1485–1496.

LeBlanc, F., D. N. Rao, and G. Commeau, 1972. Indices of atmospheric purity and flouride pollution in Arvida, Quebec. *Can. J. Bot.* 50:991–998.

Lechowicz, M. J., 1982. The effect of simulated acid precipitation on photosynthesis in the caribou lichen *Cladonia stellaris* (Opiz) Brodo. *Water Air Soil Pollut.* 18:421–430.

Lee, T., and D. H. Vitt, 1973. A preliminary study of the effects of air pollution on lichen and bryophyte vegetation near Edmonton, Alberta. In D. Hocking and D. Reiter (Eds.), *Proceedings of a Workshop on Sulphur Gas Research in Alberta*, pp. 129–141. Environment Canada, Edmonton.

Lerond, M., 1980. Lichénogéographie de las Bassee Seine: application à la cartographie de la pollution atmosphérique. *Actes Mus. Rouen* 1980(3):35–69.

Lerond, M., 1981. Les lichens épiphytes en Normandie orientale. Distribution, sociologie et application à la cartographie de la pollution atmosphérique. *Actes Mus. Rouen* 1981(1):1–299.

Lerond, M., 1985. *La Qualité de l'Air en Haute-Normandie.* Centre de Documentation sur le Milieu Naturel, Rouen.

Lindsay, D. C., 1978. The lichens of the Lickey Hills. *Proc. Bgham. Nat. Hist. Soc.* 23:249–254.

Lindsay, D. C., 1980. Lichens. In M. C. Clark (Ed.), *A Fungus Flora of Warwickshire*, pp. 232–243. British Mycological Society, London.

Lindsay, D. C., 1982. Birmingham and Warwickshire lichens: new records. *Proc. Bgham. Nat. Hist. Soc.* 24:194–198.

Löfgren, O., and R. Moberg, 1984. Oceaniska lavar i Sverige och deras tillbakagång. *Naturvårdsverket Rapport* 1819:1–50.

Marsh, J. E., and T. H. Nash III, 1979. Lichens in relation to the Four Corners Power Plant in New Mexico. *Bryologist* 82:20–28.

Marti, J., 1985. Die Toxizatät Zink, Schwefel und Stickstoffverbindungen auf Flechtensymbionten. *Bibliotheca lich., Lehre* 21:1–128.

Mathis, P. M., and G. Tomlinson, 1972. Lichens: bioassay for air pollution in a metropolitan area (Nashville, Tennessee). *J. Tennessee Acad. Sci.* 47:67–73.

Maynard, D. G., P. A. Addison, and K. A. Kennedy, 1983. Impact of elemental sulphur dust deposition on soils and vegetation of *Pinus contorta* stands in west-central Alberta, Canada. *Aquila, ser. bot.,* 19:314–325.

Mickle, J. E., 1977. A comparison of cover and distribution of corticolous macro-epiphytes in three woodlots in and north of Columbus, Ohio. *Ohio J. Sci.* 77:146–148.

Moser, T. J., T. H. Nash III, and W. D. Clark, 1980. Effects of a long-term field sulfur dioxide fumigation on arctic caribou forage lichens. *Can. J. Bot.* 58:2235–2240.

Moser, T. J., T. H. Nash III, and A. G. Olafsen, 1983. Photosynthetic recovery in arctic caribou forage lichens following a long-term field sulphur dioxide fumigation. *Can. J. Bot.* 61:367–370.

Nash, T. H., III, 1974. Lichens of the Page environs as potential indicators of air pollution. *J. Arizona Acad. Sci.* 9:97–100.

Nash, T. H., III, 1975. Influence of effluents from a zinc factory on lichens. *Ecol. Monogr.* 45:183–198.

Nash, T. H., III, 1976. Sensitivity of lichens to nitrogen dioxide fumigations. *Bryologist* 79:103–106.

Nash, T. H., III, 1988. Correlating fumigation studies with field effects. *Bibliotheca Lich.* 30:201–216.

Nash, T. H., III, and L. L. Sigal, 1979. Gross photosynthetic response of lichens to short-term ozone fumigations. *Bryologist* 82:280–285.

Nash, T. H., III, and V. Wirth (Eds.), 1988. Lichens, bryophytes and air quality. *Bibliotheca Lich.* 30:1–297.

Newberry, G., 1975. ["1974"] The influence of a sulfate-process paper mill on corticolous lichens. *Bryologist* 77:561–576.

Nieber, E. and D. H. S. Richardson, 1981. Lichens as monitors of atmospheric deposition. In S. J. Eisenreich (Ed.), *Atmospheric Pollution in Natural Waters,* pp. 339–388. Ann Arbor Science, Ann Arbor.

Nieber, E., D. H. S. Richardson, and F. D. Tomassini, 1978. Mineral uptake and release by lichens: an overview. *Bryologist* 81:226–246.

Nylander, W., 1866. Les lichens du Jardin du Luxembourg. *Bull. Soc. bot. Fr.* 13:364–372.

Pike, L. H., 1978. The importance of epiphytic lichens in mineral cycling. *Bryologist* 81:247–257.

Pike, L. H., 1981. Estimation of lichen biomass and production with special reference to the use of ratios. In D. T. Wicklow and G. C. Carroll (Eds.), *The Fungal Community,* pp. 533–552. Marcel Dekker, New York and Basel.

Pišút, I., and J. Liška, 1985. Lisjiniky Slanskych Vrchov. *Zb. slov. nar. Muz. prir. ved.* 31:27–57.

Pope, C. R., 1985. A lichen flora of the Isle of Wight. *Proc. Isle of Wight Nat. Hist. Archaeol. Soc.* 7:577–599.

Puckett, K. J., and M. A. S. Burton, 1981. The effect of trace elements on lower plants. In N. W. Lepp (Ed.), *Effects of Heavy Metal Pollution on Plants:* Vol. 2. *Metals in the environment,* pp. 213–238. Applied Science Publishers, London.

Rabe, R., and H. Wiegel, 1985. Wiederbesiedlung des Ruhrgebietsdurch Flechten zeigt Verbesserung der Luftqualität an. *Staub-Reinhalt. Luft* 45:124–126.

Richardson, D. H. S., 1975. *The Vanishing Lichens.* David and Charles, Newton Abbot.

Richardson, D. H. S., and E. Nieber, 1983. The uptake of nickel ions by lichen thalli of the genera *Umbilicaria* and *Peltigera*. *Lichenologist* 15:81–88.

Richardson, D. H. S., and C. M. Young, 1977. Lichens and vertebrates. In M. R. D. Seaward (Ed.), *Lichen Ecology*, pp. 121–144. Academic Press, London.

Roberts, B. A., and L. K. Thompson, 1980. Lichens as indicators of fluoride emissions from a phosphorous plant, Long Harbour, Newfoundland, Canada. *Can. J. Bot.* 58:2218–2228.

Robitaille, G., F. LeBlanc, and D. N. Rao, 1977. Acid rain: a factor contributing to the paucity of epiphytic cryptogams in the vicinity of a copper smelter. *Revue bryol. lichén.* 43:53–66.

Rogers, R. W., 1977. The "city effect" on lichens in the Brisbane area. *Search* 8(3):75–77.

Rose, C. I., and D. L. Hawksworth, 1981. Lichen recolonization in London's cleaner air. *Nature, Lond.* 289:289–292.

Rose, F., 1976. Lichenological indicators of age and environmental continuity in woodlands. In D. H. Brown, D. L. Hawksworth, and R. H. Bailey (Eds.), *Lichenology: Progress and Problems*, pp. 239–307. Academic Press, London.

Rose, F., and P. W. James, 1974. Regional studies on the British lichen flora I. The corticolous and lignicolous species of the New Forest, Hampshire. *Lichenologist* 6:1–72.

Ross, L. J., and T. H. Nash III, 1983. Effect of ozone on gross photosynthesis of lichens. *Envir. Exp. Bot.* 23:71–77.

Schofield, E., 1975. Some considerations on the possible effect of local and global sources of air pollution on lichens grazed by reindeer and caribou. In J. R. Luicks et al. (Eds.), *Proceedings of the First International Reindeer and Caribou Symposium*, pp. 90–94. University of Alaska, Fairbanks.

Schofield, E., and W. L. Hamilton, 1970. Probable damage to tundra biota through sulphur dioxide destruction of lichens. *Biol. Conserv.* 2:278–280.

Scotter, G. W., 1964. Effects of forest fires on the winter-range of barren-ground caribou in northern Saskatchewan. *Can. Wildlife Serv., Wildlife Manag. Bull.* (ser. I), 18:1–109.

Seaward, M. R. D., 1975. Lichen flora of the West Yorkshire conurbation. *Proc. Leeds Phil. Lit. Soc.* (sci. sect.) 10:141–208.

Seaward, M. R. D., 1980. The use of lichens as bioindicators of ameliorating environments. In R. Schubert and J. Schuh (Eds.), *Bioindikation auf der Ebene der Individuen*, pp. 17–23. Martin-Luther Universität, Halle-Wittenberg.

Seaward, M. R. D., and A. Henderson, 1984. Lichen flora of the West Yorkshire conurbation (Supplement 3, 1981–1983). *Naturalist, Hull* 109:61–65.

Seaward, M. R. D., and C. J. B. Hitch, 1982. *Atlas of the Lichens of the British Isles*, Vol. 1. Natural Environment Research Council, Cambridge, U.K.

Sheridan, R. P., C. Sanderson, and R. Kerr, 1976. Effects of pulp mill emissions on lichens in the Missoula Valley, Montana. *Bryologist* 79:248–252.

Showman, R. E., 1975. Lichens as indicators of air quality around a coal-fired power generating plant. *Bryologist* 78:1–6.

Showman, R. E., 1981. Lichen recolonization following air quality improvement. *Bryologist* 84:492–497.

Sigal, L. L., 1984. Of lichens and lepidopterans. *Bryologist* 87:66–68.

Sigal, L. L., and T. H. Nash III, 1983. Lichen communities on conifers in southern Californian mountains: an ecological study relative to oxidant air pollution. *Ecology* 64:1343–1354.

Sigal, L. L., and O. C. Taylor, 1979. Preliminary studies of the gross photosynthetic response of lichens to peroxyacetylnitrate fumigations. *Bryologist* 82:564–575.

Skorepa, A. C., A. W. Norden, and D. R. Windler, 1979. Substrate ecology of lichens in Maryland. *Castanea* 44:124–142.

Skorepa, A. C., and D. H. Vitt, 1976. *A Quantitative Study of Epiphytic Lichen Vegetation in relation to SO₂ Pollution in Western Alberta.* Environment Canada, Edmonton.

Skye, E, 1958. Luftförenigfars inverkan på busk-och bladlavfloran Kring skifferoljeverket i Närkes Kvarntorp. *Svensk bot. Tidskr.* 52:133–190.

Skye, E., 1979. Lichens as biological indicators of air pollution. *Ann. Rev. Phytopath.* 17:325–341.

Sowter, F. A., and D. L. Hawksworth, 1970. Leicestershire and Rutland cryptogamic notes I. *Trans. Leicester Lit. Phil. Soc.* 64:89–100.

Stephenson, W. R., and H. G. Merriam, 1975. Some effects of urban impact on the structure of lichen communities on trees in three deciduous woodlot types. *Urban Ecol.* 1:311–323.

Steubing, L., 1981. Ausweisung von Zonen unterschiedlicher Immissionsbelastung mittels Bioindikatoren. *Verh. Ges. Ökologie* 9:223–240.

Stringer, P. W., and M. H. L. Stringer, 1974. Air pollution and the distribution of epiphytic lichens and bryophytes in Winnipeg, Manitoba. *Bryologist* 77:405–426.

Sugiyama, K., S. Kurokawa, and G. Okada, 1976. Studies on lichens as a bioindicator of air pollution. Correlation of distribution of *Parmelia tinctorum* with SO₂ air pollution. *Jap. J. Ecol.* 26:209–212.

Taoda, H., 1980. Mapping of air pollution based on epiphytic cryptogams in Bay-Coast cities of Chiba Prefecture. In M. Numata (Ed.), *Integrated Ecological Studies in Bay Coast Cities*, pp. 1, 21–25. Chiba University, Chiba, Japan.

Taylor, R. J., 1978. Industrial impact in northwestern Whatcom County, Washington. *Water Air Soil Pollut.* 10:199–214.

Thomson, J. W., 1972. Distribution patterns of American arctic lichens. *Can. J. Bot.* 50:1135–1156.

Thrower, S. L., 1980. Air pollution and lichens in Hong Kong. *Lichenologist* 12:305–311.

Troppmair, H., 1977. Estudo biogeografico de liquens como vegetais indicadores de poluicão aerea da cidade de Campinas-SP. *Geografia* 2(4):1–38.

Türk, R., 1975. Die Veränderung der Flechtenzonen und der Luftqualität im Stadtgebiet Salzburg von den Jahren 1948/49 bis 1974/75. In E. Stuber (Ed.), *Studien über die unwelthygienisch-ökologische Situation der Stadt Salzburg*, pp. 131–135. Bundesministerium für Gesundheit und Umweltschutz, Salzburg.

Türk, R., V. Wirth, and O. L. Lange, 1974. CO₂– Gaswechsel-Untersuchungen zur SO₂ Resoteiz von Flechten. *Oecologia* 15:33–64.

Türk, R., and H. Wittmann, 1984. Atlas der aktuellen Verbreitung von Flechten in Öberosterreich. *Stapfia* 11:1–98.

Turner, D., and W. Borrer, 1839. *Specimen of a Lichenographia Britannica.* Privately printed, Yarmouth.

Vareschi, V., and E. Moreno, 1973. La contaminación en Caracas en los años 1953 y 1973. *Boln. Soc. Venez. Cienc. Nat.* 30:387–444.

Vowinckel, E., and S. Orvig, 1976). Experiments with surface heat and water budgets of the Canadian Middle North. *Tellus* 28:442–450.

Westman, L., 1975. Air pollution and vegetation around a sulphite mill at Ornskoldsvik, north Sweden. *Wahlenbergia* 2:1–146.

Wetmore, C. M., 1981. Lichens and air quality in Big Bend National Park, Texas. *Bryologist* 84:426–434.

Will-Wolfe, S., 1980. Structure of corticolous lichen communities before and after exposure to emissions from a "clean" coal-fired generating station. *Bryologist* 83:281–295.

Wirth, V., 1985. Zur Ausbreitung, Herkunft und Ökologie anthropogen geförderter Rinden-und Holzflechten. *Tuexenia* 5:523–535.

de Wit, T., 1976. Epiphytic lichens and air pollution in the Netherlands. *Bibliotheca lich., Lehre* 5:1–227.

Zanette, V. C., L. W. Aguiar, L. Martau, J. E. de A. Mariath, and H. Osorio, 1981. Estudo fitosociologica de liquens suma area localizada nos Municipos de Montenegro e Triunfo, Rio Grande de Sul, Brasil. *Iheringia* 28:107–140.

Züst, S., 1977. Die Epiphytenvegetation im Raume Zürich als Indikator den Umweltbelastung. *Veröff. geobot. Inst. Zürich* 62:1–113.

5   Biotic Impoverishment in Northern Peatlands

EVILLE GORHAM

Editor's Note: Bogs and peat and acid waters are commonly thought to be of the higher, cooler latitudes, not tropical. But peatlands and acid waters occur around the world. The traveler in the Amazon Basin, for instance, until recently restricted to its rivers, found a new world in the transition from the silt-laden water of the main stem of the Amazon or the Solimoes to the black, acid water of the Rio Negro. The traveler is blessed there with an abrupt relief from insect pests: I have slept comfortably, without screens or mosquito netting, 60 miles above Manaus in the magnificent riverine bog-swamp known by the lyrically liquid name Anavilhanas. The black water is the drainage from bog soils, extensive in that part of the basin, and supports an extraordinary fauna of herbivorous and seed-eating fishes that graze in the rich varzea forests, flooded annually to a depth of 30–50 feet in many places.

    The fact is that peatlands are widespread around the world, apparently the product of a biotically caused acidification of moist habitats that are low in nutrients. Their plant and animal communities are at once impoverished by comparison with other sites that are rich in nutrients and less acid, and yet the bogs are rich in fascinating endemics such as the seed-eating fishes of the Rio Negro. The habitat is ancient, common, widespread, important, still evolving, sometimes thought to be the product of a regressive series of changes that reduces tree growth and leads otherwise to impoverishment. The bogs of the high latitudes date in many instances from glacial times and their peat remains continuously frozen. In some circumstances the peat has been frozen long enough that the drainage pattern has developed around large patches of peat which are now elevated and frozen. A climatic warming, expected in the Arctic to be in winter more than two times the global average, may melt such deposits and speed their decay. What are the transitions under way in the northern peatlands? What is likely for the future?

    Eville Gorham, a long-time student of terrestrial and aquatic ecosystems and their responses to disturbance, has summarized the current status of the northern bog lands and the questions that arise as chronic disturbances, including the global climatic changes now under way, accumulate.

Introduction

Peatlands are predominantly northern ecosystems (Gore 1983a,b) that, since deglaciation, have developed into unique organic landforms with hydrological, biogeochemical, and biological links to both upland and

65

aquatic ecosystems. Forested peatlands are a source of wood. All types of peatland can be drained and managed for forestry and agriculture or they can be exploited destructively as a source of raw material for horticulture, home heating, power generation, and the chemical industry.

Distribution and Abundance of Peatlands and Peat

The total area of the world's peatlands (>30 cm deep) exceeds 420 million hectares (ha) and probably approaches or exceeds 500 million ha (Kivinen and Pakarinen 1980; Sjörs 1980a), about 3.8% of the world's ice-free land area. It is estimated that 384 million ha, or approximately three-quarters of the total, are in northern countries, predominantly Canada and the Soviet Union (Table 5.1).

The total amount of carbon originally present in northern peatlands is estimated to be 180–277 Gigatons (1 Gt = 10^{15} g), about 10–16% of terrestrial detrital carbon (Table 5.2). Prior to human exploitation, which

Table 5.1. *Areas of peatlands – total, drained, reclaimed, and protected – in northern countries*

Country	Total original area (10^6 ha)	Drained (%)	Protected (%)	Area used for peat production (10^3 ha)	Utilization rate Agriculture (10^3 ha/a)	Utilization rate Forestry (10^3 ha/a)
Canada	170	1	nd	8	40[b]	negligible[b]
USSR	150	9	0.9	4350	38	250
USA (Alaska)	30	nd	nd	nd	nd	nd
USA (N)[a]	6.8	10	nd	nd	nd	nd
Finland	10.4	58	2.0	20	0.1	155
Sweden	7.0	17	2.1	10	1.0	20
Norway	3.0	17	0.1	2	3.0	3
Gt. Britain	1.58	70	nd	3	10	24
Poland	1.35	94	0.4	5	4.5	15
Ireland	1.18	47	1.1	53	0.5	6
W. Germany	1.11	91	3.1	38	0	0
Iceland	1.0	nd	nd	nd	nd	nd
E. Germany	0.55	98	1.8	0.4	8.0	nd
Netherlands	0.25	(most)	nd	nd	nd	nd
Denmark	0.12	97	0.004	nd	1.0	0
TOTAL	384	7.4				

[a] Minnesota, Wisconsin, Michigan, New York, Maine, Massachusetts, New Hampshire, Connecticut, New Jersey
[b] Zoltai and Pollett (1983)
Source: Reprinted from Kivinen 1980, Kivinen and Pakarinen 1980, with permission of the publisher.

Table 5.2. *A comparison of carbon pools and fluxes in peatlands (before human exploitation) with other important pools and fluxes*

Pools		Gt (10^{15}g)
	Preindustrial	560–615
Atmosphere[a]	1980	712
	Living Plants[a]	560–830
Terrestrial biomass	Dead plant material[a]	1,750
	Northern peatlands[b]	180–277
Fluxes		Gt a^{-1}
Net primary production	All land plants[a]	53
	Northern peatlands	1.18
Peat accumulation rate	plants[c]	0.091
Fossil fuel emissions to the atmosphere	Northern peatlands[d]	5.2
	1980[a]	

[a] Bolin et al. (1983)

[b] Peatland area (3.84×10^{12} m^2) $\times$ two estimats of avg. thickness of peat (1.13 and 1.74m) $\times$ avg. bulk density (78400 g/m^3) $\times$ avg. fraction of C in peat (0.528). Average peat thickness is estimated from two sets of data that probably span the true value. According to Lappalainen (1980), the total volume of peat in Finland is 100–120 (avg. 110) $\times 10^9$ m,^{3} whereas the area of peatland is 97.4 $\times 10^9$ m^2, hence an average depth of 1.13 m. For Canada, Boville et al. (1983) estimate a total volume of 1,833 $\times 10^9$ m^3 and an area of 1,052 $\times 10^9$ m^2, hence mean depth of 1.74 m. Bulk density is the average for peat cores (top to bottom) from 17 bogs from southern Manitoba and northern Minnesota through Ontario, Quebec, and Maine to the Atlantic Provinces and Labrador (E. Gorham, unpublished). The fraction of C in dry peat (at 65°C) is that of 276 samples in peat cores (top to bottom) from 5 of the above 17 bogs.

[c] Above-ground NPP is taken as the average of 23 bog and wet tundra sites tabulated by Bradbury and Grace (1984) plus 6 bogs investigated by Grigal (1985b, Grigal, Buttleman, and Kernick 1985). Below-ground NPP is estimated by multiplying average above-ground NPP by the average *below/above* quotient for 8 sites tabulated by Bradbury and Grace (1983), who point out that below-ground data involve possibly invalid assumptions.

[d] Peatland area (3.84×10^{12} m^2) $\times$ avg. vertical peat accumulation rate (0.000575 m/a) $\times$ avg. bulk density (78,400 g/m^3) $\times$ avg. fraction of C in peat (0.528). Average vertical peat accumulation rate represents top-to-bottom data compiled by the author (from the literature and unpublished data) for 35 peatlands across Canada, and is similar to that of 37 British fen and bog peat samples from different levels at 18 sites in Britain (Walker 1970). Note that northern peatland biomass (180–277 Gt) divided by the average accumulation rate (0.091 Gt/a) yields an average age for peat deposits of 1,980–3,040 years, which seems reasonable in the light of Zoltai and Pollett's (1983) statement that although in eastern Canada peat began to form soon after the ice retreat, basal peat deposits (usually sampled near the deepest point) in northern Ontario and Manitoba are mostly less than 5,000 years old; most of those in northern Minnesota are of similar age (E. Gorham, unpublished data).

has led to drainage of about 7.4% of the total area (Table 5.1), annual peat accumulation of 0.091 Gt would have accounted for about 7.7% of annual net primary production by northern peatland plants, which, in turn, accounted for a little more than 2% of total terrestrial production. Peat

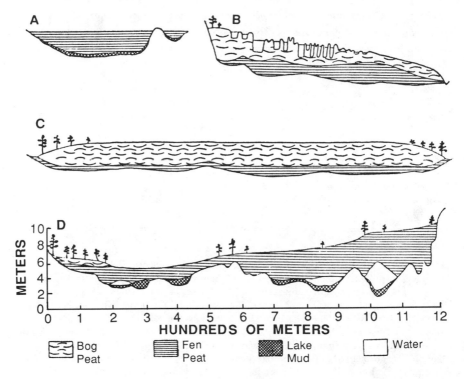

Figure 5.1. Profiles through peatlands in Sweden (vertical scale greatly exaggerated). a – classic raised bog with narrow marginal fen (*lagg*); b – sloping bog with pools; c – fen in filled-in lake, d – sloping fen with small bog, illustrating paludification outward from small filled-in lakes. (Reprinted from Sjörs 1953, with permission.)

accumulation each year tied up an amount of carbon a little less than 2% of that presently emitted to the atmosphere by combustion of fossil fuels.

The carbon total estimated above compares reasonably well with the estimate by Sjörs (1980a) of 300 Gt for the world's peat deposits, and by Armentano and Menges (1986) of 249 Gt (to 1m depth) for peatlands of the north temperate zone. Sjörs estimates the world's annual accumulation of peat at about 0.090 Gt; according to Silvola (1986) it is 0.110 Gt. Armentano and Menges estimate 0.075 Gt for the north temperate zone if all peatlands are active, 0.050 Gt if sizable areas have ceased accumulation.

Development of Northern Peatlands

Peatland can arise in two major ways (Figure 5.1) (after Sjörs 1953). One is filling in of shallow ponds and lakes due to overgrowth by floating mats of vegetation, which may be initiated or enhanced by the stream-damming activities of beaver. This process is still visible in many small ice-block lakes formed during glacial retreat and may have served as a focus for the more widespread process of paludification or swamping of upland mineral soils. Paludified peatlands developed early on freshly deglaciated, moist mineral soils and later swamped vast areas of upland forest. According to Sjörs (1983; see also Malmström 1931), peatland development is presently not very active, at least in Fennoscandia. On the other hand, Neishstadt's data (1977) suggest a fairly steady rate of expansion (about 107 km^2/a) in the world's largest peat basin throughout the last 7,000 years, after about 3–5,000 years of very slow paludification. Peat now covers at least 786,000 km^2 in West Siberia. In the James Bay Lowland of Canada (Figure 5.2), isostatic uplift has created vast areas of peatland that exhibit a striking successional sequence separated by a series of beach ridges. It ranges from freshwater marsh in areas that have emerged recently from the sea to sedge fen to wooded fen to paludified bog forest and finally to open bog in those areas that emerged earliest (Wickware, Cowell, and Sims 1980; Pala and Weischet 1982; see also Mölder and Salmi 1955).

The major characteristic of peatland development is longterm buildup of waterlogged anaerobic deposits of plant detritus that are highly organic, often well above 90% dry weight, and very wet with water usually 90–97% of volume below the water table (Clymo 1983). As organic matter increases so does cation-exchange capacity, which is saturated predominantly by base cations, especially Ca^{2+} and Mg^{2+}. This occurs as long as the peatland surface receives water that has percolated through mineral soil and is rich in bicarbonate anions. Such a peatland is said to be minerotrophic and is described as a rich fen, referring to the diversity of its flora. Fen waters are generally circumneutral to moderately acid. When the peat deposit has become sufficiently large, and is raised or domed slightly above the groundwater table, so as to be isolated from minerotrophic inputs to its surface, it is said to be ombrotrophic and is described as a bog. Bogs are strongly acid, usually below pH 4.6. Transitional areas that are boglike, but still contain a few plant species restricted to weakly minerotrophic conditions, are described as poor fens. Bogs are thus a product of autogenic succession, during which earlier plant communities deposit peat so as eventually to destroy the conditions under which they became established, and prepare the way for new colonists of succeeding communities.

The transition from fen to bog peat comes as the mineral ash content falls below about 15% dry weight; ombrotrophic bog peats commonly exhibit ash contents as low as 1–5% dry weight. The cation-exchange capacity of such bog peats is high. In the absence of minerotrophic base supply it is

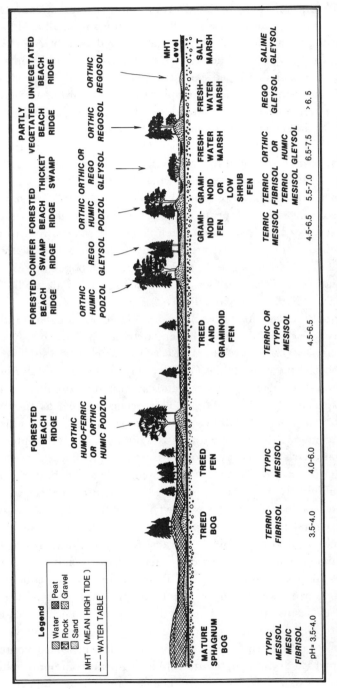

Figure 5.2. Idealized (composite) cross-section through coastal areas of southern James Bay, Canada. (Reprinted with modifications from Wickware et al. 1980, with permission.)

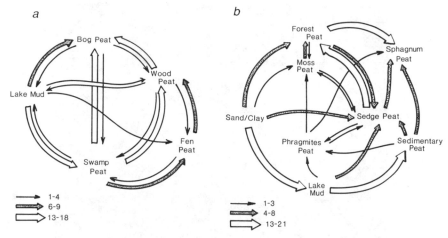

Figure 5.3. Common directions in peatland succession, revealed by stratigraphic analyses of peat cores in (a) the British Isles and (b) North America. Width of arrow represents number of cases (after Walker 1970 and Tallis 1983).

predominantly saturated by H^+ ions (Gorham 1953a, 1967; Sjörs 1961). The growth of the bog moss Sphagnum is a major generator of such H^+ ions (Clymo 1963). Generally pH is in the range 3.6–4.5, owing partly to cation-exchange processes (Clymo 1987), but more importantly to the production of colored organic acids during plant decomposition (Gorham et al. 1985; Urban, Eisenreich, and Gorham 1987a). These are dominated by fulvic and, to a lesser degree, humic acids of high molecular weight (McKnight et al. 1985). As rich fens develop through transitional poor fens into bogs, the alteration of peat and water chemistry is paralleled by changes in plant communities (Figure 5.3) that are reflected in peat stratigraphy. In Britain, reed swamp communities dominated by tall reeds such as *Phragmites australis* give way to sedge or willow/alder communities, which, in turn, may become open Sphagnum bog. In North America a more common sequence is from fen communities dominated by sedges, often present as floating mats, to wooded tamarack fens that are invaded by sphagnum mosses and gradually converted into poor fens. If the climate is sufficiently moist and the basin is large enough, these ultimately become wholly ombrotrophic, Sphagnum-dominated bogs. Such bogs are usually open in maritime regions and heavily forested by black spruce in continental regions (Glaser and Janssens 1986). The transition from fen to poor fen and from poor fen to bog is believed to be quite rapid – on the scale of decades to a few centuries (Gorham, Janssens, Wheeler, and Glaser 1987; Janssens and Gorham, unpublished data).

Figure 5.4. Large paludified patterned peatlands: (a) Central area of Red Lake
Peatland, northern Minnesota, occupying low areas of the Glacial Lake Agassiz
plain. At the center (1) is a group of ovoid, forested bog "islands," some with open
centers, separated by narrow, north-flowing fen water tracks. To the south of them
(2) is a curvilinear crested bog that runs east/west. At left (3) is a broad, east-flowing
fen water track that bifurcates northward and southward around the central bog
complex; it contains small elongated tamarack "islands" (dark on the photo). The
photo (reprinted with permission from MARKHURD Aerial Surveys, Inc.,
BRA-1237, 5-22-69) shows an area approximately 19 km across; note ditches on 1-,
2- or 3-mile grids).

Landforms

Large peatlands exhibit unique landform patterns (Heinselman 1963, 1970;
Glaser et al. 1981; Pala and Weischet 1982; Botch and Masing 1983;
Ruuhijarvi 1983; Sjörs 1983; Zoltai and Pollett 1983). Examples are shown in
Figure 5.4. Fen water tracks dominated by sedges are often characterized by
an anastomosing ridge-and-trough network oriented perpendicularly to the
direction of water flow, with ericaceous shrubs and sometimes bog birch
abundant on the ridges. In North America such water tracks may have
tamarack "islands" elongated parallel to the direction of water flow, with

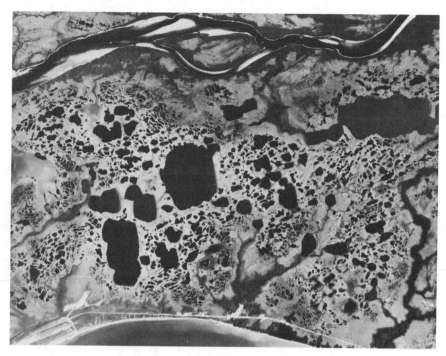

(b) Unforested bogs and marginal fens with numerous large pools at Havre St. Pierre, Quebec, at the edge of the St. Lawrence River. The photograph (reprinted with permission: part of photo no. A 244511-155, © July 23, 1976, Her Majesty the Queen in Right of Canada, reproduced from the collection to the National Air Photo Library with permission of Energy, Mines, and Resources, Canada) shows an area approximately 12 km across.

heads rounded upstream and tails pointed downstream. Bogs likewise exhibit complex structure. In maritime regions they are often centrally or excentrically domed, with a circular or subcircular pattern of connected ridges enclosing elongated troughs that are usually water-filled pools. In midcontinental North America bogs may occur as linear, crested ridges along which fingerlike forested ridges are oriented downslope, or as large, ovoid "islands" pointed slightly downstream and separated by narrow fen water tracks. Some "islands" are forested on the margin and open internally; others have an internal ridge-radiate pattern of forest and a more open margin (Glaser et al. 1981; Glaser and Janssens 1986). All of these complex patterns reflect the most delicate interaction between hydrology and vegetation in which hydrology controls the initial stages of peatland formation but is, in turn, altered profoundly by the accumulation of peat and the nature of the vegetation that deposits it.

Importance of Peatlands in Their Natural State

Peatlands are important for two reasons. First, they are unique ecosystems with distinct roles in the biology and geochemistry of the planet. Second, they are linked inextricably to both upland or upstream and especially to aquatic or downstream ecosystems in a variety of ways important to the functioning of all ecosystems.

Uniqueness of Peatland Ecosystems

Peatlands are unique in three respects. First, they have their own floras and faunas (Gore 1983a,b) that are largely, though not entirely, distinct from those of upland and aquatic ecosystems and include many rare and unusual organisms. Carnivorous plants (Drosera, Sarracenia) are among the most unusual. The bog moss Sphagnum is also an unusual plant with its network of porous, empty hyaline cells (Clymo and Hayward 1982). Second, the habitat requirements of peatland floras – waterlogged substrates that become anoxic a little below the water table once organic matter begins to accumulate – result in the buildup of organic deposits to a thickness two orders of magnitude greater than is characteristic, for example, of upland coniferous forests on well-drained soils. Third, peat buildup sequesters large amounts of the biophilic elements C, H, O, N, and to a lesser extent S and P, from their normal biogeochemical cycles for thousands of years.

Links to Other Ecosystems

Anoxia favors the emission to the atmosphere of volatile reduced forms of the biophilic elements C, N, and S, notably of the "greenhouse" gas methane (Harriss et al. 1985), which are transported to other ecosystems. Once bogs have formed, they export large amounts of complex, colored organic acids to outflow streams and lakes (Gorham et al. 1986; Urban, Eisenreich, and Gorham 1987a). These aquatic ecosystems, if they occupy soils and rocks of low base status (e.g., granites and quartzites), can by this means become strongly acidified and probably more susceptible to the ill effects of acid deposition (Gorham et al. 1987). The organic acids exported by bogs complex large amounts of trace metals, for example iron and aluminum, maintaining them in solution where otherwise they would be deposited as hydroxides in bottom sediments. Organic forms of nitrogen and sulfur also are exported in considerable quantity to downstream ecosystems.

The animals and plants of peatlands may have links to other ecosystems. Birds use them as residents and on migration (Warner and Wells 1980). Moose, deer, caribou, and reindeer inhabit them some of the time, as do beaver. Some peatland plants also occur on upland soils, notably black spruce, northern white cedar, and ericaceous heaths. Because peatlands are often resistant to the spread of fire, they may become refuges for the recolonization of burned or cut-over uplands after fire, as recognized long ago by Smith (1835; see Gorham 1955).

Human Uses for Peatlands

Peatlands have value for humanity not only as a resource to be exploited, but also as a resource to be conserved.

Values in the Natural Condition

Natural peatlands have a variety of values (Greeson, Clark, and Clark 1979; Richardson 1981). They retard stream flow and reduce flood peaks, although less than has commonly been thought (Ingram 1983). They take an important part in global chemical cycles and sequester large amounts of biophilic elements (C, N, S) from such cycles for long periods of time. As a substantial sink for atmospheric carbon, but one that can readily become an appreciable source through extensive drainage and the use of peat as a fossil fuel, peatlands are ecosystems of interest to students of the carbon cycle and its role in the atmospheric greenhouse effect (Armentano 1980; Armentano and Menges 1986). Surface peats immobilize chlorinated organic compounds of high molecular weight (DDT, PCBs, toxaphene, etc.) deposited from the atmosphere and prevent them from contaminating other ecosystems (Rapaport 1985; Rapaport and Eisenreich 1986).

Northern peatlands have long been a resource for hunters of resident or transient large mammals such as European elk, reindeer, moose, and caribou. More recently they have become valued for their aesthetic appeal and for nature study. Urban wetlands, including peatlands, are often the most "natural" ecosystems in urban areas. Boardwalks through them can enhance public appreciation of their unique nature and value.

In their natural state, peatlands are fascinating objects for scientific study, in view of their unique biota, landforms, hydrology, biogeochemistry, and patterns of development (Gorham 1982, 1986). Like lakes, peatlands record their own history in considerable detail. The macro- and microfossils preserved in peat deposits (Figure 5.5), together with their record of chemical change, provide us with a fascinating picture of vegetational succession linked to chemical changes within and beyond the peatland (see Birks and Birks 1980). Recently peat cores have provided a valuable record of changing trends of DDT deposition from the atmosphere (Rapaport et al. 1985). The linkages to other ecosystems are of scientific interest (Gorham et al. 1986). Unfortunately, the study of peatlands has lagged behind

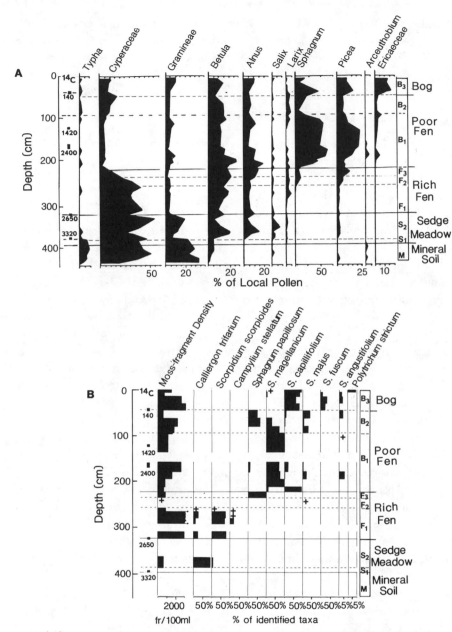

Figure 5.5. Stratigraphic succession of plant fossils in a peat core (R 8112) from a bog in the Red Lake Peatland of northern Minnesota. Pollen counts (a) are as % of local pollen (excluding *Sphagum* spores). Bryophyte counts (b) are as % of the sum of identified species.

investigation of forests, prairies, streams, and lakes. Our knowledge is fragmentary and imprecise in many respects, and has not, as yet, contributed greatly to ecosystem theory (see, however, Gorham 1953b; Heinselman 1970; Sjörs 1980b).

Peatlands can have military significance. In Napoleon's Russian campaign of 1812 the extensive peatlands of the Polesie Basin, known as the Pripet Marshes, divided the theater of operations into two fronts, the northern front being chosen for the major offensive (Chandler 1966, pp. 759–760). Today the trafficability of peatlands is of interest to the military (Dickson and Leger 1962; Harwood 1963) and to others wishing to exploit northern ecosystems, as indicated by numerous papers in the Proceedings of the Muskeg Research Conferences in Canada, published as Technical Memoranda of the Canadian National Research Council's Associate Committee on Soil and Snow Mechanics (until No. 10 in 1965) and Associate Committee on Geotechnical Research (No. 11 onward). Environmental considerations of transportation systems, pipeline building, and waste disposal are considered by Radforth and Burwash (1977), Meeres (1977), and Fee, Lawrence, and Moffat (1977), respectively.

Human Exploitation

The major uses for peatlands (Table 5.1) are for the production of fuel and horticultural peat, and, following drainage, for forestry and agriculture. Natural peatlands represent a major forest resource in Canada (Zoltai and Pollett 1983), and probably in the Soviet Union. The Soviet Union is by far the largest exploiter of peatland on a total-area basis, with about 9% of its 150 million ha drained. According to Kivinen (1980) the annual production of fuel peat was about 100 million metric tons in the late 1970s, whereas production of agricultural and horticultural peat was about 300 million m^3. In striking contrast, Botch and Masing (1983) estimated annual production of fuel peat as 60–65 million metric tons and decreasing, and agricultural and horticultural peat as 140 million tons. Drainage for forestry is important in the Soviet Union, but less so for agriculture. Canada has slightly more peatland than the Soviet Union but uses very little of it.

Countries with smaller areas of peatland have exploited more of it on a proportional basis (Table 5.1). Finland, for example, has drained about 58% of its 10.4 million ha, mainly for forestry. Great Britain has drained 70% of its 1.58 million ha, for forestry and agriculture. Poland, East Germany, West Germany, and Denmark, all with lesser areas of peatland, have drained more than 90%.

Minor uses for peat include the production of metallurgical coke, activated carbon, ethyl alcohol, hydroxy acids, furfural, waxes, bitumens, oil, and so on. (Botch and Masing 1983), and the advanced treatment of sewage wastewater (U.S. Environmental Protection Agency 1984). Many small urban peatlands have been filled in and destroyed.

Overall, about 28 million ha of northern peatlands (7.4%) have been drained (Table 5.1). For comparison, estimates of the current rate of tropical forest clearance (Brown et al. 1986) are 11 million ha (0.6%) *annually*.

Aspects of Biotic Impoverishment in Peatlands

Biotic impoverishment of an ecosystem can include a variety of processes, such as changes in species composition, particularly when they involve loss of species richness and diversity, alteration and loss of structure or function, and destabilization of interactions with other ecosystems in the biosphere. In all of these processes impoverishment can be a consequence of both natural and anthropogenic change although the latter often brings more severe effects.

Natural Aspects of Biotic Impoverishment

As an example of natural change in species diversity, the successional conversion of minerotrophic fen to ombrotrophic bog often entails a substantial loss of plant species from peatlands. Wheeler et al. (1983) list only 23 species of vascular plants in continental ombrotrophic bogs of Minnesota's Red Lake Peatland in comparison to 195 in poor and rich fens. Janssens and Glaser (1986) record 34 species of bryophytes from bogs and 81 from fens in the same peatland. Species density, the number of species per unit area, also declines as rich fens give way to poor fens and ultimately to bogs. Fen plots (10 x 10 m) in northern Minnesota normally contain 12–26 vascular taxa, whereas bog plots commonly contain 7–14 taxa (Gorham et al. 1987). Sites transitional from fen to bog, which are local in their extent and probably liable to change within decades to a few centuries (Gorham et al. 1987), contain some of the rarest plants (Figure 5.6) in Minnesota peatlands – *Juncus stygius* var. *americanus*, *Xyris montana*, and *Rhynchospora fusca*. These will disappear as sites lose weak minerotrophic inputs and become wholly ombrotrophic bogs. Whether they will colonize other transitional sites rapidly enough to maintain their presence in Minnesota depends upon the rate of natural change and on the degree of human disturbance.

Geochemical cycling within peatlands, and from them to other ecosystems, may be greatly affected by successional change. Because they receive minerotrophic inputs of plant nutrients from adjoining uplands, reed swamps and rich fens are usually more productive than ombrotrophic bogs.

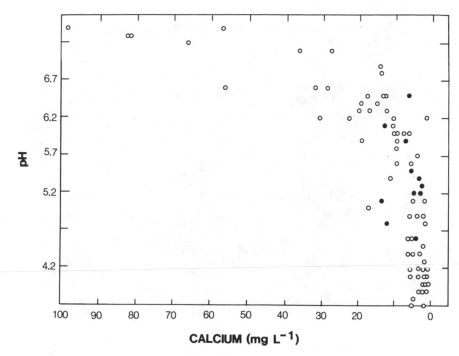

Figure 5.6. The occurrence of three rare species – *Juncus stygius* var. *americanus* (n = 5), *Xyris montana* (n = 4), and *Rhynchospora fusca* (n = 6) – in eleven sites along a minerotrophic/ombrotrophic gradient of calcium and pH in the surface waters of peatlands in northern Minnesota.

Median above-ground productivity in marshes, swamps, and fens is about 770 g/m²/a, compared to about 300 g/m²/a in bogs and wet tundra; below-ground figures are about 500 and 300 g/m²/a, respectively (Bradbury and Grace 1983). In both cases the distribution of productivity values is distinctly skewed toward low numbers. Fen peats are usually richer than bog peats in such elements as calcium, magnesium, iron, aluminum, and phosphorus, owing to minerotrophic inputs of lithophilic elements. Because rates of peat accumulation are not greatly different (Walker 1970; Gorham, unpublished data) fens will sequester larger amounts of these elements in the peat than will bogs. Verry (1975) has observed a substantially greater annual concentration, weighted for streamflow, of several elements (Si, Ca, Mg, Na) in the outflow from groundwater fens than from perched bogs in Minnesota. One element, Al, was more concentrated in the acid bog outflow, perhaps being stabilized in solution by higher concentrations of colored organic acids.

Fire is important for peatlands in their natural state. According to Wheeler

Figure 5.7. Deep irregular gully erosion of blanket bog on a gently sloping convex interfluve at Moor House in the Pennine Mountains of northern England. (Photo dated August 1, 1957, by Dr. St. Joseph, British Crown Copyright/RAF Photograph. Reproduced by permission of the Controller of Her Britannic Majesty's Stationery Office.)

et al. (1983), bogs in northern Minnesota exhibiting fire scars are characterized by a dense growth of ericaceous shrubs, whereas the normally abundant sedges, *Carex trisperma* in wooded bogs and *Carex oligosperma* in open bogs, are greatly reduced or absent.

Another aspect of successional change involves the erosion of bog peats, at least in mountainous terrain, as a natural consequence of their development. Although erosion has probably been greatly accelerated by human activity in the montane blanket bogs of Great Britain (Figure 5.7) and Ireland, it may well be the natural outcome of peat accumulation in wet climates (Kulczynski 1949; Ivanov 1981; Taylor 1983; Comeau and Beil 1984). Bog slides and bog bursts are extreme, dramatic examples of erosion, of which there are numerous historic and recent accounts (Gorham 1953b; Taylor 1983). They severely alter not only the bog but the downslope ecosystems over which peat is spread.

Climatic change may bring about loss of peatland functions. According to

Zoltai and Pollett (1983) there has been little peat accumulation for a long time in many northern Canadian peatlands owing to a lowering of temperature and the development of permafrost.

Biotic Impoverishment Directly Owing to Human Exploitation

Changes in the abundance and the diversity of plants and animals in peatlands may be slight if the disturbance is minor. Recent winter powerline construction across a very large peatland in northern Minnesota, for example, created almost no change in the open fen right-of-way. Distinct changes in wooded and shrub bog right-of-ways were recovering after a single growing season (Grigal 1985a). The bulk density of the peat in the right-of-way was only slightly affected by construction (Grigal 1983). Lumbering of forested bogs can alter peatlands to a greater degree, sometimes with a more or less natural end point, by reducing evapotrans- piration, increasing surface moisture, and accelerating the growth of sphagnum mosses (Kulczynski 1949).

Grazing, with tree felling but without drainage, can have a marked influence upon the plant communities of bogs. Kulczynski (1949) describes a case in the Polesie Basin of eastern Europe in which the original vegetation was replaced almost everywhere by a dense growth of the cotton grass (*Eriophorum vaginatum*) with occasional fen plants (e.g., *Calla palustris*) invading as a result of nitrogen manuring.

The effects of drainage, even when slight and without exploitation of the peatland, can be pronounced locally. A north-south highway built across a major, westward-flowing fen water track in the large Red Lake Peatland in northern Minnesota has dammed up drainage on its east or upstream side, and improved drainage on its west, downstream side. The ridge/trough pattern of the sedge meadow, oriented perpendicularly to the direction of water flow, has been obscured upstream but reinforced downstream where bog birch has colonized drier ridges. Where the downstream drainage effect has been severe, bog birch has colonized the troughs to produce a featureless shrub fen in place of the original patterned, shrub/sedge fen. However, Figure 5.4a shows that extensive ditching done around the time of World War I on a 1- or 2-mile grid had relatively little effect on the pattern of the Red Lake Peatland in Minnesota. This was largely because ditches were not maintained and early damming by beaver reduced their effectiveness.

When roads are built, failure to provide adequate crossdrainage by ditches and culverts frequently has a severe effect upon upstream peatland forests, either drowning out adjacent stands of timber or greatly lessening their vigor (Stoeckeler 1965). However, lowering of the water table by drainage can be beneficial to the growth of trees on peatlands (Hanell 1984). Slight lowering of water tables under natural conditions in the Red Lake Peatland during the drought of the 1930s led to considerable increase of tree-ring widths in both tamarack and black spruce (Hofstetter 1969; Tilton 1975). In contrast, intermediate levels of disturbance, such as in the long-continued burning, overgrazing, and atmospheric pollution of the southern Pennine mountains of England have resulted in a major transformation of upland blanket bogs with widespread replacement of sphagnum mosses by cotton grass (*Eriophorum vaginatum*) often accompanied by serious erosion (Tallis 1964, 1965, 1973; Ferguson et al. 1978). Many formerly common plants have become rare, and rare plants have been lost. Vegetation changes following human disturbance of peatlands in Shropshire as well as factors favoring local persistence of various peatland plants are discussed extensively by Sinker (1962), who points out the difficulties involved in the investigation of cause and effect in such circumstances. Wetland animals similarly have been exterminated from Britain through loss of habitat; Speight and Blackith (1983) list 10 such invertebrate species. Lest anyone consider such losses insignificant, we should remember that much of our understanding of genetics, including human genetics, has come from detailed study of such insignificant "nuisance" organisms as the fruit fly *Drosophila melanogaster* and the breadmold *Neurospora crassa*.

Peat mining can have much more serious results (Winkler and DeWitt 1985) unless restricted to the uppermost parts of the bog, in which case the peatland may recover at least a semblance of its original vegetation. Where peat is removed to deeper levels, a mosaic of recolonizing communities may be produced, depending on the minerotrophic quality of the newly exposed peat and the hydrologic alterations attendant upon the removal process (Poore 1956). In wet areas, as in the peat pits left by local peasantry, · regeneration can be quite rapid. Joosten (1984) gives an example of the accumulation of 60 cm of peat in 120 years.

When nearly all the peat is mined the site will usually then be afforested or cultivated with major losses of peatland biota. Urban construction by filling or paving over peatlands, though quantitatively unimportant, is the end-point of peatland destruction. Such destruction is highly significant in that awareness of peatland values by the urban populace is then lost.

Functions of peatlands are influenced by human exploitation. Silvola (1986) calculated that undisturbed pine/cotton grass/Sphagnum peatlands in Finland accumulate carbon at a rate of about 25 $g/m^2/a$. After drainage the *release* rate owing to peat oxidation may be nearly ten times as great. Armentano (1980; Armentano and Menges 1986) compiled records of peat subsidence following drainage that ranged from 0.5 to 10 cm/a for temperate peatlands, with an average of about 2 cm/a (see also Wold 1980, and Ivanov

1981, pp. 212–213). The proportion of subsidence owing to oxidation, rather than compaction by water loss, ranges from about 14% in cool-temperate Byelorussia to about 80% in warm-temperate Florida (Armentano and Menges 1986), and is much greater under crop tillage than under pasture or forestry. Assuming the minimal value of 14% oxidation loss from 2 cm of peat over 28 million ha of drained northern peatlands (7.4% of total area according to Table 5.1), carbon loss, excluding that from peat-fuel combustion, would be 0.032 Gt/a (0.28 × 10^{12} m^2 × 0.14 × 0.02m × 78400 g/m^3 BD × 0.528 C), or about 38% of the 0.084 Gt/a estimated to be still accumulating as peat each year in undrained northern peatlands. Doubling the minimal oxidation rate would double the loss to 0.064 Gt/a.

Data of Armentano and Menges (1986), using higher oxidation rates for some of the most southerly areas, yield an estimate of 0.038 Gt/a for north temperate peatlands, not greatly different from the first of those given above. They point out that a good deal of the harvested peat is used as fuel and that emissions from combusted peat will further counterbalance fixation in peatlands. Using the data for north temperate peatlands in their Table 5.4, it can be estimated that, whereas fixation in peat before human exploitation amounted to 0.050–0.075 Gt/a, depending on how many pristine peatlands were still in the accretion phase, at present the carbon balance is somewhere between a net emission of 0.0004Gt/a and a net fixation of 0.025 Gt/a. Alteration of the overall carbon balance in peatlands owing to human exploitation appears to have been substantial, and deserves much more detailed investigation.

Another consequence of peatland drainage is likely to be a marked lowering of methane emissions. In small northern Minnesota peatlands with normally high water tables, midsummer emissions ranged from 0.003 to 1.94 g CH_4/m^2/day. Half of the values were between 0.1 and 0.4 g/m^2/day (Harriss et al. 1985, and unpublished data). These are comparatively high emissions. Northern peatlands make an important contribution to the global methane flux, which is significant in the climatic greenhouse effect.

Annual runoff from a drained peatland may vary from that of the pristine site. In one well-documented case a circumneutral sedge fen with some Sphagnum was two-thirds drained by 337 m of ditches per hectare (Lundin 1984), after which the water table dropped an average of 47 cm beneath the peat surface. The peat surface itself dropped by 15–20 cm as a consequence of three years of draining. The average depth of peat was originally 3.2 m. Total solids in the drainage water increased about 10–30% during the 3-year period. Acidity changed little following drainage except after a dry period in September and October 1983 when it increased sharply (to pH 3.9) as concentrations of organic matter increased. Changes of organic and total nitrogen were small whereas ammonia-nitrogen increased slightly. Losses of nitrate-nitrogen increased from 0.1 kg/ha/a before drainage to 0.3 kg/ha/a afterward, and sulfate losses increased from 5 to 10 kg/ha/a. Calcium, potassium, and alkalinity changed little. If a peatland is originally a strongly acid bog, normally below pH 4.5, acidity may decline following drainage because the runoff passes through deeper, less acidic sedge peats, especially during periods of low flow as shown by Sallantaus (1984).

Biotic Impoverishment Indirectly Owing to Human Activities

Human activities outside the boundaries of peatlands can change their structure and function. Deforestation, cultivation, or construction on adjacent uplands may alter hydrology and add silt and plant nutrients. This can lead to regression of bog or poor fen communities to an earlier, more minerotrophic fen stage. In Minnesota, invasion of cattails into poor sedge fens is one manifestation of such a phenomenon. Direct addition of sewage waste water can have a similar effect, according to Guntenspergen and Stearns (1981), Bevis and Kadlec (1984), and Richardson and Nichols (1985). Acid mine drainage should have the reverse effect (see Barton 1978).

Acid deposition may lead to the biotic impoverishment of peatlands. Studies by Ferguson, Lee, and Bell (1978) indicate that severe acid deposition contributed to the disappearance of sphagnum mosses from peatlands in the southern Pennine mountains of England. Gorham et al. (1984, 1987) suggest that it may initiate or hasten the conversion of sedge meadows to Sphagnum bogs by stripping bases from, and thus acidifying, surface peats (see also Urban and Bayley 1986).

Concentrations of various metals, such as aluminum and iron from dustfall of cultivated soils and from gravel roads (Gorham and Tilton 1978; Gorham 1986; Urban et al. 1987b; Santelmann and Gorham 1988), have increased recently in bog mosses, surface waters, and peat cores. Others metals that have also increased include lead, copper, nickel, zinc, cadmium, arsenic, and so on, from metal smelting and fossil-fuel combustion (Rühling and Tyler 1971; Pakarinen and Tolonen 1976; Norton in press; Glooschenko 1986; Urban, Eisenreich, and Gorham 1987b; Gorham 1986 and unpublished data). Several such elements have toxic properties and probably reinforce the deleterious effects of acid deposition, although their interaction has not yet been studied in peatlands.

Chlorinated hydrocarbons of anthropogenic origin such as DDT and its alteration products, PCBs, toxaphene, and so on, had been accumulating (Figure 5.8) in surface peats, but have declined following reduction in their production and use (Rapaport 1985; Rapaport et al. 1985; Rapaport and Eisenreich 1986). These might also be expected to concentrate biologically in

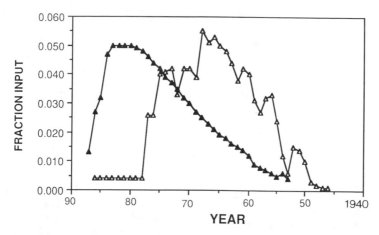

Figure 5.8. Toxaphene- and DDT-input functions (fraction of total input versus time) derived from accumulation rates in dated peat cores. (Reprinted from Rapaport and Eisenreich 1986, with permission.)

animal tissues, but whether to toxic levels in peatland animals is unknown. It is noteworthy that, despite the ban on use, fresh DDT is still being deposited at the surface of northern peatlands in the United States and Canada, coming presumably from Mexico and Central America (Rapaport et al. 1985).

Radioactive fallout, long known (Table 5.3) to accumulate to an unusual degree in the mosses and lichens common to peatlands, and in the northern food chains of which they form the base (Gorham 1958, 1959; Miettinen 1969), is again serious owing to the accident at the Chernobyl nuclear-power generator in the Soviet Union. Newspaper reports (*Minneapolis Star and Tribune* 1986) indicate that a large proportion of reindeer slaughtered in Sweden is severely contaminated by cesium-137, in some cases to more than ten times safety limits set for human consumption. The way of life of nomadic Lapp reindeer herders may be threatened because reindeer use the peatlands as one of their sources of fodder. Such effects are likely across northern Europe. Damage to other peatland biota may be expected.

Carbon dioxide enrichment of the atmosphere owing to fossil-fuel combustion may be expected to influence northern peatlands substantially through the greenhouse effect. Phytotron experiments with tundra-meadow peat cores by Billings et al. (1982, 1983) suggest that doubling atmospheric carbon dioxide will not increase photosynthetic carbon fixation sufficiently to outweigh the enhanced release of carbon dioxide by decomposition caused by

Table 5.3. *Cesium-137 in a northern food chain*

	Concentration relative to potassium (pCi/g K)
Concentrations in different types of plant (1961)	
Lichen (*Cladonia alpestris*)	63,000
Reindeer lichen (mixed)	18,000
Bog blueberry (*Vaccinium uliginosum*)	1,200
Leaves of dwarf bog birch (*Betula nana*)	440
Sedge (*Carex aquatilis*)	380
Wild grass	270
Cultivated grass	130
Leaves of upland birch (*Betula pubescens*)	36
	Body burden (mCi)
Concentrations in Finnish males (1965)	
Lapp reindeer breeders on lichen/reindeer food chain	1437
Other Lapps	545
Control group of other Finns, Helsinki	31

Source: Reprinted from Miettinen 1969, with permission.

higher temperatures and lower water tables due to pronounced climatic warming at high latitudes. Billings et al. believe that higher temperatures, coupled with falling water tables and increased oxidation of peat, might lead to "greater seasonal depth of thaw, lowering of the permafrost table (including white ice wedges), and accelerated thermokarst erosion." Major changes in peatland ecology and biogeochemistry would inevitable follow. However, the effects of greenhouse warming upon northern peatlands are not easily predicted. The development of permafrost in northern Canada 3,000–4,000 years ago apparently put an end to peat accumulation that had gone on for several thousand years previously (Zoltai and Pollett 1983). Farther north in Arctic regions where peat seldom accumulates now, peat formation was common 8,500–9,000 years ago, presumably the result of a warmer climate. Thawing of the permafrost might initiate a new phase of hydrosere succession and a further period of peat accumulation in these areas. South of the present permafrost zone, climatic warming might be expected to cause a drop in water tables, penetration of oxygen into previously anoxic peats, an increase in decomposition rate, and a substantial release of carbon dioxide to the atmosphere. However, peat accumulation rates (top to bottom) in bogs of the Red Lake Peatland in midcontinental northern Minnesota, which lie just inside the border of the forest with the prairie and have a warm summer climate, paradoxically are higher than those in maritime bogs with a cool summer climate (Gorham 1986 and unpublished data). Climatic warming will probably result in a northward shift of the major areas of peatland (Figure 5.9), with changes in the rate of

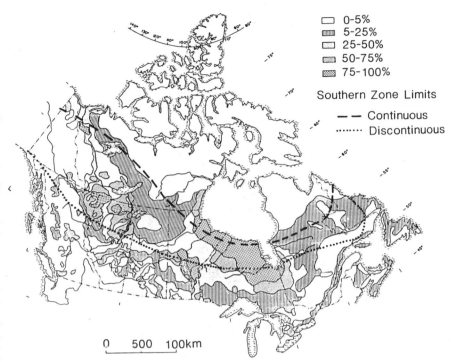

Figure 5.9. Abundance of peatland in Canada (Reprinted from Zoltai and Pollett 1983, with permission). Southern limits of permafrost are shown as − − continous and ····· discontinuous. (Reprinted from Brown 1977, with permission.)

global peat accumulation depending upon the land area suitable for peatland development.

Finally, northern peatlands are threatened with potentially substantial changes owing to large-scale engineering activities. The projected James Bay impoundment in Canada, and the possible southward diversion of large rivers flowing into the Arctic Ocean through major peatland areas of the Soviet Union, are cases in point. Both are likely to cause alterations in climate and in local hydrology that are bound to influence peatland vegetation and its dynamics in unforeseeable ways.

Studying Biotic Impoverishment

Conceptually there are three major approaches to the study of biotic impoverishment, involving (a) measurements of present system states, (b) measurements of past states of quasiequilibrium or trajectories of change, and (c) experiments. Measurements of present system states may compare water tables and flow rates, chemical outputs to air and water, chemical

storages or releases of toxins and nutrients, and population dynamics of
dominant, keystone, and endangered species in pristine peatlands with those
in peatlands subjected to varying degrees of anthropogenic impact.
Alternatively, the history of human impact on peatlands may be investigated
back to the period preceding the impact, by stratigraphic examination of
plant detritus (e.g., pollen, spores, leaf and stem fragments, diatom and
chrysophyte remains), animal fossils (e.g., tests of amoebae, ostracod or
cladoceran carapaces, chironomid head capsules, beetle remains), and
inorganic and organic chemical constituents (e.g., carbonate, organic
carbon, nitrogen, phosphorus, sulfur, calcium, iron, manganese, pore-water
pH, and conductivity). Experimental approaches include fertilization and/or
toxification of plots or whole peatlands, manipulation of water tables, peat
removal from selected areas, partial filling in of peatlands, and elimination or
introduction of selected dominant, keystone, rare (not endangered), or
invader (e.g., purple loosestrife) species. The first two approaches are useful
in sites already subjected to impact or stress. The third is useful in (a)
detailed studies of cause and effect, including mechanisms of stress or
impact, and (b) determination of the most useful early-warning indicators of
stress or impact.

Based on our knowledge of northern peatlands, several hypotheses can be
set up to guide research in biotic impoverishment:

1.   A graded series of impacts on peatlands can be identified. In descending
       order they are:
       a   in-filling,
       b   excavating,
       c   altering water tables and flows,
       d   toxification (e.g., metals, organics),
       e   enrichment (nutrients), and
       f   alteration of species composition (e.g., introduction or removal).
2   There are likely to be sudden changes in peatlands as physical (e.g., water
       table, flow) and chemical (e.g., pH/alkalinity, nutrient, toxin) thresholds
       are passed. These may be on a time scale of years (water table) to decades
       (chemical).
3   Early warning of chemical threats can be seen in rising accumulation rates
       of nutrients and/or toxins in dated peat cores.
4   Early warning of moderate biological damage can be seen in declining
       growth rings of trees and shrubs that must be calibrated, however, against
       natural declines as diameter of the tree increases. Lowering water tables
       also can lead to increased tree growth, whereas flooding will lead to a
       decrease.
5   Losses of some species – and perhaps gains by some that replace them –
       will be the earliest warning of major biological damage.
6   Bryophyte indicator species are generally likely to respond to change more
       rapidly than rooted vascular plants.
7   Changes in the biotic functions of peatland ecosystems (e.g., productivity,

deccmposition, storage of organic materials) are likely to occur much more slowly than the changes noted above, because of species replacements in major community niches.

8   Experimental studies are more likely to reveal the earliest responses to changing physical and chemical factors than comparative studies in which variations among compared sites are likely to mask them.

Conservation and Restoration of Northern Peatlands

Only a small percentage of the total area of northern peatlands is protected (Table 5.1). Even where the peatland area is small and the proportion that has been drained large, conservationists have been either unaware of the need for protection or unable to convince relevant government authorities or property owners to meet it. In some cases only depauperate fragments of the original peatlands are left, as in the Peel raised bogs of the Netherlands (Joosten 1984) and the bogs and fens of East Anglia in southeastern England (Sheail and Wells 1983). In such circumstances many rare species are eliminated from the flora and fauna. The acidophilic plants *Drosera intermedia, D. rotundifolia,* and *Narthecium ossifragum* were last recorded in Holme Fen, Huntingdonshire, England, between 1840 and 1846. Final extinction may be the result of natural causes operating upon a population reduced by human activities, as when a sudden summer flood in 1968 eliminated the large copper butterfly (*Lycaena dispar*) from Woodwalton Fen in Huntingdonshire (Duffey and Mason 1970). The reduction of biological diversity consequent upon cultivation is shown by comparing the 400 species of vascular plants now present in the preserved Woodwalton Fen with the 134 species present in a similar area of nearby fen "reclaimed" for agriculture (Sheail and Wells 1983). Acidophilic bog species requiring high water tables, such as those mentioned above, plus Sphagnum spp. and *Vaccinium oxycoccus,* disappeared first, but were followed eventually by rich-fen species such as *Cirsium dissectum* and *Parnassia palustris* once the drained fens were plowed.

As a means of forwarding the protection of internationally important peatlands, Project Telma was begun in 1966 (Bellamy and Pritchard 1973; Minnesota Department of Natural Resources 1984) by scientists in a number of different countries operating through the International Union for the Conservation of Nature and the International Biological Program. National programs were initiated in Great Britain, Ireland, Norway, Sweden, Finland, the Soviet Union, Poland, and Czechoslovakia. Project Telma is now inactive but the coordination of international conservation efforts has been taken over by a working group of Commission I of the International Peat Society (Kivinen and Pakarinen 1980). The Council of Europe has also taken an interest in European peatlands (Goodwillie 1979; cited by Kivinen and Pakarinen 1980 and by Sjörs 1980b).

There are three major problems to be faced in the conservation of peatlands. First, the attitude of the general public is that wetlands are wastelands. Developers or exploiters have fostered this view, describing their activities as "reclamation." Environmental groups have also been slow to appreciate the need for peatland protection. (Coastal and riparian wetlands have, however, received a good deal of attention, see for example Greeson et al. 1979; Richardson 1981; Wolf, Lee, and Sharitz 1986). Second, the hydrological integrity of a peatland requires protection, or at least very careful management, of adjacent uplands, or even the entire watershed. Third, once seriously damaged or destroyed, restoration is an exceedingly difficult, long-term task.

Adequate protection involves activities at several different levels: classification, inventory, research, public education, legislated protection, and environmental management of protected peatlands including their plants, animals, and surroundings. Such activities are under way in Finland (Ruuhijarvi 1978), where sites have been classified according to representativeness of various peatland types, variety of bird populations, presence of threatened plant and animal species, value in teaching and scientific research, geologic structure, and aesthetic value. Importance has been categorized as international (as in a type of peatland rare elsewhere), national, or regional. Local management is at three levels: (a) totally protected nature reserves and national parks, (b) areas managed partly in the natural state and partly for economic utilization, and (c) areas protected only from drainage. The intent is eventually to protect 700,000 ha, which is less than 7 percent of the total peatland area and compares with the 300,000 already protected in 1980 (Minnesota Department of Natural Resources 1984).

In West Germany three zones of peatland protection (Eggelsmann 1980) have been defined: (a) the central zone representing the natural area to be conserved, (b) the zone of hydrological protection buffering the central zone from alteration of its hydrology (and biota), and (c) an additional protection zone against agricultural runoff, windborne particulate pollutants, etc. Special concern has been given to determining the width of the hydrological protection zone in various types of peatland; mean widths are 30–80 m for deep raised bogs, 120–150 m for shallow raised bogs on fine sand, 200–300 m for shallow fens above coarse sand, and 350 m for spring-fens upon sand. The empirical formula used to determine the width is

$$w = 200 \times d \times k$$

where w = width of protection zone (m), d = groundwater depression between the nature reserve and the next creek or drain (m), and k = hydraulic conductivity (m/day).

In many northwestern German peatlands the flora is depauperate. Schwaar (1980) provides a list of 36 species now rare or missing. Among them are plants common to northern peatlands, such as *Andromeda polifolia, Carex aquatilis, C. chordorrhiza, C. lasiocarpa, C. limosa, C. pauciflora, Drosera anglica, D. intermedia, Ledum palustre, Menyanthes trifoliata, Narthecium ossifragum, Parnassia palustris, Rhynchospora alba,* and *Scheuchzeria palustris.* Attempts are under way to reestablish these taxa in appropriate habitats that include bogs and fens where cultivation has been abandoned, usually using seeds obtained from indigenous populations preserved in nearby botanical gardens.

Rare animals must be reintroduced into regenerating or, in some cases, into little-disturbed peatlands. The woodland caribou has been absent from peatlands in northern Minnesota for several decades. Reintroduction is hampered by the abundance on surrounding uplands of white-tailed deer that harbor a parasitic lung-worm (*Paralaphostrongylus tenuis*). This parasite is far more damaging to caribou than to the deer, which exist in much larger numbers than before European settlement (Anderson and Prestwood 1981). Further, in many cases we do not know what small animals are present in peatlands and judgments as to rarity cannot be made. Study of a small peatland in central Minnesota (Lammers 1974, 1976) revealed six new species of midges (chironomids of the group Tanypodinae) the distribution of which elsewhere is unknown. In general, the invertebrate faunas of peatlands are not well known and deserve greatly increased attention, particularly in North America.

In Minnesota the Department of Natural Resources (1984) developed a seven-step process for protection of relatively large peatlands:

1   inventory and research in different types of peatland,
2   nomination of candidate areas and assessment of data needs,
3   data collection,
4   evaluation and quantitative rating of the ecological significance of candidate areas,
5   recommendations for their protection and management,
6   review of recommendations by a committee broadly representative of such interested parties as government agencies, universities, environmental groups, and users of peat and peatlands, and
7   development of legislation for the designation, protection, and management of *core areas* and *watershed protection areas* around them.

The importance of the peatlands as habitats for 14 rare plants and 8 rare animals was considered in the evaluation, as was the presence of rare or unique "patterned" landforms alone or in peatland complexes. Stability, feasibility of protection and management, degree of present disturbance, and actual and potential scientific value were also considered. Twenty-two peatlands were identified as ecologically significant and were recommended for protection. Of these, four were already protected either as National

Wildlife Refuges or as State Wildlife Management Areas. Appropriate legislation was drafted to protect the other eighteen sites. However, owing to the depressed economic state of northern Minnesota, and to great excitement there over recent gold discoveries at Hemlo, northwestern Ontario, in a type of geological substratum that underlies many Minnesota peatlands, it has not been judged timely to introduce a bill in the state legislature. Mining interests are strongly opposed to such protection of peatlands. Small peatlands are extremely abundant in Minnesota, but are not yet under serious consideration for protection of representative or unique examples. Some work is under way to develop a rating scheme for such peatlands (E. Gorham, P. Benson-Lender, M. M. Phillips, and S. Garner, unpublished manuscripts), with a view to the eventual designation and protection of significant or unique examples as is the case with large peatlands (see Davis et al. 1983; Johansson 1985).

Conclusion

Northern peatlands comprise a unique set of ecosystems. Their ecology and biogeochemistry are of local, regional, and global significance. Biotic impoverishment of these ecosystems is a serious problem and likely to increase. Representative examples, some of very large size, deserve study, protection, and management of their surroundings. Prerequisites for better conservation of such ecosystems are: (a) inventory, (b) research, (c) public education, and (d) appropriate legislation to ensure adequate protection and management.

Acknowledgments

I thank G. M. Woodwell for suggesting the topic, J. A. Janssens and P. H. Glaser for help with the illustrations, and the National Science Foundation (Grant DEB–7922142) and the Andrew W. Mellon Foundation for support.

References

Anderson, R. C., and A. K. Prestwood, 1981. Lungworms. In W. R. Davidson, F. A. Hayes, V. F. Nettles, and F. E. Kellogg (Eds.), *Diseases and Parasites of White-Tailed Deer*, pp. 266–317. Tall Timbers Res. Sta. Misc. Publ. No. 7, Tallahassee, Fla.

Armentano, T. V., 1980. Drainage of organic soils as a factor in the world carbon cycle. *BioScience* 30:825–830.

Armentano, T. V., and E. S. Menges, 1986. Patterns of change in the carbon balance of organic soil – wetlands of the temperate zone. *J. Ecol.* 74:755–774.

Barton, P., 1978. The acid mine drainage. In J. O. Nriagu (Ed.), *Sulfur in the Environment*, Vol. 2, pp. 313–358. WileyInterscience, New York.

Bellamy, D. J., and T. Pritchard, 1973. Project "Telma": a scientific framework for conserving the world's peatlands. *Biol. Conserv.* 5:33–40.

Bevis, F. B., and R. H. Kadlec, 1984. Effect of long-term discharge of waste water on a northern Michigan wetland. In *The Ecological Impacts of Wastewater on Wetlands, an Annotated Bibliography.* Abstract no. 67. U.S. Environmental Protection Agency, EPA–905/3–84–002, Chicago.

Billings, W. D., J. O. Luken, D. A. Mortensen, and K. M. Peterson, 1982. Arctic tundra: a source or sink for atmospheric carbon dioxide in a changing environment? *Oecologia* 53:7–11.

Billings, W. D., J. O. Luken, D. A. Mortensen, and K. M. Peterson, 1983. Increasing atmospheric carbon dioxide: possible effects on arctic tundra. *Oecologia* 58:286–289.

Birks, H. J. B., and H. H. Birks, 1980. *Quaternary Paleoecology.* Edward Arnold, London.

Bolin, B., T. Rosswall, J. R. Freney, M. V. Ivanov, H. Rodhe, and J. E. Richey, 1983. C, N, P and S cycles: major reservoirs and fluxes. In B. Bolin and R. Cook (Eds.), *The Major Biogeochemical Cycles and Their Interactions,* pp. 41–65. Wiley, New York.

Botch, M. S., and V. V. Masing, 1983. Mire ecosystems in the U.S.S.R. In A. J. P. Gore (Ed.), *Ecosystems of the World, 4B, Mires: Swamp, Bog, Fen and Moor, Regional Studies,* pp. 95–152. Elsevier, New York.

Boville, B. W., R. E. Munn, and F. K. Hare, 1983. The storage of non-living carbon in boreal and Arctic zones – Canada. Final report DE–ASOI–81EV–10688, Dept. of Energy, Washington, D.C.

Bradbury, I. K., and J. Grace, 1983. Primary production in wetlands. In A. J. P. Gore (Ed.), *Ecosystems of the World, 4A, Mires: Swamp, Bog, Fen and Moor, General Studies,* pp. 285–310. Elsevier, New York.

Bramryd, T, 1980. The role of peatlands for the global carbon dioxide balance. In *Proc. 6th Int. Peat Congr.,* pp. 9–11. Duluth, Minn.

Brown, L. R., W. U. Chandler, C. Flavin, C. Pollock, S. Postel, L. Starke, and E. C. Wolfe, 1986. *State of the World.* Worldwatch Institute, Washington, D.C.

Brown, R. J. E, 1977. Muskeg and permafrost. In N. W. Radforth and C. O. Brawner (Eds.), *Muskeg and the Northern Environment in Canada,* pp. 148–163. University of Toronto Press.

Chandler, D. G, 1966. *The Campaigns of Napoleon.* Macmillan, New York.

Clymo, R. S., 1963. Ion exchange in *Sphagnum* and its relation to bog ecology. *Ann. Bot.* (Lond.), N.S. 27:309–324.

Clymo, R. S., 1983. Peat. In A. J. P. Gore (Ed.), *Ecosystems of the World, 4A, Mires: Swamp, Bog, Fen and Moor, General Studies,* pp. 159–224. Elsevier, New York.

Clymo, R. S., 1987. Interactions of *Sphagnum* with water and air. In T. C. Hutchinson and K. Meema (Eds.), *Effects of Atmospheric Pollutants on Forests, Wetlands, and Agricultural Ecosystems,* pp. 513–529. Springer-Verlag, New York.

Clymo, R. S., and P. M. Hayward, 1982. The ecology of *Sphagnum.* In A. J. E. Smith (Ed.), *Bryophyte Ecology,* pp. 229–289. Chapman and Hall, London.

Comeau, P. L., and C. E. Beil, 1984. Raised bogs on the Cape Breton Plateau. *Proc. N.S. Acad. Sci.* 34:41–81.

Davis, R. B., G. L. Jacobson, Jr., L. S. Widoff, and A. Zlotsky, 1983. Evaluation of Maine peatlands for their unique and exemplary qualities. Rept., Maine Dept. Conservation, Orono.

Dickson, W. J., and E. G. Leger, 1962. Muskeg trafficability research program, vehicle mobility laboratory, Canadian Armament Research and Development

Establishment. Nat. Res. Counc. Canada. *Tech. Mem. Assoc. Comm. Snow and Soil Mechanics* 74:1–3.

Duffey, E., and G. Mason, 1970. Some effects of summer floods on Woodwalton Fen in 1968/69. *Entomol. Gaz.* 21:23–26.

Eggelsmann, R., 1980. Hydrological aspects of peatland utilization and conservation in northwestern Germany. In *Proc. 6th Int. Peat Congr.*, pp. 28–30. Duluth, Minn.

Fee, A. E., N. A. Lawrence, and A. C. Moffatt, 1977. Waste disposal. In N. W. Radforth and C. O. Brawner (Eds.), *Muskeg and the Northern Environment in Canada*, pp. 332–351. University of Toronto Press.

Ferguson, P., J. A. Lee, and J. N. B. Bell, 1978. Effects of sulphur pollutants on the growth of *Sphagnum* species. *Envir. Pollut.* 16:151–162.

Glaser, P. H., and J. A. Janssens, 1986. Raised bogs in eastern North America: transitions in landforms and gross stratigraphy. *Can. J. Bot.* 64:395–415.

Glaser, P. H., G. A. Wheeler, E. Gorham, and H. E. Wright, 1981. The patterned mires of the Red Lake Peatland: vegetation, water chemistry, and landforms. *J. Ecol.* 69:575–599.

Glooschenko, W. A., 1986. Monitoring the atmospheric deposition of metals by use of bog vegetation and peat profiles. In J. O. Nriagu and C. I. Davidson (Eds.), *Toxic Metals in the Atmosphere*, pp. 507–533. Wiley, New York.

Goodwillie, R., 1979. European Peatlands. Mimeographed report, Eur. Comm. Conserv. Nature and Nat. Resour., Council of Europe, Strasburg. Quoted by Kivinen and Pakarinen 1980.

Gore, A. J. P. (Ed.), 1983a. *Ecosystems of the World, 4A, Mires: Swamp, Bog, Fen and Moor, General Studies*. Elsevier, New York.

Gore, A. J. P. (Ed.), 1983b. *Ecosystems of the World, 4B, Mires: Swamp, Bog, Fen and Moor, Regional Studies*. Elsevier, New York.

Gorham, E., 1953a. Chemical studies on the soils and vegetation of some waterlogged habitats in the English Lake District. *J. Ecol.* 41:345–360.

Gorham. E., 1953b. Some early ideas concerning the nature, origin and development of peatlands. *J. Ecol.* 41:257–274.

Gorham, E., 1955. Titus Smith (1768–1850), a pioneer of plant ecology in North America. *Ecology* 36:116–123.

Gorham, E., 1958. Accumulation of radioactive fallout by plants in the English Lake District. *Nature* 181:152–154.

Gorham, E., 1959. A comparison of lower and higher plants as accumulators of radioactive fallout. *Can. J. Bot.* 37:327–329.

Gorham, E., 1967. Some chemical aspects of wetland ecology. Nat. Res. Council of Canada. *Tech. Mem. Assoc. Comm. Geotech. Res.* 90:20–38.

Gorham, E., 1982. Some unsolved problems in peatland ecology. *Naturaliste Canadien* 109:533–541.

Gorham, E., 1986. The ecology and biogeochemistry of *Sphagnum* bogs in central and eastern North America. In A. D. Laderman (Ed.), *Atlantic White Cedar Wetlands*, pp. 2–15. Westview Press, Boulder, Colo.

Gorham, E., and D. L. Tilton, 1978. The mineral content of *Sphagnum fuscum* as affected by human settlement. *Can J. Bot.* 56:2755–2759.

Gorham, E., S. E. Bayley, and D. W. Schindler, 1984. The ecological effects of acid deposition upon peatlands: a neglected field of "acid-rain" research. *Can. J. Fish. Aquat. Sci.* 41:1256–1268.

Gorham, E., S. J. Eisenreich, J. Ford, and M. V. Santelmann, 1985. The chemistry of bog waters. In W. Stumm (Ed.), *Chemical Processes in Lakes*, pp. 339–362. Wiley, New York.

Gorham, E., J. K. Underwood, F. B. Martin, and J. G. Ogden III, 1986. Natural and anthropogenic causes of lake acidification in Nova Scotia. *Nature* 324:451–453.

Gorham, E., J. A. Janssens, G. A. Wheeler, and P. H. Glaser, 1987. The natural and anthropogenic acidification of peatlands. In T. C. Hutchinson and K. Meema (Eds.), *Effects of Atmospheric Pollutants on Forests, Wetlands, and Agricultural Ecosystems*, pp. 493–512. Springer-Verlag, New York.

Greeson, P. E., J. R. Clark, and J. E. Clark (Eds.), 1979. *Wetland Functions and Values: The State of Our Understanding*. Amer. Water Res. Assoc., Minneapolis, Minn.

Grigal, D. F., 1983. Impact of right-of-way construction on organic soil bulk density in the Red Lake Peatland. *Can. J. Soil Sci.* 63:557–562.

Grigal, D. F., 1985a. Impact of right-of-way construction on vegetation in the Red Lake Peatland, northern Minnesota. *Envir. Mgmt.* 9:449–454.

Grigal, D. F., 1985b. *Sphagnum* production in forested bogs of northern Minnesota. *Can. J. Bot.* 63:1204–1207.

Grigal, D. F., C. G. Buttleman, and L. K. Kernik, 1985. Biomass and productivity of the woody strata of forested bogs in northern Minnesota. *Can. J. Bot.* 63:2416–2424.

Guntenspergen, G., and F. Stearns, 1981. Ecological limitations on wetland use for waste water treatment. In B. Richardson (Ed.), *Wetland Values and Management*, pp. 273–284. Minnesota Water Planning Board.

Hanell, B., 1984. Post-drainage site index of peatlands in Sweden. Reports in Forest Ecology and Forest Soils, Swedish University of Agricultural Sciences, No. 50. (In Swedish with English summary.)

Harriss, R. C., E. Gorham, D. I. Sebacher, K. B. Bartlett, and P. Flebbe, 1985. Methane flux from northern peatlands. *Nature* 315:652–654.

Harwood, T. A., 1963. Trafficability and mobility in muskeg. In *Proc. Atlantic Prov. Regional Seminars on Organic Terrain Problems*. Nat. Res. Council of Canada. *Tech. Mem. Assoc. Comm. Soil and Snow Mechanics* 77, pp. 51–65.

Heinselman, M. L., 1963. Forest sites, bog processes and peatland types in the Glacial Lake Agassiz Region. *Ecol. Monogr.* 33:327–374.

Heinselman, M. L., 1970. Landscape evolution, peatland types, and the environment in the Lake Agassiz Peatland Natural Area, Minnesota. *Ecol. Monogr.* 40:235–261.

Hofstetter, R. H., 1969. Floristic and ecological studies of Minnesota wetlands. Ph.D. dissertation in Botany, University of Minnesota, Minneapolis.

Ingram, H. A. P., 1983. Hydrology. In A. J. P. Gore (Ed.), *Ecosystems of the World, 4A, Mires: Swamp, Bog, Fen and Moor*, pp. 67–158. Elsevier, New York.

Ivanov, K. E., 1981. *Water Movement in Mirelands*, translated from the Russian by A. Thomson and H. A. P. Ingram. Academic Press, London.

Janssens, J. A., and P. H. Glaser, 1986. The bryophyte flora and the major peat-forming mosses at Red Lake Peatland, Minn. *Can. J. Bot.* 64:427–442.

Johansson, C. E., 1985. Valuation and classification of wetlands in Sweden. *Proc. Int. Peat Soc. Symp. Peat and Environment*. Jönköping, Sweden.

Joosten, J. H. G., 1984. A 130 year micro- and macrofossil record from regeneration peat in former peasant peat pits in the Peel, The Netherlands: a paleoecological

Stoeckeler, J. H., 1965. Drainage along swamp forest roads. *J. Forestry* 63:772–776.

study with agricultural and climatological implications. *Paleogeogr. Paleoclimatol. Paleoecol.* 49:277–312.

Kivinen, E., 1980. New statistics on the utilization of peatlands in different countries. In *Proc. 6th Int. Peat Congr.*, pp. 48–51. Duluth, Minn.

Kivinen, E., and P. Pakarinen, 1980. Peatland areas and the proportion of virgin peatlands in different countries. In *Proc. 6th Int. Peat Congr.*, pp. 52–54. Duluth, Minn.

Kulczynski, S., 1949. Peat bogs of Polesie. *Mem. Acad. Polon. Sci.*, Ser. B, No. 15.

Lammers, R. K., 1974. Ecology of the Tanypodinae in a Minnesota wetland. *Verh. Int. Verein. Limnol.* 19:3142–3148.

Lammers, R. K., 1976. Plant and insect communities in a Minnesota wetland. Ph.D. dissertation in Botany, University of Minnesota.

Lappaleinen, E., 1980. The useful fuel peat resources in Finland. In *Proc. 6th Int. Peat Congr.*, pp. 59–63. Duluth, Minn.

Lundin, L., 1984. Peatland drainage – effects on the hydrology of the mire Docksmyren. Department of Physical Geography, University of Uppsala, Hydrological Division, Report Series A 1984:3. (In Swedish with English summary.)

Malmström, C., 1931. Om faran för skogsmarkens försumpning i Norrland. *Meddelanden från Statens Skogsförsöksanstalt.* 26:1–162.

McKnight, D. M., E. M. Thurman, R. L. Wershaw, and H. F. Hemond, 1985. Biogeochemistry of aquatic humus substances in Thoreau's bog, Concord, Massachusetts. *Ecology* 66:1339–1352.

Meeres, R. D., 1977. Pipelines. In N. W. Radforth and C. O. Brawner (Eds.), *Muskeg and the Northern Environment in Canada*, pp. 264–298. University of Toronto Press.

Miettinen, J. K., 1969. Enrichment of radioactivity by Arctic ecosystems in Finnish Lappland. In D. J. Nelson and R. C. Evans (Eds.), *Symposium on Radioecology*, pp. 23–31. National Bureau of Standards, Springfield, VA, CONF–670503, Biology and Medicine (TID–4500).

Minnesota Department of Natural Resources, 1984. Protection of ecologically significant peatlands in Minnesota. Prelim. Rept. St. Paul, Minn.

Minneapolis Star and Tribune, 1986. High radiation levels in reindeer threaten way of life in Lappland. 14 September, p. 28A.

Mölder, K., and M. Salmi, 1955. The general geological map of Finland, Sheet B3, Vaasa, explanation to the map of surficial deposits. Geologinen Tutkimuslaitos, Helsinki.

Neishtadt, M. I., 1977. The world's largest peat basin, its commercial potentialities and protection. *Int. Peat. Soc. Bull.* 8:37–43.

Norton, S. A., in press. Geochemistry of selected Maine peat deposits. Maine Geological Survey Bull. No. 34.

Pakarinen, P., and K. Tolonen, 1976. Regional survey of heavy metals in peat mosses *Sphagnum. Ambio* 5:38–40.

Pala, S., and W. Weischet, 1982. Toward a physiographic analysis of the Hudson–James Bay Lowland. *Naturaliste Canadien* 109:639–651.

Poore, M. E. D., 1956. The ecology of Woodwalton Fen. *J. Ecol.* 44:455–492.

Radforth, J. R., and A. L. Burwash, 1977. Transportation. In N. W. Radforth and C. O. Brawner (Eds.), *Muskeg and the Northern Environment in Canada*, pp. 249–263. University of Toronto Press.

Rapaport, R., 1985. Chlorinated hydrocarbons in peat. Ph.D. dissertation in Civil and Mineral Engineering, University of Minnesota.

Rapaport, R., N. R. Urban, P. D. Capel, J. E. Baker, B. B. Looney, S. J. Eisenreich, and E. Gorham, 1985. "New" DDT inputs to North America: atmospheric deposition. *Chemosphere* 14:1167–1173.

Rapaport, R., and S. J. Eisenreich, 1986. Atmospheric deposition of toxaphene to eastern North America derived from peat accumulation. *Atmos. Envir.* 20:2367–2379.

Richardson, B. (Ed), 1981. *Wetland Values and Management.* Minnesota Water Planning Board.

Richardson, C. J., and D. S. Nichols, 1985. Ecological analysis of wastewater management criteria in wetland ecosystems. In P. J. Godfrey, E. R. Kaynoor, S. Pelczarski, and J. Benforado (Eds.), *Ecological Considerations in Wetlands Treatment of Municipal Wastewaters*, pp. 351–391. Van Nostrand, New York.

Ruhling, A., and G. Tyler. 1071. Regional differences in the deposition of heavy metals over Scandinavia. *J. Appl. Ecol.* 8:497–507.

Ruuhijarvi, R., 1978. Basic plan for peatland preservation in Finland. *Suo* 29:1–10.

Ruuhijarvi, R., 1983. The Finnish mire types and their regional distribution. In A. J. P. Gore (Ed.), *Ecosystems of the World, 4B, Mires: Swamp, Bog, Fen and Moor, Regional Studies*, pp. 47–67. Elsevier, New York.

Sallantaus, T., 1984. Quality of runoff water from Finnish fuel peat mining areas. *Aqua Fennica* 14:223–233.

Santelmann, M. V., and E. Gorham, 1988. The influence of airborne road dust on the chemistry of *Sphagnum* mosses. *J. Ecol.* 76:1219–1231.

Schwaar, J., 1980. Possibilities of the resettlement for moribunded plant taxa. In *Proc. 6th Int. Peat Congr.* Duluth, Minn., p. 92.

Sheail, J., and T. C. E. Wells, 1983. The fenlands of Huntingdonshire, England: a case study in catastrophic change. In A. J. P. Gore (Ed.), *Ecosystems of the World, 4B, Mires: Swamp, Bog, Fen and Moor, Regional Studies*, pp. 331–393. Elsevier, New York.

Silvola, J., 1986. Carbon dioxide dynamics in mires reclaimed for forestry. *Ann. Bot. Fennici* 23:59–67.

Sinker, C. A., 1962. The north Shropshire meres and mosses: a background for ecologists. *Field Studies* 1:101–138.

Sjörs, H., 1953. Sveriges myrområden. In *Boken om Naturen*, pp. 142–143. Uddevalla.

Sjörs, H., 1961. Some chemical properties of the humus layer in Swedish natural soils. *Kungl. Skogshogsk. Skr.*, No. 37.

Sjörs, H., 1980a. Peat on earth: multiple use or conservation? *Ambio* 9:303–308.

Sjörs, H., 1980b. An arrangement of changes along gradients, with examples from succession in boreal peatland. *Vegetatio* 43:1–4.

Sjörs, H., 1983. Mires of Sweden. In A. J. P. Gore (Ed.), *Ecosystems of the World, 4B, Mires: Swamp, Bog, Fen and Moor, Regional Studies*, pp. 69–94. Elsevier, New York.

Smith, T., 1835. Conclusions on the results on the vegetation of Nova Scotia, and on vegetation, and on man in general, of certain natural and artificial causes deemed to actuate and affect them. *Loudon's Mag. Nat. Hist.* 8:641–662.

Speight, M. C. D., and R. E. Blackith, 1983. The animals. In A. J. P. Gore (Ed.), *Ecosystems of the World, 4A, Mires: Swamp, Bog, Fen and Moor, General Studies*, pp. 349–365. Elsevier, New York.

Stephens, J. C., 1974. Subsidence of organic soils in the Florida Everglades – a review and update. In P. J. Gleason (Ed.), *Environment of South Florida: Present and Past*. Miami Geol. Soc. Mem. No. 2, pp. 352–361. (Quoted by Armentano 1980.)

Tallis, J. H., 1964. Studies on southern Pennine peats: II. The pattern of erosion. *J. Ecol.* 52:333–344.

Tallis, J. H., 1965. Studies on southern Pennine peats: IV. Evidence of recent erosion. *J. Ecol.* 53:509–520.

Tallis, J. H., 1973. Studies on southern Pennine peats: V. Direct observations on peat erosion and peat hydrology at Featherbed Moss, Derbyshire. *J. Ecol.* 61:1–22.

Taylor, J. A., 1983. The peatlands of Great Britain and Ireland. In A. J. P. Gore (Ed.), *Ecosystems of the World, 4B, Mires: Swamp, Bog, Fen and Moor, Regional Studies,* pp. 1–46. Elsevier, New York.

Tilton, D. L., 1975. The growth and nutrition of tamarack, *Larix laricina.* (Du Roi) K. Koch. Ph.D dissertation in Botany, University of Minnesota.

Urban, N. R., and S. E. Bayley, 1986. The acid-base balance of peatlands: a short-term perspective. *Water Air Soil Pollut.* 30:791–800.

Urban, N. R., S. J. Eisenreich, and E. Gorham, 1987a. Proton cycling in bogs: variation in Eastern North America. In T. C. Hutchinson and K. Meema (Eds.), *Effects of Atmospheric Pollutants on Forests, Wetlands, and Agricultural Ecosystems,* pp. 517–598. Springer-Verlag, New York.

Urban, N.R., S. J. Eisenreich, and E. Gorham, 1987b. Aluminum, iron, zinc, and lead in bog waters. *Canad. J. Fish. Aquat. Sci.* 44:1165–1172.

U.S. Environmental Protection Agency, 1984. *The Ecological Impacts of Wastewater on Wetlands: An Annotated Bibliography.* EPA–905/3–84–002, Chicago.

Verry, E. S., 1975. Streamflow chemistry and nutrient yields from upland-peatland watersheds in Minnesota. *Ecology* 56:1149–1157.

Walker, D., 1970. Direction and rate in some British post-glacial hydroseres. In D. Walker and R. G. West (Eds.), *Studies in the Vegetational History of the British Isles,* pp. 117–139. Cambridge University Press.

Warner, D. W., and D. G. Wells, 1980. Bird populations and seasonal habitat use in Minnesota peatlands. In *Proc. 6th Int. Peat Congr.,* pp. 130–137. Duluth, Minn.

Wheeler, G. A., P. H. Glaser, E. Gorham, C. M. Wetmore, F. D. Bowers, and J. A. Janssens, 1983. Contributions to the flora of the Red Lake Peatland, northern Minnesota, with special attention to *Carex. Amer. Midl. Naturalist* 110:62–96.

Wickware, G. M., D. W. Cowell, and R. A. Sims, 1980. Peat resources of the Hudson Bay Lowland coastal zone. In *Proc. 6th Int. Peat Congr.,* pp. 138–143. Duluth, Minn.

Winkler, M. G., and C. B. DeWitt, 1985. Environmental impacts of peat mining in the United States: documentation for wetland conservation. *Envir. Conserv.* 12:317–330.

Wold, E., 1980. Subsidence problems on Atlantic bogs of the west coast of Norway. In *Proc. 6th Int. Peat Congr.,* pp. 499–500. Duluth, Minn.

Wolf, R. B., L. C. Lee, and R. R. Sharitz, 1986. Wetland creation and restoration in the United States from 1970 to 1985: an annotated bibliography. *Wetlands* 6:1–88.

Zoltai, S. C., 1980. An outline of the wetland regions in Canada. In C. D. A. Rubec and F. C. Pollett, (Eds.), *Proc. Workshop on Canadian Wetlands,* pp. 1–8. Environment Canada, Lands Directorate, Ecological Land Classification Series, No. 12, Ottawa.

Zoltai, S. C., and F. C. Pollett, 1983. Wetlands in Canada: their classification, distribution, and use. In A. J. P. Gore (Ed.), *Ecosystems of the World, 4B, Mires: Swamp, Bog, Fen and Moor, Regional Studies,* pp. 245–268. Elsevier, New York.

6   Climatic Change and the Survival of Forest Species

MARGARET BRYAN DAVIS

Editor's Note: Glacial advances and retreats over several hundreds of thousands of years have sorted and resorted the plant populations of the middle and high latitudes of eastern North America and have winnowed from those populations a flora of hardy survivors. The survivors among trees are almost uniquely singular species, unencumbered by dependence on other species, by the existence of a community, by a narrow dependence on edaphic perfection, or on special mechanisms for pollination or dispersal of seeds. The species of fir, spruce, birch, oak, poplar, hemlock, and pine can occur in almost any mixture in closed forests or in open woodlands, even on occasion in savannas, and on a range of habitats. To be sure, the species are not interchangeable, have different distributions and requirements and roles in succession, but, as wind-pollinated species (in contrast to tree species of the tropics that may depend on insects, birds, or mammals for pollination), they have few direct dependencies on other species that restrict them to any special community. We might go so far as to suggest that they are preadapted to climatic change as a result of selection by some of the most rapid climatic changes that we know of beyond the catastrophe of the Cretaceous/Tertiary boundary.

Margaret B. Davis, a distinguished scholar who has specialized in retrospective studies of vegetation, has addressed the challenge of estimating the rate of migration of one of these glacial survivors, *Tsuga canadensis,* under the climatic changes anticipated for the next decades. She has chosen a modest estimate of the rate of change in temperature, less than ½ the maximum thought possible in the middle and high latitudes if present trends continue. She shows why the hemlock cannot be expected to keep pace with the climatic changes, even at the lowest rates of climatic changes expected. This very careful look at the hemlock through her characteristically meticulous scrutiny may appear to establish the hemlock as a special case. It is not. It is but one example from among the flora of the recently glaciated zone of North America. It is one of the survivors of the winnowing produced by extraordinary climatic changes in this region throughout the recent glacial period. The evidence offers a glimpse of some of the more important mechanisms that sort the genes of all living systems and determine the survivors at any moment. The process of impoverishment proceeds through such trials as those outlined here for *Tsuga canadensis.*

Introduction

The fossil record provides many examples of changes in geographical distributions of plants in response to changing climate. These examples

99

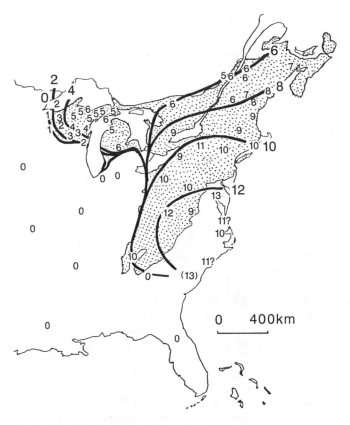

Figure 6.1. Migration map for hemlock during the Holocene, based on fossil pollen evidence. Isochrones represent the approximate position of the frontier of the continuous species population at 2,000-year intervals from 12,000 years ago (12) to the present (0). Small numbers represent the radiocarbon age (in thousands of years) at specific sites of the earliest sharply rising quantities of hemlock pollen. (Modified from Davis 1981, and Davis et al. 1986b.)

provide a basis for predicting response to future climate. The accumulation of greenhouse gasses in the atmosphere will soon cause climatic warming. With CO_2 doubling, global temperatures are expected to rise $3° \pm 1.5°C$. If emission of greenhouse gasses continues to increase at the present rate, global warming will average $0.3°C$ per decade for the next century (WMO/UNEP 1988). Can the flora adjust easily? Or will climatic change cause extinctions?

The survival of many taxa through a series of glacial-interglacial cycles during the Pleistocene suggests that most plant species in the temperate zone have been able to disperse to keep pace with climatic changes in the past. Temperate zone trees survived the last glacial maximum as small populations in refugia in southeastern United States. As the ice sheets melted and the climate warmed at the end of the glacial interval, these plants were able to disperse northward hundreds of kilometers to occupy their present-day range (Davis 1981).

The future greenhouse warming, however, differs in an important way from climatic changes in the past: the rate of change will be at least one order of magnitude more rapid. Does the fossil record give us any insight into the capacity of plant species to adjust to such rapid change? There are examples from the most recent time of relatively rapid change – the warming just at the end of the last glacial interval: in northwestern Europe fossils from warmth-requiring species of water plants and beetles (which disperse readily) are found earlier than the oldest fossils from trees. This suggests that the climate became warm enough for trees several centuries before trees began to grow on the local landscape. Dispersal of tree seeds was insufficient to track the change in temperature, or development of soils was not rapid enough to provide appropriate habitats for trees (Iversen 1954; Pennington 1986).

During most of the last 10,000 years, however, evidence for lack of equilibrium between vegetation and climate is hard to find. Papers presented at a recent symposium discussed the evidence; only a few examples could be found to support the view that seed dispersal limited the rate of range extension, and then only where large geographical barriers, such as the Great Lakes, stood in the path of expanding populations (Davis et al. 1986a; Prentice 1986; Webb 1986). Most authors were willing to concede, however, that one or more centuries may elapse before a population of trees expands as fully as the climate might allow (Davis and Botkin 1985; Brubaker 1986; Ritchie 1986). Lags of this length are long enough to be important as we consider what will happen in the twenty-first century.

An Example from the Past – Dispersal of Hemlock During the Holocene

Eastern hemlock (*Tsuga canadensis*) produces abundant pollen which is easily identifiable and will preserve in sediments. Consequently a fossil record of the density of this species through time in the forests of eastern North America is available from the quantities of pollen in sediment. Data have been compiled from the literature to show hemlock expansion northward and westward during the last 10,000 years (Figure 6.1). The isochrones on the figure show the approximate position of the leading edge of the expanding species population at 2,000-year intervals. Hemlock apparently survived the last glacial period in the eastern Appalachians or on the coastal plain or shelf. Starting 10,000 years ago, the species frontier moved northward and westward at an average rate of 20–25 km per century (Davis 1981, 1983). Detailed information from the upper Great Lakes region (Davis et al. 1986a; Davis, Mack, and Calcote 1986b; Davis, Calcote, and Mack, unpublished) show that hemlock colonized all of the eastern upper peninsula of Michigan and the northern half of the lower peninsula very quickly, between 6,000 and 5,000 radiocarbon years ago. Subsequent expansion to its present-day limit 200 km further west and south in Wisconsin took place slowly over the next 4,000 years.

Invasion of an already-forested landscape at the rate of 20-25 km per century may seem rapid for a tree that is associated with old-growth, mature forest. However, it would not be rapid enough to keep up with greenhouse warming. The spatial displacement of habitats can be visualized if one assumes the same general configuration of climate as today: with a latitudinal lapse rate in the Great Lakes region of about 100 km per degree Celsius, isotherms would be displaced northward 300 km in the next 100 years, a distance more than 10 times greater than the documented range extensions for trees in a similar time interval.

On the other hand, the observed rates of expansion are not the maximum possible if the rate of advance of trees in the past was generally controlled by climatic change (Webb 1986). Fossil data might give a better idea of maximum possible rates if there were times in the past when climate was not limiting, but instead distribution of species was limited by the capacity of the species to disperse seeds and to become established in a new area.

It seemed likely at first that the rapid colonization of eastern upper Michigan by hemlock 6,000–5,000 years ago represented such a time. In 1986 we suggested that the rapid-expansion episode resulted from chance dispersal of seeds into a region that had been favorable for hemlock for some time, but from which hemlock had been excluded due to the lack of a seed source (Davis et al. 1986a, 1987). If this interpretation were correct, the rate of colonization might represent the maximum colonization rate possible under favorable conditions, about 50,000 km^2 in 1,000 years. Yet the area is only about 500 km across, from southeast to northwest, so the rate of advance across the area still averages only about 50 km per century. Although twice as rapid as the average Holocene rate of range extension, 50 km per century is an order of magnitude too slow to keep up with climatic warming in the coming century.

More recent work suggests that hemlock populations do not expand as a continuous front but, instead, through the establishment of disjunct colonies 10 to 100 km beyond the main population. If sufficient advance colonies are established, an area can be colonized very rapidly, limited only by the rate of

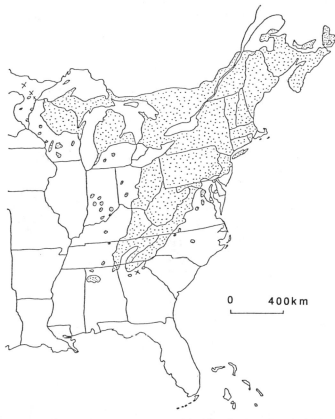

Figure 6.2. Map showing the geographical distribution of hemlock in eastern North America (modified on the basis of U.S. Land Office Survey records from Fowells 1965, p. 703). Note the large numbers of outlying colonies disjunct from the main species range.

population increase. Hemlock seeds are shed throughout the winter months, and they can apparently be carried many kilometers by winter storms. Disjunct hemlock colonies exist everywhere outside the species range limit (Figure 6.2). Some of these may represent relict populations of a once larger range (Oosting and Hess 1956). Those to the west and north, however, cannot be explained as relics because the continuous range never extended to that region (Calcote 1986; Davis et al. 1986a).

The history of two of the outlying colonies in Minnesota has been studied by R. R. Calcote (1986); his fossil pollen data show that both populations were established 1,200–2,000 years ago, at about the same time that hemlock reached the western limit of its present-day continuous range in Wisconsin. One population consists of 11 adult trees and 3 saplings; the other was about

1,000 trees, but was extirpated in the early twentieth century by logging and a subsequent fire. Pollen abundances suggest that neither population changed very much in size throughout its history. All of the Minnesota colonies grow in special microhabitats, such as north-facing slopes of ravines, or immediately adjacent to bogs (Calcote 1986).

We hypothesize, on the basis of similar persistent, but very low, pollen abundances at a number of sites in eastern upper Michigan, that similar colonies were established there between 7,000 and 6,000 years ago, through long-distance dispersal of seeds from Ontario, where hemlock had become established about 1,000 years earlier. The colonies remained small in size and presumably confined to unusual habitats (as in Minnesota) until 5,500 years ago, when a change in climate suddenly made most habitats within the region favorable to hemlock. The small colonies acted as centers of infection, permitting rapid invasion of the entire landscape and a rapid buildup of population throughout the region (Davis et al. 1986b; Davis, Calcote, and Mack unpublished).

This invasion scenario probably occurred many times during the history of the northward movement of hemlock in North America, although pollen data are not sufficiently detailed to document it in most areas. The existence of outlying colonies at present in all directions beyond the limit of continuous distribution (colonies exist in Canada, but are not shown in Figure 6.2) suggests that long-distance dispersal of seeds is a continuous process. Through time, favorable microhabitats within 50–100 km of the species limit become occupied. These isolated populations are then available as centers for colonization of the surrounding region, should the climate become more favorable.

Predicted Response to Greenhouse Warming

Information about the way in which hemlock responded to climatic changes in the past can be used to predict how hemlock might respond to climatic changes in the future. General circulation models suggest that doubled CO_2 will elevate summer temperatures in the midcontinent; some models suggest that soil moisture deficits will develop in spring and summer (Manabe and Wetherald 1987; Mitchell and Warrilow 1987). These changes are the reverse of the trend toward cooler summers and increased moisture that has characterized the upper Great Lakes region for the last 4,000 years (Webb, Cushing, and Wright 1983; Bartlein, Webb, and Fleri 1984), during which time hemlock has slowly been expanding its continuous range in Michigan and Wisconsin westward to the Apostle Islands and southward to the southern end of Green Bay.

It seems likely, therefore, that greenhouse warming will cause hemlock to contract from Minnesota and Wisconsin while its range expands northward in Canada. The process of contraction is easy to visualize, as hemlock has already been reduced in frequency by logging and fire. Reproduction is now very limited by winter browsing by deer: deer have increased in density over the past 80 years in response to the availability of fodder in second-growth aspen and birch forests (Anderson and Loucks 1979).

The expansion process is what we have been able to observe in the fossil record. By analogy, we can predict that outlying colonies of hemlock in Canada might act as centers of infection far north of the continuous range of the species. As the climate warms, these populations might expand and hemlock spread into less specialized microhabitats nearby, quickly increasing its population size to colonize the rapidly expanding area of favorable habitat.

There are a number of reasons why this scenario is unlikely. Trees growing in outlying colonies in Minnesota appear vulnerable to any and all kinds of disturbance. Of the fourteen outlying populations that have been reported by botanists or that are mentioned in historical records from the nineteenth century, only three have survived to the present (Calcote 1986). Similar patterns of human disturbance have occurred north of the hemlock range in Canada, and they have presumably had a similar effect: if the analogy with Minnesota is appropriate, the numbers of outlying colonies that might serve as centers for invasion of new areas are much reduced. The reduction of numbers of centers of infection means that colonization of a large area will occur much more slowly.

A second change involves the strength of the seed source provided by the population within the species limit. Hemlock abundance is reduced throughout its range as the result of human disturbance (Davis 1985; Davis et al., unpublished). In the Great Lakes region, logging has nearly eliminated hemlock from mixed hardwood stands (Hix and Barnes 1984); the change in abundance following logging is shown dramatically in Figure 6.3. As the entire region, except for a few scattered reserves, has been logged, hemlock is reduced in abundance everywhere and many fewer seeds are available for long-distance dispersal. The probabilities of dispersal to distant localities are correspondingly reduced.

A third change is the loss of old-growth forests, and their replacement by young successional stands. Old-growth forests have many dead logs that provide sites for the germination and growth of hemlock seedlings (Figure 6.4), whereas postlogging stands have little woody debris on the forest floor. Increased herbivory by the present-day dense populations of deer is still more important: in some areas near the Porcupine Mountains, Michigan,

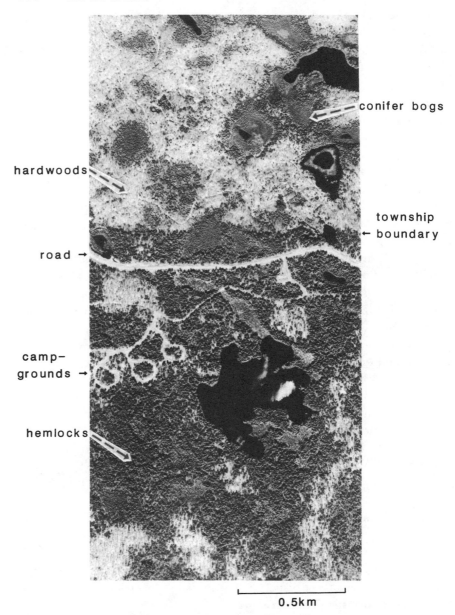

conifer bogs

hardwoods

township
← boundary

road →

camp-
grounds →

hemlocks

0.5km

Figure 6.3. Aerial photograph of the northern boundary of the Sylvania tract, northern Michigan (USDA 5–1–80). Photograph is an enhanced infrared photograph taken in the spring when leaves were still absent from the deciduous trees. Conifer stands appear as dark areas, hardwoods as light areas. The boundary between secondary forest which has grown up following logging about 50 years ago and old-growth forest that has never been clear-cut coincides with the township boundary midway across the photograph. Note that the secondary forest is mainly made up of hardwoods, whereas the old-growth forest is a mosaic of hardwood stands and hemlock stands.

Figure 6.4. Hemlock seedlings on a nurse log in an old-growth mixed hardwood–hemlock forest near Dukes, northern Michigan.

deer browsing has virtually eliminated hemlock reproduction (Frelich and Lorimer 1985).

These changes appear sufficient to reduce the potential of hemlock to invade new areas far below the rates of range extension observed in the fossil record. Yet even the maximum rate observed (for example the colonization of the eastern half of Michigan's upper peninsula) is not rapid enough to track climatic warming at 0.3°C per decade, as predicted for the twenty-first century.

Conclusions

If a dominant forest tree, one that produces abundant seed, adapted for dispersal by wind, will have difficulty dispersing rapidly enough to track future climate, how much worse is the situation for woodland herbs? We have no fossil record of small woodland species, such as trout lilies, ladies' slippers, or Trillium, and therefore we can only deduce what we can from their natural history. Unlike weedy herbs that can spread rapidly (Mack 1984), these plants produce small numbers of seeds. A few, like violets, have specialized mechanisms that propel seeds a few centimeters from the parent plant. But even those that depend on wind rather than animals for dispersal shed seed near the ground in sheltered habitats where there is little chance that seed will be carried more than a few meters. Many woodland herbs reproduce vegetatively – an effective means to increase locally but not a means for dispersal over discontinuous habitat. Because woodland habitats are fragmented, and old-growth forests are rare, the chances these plants will be able to disperse rapidly to favorable sites in climatically suitable regions appear disappearingly small.

Hemlock, despite the drop in population size since settlement, is still an abundant species with millions of individual trees spread over a wide geographical area. In contrast, many protected plant species persist only in preserves in very small populations. Without active intervention, including transplanting propagules to new preserves, it seems unlikely that plant species like these can survive a period of rapidly changing climate. Decades of active conservation and protection of rare species may prove fruitless in the face of CO_2-induced climatic change without a new strategy of management that takes problems of dispersal into account.

Summary

The fossil record shows that most forest trees were able to disperse rapidly enough to keep up with most of the climatic changes that took place in recent millennia. These changes were much more gradual than the climatic changes projected for the future. Even so, there were occasional periods of disequilibrium between plant distributions or abundances, soils, and climate that lasted a century or more. The most rapid dispersal rates known from the fossil record, however, are an order of magnitude too slow to keep up with the temperature rise expected in the coming century.

In addition, human activities have exterminated many of the outlying colonies that served in the past as advance colonists in new regions as the climate changed. Some forest trees have greatly decreased in abundance since logging, and many woodland herbs (not all, of course) have also become rare, existing today mainly in fragments of old-growth forest and in nature preserves. It seems likely that many forest trees will not be able to disperse rapidly enough to track the changing climate closely, but because of the enormous geographical range of these species, they may not become extinct. The fate of woodland herbs is much less certain, as population sizes are frequently very small, adaptations for dispersal over discontinuous habitat are fewer, and requirements for establishment are quite specific. Without active intervention, including propagation and purposeful reestablishment in new geographical regions, extensive losses of plant species are to be expected in the coming century as the result of greenhouse warming.

Acknowledgments

This work has been supported by the National Science Foundation research grants DEB84–07943 and BSR 8615196. R. R. Calcote prepared Figure 6.2.

References

Anderson, R. C., and O. L. Loucks, 1979. White-tail deer (*Odocoileus virginianus*) influence on structure and composition of *Tsuga canadensis* forests. *Journal Applied Ecology* 16:855–861.

Bartlein, P. J., T. Webb III, and E. Fleri, 1984. Holocene climatic change in the northern Midwest: pollen-derived estimates. *Quaternary Research* 22:361–374.

Brubaker, Linda B., 1986. Responses of tree populations to climatic change. *Vegetatio* 67(2):119–130.

Calcote, R. R., 1986. Hemlock in Minnesota: 1200 years as a rare species. M. S. thesis, University of Minnesota, Minneapolis.

Davis, M. B., 1981. Quaternary history and the stability of forest communities. In D. C. West, H. H. Shugart, and D. B. Botkin, (Eds.), *Forest Succession: Concepts and Application*, pp. 132–153. Springer-Verlag, New York.

Davis, M. B., 1983. Holocene vegetational history of the eastern United States. In H. E. Wright, Jr. (Ed.), *Late-Quaternary Environments of the United States*. Vol. 2: *The Holocene*, pp. 166–181. University of Minnesota Press, Minneapolis.

Davis, M. B., 1984. Climatic instability, time lags, and community disequilibrium. In Diamond, J., and T. J. Case (Eds.), *Community Ecology*, pp. 269–284. Harper and Row, New York.

Davis, M. B., 1985. History of the vegetation on the Mirror Lake watershed. In G. E. Likens (Ed.), *An Ecosystem Approach to Aquatic Ecology: Mirror Lake and Its Environment*, pp. 53–65. Springer-Verlag, New York.

Davis, M. B., 1987. Invasions of forest communities during the Holocene: beech and hemlock in the Great Lakes region. In A. J. Gray, M. J. Crawley, and P. J. Edwards (Eds.), *Colonization, Succession and Stability*. pp. 373–393. Blackwell, London.

Davis, M. B., and D. B. Botkin, 1985. Sensitivity of cool-temperature forests and their fossil pollen record to rapid temperature change. *Quaternary Research* 23:327–340.

Davis, M. B., K. D. Woods, S. L. Webb, and R. P. Futyma, 1986a. Dispersal versus climate: expansion of *Fagus* and *Tsuga* into the Upper Great Lakes region. *Vegetatio* 67:(2) 93–103.

Davis, M. B., J. H. Mack, and R. R. Calcote, 1986b. Diffusion of hemlock (*Tsuga canadensis*) into Michigan and Wisconsin during the Holocene. 71st Annual Meeting of the Ecological Society of America, Program and Abstracts, p. 128.

Davis, M. B., M. Schwartz, and K. D. Woods. Detecting a species limit from pollen grains in sediment. Unpublished manuscript.

Fowells, H. A., 1965. *Silvics of forest trees of the United States*. Agric. Handbook No. 271, U. S. Department of Agriculture, Washington, D.C.

Frelich, L. E., and C. G. Lorimer, 1985. Current and predicted long-term effects of deer browsing in hemlock forests in Michigan, USA. *Biological Conservation* 34:99–120.

Hix, D. M., and B. V. Barnes, 1984. Effects of clear-cutting on the vegetation and soil of an eastern hemlock-dominated ecosystem, western Upper Michigan. *Canadian Journal Forest Research* 14:914–923.

Iversen, J., 1954. The late-glacial flora of Denmark and its relation to climate and soil. *Denmarks geol. unders.* (Series II) 80:87–119.

Mack, R. N., 1984. Alien plant invasion into the intermountain West: a case history. In H. A. Mooney and J. A. Drake, (Eds.), *Ecology of Biological Invasions in North America and Hawaii*, pp. 191–213. Ecological Studies Vol. 58. Springer-Verlag, New York.

Manabe, S., and R. T. Wetherald, 1987. Large-scale changes of soil wetness induced by an increase in atmospheric carbon dioxide. *Journal Atmospheric Sciences* 44:1211–1235.

Mitchell, J. F. B., and D. A. Warrilow, 1987. Summer dryness in northern mid-latitudes due to increased CO_2. *Nature* 330(6145):238–240.

Oosting, H. J., and D. W. Hess, 1956. Microclimate and a relic stand of *Tsuga canadensis* in the lower Piedmont of North Carolina. *Ecology* 37:28–39.

Pennington, Winifred, 1986. Lags in adjustment of vegetation to climate caused by the pace of soil development: Evidence from Britain. *Vegetatio* 67(2):105–118.

Prentice, I. Colin, 1986. Vegetation responses to past climatic variation. *Vegetatio* 67(2):131–141.

Ritchie, J. C., 1986. Climate change and vegetation response. *Vegetatio* 67(2):65–74.

Webb, T. III, 1986. Is vegetation in equilibrium with climate? How to interpret late-Quaternary pollen data. *Vegetatio* 67(2):75–91.

Webb, T. III, E. J. Cushing, Jr., and H. E. Wright, Jr., 1983. Holocene changes in the vegetation of the Midwest. In H. E. Wright, Jr., (Ed.), *Late-Quaternary Environments of the United States*, pp. 142–165. University of Minnesota Press, Minneapolis.

WMO/UNEP, 1988. Developing Policies for Responding to Future Climatic Change. Report of the Villach–Bellagio Conferences, September–November, 1987.

7   The Atmosphere and the Future of the Biosphere: Points of Interactive Disturbance

MICHAEL OPPENHEIMER

Editor's Note: The world is changing rapidly under human influences and the changes are the enemy of life. The seriousness of the problem has remained buried until recently in the litter of aspirations for economic growth at any cost and in the convenient and comforting assumption that the biosphere is resilient, capable of absorbing any insult. Recognition of biotic impoverishment as pervasive, even global, and as a threat to economic and political security as serious as war itself is new, not yet a part of the body politic. Yet, for the environment as for any machine, once parts start breaking, damage spreads rapidly.

Michael Oppenheimer offers a physical scientist's review of the physical and chemical changes under way in our world. Although it is common to acknowledge that "everything is connected to everything else," we rarely recognize the concatenation of physical, chemical, and biotic changes in environment that make a term such as "acid rain" a reality. The complexities acknowledged by Bormann in his assertion that the decline of forests in eastern North America is not simply and certainly ascribed to air pollution become real in Oppenheimer's discussion of the mechanisms.

The effects of changes in environment appear in plants, not as a simple response to drought or heat or toxins such as ozone, but as an increase in insect or fungal damage in trees, a mysterious chlorosis, or unexplained mortality.

Repairing a troubled world will require fundamental alterations in many aspects of human behavior. The encouraging aspect is that the world is so thoroughly caught up in its own web of cause and effect that correcting one of the problems will alleviate others.

Michael Oppenheimer offers a thoughtful and probing analysis of the extraordinary array of interactions involved in generating the world's current and future problems, an analysis that hammers home the threats of business as usual and the importance of early action to set the course of human activities back on a track consistent with the limitations and demands of biotic resources. The message could scarcely be more urgent or appropriate.

Introduction

Human activity is altering the atmosphere at an increasing rate through the emission of various trace gasses. These changes enhance the greenhouse effect and cause depletion of ozone in the stratosphere. The earth will warm, climate will change globally, and ultraviolet radiation (UV-B) at the surface

111

will increase. These global changes will act on ecosystems already stressed by local and regional disruptions, such as air pollution. The interactions are the subject of this chapter.

Our approach is to describe the changes in climate, radiation, and air pollution that may occur over the next 40–80 years; secondly, to describe the pathways by which these changes in a few ecosystems will affect the biosphere interactively and occasionally synergistically; thirdly, to discuss time scales for the interactions; and, finally, to propose an agenda for research aimed at reducing these threats to the human future.

The Changing Atmosphere

Our ability to predict changes over 40–80 years is limited. The limitations are more severe when we attempt to predict biotic interactions. We know that the atmospheric concentrations of several radiatively active gasses have increased over the past century. Atmospheric carbon dioxide concentrations, for example, have increased about 25% since the preindustrial era (National Research Council 1983). The concentration of methane has been increasing recently at about 1%/year (Khalil and Rasmussen 1983; Stephens 1985); that of nitrous oxide 0.3%/year (Weiss 1983). Emissions of chlorofluorocarbons (CFC-11,12), which have no natural source, have increased by an order of magnitude over the last 30 years (Gamlen et al. 1986), leveling since about 1974, then, more recently, increasing again.

The radiative and climatic effects of these trace gasses should be determined interactively. For instance, CFCs at once trap infrared and reduce stratospheric ozone, while methane traps infrared and interferes with the ozone-depleting effects of chlorine. Ozone itself absorbs infrared radiation. Atmospheric models indicate that changes in radiatively active gas concentrations have already altered the earth's infrared budget and, possibly, the climate (Hansen et al. 1985). The combined chemical effects of these gasses on stratospheric ozone concentrations already may have led to an enhancement of UV-B at the surface (Stordal and Isaksen 1986). Discussions of these processes are available in Bolin and Cook (1983, Chapter 3) and in Malone and Roederer (1985).

Climatic changes can be predicted on the basis of a given trace gas concentration using global circulation models (GCMs) (Hansen et al. 1983). Chemical models for ozone depletion can be used to calculate changes in UV-B and certain trace-gas concentrations (Solomon and West 1985; International Conference on Health and Environmental Effects 1986). The coupling of these two types of models is the subject of current efforts.

Table 7.1 suggests the range of possible future atmospheric conditions,

Table 7.1. *Physical setting*

	(1850)	1980	2025–30	
World				
CO_2	(275)	340	450	ppm
δTeq	—	1.0 ± 0.25	3.0 ± 1.5	°K
$\delta\,\Gamma_{UV\text{-}B}$	—	0.3	18	%
SO_2-S^a	(65)	65	205	ton S $\times$ 10^6/yr
NO_x-N^d	(30)	20	65	ton N $\times$ 10^6/yr
United States				
O_3 (rural, surface)	—	100	200	%
SO_2-S^a	(<1)	13	17	ton S $\times$ 10^6/yr
NO_x-N^a	(<1)	6	9	ton N $\times$ 10^6/yr

[a] Values under (1850) reflect total natural sources of atmospheric sulfur and nitrogen, not just SO_2 and NO_x. Values for later years reflect anthropogenic SO_2 and NO_x emissions.

CO_2, δTeq, $\delta\Gamma_{UVB}$, So_s-S, NO_x-N, and δO_3 refer to the atmospheric carbon dioxide concentration, equilibrium surface temperature change, ultraviolet photoabsorption rate change for O_3 at the surface, SO_2 emissions (as sulfur), NO_x emissions (as nitrogen), and change in rural surface O_3. CO_2 concentrations, and SO_2 and NO_x emissions, are based on energy scenario projections[1] which lead to a 2.4%/yr growth rate for CO_2 emissions. (A lower growth rate of 2.1%/yr has been suggested recently.[2]) δTeq is based on this CO_2 growth rate and a set of assumptions about other trace gas growth rates.[3] In particular, CFC-11,12 emissions are assumed to grow at 3%/yr. Should the 1987 Montreal Protocol on Substances that Deplete the Ozone Layer and subsequent amendments to it prove successful, CFC emissions growth rates may, in fact, turn negative. The values in this table are therefore a worst case for CFCs, $\delta\Gamma_{UV\text{-}B}$, and O_3. The range for δTeq represents a range of predictions from current models.[4] $\delta\Gamma_{UV\text{-}B}$ is based on depletions calculated in reference c, and the photochemical rates in Whitten and Gery.[5] δO_3 was estimated from the results of photochemical smog models[6] and from the results of Whitten and Gery from the emission rates above, with the additional assumption of hydrocarbon emissions increases similar to NO_x increases.

Sources:
[1] R. M. Rotty and G. Marland, "Constraints on carbon dioxide production from fossil fuel use," paper presented at Energy/Climate Interactions Workshop Munster, Germany, March 3–8, 1980.

[2] R. M. Rotty and D. B. Reister, "Use of energy scenarios in addressing the Co_2 question." *J.A.P.C.A.* 36, 1111–1115, 1986.

[3] V. Ramanathan, R. J. Cicerone, H. B. Singh, and J. T. Kiehle, "Trace gas trends and their potential role in climate change," *J. Geophys. Res.*, 90, 5547–5566, 1985.

[4] See National Research Council 1983; Hansen et al. 1983.

[5] See Whitten and Gery 1985.

[6] J. A. Leone and J. H. Seinfeld, "Comparative analysis of chemical reaction mechanisms for photochemical smog," *Atmos. Environ.* 19, 437–464, 1985; and W. R. Stockwell, private communication.

beginning at the current time, near the ground rather than aloft. The conditions were chosen to emphasize the potential for biotic effects. Table 7.1 shows projections for global and regional anthropogenic N and S emissions, CO_2 concentrations, and regional surface ozone for the period 2025–2030. The global surface-temperature change at equilibrium and the increase in the average UV-B flux are also listed. The basis for these projections is given in footnotes in Table 7.1.

Biotic responses to such changes have not been well defined, although recent studies have taken early steps in that direction. Several investigators, including Solomon and West (1985) and the International Conference on Health and Environmental Effects (1986), as well as Emanuel, Shugart, and Stevenson (1985) and Woodwell (1983, 1989), have outlined possible migration of forests under climatic stress. Solomon and West (1985) observe that future responses of trees to temperature changes may differ from past responses because other factors, including air pollutant emissions, have changed. Svirezhev et al. (in Malone and Roederer 1985, pp. 298-313) have proposed a global model coupling changes in CO_2 and nitrogen availability in their effect on forests.

Oxidants are of particular concern to ecosystems. Oxidants such as ozone and hydrogen peroxide can form in the presence of UV-B in both the atmosphere and in surface waters, and react rapidly in chemical and biological systems. Oxidants increase with increasing emissions of NO_x and hydrocarbons, increased UV-B, and higher temperatures.

Although simulations of future urban ozone and hydrogen peroxide concentrations have been reported (Whitten and Gery 1985), rural or regional simulations, which are critical to this study, have yet to be performed. Based on simulations under current conditions, we project in Table 7.1 a substantial surface ozone increase due to the changes in the factors noted above (Stockwell 1986).

Pathways of Interaction

Atmospheric disturbances and the interactions they cause may increase or decrease effects of the separate stresses on the biosphere. Some of the interactions are illustrated in Figure 7.1. For simplicity we pick three types of ecosystems, and note the condition of the atmosphere (including climate and radiation) in which that system will exist; we outline how the changing atmosphere will affect the various components of the system such as soil, water, and the biota; and discuss interactions.

Temperate Zone Forests
The relationship of the atmosphere to the forest is determined by effects on trees, other vegetation, surface and groundwater, soils, microbes, and even

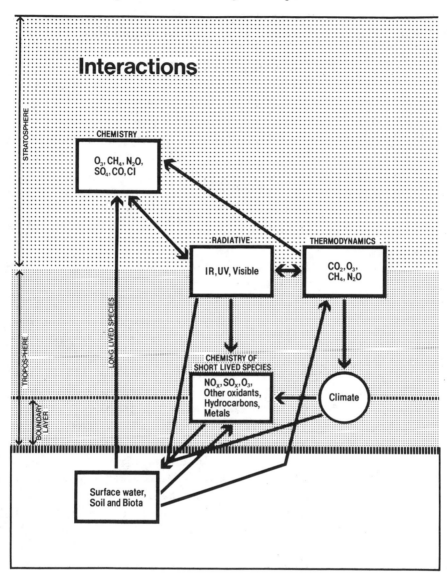

Figure 7.1. Interactions among the various components of the atmospheric system and their coupling to the earth's surface are included.

animals. The interactions are so varied and complex that one cannot be definitive about the effect of atmospheric changes. In general, increasing temperature and moisture (MacDonald 1985), and perhaps increasing carbon dioxide concentration may be expected to increase primary productivity (Pittock and Nix 1986, pp. 243–255). However, temperate zone forests in both North America and Europe are already under stress from air pollution. A variety of symptoms of this stress are observed (Tomlinson 1983; Strain and Cure 1985). At least five mechanisms have been proposed as causes of these symptoms, and several or all of these (and perhaps others) doubtless play a role. We shall describe the proposed mechanisms and determine how those mechanisms would be altered by the gradual imposition of the climatic and radiative changes we have described.

The five biogeochemical mechanisms which have been proposed as contributors to forest damage are:

1 gaseous pollutant interaction with foliage (Johnson and Siccama 1983),
2 acid precipitation (or acid fog water) surface interaction with foliage (U.S. Environmental Protection Agency 1983),
3 acid deposition and mobilization of metals in soils, subsequent biotic uptake, and associated soil nutrient impoverishment (Strain and Cure 1985),
4 toxification of soils by atmospheric deposition of metals (Fowler et al. 1980; Mallant and Salina 1985), and
5 nitrogen "overfertilization" (Heinz and Stournaras 1985).

Gaseous pollutants are phytotoxic at levels observed near urban areas (Johnson and Siccama 1983). Controlled experiments indicate that ozone, sulfur dioxide, and nitrogen oxides, alone and in combination, are capable of causing visible damage to conifers (White, Hill, and Bennett 1974; Shuett 1982; Johnson and Siccama 1983). Although no single pollutant may be capable of damaging trees at levels observed in rural areas, combinations of these gasses at low levels may act synergistically to damage trees.

As a result of the atmospheric changes anticipated (Table 7.1), damage from gaseous pollutants could increase substantially, if SO_2, O_3, and NO_x increase simultaneously. The suggestions that SO_2 reduces net photosynthesis and increases vulnerability of vegetation to climatic extremes (Schuett 1982) and insect infestation (Reich and Amundson 1985) are of particular interest.

Also of concern is the potential for phytotoxicity from H_2O_2 in droplets (U.S. Environmental Protection Agency 1983). The high solubility of H_2O_2 suggests that it may be absorbed easily by foliage. Since it is pervasive in atmospheric water droplets, and its abundance may increase several-fold under climate-radiation (CR) changes, it is a relatively near-term threat to vegetation.

Acid precipitation or acid fog may affect foliage, either synergistically with O_3 (or H_2O_2) or independently by leaching nutrients and destroying protective coatings on conifer needles. CR changes can affect this mechanism in two ways. First, due to internal reactions, atmospheric droplets and droplets on foliage are photochemical "factories" (Yang, Shelly, and Chevone 1982). CR changes will enhance droplet acidity by increasing photochemical activity inside and outside these droplets (followed by absorption). In addition, changes in precipitation frequency will alter the surface concentration of dry-deposited acids on foliage. When dry intervals lengthen, the acid stress to leaves will increase.

In some areas, the effect of acid deposition on soil chemistry will lead to increases in mobility of metals in soil solution (Graedel and Goldberg 1982). If climatic change reduces runoff, where soils are already acidic, vegetation will take up less water with lower pH and higher metal concentrations. Longterm soil nutrient impoverishment may slow where runoff decreases. However, increases in SO_2 or NO_x emissions coincident with runoff decreases could increase both nutrient loss and metal concentrations. Soil impoverishment due to acidification has been noted in Europe (Nriagu 1984), but only the most sensitive soils are seriously affected on decadal time scales.

Temperature increases due to climatic change can also enhance soil water acidification. High soil temperatures lead to rapid mineralization of humus (see Ulrich in Paces 1985). In combination with excess nitrate deposition, this process can lead to acidic discharge of nitrates into the soil solution. The associated mobilization of metals may damage vegetation. Sporadic soil water acidification during warm episodes in combination with preexisting stresses may trigger regionwide forest decline. Synergism between acid deposition and climate results because vegetation absorbs a progressively smaller fraction of available nitrogen. Most important, the increasing occurrence of "outlier" hot summers as climatic changes could increase forest decline indirectly by soil acidification, even when the mean temperature may have changed only a small amount.

Deposition of heavy metals from the atmosphere may affect vegetation, particularly in conjunction with increased mobilization due to acidification (Graedel and Goldberg 1982) and enhanced oxidation (Tomlinson 1981; Sheffield et al. 1985). No specific link with observed forest decline has been proposed for deposited metals, however.

Finally, the overfertilization of forests through excess nitrogen deposition was recently proposed as a mechanism for temperate zone forest decline (Heinz and Stournaras 1985). This suggestion partly arose from test plot experiments. The damaging nitrogen inputs exceeded observed total nitrogen throughfall in industrial regions severalfold, however, resulting in controversy over the importance of this mechanism. Nitrogen deposition also has been proposed as a stress on michorrhizal associations.

The above discussion notes two interesting pathways for stress interactions on forest ecosystems: enhanced oxidant abundances interacting with other air pollutants, both chemically and biologically, and increased temperature interacting with enhanced soil acidity to leach cations and mobilize soil metals.

The increases which may occur for H_2O_2 merit special attention. Synergistic responses with other pollutants seem likely. H_2O_2 and other oxidants also will accelerate the production of acids in leaf droplets. It has been suggested that increased CO_2 levels may reduce stomatal openings, making gaseous pollutants less damaging (Iverfeldt and Lindquist 1986), but it is unclear whether such an argument pertains to H_2O_2, which is highly soluble. Further, ozone (Pittock and Nix 1986, pp. 53-97, 1986), and perhaps H_2O_2, affect plants synergistically with acid deposited on foliage.

The increase in UV-B itself represents a significant stress on vegetation (Shriner 1978; Reich et al. 1985). Inhibition of photosynthesis, mutagenesis, changes in patterns of competition, and yield reductions are some of the changes observed (Bjorn and Borman 1983). The interaction of these changes with climate or pollutant stresses are unknown, although it is known that increased fertilization and water stress decrease UV-B sensitivity.

The stress of water availability in conjunction with that of air pollution has been postulated as a trigger for decline of temperate zone forests (Paces 1985). Climatic change offers the potential for such joint interaction in areas where soil moisture is decreasing.

We have identified ways in which temperature, soil moisture, nitrogen and sulfur deposition, and UV-B interact synergistically to stress forests. The confluence of these stresses may be expected to accelerate the change and biomass reduction already observed in temperate zone forests in industrial regions in spite of the fact that nitrogen, frequently a limiting nutrient in forest, is increasing in deposition (Teramura 1986). Mechanisms involving oxidants and nitrogen are of particular concern. Projected increased nitrogen emissions will augment nitrogen deposition and atmospheric ozone concentrations just as UV-B is stimulating ozone production. Enhanced mineralization of nitrogen threatens accelerated acidification and increased nitrogen leaching. Some drainage basins in the eastern United States already discharge a large fraction of deposited nitrogen (Serejo et al. 1984). Degradation of these systems has important downstream consequences, as discussed below. On the other hand, some feedbacks will be negative. Decay and nitrification may be slowed by acid conditions, and CO_2 increases may reduce pollutant interaction with foliage.

Acid-Sensitive Watersheds

For freshwaters in general, alterations in flow can be expected as precipitation and temperature change. Since acid anion concentrations in surface waters are determined by total deposition, it is unlikely they will undergo much change with changes in precipitation. Long-term wet deposition of sulfur is not strongly dependent on precipitation rate or volume in any case (Bolin and Cook 1983, pp. 206–207). Similarly, concentration of alkalinity is not sensitive to flow (and hence precipitation rate) under a variety of low-to-moderate flow conditions. In contrast, soil cation exchange is highly sensitive to evapotranspiration rate. Simulations (Reuss 1980) suggest that, at a fixed precipitation-acid concentration, soil solution pH varies seasonally by as much as 0.5 units, due to changes in evapotranspiration that alter acid anion concentrations in the soil solution (Bloxam, Hornbeck, and Marten 1984). Therefore, in areas where evapotranspiration increases, it can be expected that climatic change will accelerate soil and surface water acidification, even at constant acid deposition levels. This effect is enhanced with increases in sulfur dioxide and nitrogen oxide emissions. The interaction is synergistic in the sense that in the absence of mineral acids, evapotranspiration changes will have little effect on soil pH.

A temperature-dependent soil acidification due to increased nitrification has been observed by Ulrich (Paces 1985). Such a mechanism indirectly affects surface waters. Acidification of lake waters also may increase because of alterations in the chemical oxidation rate in the lake water column above sediments. The anaerobic reduction of sulfate appears to be an important source of alkalinity in many softwater lakes, sometimes contributing on the order of $\frac{1}{2}$ the alkalinity (Tirpak, personal communication). The resulting Fe-S-H_2S system is highly coupled. Intervention by increasing oxidant concentrations will enhance oxidation in bioturbed sediments, as well as in the overlying water column, resulting in increases in both sediment and H_2S oxidation from reduced form to sulfate (Schindler et al. 1986). This transformation effectively reduces alkalinity and removes Fe^{+2} from the water column, making it unavailable for pyrite formation. It appears that increasing oxidant levels resulting from UV-B and air pollutant increases may accelerate this oxidation. Whereas in situ oxidant formation is important in waters high in organic carbon (Ivanov and Freney 1983; Berner and Westrich 1985), dissolution of oxidants from the atmosphere may be an important source in other waters. A critical question is whether oxidation kinetics are controlled by dissolved oxygen, metal catalysts, or oxidants such as O_3 and H_2O_2. Direct oxidation of H_2S by H_2O_2 becomes competitive at concentrations near $10^{-5}M$ (Yang et al. 1982; Cooper and Zika 1983). Such values, although an order of magnitude higher than the limited observed values, may occur in certain freshwaters now or, perhaps, under the scenario in Table 7.1. More likely, intervention by H_2O_2 in the iron cycle will effectively inhibit sulfur reduction (Cooper and Zika 1983).

The net effect of such changes would be a decrease in freshwater alkalinity. Sulfur additions to waters are partly counteracted by increases in sulfur reduction rates, but rapidly increasing oxidant levels would again have a countervailing effect.

Increased sulfur and nitrogen emissions and deposition will obviously accelerate acidification of sensitive waters. If no further control actions are taken, for the United States, increases may be 30–50 percent after 2010 (Millero 1986). Much larger increases will occur in the lesser developed countries (see Table 7.1). Soil moisture reductions associated with climatic change will decrease pH in soil water. Enhanced oxidant levels from NO_x and hydrocarbon increases, and from UV-B enhancement, will accelerate atmospheric photochemistry and freshwater and sediment chemistry, increasing acidity and decreasing production of alkalinity.

A crude estimate based on current surface water alkalinity distributions suggests that sulfur and nitrogen deposition alone could increase by a factor of two the number of acidified lakes in the United States. Simultaneous CR changes will substantially aggravate this situation. The synergistic interactions noted above, oxidant interference with the alkalinity production, temperature-enhanced nitrification, and increased soil acidity with decreased flow, all occurring while acid deposition is increasing, may cause this value to be a significant underestimate. On the other hand, Cook (1984) has noted the potential for pH-dependent negative feedbacks in the N-cycle.

Coastal Areas

Coastal wetlands, estuaries, and the coastal ocean will bear the brunt of the combined effects of atmospheric deposition, climatic change, and enhanced UV-B. The entire physical setting in which these systems exist may change as sea level rises, erosion sets in, and salinity increases. In the long run, this process may simply eliminate many wetlands. In those that survive, substantial alterations in system biogeochemistry will occur due directly or indirectly to the UV-B increase and changes in air pollutant deposition. Estuaries will be affected by wetland alteration and by a combination of radiative and chemical changes.

From the perspective of chemical inputs, the largest effects on coastal areas may arise from nitrogen loading. Nitrogen is a limiting nutrient in some estuaries and shallow ocean areas. Although internal nitrogen from phytoplankton turnover is the major nitrogen source in the coastal ocean where upwelling is not a factor, the annual increment from deposition and riverine input is a significant source for total nitrogen demand. Atmospheric deposition is a major contributor to the nitrogen budgets of these waters. Because nitrogen in river runoff originates partly in the atmosphere, atmospheric deposition in the Baltic, for instance, may account for one-half or more of total external nitrogen sources (Malone and Roederer 1985). The same situation may characterize such estuaries as the Chesapeake Bay and the Hudson River. The change in primary production, as temperature and nitrogen flux (from atmosphere, sewage, and agriculture) increase, may lead to accelerated eutrophication with algal blooms, anoxic conditions, and large-scale biotic shifts in estuaries and shallow coastal ocean areas (Skulberg, Codd, and Carmichael 1984).

Coastal waters lie at the end of a chain that begins in forested ecosystems. The changes upstream, described below, will further increase nitrogen, sulfur, and carbon flows to coastal waters, encouraging eutrophication and sedimentation.

Increases in UV-B to some extent may counteract this change, as UV-B is known to inhibit surface productivity at least. An important effect will be the shift in plankton communities due to selective UV-B and nutrient effects. Increasing UV-B also brings photochemical changes. Most important may be the increase in hydrogen peroxide concentration in these waters. This molecule, and the associated HO_2 radical ion, are important determinants of estuarine chemistry, including sulfur utilization and metals mobility (Ivanov and Freney 1983; Berner and Westrich 1985). An increase in UV-B may change the oxidation rate in those systems. The coupling of oxidants with the global sulfur cycle in coastal waters is discussed later.

In summary, coastal areas will be seriously disturbed by the rise in sea level accompanying climatic change. These shifts will be aggravated by altered drainage of fresh water to the coast. In addition, due to upstream changes and increased deposition, C, N, S, P, and sediment additions will combine with local temperature change to encourage eutrophication. The primary synergism probably involves the combined effect of nitrogen additions, CO_2 increases, and increased temperature on productivity. However, the systems are so interactive and the perturbations so large that singling out any one mechanism appears fruitless.

Biogeochemical Cycles

The relationship of climatic change to the global carbon cycle has been discussed extensively, whereas the effects of CR changes on the sulfur and nitrogen cycles have not. We have noted some of these changes in the previous section.

The sulfur cycle is the most easily discussed because, while it is dependent on the other cycles, its potential for global regulation of these cycles is limited. Regionally the sulfur cycle is already seriously disturbed by atmospheric deposition, leading to sulfate accumulation in soils and surface water and subsequent acidification. It is less well understood that CR changes may affect the sulfur cycle. For instance, the sulfur emission rates of soils (as CS_2 and OCS) are strongly dependent on temperature, varying by twofold or more for a 5°C change (Bolin and Cook 1983, Chapter 14). The increasing anthropogenic sulfur load, now roughly equal to natural emissions, also may cause increased biotic emissions of reduced sulfur from soils (Adams et al. 1981). As temperature and redox balances are altered, freshwater H_2S emissions may also increase, shifting the disposition of sulfur runoff from pyrite to gaseous form. Due to enhanced oxidant levels this sulfur may be reoxidized. The greatest biological effect of sulfur cycle alteration may be associated with increased acidification caused by loss of alkalinity from net sulfur reduction in acid-sensitive waters. Emissions of reduced sulfur from coastal wetlands may increase due to eutrophication and increased sedimentation (Adams et al. 1981), but wetland loss and increased oxidant levels will counteract this change. Parts of the global sulfur cycle will be massively disturbed in any case.

Another important question relates to CR effects on marine photoplankton that reduce sulfates in sea salt. If, as Charlson has noted (Bolin and Cook 1983, Chapter 7), these species control remote fine aerosol concentrations and droplet nucleation, then both UV-B and temperature changes could alter global weather since the microbial reduction rate is bound to be affected.

The perturbation of the nitrogen cycle by CR changes is less straightforward than the sulfur–CR relation. Nitrogen and CO_2 may alter primary production synergistically, which will, in turn, affect the nitrogen cycle. The nitrogen cycle has already been altered both globally and regionally (Charlson et al. 1986), by anthropogenic inputs comparable to, or greater than, natural inputs, to both rivers and the atmosphere. In remote forests, internal sources are 10–30 times inputs and outputs. However, in temperate zone forests in industrial regions, nitrogen uptake accounts for about 50–60 kg NO_3/ha/yr whereas only 45 kg/ha/yr is cycled internally. Deposition is as high as 50–100 kg at higher, and 10–20 at lower, elevations. Nitrogen deposition thus plays an important role in determining the leaching that occurs in some forests.

Oceans have a substantial nitrogen reserve. When both direct deposition to the ocean surface and the anthropogenic component of river runoff are considered, however, the anthropogenic input is currently within a factor of two of other inputs originating on land. For the ocean as a whole, these inputs are on the order of 1 percent of annual nitrogen requirements and are small compared to the internal pool (Bolin and Cook 1983, Chapter 12; Woodwell 1983). However, in estuaries, coastal regions, and relatively enclosed seas such as the Baltic, compared to the local reservoir, the anthropogenic nitrogen input may be large, leading to eutrophication.

How will CR changes affect the nitrogen cycle? First, coastal primary production will rise as temperature, CO_2 concentration, and nitrogen flux increase (with growing deposition and runoff from sewage, agriculture, and degrading forests). It is important to note that this change is more than additive (Malone and Roederer 1985). Second, terrestrial systems respond to disturbance by increasing respiration relative to primary production (Bolin and Cook 1983, Chapter 2). This will be particularly true of the anticipated climate disturbance since its rate of change will far exceed normal migration rates for forests (Bolin and Cook 1983, Chapter 11; Woodwell 1983). Disturbance by either air pollution, climate, or other factors thus may be expected to accelerate nitrogen mineralization and flux (and perhaps phosphorous flux) from terrestrial systems. Such releases are, of course, self-limiting, either through loss of the terrestrial nitrogen pool or forest recovery, if any, after disturbance ceases.

Time Scales: A Microscopic View

The major premise of this article is that ecosystems will be disturbed simultaneously by climatic change, increases in ultraviolet flux, and air pollution, and that some systems are already under severe stress, having been disturbed by air pollution and other anthropogenic effects. Thus, the time scale for change in natural systems will not be based on climate or UV-B alone. Rather, the time scale is determined by the superposition of these disturbances. Due to synergistic interactions, this superposition may not be linear. From the perspective of global cycles, disturbance due to climate is not occurring in relationship to fixed cycles, but to those that are evolving. Furthermore, the pre-CR changes are already substantial and may be expected to progress in such ecosystems as temperate zone forests. This realization casts doubt on approaches that analyze climate effects as a stress on fixed systems.

By interacting at the biological level, the effects of simultaneous stresses may reinforce or cancel one another. Examples of both cases have been presented.

The concept of a time scale for change at a global scale has been developed by others (Malone and Roederer 1985). Two other levels on which to examine the questions of time scales are those of the individual ecosystem and the local biogeochemical level.

A substantial literature exists on the rate at which individual systems respond to climate shifts (M. Davis, this volume). A few studies exist on the rates of change in ecosystems under atmospheric stresses, such as radiation and intense air pollution. For instance, a time scale for response of surface waters to acid deposition stress can be inferred from paleolimnological and intentional alteration studies. Different components of the system respond on different time scales. In the case of acid deposition and watersheds, the biological system decays rapidly, in less than a decade, while the associated chemical system takes decades or longer to equilibrate. In the case of forests, we are in the course of determining the biological response time scale to air pollution, but it apparently is less than four decades. Based on Central European observations since 1978, a linear time scale seems inappropriate. Estuarine response times to stresses such as augmented nitrogen loading appear to be on the order of three or four decades as well, based on the Chesapeake Bay experience.

How can we augment these time scales to account for CR changes? We can distinguish two types of change. Radiative changes will be continuous. For oxidants, excursions from the long-term mean may not be large compared to the predicted systematic change, so their concentrations may be viewed as increasing monotonically. Biologically, the importance of event versus average doses is problematic. Although no adequate dose-response curves for the individual or synergistic pollutant effects on forest exist, it may be presumed at first approximation that an increase in oxidants will accelerate biological time scales in forests at least proportionately to their concentrations. The inference from oxidant enhancements in Table 7.1 is that the rate of oxidant-related forest decline may double in industrial areas by the year 2030.

In contrast, temperature and precipitation changes will be manifest on an event basis and are biologically important on that basis. Therefore, the time scale change should be defined by a non-linear model. As several investigators have shown (Graedel and Goldberg 1982), the frequency of outliers may be expected to increase more rapidly than the mean. For forests, at least, this pattern suggests possible triggering events at higher temperatures in the course of a few decades. Continuous air pollution and oxidant changes will accelerate the current decline and set the stage for a large-scale decline based on climate events. It is not unreasonable to imagine a confluence of these stresses around the beginning of the next century.

Estuaries and fresh waters in isolation may respond more continuously. They are, however, strongly coupled to the forest-terrestrial ecosystem so the time scales are, in fact, tightly coupled. For instance, forest decline and nitrogen discharge will immediately affect freshwater and estuarine biochemistry.

Summary

Changes in CR properties affecting the earth surface may substantially alter ecosystems and biogeochemical cycles by the middle of the next century.

With regard to biogeochemical cycles, these changes (in temperature and oxidant levels) will generally accelerate the loss of carbon, sulfur, and nitrogen from terrestrial reservoirs. The most prominent actor is the effect of increased levels of atmospheric oxidants. Increased oxidants will:

1   interfere in the sulfur cycle, increasing freshwater acidification;
2   increase solubilization and mobilization of some metals;
3   act as a phytotoxin;
4   indirectly enhance nitrogen mineralization and loss from forests due to the degrading consequences of phytoxicity;
5   enhance carbon and nitrogen respiration from soils by accelerating decomposition; and
6   enhance sediment oxidation (as do increased nitrates and sulfates).

Ecosystem disturbance from climatic change also will increase soil carbon respiration. Respiration will exceed production due to the long equilibration time for terrestrial systems, and forests may experience decline. It is likely that nitrogen loss will increase with respiration due to climate disturbance since nitrate fluxes increase markedly in disturbed forests (Bolin and Cook 1983, Chapter 7). Mineralization will accelerate in the warmer, wetter soils brought about by forest decline and, in some areas, directly by climatic change.

On the other hand, ocean surface flora experiencing a nitrogen surge from these changes and from direct deposition equilibrate rapidly. They may respond to these changes by increased productivity leading to local coastal eutrophication as production shifts from land to sea. By a shift to anoxic conditions, such productivity may also accelerate ocean sulfur release. Over a much longer time scale, this process again can withdraw substantial carbon from the atmosphere. Biota (land plus sea), needed as a carbon reservoir in the short term, may experience a net decline.

To some extent, these changes occur synergistically. We have proposed several specific mechanisms to illustrate these synergisms. Climate and UV-B changes fit into a pattern of preexisting disturbances, the effects of which will be accelerated. Our overall conclusion is that those interactive changes may move nutrients from land to sea, increasing biota at sea, but sharply decreasing them on land.

Research Priorities and Warming Signals

The scope of research needed to elucidate the interactions of local and global stresses on ecosystems is extremely broad. The recently proposed International Geosphere–Biosphere Program is a step in the right direction. However, something more specific is required. The thrust of this chapter is that preexisting local stresses will be accelerated by climate and UV-B changes. Due to the prevalence of preexisting stresses, for many ecosystems the effects of climatic change cannot be studied in isolation. Midlatitude forests in industrial regions now appear stressed by current atmosphere and ozone. As these stresses increase and as UV-B and climate change, these forests may continuously decline. Such changes have implications for fresh waters and for the coastal zone. We suggest that these forests are an appropriate location for an intensive research watch. Estuaries are another such proposed location. As outflow points for the discharges from terrestrial ecosystems, including nutrients from stressed forests and industrial toxins, and as ecosystems that will bear the direct impacts of sea level rise, these estuarine systems may relatively soon be expected to register the local effects of global change.

Research on some specific processes is also of great importance. This includes investigation of multipollutant stress on vegetation with particular emphasis on the role of hydrogen peroxide; effects of nutrient changes, CO_2 changes, and soil and atmospheric chemistry changes on decomposers and nitrogen-cycling microbes; and the effects of UV-B on plankton communities under stress from nutrient changes and toxic chemical inputs.

Conclusion

Ecosystems that already are stressed (and changing) due to local and regional anthropogenic pressures, including air pollution, may shortly experience further stress from the global consequences of UV-B increases and climatic change. The global changes will interact with regional stresses. These interactions may be synergistic in some cases, accelerating changes already under way. Among these are multipollutant stress on vegetation, climate-related soil acidification, and sea-level-rise stress on nutrient-enriched estuaries. Some of these interactions, such as the direct effect of CO_2 on foliage, potentially reducing air pollutant stress, may be inhibitory. Because ecosystems are already changing rapidly, and because synergisms are inherently non-linear and theoretically can lead to instabilities, the relevance of equilibrium models is in doubt. Furthermore, since the change in many environmental variables must be taken into account, controlled studies will become more complex.

A program of research, focused on determining rates of change in a particular ecosystem has been proposed. Unless we act quickly, our ability to organize such research may lag behind the changes.

Acknowledgments

Portions of this paper are reprinted by permission of Climatic Change, National Center for Atmospheric Research.

References

Acid Rain and Transported Air Pollutants: Implications for Public Policy. Washington, D.C., U.S. Congress, Office of Technology Assessment, 1984.

Adams, D. F., S. O. Farwell, M. R. Peck, and E. Robinson, 1981. Biogenic sulfur gas emissions from soils in eastern and southeastern United States. *J.A.P.C.A.* 31:1083–1089.

Ashcraft, P. G., and J. E. Hansen, 1985. *Effect of Doubled CO₂ on Severity of Summers in the United States.* Beltsville, Maryland, Goddard Inst. for Space Studies, June.

Berner, R. A., and J. T. Westrich, 1985. Bioturbation and the early diagnosis of carbon and sulfur. *Am. J. Sci.* 285:193–206.

Bjorn, L. O., and J. F. Bormon (Eds.), 1983. Proceedings of the International Workshop on the Effects of Ultraviolet Radiation on Plants. *Physiologic Planetarium* 58:349–450.

Bloxam, R. M., J. W. Hornbeck, and C. W. Marten, 1984. The influence of storm characteristics on sulfate in precipitation. *Water, Air, Soil Pollution* 23:359–374.

Bolin, B., and R. B. Cook (Eds.), 1983. *The Major Biogeochemical Cycles and Their Interactions, Scope 21.* Wiley, New York.

Caldwell, M. M., 1979. Plant life and ultraviolet radiation: some perspective in the history of the Earth's UV climate. *BioScience* 29:520–525.

Charlson, R., S. F. Warren, J. Lovelock, and M. O. Andrae, 1986. On the feedback of dionethylsulfide from biota, cloud condensation nuclei, and climate. *EOS* 67:869.

Cooper, W. J., and R. G. Zika, 1983. Photochemical formation of hydrogen peroxide in surface and groundwaters exposed to sunlight. *Science* 220:711–712.

Cosby, B. J., G. M. Hornberger, J. N. Galloway, and R. F. Wright, 1985. Timescales for catchment acidification. *Environ. Sci. and Tech.* 19:1144–1149.

Emanuel, W. R., H. H. Shugart, and M. L. Stevenson, 1985. Climate change and the broadscale distribution of terrestrial ecosystem complexes. *Climate Change* 7:29–43.

Fowler, D. J., J. N. Cape, J. A. Nicolso, J. W. Kinnaird, and I. S. Paterson, 1980. The influence of a polluted atmosphere on cuticle degradation in Scots pine (*Pinus sylvestris*). In D. Drablos and A. Tollan, (Eds.), *Proc. Intl. Conf. Ecol. Impacts Acid Precip.* SNSF project, Oslo, March 11–14.

Friedland, A. J., R. A. Gregory, L. Karenlampi, and A. H. Johnson, 1986. Winter damage to foliage as a factor in red spruce decline. *Can. J. Forest Res.* (in press).

Gamlen, R. H., B. C. Lane, P. M. Midgeley, and J. M. Steed, 1986. The production and release to the atmosphere of CCl3F and CCl2FF2 (chlorofluorocarbons CFC11 and CFC12). *Atmospheric Environ.* 20:1077–1085.

Graedel, T. E., and K. I. Goldberg, 1982. Kinetic studies of raindrop chemistry. I. Inorganic and organic processes. *J. Geophys. Res.* 88(10):865–821.

Hansen, J., G. Russell, A. Lacis, I. Fung, and D. Rind, 1985. Climate response times: dependence on climate sensitivity and ocean mixing. *Science* 229:857–859.

Hansen, J., G. Russell, D. Rind, D. Stone, A. Lacis, S. Lebedeff, R. Ruedy, and L. Travis, 1983. Efficient three-dimensional global models for climate studies: Models I and II. *Mon. Weath. Rev.* 111:609–662.

Heinz, F., and C. Stournaras, 1985. Potentially toxic concentrations of triethyl lead in Black Forest rainwater samples. *Nature* 317:714–715.

International Conference on Health and Environmental Effects of Ozone Modification and Climate Change, 1986. *Atmospheric carbon dioxide change: agent of future forest growth or decline*, pp. 16–20. Arlington, Va., June.

Ivanov, M. V., and J. R. Freney (Eds.), 1983. *The Global Biogeochemical Sulfur Cycle.* Wiley, New York.

Iverfeldt, A., and O. Lindquist, 1986. Atmospheric oxidation of elemental mercury by ozone in the aqueous phase. *Atm. Env.* 20:1567–1573.

Johnson, A. H., and T. G. Siccama, 1983. Acid deposition and forest decline. *Environ. Sci. and Tech.* 17:294a–305a.

Khalil M. A. K., and R. A. Rasmussen, 1983. Increase and seasonal cycles of nitrous oxide in the Earth's atmosphere. *Tellus* 35B:161–169.

MacDonald, G. J., 1985. *Climate Change and Acid Rain.* MITRE Corp., McLean, Va.

Mallant, R. K. A. M., and J. Salina, 1985. Experiments on H_2O_2-containing fog exposures of young trees. Symposium on Aerosols, Williamsburg, Va., pp. 19–24, May.

Malon, T. F., and J. G., Roederer (Eds.), 1985. *Global Change*, pp. 75–126. Cambridge University Press.

Mearns, L. O., R. W. Katz, and S. H. Schneider, 1984. Extreme high temperature events: changes in their probabilities with changes in mean temperature. *J. Climate Appl. Meteor.* 23:1601–1613.

Millero, F. J., 1986. The thermodynamics and kinetics of the hydrogen sulfate system in natural waters. *Marine Chemistry* 18:121–147.

National Research Council, 1983. *Changing Climate.* National Academy Press, Washington, D.C.

Nriagu, J. O. (Ed.), 1984. *Changing Metal Cycles and Human Health.* Berlin, Springer-Verlag.

Paces, T., 1985. Sources of acidification in Central Europe estimated from elemental budgets in small basins. *Nature* 315:31–36.

Pittock, A. B., and H. A. Nix, 1986. The effect of changing climate on Australian biomass production: a preliminary study. *Climate Change* 8:243–255.

Reich, P. B., and R. G. Amundson, 1985. Ambient levels of ozone reduce net photosynthesis in tree and crop species. *Science* 230:566–570.

Reich, P. B., A. W. Schuettle, H. F. Stroo, J. Troiano, and R. G. Amundson, 1985. Effects of O_3, SO_2 and acid rain on mychorrhizal infection in northern red oak seedlings. *Can. J. Bot.* 63:2049–2055.

Reuss, J. O., 1980. Simulation of soil nutrient losses resulting from rainfall acidity. *Ecological Modeling* 11:15–38.

Schindler, D. W., M. A. Turner, M. P. Stainton, and G. A. Linsey, 1986. Natural sources of acid neutralizing capacity in low alkalinity lakes of the Precambrian shield. *Science* 232:844–847.

Serejo, A., K. Wagener, and H. Leith, 1984. Deposition anthropogenen Nitrats als Vermutliche Ursache fur die Wachstums Zunahme Beobachtet and Europaischen Eichen. In H. Leith, R. Fantechi, H. Schmutzler (Eds.), *Interactions between Climate* and *Biosphere.* Lisse, Netherlands, Swets and Zeitlinger.

Sheffield, R. M., N. D. Cost, W. A. Bechtold, and J. P. McClure, 1985. *Pine growth reductions in the Southeast.* U.S. Dept. of Agriculture, Resource Bulletin SE–83, Southeastern Forest Experiment Station, Asheville, N.C., November.

Shriner, D. S., 1978. Interactions between acidic precipitation and SO_2 or O_3 on plant response. *Phytopath. News* 12:153.

Shuett, P., 1982. The disease picture – different species of trees but identical symptoms. *Bild der Wissenschaft* 12:86–100.

Skulberg, O. M., G. A. Codd, and W. W. Carmichael, 1984. Bluegreen algae blooms in Europe: a growing problem. *Ambio* 13:244–247.

Solomon, A. M., and D. C. West, 1985. In M. R. White, (Ed.), *Potential Responses of Forests of CO2–Induced Climate Change in Characterization of Information Requirements for Studies of CO2 Effects: Water Resources, Agriculture, Forests and Human Health,* pp. 145–169. U.S. D.O.E./ER–0236. Washington, D.C., U.S. Dept. of Energy,

Stephens, E. R., 1985. Tropospheric methane: concentrations between 1963 and 1970. *J. Geophys. Res.* 90:13076–13080.

Stockwell, W. R., 1986. A homogeneous gas phase mechanism for use in a regional acid deposition model. *Atmospheric Environ.* 20:1615–1632.

Stordal, F., and I. S. A. Isaksen, 1986. Ozone Perturbations Due to Increases in N_2O, CH_4 and Chlorocarbons: Two Dimensional Time Dependent Calculations. Preprint, May.

Strain, B. R., and J. D. Cure (Eds.), 1985. *Direct Effects of Increasing Carbon Dioxide on Vegetation.* U.S.D.O.E./ER–0238. Washington, D.C., U.S. Dept. of Energy, December.

Teramura, A. H., 1986. Overview of our current state of knowledge of UV effects on plants. Intl. Conf. Health Environ. Effects of Ozone Modification and Climate Change, Arlington, Va., pp. 16–20, June.

Tomlinson II, G. H., 1981. *Dieback of forests – continuing observations, May and June, 1981.* Research Center, Senneterr, Quebec.

Tomlinson II, G. H., 1983. Air pollutants and forest decline. *Environ. Sci. and Tech.* 17:246a–256a.

U.S. Environmental Protection Agency, 1983. U.S.–Canada Memorandum of Intent on Transboundary Air Pollution, Working Group I, pp. 4.1–4.38, Jan.

Watson, R. T., J. J. Prather, and M. J. Kurylo, 1988. *Present State of Knowledge of the Upper Atmosphere 1988: an Assessment Report.* NASA Reference Publication 1208, August.

Weiss, R. F. The temporal and spatial distribution of trophospheric nitrous oxide. *J. Geophys. Res.* 86:7185–7195.

White, K. L., A. C. Hill, and J. H. Bennett, 1974. Synergistic inhibition of apparent photosynthesis rate of alfalfa by combinations of sulfur dioxide and nitrogen dioxide. *Environ. Sci. and Tech.* 8:574–576.

Whitten, G. Z., and M. W. Gery, 1985. Effects on urban smog resulting from changes in the stratospheric ozone layer and in global temperature. U.S. Environmental Protection Agency. Workshop on Global Atmospheric Change and E.P.A. Planning, Raleigh, N.C., November.

Wigley, T. M. K., 1985. Impact of extreme events. *Nature* 316:106–107.

Woodwell, G. M., 1983. Biotic effects on the concentration of atmospheric carbon dioxide: a review and projection. In *Changing Climate.* NAS Press, Washington, D.C.

Woodwell, G. M., 1989. The warming of the industrialized latitudes, 1985–2050, causes and consequences. *Climatic Change Journal* 15:31–50.

Yang, Y-S., J. M. Shelly, and B. I. Chevone, 1982. Clonal response of eastern white pine to low doses of O_3, SO_2 and NO_2 singly and in combination. *Can. J. For. Res.* 17:803–808.

Part II

Chronic Disturbance and Natural
Ecosystems: Forests

8   The Restoration of Nonsuch Island as a Living Museum of Bermuda's Precolonial Terrestrial Biome

DAVID B. WINGATE

Editor's Note: Is it possible to restore an impoverished landscape? What if the landscape is insular, the vegetation has been the victim of goats and other insults compounded with introductions of exotics, including disease, to the point where species have been lost? Is there a possibility of rebuilding a stable community that will have the resilience and vigor of the original? The answer has implications for a globe now wracked regionally by waves of impoverishment without obvious end.

David B. Wingate is one of the few ecologists who has addressed this challenge. He has been successful because he is an extraordinary naturalist with the knowledge, energy, interest, will, and the opportunity to divine the details of the structure, function, and successional relationships of the original vegetation of Bermuda. He tells here the story of how he has reconstructed it on Nonsuch Island. To the extent possible, he has also reestablished the animal community as well, although extinctions and introductions make the reconstruction partial.

The story is unique and delightful. Told here in flowing prose, it is as rich in lessons in ecology as any lifetime could be. And yet, the history of Bermuda is short. It was inundated during the interglacial periods and its biota prior to human settlement in the seventeenth century was limited, even for an oceanic island. One cannot help but wonder what the role of the indigenous biota would be on this island landscape if the island were not a recreational fairyland, but dependent on intrinsic resources for energy and the sustenance of its populace.

Introduction

Bermuda is the world's most densely populated oceanic island, and its indigenous terrestrial ecosystem has been drastically modified. Nevertheless some of the endemic flora and fauna have survived, and the rediscovery of the endemic Bermuda petrel or cahow in 1951 resulted in the establishment of the 10 ha Castle Harbour Island National Park. The largest island, Nonsuch (6 ha) was selected in 1962 for restoration as a living museum of the terrestrial biome because of its isolation and because its diverse topography is representative of most Bermuda habitats. Nonsuch was a desert island when the project began. It had been ravaged by feral goats, dogs, and rats, and its forest of Bermuda cedar had been killed by a scale-insect epidemic between 1947 and 1951. Restoration has involved the elimination and/or

133

exclusion of exotic species, the reintroduction of native fauna, reforestation with indigenous flora, and the artificial creation of additional habitats and niches to accommodate endangered species. The island's small size and isolation have made possible the elimination or exclusion of most exotic species including rats, and the restored native flora, including the Bermuda Cedar, has thrived in the absence of exotic competitors. Species successfully reintroduced include the endemic race of the white-eyed vireo from Bermuda's main island and the yellow-crowned night heron from Florida. Other experimental reintroductions from abroad include the green turtle and the West Indian top shell. Habitat manipulation has included the construction of two ponds to allow the establishment of native wetland species. The development of a "baffler" to eliminate nest-site competition with the white-tailed tropicbird, and of artificial burrows to increase the availability of nesting sites, have enabled the cahow to increase with the potential for a large population. The advantages and limitations of satellite islands for endangered-species conservation are discussed in the light of the Nonsuch Island experience.

Oceanic islands have been recognized as crucibles of rapid speciation in the grand process of evolution ever since the publication of Charles Darwin's *Origin of Species*. More recently, they have also been identified as having the highest species-extinction rates following the era of rapid colonial expansion and subjugation of remote corners of the planet by European nation-states since the fifteenth century (see IUCN Red Data Book Series including King 1981). Not so generally recognized is the fact that many of the unique and endangered species which still survive on islands are dependent for their survival not so much on the main islands of the group, where they evolved, but on small adjacent satellite islets which have by chance escaped the main thrust of exploitation and exotic introductions. This is especially true of seabirds and other marine-living species which are dependent on islands only for breeding. Cousin Island in the Seychelles and Boatswain Bird Island off Ascension Island are two examples which come immediately to mind, but there are numerous others.

This chapter examines the potentials and limitations of small satellite islands for conserving endangered species or aiding their restoration by detailing the Cahow conservation project and the Nonsuch Island "living museum" project, which have been under way on the Castle Harbour Islands of Bermuda since 1951 and 1962, respectively.

These projects are possibly unique in that they have involved the successful long-term rehabilitation of an indigenous oceanic island ecosystem on a group of satellite islets where that ecosystem had been almost obliterated.

Historical Background

The isolated oceanic island of Bermuda is located at 32° 17'N and 64° 45'W in the Atlantic. It is the most northerly coral atoll in the world, a circumstance made possible by the warming effects of the Gulf Stream. The emergent land area, totaling 53 km^2, consists of one large island and numerous closely adjacent small islands on the southeastern rim of the shallowly submerged Bermuda volcanic platform (775 km^2). The topography is hilly and is formed from beach-derived calcareous sediments deposited as dunes by the wind and cemented to form aeolionite (Bretz 1960; Land and Mackenzie 1970). Brackish, peat-filled marshes occupy some of the deeper interdune valleys, and small areas of mangrove occupy the sheltered coves.

At the time of its discovery by European explorers in the early sixteenth century, Bermuda had no indigenous human inhabitants or other mammals. The fauna was dominated by large nesting colonies of seabirds, notably the endemic Bermuda petrel or cahow (*Pterodroma cahow*), the Audubon shearwater (*Puffinus l'herminieri*), the white-tailed tropicbird (*Phaethon lepturus catesbyi*), various terns (*Sterna* spp.), noddies (*Anous stolidus*), and boobies (*Sula* spp.) (Lefroy 1877; Verrill 1902a, b). There were also a few extremely tame endemic landbirds and marsh birds, now known only from the early historic accounts and the largely undescribed subfossil remains preserved in limestone caves (Shufeldt 1916, 1922; Wetmore 1960, 1962; Wingate, unpublished). The only non-flying, non-marine vertebrate was the rock lizard (*Eumeces longirostris*), an endemic skink (Wingate 1965). The relatively impoverished flora, with 8 percent endemism, was dominated by Bermuda cedar (*Juniperus bermudiana*), Bermuda palmetto (*Sabal bermudana*), and a few species of woody shrubs, which together formed a dense evergreen forest over most of the island (Britton 1918).

Permanent human settlement did not begin until 1612 when a British colony was established. By that date pigs (*Sus scrofa*), which had been released by Spanish voyagers about 1500, had already decimated the seabirds on the main island. *Rattus rattus* (and probably *Mus musculus*) arrived accidentally in 1613, and domestic cats and dogs were introduced at about the same time. The impact of these new predators, combined with extensive burning and deforestation for tobacco cultivation during the first two decades of settlement, reduced the seabird population to a pitiful remnant and caused the rapid extinction of most landbirds. Thereafter, changes in the native fauna and flora appear to have occurred at a more gradual pace. However, the period from 1680 to 1840 is poorly documented. The small size of Bermuda enabled the settlers to exterminate the feral pigs before 1630, and rabbits, goats, and other ungulates were never permitted to become feral except on a few small harbor islands. The brown rat (*Rattus norvegicus*) probably became established in the eighteenth century, but was not specifically recorded before 1840 (Jones 1859).

Prior to the nineteenth century, the human population never grew beyond 10,000 and was supported primarily by shipbuilding and sea trading. Following the American War of Independence however, Bermuda became of great strategic importance to Great Britain, and vast sums were spent in fortifying and garrisoning the island as a "Gibraltar of the West." This not only stimulated a rapid population growth which has continued up to the present, but also laid the cultural foundation for a more sophisticated economy based initially on agriculture and tourism and more recently on tourism and international "offshore" company business (Hayward et al. 1981). The island presently enjoys one of the highest standards of living in the world, and threats to the remaining natural resources come mainly from the excesses of luxury developments, for there is no poor population dependent directly on Bermuda's resources for subsistence, as is the case with most developing nations.

The natural history has been well documented since 1840, at first by governors and officers in the British military and colonial service and later by local naturalists and scientists from American and European universities. Increased communication with the outside world resulted in a new wave of faunal and floral introductions during the Victorian era, but most of these were relatively benign and their impact on surviving native species was cumulative rather than catastrophic. The most notable exception was the house sparrow (*Passer domesticus*), introduced in 1870–1874, which caused a drastic decline in the native cavity-nesting eastern bluebird (*Sialia sialis*) through competition for nest sites (Bradlee et al. 1931).

It was not until 1940 that the deterioration of Bermuda's remaining native heritage accelerated sufficiently to arouse public concern for conservation action. From 1941 to 1943, as part of a wartime land-lease agreement between the United States and Great Britain, portions of the island were leased for the construction of an airport and naval base. The dredging for this destroyed many small islands, including Cooper's Island (31 ha) in Castle Harbour, and increased Bermuda's land area by more than 6 percent. The opening of the new airport to commercial air traffic after the war stimulated an unprecedented growth in tourism and a boom in hotel and house construction, all of which was facilitated by modern construction equipment such as bulldozers. By 1982 new housing units were being built at a rate of over 300 per year, and Bermuda had become the most densely crowded oceanic island in the world, with a housing density of more than 5 per ha and a human population density of 12 per ha. The endemic *Juniperus bermudiana* forest remained dominant, forming a virtual monoculture until 1946, but two accidentally introduced scale insect pests destroyed 96 percent of the forest before 1951 (Challinor and Wingate 1971). This disaster stimulated a major reforestation effort by the government, but the use of "exotic" species was emphasized so heavily in this program that naturalized introductions and garden ornamentals now comprise more than 90 percent of the flora biomass (Wingate, unpublished).

The landbird fauna suffered equally dramatic changes after 1950 (Wingate 1973). The rapid urbanization and floral changes favored natural colonization by mourning doves (*Zenaida macroura*) and starlings (*Sturnus vulgaris*) from the American continent, and in 1957 the kiskadee flycatcher (*Pitangus sulphuratus*) was deliberately introduced from Trinidad as part of a government-sponsored biological control program. All three species increased rapidly during the 1960s, while the native birds suffered a further decline. By 1980 urban habitat was sufficiently prevalent to allow a population explosion of the domestic pigeon (*Columba livia*), which now competes with Tropicbirds for nest sites in the coastal cliffs.

The loss of Bermuda's cedar forest and the unexpected rediscovery of the cahow (Murphy and Mowbray 1951) became the chief catalysts for government involvement in conservation on Bermuda. Although non-government organizations such as the Bermuda National Trust and the Bermuda Audubon Society still play a primary role in the establishment of nature reserves, the government parks system now covers more than 242 ha including the Castle Harbour group of islands (Jones 1979). In 1966 the government also established a Conservation Division within the Department of Agriculture and Fisheries with a mandate to protect and restore habitats of indigenous flora and fauna.

The Living Museum Project on Nonsuch Island

Origins and Methods

The Castle Harbour Islands National Park consists of nine small islands totaling 10 ha within an area of approximately 2 km^2 at the eastern end of Bermuda (Figure 8.1). Nonsuch Island (6 ha) is the largest and once served as a quarantine hospital for yellow fever. In 1962 I moved to that island as warden in charge of the conservation program for the cahow. The idea of managing Nonsuch as a living museum of Bermuda's precolonial terrestrial biome was conceived at that time, and after 1966 it received full government recognition and support as a project of the Conservation Division.

Nonsuch was ideally suited for such a project because its size and diverse topography made it potentially capable of representing most of the habitat

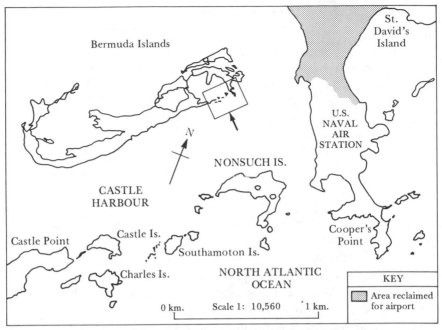

Figure 8.1. Location of Nonsuch Island and the other Castle Harbour Islands in Bermuda.

Figure 8.2. Bermuda cedar forest above North Cove Beach on Nonsuch Island in 1945 before the scale-insect epidemic. Photo by Fred Hamilton, 1945, courtesy of the Bermuda National Trust.

types found on the main island of Bermuda. Also it was sufficiently isolated from the main island to permit the exclusion by quarantine measures of most of the exotic species which had become naturalized on the main island. Indeed, at that time many of the exotic introductions had not reached the Castle Harbour Islands, making them the only sanctuary for the cahow and the last area on Bermuda where the endemic skink remained abundant.

Nevertheless, when the project began, Nonsuch itself was essentially a desert island. Its dense evergreen forest of *Juniperus bermudiana*, which had formed a monoculture until 1947 (Figure 8.2), had been totally destroyed by the scale-insect epidemic before 1953. By 1962 free-roaming goats had further reduced the flora to a herbaceous cover virtually devoid of landbirds (Figure 8.3).

Figure 8.3. Nonsuch Island forest restoration. Early stages showing palmettos and silverwoods under the standing dead trees of Bermuda cedars killed by a scale epidemic of the late 1940s. Young casuarina visible in background. Photo by David B. Wingate, 1967.

The living museum project is best described, therefore, as a long-term experiment in restoration. This restoration has been based on a review of all previous literature on the natural history of Bermuda, together with first-hand study of the few intact remnants of the indigenous floral communities on Bermuda's main island.

The work has proceeded in three ways:

1   Introduced and naturalized "exotics" have been eliminated by selective culling, insofar as possible, or prevented from colonizing by the imposition of quarantine measures.

2   Missing elements of the indigenous floral and faunal communities have been reintroduced from Bermuda's main island or from other parts of their native range abroad, as necessary, and habitat restoration has been accelerated by mass reforestation with nursery-propagated native trees and shrubs, all planted in their appropriate niches at the appropriate spacing.

3   Additional habitats and ecological niches have been created artificially by modifying the topography and making use of human-made structures and manipulative techniques.

Elimination and Exclusion of Exotic Species

Flora

In 1962 Nonsuch had not yet been colonized by the majority of exotic trees, shrubs, and forbs which now dominate Bermuda's main island. Indeed, only five naturalized species were sufficiently aggressive on Nonsuch to pose a threat to the native flora, and all were eliminated or reduced to insignificance by selective culling before 1966. Three of these continue to reach the island via bird droppings from a night roost of starlings, but are prevented from establishing by a continuing culling program. A small number of cosmopolitan forbs and grasses which disperse by burrs or wind cannot be readily eliminated from the island, but these only compete with native species along the mown trailways.

Fauna

Of the fifteen introduced terrestrial vertebrate species which are currently naturalized on Bermuda, only five species of birds, the two *Rattus* species, and the Jamaican anole (*Anolis grahami*) had succeeded in establishing on Nonsuch before the project began. Goats were removed from the island in 1962 and domestic dogs and cats are now excluded under the management regulations. Quarantine measures have effectively excluded the toad (*Bufo marinus*), two whistling frogs (*Eleutherodactylus johnstonei* and *E. gossei*), two species of lizard (*Anolis leachii* and *A. roquet*), and the house mouse (*Mus musculus*). Of these, only the toad regularly makes the water crossing by swimming from Cooper's Point at an average rate of three per year, but the immigrants have so far been detected by night searches and removed before they could reproduce.

Rats of both species have been totally eliminated by the use of bait stations containing anticoagulant rodenticides, either Warfarin in cornmeal or diphacinone in wax-impregnated blocks of grain. The stations are spaced at 40 m intervals throughout the island. Because rats are strong swimmers and Nonsuch is only 170m from the nearest source of reinfestation on Cooper's Point, the island is recolonized at rare intervals. No attempt has been made to eliminate house sparrows, starlings, or European goldfinches (*Carduelis carduelis*) because they are too abundant and mobile. Starlings use the island mainly for cliff nesting and more recently for night roosting in the restored forest, but they feed mainly on the main island. House sparrows are relatively uncommon in the restored native habitats and the goldfinches, though abundant, occupy a seed-eating niche which became vacant with the extinction of native finches in the seventeenth century. The only introduced bird that poses a significant threat to the living museum project (by virtue of its potentially heavy predation on the endemic skink and a native cicada, *Tibicen* sp.) is the kiskadee. Although kiskadees are abundant on the main island, they are relatively sedentary, and their rate of immigration to Nonsuch is sufficiently low (less than 50/year) that it has been feasible to prevent them from establishing by shooting. Partly as a result of this control program, Nonsuch is now the only place on Bermuda where the native cicada survives and the only place where the skink remains common.

An attempt to eliminate the lizard *Anolis grahami* by intensive culling was unsuccessful. Culling began in 1963 when the population was still small and localized, but was discontinued in 1972 when the forest cover became too dense and it became apparent that the population was increasing and spreading anyway. By 1980 the population density was comparable to that on the main island.

Deliberate Reintroductions and Habitat Restoration

Flora

The most urgent task of the living museum project was a general reforestation program to replace the windbreak and wildlife habitat lost when the cedar forest was destroyed. The dead cedars were left standing because of their historic and aesthetic interest, and for the windbreak and rigid support for other vegetation that their highly durable timber still provided. Most of these trees were still standing in 1982.

Figure 8.4a. Nonsuch Island. View along main path in 1964 showing dead cedars killed by scale epidemic in late 1940s. Note initial stage of reforestation: seedling palmettos amidst the St. Augustine grass cover. Photo by David B. Wingate.

In 1966–1967 two rapid-growing and evergreen exotic species, the tamarisk (*Tamarix gallica*) and the casuarina (*Casuarina equisetifolia*), were planted around the periphery of the island to provide a temporary windbreak while the slower-growing native species became established. These exotics were selected because they do not self-seed in Bermuda's soils and thus could easily be eliminated by girdling when they had served their purpose. The initial native planting of approximately 6,000 trees and shrubs between 1963 and 1968 involved all species which are known to have formed the canopy of Bermuda's precolonial forest, except the Bermuda cedar. The main species planted were Bermuda palmetto, Bermuda olivewood (*Cassine laneanum*), sea grape (*Coccoloba uvifera*), buttonwood (*Conocarpus erecta*), forestiera (*Forestiera segregata*), white stopper (*Eugenia axillaris*), Jamaica dogwood (*Dodonaea jamaicensis*), and yellow-wood (*Zanthoxylum flavum*). Cedars were not used in the initial planting because seedlings available at that time were not able to withstand scale-insect attack. By 1970, however, a scale-tolerant strain, aided also by the deliberate introduction of specific biological control insects, was becoming prevalent again on the main island. Six hundred cedar

Figure 8.4b. Same view as Figure 8.4a in 1987. Restored forest along main path. Visible in picture are palmettos, olivewood, Jamaica dogwood, and Bermuda cedar. Photo by David B. Wingate.

seedlings were propagated from seed in that year and planted on Nonsuch in 1972. Although less than half of these have survived, the healthiest specimens have rapidly overtaken the other native trees in height and now form a significant part of the canopy over 20 percent of the island.

It took 10 years for the native plantings to form a thicket and another 10 before a proper canopy was established (Figures 8.4a, b), which then allowed the introduction of more fragile and shade-loving native understory species.

One measure of success of the reforestation effort since 1980 has been the vigorous regeneration from seed of all species which is taking place naturally in the absence of exotic plant competitors.

Fauna

With the exception of the Eastern Bluebird, the accelerated restoration of the native forest by reforestation enabled surviving species of indigenous fauna to recover on or to recolonize Nonsuch Island naturally. Only the endemic race of the White-Eyed Vireo (*Vireo griseus bermudianus*) required deliberate reintroduction from Bermuda's mainland in order to achieve recolonization within a reasonable time. This sedentary forestdependent species died out on Nonsuch in 1963 due to the loss of the cedar forest and the effects of a hurricane. Three pairs were netted on Bermuda's mainland and released on Nonsuch in 1972. In the absence of mammal predators and Kiskadees the vireo quickly attained a population density almost twice as high as in the equivalent habitat on the main island. This population is also beginning to exhibit tamer behavior and a greater tendency to feed on or near the ground.

Reintroductions are now being attempted with species which were extirpated entirely from Bermuda in the early colonial period. Herons of various species were recorded as resident by the early settlers. One of them has recently been identified from subfossils as an undescribed race of the Yellow-Crowned Night Heron (*Nycticorax violacea*), which was adapted for feeding on landcrabs. Between 1976 and 1978, forty-four nestlings of the nominate race were transported to Bermuda from Tampa Bay, Florida, and weaned into the wild at Nonsuch on a diet of native land crabs (*Gecarcinus lateralis*). A majority survived and remained resident, feeding almost exclusively on land crabs, which are abundant on the Castle Harbour Islands. Successful breeding was subsequently confirmed on a larger nature reserve on the main island in 1980, and at least 16 pairs were breeding there by 1982 (Wingate 1982).

Early historical accounts also confirm that Bermuda supported a major nesting rookery for green turtles (*Chelonia mydas*). Bermudan waters still support a large population of immigrant juveniles from elsewhere, but the population which used to breed on Bermuda was reduced to insignificant numbers as early as 1620 and was totally exterminated before the mid-1950s. An experimental attempt to reestablish a breeding rookery has been under way since 1967 by transplanting clutches of eggs from Tortuguero, Costa Rica, and allowing the hatchlings to swim to sea from South Beach on Nonsuch. Approximately 16,000 hatchlings were released to sea between 1967 and 1979, but it may take several more years before the outcome of the experiment is determined because green turtles may take up to 25 years to reach maturity. The Top Shell (*Cittarium pica*), a large marine gastropod, is another species which was apparently extirpated on Bermuda by overharvesting before the nineteenth century. In 1982, eighty-two individuals of the species were reintroduced to the intertidal zone of Nonsuch from the southern Bahama Islands (Bickley and Rand 1982). The survival rate during the first year was 70 percent and all of the survivors grew rapidly. If the reintroduction proves successful, this species will once more provide shells for the native Land Hermit Crab (*Coenobita diogenes*), which has become increasingly rare on Bermuda since the original population of Top Shells was extirpated.

Habitat Restoration with the Aid of Human-Made Structures and Manipulative Procedures

Cahow Conservation Program

The history of the Cahow has been thoroughly documented by Verrill (1920b), Murphy and Mowbray (1951), and Zimmerman (1975). Suffice it to say here that a combination of factors so decimated the Cahow population after human settlement of Bermuda that the birds were ultimately restricted to four of the smallest Castle Harbour Islands, totaling less than 1 ha. But even these islets were marginal breeding habitat because they were accessible to rats and were so eroded that they lacked sufficient soil to enable the birds to excavate nesting burrows. As a consequence the Cahows were forced to nest in the few deep natural holes and crevices in the cliffs, but these also happened to be the optimum breeding habitat of the white-tailed tropic bird. The resulting nest-site competition invariably favored the later-nesting and larger tropicbirds, and was causing the deaths of more than 60 percent of Cahow chicks when the population was first rediscovered.

In addition to the rat-elimination procedure described above, two manipulative procedures have been developed since 1954 to overcome this problem and to increase the number of safe nesting sites (Wingate 1978). In 1954 Richard Thorsell and Louis Mowbray devised an artificial entrance for the Cahow nesting crevices which they called a "baffler." This excludes the larger Tropicbird by taking advantage of the size difference, in the same way that a 4 cm entrance hole on a bluebird nest box excludes the larger starling. Since 1961 the baffler has completely prevented mortality from tropic birds, effectively trebling the Cahows' reproductive success.

The second manipulative technique has been the construction of artificial nesting burrows on the level tops of the Cahow nesting islets. This has been done in an effort to reestablish the original separation in breeding niches between the soil-burrowing Cahow and the cliff-nesting tropic bird. The burrows are made by excavating trenches into the soft rock with a mattock and roofing them over with concrete. Their major advantage is that they can be added as required, built anywhere, and duplicated indefinitely until they completely saturate the smaller islands. Now that nest sites are no longer a limiting factor and full protection is afforded from predators and competitors, the Cahow population has responded with a gradual but accelerating increase from 18 pairs in 1962 to 46 pairs in 1989. Ultimately, this increasing population is expected to spill over onto the larger neighboring soil-covered islands such as Nonsuch, where soil burrowing will once again become possible. Nonsuch Island could easily accommodate a naturally burrowing population in excess of 1,000 pairs, but the use of artificial burrows could increase the potential to many thousands.

Creation of Marsh Habitats

One major factor limiting the scope of the living museum project when it began on Nonsuch was the lack of any natural marshland or ponds on the island. By chance, the topography of Nonsuch made it possible to create two small ponds, one providing saltmarsh/mangrove habitat and the other freshwater marsh habitat, by comparatively minor enhancement of two natural swales or valleys. In 1975 the availability of funds and equipment made it possible to develop both ponds simultaneously. The slightly tidal saltmarsh pond was created by excavating an area of 30,000 m^2 behind the South Beach dune to a depth of 50 cm below the water table. The freshwater pond (Figure 8.5) was created by deepening a natural swale between two hills, installing a 25 × 55 m impermeable PVC liner, and covering it with a 40 cm layer of soil. The resulting impermeable basin filled naturally with rainwater because the annual rainfall exceeds the evaporation rate on Bermuda (Macky 1957).

Completion of these ponds made it possible to introduce the native flora and fauna associated with such habitats on Bermuda's mainland, and was regarded as a necessary prerequisite to the reintroduction of the Yellow-crowned Night Heron. With the exception of the slow-growing mangroves, mature communities essentially indistinguishable from their counterparts on the main island were established in these ponds within 3 years (Figure 8.5). One species successfully introduced to the brackish pond in 1976 was an endemic killifish (*Fundulus bermudae*), known only from two other inland ponds on Bermuda (Beebe and TeeVan 1933).

At least two other rare and localized native species are expected to benefit significantly from the creation of these ponds. The giant land crab (*Cardisoma quanhami*), limited to two small colonies in mainland mangrove swamp, was successfully introduced to the saltmarsh pond in 1980. The moorhen (*Gallinula chloropus cachinnans*), which presently numbers less than fifteen breeding pairs on the main island, is expected to breed on the freshwater pond if it can be deliberately introduced, and it may even colonize Nonsuch naturally. In the absence of mammalian predators, its high reproductive potential could result in good breeding success and provide a boost to the main population by dispersal from Nonsuch.

Discussion

There are two important features of the living museum nature reserve described in this paper. Firstly, it is concerned with restoring a whole

Figure 8.5. Freshwater Marsh on Nonsuch Island. Note restored cedar, palmettos, and olivewood stands in background. The taller dead stems are casuarina, phased out and killed by girdling.

ecosystem rather than any particular component species. This is advantageous because of commensal relationships which might not be anticipated beforehand. Secondly, it exploits the isolation and manageable size of small islands in order to maintain, readjust, or enhance species and habitats in a way that is either self-sustaining, or at least sustainable, in the long term with a minimum of energy input.

The achievements of the Cahow and living museum projects on the Castle Harbour Islands demonstrate that satellite islands can play a unique and vital role in the conservation of endangered species, provided that they are sufficiently isolated from the parent island and are representative of at least some of its habitats.

In the case of seabirds and other marine animals which need land only for breeding and which are colonial nesters, satellite islands are theoretically capable of supporting the entire world population. The Castle Harbour Islands, for example, are the only remaining breeding stations for the Cahow, but clearly have the potential to support a large and viable population with the aid of bafflers and artificial burrows. These islands also support a stable population of more than 500 nesting pairs of white-tailed tropic bird, which represents approximately 15 percent of Bermuda's total breeding population. This is significant, too, in view of the fact that the bulk of the population, which nests on cliffs on the main island, is declining.

Satellite islands can likewise perform a vital role as predator-free or competitor-free sanctuaries for species entirely terrestrial in habit. However, in this case the size of the island can be a serious limiting factor for two reasons.

First, small size may limit the number or diversity of habitats, so precluding the establishment of certain species altogether. An extreme example of this problem would be a mountainous oceanic islet with a low satellite islet which could not be used as a refuge for endangered cloud forest species. Even Nonsuch, which is fairly representative of Bermuda, has problems of this type. Its small size places it entirely within the coastal distribution of the soil-burrowing land crab and greatly increases exposure to wind and salt spray during gales. Although these factors did not prevent the artificial creation of self-sustaining marshlands, it has precluded the creation of a typical inland valley habitat because some of the component species cannot survive the combined stress of salt spray and burrowing by land crabs. Such species could only be maintained on Nonsuch by continuous and intensive horticultural care, thus blurring the important distinction between a living museum nature reserve and a botanical garden or zoo.

Secondly, small size may preclude large species with large foraging territories from maintaining viable populations on the island. Although the endemic rock lizard has a sufficiently large population on Nonsuch to survive in isolation indefinitely, it is extremely doubtful whether the White-Eyed Vireo could do the same if it became extinct elsewhere on Bermuda, because Nonsuch is capable of supporting only ten breeding pairs.

Nevertheless, small satellite islands free of predators or competitors can still provide a crucial *temporary* role in a crisis, even for species with large territories in relation to the size of the island. The case history of the reintroduction of Yellow-Crowned Night Herons is pertinent here because it revealed that Nonsuch Island by itself was not sufficient to meet the herons' breeding requirements. The success of the project was ultimately dependent on their access to a much larger reserve on the main island.

If there is a moral in these examples, it is that satellite islands may assist in the preservation of unique island ecosystems, but they are no substitute for, and should not become an excuse to neglect, the greater challenge of establishment or rehabilitation of large reserves on the parent islands themselves. Rather, the operative principles of the satellite island approach should be employed wherever possible in the design of those large reserves on the parent island.

In order to illustrate how this might be done I offer the following proposal involving Cooper's Headland on the eastern boundary of the Castle Harbour Islands National Park. Prior to its connection to St. David's Island with dredged fill during the construction of the airport in 1943 (Figure 8.1), Cooper's Point was an island of 31 ha separated from St. David's Island by a water gap of 700 m. This island was part of the land leased to the United States for a military base in 1941 for a period of 99 years. Much of it has since been bulldozed, quarried, or otherwise modified for a variety of installations, including storage bunkers, a 4 ha concrete water catchment, and a NASA tracking station. Nevertheless, the headland has not been used for residential development, and even today the greater part of its varied coastline (which includes 7 percent of Bermuda's total beach area), together with about 2 ha of sheltered inland habitat, remains unspoiled and dominated by native species.

Assuming that the formidable political and planning problems of handing Cooper's Island back to Bermuda and relocating its vital installations elsewhere could be overcome, it would be a comparatively easy engineering task thereafter to isolate the island again by dredging a wide channel through the reclaimed area. It could then be restored as an extension of the living museum project within an expanded Castle Harbour Islands National Park. Considering what has been achieved on Nonsuch with only one-fifth of the land area, the potential of Cooper's Island as a living museum would be almost unlimited.

Acknowledgments

Since 1951 the Cahow conservation program and some of the research on Nonsuch have been partly funded by grants from the New York Zoological Society. I have been employed as Conservation Officer in the Bermuda Government Department of Agriculture and Fisheries since 1966, and most of the work on Nonsuch Island has been supported by the Bermuda government since then. The Caribbean Conservation Corporation provided funding, and the funding of Dr. H. Clay Frick has played a leading role in the Green Turtle rookery restoration experiments since 1967. Numerous other friends and colleagues from the Department of Agriculture, the Bermuda Biological Station, and research institutions abroad have provided encouragement, scientific advice, and voluntary assistance over the years.

This paper is reprinted with the permission of the International Council for Bird Preservation (Technical Publication 3, 1985).

References

Beebe, W., and J. TeeVan, 1933. *Field Book of the Shore Fishes of Bermuda*. G. P. Putman's Sons. New York and London.

Bickley, E., and T. G. Rand, 1982. Reintroduction of West Indian top shells on Bermuda. *Dept. Agri., and Fish. Bull.* 53:64–66.

Bradlee, T. S., L. L. Mowbray, and W. F. Eaton, 1931. A list of birds recorded from the Bermudas. *Proc. Boston Soc. Nat. Hist.* 39:279–382.

Bretz, J. H., 1960. Bermuda: a partially drowned, late mature, Pleistocene karst. *Bull. Geol. Soc. Amer.* 71:1729–1754.

Britton, N. L., 1918. *Flora of Bermuda*. Hafner Publ., New York and London.

Challinor, D., and D. B. Wingate, 1971. The struggle for survival of the Bermuda Cedar. *Biol. Conserv.* 3:220–222.

Hayward, S. J., V. H. Gomez, and J. W. Sterrer, (Eds.) 1981. *Bermuda's Delicate Balance*. Bermuda Biol. Station for Research Inc., Spec. Publ. No. 20.

Jones, J. H., 1979. *The Guide to Bermuda's Public Parks and Beaches*. Dept. Agric., and Fish. Publ. Island Press Ltd, Hamilton.

Jones, J. M. 1859. *The Naturalist in Bermuda*. Reeves and Turner, London.

King, W. B., 1981. *Endangerd Birds of the World: ICBP Bird Red Data Book*. Smithsonian Inst. Press, Washington, D.C.

Land, L. S., and F. T. Mackenzie, 1970. *Field Guide to Bermuda's Geology*. Bermuda Biol. Station for Research Inc. Spec. Publ. No. 4.

Lefroy, J. H. 1877. *Memorials of the Discovery and Early Settlement of the Bermudas or Somers Islands 1511–1687: Compiled from the Colonial Records and Other Original Sources*. Vols. 1 and 2. Longmans, Green, and Co., London.

Macky, W. A., 1957. The rainfall of Bermuda. Bermuda Meteorological Office Technical Note No. 8.

Murphy, R. C., and L. S. Mowbray, 1951. New light on the Cahow (*Pterodroma cahow*). *Auk* 68:266–280.

Shufeldt, R. W., 1916. The bird caves of the Bermudas and their former inhabitats. *Ibis* 10:623–635.

Shuefeldt, R. W., 1922. A comparative study of some subfossil remains of birds from Bermuda, including the "Cahow." *Ann. Carnegie Mus.* 13:333–418.

Verrill, A. E., 1902a. *The Bermuda Islands*. Reprinted from the Transactions of the Connecticut Acad. Sci. Vol. 11, with some changes. New Haven, Conn.

Verrill, A. E., 1902b. The "Cahow" of the Bermudas, an extinct bird. *Ann. Mag. Nat. Hist.* 7:26–31.

Wetmore, A., 1960. Pleistocene birds in Bermuda. *Smithsonian Misc. Collections* 140:1–11.

Wetmore, A., 1962. Notes on fossil and subfossil birds. *Smithsonian Misc. Collection* 145:1–17.

Wingate, D. B., 1965. Terrestrial herpetofauna of Bermuda. *Herpetololgica* 21:202–218.

Wingate, D. B., 1973. *A Checklist and Guide to the Birds of Bermuda*. Bermuda Press Ltd., Hamilton.

Wingate, D. B., 1978. Excluding competitors from Bermuda Petrel nesting burrows. In S. A. Temple (Ed.), *Endangered Birds: Management Techniques for Preserving Threatened Species*. University of Wisconsin Press, Madison.

Wingate, D. B., 1982. Successful re-introduction of the Yellow-Crowned Night Heron as a nesting resident on Bermuda. *Colonial Waterbirds* 5:104–115.

Zimmerman, D. R., 1975. *To Save a Bird in Peril*. Coward, McCann, and Geoghegan Inc., New York.

9 Patterns of Impoverishment in Natural Communities: Case History Studies in Forest Ecosystems – New Zealand

A. F. MARK AND G. D. McSWEENEY

Editor's Note: New Zealand, isolated 80 million years ago by the vagaries of continental drift, blessed with a high degree of endemism as a result of the isolation, and protected from human depredations until about 1,000 years ago, offers a window on the effects of rampant mismanagement of an especially vulnerable flora and fauna. The most conspicuous transition was the destruction of the lowland forests by Polynesian settlers and the replacement of the forests with fernlands, shrublands, and tussock grasslands. But the introduction of exotic mammals, apart from humans, has been an almost equivalently destructive force, changing plant and animal communities throughout the islands. The changes have been the more profound in that the indigenous plants and animals were of the large-bodied, slowly reproducing forms that are most vulnerable to disruptions.

The principal solution advanced by Mark and McSweeney is a more elaborate system of reserves. The lessons from New Zealand are many and rich. The danger is that they will be seen as peculiar to that entrancing place and not the window on the world that they are.

Introduction

The continuous isolation of New Zealand since its separation from the Gondwanaland supercontinent during the upper Cretaceous era has allowed preservation of unique archaic elements among its limited indigenous biota.

Three periods in the recent past have had important influences on the current biota. Some of the ancient biota became extinct during the Pleistocene glaciations. About 1,000 years ago, soon after Polynesian settlement, fires in the drier rain shadow regions of the South Island reduced the forested area from *c.* 78% to *c.* 53%. Habitat destruction, hunting, and predation by the Polynesian rat and dog caused further extinctions and other changes.

Over the last two centuries, European occupation has been more destructive. Forest area has now been reduced to 23% and both intentional and accidental introduction of exotic plants and animals has brought further problems. Biotic depletion is now beginning to be controlled through a range of conservation measures promoted by greater public awareness and political action through citizen conservation movements.

151

Biotic impoverishment of New Zealand's forest ecosystems can be treated in three chronological phases:

1   the prehuman period;
2   the millennium of human occupation by Polynesians; and
3   the last two centuries under increasing European influence.

Phase 1: The Prehuman Period of New Zealand's History

New Zealand originated from the southern supercontinent of Gondwana-land. Separation from the larger land mass in the upper Cretaceous, 80 million years ago, subsequent continued isolation, and the persistence of terrestrial habitats (Stevens 1985) endowed New Zealand with a small, but distinctive and generally archaic biota (Fleming 1962, 1975; Enting and Molloy 1982).

Forests occupied about 78 percent of New Zealand's 268,000 km^2 prior to the arrival of the first humans about a millennium ago (Figure 9.1). These forests persist today, albeit over a vastly reduced area. Their biota more closely resembles the ancient Mesozoic forests of Gondwanaland than those of any other southern land mass (Fleming 1977). The ancestors of many members of the contemporary evergreen indigenous forest flora (Wardle, Bulfin, and Dugdale 1983) – particularly the dominants, kauri (*Agathis australis*, Araucariaceae), celery pines (*Phyllocladus* spp.), and other podo-carps (Podocarpaceae), and southern beeches (*Nothofagus* spp.); as well as some of the more minor groups, *Pseudowintera* (Winteraceae), the Proteaceae, and a genus of Psilotales (Tmesipteris) – undoubtedly existed when the islands were separated from Gondwanaland.

New Zealand's distinctive prehuman land fauna reflected the timing of its separating from the larger land masses (Fleming 1975). Many of these animals are now extinct. About 300 species of land birds, 40 reptilian species, and 3 amphibians remain. The separation of the country from Gondwana-land must have preceded the dispersal of snakes and terrestrial mammals. The only subsequent vertebrate migrants were birds and three species of bats. The archaic (Gondwana) element of the fauna is also shared by many invertebrates, particularly land snails (Climo 1975), arachnids (Forster 1975), and a wide range of insects (Watt 1975).

Over the millennia, the original inhabitants along with occasional colonists established and evolved on an archipelago which ranged in climate from warm-subtropical to cold-temperate and allowed forests to persist (Fleming 1975). The land mass was of low relief throughout most of the Tertiary era, and was subsequently uplifted in the early Quaternary. This

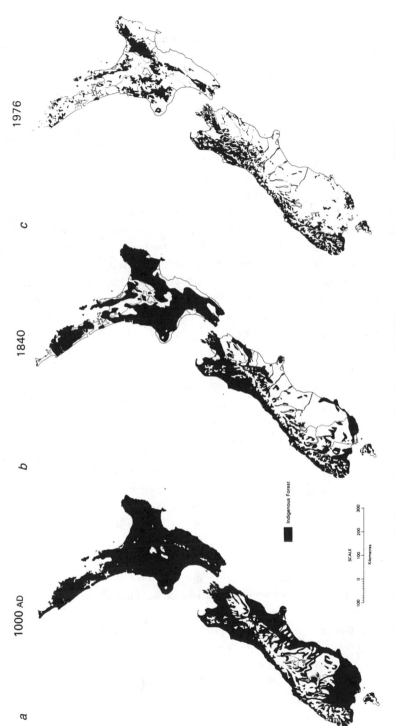

1000 AD

1840

1976

a

b

c

■ Indigenous Forest

SCALE

100   0   100   200   300

Kilometres

Figure 9.1. Estimated indigenous forest cover in New Zealand (a) 1000 A.D. (prior to human settlement), (b) 1840 A.D. (prior to European settlement), and (c) 1976, based on New Zealand Forest Service information. (Reprinted with permission from Froud et al. 1985.)

movement was concentrated along the boundary between two converging crustal plates, the Indian–Australian and Pacific Plates. Their boundary virtually bisects the North and South Islands close to the main axial mountain ranges. Movement has resulted in a lateral displacement along the Alpine Fault of some 480 km (Stevens 1985). Subsequent erosion, particularly as the climate cooled with the onset of the Pleistocene and during postglacial times, has produced extensive areas of outwash gravels. Although uplift continues at a maximum rate of 17 mm/yr (Wellman 1979), the main axial ranges are now in a steady state with the rate of erosion matching the rate of uplift. These erosional processes, combined with localized volcanism and precipitation which can reach 12,000 mm on windward slopes, have created an extremely dynamic landscape. Today, mainland New Zealand varies from warm-temperate in the far north (34° S) to cool-temperate in the south (47° S). Apart from the subcontinental basins to the leeward of the South Island's Southern Alps, areas below the regional treeline (which ranges from 1,400 to 900 m depending largely on latitude) are characterized by a forest climate. The North Island is typically hilly and partly mountainous, but much less so than the South Island where several peaks exceed 3,000 m. The highest, Mt. Cook, reaches 3,764 m. There are extensive permanent snow fields down to 2,000–2,400 m.

During the Quaternary when climates cooled, the forest flora lost some genera, Cocos for example, and many warmth-dependent species. Based on pollen forms, among the plants (Fleming 1975) Bombax, Cupania, Ephedra, Microcachrys, Casuarina, and the Brassii southern beeches were lost as were a number of species of birds (Fleming 1962a). Rising seas associated with the interglacial periods of the Pleistocene inundated low-lying areas, causing sections of higher land to become islands. Isolated on these islands there evolved many new species, subspecies (Fleming 1962c), and, among some invertebrates, even subgenera (Climo 1975). For thousands of years after human habitation had modified much of the rest of the world, the environment of New Zealand developed unaffected by terrestrial mammals, including humanity.

Free from browsing and predatory mammals and continuously isolated by sea, New Zealand's biota evolved its distinctive, indeed unique, character marked by high levels of endemism in all major groups (Table 9.1). Primeval forest plants flourished. Some birds became ground-dwelling, flightless, and adapted to ecological niches that elsewhere would have been exploited by mammals. Other vertebrates and even large insects such as the flightless giant wetas (Henicidae) also utilized such habitats (Watt 1975). Three ancient frogs still survive (Bull and Whittaker 1973) as does the tuatara (*Sphenodon punctatus*), the sole remnant of a reptilian order (Rhynchocephalia) that disappeared elsewhere about 100 million years ago (Crook 1975).

Table 9.1. *Numbers of native and introduced species of main plant and animal groups in New Zealand with the status of native species in these groups*

Group	Number of species		Status of native species		
	Native	Introduced	% Endemic	Threatened	Endangered
1. Mosses and ferns	1,170	38	35	12	Unknown
2. Conifers	20	30	100	0	0
3. Flowering plants	1,813	1,700	81	250	39
4. Invertebrates – worms, snails, spiders, and insects	12,658	1,212	94	184	Unknown
5. Lower vertebrates – freshwater fish, frogs, and lizards	68	7	95	18	0
6. Higher vertebrates – birds and mammals	192	66	53	22	6

Source: Reprinted by permission from Nature Conservation Council (1981).

Today New Zealand's indigenous land and freshwater birds are reduced to 65 species, most of which are forest dwellers. Fifty-seven percent of these are endemic, although the proportion reaches 70 percent if subfossil and recently extinct species are included. Ratites – including the still extant kiwi, Apteryx (Reid and Williams 1975), and the giant moas, Dinornithidae, which became extinct during the period of pre-European Polynesian occupation – formed part of the archaic element before the isolation of New Zealand in the late Cretaceous (Oliver 1949; Fleming 1962a, 1962b). Other archaic birds include the now very localized wattle birds with three monotypic genera in the endemic family Callaeatidae, the extinct thrushes (Trimagra), the extinct giant, meter-tall, rail (Aptornis), the near-extinct, almost flightless, nocturnal ground parrot or kakapo (*Strigops habroptilus*), and the New Zealand wrens (Acanthisittidae). Forest birds still endemic at the specific or generic level include the kaka parrot (*Nestor meridionalis*) and the related unique alpine parrot, the kea (*Nestor notabilis*), parakeets (Cyanoramphus), a large pigeon (*Hemiphaga novaeseelandiae*), an owl (*Ninox novaeseelandiae*), a falcon (*Falco novaeseelandiae*), three honeyeaters (Meliphagidae), and the flightless rails (*Gallirallus* spp. and *Notornis mantelli*, takahe). A few species such as the kingfisher and the migratory cuckoos extend beyond New Zealand. Many bird species are self-introduced from Australia, arriving on the prevailing westerly wind and exploiting habitats arising from human settlement. Eight species of Australian birds have reached New Zealand unassisted since European settlement. Others like the pukeko and white heron, being indistinguishable from their Australian counterparts, are still regarded as relatively recent (though pre-European) colonists (Fleming 1962b). Extinctions have been more frequent among endemic bird species than among those presumed to be recent arrivals still having close relatives in Australia (McDowall 1969).

There are a number of features characteristic of indigenous vertebrate fauna, particularly the archaic element of the avifauna and much of the indigenous flora as well. They include low reproductivity, or slow seedling growth, extraordinary longevity, and, for the birds, long nesting periods, large eggs, long incubation periods, long family periods, year-round site fidelity, no migration, early pair bonding, mate fidelity, flightlessness, and melanism. Most of these are features of equilibrium (K-strategy) rather than opportunist (r-strategy) species. The plants have a high proportion of species with palatable foliage or bark, and shallow feeding roots. Many of both the flora and fauna (Table 9.1) are on current "rare and endangered species" lists. Williams and Given (1981) cite 21 birds, 10 reptiles, 3 amphibians, 5 fish, 1 mammal, and 66 vascular plants.

Phase 2: The Polynesian Era

This phase began with the arrival of Polynesian settlers about 1,000 years ago. Their widespread use of fire was much more destructive of the forest (Molloy et al. 1963) than previous natural fires and local volcanism had been. The combination of the burning of the forests, the introduction of the kiore or Polynesian rat (*Rattus exulans*) and the Polynesian dog (*Canis familiaris*), and the practice of hunting eliminated many bird species. The forest cover was reduced to about 53 percent (Figure 9.1) and was displaced by fernland, shrubland, and tussock grassland. Fire was particularly destructive of the drier forests of central and eastern South Island in the rain shadow of the Southern Alps (Molloy et al. 1963). The practice of burning was continued up to the period of European settlement. In 1769, when off the east coast of the South Island, British explorer James Cook recorded in his diary that he had observed great palls of smoke coming from the interior.

During the Polynesian period all of the 12 to 24 species (six genera) of moa – ratite ground-dwelling birds that reached to 4 m in height, weighed up to 300 kg, and occupied several niches – were exterminated. Some survived as late as the early eighteenth century. Samples of gizzard contents indicate a diet made up of mainly twigs but also some leaves, fruit, and seed of mostly forest or forest margin species (Burrows 1980; Burrows et al. 1981; Anderson 1983). The role of moas in the evolution of the divaricating shrub form, a pronounced feature of New Zealand's woody flora, is still debated (Greenwood and Atkinson 1977; McGlone and Webb 1981; Wardle 1985). Other extinctions attributed to Polynesians include seven waterfowl, six rails, two hawks, two eagles – including Harpagornis, with a 2–3 m wing span and 10–12 kg body weight – one snipe, and one crow. The total comes to 45 species. Many of the remains of these species are associated with Polynesian middens or campsites (Kinsky 1970).

The Maori dog became extinct in the wild during the Polynesian era. The kiore has persisted and adversely affects populations of tuatara (Crook 1973a), lizards (Whittaker 1973), and *Leiopelma* frogs (Bull and Whittaker 1975); *L. hamiltoni* is now confined to two offshore islands where they occupy an area of < 20 ha. Crook cites evidence of recruitment failure in tuataras on seven of twenty-three island populations which could be attributed, in almost all cases, to the Polynesian rat.

Phase 3: The European Period

The period of European settlement (Phase 3) has brought even more disastrous changes than that of the Polynesians. European colonization of New Zealand was rapid. The settlers were largely ignorant of, or indifferent to, the unique nature of their new landscape, on which they attempted to impose a European imprint. Vast areas of forest were wastefully logged, burned, and cleared for pasture (Nicholls 1980). Such actions, in combination with the introduction of numerous animals, caused further massive reduction in forest cover (Figure 9.1) and a serious decline in the variety and abundance of the flora (Given 1981) during the nineteenth century.

Among the introduced animals were several species of deer, the Australian brush-tailed possum (*Trichosurus vulpecula*), feral goats, and pigs. These animals, in various combinations, destroyed or modified countless forest habitats. A number of new predators – including mustelids (especially stoats); rats, both the ship rat (*R. rattus*) and the Norwegian rat (*R. norvegicus*); and feral cats – devastated native bird populations, particularly the ground dwellers (King 1984). Some 33 species of foreign terrestrial mammals are now well established in the wild in New Zealand. Nineteen of them occupy forest habitats (Gibb and Flux 1973; Mark 1984). Numerous other attempts at introductions have proved unsuccessful. The forays of collectors have contributed to the demise of such rarities as the huia (*Heteralocha acutirostris*), which has been extinct since about 1907, and the stitchbird (*Notiomystis cincta*), now confined to offshore islands.

After less than a century of European settlement the toll for the New Zealand region was seven species of birds driven extinct. A further 23 species or subspecies had become endangered or rare. Significantly, endemic species have experienced an extinction rate about eight times that of the total indigenous species (Mills and Williams 1979). The principles of island biogeography apply to indigenous birds in New Zealand forests (see Figure 9.4). Fewer than a dozen of the 77 native land and freshwater breeding bird species survive in abundance in most of the remaining forests. By contrast, 10 of the 36 species of exotic birds now established in New Zealand are common in lowland forests. Some of them have been credited with widening the distribution of indigenous plants through seed dispersal (Baylis 1986). Most wild animal introductions were intentional, although some, like rats, came by accident. Others escaped from domestication. Introductions had virtually ceased by about 1920. Yet despite the documentation and widespread concern regarding the effects of previous introductions, recently mink and chinchilla have been approved for fur farming, and commercial farming of once-wild stocks of deer and possum is likely to result in their escape into forested regions they have not yet reached.

Pastoral and industrial development and forestry during this century has further reduced the area and integrity of indigenous forest communities (Given 1981). By the mid-1970s indigenous forest covered approximately 23 percent of the land area (Figure 9.1). Several remnants of ancient flora and fauna have been eliminated from the mainland altogether. Even so, about 12 percent of the land area is formally protected in 10 national parks and some 1,660 reserves (Mark 1985). Indigenous forests are well represented in these reservations but they are mostly steepland protection-type mountain vegetation. This kind of land area has been formally reserved in preference to land with value for economic use (Kelly 1980). However, reserves are often on atypical sites or are small, barely viable stands close to urban areas or they form narrow scenic corridors along major traffic routes (Mark 1985).

There are several offshore and outlying islands which have remained virtually unmodified by settlement and are still the last refuges for biota such as the tuatara (Crook 1975), some lizards, frogs (Bull and Whittaker 1975), and several birds (King 1984) that have become extinct or seriously threatened on the mainland. They are also sanctuaries for transferred populations of endangered mainland bird species. Some islands recently have been successfully cleared of predators in preparation for the transfer of threatened mainland birds (King 1984). On certain islands, as on Secretary Island in Fiordland National Park, red deer (*Cervus elaphus*) have become established within the last two decades and have defeated attempts at eradication. The highly selective browsing which characterizes the establishment and rapid growth phases of deer has been described (Mark and Baylis 1975, 1982). Deer continue to eliminate their preferred forage species on the island (Mark 1988) and are impairing the habitat of several indigenous ground-dwelling invertebrates. Other studies in Fiordland have documented the preferences and effects of deer in already modified forest (Wardle et al. 1971). Comparisons of the flora and vegetation on deer-free islands and adjacent mainland areas where forests have been modified by deer have served to highlight the devastating effects of both red deer (Johnson 1972) and white tail or Virginian deer (Veblen and Stewart 1980). Recently the need to add lowland indigenous forests to the national park and reserve system has become accepted, and has been a major factor in decisions to enlarge Westland National Park (addition of 25,000 ha) and to create a Paparoa National Park (30,000 ha) and a Whanganui National Park (79,000 ha). Political commitments have also been made to protect all the remaining unlogged indigenous state forest in the North Island.

Damage to indigenous ecosystems ranging from plant community to faunal habitats is attributed to the brush-tailed possum (*Tricosurus vulpecula*) as well as to deer. Notable are serious canopy dieback and mortality caused by defoliation in the rata-kamahi broadleaved montane forest in the central Westland region of the South Island especially where these species often occur as relatively even-aged stands following natural site disturbance. The older stands, dominated by southern rata, *Metrosideros umbellata* (Myrtaceae) are particularly vulnerable where defoliation by possums (Fitzgerald and Wardle 1979) appears to reduce to critical levels the ratio of green to non-green tissue in mature trees (Payton 1984a, b, 1988). The dynamic processes of the stands of this forest association (Stewart and Veblen 1982) appear to contribute significantly to this mortality (Veblen and Stewart 1982). Possums also have been implicated in the virtual disappearance from many regions of some mistletoe species (*Peraxilla [= Elytranthe] colensoi* and *P. tetraptera*) that usually parasitize the beeches (*Nothofagus* spp.).

A recent comprehensive ecological study of the decline of the threatened North Island kokako *Callaeas cinerea*, a wattlebird, revealed that possums, red deer, and feral goats (*Capra hircus*) have seriously impoverished its habitat by depleting many of its food plants. There is a considerable overlap between the diet of kokako and that of the three mammalian browsers which has aggravated the problems of forest clearance, selective logging, and introduced predators (Leathwick et al. 1983). Habitat modification and competition from red deer for a limited range of diet have also been invoked in the continued decline of the endangered flightless gallinule, the takahe, *Notornis mantelli* throughout its range in forest and tussock grasslands of the Murchison Mountains in Fiordland National Park (Mills and Mark 1977).

Recently, due to drastic reductions in the deer population, there has been some resurgence in takahe numbers. Success in rearing of captive chicks will permit supplementation of the wild population (Dr. J. A. Mills, personal communication).

Continued destruction of habitat through forest clearance and browsing by introduced herbivores is considered a greater threat to the remaining indigenous fauna than the impact of introduced predators (King 1984). This supposition also applies to the survival of several of New Zealand's relatively few native freshwater fishes which are largely restricted to streams flowing through forests. These species usually disappear from cleared areas (McDowall 1973). Three species of the indigenous genus *Galaxias* which, as migrating juveniles, support an important commercial and recreational "whitebait" fishery, are particularly affected. The fishery has declined in many parts of New Zealand.

Forest insect fauna is relatively rich and complex. This is particularly true of the saprophages in decaying plant debris and bryophyte communities: there are 16 orders of terrestrial insects (some 3,000 species of Coleoptera alone), abundant molluscs, and several crustacean orders (Cladocera, Ostracoda, Isopoda, and Amphipoda amongst others), as well as primitive spiders, primitive harvestmen (Cyphophthalmi), and the relict Peripatus and earthworms which can reach 140 cm in length. More than 150 species or c. 11% of the total indigenous Lepidoptera inhabit the forest litter and have larvae that feed on the litter. Less than 10% of this fauna survives replacement of the indigenous forest cover by exotic vegetation. By contrast, the arboreal phytophagous insect fauna is relatively impoverished.

The principal habitat loss has been lowland forest (for definition, see Froude et al. 1985), which reflects their accessibility, more fertile soils, and favorable climatic conditions. Upland and steepland forest, though important for water and soil conservation, are less diverse biologically than the lowland forests due to colder conditions and impoverished soils. They are generally less heavily timbered.

New Zealand soils are largely derived from sedimentary rocks inherently low in phosphorus and cations. Today, depositional surfaces cover most of the lowlands. Most of these are postglacial alluvium which, even in areas subject to intense leaching, is usually free draining and comparatively high in available phosphorus, cations, and nitrogen. The lowland alluvial surfaces matched the recent volcanic ash surfaces of the central North Island in supporting the tallest and most species-rich forests in the country. There is increasing evidence that the vertebrate and invertebrate fauna of these alluvial surfaces are equally rich and diverse. Hackwell and Dawson (1982) have concluded that the preferred habitat of the majority of the New Zealand forest biota is low-altitude forest. Among the indigenous woody flora 35% of the forest species occur only in lowlands while another 53% are found in both lowland and montane forests. Only 12% of the woody forest species are confined to the montane or subalpine zones.

Of the 700 described indigenous species of mollusca, a remarkably high number in relation to the country's small land area, many of the terrestrial species are confined to the lowlands. The majority of species of the large carnivorous landsnail genus *Powelliphanta* are confined to small areas generally at low altitudes. The numbers and distribution of these snails have declined rapidly since European settlement as a result of clearance of their alluvial forest habitat, habitat modification, and predation by introduced rodents, hedgehogs, and pigs (Climo 1975).

The distribution of indigenous insects suggests that most of them evolved in lowland forest to which for the most part they are still primarily adapted. Of the 60 known species of Anthribids (Coleoptera) in New Zealand, 29 have never been collected above 500 m above sea and only 12 have been found above 1,000 m. The greatest altitude at which any endemic anthribid species has been collected is 1,025 m (Dr. L. Roberts, D.S.I.R. Entomology Division, personal communication). There is clear evidence that quality of the lowland habitat influences insect diversity and richness. Dugdale (1974) and McColl (1974) showed that low-altitude podocarp–beech forests on good soils with the greatest diversity of plant species (forest type PB1) also had the greatest diversity of forest floor invertebrates. Pure beech forests (type B2) and podocarp–hardwood forests had fewer insect species than the podocarp–beech forests. Even lower numbers of insects were found in the logged stands. Mature plantations of *Pinus radiata* and *P. laricio* had diversity values at or below those of logged stands and never attained the level of the original forest type that the exotic plantations replaced (Figure 9.2).

Most bird species occur in a range of forest habitats and have a distinct preference for the lowland forest on a year-round basis. This preference is particularly marked for fruit- and nectar-eating species in late winter and spring and is pronounced in the bellbird (*Anthornis melanura*), tui (*Prosthemadera novaeseelandiae*), New Zealand pigeon (*Hemiphaga novaeseelandiae*), tit (*Petroica macrocephala*), and warbler (*Gerygone igata*). Figure 9.3 shows the altitudinal distribution of some bird species in beech–podocarp forests of western Southland. Five-minute count surveys indicate that the quality of low-altitude forest habitat also influences the richness of the bird fauna. Over two years, a monthly survey of birds in four lowland sites below 270 m elevation at the Franz Josef Glacier on the West Coast of the South Island showed significantly higher numbers of birds in lowland forest on fertile soils (alluvium and colluvium) compared to forests at similar altitudes on less

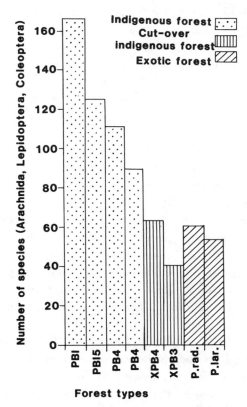

Figure 9.2. Diversity of certain forest-floor invertebrates of selected forest types in North Westland New Zealand (from Dugdale 1974). Forest types are as follows: *PB1* *Nothofagus fusca* on alluvial flats with groups of *Dacrydium cupressinum* and *Dacrycarpus dacrydioides;* subdominant *Nothofagus menziesil* and local riparian *N. solandri* var. *cliffortioides*. *PB3* A semibog terrace association with groups of usually small *Dacrydium cupressinum* and *Dacrycarpus dacrydioides* with equally variable understories of Nothofagus, generally *N. solandri* var. *cliffortioides* and *N. menziesii*. Enclaves of Leptospermum scrub common. *PB4* Complex mixtures on poorly drained terraces, principally small *Dacrydium cupressinum, Dacrycarpus dacrydioides, Libocedrus bidwillii,* with *Phyllocladus alpinus, Lagarostrobos colensoi, Lepidothamnus intermedius, Halocarpus biformis, Elaeocarpus hookerianus, Leptospermum scoparium, Nothofagus solandri* var. *cliffortioides*. Local *N. truncata, N. fusca* or *N. menziesil* usually stunted. *PB15* A general hillcountry type of *N. fusca* stunted; and rather more localized *N. truncata* and *N. menziesii* with *Decrydium cupressinum* and *Prumnopitys ferruginea, Podocarpus hallii, Metrosideros umbellata, Weinmannia racemosa,* and *Quintinia acutifolia* common throughout. *X* denotes a logged forest. *P. rad.* and *P. lar.* are exotic plantations of *Pinus radiata* and *P. laricio,* respectively.

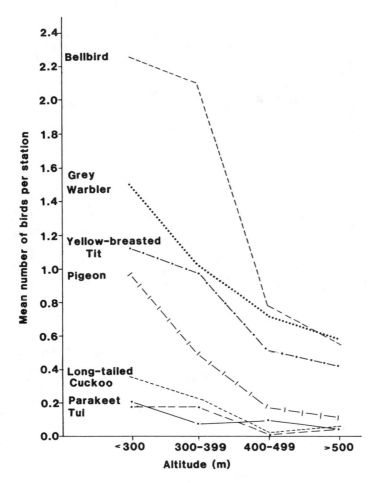

Figure 9.3. Altitudinal distribution of some indigenous bird species in Longwood State Forest, Southland (from Best and Ogle 1979).

fertile glacial moraines (Figure 9.4). The pattern was similar for insectivorous birds (tit, warbler) and fructivorous birds particularly the tui, New Zealand pigeon, and bellbird (Figure 9.5).

Low-altitude forest throughout New Zealand has borne the brunt of European settlement and forest clearance for agriculture and timber production. Of the 6.2 million hectares of indigenous forest that remains, fully 69% of it is steepland protection forest. A further 11.6% is logged lowland forest. Whereas in prehuman New Zealand, lowland forest predominated (for definition, see Froude et al. 1985), today unlogged lowland forest forms a mere 19% (1.198×10^6 ha) of the total (Froude et al. 1985). Only about 20% of this is legally protected in national parks and reserves. The west coast of the South Island contains over half of the

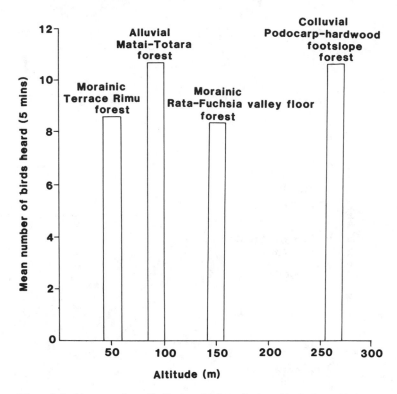

Figure 9.4. Mean number of indigenous bird species heard in 5 minute bird counts conducted monthly over a 24-month period in 1980–1982 at Franz Josef Glacier, South Westland, South Island. The bird species included bellbird, tui, New Zealand pigeon, warbler, tit, kaka, parakeet, silvereye, fantail, brown creeper, shining cuckoo, long-tailed cuckoo, and rifleman.

remaining lowland native forests and provides the best opportunity to preserve forest species and habitat lost elsewhere. Three sample case studies involving serious depletion of lowland forest ecosystems follow: (a) matai–totara forests on alluvial sites, (b) kahikatea forests, and (c) kauri forest.

Lowland Forest: Three Case Studies

Alluvial Matai–Totara Forests
Although the lowland forests received the brunt of clearance and modification as a result of logging, the impact was not evenly distributed. Lowland forests on the richest soils were priority areas for logging and clearing.

Totara (*Podocarpus totara*), which grows on well-drained alluvial soils, was targeted because of its durable timber useful for fencing and building materials. Unlike many New Zealand rainforests, the totara forest was

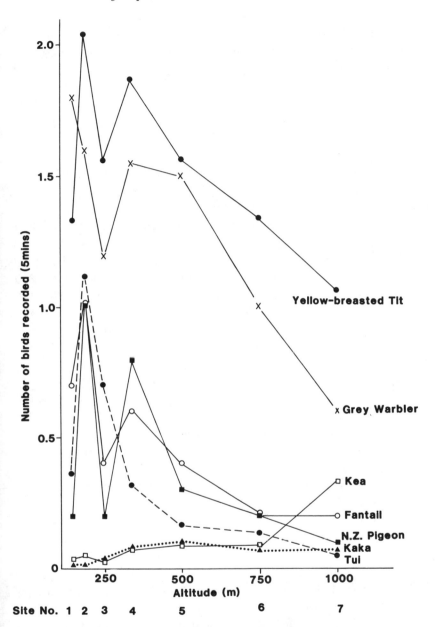

Figure 9.5. Numbers of selected bird species per 5-minute bird counts at seven stations along an altitudinal transect from 50 to 1,000-m elevation at Franz Josef Glacier, South Westland, South Island. Each point is the mean of 24 monthly counts over a 2-year period.

flammable. Wildfires of the pioneers had destroyed huge areas prior to the timber being extracted. Totara usually grows in association with another podocarp, matai (*Prumnopitys taxifolia*), and a diversity of pioneering shrub species which include a large proportion of the 54 species of small-leaved divaricating shrubs with closely interlaced and wiry branches described by Greenwood and Atkinson (1977). These shrubs favor fertile soils derived from river alluvium, talus, or volcanic ash. Such highly productive associations likely supported the largest numbers of browsing moas, a pressure which may have favored the evolution of this distinctive shrub form as a mechanism of browse resistance. These habitats support a high density of bird species in comparison to other lowland forest sites.

Totara−matai forests on alluvium have now disappeared from most of New Zealand. Tiny remnants survive in reserves. The only significant remaining stands are in the South Westland region of the South Island where farming has been hampered by poor access and high rainfall. Yet even in this region these forests largely have been eliminated. Of an estimated total area of totara-matai prior to European settlement of 43,476 ha, only 608 ha or 1.4% persists, the largest stand of which is 67 ha (McSweeney 1983b). Recent studies suggest that this type of forest contains plant species of restricted distribution which are uniquely adapted to inundation by alluvium and host to native bird species at critical times when fruit and nectar are not available in adjoining forests on older more impoverished soils.

Totara−matai forests are vulnerable to browsing domestic stock, especially cattle, as well as to introduced wild animals like deer and possum, all of which seek foliage high in nitrogen and phosphorus. As farming dominates on virtually all the recent alluvial soils along rivers there is little scope for successional establishment of matai−totara forests in the future.

Kahikatea Forests

Wetter alluvial soils and swamp margins provide a habitat for New Zealand's tallest tree, the podocarp *Dacrycarpus dacrydioides* or kahikatea. Kahikatea forests grow in two distinct associations. There are almost pure stands in and around swamps where they form a tangled root platform that allows the forest stands virtually to float over mud and water. On alluvial flats and volcanic pumice and ash it grows in association with other podocarps. Formerly extensive throughout the country, kahikatea, like totara−matai, was exploited for timber and for the fertile soils where it grows. With drainage these soils became ideal for dairy farming.

Kahikatea forests are associated with a range of other water-tolerant plant species; *Phormium tenax* (flax), *Astelia grandis*, *Freycinetia bauriana* spp. *Banksii*, *Laurelia novae zelandiae* (pukatea), *Schyzigium maire* (swamp maire), and distinctive epiphytes such as *Pittosporum cornifolium*. The forests are important wildlife habitat. Freshwater wetlands surrounding kahikatea stands host wetland birds such as bittern (*Botaurus stellaris poiciloptilus*), spotless and marsh crake (*Porzana tabuensis plumbea* and *P. pusilla affinis*), and fernbird (*Bowdleria punctata*). Native galaxid fish including the rare giant kokopu and the unusual aestivating brown and black mudfish inhabit kahikatea–flax swamps. Today the clearance and drainage of these forests and their associated wetlands has proceeded to the extent that many of these bird and fish species are extinct regionally and are threatened everywhere.

The Maori called kahikatea the food basket of the forest. It yielded food for both human consumption and birds. The kahikatea fruits heavily every two to three years. Up to 14,000 of the large fleshy fruits have been collected from a square meter of forest floor – an estimated 800 kg per tree (Beveridge 1973). Recent surveys in South Westland indicate kahikatea fruit as a major food source for the parakeet (*Cyanoramphus novaeseelandiae*), tui, pigeon, and kaka (*Nestor meridionalis*) (McSweeney 1983a; Mr. C. O'Donnell, personal communication). There is also increasing evidence that New Zealand's endemic species of bat, the only native mammal, favor the kahikatea forest. The short-tailed bat (*Mystacinea tuberculata*) is the sole member of the endemic family Mystacinidae. Both the short- and the long-tailed bat *Chalinolobus tuberculatus* were formerly widespread throughout the country but now have disappeared from many districts. They have not adapted to farmland. Even in native forest they are more scarce than formerly. Mystacinea feeds seasonally on forest fruits, pollen, and nectar as well as on insects. It is found predominantly in podocarp, particularly kahikatea forest, the soft timber of which provides nest sites.

There has been, so far, no detailed national survey of either the former or the present extent of kahikatea forests. Based on soil types and historical records, it is probable that 95% of kahikatea stands have been cleared. The Forest Service estimates that 12,500 ha of mature dense kahikatea remains, 80% of which is in South Westland. Other estimates are considerably lower.

The extent of freshwater wetlands, with which the kahikatea is closely associated, has been reduced by an estimated 90% since European settlement (Stephenson et al. 1983). Moreover, there is little scope for expanding kahikatea forests in the future despite pleas for its protection (e.g., Wardle 1974). Decisions on the future of most of the remaining kahikatea forest are likely to be made by the government in the near future.

Kauri Forest Exploitation and Fragmentation

Whereas kahikatea and matai–totara stands were cleared as much for access to farmland as for timber, kauri was favored for timber and was ruthlessly exploited from the time of earliest European settlement. Kauri is indigenous to the northern half of the North Island. In pre-European times kauri forests extended over 1.5 million hectares. Today they cover only 67,144 hectares which represents a 95% loss. Of the remaining area, 11% (7,455 ha) are mature stands. The balance of 59,679 ha is second-growth stands (Froude et al. 1985). Such destruction is unparalleled in New Zealand's history and represents severe biotic impoverishment. The New Zealand Red Data Book (Williams and Given 1981) lists nine plant species as threatened through the exploitation of kauri forest. Even many of the forest remnants which contain distribution limits of more common species are vulnerable to clearance as has been shown by Wildlife Service surveys of Northland province for the five-year period 1978–1983. Seven and one-half percent (13,153 ha) of the indigenous, mostly privately owned, forest was cleared for farming and for exotic forestry. The loss is equally alarming at a regional level. In the Rodney Ecological District, a 1984 survey revealed that 10.7% (3,760 ha) of the indigenous forest and scrub recorded in 1977–1979 had been destroyed in the ensuing six-year period. This included 8.6% of the total forest area and 16.3% of the area in shrubland. There are serious doubts about the ability of many of the fragmented forest remnants to sustain their natural comple- ment of plant and animal species in the long term. Small remnant reserves elsewhere in New Zealand like Riccarton Bush kahikatea forest in Canterbury (7 ha) and Keebles Bush in Manawatu (5 ha) contain many species that are represented by a single individual – for example, *Ripogonum scandens* (supplejack), *Rhopalostylis sapida* (nikau), *Prumnopitys taxifolia* (matai). Because the surrounding areas are deforested the bush remnants function essentially as islands. Without human intervention it is unlikely that such species will survive. Natural relaxation to a complement of species characteristic of a small island is most probable (MacArthur and Wilson 1967). Wildlife surveys in Northland have already confirmed a pattern for wildlife that is anticipated for plant species as well (Ogle 1982). As for specific islands (East and Williams 1984), the survey found that certain bird species (kokako, kaka, parakeet) were restricted to the largest remnants of forest. They had disappeared from the smaller remnants where only the more generalist birds, such as fantail and warbler, which are not restricted to forest habitats, survived (Hackwell and Dawson 1982).

Recent Developments in Conservation

Public support for conservation has been significant in New Zealand for at least a century, leading to the establishment of national parks, reserves, and sanctuaries and a national system of catchment authorities. It was not until the 1970s, however, that the cause gained sufficient political strength to ensure that economically significant resources may be set aside from exploitation for conservation purposes. The resurgence of the conservation movement dates from a successful campaign in 1972 to save Lake Manapouri in Fiordland National Park from inundation by a hydroelectric development project. In 1976 the Maruia Declaration, a petition bearing the signatures of almost a quarter of the adult population, who sought better protection for indigenous forests, was presented to Parliament. Popular conservation movements experienced rapid membership growth as they mounted organized campaigns to protect indigenous forests, expand national parks, and gain protection for rivers, wetlands, and tussock grasslands. The support of the scientific community has been important to the development of procedures for systematic identification of a representative system of protected natural areas, initially on public lands and subsequently on land of all tenures throughout New Zealand. The future of the Protected Natural Areas Programme is, however, in doubt because of inadequate funding.

There has been progressive governmental response to political pressures for habitat conservation (Froude et al. 1985). In 1975 a management policy for indigenous State forests was introduced, the principal effect of which was to curb forest clearance, although it was not fully effective until 1985. In 1978 the government removed price control from native timbers and considerably reduced cutting levels in indigenous state forests. The effect was to remove native timbers from the bulk commodity markets for general construction materials and reposition them in small-volume, high-value markets for furniture and decorative paneling. Rewriting of the Forests Act in 1976 and the National Parks Act in 1980 removed the priority emphasis on timber production in the forests and scenic grandeur for the parks, introducing in each case-specific reference to scientific and particularly to ecological values. This cleared the way for expanded programs of habitat reservation based on ecological criteria under both acts.

A strong emphasis on reducing government intervention in the economy followed the election in 1984. This proved to be markedly beneficial to habitat conservation in most areas. Two major policy thrusts were particularly significant. The first was the systematic removal of subsidies for natural resource exploitation. This included non-renewal of the land-development encouragement loan scheme, the phasing out of the supplementary minimum price scheme for sheep farming, wetland drainage subsidies, forestry and farm development tax incentives, and concessional loans for local authority hydroelectric development. The second policy thrust was to place state trading activities on a commercial basis, eliminating hidden subsidies which had previously been a major feature of state involvement in resource development. The citizen conservation movement strongly supported the division of the Forest Service and Lands and Survey Department, vesting much of their lands in a new non-production Conservation Department, their production lands in state-owned Forestry and Lands Corporations, and their regulatory activities in small separate agencies. The resulting re-allocation of public land holdings has been favorable to the conservation of indigenous ecosystems, particularly forests. Large areas on which production was planned or was being subsidized were released from production zoning and vested in the new Department of Conservation. The coastline and wetlands, both estuarine and freshwater, will benefit from allocation to the new department which will have a statutory emphasis on maintaining the natural state of these areas. Established legal rights held by grazing interests have led to a less satisfactory outcome so far for tussock grasslands, but sizable areas are expected to be allocated to dominantly conservation uses over the next five years. Meanwhile the emphasis on commercial returns for state trading enterprises has drastically curbed state-sponsored agricultural land development, commercial tree planting, and irrigation projects.

Discussion and Conclusions

It is a strong indictment of the European settlers that 11 percent of the world's 318 currently endangered bird species and subspecies are native to New Zealand. Despite the allocation of protected natural areas (c. 12% or 32,160 km^2), important habitats remain inadequately represented, particularly lowland forest rich in biota. While legislation under the Wildlife Act attempts to protect nearly all native vertebrates and several invertebrates, the administering Wildlife Service has had only limited success in dealings with private land owners and even with government departments administering public land. This situation is expected to improve with the creation of the Department of Conservation which will administer most public land with natural values, and a recent amendment to the Public Works Act which empowers the government to acquire habitats for general reserve purposes.

Over the last two decades commercial hunting of some wild animals, particularly red deer, has greatly reduced their numbers. Public concern over continued exploitation and development of the land resources, especially indigenous forests, has enabled conservation groups to be more effective politically. They have achieved retention and even reservation of some of the few remaining large areas in addition to many smaller areas of lowland indigenous forest.

A Protected Natural Areas Program on an Ecological District basis

(Simpson 1982) has begun surveys to identify a representative system of reserves now provided for by legislation. The government's environmental administration is being reorganized, largely in the interests of conservation. This program, including the ecological district concept and more appropriate criteria for identifying and defining a representative reserves system, was foreshadowed in the mid-1970s with an exercise in reserving extensive areas of indigenous state forest, much of which had been proposed for exploitation and conversion to exotic forestry (Mark 1985). Despite an enlightened approach, the realization of a representative reserves system was constrained by both prior developments and competing demands (Figure 9.6). Rapidly expanding tourism, including nature tourism, is being used to promote the conservation of additional natural areas. There is considerable opposition to nature conservation from the development lobby and from recreational hunters who demand several species of introduced wild animals on managed public lands. The hunters have achieved this officially in several areas, some of which adjoin reserve land. There are also a few biologists who are equivocal in claiming that New Zealand "will come of age ecologically when western man and his animal introductions are regarded as part of the natural environment" (Gibb and Flux 1973). We reject this attitude as it ignores the great loss of diversity and historical record that such action would inevitably entail. Continued effort is essential to retain New Zealand's unique component of the world's biological heritage.

References

Anderson, A., 1983. *When All the Moa-Ovens Grew Cold: Nine Centuries of Changing Fortune for the Southern Maori*. Otago Heritage Books, Dunedin.

Baylis, G. T. S., 1986. Widened seed dispersal at the Three Kings Islands attributed to naturalised birds. In *The Offshore Islands of Northern New Zealand*, pp. 41–45. Department of Lands and Survey Information Series No. 16.

Best, H. A., and C. C. Ogle, 1979. *Birdlife of the Western Southland Beech Project Area*. Wildlife Service Fauna Survey Unit Report No. 16. New Zealand Department of Internal Affairs, Wellington.

Beveridge, A. E., 1973. Regeneration of podocarps in a central North Island forest. *New Zealand Journal of Forestry* 18:23–35.

Bull, P. C., and A. H. Whittaker, 1975. The amphibians, reptiles, birds and mammals. In G. Kuschel (Ed.), *Biogeography and Ecology in New Zealand*, pp. 231–276. W. Junk, The Hague.

Burrows, C. J., 1980. Diet of New Zealand dinornithiformes. *Naturwissenschaften* 67:151–153.

Burrows, C. J., B. McCulloch, and M. M. Trotter, 1981. The diet of moas based on gizzard content samples from Pyramid Valley, North Canterbury and Scaife's Lagoon, Lake Wanaka, Otago. *Records of the Canterbury Museum* 9:309–336.

Climo, F. M., 1975. The land snail fauna. In G. Kuschel (Ed.), *Biogeography and*

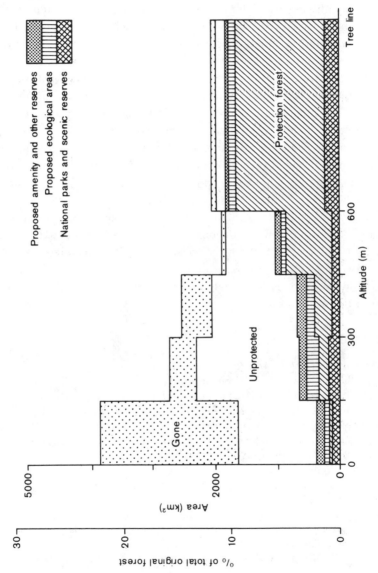

Figure 9.6. The altitudinal distribution of forests north of the Cook River in Westland in pre-European times and now (1978) showing the proposed uses, in particular the pattern of ecological areas proposed by the Scientific Co-ordinating Committee (from Dawson and Hackwell via Mark 1985).

Ecology in New Zealand, pp. 459–492. W. Junk, The Hague.

Crook, I. G., 1973a. The tuatara. In G. Kuschel (Ed.), *Biogeography and Ecology in New Zealand*, pp. 331–352. W. Junk, The Hague.

Crook, I. G., 1973b. The tuatara, *Sphenodon punctatus* Gray, on islands with and without populations of the Polynesian rat, *Rattus exulans* (Peale). *Proceedings of the New Zealand Ecological Society* 20:115–120.

Crook, I. G., 1975. The tuatara. In G. Kuschel (Ed.), *Biogeography and Ecology in New Zealand*, pp. 331–352. W. Junk, The Hague.

Dugdale, J. S., 1974. Arthropod species composition of the beech forest floor. *Beech Research News* 1:25–27.

East, R., and G. R. Williams, 1984. Island biogeography and the conservation of New Zealand's indigenous forest-dwelling avifauna. *New Zealand Journal of Ecology* 7:27–35.

Enting, B., and L. Molloy, 1982. *The Ancient Islands: New Zealand's Natural Environments*. Port Nicholson, Wellington.

Fitzgerald, A. E., and P. Wardle, 1979. Food of the oppossum *Trichosurus vulpecula* Kerr in the Waiho Valley, South Westland. *New Zealand Journal of Zoology* 6:339–345.

Fleming, C. A., 1962a. The extinction of the moas and other animals during the Holocene Period. *Notornis* 10:113–117.

Fleming, C. A., 1962b. History of the New Zealand land bird fauna. *Notornis* 9:270–274.

Fleming, C. A., 1962c. New Zealand biogeography – a palaeontologist's approach. *Tuatara* 10:53–108

Fleming, C. A., 1975. The geological history of New Zealand and its biota. In G. Kuschel (Ed.), *Biogeography and Ecology in New Zealand*, pp. 1–86. W. Junk, The Hague.

Fleming, C. A., 1977. The history of life in New Zealand forests. *New Zealand Journal of Forestry* 22:249–262.

Forster, R. R., 1975. The spiders and harvestmen. In G. Kuschel (Ed.), *Biogeography and Ecology in New Zealand*, pp. 493–505. W. Junk, The Hague.

Froude, V., A. Gibson, and W. Carlin, 1985. *Indigenous Forests of New Zealand: Environmental Issues and Options*. Commission for the Environment, Wellington.

Gibb, J. A., and J. E. C. Flux, 1973. Mammals. In G. R. Williams (Ed.), *The Natural History of New Zealand*, pp. 334–371. Reed, Wellington.

Given, D. R., 1981. *Rare and Endangered Plants of New Zealand*. Reed, Wellington.

Greenwood, R. M., and I. A. E. Atkinson, 1977. Evolution of divaricating plants in New Zealand in relation to moa-browsing. *Proceedings of the New Zealand Ecological Society* 24:21–33.

Hackwell, K. R., and D. S. Dawson, 1982. A review of the importance of different New Zealand forest habitats for biota. Ecology Division, Department of Scientific and Industrial Research. Unpublished report.

Johnson, P. N., 1972. Applied ecological studies of shoreline vegetation at Lakes Manapouri and Te Anau, Fiordland Part 1: Vegetation of Lake Manapouri shoreline. *Proceedings of the New Zealand Ecological Society* 19:109–119.

Kelly, G. C., 1980. Landscape and nature conservation. In *Land Alone Endures: Land Use and the Role of Research*. Department of Scientific and Industrial Research Discussion Paper No. 3, p. 63-87. Wellington.

King, C., 1984. *Immigrant Killers: Introduced Predators and the Conservation of Birds in New Zealand.* Oxford University Press, Auckland.

Kinsky, F. C. (Ed.), 1970. *Annotated Check List of the Birds of New Zealand.* New Zealand Ornithōlogical Society. Reed, Wellington.

Leathwick, J. R., J. R. Hay, and A. E. Fitzgerald, 1983. The influence of browsing by introduced mammals on the decline of North Island kokako. *New Zealand Journal of Ecology* 6:55–70.

MacArthur, R.H., and E. O. Wilson, 1967. *The Theory of Island Biogeography.* Princeton University Press, Princeton, New Jersey.

McColl, H. P., 1974. The arthropods of the floors of six forest types on the West Coast South Island: a preliminary report. *Proceedings of the New Zealand Ecological Society* 21:11–20.

McDowall, R. M., 1969. Extinction and endemism in New Zealand land birds. *Tuatara* 17:1–12.

McDowall, R. M., 1973. *The Freshwater Fishes of New Zealand.* Reed, Wellington.

McGlone, M. S., and C. J. Webb, 1981. Selective forces influencing the evolution of divaricating plants. *New Zealand Journal of Ecology* 4:20–28.

McSweeney, G. D., 1983a. Seasonal bird movement in relation to altitude in the podocarp–hardwood forests of South Westland. *New Zealand Journal of Ecology* 7:201.

McSweeney, G. D., 1983b. Matai–totara flood plain forests in South Westland. *New Zealand Journal of Ecology* 5:121–128.

Mark, A. F., 1984. Effects of introduced mammals on natural ecosystem values in New Zealand. In *Protection and Parks – Essays in the Preservation of Natural Values in Protected Areas*, pp. 7–14. Lands and Survey Department, Wellington.

Mark, A. F., 1985. The botanical component of conservation in New Zealand. *New Zealand Journal of Botany* 23:789–810.

Mark, A. F., 1988. Responses of indigenous vegetation to contrasting trends in utilization by red deer, in two southwestern New Zealand National Parks. In M. R. Rudge (Ed.), *Moas, Mammals and Man.* New Zealand Ecological Society 12 (Supp.) 103–114.

Mark, A. F., and G. T. S. Baylis, 1975. Impact of deer on Secretary Island, Fiordland, New Zealand. *Proceedings of the New Zealand Ecological Society* 22:19–24.

Mark, A. F., and G. T. S. Baylis, 1982. Further studies on the impact of deer on Secretary Island, Fiordland, New Zealand. *New Zealand Journal of Ecology* 5:67–75.

Mills, J. A., and A. F. Mark, 1977. Food preferences of takahe in Fiordland National Park, New Zealand, and the effect of competition from introduced red deer. *Journal of Animal Ecology* 46:939–958.

Mills, J. A., and G. R. Williams, 1979. The status of endangered New Zealand birds. In *The Status of Endangered Australian Wildlife*, pp. 147–168. Royal Zoological Society of South Australia.

Molloy, B. P. J., C. J. Burrows, J. E. Cox, J. A. Johnston, and P. Wardle, 1963. Distribution of subfossil forest remains, eastern South Island, New Zealand. *New Zealand Journal of Botany* 1:68–77.

Nature Conservation Council, 1981. *Integrating Conservation and Development: A Proposal for a New Zealand Conservation Strategy.* Nature Conservation Council, Wellington.

Nicholls, J. L., 1980. The past and present extent of New Zealand's indigenous forests. *Environmental Conservation* 17:309-310.

Ogle, C. C., 1982. *Wildlife and Wildlife Values of Northland*. New Zealand Wildlife Service. Fauna Survey Unit Report No. 30. Department of Internal Affairs, Wellington.

Oliver, W. R. B., 1949. The moas of New Zealand and Australia. *Dominion Museum Bulletin* 15.

Payton, I. J., 1984a. Southern rata (*Metrosideros umbellata* Cav.) mortality in Westland, New Zealand. In H. Turner and W. Tranquillini. (Eds.), *Establishment and Tending of Subalpine Forest: Research and Management*, pp. 207–214. Proceedings 3rd IUFRO Workshop.

Payton, I. J., 1984b. Defoliation as a means of assessing browsing tolerance in southern rata (*Metrosideros umbellata* Cav.). *Pacific Science* 37:443–452.

Payton, I. J., 1988. Canopy closure, a factor in rata (*Metrosideros*) – kamahi (*Weinmannia*) forest dieback in Westland, New Zealand. *New Zealand Journal of Ecology* 11:39–50.

Reid, B., and G. R. Williams, 1975. The kiwi. In G. Kuschel (Ed.), *Biogeography and Ecology in New Zealand*, pp. 301–330. W. Junk, The Hague.

Simpson, P., 1982. *Ecological Regions and Districts of New Zealand: A Natural Subdivision*. Department of Scientific and Industrial Research Biological Resources Centre Publication 1. Wellington.

Stephenson, G. K., B. Card, A. F. Mark, R. McLean, K. Thompson, and R. M. Priest, 1983. *Wetlands: A Diminishing Resource*. Report for the Environmental Council. National Water and Soil Conservation Organisation Miscellaneous Publication 58.

Stevens, G., 1985. *Lands in Collision: Discovering New Zealand's Past Geography*. New Zealand Geological Survey, Department of Scientific and Industrial Research, Wellington.

Stewart, G. H., and T. T. Veblen, 1982. Regeneration patterns in rata (*Metrosideros umbellata*)–kamahi (*Weinmannia racemosa*) forest in central Westland, New Zealand. *New Zealand Journal of Botany* 20:55–72.

Veblen, T. T., and G. H. Stewart, 1980. Comparison of forest structure and regeneration on Bench and Stewart Islands, New Zealand. *New Zealand Journal of Ecology* 3:50–68.

Veblen, T. T., and G. H. Stewart, 1982. The effects of introduced wild animals on New Zealand forests. *Annals of the Association of American Geographers* 72:372–397.

Wardle, P., J. Hayward, and J. Herbert, 1971. Forests and scrubland in northern Fiordland, New Zealand. *New Zealand Journal of Forestry Science* 1:80–115.

Wardle, P., 1974. The kahikatea (*Dacrycarpus dacrydioides*) forest of South Westland. *Proceedings of the New Zealand Ecological Society* 21:62–71.

Wardle, P., 1985. Environmental influences on the vegetation of New Zealand. *New Zealand Journal of Botany* 23:773–788.

Wardle, P., M. J. A. Bulfin, and J. Dugdale, 1983. Temperate broad-leaved evergreen forests of New Zealand. In J. D. Ovington (Ed.), *Temperate Broad-Leaved Evergreen Forests*, pp. 33–71. Elsevier, Amsterdam.

Watt, J. C., 1975. The terrestrial insects. In G. Kuschel (Ed.), *Biogeography and Ecology in New Zealand*, pp. 507–535. W. Junk, The Hague.

Wellman, H. W., 1979. *The Origin of the Southern Alps*. Royal Society of New Zealand Bulletin 18.

Whittaker, A. H., 1973. Lizard populations on islands with and without Polynesian rats, *Rattus exulans* (Peale). *Proceedings of the New Zealand Ecological Society* 20:121–130.

Williams, G. R., and D. R. Given, 1981. *The Red Data Book of New Zealand: Rare and Endangered Species of Endemic Terrestrial Vertebrates and Vascular Plants.* Nature Conservation Council, Wellington.

10   Changes in the Eucalypt Forests of Australia as a Result of Human Disturbance

R. L. SPECHT

Editor's Note: The eucalypt forests of Australia have evolved to occupy a narrow habitat of restricted nutrient and water availability. They have proven vulnerable to fire, the introduction of exotics, and to the eutrophication that accompanies human activities. They are also vulnerable to a host of aggressive, introduced annuals that are more responsive to the nutrients and that carry fires through the forest at unusual times and in novel ways. The effect is the replacement of the forest by grasslands made up of exotics, a pattern of impoverishment now recognized as common around the world. But the special sensitivity of these forests and those of New Zealand sets them apart as a lesson in both the details of evolution and in the importance of knowledge of those details in management of a potentially rich, productive, and enduring resource that is now rapidly being lost. The loss is through a classical series of stages of impoverishment and results in a conspicuous loss in the capacity of the land for support of people.

R. L. Specht is a distinguished ecologist, long a student of the vegetation of Australia. He writes here about the transitions he has observed in forests in response to cumulative human disturbance.

Introduction

Eucalypt Forests/Woodlands in Australia

Only a quarter of the continent of Australia has the subhumid to perhumid climate favorable to eucalypt-dominated open-forests and woodlands (Table 10.1 and Figure 10.1). The perhumid zone, with an evaporative coefficient $(k)^1$ between 0.075 and 0.100 and an annual moisture index $(AMI)^2$ between 0.70 and 0.95 (Specht 1972a), supports a tall open-forest dominated by *Eucalyptus* spp., 30–100 m in height. The formation is often found on deep red earths (krasnozems), with high water-storage capacity and relatively high levels of soil nutrients, although mineral deficiencies of P, Mo, and K have been recorded. Tree- and ground-ferns tend to flourish on these soils. The tall open-forests on less fertile soils are lower in height and the ferny ground stratum is replaced by a wealth of tall sclerophyll shrubs (Specht 1981b).

In the humid zone, with an evaporative coefficient between 0.055 and 0.075 and an annual moisture index between 0.55 and 0.85, the eucalypt

177

Table 10.1. *Structural formations dominated by* Eucalyptus *spp. in Australia*

Structural formations		Area (km²)	% Total area
Specht (1970)	Williams (1955)		
Tall open forest Ht > 30 m FPC 30–70%	Wet sclerophyll forest	126,514	1.6
Open forest Ht 10–30 m FPC 30–70%	Tropical layered forest Dry sclerophyll forest	60,622 217,560	
	Subtotal	278,182	3.6
Woodland Ht 10–30 m FPC 10–30%	Tropical deciduous woodland Tropical woodland (mixed) Tropical layered woodland Mixed coastal woodland Temperate woodland (mixed)	28,866 864,134 32,870 57,762 390,722	
	Subtotal	1,374,354	17.8
Low woodland Ht < 10 m FPC 10–30%	Low shrub woodland Low arid woodland	57,612 312,563	
	Subtotal	370,175	4.8
Total		2,149,225	27.8

Source: Reprinted from Specht et al. 1974, with permission.

open-forest is less than 30 m in height. As in the perhumid zone, the development of the understory is related to soil nutrient levels. A grassy ground stratum is associated with relatively fertile soils. Sclerophyll shrubs develop on infertile soils (Specht 1981b).

Eucalypt trees extend into the subhumid zone with an evaporative coefficient between 0.045 and 0.055 and an annual moisture index between 0.35 and 0.75. Here, the spacing of the trees becomes more open (foliage projective cover FPC less than 30 percent) and the trees are shorter in stature. Depending on soil fertility, a savanna woodland or a sclerophyll woodland formation develops. In recent years, detailed accounts of the structure, floristics, and ecology of eucalypt forests and woodlands have been compiled by Ashton (1981b), Gill (1981c), Gillison and Walker (1981), Groves (1981), Bourlière (1983), Gillison (1983), Mott et al. (1985), Tothill and Mott (1985), and Clifford and Specht (1986).

During the Tertiary, much of the Australian continent was covered by lateritic podzolic soils. It was on these infertile podzolic soils and their

Tall open-forest

open-forest & woodland
(sclerophyll understory)

open-forest & woodland
(savanna understory)

Figure 10.1. Distribution of open forests and woodlands dominated by *Eucalyptus* spp. in Australia (after Specht 1981b).

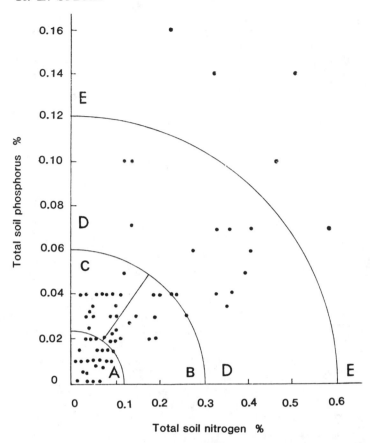

Figure 10.2. Edaphic range of Australian plant communities, with respect to total nitrogen (%) and total phosphorus (%) in surface soil.
Zone A: Sclerophyll (heathy) communities. Acacia shrublands and Triodia hummock grasslands. *Zone B*: Savanna communities, including grassy open forests/woodlands on lateritic earths. *Zone C*: Chenopod and Stipa–Aristida communities. *Zone D*: Grasslands on cracking clays; wet sclerophyll forests–rain forests on krasnozems.

derivatives that the flora of the eucalypt forests and woodlands evolved. Today most of the forested landscape is covered by these oligotrophic ecosystems, dominated by *Eucalyptus* spp. (Figure 10.2). These nutrient-poor ecosystems are now in danger of "nutrient pollution" from a wide range of human activities.

Human Disturbance in Eucalypt Forests/Woodlands

Over the last 200 years European immigrants and their descendants have exerted increasing pressure on the eucalypt forests/woodlands of Australia.

Figure 10.3. Chronic disturbance of forested hills at Queenstown, Tasmania, caused by SO_2 pollution from copper smelter ($\pm$ fire). Photo by J. S. Turner, March 1963; reprinted with permission.

The subhumid to perhumid climatic zones favored agriculture on more fertile soils and silviculture, in particular *Pinus radiata* and *P. elliottii* plantations, on infertile soils. In the 1930s through the 1950s, with the discovery of trace-element deficiencies in many infertile soils and increased farm mechanization, pasture areas expanded rapidly. Very few native eucalypt forests and woodlands have been left undisturbed.

Small areas of forest have been subjected to the chronic disturbance of SO_2 pollution (Figure 10.3) and overgrazing (Figure 10.4). The most severe destruction has come from clearing the forests for urban and rural development.

As rural and urban development has expanded, engulfing eucalypt forests and woodlands, disturbance has increased in the remnants of original vegetation. For example:

1   The frequency of devastating bush-fires, which often affect crown, timber, and ground strata has increased.

2   Introduced, often annual, herbs and grasses have invaded the understory, especially the ground stratum of the more-fertile savanna forests/ woodlands, already disturbed by overgrazing. Nutrient improvement at the periphery and along roadways in infertile sclerophyll forests/woodlands has led to similar invasions.

3   Forest root pathogens, such as the introduced *Phytophthora cinnamomi*, have

Figure 10.4. Chronic disturbance (destruction of original forest vegetation) of Philip Island, near Norfolk Island, caused by overgrazing by pigs, goats, and rabbits introduced by the prison authorities of Norfolk Island during the 1800s (Turner et al. 1968). Photo by J. S. Turner, November 1967; reprinted with permission.

        affected large areas of eucalypt forest leading to the death of trees and shrubs (Figure 10.5).

4   "Dieback" of eucalypt has increased across southern Australia when isolated stands of aging trees are weakened by drought, fungal pathogens, insect pests, and possibly phosphorus toxicity from fertilized rural land nearby (Figure 10.6).

5   Reduced foliage cover of evergreen overstory and understory species and associated litter cover has led to increased surface runoff and soil erosion.

6   Loss of trees from the landscape has increased water movement through the soil profile, leaching cyclic salt accumulated in the deeper horizons of the soil. Sodium chloride, thus leached, approaches the surface at low altitudes in the landscape causing salinity problems.

Fire in Eucalypt Forests and Woodlands

Fire has been a major factor affecting eucalypt forests since the human occupation of Australia 40,000 years ago (Ashton 1981a; Christensen et al. 1981; Specht 1981a; Stocker and Mott 1981; Walker 1981; Lacey et al. 1982). Charcoal particles recorded in the lacustrine sediments of Lake George, near Canberra, indicate that fires became increasingly frequent about 130,000

Figure 10.5. Jarrah (*Eucalyptus marginata*) dieback, caused by *Phytophthora cinnamomi*, in southwest Western Australia. Photo by F. R. Wylie, reprinted with permission.

Figure 10.6. Dieback in eucalypt forests in rural areas of the New England District, New South Wales. Photo by F. R. Wylie, reprinted with permission.

years B.P. (before present), as eucalypt forests replaced savanna communities dominated by trees of casuarina (Singh and Geissler 1985). These authors suggest that the sudden change to "fire-tolerant" eucalypt communities may have been the result of early aboriginal burning which would have predated the oldest archeological data of 40,000 years B.P. More probably, the change in vegetation was caused by a climatic change, paralleling the present change in distribution of eucalypt- and casuarina- dominated communities of the Mt. Lofty Ranges, South Australia; eucalypt seedlings now fail to become established on the frost-prone hills of the eastern scarp and the Mid-North (Specht 1972b). The greater annual growth of the eucalypt communities in relatively frostfree areas, in addition to the aromatic oils in the leaves of the family Myrtaceae, make them more fire-prone than the stunted grasslands with scattered trees of *Allocasuarina verticillata* (syn. *Casuarina stricta*).

Fire appears to have been part of the Australian landscape for a long time, predating the aborigines. In the last 100 years, fires have increased in frequency and severity. Vines (1969) noted that "potentially bad fire seasons" tend to occur about once every three years, "bad fires" every six or seven, and "very bad fires" every thirteen years, probably associated with periodic climatic cycles. These fires are mostly of human origin. In Victoria only 10–20 percent are caused by lightning (Gill 1981a).

It would appear that the eucalypt forest vegetation is very resilient and regenerates rapidly after fire (Gill et al. 1981). Shortly after a high-energy crown fire, epicormic buds will sprout from trunk or lignotuber of most eucalypt trees to renew the overstory foliage canopy. Many ground-stratum species resprout from underground organs: sclerophyll shrubs and evergreen hemicryptophytes in the sclerophyll forests; grasses and herbs in the savanna forests.

It is only in the tall open-forests with *Eucalyptus* species lacking lignotubers that death of the giant (> 30 m) trees occurs after fire. Regeneration occurs only via seedlings.

High-energy fires, generated in the understory, will damage foliage crowns and trunks of *Eucalyptus* spp., reducing annual timber production. Vast conflagrations cause immeasurable damage to lives and property. Regular control burning, using low-energy ground fires, is aimed at reducing these hazards.

It would appear that Eucalyptus forests have a remarkable ability to regenerate after even the hottest fire. Infertile soils become much more fertile after fire due to the "ash-bed effect" (Humphreys and Craig 1981). Shortly after a fire the species richness of community reaches its highest observable count. As the overstory species grow, understory species are slowly and successively eliminated (Figure 10.7). Regeneration after fire depends on the

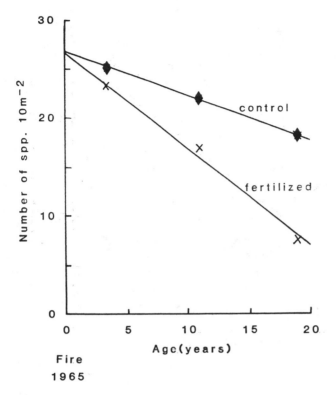

Figure 10.7. Decrease in species richness of the understory of a subtropical eucalypt open forest (Stradbroke Island), regenerating after fire, unfertilized and with added fertilizer (required by pasture plants and crops).

supply of seed. Fires at too-frequent intervals can destroy seed regenerators (e.g., eucalypts in the tall open-forest) which have had too little time to set seed. On the other hand, senescing vegetation may no longer contain viable seed or rootstock regenerators.

The decline in understory species richness in postfire succession (Figure 10.7) is affected by the regenerating overstory foliage cover (Specht and Specht, 1989b). Development of overstory foliage cover is accelerated by phosphorus fertilizer, and decline in species richness is thus accelerated (Figure 10.7).

In mature eucalypt forests, surface runoff could account for less than 1 percent of measured stream flow (Bren and Leitch 1986). Soil erosion is minimal. Immediately after a bushfire, storm rainfall on a desiccated, hydrophobic, soil surface, will induce considerable surface runoff and soil erosion (McArthur 1964; McArthur and Cheney 1965; Gilmour 1968; Brown 1972; Humphreys and Craig 1981). Once the soil surface is moistened, surface runoff from the burnt forest is essentially the same as that from the mature forest (Bren and Leitch 1986). Some three to five years must elapse before the regenerating eucalypt forest reaches maximum overstory/understory foliage cover. During that time, stream flow (the excess of water lost by soil drainage and seepage from the regenerating forest) will be higher than prefire (Langford 1976). In the humid-to-subhumid zones, the canopy of fire-tolerant *Eucalyptus* spp. regenerates rapidly from epicormic buds, restoring the evaporative canopy, and hence stream flow, to the prefire condition. In the perhumid zone, the densely packed foliage canopy of regrowth forests, with seed-regenerating *Eucalyptus* spp., 1,730 pole stems per hectare at 25 years, increases evapotranspiration at the expense of stream flow (Langford 1976).

In summary, eucalypt forests are generally resilient to fire; they regenerate rapidly by seedling, rootstock, and trunk regenerators (Gill 1981b). Surface runoff and associated soil erosion is minimal except immediately after the fire: evapotranspiration and stream flow fluctuate according to the regeneration patterns of overstory and understory foliage. High-intensity fires reduce annual timber production but production levels can be maintained after low-intensity control burns. Species richness of the understory is stimulated by fire. Species are lost only occasionally by too frequent or too long delayed fires. Frequent fires, although serious in Australian eucalypt forests and woodlands, have not caused widespread degradation of these communities.

Degradation of Eucalypt Forests and Woodlands

Although frequent fires may not cause widespread degradation of eucalypt forests, such disturbance can cause localized degeneration within the forest. Pathogens, competitive weeds, and pests gain a foothold and gradually increase the area of degeneration.

In south-eastern Australia, repeated fires may be detrimental to the survival of seed regenerators such as perhumid *Eucalyptus* spp. and many species of *Acacia, Banksia*, and *Hakea*. Even rootstock regenerators occasionally germinate from seed after fire although the regenerating seedlings/saplings are vulnerable to subsequent fires. Eventually, without fire, only aged, often badly fire-scarred, trees may survive. These weakened trees degenerate to form a gap in the forest.

Repeated fires in the savanna forest/woodlands of monsoonal northern Australia, have stimulated the growth of tall (1–4 m) annual grasses like *Sorghum intrans* and *Heteropogon contortus*. During the wet season, rapid growth masks the lower-growing perennial grasses and herbs and increases the fire hazard during the dry season. Repeated, high-energy conflagrations appear detrimental to midstratum trees and shrubs and cause considerable damage to stems of upper-stratum trees (Lacey et al. 1982). Gaps in the eucalypt communities become more frequent as senescent and degeneration phases are accelerated (Watt 1947).

Most forest fires can be attributed to human agencies. Such activities as timber extraction, selective clearing, cattle grazing, road-making, and rubbish disposal accelerate the degeneration of eucalypt forests and lead to an extensive mosaic of "gaps." In the extreme case, rural and urban developments have left only islands of original forests or shade trees scattered across farms.

Seeds stored in capsules in the canopy of eucalypt trees are released following fire. Many germinate during the following wet season. Survival tends to be greatest in gaps where competition between eucalypt seedlings, microflora (Warcup 1981), and ants (O'Dowd and Gill 1984) is reduced. Reduced competition with microorganisms and the increased fertility of the ash-bed (Humphrey and Craig 1981) also favor the germination of seasonal short-lived herbaceous plants, including introduced weeds, which are rare in the mature eucalypt communities. In the winter rainfall zone of southern Australia, these seasonal herbaceous species flourish during spring (Figure 10.8), using water and nutrient resources some months before the long-lived native sclerophyll or savanna species begin shoot growth (Specht and Rayson 1957; Specht 1975).

Most of the long-lived native species appear to have evolved during the Tertiary when the climate of Australia favored the development of lateritic podzols and lateritic earths low in plant nutrients (Figure 10.2). The growth response of these species to such added fertilizer as localized ash accumulation or nutrient accumulation from garbage or road works is minimal (Figure 10.9) compared to that of introduced weeds (Specht 1963; Heddle and Specht 1975). It would appear that plants invading disturbed areas within eucalypt communities have a strong competitive advantage over regenerating native seedlings due to earlier and greater shoot growth. Many invaders are herbaceous and attract herbivores, increasing site disturbance. Seedlings of long-lived native species are in danger in disturbed areas in which nutrients have increased soil fertility. Seedlings of many species are sensitive to phosphorus toxicity (Ozanne and Specht 1981), an imbalance between levels of phosphorus and nitrogen in the substrate as nitrogen is lost from the ecosystem during fire. In the undisturbed forest, increased nutrient levels accelerate postfire development of overstory cover, causing a more rapid decline in species richness of the understory (Figure 10.7).

Unstable gaps, which are increasing in frequency in eucalypt communities, become centers for invading root pathogens (e.g., *Phytophthora cinnamomi*)

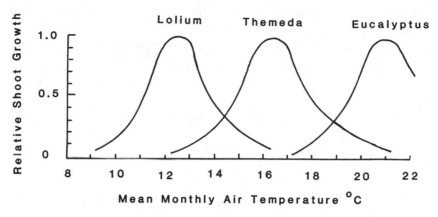

Figure 10.8. Seasonal shoot growth of invading plants (e.g., lolium), compared with native dominance (*Eucalyptus* spp., *Banksia* spp.) and the native grass (*Themeda triandra*), in the mediterranean-climate zone of southern Australia.

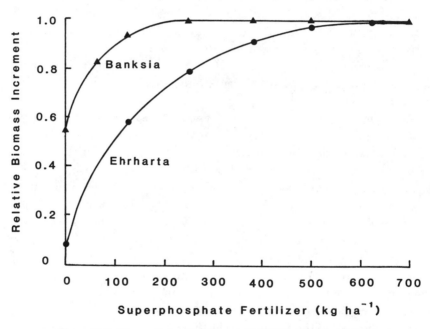

Figure 10.9. Biomass increment due to added superphosphate fertilizer of *Banksia ornata* (a long-lived native shrub) and invading plants (*Ehrharta calycina*) in the mediterranean-climate zone of southern Australia.

Table 10.2. *Some factors associated with rural dieback of eucalypts*

Defoliation or other insect damage	All states
Drought	N.S.Wales, Qld., Tas., Vic.
Mistletoe	N.S.Wales, Vic., W.Aust.
Phytophthora cinnamomi	Vic., W.Aust.
Possum damage	Vic.
Soil salinity	Qld., S.Aust., Vic., W.Aust.
Tree age	All states

Source: After Kile 1981.

and insect defoliation (Table 10.2). The development of an increased depth of foliage canopy on trees at the edge of the gap increases not only the amount of photosynthesis per tree but also the production of new foliage shoots and flowers (Davie 1982; A. Specht 1985; Specht 1986). These developing organs, which are richer in nutrients than mature sclerophyllous leaves, are much more attractive to insect and vertebrate consumers (Kikkawa et al. 1979). Landsberg and Wylie (1983) reported increased insect attack on trees with higher foliar nutrients at the edge of subtropical eucalypt forests. Increased growth of the foliage canopy is even more apparent in isolated clumps of trees in rural and urban areas. Repeated insect defoliation of young shoots has led to widespread dieback in the New England Tableland of New South Wales and other areas of Australia (Old et al. 1981).

Land use practices that result in the movement of soil by animals or vehicles, for example, can aid the spread of root pathogens (Brown 1976; Shea 1982). The introduced root pathogen (*Phytophthora cinnamomi*) is causing dieback and destruction of the jarrah forests (*Eucalyptus marginata* and associated tall shrubs of *Banksia grandis*) in Western Australia. The jarrah forest appears to be degenerating into a low sclerophyllous grassland/ heathland. It is possible that fire could be used to reduce disease susceptibility in jarrah forests, by (a) reducing the susceptible food base (*Banksia grandis*) available to the pathogen (Shea 1982) and (b) creating a soil environment unfavorable for pathogen survival and reproduction by increasing the rhizosphere flora associated with woody legumes, *Acacia* spp., for example (Malajczuk and Glenn 1981; Shea 1982).

Soil Erosion

The degradation of eucalypt communities to low sclerophyllous grasslands/ heathlands on soils of low fertility or to annual grasslands/herblands on soils of medium fertility appears to be increasing throughout Australia. Eucalypt communities have already been lost from cropping lands, except along roadsides and in a few small reserves. Formerly, the tree canopy absorbed much of the energy of heavy rainstorms and protected the soil surface between the plants of the ground stratum from erosion. Surface runoff accounted for less than 1 percent of measured stream flow (Bren and Leitch 1986).

Decrease in tree canopy may enable understory foliage cover to increase so that the sum of overstory and understory foliage cover remains constant (Specht and Morgan 1981; Specht 1983). Short-lived, seasonal herbaceous plants which attract grazing animals during the wet growing season may spring up but then die off during the dry season exposing the soil surface to erosion. Soil erosion is accelerating throughout the non-arid zone, the landscape which formerly supported eucalypt communities. In a report on *A Soil Conservation Policy in Australia* (Anonymous 1978), the following statistics on water erosion were assembled (for June 1975):

Grazing land	364,000 km^2 out of	1,337,000 km^2
Extensive cropping land	206,000 km^2 out of	443,000 km^2
Intensive cropping land	7,000 km^2 out of	24,000 km^2
Total	577,000 km^2 out of	1,804,000 km^2

Wind erosion, vegetation degradation or dieback, and salinity were reported to affect another 238,000 km^2 of the non-arid zone. Erosion, some severe, was reported in 49 percent of the 3,356,000 km^2 of the arid rangelands.

Secondary Salinization

The loss of deep-rooted trees from the landscape reduces the rooting depth of the plant community to relatively shallow-rooted shrubs, grasses, and herbs. With soil water storage (*S*max) reduced within the rooting zone, more excess water can percolate as drainage into lower levels in the landscape. Figures 10.10 and 10.11 illustrate the increase in drainage resulting from reduced *S*max in the humid, subhumid, and semiarid zones of southern Australia.

It is unfortunate that the soils of many areas of Australia have saline or sodic properties (Northcote and Skene 1972), probably due to cyclic salt (sodium chloride) accretion during arid periods since the Miocene. The increase in drainage water following clearing of the Eucalyptus forests promotes leaching of the accumulated soluble salts, mainly sodium chloride. Increased water flow following clearing is responsible for rising water tables and for seepage into low-lying areas. Secondary salinization follows, leading

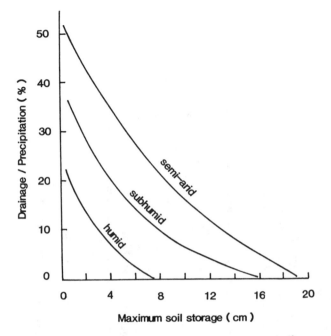

Figure 10.10. Annual estimates of drainage from soils with increasing soil storage capacity (*S*max) in the humid, subhumid, and semiarid zones of southern Australia (calculated using the water-balance equation in Specht 1972a, with permission).

to the replacement of the Eucalyptus-dominated forested wetlands by halophytic vegetation.

Dryland salinization has affected about 4,260 km^2 of agricultural land throughout Australia (Peck et al. 1983). Over half of this area (2,420 km^2) is in southwest Western Australia; a quarter of the area is in the regions of the Murray–Darling rivers (620 km^2) and the southeast coast (620 km^2). Methods for reclamation of such "scalded" areas are based on grazing control, suitable cultivation, and the use of salt-tolerant plants.

Possible Solutions

Urban and rural developments and, more recently, open-cut mining have led to the complete destruction of large areas of Australian eucalypt forests and woodlands. Only remnants of the original vegetation remain along roadsides and in patches throughout the landscape. In the past, in a few small areas, uncontrolled SO_2 effluent from copper smelters has contributed to the destruction. Now soil erosion and secondary salinization are common. Soil contour banks are being constructed to reduce surface runoff and soil

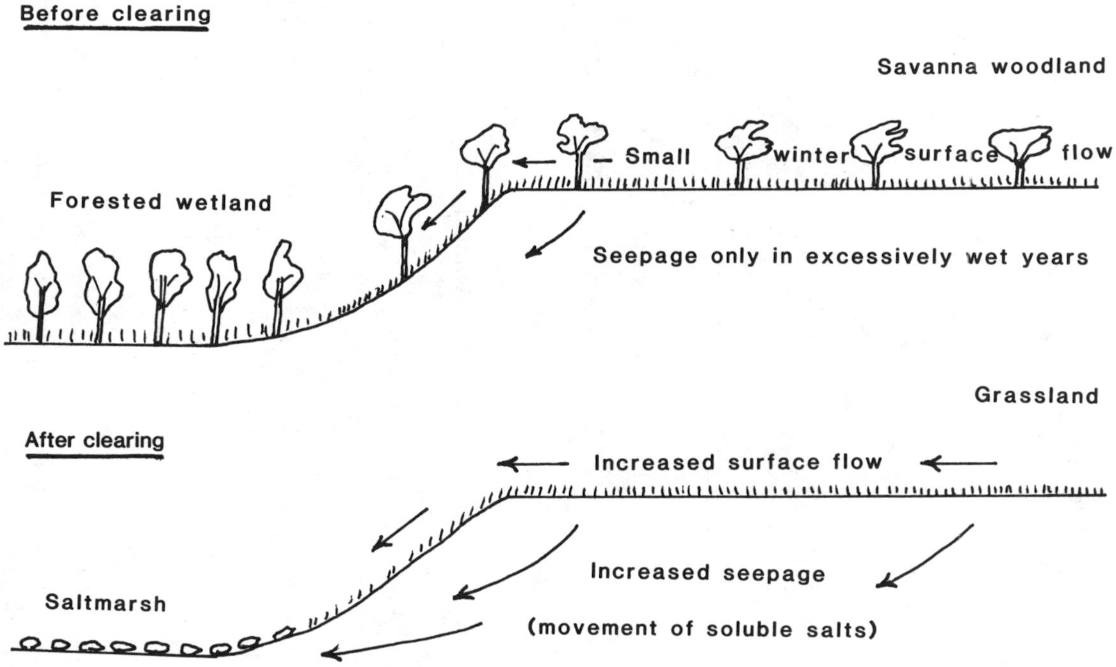

Figure 10.11. The effect of clearing eucalypt woodland on water movement in the soil.

erosion. Tree planting is being fostered by the "Greening Australia" campaign in an effort to beautify the landscape and to restore some balance between overstory and understory, thus reducing surface runoff, soil erosion, deep soil drainage, and leaching of soluble salts. Agroforestry experiments to establish the optimal balance between trees and pastures/crops are being encouraged. Research to reclaim salt-scalded areas, which are currently dominated by halophytes, is focused on drainage technology and the development of salt-tolerant tree, pasture, and crop species.

The remaining areas of eucalypt forests and woodlands appear to be slowly degrading (the creeping degradation as defined by Bormann, this volume) as the frequencies of fire, drought, overgrazing, introduced plants, root pathogens, and insect pests increase. A National System of Ecological Reserves (Specht et al. 1974; Fenner 1975) will conserve representative examples of the different eucalypt communities in tropical, subtropical, and temperate Australia. Management plans are needed to maintain long-term ecosystem stability for conservation reserves, as well as for forest reserves and timbered rangelands.

Low-energy fires during cool seasons of the year can reduce understory fuel loads and prevent high-energy summer bush fires (Walker 1981). In monsoonal Australia, the fuel load of tall annual grasses can be removed from the eucalypt communities by early summer burns just after seeds have germinated (Bailey et al., in preparation). Unfortunately, during a season when fires are rare, low-energy fires may fail to release seeds from woody fruits (e.g., *Eucalyptus, Banksia, Hakea, Leptospermum,* etc.) or to stimulate germination of "hard-seeded" species (e.g., *Acacia* spp.). Thus seedlings of trees and shrubs, which germinated a few months prior to the beginning of the wet season, may be too small to survive the fire. Seedlings germinating after low energy fires have to survive the following dry season. As many *Eucalyptus* species are both fire-tolerant and long-lived (200–400 years), degeneration–regeneration phases in the forests are difficult to quantify. Gaps in the eucalypt communities are associated with reduced competition and increased ash-bed nutrients. Invasions of short-lived herbaceous plants – including introduced plants – root pathogens, and insect pests have occurred. An important management strategy should be to minimize such invasions.

Multiple use of eucalypt forests has been advocated over the last 20 years, but land use for both timber production and grazing may eventually lead to the dieback problem so widespread in rural Australia. Management of forest reserves continues to focus on timber production, ignoring the understory. Management of forested rangelands focuses on herbage production, ignoring the overstory.

Much of the eucalypt forests and woodlands in the Australian landscape exist on soils very low to low in plant nutrients (Figure 10.2). It would appear that any perturbation increasing the fertility of a forest gap may lead to invasion. To reverse this trend, top-dressing gaps and roadside verges with kaolinitic clay, which binds phosphates and molybdates in unavailable form, has been suggested (Ozanne and Specht 1981; Specht 1981d). This solution would be practical for conservation reserves only. It would not be economical for forest reserves and forested rangelands.

Notes

1. Evaporative coefficient (k) expresses the ratio of actual to potential water conductance through an evergreen plant community for a particular annual cycle of evaporation.
2. Annual moisture index (AMI) expresses the mean monthly ratio of actual to potential evapotranspiration.

References

Anonymous, 1978. *A basis for soil conservation policy in Australia*. Commonwealth and State Government Collaborative Soil Conservation Study 1975–77, Report 1, Dept. Environment, Housing and Community Development, Aust. Govt. Publ. Serv., Canberra, Aust.

Ashton, D. H., 1981a. Fire in tall open-forests (wet sclerophyll forests). In A. M. Gill, R. H. Groves, and I. R. Noble, (Eds.), *Fire and the Australian Biota*, pp. 339–366. Aust. Acad. Sci., Canberra, Aust.

Ashton, D. H., 1981b. Tall open-forests, In R. H. Groves, (Ed.), *Australian Vegetation*, pp. 121–151. Cambridge University Press.

Bailey, B., J. Day, and K. Duggan, in prep. Wet season burning for fire management in Kakadu National Park. A preliminary study.

Bourliére, F. (Ed.), 1983. *Ecosystems of the World: Vol. 13. Tropical Savannas*. Elsevier, Amsterdam.

Bren, L. J., and C. J. Leitch, 1986. Rainfall and water yields of three small, forested catchments in north-east Victoria and relation to flow of local rivers. *Proc. R. Soc. Vict.* 98:19–29.

Brown, B. N., 1976. *Phytophthora cinnamomi* associated with patch death in tropical rainforests in Queensland. *Aust. Plant Path. Soc. Newsl.* 5:1–4.

Brown, J. A. H., 1972. Hydrologic effects of a bushfire in a catchment in south-eastern New South Wales. *J. Hydrol.* 15:77–96.

Christensen, P., H. Recher, and J. Hoare, 1981. Responses of open forest to fire regimes. In A. M. Gill, R. H. Groves, and I. R. Noble, (Eds.), *Fire and the Australian Biota*, pp. 367–393. Aust. Acad. Sci., Canberra, Aust.

Clifford, H. T., and R. L. Specht (Eds.), 1986. *Tropical Plant Communities: Their Resilience, Functioning and Management in Northern Australia*. Botany Dept., University of Queensland, St. Lucia, Qld.

Davie, J. D. S., 1982. Pattern and process in the mangrove ecosystems of Moreton Bay, southeastern Queensland. Ph.D. dissertation, University of Queensland, St. Lucia.

Fenner, F. (Ed.), 1975. *A national system of ecological reserves in Australia*. Aust. Acad. Sci. Rep. No. 19, Canberra, Aust.

Gill, A. M., 1981a. Post-settlement fire history in Victorian landscapes. In A. M. Gill, R. H. Groves, and I. R. Noble, (Eds.), *Fire and the Australian Biota*, pp. 77–98. Aust. Acad. Sci., Canberra, Aust.

Gill, A. M., 1981b. Adaptive responses of Australian vascular plant species to fires. In A. M. Gill, R. H. Groves, and I. R. Noble (Eds.), *Fire and the Australian Biota*, pp. 243–272. Aust. Acad. Sci., Canberra, Aust.

Gill, A. M., 1981c. Pattern and processes in open-forests of Eucalyptus in southern Australia. In R. H. Groves (Ed.), *Australian Vegetation*, pp. 152–176. Cambridge University Press.

Gill, A. M., R. H. Groves, and I. R. Noble (Eds.), 1981. *Fire and the Australian Biota*. Aust. Acad. Sci., Canberra, Aust.

Gillison, A. N., 1983. Tropical savannas of Australia and the southwest Pacific. In F. Bourlière (Ed.), *Ecosystems of the World:* Vol. 13. *Tropical Savannas*, pp. 183–243. Elsevier, Amsterdam.

Gillison, A. N., and J. Walker, 1981. Woodlands. In R. H. Groves (Ed.), *Australian Vegetation*, pp. 177–197. Cambridge University Press.

Gilmour, D. A., 1968. Hydrological investigations of the soil and vegetation types in the lower Cotter catchment. *Aust. For.* 32:243–256.

Groves, R. H. (Ed.), 1981. *Australian Vegetation*. Cambridge University Press.

Heddle, E. M., and R. L. Specht, 1975. Dark Island heath (Ninety-Mile Plain, South Australia). VIII. The effect of fertilizers on composition and growth, 1950–1972. *Aust. J. Bot.* 23:151–164.

Humphreys, F. R., and F. G. Craig, 1981. Effects of fire on soil chemical, structural and hydrological properties. In A. M. Gill, R. H. Groves, and I. R. Noble (Eds.), *Fire and the Australian Biota*, pp. 177–200. Aust. Acad. Sci., Canberra, Aust.

Kikkawa, J., G. J. Ingram, and P. D. Dwyer, 1979. The vertebrate fauna of Australian heathlands – an evolutionary perspective. In R. L. Specht (Ed.), *Ecosystems of the World:* Vol. 9A. *Heathlands and Related Shrublands. Descriptive Studies*, pp. 231–279. Elsevier, Amsterdam.

Kile, G. A., 1981. An overview of eucalypt dieback in rural Australia. In K. M. Old, G. A. Kile, and C. P. Ohmart (Eds.), *Eucalypt Dieback in Forests and Woodlands*, pp. 13–26. Commonwealth Scientific and Industrial Res. Org., Melbourne, Australia.

Lacey, C. J., J. Walker, and I. R. Noble, 1982. Fire in Australian tropical savannas. In B. J. Huntley, and B. H. Walker (Eds.), *Ecology of Tropical Savannas*, pp. 241–272. Springer-Verlag, Berlin.

Landsberg, J., and F. R. Wylie, 1983. Water stress, leaf nutrients and defoliation: a model of dieback of rural eucalypts. *Aust. J. Ecol.* 8:27–41.

Langford, K. J., 1976. Changes in yield of water following a bushfire in a forest of *Eucalyptus regnans. J. Hydrol.* 29:87–114.

Malajczuk, N., and A. R. Glenn, 1981. *Phytophthora cinnamomi* – a threat to the heathlands. In R. L. Specht (Ed.), *Ecosystems of the World:* Vol. 9B. *Heathlands and Related Shrublands. Analytical Studies*, pp. 241–247. Elsevier, Amsterdam.

McArthur, A. G., 1964. Streamflow characteristics of forested catchments. *Aust. For.* 28:106–118.

McArthur, A. G., and N. P. Cheney, 1965. The effect of management practice on streamflow and sedimentation from forested catchments. *J. Inst. Engs. Aust.* 37:417–425.

Mott. J. J., J. Williams, M. H. Andrew, and A. N. Gillison, 1985. Australian savanna ecosystems. In J. C. Tothill and J. J. Mott (Eds.), *Ecology and Management of the World's Savannas*, pp. 56–82. Aust. Acad. Sci., Canberra, Aust.

Northcote, K. H., and J. K. M. Skene, 1972. *Australian Soils with Saline and Sodic Properties.* Commonwealth Scientific and Industrial Res. Org., Melbourne, Australia. Soil Publ. No. 27.

O'Dowd, D., and A. M. Gill, 1984. Mass reproduction of *Eucalyptus delegatensis.* Predator satiation and site alteration following fire. In B. Dell (Ed.), *MEDECOS IV. Proceedings of the 4th International Conference on Mediterranean Ecosystems*, pp. 132–133. Botany Dept., University of Western Australia, Nedlands, W. Aust.

Old, K. M., G. A. Kile, and C. P. Ohmart (Eds.), 1981. *Eucalypt Dieback in Forests and Woodlands*, Commonwealth Scientific and Industrial Res. Org., Melbourne, Australia.

Ozanne, P. G., and R. L. Specht, 1981. Mineral nutrition of heathlands: phosphorus toxicity. In R. L. Specht (Ed.), *Ecosystems of the World:* Vol. 9B. *Heathlands and Related Shrublands. Analytical Studies*, pp. 209–213. Elsevier, Amsterdam.

Peck. A. J., J. F. Thomas, and D. R. Williamson, 1983. *Salinity issues: effects of man on salinity in Australia.* (Water 2000: Consultants Report No. 8, Dept. Resources and Energy). Aust. Govt. Publ. Service, Canberra, Aust.

Shea, S. R., 1982. Multiple use management in a Mediterranean ecosystem – the jarrah forest, a case study. In C. E. Conrad, and W. C. Oechel (Eds.), *Dynamics and Management of Mediterranean-Type Ecosystems*, pp. 49–55. U.S.D.A. Forest Service, Pacific Southwest Forest and Range Experiment Station, Gen. Tech. Rep. PSW–58. Berkeley, Cal.

Singh, G., and E. A. Geissler, 1985. Late Cainozoic history of vegetation, fire, lake levels and climate, at Lake George, New South Wales, Australia. *Phil. Trans. R. Soc. Lond.* B311:379–447.

Specht, A., 1985. Temperature effects on eucalypt shoot growth in the Brisbane region. Ph.D. dissertation, University of Queensland.

Specht, R. L., 1963. Dark Island heath (Ninety-Mile Plain, South Australia). VII. The effect of fertilizers on composition and growth, 1950–60. *Aust. J. Bot.* 11: 67–94.

Specht, R. L., 1970. Vegetation. In G. W. Leeper (Ed.), *The Australian Environment*, 4th ed., pp. 44–67. Commonwealth Scientific and Industrial Res. Org., Melbourne, Australia.

Specht, R. L., 1972a. Water use by perennial evergreen plant communities in Australia and Papua New Guinea. *Aust. J. Bot.* 20:273–299.

Specht, R. L., 1972b. *Vegetation of South Australia*, 2nd Ed. Govt. Printer, Adelaide, South Aust.

Specht, R. L., 1975. A heritage inverted: our flora endangered. *Search* 6:472–477.

Specht, R. L., 1981a. Responses to fires of heathlands and related shrublands. In A. M. Gill, R. H. Groves, and I. R. Noble (Eds.), *Fire and the Australian Biota*, pp. 395–415. Aust. Acad. Sci., Canberra, Aust.

Specht. R. L., 1981b. Major vegetation formations in Australia. In A. Keast (Ed.), *Ecological Biogeography of Australia*, pp. 163–297. Junk, The Hague.

Specht, R. L., 1981c. Evolution of the Australian flora: some generalizations. In A.

Keast (Ed.), *Ecological Biogeography of Australia*, pp. 783–805. Junk, The Hague.

Specht, R. L., 1981d. Conservation: Australian heathlands. In R. L. Specht (Ed.), *Ecosystems of the World:* Vol. 9B. *Heathlands and Related Shrublands. Analytical Studies*, pp. 235–240. Elsevier, Amsterdam.

Specht, R. L., 1983. Foliage projective covers of overstorey and understorey strata of mature vegetation in Australia. *Aust. J. Ecol.* 8:433–439.

Specht, R. L., 1986. Functioning of tropical plant communities. 6. Phenology. In H. T. Clifford, and R. L. Specht (Eds.), *Tropical Plant Communities, Their Resilience, Functioning and Management in Northern Australia*, pp. 78–90. Botany Dept, University of Queensland, St. Lucia, Qld.

Specht, R. L., and P. Rayson, 1957. Dark Island heath (Ninety-Mile Plain, South Australia). I. Definition of the ecosystem. *Aust. J. Bot.* 5:52–85.

Specht, R. L., E. M. Roe, and V. H. Boughton (Eds.), 1974. Conservation of major plant communities in Australia and Papua New Guinea. *Aust. J. Bot. Suppl.* 7:1–667.

Specht, R. L., and D. G. Morgan, 1981. The balance between the foliage projective covers of overstorey and understorey strata in Australian vegetation. *Aust. J. Ecol.* 6:193–202.

Specht, R. L., and A. Specht, 1989a. Canopy structure in Eucalyptus-dominated communities in Australia along climatic gradients. *Oecologia Plantarum.* 10:191–213.

Specht, R. L., and A. Specht, 1989b. Species richness of sclerophyll (heathy) plant communities in Australia – the influence of overstorey cover. *Aust. J. Bot.* 37:337–350.

Specht, R. L., and A. Specht, 1989c. Species richness of overstorey strata in Australian plant communities – the influence of overstorey growth rates. *Aust. J. Bot.* 37:321–336.

Stocker, G. C., and J. J. Mott, 1981. Fire in the tropical forests and woodlands of Northern Australia. In A. M. Gill, R. H. Groves, and I. R. Noble (Eds.), *Fire and the Australian Biota*, pp. 425–439. Aust. Acad. Sci., Canberra, Aust.

Tothill, J. C., and J. J. Mott (Eds.), 1985. *Ecology and Management of the World's Savannas.* Aust. Acad. Sci., Canberra, Aust.

Turner, J. S., C. N. Smithers, and R. D. Hoogland, 1968. *The conservation of Norfolk Island.* Aust. Conserv. Found. Spec. Publ. No. 1.

Vines, R. G., 1969. A survey of forest fire danger in Victoria (1937–1969). *Aust. For. Res.* 4:39–44.

Walker, J., 1981. Fuel dynamics in Australian vegetation. In A. M. Gill, R. H. Groves, and I. R. Noble (Eds.), *Fire and the Australian Biota*, pp. 101–127. Aust. Acad. Sci., Canberra, Aust.

Warcup, J. H., 1981. Effect of fire on the soil microflora and other non-vascular plants. In A. M. Gill, R. H. Groves, and I. R. Noble (Eds.), *Fire and the Australian Biota*, pp. 203–214. Aust. Acad. Sci., Canberra, Aust.

Watt, A. S., 1947. Pattern and process in the plant community. *J. Ecol.* 35:1–22.

Williams, R. J., 1955. Vegetation regions of Australia. *Atlas of Australian Resources.* Dept. Nat. Dev., Canberra, Aust.

11   Impoverishment in Pacific Island Forests

DIETER MUELLER-DOMBOIS

Editor's Note: Islands have provided some of the most fundamental of insights into evolution and ecology while bearing some of the greatest burdens of human depredation. What biologist can remain long innocent of the saga of Darwin's finches as spun out by Darwin himself and David Lack and others who have been puzzled by the diversity of life of the Galapagos? Whose curiosity is not piqued by the biotic anomalies of New Zealand, Australia, Madagascar, Easter Island, Surtsey? And yet, while scholars have found extraordinary insights in the biota of islands, the biota was often devastated early in the period of human expansion through the introduction of goats or other ungulates thought to benefit seamen on future visits.

Both the puzzles and the depredations grow more complicated as human influences spread. Dieter Mueller-Dombois addresses the current transitions in the forests of Pacific Islands. He describes the rain forests of the Hawaiian Islands as "originally impoverished and secondarily enriched." They were impoverished by comparison with other large islands of the Pacific that are closer to continental areas of higher diversity; they have been enriched by high endemism, a product of their insularity and period of isolation. Mueller-Dombois introduces a concept new in this treatment, progressive development through a peak period of a thousand years or more followed by regression as soils deteriorate.

In the Hawaiian Islands as in so many other places around the world, the history of land and vegetation and the special circumstances of the region have produced a vegetation that is vulnerable to disturbance, including the introduction of exotics. Grasses such as the broomsedge, *Andropogon virginicus*, are especially insidious, opening the forest to fire and invasion by other exotics. The result is the systematic, irreversible replacement of the native forest by lesser vegetation, often exotics that form a novel grassland.

Introduction

The forests of islands are commonly more vulnerable to disturbance than are continental forests. Three factors contribute to this sensitivity. Insularity restricts the area of forests, often has protected the forests from human disturbances over long periods (Mueller-Dombois et al. 1981), and has limited the availability of species. This third factor, impoverishment relative to continental forests with similar climate and soils, is a function of distance to biotic centers that were the source of the insular forests.

199

Disturbance brings changes, some of which constitute further impoverishment. Conspicuous examples include the recent logging of a small remnant of an original lowland tropical rain forest in Hawaii (Holden 1985; Mueller-Dombois 1985) and the effects of introducing ungulates without biological controls (Mueller-Dombois and Spatz 1975; Stone and Scott 1985; Williams 1985). Island communities are easily destroyed or pushed off balance by such drastic measures.

As yet we know little about resilience to various natural and more subtle human disturbances and have little basis for measurement of such changes. If we are to use community and species dynamics as indicators of human-induced changes, we must first understand the patterns and processes that have evolved under natural conditions. Island ecosystems may be of particular interest because of their simplified structure and their location remote from centers of industrial pollution.

I will first briefly compare the Hawaiian rain forest with other Pacific island forests. Then I will highlight three hypotheses relating to the dynamics of island species. This will be followed by a characterization of ecosystem development and secondary succession under natural conditions. Finally, I will address important aspects of human-induced impoverishment and draw some conclusions.

The Hawaiian Rain Forest in Comparison to Other Island Forests

When one travels from the Hawaiian Islands, which are by comparison isolated far from continental land masses, to the other large islands in the Pacific, one finds biotic enrichment in species diversity and life forms in ecosystems that seem otherwise equivalent. The lowland and montane rain forest in Hawaii contains, as a rule, only one canopy species, *Metrosideros polymorpha*. In certain habitats a second species, *Acacia koa*, is added. Occasionally, a few other species join the canopy guild; these include *Myrsine lessertiana*, *Ilex anomala*, *Coprosma ochracea*, and *Cheirodendron trigynum* among others. In Samoa the rain forest usually has more canopy species; in Fiji one can speak of a multiple-species rain forest where an important tree life form is the tall-growing conifer *Agathis vitiensis*. Canopy species diversity increases further in the Solomon Islands, and in Papua New Guinea the tall-growing *Araucaria hunsteinii* forms an impressive emergent canopy tree towering up to 30 m above the multiple-species hardwood canopy. This enrichment of canopy species is accompanied by an increase in canopy stature. In Hawaii the taller native trees may reach up to 25 m (maximally 30 m) in favorable habitats, but usually Hawaiian forests are of lower stature, around 10–15 m.

In Fiji, many canopy trees attain 35 m in height, and in the Solomon Islands and in Papua New Guinea they can grow to 40–50 m heights. It seems logical that this trend is associated with an increase in woody plant biomass. In relationship to other big islands in the Pacific, the Hawaiian Islands have an impoverished tree flora.

A similar relationship holds for the undergrowth vegetation. Ferns are prevalent in the Hawaiian forest, particularly tree ferns of the genus *Cibotium*. There are, in addition, a number of smaller-statured woody species, small trees, and arborescent shrubs. Ferns assume a less important role in the rain forests of the southwestern Pacific. Instead there is a greater diversity of woody and herbaceous undergrowth species, and one commonly finds canopy species in the undergrowth as saplings, a situation rather rare in Hawaii.

The Hawaiian rain forest can be seen as a biogeographically impoverished outlier of the Old World Tropics. Its biota has been characterized as "disharmonic" because of the underrepresentation of certain taxa. For example, totally absent are conifers, Fagaceae, Aceraceae, Bignoniaceae, Moraceae, and Cunoniaceae.

The fact of Hawaii's original taxonomic impoverishment is, at the same time, a source of enrichment, that of high endemism. It has been estimated by Fosberg (1948) that the native Hawaiian flora of approximately 1,500 species of flowering plants evolved from only 272 original arrival forms, resulting in an unusually high rate of endemism. The Hawaiian Island rain forest can thus be characterized as an originally impoverished and secondarily enriched ecosystem. To different degrees this can be said of all forests on oceanic islands.

Dynamics of Island Species: Three Hypotheses

Many attempts have been and are being made to characterize island species. Earlier workers have developed conflicting hypotheses explaining the behavior of island species.

For example, after the turn of the present century, when a large area of Metrosideros rain forest on the Island of Maui exhibited massive dieback, Lyon (1909) thought that the forest was dying from an introduced disease. Lyon and other investigators spent several years searching for a disease or insect pest. In spite of a thorough investigation no causative biotic agent could be identified. At the end of these studies, Lyon (1918, 1919) concluded that the Metrosideros and some of the associated tree species were dying because of soil toxification associated with soil aging. He thought that particularly reducing iron, which develops in tropical soils derived from basalt under poor drainage conditions, was the cause. He proposed that, because the Hawaiian flora is an impoverished outlier of a continental vegetation, it consisted mostly of colonizers and was missing the climax species component. He suggested that species from other tropical areas be introduced and planted on the windward slopes to save the Hawaiian watersheds. A decade later the Territorial Forestry Office followed Lyon's recommendation and planted about half of the Maui dieback area to the Australian tree species *Eucalyptus robusta* and *Melaleuca quinquenervia* (Holt 1983).

A totally different conclusion was drawn by Egler (1942) and later by Hatheway (1952). Both authors had made observations on the tenacity of indigenous tree species in areas under chronic stress from grazing and other human-induced disturbances. They concluded that native species would come back into dominance to the exclusion of alien invaders provided that native systems were protected from further disturbances. Egler and Hatheway thought that native species dynamics were characterized as climax species or, in more recent terminology, as species with *K* strategies.

A third hypothesis, based more on evolutionary thinking, is that of Carlquist (1965, 1980) and others. Carlquist suggested that island species gradually lose both their former colonizing capacity and their competitive ability in the less stressful island environment. On this basis he predicted eventual extinction in the competitive struggle with alien species. This could be termed a theory of chronic impoverishment, as the invasion of alien species into native communities must be considered an impoverishment not an enrichment.

Soil Aging, Ecosystem Development, and Retrogression

Lyon was correct in that soil aging in the Hawaiian rain forest is associated with soil toxicity. Soil acidity increases in the course of time to pH values of < 4. Such low pH values promote Al, Fe, and Mn toxicity, a fact generally known (Etherington 1982) and documented for Hawaii (Balakrishnan and Mueller-Dombois 1983). However, Lyon was incorrect in suggesting that the Hawaiian vegetation was not adapted to aging soils. Soils at least 3 million years old, on the Island of Kauai, still support closed and functioning Metrosideros-dominated rain forests. These forests are of lower stature than those on younger soils.

Soil development in the Hawaiian rain forest biome can be described as initially following a progressive trend until 1,000–2,000 years of age. Thereafter it follows a regressive trend (Figure 11.1). The progressive trend can be recognized by an increase of biophilic nutrient availability, primarily on

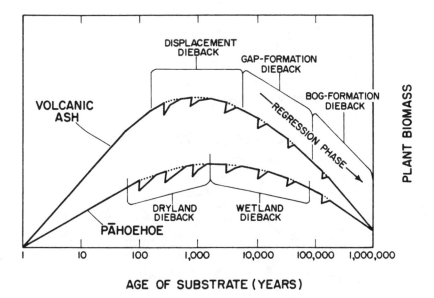

Figure 11.1. A general hypothesis of soil development in the Hawaiian rain forest. After a few thousand years the soils become impoverished of nutrients with increasing acidification and toxification. Different forms of *Metrosideros* dieback are associated with different stages of soil development. (Reprinted with modification from Mueller-Dombois 1986, with permission from the *Annual Review of Ecology & Systematics*, Vol. 17 © 1986 by Annual Reviews, Inc.)

account of nitrogen (Vitousek et al. 1983). Thereafter, nutrient availability decreases in association with increasing soil acidity. The trend is reflected in the plant biomass which goes up in the progressive phase and down during the regressive phase. Superimposed on this trend is the primary succession of the Hawaiian rain forest. It begins on new volcanic substrates on the Island of Hawaii. Atkinson (1970) estimated that it takes roughly 400 years for a closed Metrosideros–Cibotium forest to develop.

However, primary succession does not end with the closed forest. Instead it seems to go on in the form of periodic canopy or stand-level dieback and recovery sequences. The predisposing cause for stand-level dieback appears to be the cohort nature of most Metrosideros forest stands. After canopy closure of the first-generation forest, Metrosideros regeneration is confined to small seedlings that remain small and turn over under the canopy without reaching the sapling life stage until the canopy collapses. Figure 11.2 shows a model, recently synthesized from a large number of population-structure analyses under dieback and closed Metrosideros canopies. In previous studies (Mueller-Dombois et al. 1980; Mueller-Dombois 1981a), we have

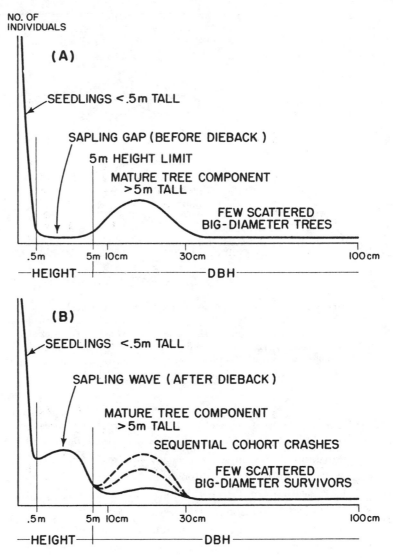

Figure 11.2. A model of the population structure of a closed *Metrosideros polymorpha* rain forest before (a), and after (b), canopy dieback. (Reprinted from Mueller-Dombois 1987, with permission from *BioScience*, © 1987.)

recognized five dieback types in relation to the type of habitat and stand structure as wetland, dryland, displacement, gap-formation, and bog-formation diebacks. Their position is indicated on Figure 11.1 along the primary successional gradient. Displacement dieback involves the quantitative displacement of Metrosideros canopy trees in the eutrophic ash phase of ecosystem development. In this phase, the undergrowth tree ferns are so vigorous that regeneration of the relatively shade-intolerant Metrosideros is not able to penetrate the tree-fern canopy unless individuals germinate as epiphytes on tree-fern trunks (Burton and Mueller-Dombois 1984). Bog-formation dieback occurs during the nutrient impoverishment phase of soil development. Metrosideros recovery becomes more sporadic. Trees become stunted, eventually to dwarf forms, and finally are eliminated.

Secondary Successional Dynamics in Forests Impoverished of Canopy Species

It is currently hypothesized that the large areas of stand-level or canopy dieback that repeatedly occur in the Hawaiian rain forest are due to three factors that work in chronosequence:

1   A catastrophic disturbance such as a new lava flow, ash blanket deposit, or hurricane destroys a former forest segment giving rise to a new one comprised of a large cohort of Metrosideros individuals.

2   When such disturbances do not recur during the life span of such a Metrosideros cohort stand, the stand is more sensitive to fluctuating climatic disturbances. These occur in intervals of several years and seem to become effective through the soil moisture regime in the form of temporary floods or droughts (Mueller-Dombois 1986). Such strongly fluctuating site factors may upset the forest sufficiently for it to go into a synchronized dieback over a certain area, such as that of a physically uniform lava flow.

3   Following canopy collapse, which does not affect stands in younger stages to the same extent, reproduction in the form of sapling stand development follows the senescent cohort.

Similar forms of dieback have been noted in monodominant or canopy-species-impoverished forests in other Pacific islands. Examples are documented by Stewart and Veblen (1983) in Metrosideros forests of New Zealand, by Wardle and Allen (1983) in *Nothofagus* forests of New Zealand, and by Arentz (1983) in *Nothofagus* forests of Papua New Guinea.

In Hawaii we discovered that there is a turnover of Metrosideros races, from the pubescent leaved forms to glabrous leaved forms along the primary successional gradient (Stemmermann 1983, 1986). The existence of successional ecotypes of Metrosideros is further evidence against Lyon's hypothesis of a failure of this species to adapt to aging soils. Moreover, the prevalence of native Hawaiian species in primary successional habitats can be taken as evidence against the idea that the Hawaiian tree flora is made up mostly of climax species.

Human-Induced Impoverishment in Island Forests

One of the major factors of human-induced impoverishment is the invasion of alien species into native communities. Another is the fragmentation of native habitat into increasingly smaller segments.

Calquist's thesis that island species lose their colonizing capacity is not supported by the fact that lava flows, ash-blanket deposits, and other open sites such as landslides and right-of-ways in the rain forest are often dominantly invaded by native species. However, it is true that the native Hawaiian flora contains few ruderals or species of weedy character. A major reason for this is probably the absence of grazing and browsing animals as an evolutionary stress factor. Limited occurrence of fires before human occupation (Mueller-Dombois 1981b) is probably another.

Loss of competitive capacity is difficult to estimate since this attribute cannot be properly defined outside the context of the habitat where the interaction takes place. Egler (1942) and Hatheway (1952) do not agree with Carlquist. Hatheway's plots on northern Oahu were reassessed by Wirawan (1974) after 20 years. He found all native tree species to be still present and actively reproducing on Hatheway's sites. He found all the alien species were also still present and without any indication that they would be subdued by the natives.

Invading alien species can be roughly grouped into two kinds; those that invade physically disturbed habitats, and those that invade undisturbed communities. By far the majority of disruptive aliens is in the first category, but there are a few that penetrate into undisturbed communities. An example is the western Mediterranean tree *Myrica faya*, which, over the last two decades, has become a very aggressive invader in early primary successional habitats (i.e., ash-blanket deposits) in Hawaii Volcanoes National Park. This tree fixes large amounts of nitrogen in symbiosis with Frankia. It has the capacity to change drastically the early successional environment of the developing Metrosideros ecosystem which typically has a very low nitrogen supply. Other examples are the strawberry guava (*Psidium cattleianum*) and Koster's curse (*Clidemia hirta*). However, all three of these successful invaders of physically undisturbed rain forest sites would not be able to do so without introduced alien birds which carry their seeds into the native forest.

This point is important. Successful invaders are often successful only because of other alien species which further support the anthropogenically induced process of impoverishment. ·

In some cases, introduction of alien species has led to landscape damage such as accelerated erosion. For example, broomsedge (*Andropogon virginicus*) has become established in former rain-forest habitat on abandoned fields on Oahu. It has maintained the summer and winter phenology from its native habitat in the eastern and southeastern United States by undergoing dormancy during the winter months in Hawaii, when rainfall increases and evergreen tropical rain forest plants remain productive. Because of this change in the vegetation, runoff and erosion are increased (Mueller-Dombois 1973). Moreover, broomsedge, like several other invasive grasses (*Pennisetum rupellum, Melinis minutiflora, Andropogon glomeratus*), completely changes ecosystem-level influences by inviting frequent fires, a stress to which the native biota is poorly adapted.

However, aggressive alien plants often lose their superiority in such extreme habitats as new lava flows (Smathers and Mueller-Dombois 1974), soils with aluminum toxicity (Gerrish and Mueller-Dombois 1980), or montane bogs (Canfield 1986), where the native plants retain an advantage.

Fragmentation of rain forest habitat is another factor accelerating human-induced impoverishment. The fragmentation is particularly critical because of the irregular mosaic of cohort stands which form the canopy matrix of the Hawaiian rain forest. Large-stand segments appear to be in the same age state. Their canopy can break down more or less synchronously in the senescing life stage because of climatic instabilities. Stands in the dieback phase are particularly prone to invasion by alien heliophytes.

Further human-induced fragmentation of the montane rain-forest biome in Hawaii can easily tip the balance from a "shifting mosaic steady state" (as defined by Bormann and Likens 1979) to a "non-equilibrium landscape" (as defined by Shugart and West 1981).

Conclusion

Pacific island forests can be characterized as biogeographically impoverished but evolutionarily enriched ecosystems. Since they are naturally impoverished in various degrees by lower biotic diversity relative to that of corresponding continental forests, they can be viewed as examples of what may happen in human-impoverished continental forests. For example, a reduction in the number of species in the canopy guild and a reduction in successionally functional tree life forms will make a forest biome more fragile, or less resilient, to environmental disturbances.

Such impoverishment has occurred in Europe in many areas in which forest management has favored a few successful commercial tree species planted in large artificial cohorts over square kilometers of forest land.

Now these forests are affected by new human-induced stresses. It is widely believed that air pollution is causing forest breakdown (Schütt and Cowling

1985). The new European dieback may have its predisposing cause, however, in the artificial cohort stands which functionally resemble the natural cohort stands found in several Pacific island forests. Air pollution undoubtedly presents a new human-induced stress, but it seems an overburden on an earlier impoverishment imposed by human intervention. There is clearly a parallel to the biogeographically imposed natural biotic impoverishment as found in indigenous Pacific island forests.

Acknowledgment

This paper was prepared and presented with support from National Science Foundation Grant BSR84–16176.

References

Atkinson, I. A. E., 1970. Successional trends in the coastal and lowland forest of Mauna Loa and Kilauea Volcanoes, Hawaii. *Pacific Science* 24:387–400.

Arentz, F., 1983. *Nothofagus* dieback on Mt. Giluwe, Papua New Guinea. *Pacific Science* 37(4):453–458.

Balakrishnan, N., and D. Mueller-Dombois, 1983. Nutrient studies in relation to habitat types and canopy dieback in the montane rain forest ecosystem, Island of Hawaii. *Pacific Science* 37(4):339–359.

Bormann, F. H., and G. E. Likens, 1979. *Pattern and Process in a Forested Ecosystem.* Springer-Verlag, New York. Second corrected printing 1981.

Burton, P. J., and D. Mueller-Dombois, 1984. Response of *Metrosideros polymorpha* seedlings to experimental canopy opening. *Ecology* 65(3):779–791.

Canfield, J. E., 1986. The role of edaphic factors and plant water relations in plant distribution in the bog/wet forest complex of Alakai Swamp, Kauai, Hawaii. Ph.D. dissertation, University of Hawaii, Honolulu.

Carlquist, S., 1965. *Island Life, a Natural History of the Islands of the World.* The Natural History Press, Garden City, New York.

Carlquist, S., 1980. *Hawaii, a Natural History.* 2nd ed. Printed for Pacific Tropical Botanical Gardens by S. B. Printers, Inc., Honolulu.

Egler, F. E., 1942. Indigen versus alien in the development of arid Hawaiian vegetation. *Ecology* 23:14–23.

Etherington, J. R., 1982. *Environment and Plant Ecology,* 2nd ed. Wiley, New York.

Fosberg, F. R., 1948. Derivation of the flora of the Hawaiian Islands. In E. C. Zimmerman (Ed.), *Insects of Hawaii*, Vol. 1, pp. 107–110. University of Hawaii Press, Honolulu.

Gerrish, G., and D. Mueller-Dombois, 1980. Behavior of native and non-native plants in two tropical rain forests on Oahu, Hawaiian Islands. *Phytocoenologia* 8(2):237–295.

Hatheway, W. H., 1952. Composition of certain native dry forests: Mokuleia, Oahu, T. H. *Ecol. Monogr.* 22:153–168.

Holden, C., 1985. Hawaiian rainforest being felled. *Science* 228(4703):1073–1074.

Holt, R. A., 1983. *The Maui forest trouble: a literature review and proposal for research.* Hawaii Bot. Science Paper No. 42. Honolulu.

Lyon, H. L., 1909. The forest disease on Maui. *Hawaiian Planter's Record* 1(4):151–159.

Lyon, H. L., 1918. The forests of Hawaii. *Hawaiian Planter's Record* 20:276–281.

Lyon, H. L., 1919. Some observations on the forest problems of Hawaii. *Hawaiian Planter's Record* 21:289–300.

Mueller-Dombois, D., 1973. A non-adapted vegetation interferes with water removal in a tropical rain forest area in Hawaii. *Tropical Ecology* 14(1):1–18.

Mueller-Dombois, D., 1981a. *Spatial variation and succession in tropical island rain forests: a progress report.* Hawaii Bot. Science Paper No. 41. Honolulu.

Mueller-Dombois, D., 1981b. Fire in tropical exosystems. In H. A. Mooney. T. M. Bonnickson, N. L. Christensen, J. E. Lotan, and W. A. Reiners (Eds.), *Fire Regimes and Ecosystem Properties,* pp. 137–176. USDA Gen. Tech. Report WO–26.

Mueller-Dombois, D., 1985. The biological resource value of native forest in Hawaii with special reference to the tropical lowland rain forest at Kalapana. 'Elepaio, *J. of Hawaii Audubon Society* 45(10):95–101.

Mueller-Dombois, D., 1986. Perspectives for an etiology of stand-level dieback. *Ann. Rev. Ecol. Syst.* 17:221–243.

Mueller-Dombois, D., 1987. Natural dieback in forests. *BioScience.* 37(8):575–583.

Mueller-Dombois, D., and G. Spatz, 1975. The influence of feral goats on the lowland vegetation in Hawaii Volcanoes National Park. *Phytocoenologia* 3(1):1–29.

Mueller-Dombois, D., J. D. Jacobi, R. G. Cooray, and N. Balakrishnan, 1980. *'Ōhi'a rain forest study: ecological investigations of the 'ōhi'a dieback problem in Hawaii.* Coll. Trop. Agric. and Human Resources. Hawaii Ag. Expt. Sta. Miscell. Public. 183.

Mueller-Dombois, D., K. W. Bridges, and H. L. Carson (Eds.), 1981. *Island Ecosystems: Biological Organization in Selected Hawaiian Communities.* US/IBP Synthesis Series 15. HutchinsonRoss/Academic Press.

Schütt, P., and E. B. Cowling 1985. Waldsterben, a general decline of forests in Central Europe: symptoms, development, and possible causes. *Plant Disease* 69(7):548–558.

Shugart, H. H., and D. C. West, 1981. Long-term dynamics of forest ecosystems. *Am. Scientist* 69:647–652.

Smathers, G. A., and D. Mueller-Dombois, 1974. *Invasion and recovery of vegetation after a volcanic eruption in Hawaii.* National Park Service Sci. Monogr. Series No. 5.

Stemmermann, L., 1983. Ecological studies of Hawaiian *Metrosideros* in a successional context. *Pacific Science* 37(4):361–373.

Stemmermann, L., 1986. Ecological studies of 'ōhi'a varieties (*Metrosideros polymorpha* Myrtaceae), the dominants in successional communities of Hawaiian rain forests. Ph.D. dissertation. University of Hawaii, Honolulu.

Stewart, G. H., and T. T. Veblen, 1983. Forest instability and canopy tree mortality in Westland, New Zealand. *Pacific Science* 37(4):427–431.

Stone, C. P., and J. M. Scott (Eds.), 1985. *Hawaii's Terrestrial Ecosystems: Preservation and Management.* University of Hawaii Press, Honolulu.

Wardle, J. A., and R. B. Allen, 1983. Dieback in New Zealand *Nothofagus* forests. *Pacific Science* 37(4):397–404.

Williams, J., 1985. The lowland dry forest and scrub in Hawaii Volcanoes National Park: current status and developmental trends in a stressed ecosystem. M. Sc.

thesis. University of Hawaii, Honolulu.

Wirawan, N., 1974. *Floristic and structural development of native dry forest stands at Mokuleia, NW Oahu.* University of Hawaii IBP Island Ecos. Tech. Rep. no. 34. Honolulu.

Vitousek, P. M., K. Van Cleve, N. Balakrishnan, and D. MuellerDombois, 1983. Soil development and nitrogen turnover in montane rainforest soils on Hawaii. *Biotropica* 15(4):268–274.

12   Deforestation in Brazilian Amazonia

PHILIP M. FEARNSIDE

Editor's Note: Why are ecologists concerned about the imminent destruction of the last of the tropical forests?

The answers are legion, so many as to seem diffuse, so powerful as to seem exaggerated and shrill, so fundamental as to seem obvious, and so demanding as to seem preemptive.

Forests are the great biotic flywheel that keeps the biosphere functioning more or less predictably. They are the major biotic component of the global carbon cycle, contain about three times as much carbon as the atmosphere, and their destruction contributes directly to the warming of the earth. Their presence determines the reflectivity of the earth over large areas, energy balance, water balance, nutrient fluxes, and air and water flows. They are, moreover, the major reservoir of biotic diversity on land: there is no habitat richer in species, none more promising as a source of succor for a swelling, scrambling, grasping human population uncertain as to where its great hopes lie. And yet, no habitat is being addressed more rapaciously than the tropical forests of Brazil.

Philip Fearnside is an ecologist with many years' experience in research, writing, and teaching in Brazil. He writes here about one of the world's greatest tragedies and touches on the transitions in plant communities that accompany the process around the world. The shift from forest to grassland or lesser communities is common here as elsewhere under chronic disruption. The great bamboo stands of Asia are a part of the transition, remnants of what once was .... and might be again, given insight, wisdom, and restraint beyond the current measure.

The final destruction of the earth's remaining tropical forests is the most recent and least justifiable act of rapine being visited on an earth otherwise already reeling from human depravity. Barbara Tuchman has called persistence in such acts that are clearly not in the common interest "folly," a most charitable term. Philip Fearnside not only spins out a contemporary estimate of the rate of deforestation in the Brazilian Amazon, but offers an analysis of the causes, shows the complicity of government and the international development agencies, and shows as well the consequences of the current patterns of land management for agriculture and on the potential for recovery of a productive vegetation. The connection between biotic impoverishment and personal and national impoverishment has seldom been better made.

Introduction

The extent and rate of rainforest clearing in Brazilian Amazonia provide ample cause for fear about the forest's future. Although clearings are still

211

small relative to the region's total area, the explosive surge of clearing in recent years has followed a pattern that would lead to disappearance of the forest within a few years if continued unchanged. Deforestation is concentrated in certain parts of the region, especially Mato Grosso, Rondônia, Acre, and southern Pará.

Reasons dominating the deforestation process vary in different parts of Amazonia. Migration of small farmers is most important in Rondônia and eastern Acre; large cattle ranchers are the principal agents elsewhere. Deforestation for cattle pasture is used by speculators to secure their land claims. Positive feedback relationships linking road building to population increase, agricultural profits, and speculative land values all lead to increased deforestation. Deforestation for low-yielding cattle pasture has also been a contributor to Brazil's high inflation, adding to the motivation for land speculation. These vicious cycles fuel accelerating deforestation.

Very little stands in the way of continued rapid clearing. Lack of sufficient capital and labor can temporarily slow the rate at which deforesters can realize their plans, but the deforestation process will run to completion unless fundamental changes are made in the structure of the system underlying forest clearing. While many events in Amazonian deforestation are beyond the government's control, key points within the government's domain include granting land titles on the basis of deforestation, programs of special loans and tax incentives for land uses requiring deforestation, and construction and improvement of highways. The frenzied rate of deforestation in the region today indicates the need for speedy government action to contain the process.

Deforestation Patterns and Trends

Brazil's Amazon forest is being destroyed at a galloping rate. The seemingly endless expanse of trees still existing cannot delay the forest's destruction by more than a brief moment in historical terms. It is of little importance whether 20 or 60 years pass before we come to the last tree. The essential point is the decision about what kind of world future generations will inherit: Will the Amazon forest survive?

The sharp disagreements concerning the area currently deforested in the Brazilian Amazon are partly rooted in limitations of existing data and, more importantly, in interpretation of these data. Both under- and overstatements of the extent of deforestation have resulted. Understatements have resulted from early studies of LANDSAT satellite images that suffered from the images' being out of date and unreliable for areas deforested for more than a few years. In addition, the numbers were generally presented to emphasize the least alarming and least important aspects of the results.

In 1980 Brazil's National Institute for Space Research (INPE) revealed a study of images of the Amazon taken in 1975 and 1978 (Tardin et al. 1980). This study created the widespread impression that only 1.55 percent of the Legal Amazon had been cleared, substantially underestimating the deforestation that had occurred up to that time – a fact easily deduced from a comparison between results of the satellite study and what is known from direct ground observations. The *Zona Bragantina* in the state of Pará is the best example: the 30,000 km^2 surrounding the city of Bragança (Figure 12.1) was completely deforested by the early 1900s by colonists furnishing food, charcoal, and other products to the city of Belém (Egler 1961; Penteado 1967; Sioli 1973). This area alone represents over three times the area indicated as deforested by 1975 in Pará. Disturbed areas not completely deforested (such as forests where loggers have removed the more valuable trees) are not easily identified in LANDSAT studies even though more recent reports refer to "altered" instead of "deforested" areas. The areas that are disturbed but not yet deforested are at present relatively rare in the Amazon in comparison with other parts of the world, but this situation is changing rapidly as the pace of logging increases.

Although studies of LANDSAT images have underestimated the extent of deforestation in the Amazon, it is still true clearings represent only a fraction of the region's 5 million km^2 total area. Despite Amazonia's vastness, it is nonetheless finite, and can therefore be destroyed. This becomes clear when one considers the rate of deforestation indicated by satellite data, instead of being concerned only with the area deforested at any given time.

The shape of the growth curve of the deforested area is crucial – the most dangerous tendency is exponential increase. The best illustration is inflation. Who in Brazil ten or fifteen years ago would have imagined prices would be hundreds of times higher today? The difficulty of intuitively understanding exponential change is great, even for us, who live daily with a phenomenon such as inflation. Thus, for many people, it seems impossible that the relatively small deforested area of the Amazon today could increase within a few years to the point of encompassing the whole region. This is precisely what would occur if deforestation were to increase in an uninterrupted exponential fashion, as inflation has. The same lack of understanding caused many people to be surprised when the forests in Brazil's Central-South states disappeared in less than a generation.

To evaluate the growth curve of the deforested areas, it is necessary to measure them in successive years. In the case of the Amazon, data of this type are very scarce. One attempt (Fearnside 1982) used information from

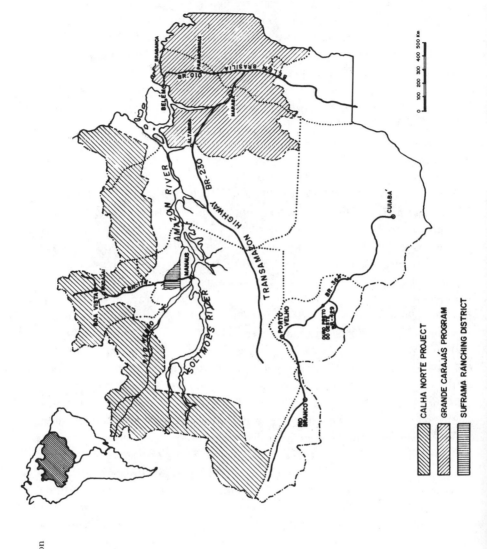

Figure 12.1. Brazil's Legal Amazon region.

CALHA NORTE PROJECT

GRANDE CARAJÁS PROGRAM

SUFRAMA RANCHING DISTRICT

Table 12.1. *Deforestation in Brazil's Legal Amazon region: Two recent satellite measurements for each state, with linear projection to 1988*

State	Land area (km²)	Year	Area cleared (km²)	Source	Year	Area cleared (km²)	Source	Estimated area cleared by 1988 (km²)	(%)
Acre	152,589	1980	4,627	(a)	1987	8,133	(b)	8,634	5.7
Amapá	139,068	1975	153	(c)	1978	171	(c)	231	0.2
Amazonas	1,558,987	1975	784	(c)	1978	1,791	(c)	5,150	0.3
Goiás[a]	285,793	1978	7,209	(c)	1980	9,120	(a)	16,768	5.9
Maranhão[a]	257,451	1978	7,334	(c)	1980	10,671	(a)	24,019	9.3
Mato Grosso	881,001	1980	52,786	(d)	1983	89,903	(e)	151,766	17.2
Pará	1,227,530	1980	33,914	(f)	1986	119,561	(g)	148,111	12.1
Rondônia	243,044	1985	27,658	(h)	1987	36,900	(i)	41,521	17.1
Roraima	230,104	1978	144	(c)	1981	1,170	(j)	3,565	1.6
Total	4,975,567							399,765	8.0

[a] Only the portions of these states included in the Legal Amazon.

Sources:
(a) Acre 1980 estimate from Brazil, Ministério da Agricultura, IBDF, 1982c based on LANDSAT-MSS. A value of 5,269 km² for 1985 deforestation in Acre (Malingreau and Tucker 1988) was not used because only the eastern ⅔ of the state is covered by the AVHRR image interpreted by these authors.
(b) IBDF, Brasília (estimate made using LANDSAT-TM).
(c) Tardin et al. 1980 (estimate made using LANDSAT-MSS).
(d) Brazil, Ministério da Agricultura, IBDF, 1982b (estimate made using LANDSAT-MSS).
(e) LANDSAT-MSS data for 1983 are available only for the western portion of Mato Grosso (227,996 km²) interpreted for the POLONOROESTE Program (Brazil, Ministério da Agricultura, IBDF, 1985). The projection was made separately for the western and eastern portions of the state, using values for 1978 and 1980 for the eastern portion, and 1980 and 1983 for the western portion. The 1978 and 1980 values for eastern Mato Grosso (24,084 km² and 40,700 km² cleared, respectively) are approximations made assuming the same percentage deforested as in the state as a whole (Brazil, Ministério da Agricultura, IBDF, 1982a; Tardin et al. 1980). The 1980 western Mato Grosso value (12,086 km²) was derived in the same way.
(f) Brazil, Ministério da Agricultura, IBDF, 1983c (estimate made using LANDSAT-MSS).
(g) SUDAM, Belém (estimate made using LANDSAT-TM).
(h) Malingreau and Tucker 1988 (estimate made using AVHRR 1.1-km resolution data).
(i) Jean-Paul Malingreau, personal communication, in 1988 (based on AVHRR 1.1-km resolution data).
(j) Brazil, Ministério da Agricultura, IBDF, 1983a (estimate made from LANDSAT-MSS images, using 2 scenes from 1980, 6 from 1981, and 2 from 1982; p. 33. The date is therefore considered as 1981, rather than the 1982 date assigned by IBDF; p. 74.

LANDSAT images for three areas where the government settled small farmers and one area of large cattle ranches in Rondônia for the period 1973–1978. The data suggest the trend is better described as exponential rather than linear.

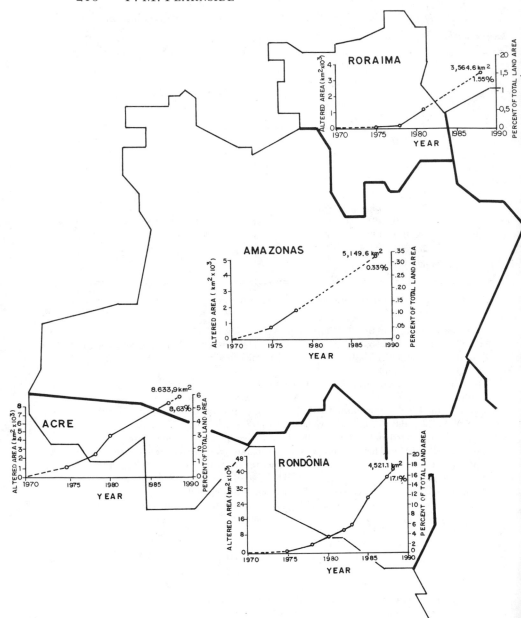

Figure 12.2. Trends in deforested areas derived from satellite data. Growth is
especially rapid in Rondônia and Mato Grosso. The beginning of the curves is shown
as a broken line since LANDSAT data for 1970 do not exist. (Updated from
Fearnside 1986b.) See note for data sources.

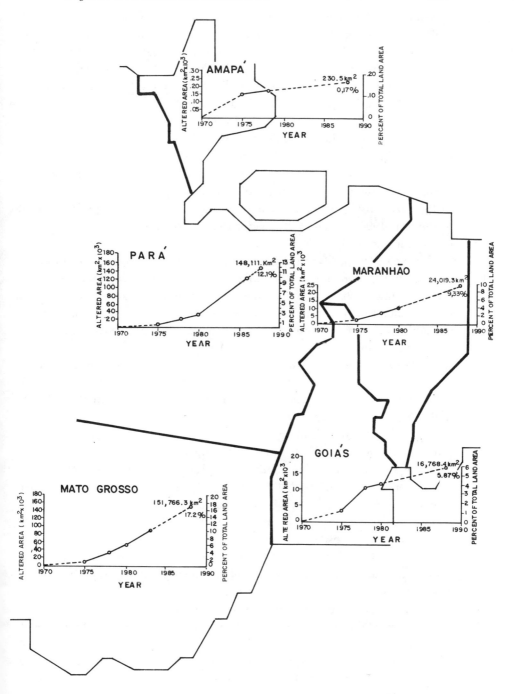

Available information for each state and territory is listed in Table 12.1 and graphed in Figure 12.2.[1] To better visualize the trends, the horizontal axes of the graphs begin in 1970. We know deforested areas were relatively small at that time based on the RADAMBRASIL Project's mosaic of radar images taken in 1971–1972 (Brazil, Presidência da República, DNPM, Projeto RADAMBRASIL, 1973–1979). For purposes of comparison with later LANDSAT data we can consider the open area in 1970 negligible, taking into account the method's inability to identify deforested areas under old second growth, as was apparent in the case of Pará's *Zona Bragantina*. The fact that deforested areas really did exist in 1970 only increases the exponential rate implied by the graphs in Figure 12.2, where the open areas in 1970 are considered zero. The axes are presented in the graphs extending to the year 1990 to remind the reader that the data already are out of date due to the extremely rapid pace of events.

The results presented in Figure 12.2 indicate explosive deforestation – apparently exponential – in Rondônia and Mato Grosso. In other states, the increase may not have been exponential; it is nevertheless very rapid. The deforestation rate in Rondônia declined slightly after 1985, partly as a result of migrants moving on to more distant frontiers in Acre and Roraima, and partly from a decrease in the number of migrants entering Rondônia from Mato Grosso. The increasing movement of migrants from Rondônia to Roraima – one of the federative units with no recent data available – means deforestation there has progressed further than the results in Figure 12.2 indicate.

Some satellite-interpretation techniques have led to the opposite impression: that the areas deforested are much larger than those shown in Figure 12.2. An INPE study of areas burning in 1987, using the AVHRR on the NOAA–9 satellite, indicated 204,000 km^2 (20 million ha) burning in an area roughly corresponding to the Legal Amazon, of which 80,000 km^2 (8 million ha) were in the portion of the area classified as dense forest (Setzer et al. 1988). Several reasons explain why these numbers are much higher than the 35,000 km^2 (3.5 million ha) calculated in Table 12.1 as the annual rate of deforestation in 1987. First, burning is not the same thing as deforestation: cattle pasture, secondary forest, and especially *cerrado* (savanna) vegetation of Mato Grosso and Goiás are burned without adding to deforestation. Second, part of the area yielding the 204,000 km^2 value lies outside the Legal Amazon (the 427,331 km^2 that make up the non-Amazonian portions of Maranhão and Goiás), and these largely occupied areas are mostly pasture and *cerrado*. On the other hand, the inclusion of non-Amazonian areas is partly compensated by not including Roraima and Amapá, with a combined area roughly the same as the non-Amazonian portions of Maranhão and

Goiás (areas north of the equator were not covered by the AVHRR image used). These two reasons account for the great difference between the 204,000 km² value for the Legal Amazon and the 80,000 km² value for dense forest. The difference between the 80,000 km² registered as burning in dense forest and the 35,000 km² annual deforestation calculated in Table 12.1 is probably in large part due to saturation of the sensor, or the phenomenon of triggering the heat-measuring device to indicate that the whole of a picture element is burning when only a small fraction is, in fact, on fire. The AVHRR images used are composed of small squares or picture elements (pixels), each 1.1 km on a side. At a temperature of 825°K (602°C), a 1 m wide flame front only 30 m long is sufficient to trigger the sensor's 300°K threshold to indicate the entire 1.2×10^6 m² pixel as burning (Robinson, in press). Therefore, the pixels that are triggered when less than half of their area is burning will lead to an overestimate. In the INPE study, a correction factor of 70% was applied to compensate for partially burned pixels (A. Setzer, personal communication). However, it is difficult to derive a constant correction factor that adequately represents this effect because the relationship of area burning to the triggering of the sensor varies tremendously with fire temperature, and fire temperature varies with time of day and local conditions.

The best evidence that the measurements made of areas burning are overestimates of deforestation is the discrepancy between the burning estimate and an AVHRR measurement of deforested area made in Rondônia in the same year (1987). The AVHRR image interpreted by Jean-Paul Malingreau (personal communication) indicated that 36,900 km², or 15.1% of the state, had been deforested (see Table 12.1). The INPE study of burning indicated that 45,452 km² (18.7% of the state) was burning in 1987 (Setzer et al. 1988, p. 28). Area deforested is cumulative since the beginning of occupation of the state, and is of necessity much larger than the area burned in any given year. Pastures can only be reburned every 2–3 years, since the settlers must maintain part of their pasture unburned in order to sustain their cattle while part of the lot is burned. If 18.7% of Rondônia were burning in 1987, this would imply that at least 40% of the state had been deforested by that year. The discrepancy between a value on the order of 40% and the 15.1% obtained for deforested area when sensing reflected solar radiation rather than the heat produced directly by the flames is of roughly the same proportion as the difference between the 80,000 km² and 35,000 km² estimates for Legal Amazonia.

It should be emphasized that even though the deforested area is less than the INPE burning study indicated, the rate of deforestation is extremely rapid and the areas affected are immense. Worse still, the 1987 AVHRR image for deforestation in Rondônia mentioned above indicated the beginning of clearing along the BR–429 Highway, penetrating the half of Rondônia represented by the Guaporé River valley, which until then was virtually untouched. No soils in the area are classified as good for agriculture (Fearnside 1986a). This event is much more grave than would be the addition of the same amount of clearing to the already occupied areas along the BR–364 Highway. The danger is great that the BR–429 Highway will bring uncontrolled deforestation to the remainder of Rondônia.

An estimate for 1988 deforestation made by the World Bank (Mahar, 1988, p. 5) concludes that 12% of the region had been cleared by that year – a higher percentage than the 8% value from the present study. The World Bank estimate is based on LANDSAT data, but the report does not specify the years of the images and the means of projection (because the report was released in June 1988 – the beginning of the dry season – all of its 1988 values are undoubtedly projections). Some of the values conflict with those obtained from recent LANDSAT studies: 12.8% for Acre being higher and 9.6% for Pará being lower than those reported in Table 12.1. Qualitative assessment of a mosaic of 1986 and 1987 LANDSAT-TM images mounted by INPE (Brazil, Ministério da Ciência e Tecnologia, INPE 1988) suggests that the 6.8% reported as cleared by 1988 in the state of Amazonas is much too high. Because of the vast size of Amazonas, this state alone accounts for more than half of the difference between the regional totals Mahar (1988) reports and those of the present study. Both the World Bank estimate and the present one lead to the same conclusion: the deforested area in Brazil's Legal Amazon is still relatively small, but is expanding explosively.

Data indicating that only a small fraction of the region has been deforested so far are quite deceptive as an indication of the impact of deforestation in the affected zones. Deforestation is highly concentrated in a few foci of human activity. These foci are strongly affected, while many other areas are not significantly altered. The deforestation foci are concentrated along the Belém–Brasília Highway (which cuts through Pará, Maranhão, and Goiás); in the states of Mato Grosso, Rondônia, and Acre; in smaller areas along the Transamazon Highway in Pará; and in the SUFRAMA (Manaus Free Trade Zone Superintendency) Agriculture and Cattle-Ranching District in Amazonas.

The spatial distribution of deforestation, when mapped in quadrats of one degree of latitude by one degree of longitude, shows clearly the concentration of deforestation in the areas mentioned above (Fearnside 1986b). The routes of the principal highways in the region appear outlined in deforestation. The close association of deforestation with roads is a reflection of some of the principal causes of the current explosive trends, and is also an indication of what governmental actions would be most effective in reducing these rates.

Motives for Deforestation

The process of deforestation in Amazonia has two distinct components: the appearance of new deforestation foci, and the expansion of open areas inside already-existing foci. Within these foci are distinct influences from establishment of more properties and from the pattern of deforestation within already-occupied properties. The kind of increase in deforested areas, therefore, depends on the history of any given place as a focus of deforestation and on the dominant forces affecting clearing in the area.

The formation of new foci has been strongly influenced by governmental decisions over the past decades. Construction of the Belém–Brasília Highway (BR–010) in 1960, its improvement for year-round traffic in 1967, and its paving in 1974 were significant milestones in creating the Amazon's largest deforestation nucleus. The cleared area in this nucleus in southern Pará and in northern Mato Grosso enlarged significantly in recent years. Construction of the Cuiabá–Porto Velho Highway (BR–364) in 1967 initiated another focus, and its paving in 1984 brought even more rapid expansion.

Deforestation has been indirectly stimulated by the government through programs to attract new migrants from other parts of the country, along with establishment of settlements and improvement of access roads. These programs have multiplied as a result of the increase in federative units in Amazonia and the elevation of "territories" to the status of "states." The proliferation of new political units results from interior areas of the Amazon having almost always lent their support to incumbent governments, making it advantageous for any party in power to increase the political representation of these areas. The principal criterion for creating new territories and states is population increase, a factor leading directly to deforestation. In the early 1980s, for example, the governor of Rondônia launched a national media campaign to promote the "fertile land" there, which, in reality, represents under 10% of the area, almost all in already-occupied zones. The campaign was strongest just preceding transformation of that territory into a state in 1982. In 1983, the government of Roraima published paid advertisements in Brazilian newsmagazines stating: "Thanks to its very rapid growth in the past four years, Roraima is almost ready to become the twenty-fourth state of Brazil." The text explained: "this dizzying expansion is due to the policy of attracting colonists. In four years – 1979 to 1983 – the government of Roraima distributed no less than one million hectares of land to ten thousand families. With this, the population has more than doubled in this period" (*Veja*, 13 April 1983). In recent years the press has reported various government plans to create new federal territories in the southern, central, and western parts of Pará and in the southwestern and western portions of Amazonas.

The paving of the Marechal Rondon or Cuiabá–Porto Velho Highway (BR–364) in 1984, with financing from the World Bank, removed a great impediment to population flow to western Amazonia, thus increasing the probability that heretofore untouched areas in the upper Rio Solimões (Upper Amazon) and Rio Negro drainage basins will be felled. Reconstruction and paving of BR–364 from Porto Velho (Rondônia) to Rio Branco (Acre) began in 1986, with financing from the Interamerican Development Bank. Disbursement of funds was suspended because of public concern in North America over the project's potential environmental impacts. Disbursements were resumed in 1988 coincident with announcement of the Brazilian government's "Our Nature" program establishing a series of committees and suspending for 90 days the export of logs and the approval of new ranching incentives. Opening Acre to rapid settlement can be expected to play a key role in bringing the Amazon as a whole into an accelerated phase of deforestation. Discovery of oil and gas fields in the Juruá and Urucu River valleys has added to the pressure for road construction in western Amazonas, which could become the next destination for the influx of migrants no longer finding land in Rondônia and Acre.

Migration to the Amazon has caused a rate of population increase far above the national average, reaching the highest values in places receiving the largest fluxes, such as Rondônia. The population of Brazil's Northern Region grew at 4.9%/year (continuous exponential rate) between the censuses of 1970 and 1980, compared with 2.5%/year in Brazil and 14.9% in Rondônia! In this state the deforested area increased at a rate of 37% per year between 1975 and 1980 (Figure 12.2), indicating deforestation reached rates even higher than population growth. This suggests that the arrival of migrants explains only a part of the phenomenon of explosive deforestation.

Even so, the arrival of new inhabitants is fundamental. Deforestation patterns in 100-hectare lots in the Ouro Preto Integrated Colonization Project (PIC) in Rondônia are being observed as part of INPA's Carrying Capacity Estimation of Amazonian Agro-Ecosystems Project. In eighteen lots that had only one owner over a 10-year period, the cumulative area deforested, on the average, increased linearly until the sixth year of occupation, after which it increased much more slowly (Figure 12.3). The replacement of original colonists by new owners who bought lots secondhand has a great impact on deforestation – new owners increase the pace of deforestation after purchasing the lot. A comparison between 23 original

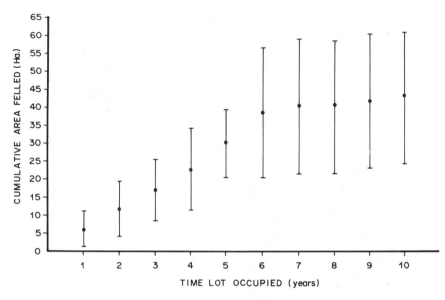

Figure 12.3. Observed felling in Ouro Preto, Rondônia, in a cohort of lots occupied by their original owners. (Reprinted from Fearnside 1984a, with permission from Leeds Philosophical and Literary Society.)

colonists and 97 new colonists in the Ouro Preto PIC indicated that, in the first four years after purchasing a lot, the new owner deforests, on the average, at an annual rate almost twice that of the original colonist (Figure 12.4). Therefore, the process of replacing original colonists with new owners, already well on its way both in Rondônia and on the Transamazon Highway, contributes to accelerating deforestation in these areas.

Pasture plays a central role in accelerating deforestation, both for small colonists and for large landowners and speculators (Fearnside 1983). Even in official settlement areas in Rondônia – where almost all of the government effort in agricultural extension, credit, and advertising is focused on promoting perennial crops – it is pasture that occupies the greatest area. For the small colonist, planting pasture is both a cause and a result of rapid deforestation. The colonist cutting forest for an annual crop can expect only one or two harvests before the decline in yields makes continued planting less attractive than the option of cutting a new area. When annual crop production is halted in any given field, the colonist is usually forced to choose between planting grass and temporarily abandoning the area to secondary forest. Other options, such as planting perennial crops, demand a much larger labor and capital investment. Pasture offers the advantage, in comparison with secondary forest, of producing some income, even if only a small amount, from the cattle raised by the colonist or from leasing the pasture.

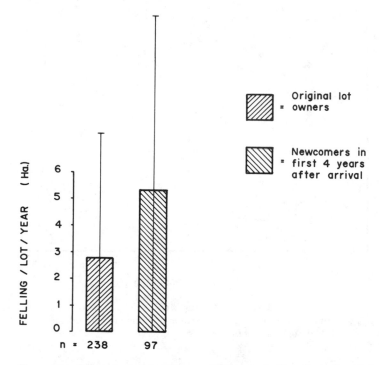

Figure 12.4. Effect of colonist turnover on felling rates in Ouro Preto, Rondônia, 1978–1981. (Reprinted from Fearnside 1984a, with permission from Leeds Philosophical and Literary Society.)

Much more important is the value that pasture grass adds to a lot's price when the land is sold. Much of the money colonists receive as the fruit of their labors in the colonization areas comes not from agricultural production, but from the eventual sale of the lot for a higher price.

Real estate speculation is a major force driving deforestation in the Brazilian Amazon and pasture has a central role in this system: besides increasing land value of legalized lots, deforestation followed by planting pasture is the method most often used both by small *posseiros* (squatters), not always thinking of speculation afterwards, and by large *grileiros* (land grabbers), attracted primarily by speculative opportunities. The centuries-old legal practice in the Brazilian Amazon is to grant the right of possession to whoever deforests a piece of land (Fearnside 1979a). Such rights of possession are eventually transformed into full rights of ownership. Pasture represents the easiest way to occupy an extensive area, thus considerably increasing the impact of a small population on deforestation.

Land speculation in the Amazon has yielded spectacular profits in recent years, far surpassing the income obtainable from agricultural production (Mahar 1979; Hecht 1985; Hecht et al. 1988a). Increase in land prices is linked to the function of real estate as protection against inflation. The prospect of reselling the land makes land buyers willing to pay prices far above those that expected production could justify. Land becomes something similar to gold or rare stamps, whose value is not based on utility as an input to production. Could it be that, in the future, the speculative value of land in the Amazon might crash, as sometimes happens with the prices of stocks? This is an important question, since the outlook for sustained production is very doubtful. The pastures being planted in Amazonia have dismal prospects for sustaining cattle production because of decline in the soil's level of available phosphorus, soil compaction, and the invasion of inedible secondary vegetation (Fearnside 1979b, 1980, 1985a; Hecht 1981, 1984). Limited and poorly located deposits of phosphates (de Lima 1976) make official plans for widespread fertilization of pasture unrealistic (Fearnside 1988b).

Financial incentives also continue to contribute to the deforestation, despite the myth these incentives ceased to be important following the 1979 decision of the Superintendency for the Development of the Amazon (SUDAM) to stop approving incentives for new cattle projects in parts of the Amazon classified as "dense forest." New projects continue to be approved in the areas of "transition forest," located between the Amazon forest and the *cerrado* (Central Brazilian scrubland), contributing to intense deforestation in southern Pará and northern Mato Grosso. Old projects in dense forests continue to receive incentives for deforestation. Even the policy of denying new incentives to dense forest areas has not always been followed: according to Fernando Campano (a member of the Consulting Council of SUDAM's Renewable Resources Department), a large cattle project was approved for Acre, completely within the supposedly protected dense forest zone (F. Campano, statement at the Interciencia Association Symposium on Amazonia, Belém, October 1983). The *Nossa Natureza* (Our Nature) program announced on 12 October 1988 does little to stem the flow of incentives: the program only suspends *new* incentives for ranching, and this only for a period of 90 days (later renewed for an additional 90 days). Generous governmental incentives make it possible for many projects to continue clearing pastures even after low beef production would have bankrupted any undertaking whose profits depended on agronomic results.

Deforestation for subsistence production is currently of little importance in the Brazilian Amazon when compared with other factors, but it may become more significant if the population continues to grow. Because settlement schemes are almost always unsustainable, even more deforestation occurs as farmers and ranchers clear new areas when production ceases in already-cleared areas. Increasing output or sustainability of agricultural systems would not necessarily decrease deforestation rates, however, because very little clearing now occurring in Brazilian Amazonia is the handiwork of traditional farmers who limit their activities when subsistence demands are satisfied (Fearnside 1987a).

Felling for commercial crop production occupies a larger area than subsistence agriculture, even for food crops such as rice, also planted for direct consumption. Loans from special financing programs have encouraged clearing, as happened in the colonization areas of the Transamazon Highway and Rondônia, for both annual and perennial crops. In assessing the motivation for the crops planted, or the pasture often replacing them, the speculative value of the land is inseparable from the value of the commercial production.

Inflation and deforestation for pasture are linked in a vicious cycle of positive feedback. Money invested in establishing and maintaining cattle ranches (including the vast pyramid of support activities) creates demand for products, but low pasture yields mean little is added to the marketplace for people to buy with the salaries they receive. Raising demand without increasing supply results in rising prices. Like any large investment that does not contribute to the economy, implanting vast areas of low-productivity cattle pasture is an inflationary factor (Fearnside 1987b). Inflation, in turn, motivates speculation in Amazonian real estate – investments that are protected by planting more pasture.

How can these processes of Amazon forest destruction be controlled? The minuscule amount of funds and personnel currently allocated to enforce environmental regulations indicates the Brazilian government is not taking deforestation control seriously. Infringement on parks and reserves is common whenever they stand in the way of new highways or other development projects (see Câmara 1983; Werneck 1983; Fearnside and Ferreira 1984). The deforestation problem must be elevated to a higher position in the hierarchy of national priorities, but various obstacles would still remain even after the rationality of such a change is recognized.

One fundamental problem impeding control of deforestation is the current distribution of the costs and benefits of forest destruction. The groups and individuals profiting from deforestation are generally not the same ones that pay the resulting environmental, social, and financial costs. Profits are often channeled to beneficiaries outside the Amazon region. Besides this, the benefits are concentrated, while the costs are distributed among many: this is the classic formula of the "tragedy of the commons" (Hardin 1968). Under these conditions, destruction continues to be completely rational in economic terms even if the total cost were much greater than the benefits. On the other hand, some costs are concentrated, with the benefits accruing to larger, more influential groups, as in the case of land seized from indigenous tribes.

Another factor that impedes controlling deforestation is the monetary nature of the benefits, while the costs, being environmental and human, are more difficult to quantify. The non-monetary costs, unfortunately, are no less real than the monetary ones (for a review of environmental impacts of deforestation, see Fearnside 1985b).

The fact that felling forest brings immediate profits – while many of the costs will only be paid by future generations – is one of the most fundamental aspects of the problem. In the middle of the economic crisis Brazil faced in July 1983, Rondônia, Mato Grosso, and Roraima were the only federative units whose monthly income from the tax on circulation of merchandise (ICM) grew more than inflation. It is probably not a coincidence the ICM, considered one of the best indices of economic activity, has increased most where deforestation is most explosive. This encouraging picture of immediate profits, however, should be evaluated by taking into account the heavy costs following massive deforestation.

The discount rate is a part of the very structure of decision making that renders inviable many potentially renewable systems of resources management (Fearnside 1989a). The discount rate – the speed at which future profits and costs have their weights diminished in calculating the net present value of each option – is an index that depends on the income potentially earned in alternative investments. No logical connection exists between the discount rate and the biological rates (such as the rate of growth of a tree in the forest) that limit the rate of return from sustained exploitation of biological resources (Fife 1971; Clark 1973, 1976). Rational use of the Amazon forest would generate only a slow return.

Human population growth in the Amazon region could also frustrate any policy designed to control deforestation. Population growth is attributed to two causes: reproduction above mortality rate and entrance of new migrants. The flow of new migrants now greatly surpasses the impact of reproduction, but in the long term both must reach an equilibrium. The capacity of Amazonia to absorb population in a sustainable manner is very limited: the social problems motivating the rush of migrants to the region must be solved in the source areas themselves (Fearnside 1986c).

The expulsion of small agriculturalists by land concentration both in the Amazon and outside it, together with the existence of a large landless rural population, makes finding a definitive solution to the deforestation problem extremely difficult. The land tenure system in Amazonia, based on deforestation, would have to be modified to make using the forest possible without clearing it. Since the tradition of legalizing land claims established by deforestation is an important factor in alleviating the impact of extreme social inequalities and the expulsion of rural population, solutions for these problems would have to be implemented at the same time.

Future Pressures for Deforestation

What forces, besides the current ones, could influence Amazonian deforestation in the future? Commercial logging, until recently affecting a relatively small fraction of the region, is rapidly becoming a substantial source of disturbance. At the moment, world markets for tropical hardwoods are being supplied principally by forest destruction in southeast Asia (Ranjitsinh 1979; Myers 1980a, 1980b).

The Asian tropical forests are dominated by a single family of trees, Dipterocarpaceae, and almost all produce high-quality lumber. Due to their more homogeneous character, the Asian forests are much more easily used for industrial purposes than is the Amazon forest. At the present pace, virtually all of Asia's tropical forests will be destroyed before the end of the century, and, according to tropical wood merchants, commercial volumes of hardwood from Asia could be insignificant by the early 1990s. This means large lumber firms, currently much more active in Asia than in tropical America, are likely to transfer their attention to Amazonia. Many forests intensively exploited by these firms are left in a heavily altered state with little chance of recuperation, even without having been cut down by clear-cutting or burning. This form of destruction will increase substantially in the Amazon. More advanced methods using a larger number of species to make fuelwood chips, pulp, plywood, particle board, or other wood products would also increase the areas clear-cut.

Another potential cause of large-scale destruction is the making of charcoal (Fearnside and Rankin 1982). Wood is now being collected from native forest to supply a pig-iron industry in conjunction with the Grande Carajás Program. In 1986, seven pig-iron plants were approved for financial incentives from the Grande Carajás Program, with a combined annual demand for 705,000 metric tons (Brazil, Presidência da República, SE-PLAN/PGC/SUDAM/CODEBAR, 1986:3). In addition, two iron-alloy plants requiring an annual total of 300,000 metric tons and two cement plants together requiring annually 82,000 metric tons were approved at the same time. Planned expansion to 20 pig-iron plants would bring the yearly total for charcoal demand to 2.4 million metric tons (Fearnside 1988a, 1989b). Recent statements by the Grande Carajás Interministerial Commission concerning planned smelters imply a charcoal demand double this amount, enough to consume 1000 km^2 of surrounding forest per year. The Carajás iron deposit contains 18 billion metric tons of high grade (67 percent Fe) ore – by far the world's largest, sufficient to sustain mining at current rates for at least 250 years (see Fearnside 1986e). Only a tiny fraction is to be smelted in the area: the potential for expansion of smelting activity is limited only by the amount of available charcoal (i.e., by the amount of forest to be sacrificed). The first plant began operation on 8 January 1988. No environmental studies were done or impact statement prepared; it has not yet even been decided how much charcoal would be produced from plantations and how much harvested from native forest. Approval of the incentives, construction of the smelters, and the beginning of operation all occurred after 23 January 1986, when environmental impact statements became a requirement in Brazil. The pig-iron program also illustrates several ways potential environmental impacts of major development projects escape the environmental review processes of multilateral lending agencies such as the World Bank, which financed the Carajás railway and mine (Fearnside 1987c).

Many sources of forest loss are increasing in importance. Mining activity, with its associated population concentrations, should increase considerably in the future. The invasion of Amerindian reserves spearheaded by free-lance gold prospectors (*garimpeiros*) is already a major concern; the continuing, officially condoned assault on Yanomami tribal areas in Roraima is the best-known case. Another growing factor is military bases with roads and settlements, especially in the Calha Norte Program along Brazil's borders with neighboring Amazonian countries (see Fearnside 1990). Yet another source of forest loss is hydroelectric development, plans for which imply flooding 2 percent of Brazil's Legal Amazon (Brazil, Ministério das Minas e Energia, ELETROBRAS 1987). The rapidly increasing rate of forest loss throughout the region means that vegetation replacing Amazonian forest is likely to become increasingly important in determining the global impact of deforestation.

Vegetation Replacing Amazonian Forest

Cattle pasture is the land use replacing almost all forest felled in Brazilian Amazonia. Small farmers often plant annual crops such as rice, maize, and manioc (cassava) for one to three years before planting pasture, whereas large ranchers plant pasture directly after felling. The cattle pastures become degraded over the course of a decade or two, depending on the efforts undertaken by the land owner in combatting invading weeds and secondary forest vegetation. Small areas near dwellings or public roadways may receive special treatment beyond that justified by the beef produced if viewed as a return on investment in pasture maintenance. For larger areas, however, the poor prospects of degraded pastures often lead to effective abandonment (although land owners are often careful not to refer to their pastures as "abandoned" or as secondary forest).

Pasture degradation results from loss of soil fertility through erosion and leaching and from fixation of phosphorus in forms unavailable to plants. Soil compaction inhibits growth of pasture grasses. The decomposition of the unburned biomass from the original forest, and forest roots in the soil, removes this source of soil fertility after about a decade (Hecht 1983). Measurements of pasture dry-weight production over a 2-year period in Rondônia have shown a 12-year-old pasture produces at about half the rate of a 3-year-old pasture (Fearnside et al., in preparation).

The types of vegetation following the degraded pasture vary widely in different parts of Amazonia and in fields with different histories. Degraded pastures undergo a secondary succession quite distinct from that in shifting cultivation fallows. In succession after shifting cultivation, woody vegetation quickly recolonizes the sites (Uhl 1987). The intensity of use greatly influences the species and rate of recovery. Stump sprouts are important in the case of first-cycle fallows if unburned or if burning is light. In Altamira (Pará) and Ouro Preto do Oeste (Rondônia), fields that were fallowed after burning the forest and a single crop of rice showed that a general relationship exists between growth rate and soil quality. One would expect that soil degradation from extended use with inadequate fallows would therefore lead to reduced rates of recovery, making a longer fallow necessary to achieve the same effect. The relatively fast biomass recovery on shifting cultivation sites (such as the fallows in Africa studied by Bartholomew et al. 1953; cited by Lugo and Brown 1981, 1982) would reduce the contribution of Amazonian deforestation to the global greenhouse effect if these recovery rates applied to deforested areas in Brazil. Lugo and Brown (1981, 1982) have argued this is the case. Unfortunately, most deforestation in Amazonia is for cattle pasture, which regenerates much more slowly when abandoned. The large difference in biomass between forest and pasture means carbon release to the atmosphere from Amazonian deforestation could be a major contributor to the greenhouse effect over the coming decades (Fearnside 1985c, 1986d, 1987d).

Secondary vegetation in abandoned pastures grows much more slowly if the pasture has been heavily used prior to abandonment. In Parágominas (Pará), Uhl et al. (1988) found that 8 years after abandonment (defined as the date of last weeding or burning), lightly used pastures (areas never weeded, with no or little grazing, and abandoned shortly after formation) had approximately twice the plant biomass as moderately used pastures (areas abandoned 6–12 years after formation, with grazing, weed cutting, and burning every 2–3 years). The lightly used pasture sites had about seventeen times more biomass than a heavily used site (an area undergoing bulldozing and windrowing after several years of maintenance under the "moderate use" techniques). Light, moderate, and heavy use accounted for approximately 20%, 70%, and 10% respectively of the pastures in the Parágominas area.

Between Paragominas and Mato Grosso lies a wide strip where succession in abandoned pastures follows a different course. From Maranhão to the Marabá area in Pará, pastures are often completely displaced after a few years by solid stands of babaçu (*Attalea speciosa* or *Orbignya phalerata*). These palms occur naturally in pure stands in parts of Maranhão outside of dense forest, and in the forest areas of Maranhão and central Pará they are present at low density in the original forest. They are highly resistant to fire and propagate quickly as the pastures are reburned. Their hard trunks have earned them the name of "quebra machado" (axe breaker), and have discouraged cutting them back. Although babaçu forms the basis of local industry in Maranhão (Hecht et al. 1988a), it is regarded strictly as a weed in Pará. Vast expanses of abandoned pastures in the Marabá area are virtually impenetrable stands of this palm; the problem is increasing 500 km further west in the Altamira area.

In Roraima, the related inajá palm (*Attalea regia*) plays a role very similar to babaçu. Pure stands have taken over many pastures in the area of Mucajaí. Inajá palms invade only pastures planted in formerly forested areas – not Roraima's extensive "natural" grasslands.

Some areas of very highly degraded pasture are taken over by a low mint (Labiaceae), inedible to cattle. This has been the fate of pastures in areas near Altamira (Pará) that were cleared in the first four decades of this century (Fearnside 1980).

It is possible the course of succession in degraded pastures could change to favor unpalatable grasses rather than woody secondary forest. Forest recovery in highly degraded pastures is extremely slow unless special countermeasures are taken, because repeated fire and hostile conditions present formidable barriers to tree seed dispersal and seedling establishment (Nepstad et al., in preparation). In some highly degraded pastures in Acre, for example, a grass known locally as "rabo de cavalo" (*Andropogon* spp.) dominates. In the Gran Pajonal region of Peru, *Imperata brasiliensis* dominates shifting cultivation succession (Scott 1978). This is a less aggressive grass than its notorious relative, *Imperata cylindrica*, which dominated succession in southeast Asia (see UNESCO/UNEP/UN-FAO 1978, p. 224). The tendency

of woody species to dominate secondary succession in Amazonia is presently
a major difference between South America and Asia, but nothing guarantees
the woody successional path will always predominate in Amazonia. *"Sapé"*
(*Imperata brasiliensis*) is frequent as the successional route in indigenous
shifting cultivation fallows in dense forest areas near the *cerrado* edge in
northern Mato Grosso (R. L. Carneiro, personal communication). Dense
forest trees near the southern edge of their distribution may be nearer to
their limits of tolerance for water stress, making these trees more easily
displaced by grass than is the case farther north. Widespread deforestation in the future is expected to lengthen the dry season because of reduced
evapotranspiration (Salati et al. 1979; Salati and Vose 1984). The change in
precipitation patterns, especially during the periodic droughts naturally
occurring even in the absence of massive deforestation, could alter successional patterns to favor a grassland or savanna dysclimax (Fearnside 1985b).
In addition to greater impact on the greenhouse effect, the shift to grass
would further aggravate the disruption of the region's hydrological cycle –
thereby forming a positive feedback loop that would continue to degrade the
remaining remnants of forest (Fearnside 1985b).

Fire entry into unfelled forest, which occurred on a large scale in Borneo during the 1982–1983 El Niño drought (Malingreau et al. 1985)
could become an additional major factor hastening the demise of the remaining forest in Amazonia. Increased perturbation from selective logging,
a practice already facilitating entry of fire into uncleared forest in Amazonia
(Uhl and Buschbacher 1985), could allow fire to deliver a coup de grace
to the remaining patches of forests much more quickly than is commonly
imagined.

Conclusion

Deforestation threatens to convert the remainder of Brazil's Amazon forest
into degraded cattle pastures with little economic or other value. The
succession following cattle pasture varies, but all compare poorly with the
original forest in terms of biological richness and performance of the forest's
environmental functions. Among the expected impacts of widespread conversion of forest to pasture are regional drying through reduced evapotranspiration and global warming through the greenhouse effect.

It is clear the range of problems that need to be solved to slow
deforestation in the Amazon is enormous. Brazil must face all of these
problems both present and future if destruction of the Amazon forest is to be
avoided. Root causes of deforestation must be addressed, rather than
restricting action to the more superficial symptoms.

Very little now stands in the way of massive increase in deforested areas. Limited amounts of capital, especially in Brazil's current crisis, can temporarily slow the rate deforesters are able to realize their plans, but the deforestation process will run to completion unless fundamental changes are made in the structure of the system underlying clearing.

Many events in the process of Amazonian deforestation are beyond governmental control. Decrees prohibiting deforestation, such as Law 7511 of 7 July 1986, have minimal effect on landclearing decisions made by farmers or ranchers living many kilometers from major roads and cities, and spread over a region as vast as Amazonia. Some key points in the system, however, are subject to governmental control. The granting of land titles, with its associated criteria of land "improvement" through deforestation, is entirely a government activity. The government also is responsible for the programs granting special loans and tax incentives for agriculture and cattle-ranching activities requiring felling. Above all, only the government builds highways. Were the government to build and improve fewer highways in Amazonia, the vicious cycle of highway construction, population immigration, and deforestation would be broken.

Current deforestation rates indicate such changes would have to be made without delay. In the face of such a daunting array of problems, paralysis is frequent: either accepting destruction as inevitable, or considering as useless any actions less extreme than a complete restructuring of society. Parálysis, whatever its rationalization, is the most certain path to a future without an Amazon forest.

Acknowledgments

My research in Rondônia is funded by the Science and Technology Component of Projeto POLONOROESTE. J. G. Gunn, A. Setzer, and S. Wilson provided useful comments on the manuscript. I thank the Sociedade Brasileira para o Progresso da Ciência (SBPC) for permission to use portions of the translation from *Ciência Hoje* (Fearnside 1984b), the Leeds Philosophical and Literary Society for permission to use Figures 12.3 and 12.4 (Fearnside 1984a), and the Royal Swedish Academy of Sciences for permission to use Figure 12.2 (Fearnside 1986c).

Note

1. Deforestation data references for Figure 12.2: All 1975 and 1978 data from Tardin et al. 1980 based on LANDSAT-MSS. All available data for Amapá and Amazonas are explained in Table 12.1. For the remaining states, values in Figure 12.2 exclusive of the last two years of data (which are presented in Table 12.1) are: Acre 1975 (1,166 km^2), 1978 (2,465 km^2); Goiás (Amazonian portion) 1975 (3,299 km^2); Maranhão (Amazonian portion) 1975 (2,941 km^2);

Mato Grosso 1975 (9,781 km²), 1978 (30,369 km²); Pará 1975 (9,948 km²), 1978 (24,949 km²); Rondônia 1975 (1,217 km²), 1978 (4,185 km²); 1980 (7,579 km²) based on LANDSAT-MSS (Brazil, Ministério da Agricultura, IBDF, 1982b); 1982 (11,400 km²) based on AVHRR 1.1 km resolution data (Woodwell et al. 1986, p. 252); 1983 (13,955 km²) based on LANDSAT-MSS (Brazil, Ministério da Agricultura, IBDF 1985); Roraima 1975 (55 km²).

References

Bartholomew, W. V., J. Meyer, and H. Laudelout, 1953. Mineral nutrient immobilization under forest and grass fallow in the Yangambi (Belgian Congo) region. Publication de l'Institut Nacional pour l'Etude Agronomique du Congo Belge. *Série Scientifique* No. 57.

Brazil, Ministério da Agricultura, Instituto Brasileiro de Desenvolvimento Florestal (IBDF), 1982a. *Alteração da Cobertura Vegetal Natural do Estado de Mato Grosso: Relatório Técnico.* IBDF, Brasília.

Brazil, Ministério da Agricultura, Instituto Brasileiro de Desenvolvimento Florestal (IBDF), 1982b. *Alteração da Cobertura Vegetal Natural do Estado de Rondônia: Relatório Técnico.* IBDF, Brasília.

Brazil, Ministério da Agricultura, Instituto Brasileiro de Desenvolvimento Florestal (IBDF), 1982c. *Alteração da Cobertura Vegetal Natural do Estado de Acre: Relatório Técnico.* IBDF, Brasília.

Brazil, Ministério da Agricultura, Instituto Brasileiro de Desenvolvimento Florestal (IBDF), 1983a. *Alteração da Cobertura Vegetal Natural do Território de Roraima: Anexo Relatório Técnico.* IBDF, Brasília.

Brazil, Ministério da Agricultura, Instituto Brasileiro de Desenvolvimento Florestal (IBDF), 1983b. *Alteração da Cobertura Vegetal Natural do Território de Amapá.* (Relatório No. 3 Convênio IBDF/SUDAM), IBDF, Brasília.

Brazil, Ministério da Agricultura, Instituto Brasileiro de Desenvolvimento Florestal (IBDF), 1983c. *Desenvolvimento Florestal do Brasil.* PNUD/FAO/BRA–82–008, Folha Informativa No. 5. IBDF, Brasília.

Brazil, Ministério da Agricultura, Instituto Brasileiro de Desenvolvimento Florestal (IBDF), 1985. *Monitoramento da Alteração da Cobertura Vegetal Natural da Area do Programa POLONOROESTE nos Estados de Rondônia e Mato Grosso: Relatório Técnico.* IBDF, Brasília.

Brazil, Ministério da Ciência e Tecnologia, Instituto de Pesquisas Espaciais (INPE), 1988. Região Norte. (Mosaic of 1986 and 1987 LANDSAT–TM images). INPE, São José dos Campos, São Paulo.

Brazil, Ministério das Minas e Energia, ELETROBRAS, 1987. *Plano Nacional de Energia Elétrica 1987/2010: Plano 2010: Relatório Geral (Dezembro 1987).* Centrais Elétricas Brasileiras S.A. (ELETROBRAS), Rio de Janeiro.

Brazil, Ministério das Minas e Energia, Projeto RADAMBRASIL, 1973–1982. *Levantamento de Recursos Naturais,* Vols. 1–23. Departamento Nacional de Produção Mineral, Rio de Janeiro.

Brazil, Presidência da República, Secretaria de Planejamento (SEPLAN), Programa Grande Carajás (PGC), Companhia de Desenvolvimento de Barcarena

(CODEBAR) and Ministério do Interior, Superintêndencia de Desenvolvimento da Amazônia (SUDAM), 1986. *Problematica do Carvão Vegetal na Area do Programa Grande Carajás*. CODEBAR/SUDAM, Belém.

Câmara, I. de G., 1983. Araguaia: Uma estrada contra o parque. *Ciência Hoje* 1(4):67–68.

Clark, C. W., 1973. The economics of overexploitation, *Science* 181:630–634.

Clark, C. W., 1976. *Mathematical Bioeconomics: The Optimal Management of Renewable Resources*. Wiley-Interscience, New York.

de Lima, J. M. G., 1976. *Perfil Analítico dos Fertilizantes Fosfatados*. Ministério das Minas e Energia, Departmento Nacional de Produção Mineral (DNPM) Boletim No. 39. DNPM, Brasília.

Egler, E. G., 1961. A Zona Bragantina do Estado do Pará. *Revista Brasileira de Geografia* 23(3):527–555.

Fearnside, P. M., 1979a. The development of the Amazon rain forest: priority problems for the formulation of guidelines. *Interciencia* 4(6):338–343.

Fearnside, P. M., 1979b. Cattle yield prediction for the Transamazon Highway of Brazil. *Interciencia* 4(4):220–225.

Fearnside, P. M., 1980. The effects of cattle pastures on soil fertility in the Brazilian Amazon: consequences for beef production sustainability. *Tropical Ecology* 21(1):125–137.

Fearnside, P. M., 1982. Deforestation in the Brazilian Amazon: how fast is it occurring? *Interciencia* 7(2):82–88.

Fearnside, P. M., 1983. Land use trends in the Brazilian Amazon Region as factors in accelerating deforestation. *Environmental Conservation* 10(2):141–148.

Fearnside, P. M., 1984a. Land clearing behaviour in small farmer settlement schemes in the Brazilian Amazon and its relation to human carrying capacity. In A. C. Chadwick and S. L. Sutton (Eds.), *Tropical Rain Forest: The Leeds Symposium*, pp. 255–271. Leeds Philosophical and Literary Society, Leeds, U.K.

Fearnside, P. M., 1984b. A floresta vai acabar? *Ciência Hoje* 2(10):42–52.

Fearnside, P. M., 1985a. Agriculture in Amazonia. In G. T. Prance and T. E. Lovejoy (Eds.), *Key Environments: Amazonia*, pp. 393-418. Pergamon Press, Oxford, U.K.

Fearnside, P. M., 1985b. Environmental change and deforestation in the Brazilian Amazon. In J. Hemming (Ed.), *Change in the Amazon Basin: Man's Impact on Forests and Rivers*, pp. 70–89. Manchester University Press, Manchester, U.K.

Fearnside, P. M., 1985c. Brazil's Amazon forest and the global carbon problem. *Interciencia* 10(4):179–186.

Fearnside, P. M., 1986a. Settlement in Rondônia and the token role of science and technology in Brazil's Amazonian development planning. *Interciencia* 11(5):229–236.

Fearnside, P. M., 1986b. Spatial concentration of deforestation in the Brazilian Amazon. *Ambio* 15(2):74–81.

Fearnside, P. M., 1986c. *Human Carrying Capacity of the Brazilian Rainforest*. Columbia University Press, New York.

Fearnside, P. M., 1986d. Brazil's Amazon forest and the global carbon problem: reply to Lugo and Brown. *Interciencia* 11(2):58–64.

Fearnside, P. M., 1986e. Agricultural plans for Brazil's Grande Carajás Program: lost opportunity for sustainable development? *World Development* 14(3):385–409.

Fearnside. P. M., 1987a. Rethinking continous cultivation in Amazonia. *BioScience* 37(3):209–214.

Fearnside, P. M., 1987b. Causes of deforestation in the Brazilian Amazon. In R. F. Dickinson (Ed.), *The Geophysiology of Amazonia: Vegetation and Climate Interactions*, pp. 37–53. Wiley, New York.

Fearnside, P. M., 1987c. Deforestation and international economic development projects in Brazilian Amazonia. *Conservation Biology* 1(3):241–221.

Fearnside, P. M., 1987d. Summary of progress in quantifying the potential contribution of Amazonian deforestation to the global carbon problem. In D. Athié, T. E. Lovejoy, and P. de M. Oyens (Eds.), *Proceedings of the Workshop on Biogeochemistry of Tropical Rain Forests: Problems for Research*, pp. 75–82. Universidade de São Paulo, Centro de Energia Nuclear na Agricultura (CENA), Piracicaba, São Paulo.

Fearnside, P. M., 1988a. Jari at age 19: lessons for Brazil's silvicultural plans at Carajás. *Interciencia* 13(1):12–24.

Fearnside, P. M., 1988b. An ecological analysis of predominant land uses in the Brazilian Amazon. *The Environmentalist* 8(11):281–300.

Fearnside, P. M., 1989a. Forest management in Amazonia: the need for new criteria in evaluating economic development options. *Forest Ecology and Management* 27:61–79.

Fearnside, P. M., 1989b. The charcoal of Carajás: pig-iron smelting threatens the forests of Brazil's eastern Amazon region. *Ambio* 18(2):141–143.

Fearnside, P. M., 1990. Environmental destruction in the Brazilian Amazon. In A. Hall and D. Goodman (Eds.), *The Future of Amazonia: Destruction or Sustainable Development*. Macmillan, London, U.K.

Fearnside, P. M., and G. de L. Ferreira, 1984. Roads in Rondônia: highway construction and the farce of unprotected forest reserves in Brazil's Amazonian forest. *Environmental Conservation* 11(4):358–360.

Fearnside, P. M., N. Leal Filho, P. M. L. A. Graça, G. L. Ferreira, R. A. Custodio, and F. J. A. Rodrigues. Pasture biomass and productivity in Brazilian Amazonia (in preparation).

Fearnside, P. M., and J. M. Rankin, 1982. Jari and Carajás: the uncertain future of large silvicultural plantations in the Amazon. *Interciencia* 7(6):326–328.

Fife, D., 1971. Killing the goose. *Environment* 13(3):20–27.

Hardin, G., 1968. The tragedy of the commons. *Science* 162:1243-1248.

Hecht, S. B., 1981. Deforestation in the Amazon basin: practice, theory and soil resource effects. *Studies in Third World Societies* 13:61–108.

Hecht, S. B., 1983. Cattle ranching in the eastern Amazon: environmental and social implications. In E. F. Moran (Ed.), *The Dilemma of Amazonian Development*, pp. 155–188. Westview Press, Boulder, Colorado.

Hecht, S. B., 1984. Cattle ranching in Amazonia: political and ecological implications. In M. Schmink and C. H. Wood (Eds.), *Frontier Expansion in Amazonia*, pp. 366–398. University Presses of Florida, Gainesville.

Hecht, S. B., 1985. Environment, development and politics: capital accumulation and the livestock sector in eastern Amazonia. *World Development* 13(6):663–684.

Hecht, S. B., A. B. Anderson, and P. May, 1988a. The subsidy from nature: shifting cultivation, successional palm forests, and rural development. *Human Organization* 47(1):25–35.

Hecht, S. B., R. B. Norgaard, and G. Possio, 1988b. The economics of cattle ranching in eastern Amazonia. *Interciencia* 13(5):233-240.

Lugo, A. E., and S. Brown, 1981. Tropical lands: popular misconceptions. *Mazingira* 5(2):10–19.

Lugo, A. E., and S. Brown, 1982. Conversion of tropical moist forests: a critique. *Interciencia* 7(2):93–98.

Mahar, D. J., 1979. *Frontier Development Policy in Brazil: A Study of Amazonia.* Praeger, New York.

Mahar, D. J., 1988. *Government Policies and Deforestation in Brazil's Amazon Region.* The World Bank, Washington, D.C.

Malingreau, J. P., G. Stephens, and L. Fellows, 1985. Remote sensing of forest fires: Kalimantan and North Borneo in 1982-83. *Ambio* 14(6):314–321.

Malingreau, J. P., and C. J. Tucker, 1988. Large-scale deforestation in the southeastern Amazon basin of Brazil. *Ambio* 17(1):49–55.

Myers, N., 1980a. *Conversion of Tropical Moist Forests.* National Academy of Sciences Press, Washington, D.C.

Myers, N., 1980b. The present status and future prospects of tropical moist forests. *Environmental Conservation* 7(2):101–114.

Nepstad, D., C. Uhl, and E. A. Serrão, in press. Surmounting barriers to forest regeneration in abandoned, highly degraded pastures (Parágominas, Pará, Brazil). In A. B. Anderson (Ed.), *Alternatives to Deforestation: Steps toward Sustainable Land Use in Amazonia.* Columbia University Press, New York.

Penteado, A. R., 1967. *Problemas de Colonização e de Uso da Terra na Região Bragantina do Estado do Pará.* Universidade Federal do Pará, Belém.

Ranjitsinh, M. K., 1979. Forest destruction in Asia and the South Pacific. *Ambio* 8(5):192–201.

Robinson, J. M., in press. Fire from space: global fire evaluation using IR remote sensing. *International Journal of Remote Sensing.*

Salati, E., A. Dall'Olio, E. Matusi, and J. R. Gat.1979. Recycling of water in the Brazilian Amazon Basin: an isotopic study. *Water Resources Research* 15:1250–1258.

Salati, E., and P. E. Vose, 1984. Amazon Basin: a system in equilibrium. *Science* 225:129–138.

Scott, G. A. J., 1978. *Grassland Development in the Gran Pajonal of Eastern Peru: A Study of Soil-Vegetation Nutrient Systems.* Hawaii Monographs in Geography, No. 1. University of Hawaii at Manoa, Department of Geography, Honolulu.

Setzer, A. W., M. C. Pereira, A. C. Pereira Júnior, and S. A. O. Almeida, 1988. *Relatório de Atividades do Projeto IBDF-INPE "SEQE" – Ano 1987.* Instituto de Pesquisas Espaciais (INPE), Pub. No. INPE–4534–RPE/565. INPE, São José dos Campos, São Paulo.

Sioli, H., 1973. Recent human activities in the Brazilian Amazon Region and their ecological effects. In B. J. Meggers, E. S. Ayensu, and W. D. Duckworth (Eds.), *Tropical Forest Ecosystems in Africa and South America: A Comparative Review*, pp. 321–334. Smithsonian Institution Press, Washington, D.C.

Tardin, A. T., D. C. L. Lee, R. J. R. Santos, O. R. de Assis, M. P. dos Santos Barbosa, M. de Lourdes Moreira, M. T. Pereira, D. Silva, and C. P. dos Santos Filho, 1980. *Subprojeto Desmatamento, Convênio IBDF/CNPq–INPE 1979.* Instituto Nacional de Pesquisas Espaciais-INPE, Relatório INPE–1649–RPE/103, São José dos Campos, São Paulo.

Uhl, C., 1987. Factors controlling succession following slash-and-burn agriculture in Amazonia. *Journal of Ecology* 75:377-407.

Uhl, C., and R. Buschbacher, 1985. A disturbing synergism between cattle-ranching, burning practices and selective tree harvesting in the eastern Amazon. *Biotropica* 17(4):265–268.

Uhl, C., R. Buschbacher, and E. A. S. Serrão, 1988. Abandoned pastures in eastern Amazonia. I. Patterns of plant succession. *Journal of Ecology* 76:633–681.

United Nations Educational Scientific and Cultural Organization (UNESCO)/ United Nations Environmental Programme (UNEP)/United Nations Food and Agricultural Organization (UN-FAO), 1978. *Tropical Forest Ecosystems: A State of Knowledge Report*. UNESCO, Paris.

Veja (São Paulo) 13 April 1983. "A fronteira do futuro," pp. 95-97. Advertisement from the Government of Roraima.

Werneck, H. F., 1983. A quem serve a nova estrada? *Ciência Hoje* 1(4):68–69.

Woodwell, G. M., R. A. Houghton, T. A. Stone, and A. B. Park, 1986. Changes in the area of forests in Rondônia, Amazon Basin, measured by satellite imagery. In J. R. Trabalka and D. E. Reichle (Eds.), *The Changing Carbon Cycle: A Global Analysis*, pp. 242–257. Springer-Verlag, New York.

13 Incentives for Sustainable Forest Management

ROBERT REPETTO

Editor's Note: Economic gradients usually dominate in determining details of the management of resources, including land and forests. One of the most important examples is the influence that inexpensive oil and cheap transportation have had on the use and value of land and the size and shape of cities in the United States and eleswhere. Cheap energy has enabled the spread of dwellings across the landscape; has raised the value of rural land for housing beyond its value for farm, pasture, or forest; and has favored massive agricultural enterprises far from markets. The management of forests, too, has yielded again and again to economic gradients that place a hundred years' experience with research in forestry secondary to the expense of harvesting. Monster clipping machines now wander across the landscape, mowing forests in acre increments, building clearcuts on clearcuts no matter what science and common sense might dictate.

Robert Repetto, an economist on the staff of the World Resources Institute, examines in lucid detail the economic forces that are currently leading to deforestation around the world. Most such gradients are artificial, sometimes flagrantly corrupt, often established or condoned by governments for the advantage of some favored few at public expense. One of the most flagrant examples is the practice of the U.S Forest Service of supporting "logging on over a hundred million acres of national forests that are economically unfit for sustained timber production.... The timber is sold at prices that do not cover governmental expenses, with a cost to the taxpayers of a hundred million dollars a year." Similar policies by other nations subsidize deforestation around the world. The effects of deforestation have been widely recognized as profound, but the general perception that deforestation is necessary to make way for a more productive use of the land in agriculture has prevailed until now. That there are limits to the value of the transition was recognized long ago, and many efforts have been made to preserve forests for game, for drainage basins, for fuel, lumber, parks, for local climatic modification, and for preservation of water courses, among other reasons. The recent recognition that deforestation globally is bringing a wave of biotic impoverishment of frightening proportions is stirring steps internationally and nationally toward reason in the form of concern about climatic changes, the loss of species, and the loss of the potential for the land, even the earth as a whole, for support of life.

The concern comes late and the prospect is depressing but not hopeless. While it is true that many nations, including some of the world's richest at the moment, seem intent on destroying as rapidly as possible one of their most important and broadly useful resources, the causes of the destruction are also clear. The economic gradients that are so effective in destruction can be adjusted to favor preservation and

239

management for long-term use as forests. The challenge remains to establish both the technical and social need and the political strength to deflect avarice and the governmental corruption that feeds it.

Scholars have been slow in defining objectives here: How much forest? What is a wholesome ratio of forest to agriculture to other uses of the land? Will the ratio be different in the tropics from the temperate zone? One guesses that a ratio of forested land or other natural ecosystem to disturbed land in excess of 75% might be appropriate, but where's the argument, now that the issue is open?

Introduction

The causes of rapid deforestation in the Third World are deeply rooted in development patterns that include rapid population growth, the concentration of landholding, and the slow growth of employment. Exploitation of the forest is intense. For hundreds of millions of people it is integral to their struggle for survival. Rural populations invade the forests in search of fuel, fodder, and cropland. Governments, impelled to raise foreign exchange earnings with domestic revenues, turn to the forests as a resource to be readily exploited. Under this relentless assault, the forest area in the Third World has shrunk by nearly half during this century. Every year more than 11 million hectares are deforested. The rate is increasing in most developing countries. While some forest clearance leaves farmers and ranchers with viable agricultural holdings, it often results in degraded soils, increased erosion and siltation, a growing shortage of wood products, and a shrinking habitat for uncounted plant and animal species (World Resources Institute 1985).

Much deforestation stems from governmental policies toward forest exploitation and competing land uses. Investment incentives, tax and credit subsidies, farm pricing policies, and the terms of logging concessions in public forests often intensify forest exploitation.

In most Third World countries, governments have taken over forest management, replacing indigenous communities who used the forests in accordance with traditional practices. Over 80% of the closed forest area in the Third World is public land (Lanly 1982). Much of the remaining forests are public in industrialized countries as well. Because private commercial forestry involves long-term growing assets, profit-oriented decisions are affected by credit costs, inflation, taxes on land and capital gains, and other policy parameters. In law and in fact, governments set the conditions for the exploitation and use of public forests.

One widely accepted criterion for forest management is the maximizing of total benefit from *all* possible commodity and non-commodity uses over the long run – discounting future benefits at an appropriate interest rate –

whether or not those benefits are reflected in market transactions. Governmental policies frequently violate this criterion. By manipulating tax codes, public credits, and charges for the use of public lands, they typically create fiscal burdens for taxpayers, sacrificing both long-term economic welfare and wasting forest resources. Improving the framework for such policies could promote more nearly sustainable forest development in the form of greater long-term economic benefits, more effective resource conservation, and reduced fiscal burdens on governments. Without such policy improvements, expanded public investment programs in forestry are unlikely to succeed.

Forest-Sector Policies

Rent-Seeking in Timber Concessions

Many countries, once well endowed with timber resources, have promoted rapid forest depletion by conceding most of their economic value to logging contractors on public lands. The considerable "stumpage value"[1] of an accessible virgin forest of commercial species is an economic rent, a value in excess of the costs of marketing trees as logs or wood products, including a return on the necessary investment. It can be captured by governments through royalties, land rents, license fees, and various harvest taxes as a return on the country's natural resource endowment. If not so captured, it provides greater than normal profits for the timber contractor, and a cushion for defraying excess costs.

Most forest-rich countries have failed to acquire such rents for the public treasury, and have thereby set off races by private contractors for (aptly named) "timber concessions." This rent-seeking behavior has generated the "timber booms" experienced by many countries. Many governments have reinforced such an incentive by entering into agreements with concessionaires, not through competitive bidding which would increase the government's share of the rents, but on the basis of standard terms or individually negotiated agreements. Potential investors rush into agreements before others take up all the favorable sites.

The Ivory Coast provides an extreme example. Despite ad valorem export taxes that ranged from 25% of f.o.b. (free-onboard) value for low-valued species to 45% for highly prized varieties, the estimated rents left to concessionaires in the early 1970s exceeded $40 per cubic meter for the most valuable species, $30 for moderately valued species, and $20 for low-valued varieties (Gillis 1985c). Between 1965 and 1972 concession agreements were signed for more than two-thirds of all productive forests. Since then, the deforestation rate has accelerated from 3.9% annually of the total forest area in the late 1960s to 5% in the late 1970s to an estimated 7% today. Timber contractors have virtually exhausted the more valuable species. Shifting cultivators have moved in behind them to clear the depleted forests. By 1985 Ivorian forests had shrunk to 22% of their extent 30 years earlier (Gillis 1985c).

Detailed estimates for Indonesia illustrate the size and disposition of rents. Between 1979 and 1982 log exports from Sumatra and Kalimantan, two main concession areas, generated potential rents averaging $61 per cubic meter exported. This is the difference between the average export value of the logs and the total costs of harvesting and moving them to the ports (exclusive of taxes and fees). Total identifiable governmental revenues, including timber royalties, land taxes, reforestation fees, and other charges, averaged $30 per cubic meter. The government captured only 50% of the rents from log exports.

Timber exported in the form of sawn logs received even more favorable treatment, due to lower tax rates intended to encourage local processing. The government captured less than 25% of the rents generated by Indonesian logs exported as sawn timber.

Between 1979 and 1982 the total economic rents generated by logging for milling and direct export exceeded $4.9 billion. Of this, the government's official share was $1.6 billion. One-half billion dollars of potential profits were lost because high-cost domestic processing lowered profit margins. The rest, $2.8 billion or $700 million annually, went to private parties. Largely due to strong profit incentives, by 1983 the area under concession agreements or being awarded to applicants was 65.4 million hectares, 1.4 million hectares *more* than the actual total area of production forests in the country (Gillis 1985b).

In Ghana, for 1971–1974, before tax and foreign-exchange administration deteriorated too badly, rents per cubic meter averaged $28 for mahogany (meranti) and $79 for afformosia. Only 38% of these rents were captured by the Ghanaian government through forest charges, even though log production reached a maximum in those years. Much of the virgin forest was destroyed as annual deforestation reached an estimated 45,000 hectares per year (Gillis 1985a).

In the Philippines, between 1979 and 1982, the forest sector generated more than a billion dollars in rents. Larger potential rents, approximately 1.5 billion, were reduced because an increasing volume of exportable logs was converted to plywood in such inefficient mills that each log exported as plywood brought a lower net return than the same log would have had if exported as sawn timber or without processing. The government's total revenues over these years from export taxes and forest charges was $140 million, less than 10% of potential rents and 14% of actual available rents (Boado 1985). The rest, more than $800 million, was retained by exploiters of the forest resource. Moreover, it appears that before 1979, when more timber was harvested in the Philippines, the government's share of rents was even lower. From 1979 to 1982 forest charges and export taxes totalled 11% of the value of forest product exports. In the preceding five years, they came only to 8%.

In addition, many governments increase contractors' profits on timber from public lands by assuming some of the timber-marketing costs, including costs of constructing trunk roads, port facilities, and other infrastructure; costs of surveying, marking, and grading salable timber; and the environmental costs of timber operations. In extreme cases, this results in a commercial harvest of timber with negative rent; the timber not being worth the cost of marketing. For example, the United States Forest Service supports logging on over 100 million acres of national forest that are economically unfit for sustained timber production, thereby impairing recreational uses and wildlife habitat. The timber is sold at prices that do not cover governmental expenses, with a cost to taxpayers of over $100 million dollars a year (Repetto 1983).

Governments compound this incentive by requiring concessionaires to begin harvesting sites within a stipulated time, and by limiting agreements to periods much shorter than a single forest rotation. In the Malaysian state of Sabah, for example, half of all timber leases are for 21 years. Most of the remainder are for only 10 years, and 5% for just 1 (Gillis 1985d). These conditions prevent concessionaires from stockpiling leases, but result in a faster harvest schedule and less concern for future productivity than that of a private investor owning the land and timber outright.

The Structure of Forest Revenue Systems

Governments affect the pace of deforestation not only through the level of user charges, but by the form those charges take. Most forest charges are based on the volume of timber removed, not the volume of merchantable timber in the tract. This encourages licensees to take only the most valuable stems. As a result a larger area must be harvested to meet timber demand and remaining trees are usually severely damaged during logging. In Sabah, between 45% and 74% of trees remaining after a harvesting operation are substantially damaged or destroyed (Gillis 1985d). In Indonesia, damages fall in the same range.

In tropical rain forests, which contain many species, this "high-grading" is a serious problem. When an area has been cut over twice in this way, the

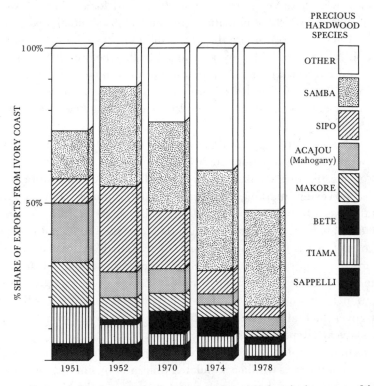

Figure 13.1. Evolution of precious hardwood species' share in the exports of the Ivory Coast, 1951–1978.

number of potentially valuable trees left is usually quite low. Figure 13.1 depicts the dramatic depletion of highly valued species, including ebony and mahogany, from the forests of the Ivory Coast, and the rising percentage of "other" low-valued trees in timber exports: between 1962 and 1978 these residual species rose from 15 to over 50% of the harvest as the prized woods became ever more scarce.

Flat charges per cubic meter harvested provide licensees the strongest incentive for high-grading, unless they are finely differentiated by species, grade, and site condition. The reason is simple: trees with a stumpage value less than the forest charge are worthless to the licensee, and can be left or destroyed with impunity. In the Philippines, an almost uniform specific royalty that tends to encourage high-grading is the main charge.

Finely differentiated fees are beyond the administrative capabilities of most tropical countries, and are not widely used.[2] However, Sarawak, which imposes specific charges that vary considerably by species with much lower rates on low-valued trees, suffers only half as much residual tree damage from logging operations as either nearby Sabah or Indonesia (Gillis 1985d). Revenue systems based on ad valorem charges, income taxes, or site rents also promote more complete utilization of the growing timber, because even inferior trees are more likely to have some positive after-tax value to the licensee.

Enforcement of concession agreements, although inherently difficult, is at least as important as their stipulations. Events in vast, remote forests are far removed from public scrutiny. Government agents are few, and timber rents provide ample funds with which to suborn them. In many countries, concessionaires have been closely linked to political or military leaders. When concession terms are not adequately enforced, licensees can cut costs and raise profits at the expense of the government and the forest base. In the Ivory Coast, harvest methods were not prescribed in concession agreements until 1972. Thereafter, "through the 1970s, forestry officials lacked the resources and information to determine and enforce annual allowable cuts or the obligatory removal of secondary species, or to verify the working programs of logging companies. As a result, concessionaires were not obliged to follow any particular technique of selection, nor any particular cutting method" (Gillis 1985c). In Indonesia and the Philippines evasion of harvesting regulations, export restrictions, and fees has been widespread.

Incentives for Wood-Processing Industries
Although processing reduces shipping costs, log-exporting countries have had to struggle to establish local wood-processing industries because industrial country tariffs are much higher on imports of processed wood products than on logs. In response, log-exporting countries have reduced or waived export taxes on processed wood and offered substantial investment incentives. For example, Ghana enacted log export bans (none of which was fully enforced); exempted plywood and other wood products from export taxes (which were far less onerous than the overvaluation of the exchange rate); granted long-term loans to mills at zero or negative real interest rates;[3] and granted a 50% rebate on income-tax liabilities to firms that exported more than 25% of output. By 1982 these policies had created a domestic industry of 95 sawmills, 10 veneer and plywood plants, and 30 wood-processing plants (Gillis 1985a).

These incentives can increase local employment and income, but at a heavy cost in lost revenues and faster deforestation. In Ghana, the Ivory Coast, and Indonesia, many of the mills built in response to these inducements have been small and inefficient. Ghanaian plymills use 2.2 cubic meters of log inputs per cubic meter of output, compared to 2:1 in

Korean and Taiwanese mills and 1.8:1 in Japanese mills. Wasteful milling means that many more logs must be harvested to meet any level of final demand.

Furthermore, once local mills have been built with official encouragement, governments are reluctant to reduce their log supply, whatever the economic or ecological reasons for reducing the harvest. In the United States, the U.S. Forest Service continues to harvest timber in Alaskan national forests unsuitable for commercial production at a cost to the taxpayer of ninety-eight cents for every dollar spent to produce timber, mainly to supply local mills dependent on logs from the national forests (Repetto 1983).

Indonesia's experience illustrates both the risks to the forest and the fiscal costs of ambitious forest-based industrialization. In 1983 the government raised the log-export tax rate to 20%, but exempted most sawn timber and all plywood. Mills were exempted from income taxes for periods of 5 or 6 years. With these incentives and the impending log-export ban, the number of operating or planned sawmills and plymills jumped from 16 in 1977 to 182 in 1983. By 1988 plymills with a total capacity for processing 20 million cubic meters of logs per year were in operation. Sawmills are expected to use another 18 million cubic meters. Only 1 million cubic meters of logs will be supplied by teak plantations on Java. Thirty-seven million must come from the forests, an annual harvest level 50% greater than the maximum reached in the 1970s, when log exports peaked. According to government forestry plans, log harvests to feed the mills are expected to rise throughout the 1990s as well.

Because conversion is inefficient (2.3:1 for plymills and 1.75:1 for sawmills) mill jobs are costly. Although a cubic meter of plywood exported in 1983 brought $250, its value, in terms of the logs used as raw materials, was only $109, and raw logs could be exported for $100 per cubic meter. Plymills added only $9 in domestic value added for every cubic meter of logs used. The government sacrificed $20 per cubic meter of logs diverted to plymills by waiving export taxes, paid mostly by foreign buyers or concessionaires. If conversion remains so inefficient, in 1988 the revenue loss will mount to $400 million annually. Because sawn timber exported in 1983 brought only $155, a cubic meter of logs that could be exported for $100 brought $89 if sawn locally. The government sacrificed $20 in export taxes in order to *lose* $11 in value added per cubic meter of logs sawn at home.

Inefficient processing drastically reduced the rents from Indonesia's forests by absorbing potential profits into higher costs. In 1983, for example, plywood exports worth $109 per cubic meter of processed logs cost $133 to produce, feasible only because of the government's financial incentives. Rents were *minus* $24 per cubic meters of logs used by plymills, compared with $53 if directly exported and $23 if used in sawmills (Gillis 1985b). Both economic losses and wasted resources resulted from inefficient domestic processing.

Industrialization policies raise the same issues in other countries. Sarawak, for example, has fostered considerable plymill and sawmill capacity by waiving the export tax on sawn timber. Like Indonesia, the government has paid heavily in forgone revenues for a marginal gain in domestic value added. In the Philippines, wood-processing industries have been protected by differential export taxes and plymills have absorbed a substantial fraction of available rents in inefficient operations. In the Ivory Coast, plymills have been erected by timber concessionaires mainly to obtain log-export quotas, but are inefficient, with conversion ratios of about 2.5:1. Because ad valorem export taxes on plywood are only 1% and 2% for low- and high-valued species, respectively, compared to 25% and 45% for raw logs, domestic processing actually sacrifices government revenues. For mahogany, more that $40 in export taxes are forgone for every $20 of extra domestic value added generated when a cubic meter of log is processed into plywood (Gillis 1985c).

Countries with forest resources have reinforced such differential forest taxes with other incentives for domestic processing. During the 1970s, for example, Brazil offered wood-processing industries in the Amazon tax credits on investments in approved projects, of up to 50% of their total income-tax liability and 75% of the total project costs. Between 1965 and 1983, about one-half billion dollars of such funds were invested in wood-processing industries, 35% of all tax-credit funds committed to Amazonian investments (Browder 1985). Investors could also deduct from taxable income 75% of the value of their purchases of shares in an investment fund, Fondo de Investimento da Amazonia (FINAM), which in turn would invest in their approved projects. These two provisions ensured that firms with tax liabilities could obtain most of the capital costs of Amazonian investments from the government. In addition, approved projects could get partial or complete income-tax holidays for up to 15 years. By 1983, the agency administering these incentive programs had granted tax holidays to 260 wood-processing firms in the Amazon. Finally, from 1981 to 1985 Amazonian forest-product producers and traders could borrow up to 100% of their prior year's exports at interest rates up to 30 percentage points below Brazil's rapid inflation rate (Hecht 1985).

In summary, the combined effects of overly generous logging agreements, which leave most of the rents from logging virgin forests to concession-aires, and excessive incentives to forest-product industries, which encourage inefficient investment in wood-processing capacity, increase the log harvest well beyond what it would be otherwise. Poorly drafted and insufficiently enforced forestry stipulations are inadequate to ensure sustainable forestry practices in the face of such powerful incentives. Forest stocks are depleted, yet neither the government treasury nor the national economy benefit from the exploitation.

Indeed, many unmeasured costs further reduce benefits. In all Third World countries, settlers and shifting cultivators follow the logging roads after the harvest, completing the process of forest clearance. Deforestation by timber operations and shifting cultivators are closely interlinked.

Forest clearance reduces the output of many valuable non-timber forest products. The exports from Indonesia of such products as rattan, resin, honey, natural silk, sandalwood, nuts and fruits, and a variety of cosmetic and pharmaceutical products were $120 million in 1982 in spite of very little development effort (Gillis 1985b).

In addition, overall ecological losses are severe. The most dramatic of these occurred in Indonesia and Sabah during the 1982 drought. An area as large as Belgium in East Kalimantan was destroyed by the worst forest fire in history. Estimated losses in Sabah are in the millions of hectares. In both countries destruction was especially severe in logged areas, where dead trees and litter provided fuel to ignite live tress. Damage to unlogged areas was slight. Further unpriced costs of forest exploitation include soil erosion and compaction, river siltation, flooding, and the destruction of the habitats of indigenous peoples and species.

Policies Outside the Forest Sector

Many forest-rich countries use incentives to encourage the conversion of forest lands to other uses. Such conversion to more economic usage will take place over time anyway as, for example, farms displace forests in countries with growing rural populations. In developed countries, in areas where farming is now uneconomic, reforestation indicates that market forces can move in both directions. Government incentives are often so large, however, that they encourage intrinsically uneconomic activities or push competing land uses beyond the limits of economic rationality.

Incentives take several forms. Governments may subsidize a competing activity directly through spending on infrastructure, grants to settlers, or budgetary losses in state enterprises. Governments may support private investors through low-interest loans and tax breaks. In some countries, property rights to forest land can be established only by clearing and converting it to another use. All such measures shift the margin of relative profitability between forestry and competing land uses, encouraging more-rapid forest conversion.

Land-tenure issues are important. In the Malaysian state of Sabah, for example, any citizen who clears and cultivates a piece of forest land can get title to it (Gillis 1985d). This rule expands the area of shifting cultivation. After timber concessionaires open up forest tracts, natives clear and claim the logged-over areas. In other countries, the Philippines for example, land claims based on forest clearance involve not only shifting cultivators, but also large livestock operations.

Many governments promote and subsidize farm settlement in forested areas with help from multilateral banks and bilateral aid agencies. In Indonesia, the "transmigration" of settlers from Java to the outer islands has long been government policy. In the 1970s almost 1 million people were moved, at a per family cost of several thousand dollars. The government plans to resettle about 5 million people between 1983 and 1988. The costs have risen to $10,000 per household, although GNP per capita is only $560 per year and total annual investment per capita is only $125. World Bank loans for Indonesia's transmigration program total hundreds of millions of dollars.

Many settlements have failed in the past, in part because the agricultural capabilities of the Outer Island soils, most of which are nutrient-poor, easily leached, and erodible, were overestimated. Low population densities reflect limited agricultural potential of the Outer Islands just as the historically dense population of Java is based on the deep, fertile, volcanic soils (Repetto 1986). Eighty percent of future transmigrants are to be settled in logged and unlogged forest to grow oil palm, rubber, and other commercial tree crops for supplementing subsistence crops. This plan may avert the crop failures, soil depletion, and marketing gaps that have defeated efforts to introduce Javanese rice culture in ecologically unsuitable areas. If targets are met, 3 million hectares of forest, an area equal to 5% of all productive forests, will be converted by 1988 (Gillis 1985b).

Incentives for Forest Conversion

In addition to sponsoring agricultural settlement directly, many governments have generously subsidized other activities that encroach on the forests. In Latin America, incentives for cattle ranching have caused the conversion of vast forest areas to ranches, many of which not only have been uneconomic, but also probably would not have been undertaken at all without heavy subsidies and the speculative hope of rising land prices. Unproductive and deteriorating pastures distant from markets have not supported enough cattle to justify either establishing or maintaining them.

Table 13.1. *Structure of costs and revenues for
typical government-supported cattle ranches in the
Brazilian Amazon*

		US$/hectare
I.	Capital costs	
	1. Land acquisition[a]	31.70
	2. Forest clearance[b]	65.95
	3. Pasture establishment[c]	26.36
	4. Fencing[b]	19.38
	5. Road building[b]	6.31
	6. Miscellaneous construction[b]	1.25
	7. Cattle acquisition[c]	90.87
II.	Annual operating costs	
	1. Labor costs	5.23
	2. Herd maintenance	4.25
	3. Pasture maintenance	9.47
	4. Facility maintenance	14.87
	5. Administration	0.82
III.	Average revenues from cattle sales	22.50

[a] Typical ranch size is 49,500 ha, although average area of
pasturage is 10,500 hectares.
[b] Estimates applied to schedule of pasture creation and stock
increase.
[c] Based on an initial herd of 4,000 head.

Source: Based on survey data of 24 SUDAM-assisted ranches in
John Browder, "Subsidies, deforestation, and the forest sector in
the Brazilian Amazon," paper prepared for the World
Resources Institute, Washington, D.C., December 1985.

Under minimal management and without adequate fertilization, once tree
cover has been removed, many of the soils converted to pasture have
deteriorated through leaching of nutrients and invasion by weed species.
Failed ranches have been sold or abandoned even as new lands are cleared
for tax benefits.

In Brazil, the cattle herd in the Amazon had reached almost 9 million head
by 1980. At an average stocking rate of 1 head per hectare, cattle ranching
had accounted for 72% of all the forest alteration detected by LANDSAT
monitoring up to that time (Browder 1985). By 1983 there were 470 cattle
projects approved by SUDAM as eligible for financial assistance. They had
taken more than $500 million in tax forgiveness. Although relatively few in
number, their large average size – over 49,000 hectares – accounted for more
than one-third of the total area converted to ranching (Browder 1985).

The overall economic worth of these large SUDAM-assisted ranching projects is questionable. Fiscal incentives increase the rate of return to the private investor far above that of the project itself. In a recent World Resources Institute analysis, survey data on costs and revenues in a sample of 24 large-scale, government-supported cattle ranches were merged to derive a typical economic profile, presented in Table 13.1 (Browder 1985).

The economic value of such a livestock project was contrasted with its value to a private investor taking advantage of the incentives available in the Amazon in the late 1970s, which for approved projects continue to the present. These incentives have included (a) income-tax holidays extending up to ten years, (b) provision for offsetting tax losses against taxable income from other enterprises, (c) provision for accelerated write-offs of buildings, equipment, and other depreciating assets, (d) tax credits for investments in approved projects in the Amazon region of up to 75% of total investment costs, (e) subsidized loans for remaining capital and operating expenses at real interest rates that were negative, on average, by at least 15 percentage points during the late 1970s.

The Brazilian government, with these incentives, financed by far the greater share of approved livestock investments through forgone tax receipts and loans that could be repaid in inflated currency. Moreover, the Brazilian government bore a substantial share of the operating losses by allowing investors to write them off against other taxable income. Private investors could shelter outside income by acquiring cattle ranches in the Amazon with very little equity investment, and hope to take advantage of rising land prices for an ultimate capital gain.

Economic analysis of the typical cattle project described above demonstrates that even under optimistic assumptions, from a national perspective it is an extremely poor investment. The first panel of Table 13.2 shows that in the base case, which assumes a 15-year project life after which land, cattle, and equipment are sold, an annual rise in land prices 2% above the rate of general inflation, and a real discount rate of about 5%, the net present value of the investment is a *loss* equal to 55% of total investment costs. For a typical ranch economic losses are $2.8 million out of the $5.1 million investment. Sensitivity analysis shows that even if land prices rose annually at 5% above the rate of inflation, the typical project would still lose 45% of investment capital. Even if cattle prices were double the reported average figure, the project would only be marginally viable. Such ranches, which converted large areas of tropical forest to pastures, have been intrinsically bad investments.

The second panel of Table 13.2 explains why these investments nonetheless went ahead. It presents their returns, not to the national economy, but to the private entrepreneur able to take advantage of all the

Table 13.2. *Economic and financial analysis of government-assisted cattle ranches in the Brazilian Amazon*

	Net present value ($ mil.)	Total investment outlay ($ mil.)	NPV % investment outlay
I. Economic analysis			
A. Base case	−2,824,000	5,143,700	−.55
B. Sensitivity analysis			
1. Cattle prices assumed doubled	511,380	5,143,700	+.10
2. Land prices assumed rising 5%/year more than general inflation rate	−2,300,370	5,143,700	−.45
II. Financial analysis			
A. Reflecting all investor incentives: tax credits, deductions, and subsidized loans	1,875,400	753,650	+2.49
B. Sensitivity analysis			
1. Interest rate subsidies eliminated	849,000	753,650	1.13
2. Deductibility of losses against other taxable income eliminated	−658,500	753,650	−0.87

Sources: Analysis based on survey data of 24 SUDAM-assisted ranches in John O. Browder, "Subsidies, deforestation, and the forest sector in the Brazilian Amazon," paper prepared for the World Resources Institute, Washington, D.C., December 1985.

incentives. Though intrinsically uneconomic, the typical project has a present value to the private investor equal to 249% of the investor's equity contribution, at a real discount rate of 5%. Sensitivity analysis shows that this present value remains positive if interest-rate subsidies are removed, but turns into a loss if provisions for offsetting operating losses against other income are also withdrawn. The implication is that government policy made profitable investments that led to the conversion of large areas of tropical forests to pasturage of low productivity and livestock operations of no economic value.

This experience represents an extreme example of the scope for policy reform. In fact, the Brazilian government has modified the policies described above, slowing or halting the approval of new livestock projects and reducing the extent of financial incentives. Rural interest rates have been indexed and raised above the rate of inflation, and tax incentives have been reduced. However, strong incentives for investment which separate returns on ecologically risky investments in the Amazon to the national economy and those to the private entrepreneur still exist.

Conclusions

Forestry policies leading to rapid depletion involve inappropriate forest-revenue systems that (a) leave enormous economic rents to concessionaires and other timber exploiters, (b) provide concessionaires little reason to practice sustainable long-term forestry, and (c) encourage highly selective harvesting of tropical forests with undue wastage of remaining trees. Inadequate enforcement of forestry stipulations and underemphasis on non-timber products obtained from tropical forests reinforce these consequences.

In an attempt to increase local employment and income, through differential taxation and investment incentives, governments have overprotected domestic milling and wood processing industries. This has encouraged large, inefficient industries to spring into existence. Inefficient conversion rates mean that many more logs must be processed to satisfy a given demand for wood products. Moreover, once established with government encouragement, local industries exert a strong pressure for a continuing harvest of logs in order to use their capacity fully, whatever the case for conservation.

Generous government subsidies to competing land uses result in rapid conversion of forest lands, often to uses that are economically inferior, even non-viable without continuing government support. Large-scale agricultural settlements in formerly forested areas, carried out at great cost to the government, have failed in several countries after huge areas have been cut. In Latin America, generous incentives for extensive cattle ranches have acted as convenient tax shelters for corporations and for wealthy investors. Although investors have gained, the ranches have often failed both economically and ecologically.

Although all these policies have been adopted in the name of development, the issue is not between economic development and resource conservation. Such policies are unsuccessful in terms of economic development alone. They result, in fact, in huge economic losses that include wastage of resources, excessive costs, reductions in potential profits and net foreign-exchange earnings, loss of badly needed government revenues, and unearned windfalls for a favored few businesses and individuals.

They also result in severe environmental losses: unnecessary destruction and depletion of valuable forest resources; displacement of indigenous peoples; degradation of soils, waters, and ecosystems; and loss of habitat for many wildlife species. Both development and environmental goals can be served by policy improvements to promote sustainable forest development. It is by no means too late. Although there are many countries, such as Liberia, the Ivory Coast, and the Philippines, where the rain forest has been extensively disturbed or virtually destroyed, there are others – Brazil and Indonesia, for example – where huge forests remain. In other countries, such as Gabon, the Congo, and Zaire, most forests are still untouched. In some of these countries, it is inaccessibility rather than policy that effectively restrains the timber harvest. That inaccessibility is steadily eroding. Enacting rational policies toward forest exploitation, forest-based industrialization, and conversion of forests to other land uses is essential to conserve these important resources and forestall serious economic and fiscal losses.

Notes

1. A standing tree's stumpage value is its implicit market worth, estimated by subtracting from the market value of the wood products that can be derived from it all the costs of harvesting, transporting to mill, and processing.
2. Ironically, Ghana, where forestry administration has been relatively weak, operates an effectively differentiated system of specific royalties. A different royalty rate applies to each of thirty-nine commercial species, and rates are charged per tree (rather than per cubic meter) harvested. The effect of this system is to encourage loggers to harvest a variety of species, to harvest large trees and thereby open the forest canopy for regeneration, and to utilize each stem cut as fully as possible. Unfortunately, since Ghana has almost no virgin production forests left, these beneficial effects cannot be fully realized there.
3. A loan which has a negative real interest rate is one on which the nominal rate of interest charged is less than the trend rate of inflation. With such a loan, the borrower could invest in any asset appreciating at the rate of inflation, sell it when the loan is due, repay the loan with interest, and make a profit.

References

Boado, E. L., 1985. Policies affecting forest use in the Philippines. Paper prepared for the World Resources Institute, Washington, D.C.

Browder, J. O., 1985. Subsidies, deforestation, and the forest sector in the Brazilian Amazon. Paper prepared for the World Resources Institute.

Gillis, M. 1985a. Ghana: public policies, resource management, and the tropical forest. Paper prepared for the World Resources Institute, Washington, D.C.

Gillis, M., 1985b. Indonesia: public policies, resource management, and the tropical forest. Paper prepared for the World Resources Institute, Washington, D.C.

Gillis, M., 1985c. Ivory Coast: public policies, resource management and the tropical forest. Paper prepared for the World Resource Institute, Washington, D.C.

Gillis, M. 1985d. Malaysia: public policies, resource management and the tropical forest in Sabah, Peninsular Malaysia and Sarawak. Paper prepared for the World Resources Institute, Washington, D.C.

Hecht, S., 1985. Dynamics of deforestation in the Amazon. Paper prepared for the World Resources Institute, Washington, D.C.

Lanly, J.-P., 1982. *Tropical Forest Resources*. Forest paper No. 30, Food and Agriculture Organization of the United Nations, Rome.

Repetto, R., 1983. *Subsidized Timber Sales from National Forest Lands in the United States*. World Resources Institute, Washington, D.C.

Repetto, R., 1986. Soil loss and population pressure on Java. *Ambio I*, 15(1):14–18.

World Resources Institute, Washington, D.C., 1985. *Tropical Forests: A Call to Action*. Part 1, p. 10.

Part III
Chronic Disturbance and Natural Ecosystems: Woodlands, Grasslands, and Tundra

14 Changes in the Mediterranean Vegetation of Israel in Response to Human Habitation and Land Use

ZEV NAVEH AND PUA KUTIEL

Editor's Note: Ecologists normally think of evolution as independent of human influences. But people have been around for at least 2 million years, long enough to have influenced not only the landscape but evolution itself.

Naveh, a landscape ecologist, shows how long habitation of the Mediterranean Basin has affected both species and the structure of the communities of this region. The vegetation of the basin is both unique in having evolved over many thousands of years with dense human populations and, strangely, common to the point of illustrating the central principle of impoverishment.

The story is fascinating but not elevating: the human role has been persistent, unrelieved, continuous pressure toward impoverishment. The evolutionary response has been, not surprisingly, adaptation in the pattern now so familiar in these pages. Where we started on this path is obscure, buried in geological history hundreds of thousands of years back and interpretable in more recent times only from such fragmentary documents as the records of the rain of pollen left in special places such as bogs.

Naveh brings a lifetime of research and intimate knowlege of the region to bear on the history and development of the Mediterranean vegetation.

When the Holy One, blessed be He, created the first man, He took him and warned him: "See my works, how beautiful and perfect they are, and all I created – I created for you. Beware lest you spoil and destroy my world, for if you spoil it, there is no one to repair it after you."
(Great Midrash on the Book of Ecclesiastes, Kohelet Rabba 7, 28 – Talmud).

Introduction

The Mediterranean Basin, Israel especially, provides an unparalleled example of the complex, far-reaching effects of chronic human-induced disturbance of landscapes and their vegetation. No other region of the world has endured so long and intensive a period of disturbance; no other region has had the unfortunate combination of a vulnerable environment and a history of human misuse of the land from the Pleistocene through the present. The effect is soil erosion, nutrient depletion, and landscape desiccation. Nowhere else are the combined dangers of traditional and

259

neotechnological pressures from expanding populations, tourism, and urban–industrial development more threatening to the future of the organic world.

At the same time, no other region has shown the resilience or the soil-building capacities of the native vegetation more strikingly than the denuded Mediterranean uplands. Nowhere else has it been more convincingly demonstrated that humanity has not only the power to destroy its habitat and deplete its flora and fauna, but also, with sufficient motivation and skill, to reclaim it.

The human role in the Mediterranean has not always been destructive as has so often been claimed. In this chapter, we discuss the decisive role of chronic anthropogenic disturbances in shaping the rich seminatural and agropastoral landscapes and their vegetation. The analysis will lead to a reconsideration of the deterministic relay-floristic climax and succession concepts which, until recently, have dominated the study of Mediterranean vegetation dynamics in Israel and elsewhere (Di Castri 1981). Although our examples of these processes are from Israel, they apply to the Mediterranean in general and to the drier eastern Mediterranean and Levant in particular.

Ecological Characteristics

Israel is on the eastern shore of the Mediterranean Sea, on the driest equatorward border of the Mediterranean climatic zone and the southwest corner of Asia. The region is a meeting ground of plants, animals, and people of three continents, and a land bridge between two oceans. Israel's location has made it a battleground between powerful political centers in the north and south and between the "sown and the desert" (Reifenberg 1955).

Israel has four bioclimatic and phytogeographic regions:

1   the extremely arid zones of the Negev in the south with Saharo-Arabian desert vegetation;
2   the mildly arid zone with Irano-Turanian steppe vegetation, marginal for stable, rain-fed agriculture, in the northern Negev and the eastern slopes of the Galilee and Sumarian mountains;
3   the transitional, semiarid zone on the xeric borders of the Mediterranean phytogeographic region;
4   the proper subhumid Mediterranean zone of Central and North Israel, to which this discussion chiefly will be devoted.

This fourth zone comprises about 35% of Israel's (pre-1967) land area of 21,147 km^2. It contains the main population and industrial centers and supports most of the agriculture. It contains, as well, 75% of the planted forests and all of the natural forests, amounting together to about 100,100 ha.

With the exception of the narrow belt of coastal sand dunes, it is part of the so-called Sclerophyll Forest Zone with its degradation stages, where broadleaved, evergreen trees and shrubs with thick but mostly leathery leaves (*sclerophylls*) reach optimum development. Outside the Mediterranean Basin the closest ecological counterparts are the broadleaved sclerophyll shrublands and woodlands in central and southern California and in similar bioclimatic regions in central Chile (Di Castri 1981).

Three main physiographic–lithological units can be distinguished:

1   the coastal belt with light-to-medium, chiefly arable soils, derived mainly from aeolian sand sediments, at present densely populated and urbanized;

2   the mountainous belt, rising to about 1000 m having various Cretaceous and Eocene calcareous rocks, including hard limestone and dolomite with terra rossa and dark rendzina soils, and chalk and marls with pale rendzinas, as well as basaltic soils of volcanic origin;

3   the valleys, plains, and plateau regions, including the southern and eastern parts of the coastal plains as well as basaltic plateau in the north; these valleys are usually covered by fine silty clayey aeolian or alluvial material and are all cultivated.

The Mediterranean zone of Israel is well within the 400–800 mm isohyets of annual rainfall between October and May. The bulk of the precipitation is in winter between December and February. There are tendencies for violent autumn and early winter storms after several months of drought. These can reach intensities of 100 mm per hour even in drier regions, creating severe erosion on bare and denuded slopes.

Intra- and interseasonal rainfall variability is high. Relative variability as measured by mean deviation from the longtime average within this zone is 20–30% (Kaznelson 1956). In the Lower Galilee it varies from 46% in the highest rainfall month (January) to 113% in October, 77% in November, and 88% in April – the critical early and late rainfall seasons (Naveh 1967). The annual fluctuations in phytomass production are even greater and can differ by 400% between favorable versus dry years, depending chiefly on differences in seasonal distribution rather than on differences in total rainfall (Naveh 1982). Summers are dry and hot, the typical "Mediterranean fire bioclimate," in which acute fire hazards prevail in the open landscape for 150 to 200 days (Naveh 1973).

With the exception of the rapidly vanishing coastal dunes and undrained wetlands and marshes, the non-cultivable upland ecosystems are, in Israel and elsewhere, the last refuges of spontaneously occurring and reproducing natural Mediterranean plants and animals (for further definitions of naturalness see below). Wherever these lands have not yet been converted into dense pine or eucalyptus forests or depleted into scrub or asphodel and

Table 14.1. *Comparative floristic species richness of Mediterranean landscapes*

Country	Surface area in Mediterranean region	Approximate number of species	Species: Area/ratio
Portugal	70,000	2,500	0,036
Spain	400,000	6,000	0,015
Italy	200,000	3,500	0,017
France	50,000	3,000	0,06
Yugoslavia	40,000	2,500	0,06
Greece	100,000	4,000	0,04
Turkey	480,000	5,000	0,01
Cyprus	9,000	1,800	0,2
Israel	10,000	1,500	0,15

rock deserts, they are distinguished by great biological and ecological diversity. This is the result of the great heterogeneity of a rugged and rocky terrain and the long history of fire and human-induced disturbances over hundreds of thousands of years. Relative to its small area (Table 14.1), Israel, after Cyprus, has the greatest Mediterranean floristic wealth.

The vegetation of the Mediterranean zone of Israel has been described in detail by Zohary (1962) and that of the Mediterranean in general by Di Castri, Goodall, and Specht (1981) in a recent compilation on Mediterranean shrubland ecosystems. The vegetation consists chiefly of complex mosaics of regenerating and degrading patches. Depending on site conditions and past and present land-use pressures, the patch types range from rich, productive open grasslands and woodlands to severely depleted dwarf shrub communities ("batha" or phrygana) and denuded rock deserts; from rich multilayered, semiopen shrublands and forests to one-to-two-layered, closed, tall shrublands (so-called maquis or mattoral). The latter consist of chiefly evergreen sclerophyll phanerophytes and are dominated by *Quercus calliprinos* ("Kermes oak") in Israel.

Most of these sclerophyll trees and shrubs are distinguished by dual root systems that can spread horizontally and penetrate deeply into rock cracks, resprouting after fire, grazing, or cutting. They respond favorably to pruning and coppicing on one stem. If resprouting from suckers is prevented they soon attain the stature of small trees. In this way closed, one-layered, very fire-prone, and unproductive shrub thickets can be converted into rich, multilayered parklike groves and woodlands. This, apparently, was the way sacred oak groves, mistakenly regarded as remnants of "climax oak communities," have been created in cemeteries.

In the slightly drier and warmer conditions in the coastal foothills and lower mountain elevation, the natural potential vegetation is parklike, dominated by scattered *Ceratonia siliqua,* the valuable carob tree, with a few *Olivea europea,* the native olive tree, and with a rich shrub and grass understory dominated by *Pistacia lentiscus,* the Eumediterranean "Mastic."

Another important formation in the drier foothills consists of deciduous tabor oak (*Quercus ithaburense*) woodlands with a rich herbaceous understory dominated chiefly by annual plants and resembling in many aspects the blue oak (*Q. douglasii*) woodlands in California (Naveh 1967).

The most productive herbaceous plant communities, with annual forage production of 3,000 kg/ha and more, can be found in drier sub-Mediterranean conditions on fertile rendzinas and basaltic soils which are rich in phosphate and conducive to vigorous growth of valuable pasture plants. The poorer, highly calcareous pale rendzinas (as well as the poor brown soils from granitic rocks, sandstone, and metamorphic rocks in other Mediterranean countries) are much less fertile and are highly erodible. On these soils, the predominant woody plants are xerophytic phanerophytes and chamaephytes, including many unpalatable, aromatic *Labiatae* and also *Cistus* species. Batha or phrygana formations with these plants occupy large areas in many Mediterranean countries and are favored by frequent burning and heavy grazing. Conversion into more valuable ecosystems should be considered.

In this chapter, vegetation types are defined according to Westhoff (1983) as *natural* if not influenced by humanity; as *subnatural* if influenced to a degree, but retaining structural vegetation formation type; as *seminatural* if most flora and fauna are largely spontaneous, but the vegetation structure has been altered; and as *agricultural* if dominant species have been replaced.

In the agropastoral Mediterranean landscape the seminatural vegetation, utilized as "natural pastures" ("ranges" in North American terminology), is closely interwoven with the agricultural vegetation of cultivated fields and plantations.

Major Phases in Human-Induced Changes in the Mediterranean Vegetation of Israel

Several accounts have been published on the history of Mediterranean lands and their vegetation in Israel and the Levant (Lowdermilk 1944; Reifenberg 1955; Mikesell 1969; and others).

More recently, Thirgood (1981) described the sad history of the resource depletion of Mediterranean forests. Le Houerou (1981) reviewed the impact of humanity and livestock, and Trabaud (1981) that of humanity and fire.

The history of the flora and vegetation and human disturbances in the Mediterranean has been recently reviewed by Pons and Quezel (1985).

In discussing human–vegetation relations in the Middle East including Israel, Zohary (1983) claimed that the effects of humanity far exceeded the destruction from Pleistocene climatic changes. However, Horvat, Glavac, and Ellenberg (1974), in describing changes in Mediterranean vegetation in prehistoric and historic times in southeast Europe, called humanity "the codesigner of the plant canopy." Pignatti (1983) emphasized the human role in the evolution of new habitats and in stimulating the evolution of flora. DiCastri (1981) stated that human beings have coevolved with these ecosystems and coevolutionary features are present in a number of ecological and cultural characters in this region.

Three major periods of human-induced changes in the vegetation of Israel and the Mediterranean in general can be distinguished. These can be further subdivided into several phases. An updated and modified version of an earlier review by Naveh and Dan (1973) on human degradation of Mediterranean landscapes will be used for this purpose.

These periods are:

1   A very long preagricultural period during the Pleistocene which marked the coevolution of Mediterranean peoples and their subnatural and seminatural landscapes and vegetation formations, and which led to the domestication of plants and animals.

2   A long prehistoric and historic agricultural period, during which the agropastoral cultural landscape was shaped, reached its peak, then gradually declined, and seminatural vegetation formations were maintained in a metastable state.

3   A recent brief neotechnological period of increasing intensification and expansion of agricultural and urban-industrial development that caused the biological and cultural impoverishment of the Mediterranean landscape.

The Coevolution of Mediterranean Peoples and the Subnatural and Seminatural Landscape and Its Vegetation

The Mediterranean geoflora since Cretaceous times has evolved from the Tertiary, Indo-Malesian, Paleo-African, and mesogean stock (Zohary 1974). The sclerophyll woody species were apparently best adapted to climatic patterns of increasing drought and lower winter temperatures that developed during the Pleistocene. Most herbaceous species evolved in this period. These now constitute up to 50 percent of all species (Pignatti 1978), more in the drier parts, including Israel. Paleobotanists differ in defining the climatic fluctuations during the Pleistocene, however, and are not yet able to provide a detailed and continuous historical scheme of taxa and communities of this ancient vegetation. According to Pons and Quezel (1985), the first

Mediterranean vegetation communities arose during the Middle Pliocene on low hillsides with dry calcareous soils.

Mediterranean landscapes in Israel and elsewhere gained the present high, sharply folded, and faulted geomorphological forms of mountains and hills, often close to the coast, by violent uplifting during the late Tertiary and early Quarternary periods. Their final shaping was a result of tectonic and volcanic activities during the Pleistocene, followed by increasing diversification of local site conditions.

From the Middle Pleistocene onward, geological and biological landscape evolution coincided with the major phases of the biological and cultural evolution of humans. The Paleolithic *Homo erectus* hunter and food gatherer was followed by the more advanced Mesolithic Neanderthaloid, subsequently by the intensively food collecting Epipaleolithic *Homo sapiens* and finally by the food-producing Neolithic *Homo sapiens sapiens*.

Coevolution is an evolutionary process in which the establishment of a symbiotic relationship between organisms, increasing the fitness of all involved, brings about changes in the traits of the organisms (Rindos 1984). Applying the definition of Stebbins (1982) for coevolution, as the simultaneous evolution of two genetically independent but ecologically interdependent lines via both biological and cultural templates, these closely coupled processes can be seen in the coevolution of Mediterranean peoples and the subnatural and seminatural vegetation.

Such coevolution has been described in more detail for Mt. Carmel (Naveh 1984), where some of the crucial stages have been documented by archaeological findings. The imprint remains on the present agropastoral, cultural landscape and the seminatural vegetation types. The process can be roughly subdivided into three major phases, corresponding to the major cultural stages in the Pleistocene.

The Early Phase of Coevolution. During the 300,000–500,000 years of the Late Acheulian and Middle Paleolithic in the Levant, disturbances by emerging Mediterranean peoples were probably confined to widely scattered habitations.

However, tectonics and erosion have obliterated most archeological evidence of the Pleistocene. Our knowledge of the early history of the Near East and Israel's Paleolithic peoples in the Lower and Middle Pleistocene is confined to findings of surface concentrations of isolated handaxes and many rolled or fresh Acheulian artifacts in wadi gravels or river terraces, and to infrequent in situ occurrences in riverine situations, lacustrine and marshy environments, and cave sites (Bar Joseph 1984). No ash deposits and sparse floral remains have been detected in open in situ habitations. Even recent, sophisticated flooding methods have not provided large samples of vegetal relics in shallow and eroded Mediterranean upland soils, especially terra rossa in which preservation is very poor. In the specific climatic and edaphic conditions of Mediterranean uplands most of the ashes of forest and brush fires are washed away by the first heavy rains, and remnants become intimately mixed with the thin upper layer of humus-rich terra rossa or rendzina soils (Naveh 1973). We can hardly expect to find archaeological evidence of such fires, especially since these slopes underwent severe geological erosion and morphotectonic upheavals. Even in the caves most traces of hearths have probably been erased by erosion and by changes in sea level followed by sedimentation.

Rindos (1984) has discussed the close interrelationships between Paleolithic populations and the plants near their habitations. He considered this relationship as the first step of "incidental domestication" in the origins of agriculture. The process can be traced in Africa for both the chimpanzee and the hunting–gathering bushman. Rindos concluded that there is no evidence for the emergence of hunting at the origin of humanity.

In describing early human evolution, Leakey and Lewin (1979) stated that it would be foolish to ignore the lessons that contemporary societies of hunters and gatherers, of which only a few hundred thousand remain, could teach us. On the basis of the importance of plants in their diets and economies, time spent on food collecting, and the tools used (mostly made of wood and therefore perishable), they concluded that it would be more accurate to refer to these people, as well as to their Paleolithic ancestors, as gatherers–hunters and not hunters–gatherers. For the same reason we should not underestimate either their effect on the immediate environment or that of their grazing animals (Sauer 1961). Rindos (1984) emphasized the interaction between the creation and maintenance of anthropogenic environments and other cultural traits. He stated (p. 137): "The habitual destruction or preservation of species will have major effects on the floristic structure of the region, and eventually on the directions open in plant evolution. Such habitual activities, passed as a cultural trait, are inseparable from human language."

Contrary to these findings, Pons and Quezel (1985) began their description of the history of human disturbances in the Mediterranean with postglacial times, some 10,000 years ago. They believed that (p. 35): "Early man was a hunter and a gatherer, and had relatively little influence on natural vegetation."

Fire was yet another important disturbance in Israel and elsewhere in the Mediterranean region. It played an important role not only in the evolution of natural vegetation, comparable to that in the California Madro-tertian geoflora (Axelrod 1958), but also in the cultural evolution of the paloeolithic hunter-gatherers. As described in more detail for Mt. Carmel (Naveh 1984), fire served as the first source of energy for heating and cooking. It was used to open dense forests and shrublands to create more accessible and richer ecotones for better hunting.

In recent archeological findings in the Petralona limestone cave in northern Greece, the use of fire by Acheulian hunter-gatherers has been dated back to about 1 million years in the lowest levels and 500,000–600,000 years in upper levels. This cave provides the oldest proof of fire culture in the world (Ikeya and Poulianos 1979). The early use of fire probably coincided with the widespread occurrence of wildfires caused by volcanic activity and lightning. Such fires apparently accompanied the establishment of Mediterranean rainfall patterns during the drier interpluvial periods of the Middle and Upper Pleistocene (Rosenan, personal communication). As reviewed by Perles (1977), human use of fire is documented by findings from later Acheulian and Mousterian cultures in southern France, Greece, Spain, and Israel.

The oldest and most intensively explored Lower Paleolithic findings in Israel and the Levant are from Ubeidiya, near Lake Kinnereth in the Jordan Valley, 160–220 m below sea level. They have been summarized recently by Bar Joseph (1984). The exposed layers with stone artifacts and bones are dated later than 700,000 years. The paleoenvironment included a hilly area, covered with mixed Mediterranean forest and, according to palynological evidence from Lacustrine sediments, with a preponderance of sclerophyll phanerophytes, such as Quercus and Pistacia (Horowitz 1979). The rich fauna (with not less than 45 mammal species) exhibited the transition from early Lower Pleistocene to Middle–Upper Pleistocene faunas. The dominant mammals and rodents of the forest indicated that the climate was more humid and cooler than that of the Jordan Valley today.

The first archeological evidence of fire and its use by *Homo erectus* from Clark's (1966) studies of other Acheulian occupations in this region was a later Acheulian assemblage near Jisr Banaat Yacub in the Hula Valley. Here Stekelis (1960) found burned fibia fractures together with bifaces and flake cleavers made of basalt.

The lithic Acheulian assemblages of Ubeidiya and Jisr Banaat Yacub show African similarities or even origin. According to Bar Joseph (1984) it was during the early Upper Pleistocene that the special character of the early Mediterranean and Levant stone cultures emerged, exhibiting special adaptation to these environments. This period marked the beginning of major coevolution with gradual intensification of human disturbances and more sophisticated use of fire by Mousterian gatherer-hunters and their more advanced Levallois stone tool techniques.

We have more archeological information of the rich fauna and flora, including pollen analyses from the Tabun cave at Mt. Carmel, for this period. The cave was formed by the dissolution of a Cenomanian reef core in the early or middle Pleistocene. Sediments and recent palynological findings have been described in detail by Jelinek (1981) and Horowitz (1979).

The earliest sediments of the last (glacial) interpluvial contain low percentages of arboreal pollen, very high percentages of Chenopodiaceae in relation to Gramineae and Cyperaceae, and high percentages of Compositae. They indicate a drier climate and probably closer proximity to the sea, as compared with later samples from Beds D and C of the early Würm pluvial about 60,000-70,000 years ago, which contained higher arboreal pollen percentages, rich in Quercus and Pinus together with Picea, Pistacia, olives and cypress pollen, much Gramineae, Cyperaceae, and other herbaceous components. With the onset of pluvial climatic conditions, the sea apparently retreated and forests, swamps, and marshes developed (Horowitz 1979). Such rich herbaceous flora, dominated by Gramineae, can be found today on open grassy sites on the Carmel slopes (Table 14.2) and may have formed a dense, rich understory of fire-opened forests and woodlands, especially if the latter consisted of deciduous *Q. ithaburensis* or other, more mesic, oaks.

Of special interest, in our opinion, are the lowest non-arboreal samples, collected from the base of the sequences in Bed F, with a greatly differing composition. In one, *Scabiosa prolifera* made up 50 percent of the pollens; in another, Compositae were dominant; and in the third, Compositae and Gramineae. Similar assemblages of herbaceous plants can be found today in close proximity to the cave and at other open, nutrient-rich sites. We assume that the presence of such a community indicates early human habitation and waste disposal.

Such data are the first archeological evidence in Israel of a further stage in the coevolutionary process which Rindos (1984) called "specialized domestication," in which differential human destruction or protection of various plant species set the stage for the development of complex agricultural systems.

From the Tabun cave we have archeological evidence of human-made fire from reddened earth, ash, and hearth, and a rich faunal bone collection. A nearly complete skeleton of a woman was found in the younger Mousterian layers, 70,000–90,000 years old. It was identified as belonging to the Neanderthaloids of the Middle Paleolithic. The upper Mousterian layer showed indication of repeated burning of the whole cave surface. According to Prof. A. Ronen (personal communication), this could have been caused by accumulation of wind-blown ash deposits of fire from the woody vegetation canopy surrounding the cave.

Similar evidence for the use of fire by Mediterranean Mousterian cultures

Table 14.2. *Vascular plant species of the surroundings of Nahal Sefunim in spring 1982, and their value for human consumption*

	Woody plants		
Trees			
1. *Arbutus andrachne*	F		W
2. *Ceratonia siliqua*	F!	P!Br	W
3. *Cercis siliquastrum*	Fl, F	Br	W
4. *Crategus aronia*	F	Br	W
5. *Laurus nobilis*	L	Br	W
6. *Olea europea*	F!	Br	W!
7. *Phyllirea media*		Br	W!
8. *Pinus halepensis*			W!
9. *Pistacia palaestina*	F	Br!	W
10. *Styrax officinalis*			W
11. *Quercus calliprinos*	F	Br!	W!
Shrubs			
1. *Calycotome villosa*	Fl	Br	W
2. *Genista fasselata*			W
3. *Pistacia lentiscus*	F	Br	W
4. *Rhamnus alaternus*		Br	W
5. *Rhamnus palaestina*	F	Br	W
6. *Ruscus aculeatus*	L		
7. *Ruta graveolens*			
Climbers			
1. *Aristolochia sempervirens*			
2. *Asparagus aphyllus*	Sh		
3. *Bryonia syriaca*			
4. *Clematis cirrhosa*			
5. *Ephedra campylopoda*			
6. *Lonicera etrusca*			
7. *Rubia tenuifolia*			
8. *Smilax aspera*	Sh		
9. *Tamus communis*	Sh		
Dwarfshrubs			
1. *Ajuga chisa*			
2. *Ballota saxatilis*			
3. *Cistus salvifolius*	L		
4. *Cistus villosus*	L		
5. *Coridothymus capitatus*	L		
6. *Eurphorbia hierosolymitana*			
7. *Fumana arabica*			
8. *Fumana thymifolia*			
9. *Hypericum thymifolium*			
10. *Majorana syriaca*	L		
11. *Melissa officinalis*	L		
12. *Micromeria fruticosa*	L		
13. *Micromeria myrtifolia*			
14. *Micromeria nervosa*			

Table 14.2. *(cont.)*

15. *Osyris alba*			
16. *Phlomis viscosa*			
17. *Prasium majus*			
18. *Salvia fruticosa*	L		
19. *Sarcopoterium spinosum*		Br	W
20. *Satureja thymbra*	L		
21. *Stachys palaestina*			
22. *Stachys distans*			
23. *Teucrium creticum*	L		
24. *Teucrium divaricatum*			
25. *Varthemia iphionides*			

Total Woody Species   52

Herbaceous plants

Geophytes

1. *Allium neapolitanum*	
2. *Allium stamineum*	
3. *Allium trifoliatum*	
4. *Anacamptis pyramidalis*	
5. *Anemona coronaria*	
6. *Arisarum vulgare*	L
7. *Arum dioscioridis*	L
8. *Asphodelus microcarpus*	B
9. *Bellavalia flexuosa*	
10. *Cephalantera longifolia*	
11. *Colchicum steveni*	
12. *Crocus hyemalis*	B
13. *Cyclamen persicum*	L, Fl
14. *Gagea chlorantha*	
15. *Gagea commutata*	
16. *Gladiolus italicus*	
17. *Limodorum abortivum*	
18. *Muscaris parviflorum*	
19. *Narcisus tazetta*	
20. *Ophrys carmeli*	B
21. *Ophrys bornmuelleri*	B
22. *Ophrys fleischmanii*	B
23. *Ophrys galilaea*	B
24. *Ophrys transhyrcana*	B
25. *Orchis caspia*	B
26. *Orchis galilaea*	B
27. *Orchis tridentata*	B
28. *Ornithogalum montanum*	
29. *Ornithogalum narbonense*	
30. *Pancratium parviflorum*	
31. *Ranunculus asiaticus*	
32. *Romulea phoenicia*	
33. *Scilla autumnalis*	

Table 14.2. *(cont.)*

34. *Scilla hyacinthoides*		
35. *Serapias vomeracea*	B	
36. *Fritillaria persica*		
37. *Tulipa montana*	B	

Grasses

1. *Aegilops ovata*	S	P
2. *Andropogon distachyus*		P!
3. *Avena sterilis*		P!
4. *Bromus alopecurus*		P
5. *Bromus syriaca*		P
6. *Catapodium rigidum*		P
7. *Dactylis glomerata*		P!
8. *Hordeum bulbosum*	S, B	P!
9. *Hordeum spontaneum*	S	P!
10. *Hyparrhenia hirta*		P
11. *Lopochloa phleoides*		P
12. *Phleum subulatum*		P
13. *Piptatherum miliaceaum*		P!
14. *Piptatherum blancheanum*		P!
15. *Stipa bromoides*		P
16. *Trachynia distachya*		P

Legumes

1. *Anthyllis tetraphylla*		P
2. *Coronilla cretica*		P
3. *Hippocrepis unisiliquosa*		P
4. *Hymenocarpus circinnatus*	S	P
5. *Lathyrus blepharicarpus*	S	P
6. *Lotus peregrinus*		P
7. *Medicago orbicularis*		P!
8. *Medicago scutellata*		P!
9. *Medicago polymorpha*		P!
10. *Onobrychis squarrosa*		P
11. *Pisum elatus*	S, L	P
12. *Scorpiurus muricatus*		P!
13. *Tetragonolobus paleastinus*		P!
14. *Trifolium campestre*		P!
15. *Trifolium clusii*		P
16. *Trifolium clypeatum*		P!
17. *Trifolium stellatum*		P
18. *Vica hybrida*	S	P!
19. *Vicia narbonensis*		

Compositae

1. *Anthemis melanolepis*		
2. *Anthemis* spp.		
3. *Atractylis comosa*		
4. *Bellis silvestris*		
5. *Calendula arvensis*	L	P
6. *Carduus argentatus*	L	

Table 14.2. *(cont.)*

7. *Carlina involucrata*	L	
8. *Catananche lutea*		P
9. *Cichorium pumilum*	L, S	P
10. *Centaurea cyanoides*		
11. *Cirsium phyllocephalum*		
12. *Crepis hierosolymitana*		
13. *Crepis palaestina*		
14. *Crepis sancta*		
15. *Crupina crupinastrum*		
16. *Echinops* spp.		
17. *Filago eriocephala*		
18. *Gundelia tournefortii*	C	
19. *Hedypnois cretica*		P
20. *Inula viscosa*	L, C	
21. *Notobasis syriaca*		P
22. *Pallemis spinosa*		
23. *Rhagadiolus stellatus*		P
24. *Scorzonera papposa*	B	P
25. *Senecio vernalis*		P
26. *Tolpis virgata*		P
27. *Trincia tuberosa*		P

Miscellaneous Herbs

1. *Adonis aestivalis*		
2. *Ainsworthia cordata*		
3. *Alcea acaulis*	L, S	
4. *Alcea setosa*	L, S	
5. *Alyssum minus*		
6. *Anagallis arvensis*	L	
7. *Anchusa aegyptiaca*		
8. *Anchusa hybrida*		
9. *Anchusa strigosa*		
10. *Artedia squamata*		
11. *Biscutella didyma*		
12. *Bupleurum cretica*		
13. *Bupleurum lancifolium*		
14. *Bupleurum nodiflorum*		
15. *Campanula rapunculus*		
16. *Capsella bursa-pastoris*	L	
17. *Cephalaria joppica*		
18. *Ceratocapnus palaestinus*		
19. *Chaetosciadium trichospermum*		
20. *Convolvulus caelesyriacus*		P
21. *Crucianella maritima*		
22. *Daucus carota*	R	
23. *Dianthus pendulus*		
24. *Dianthus stricyus*		
25. *Erodium gruinum*		P
26. *Erodium moschatum*		P
27. *Erophila minima*		

Table 14.2. *(cont.)*

28. *Eryngium billardieri*			
29. *Ferula tingitana*			
30. *Foeniculum vulgare*	L		
31. *Galium bisiferum*			
32. *Geranium molle*			P
33. *Geranium purpureum*			P
34. *Geranium rotundifolium*			P
35. *Helichrysum sanguineum*			
36. *Heptaptera crenata*			
37. *Hirschfeldia incana*			
38. *Hyoscyamus aureus*			
39. *Hypericum lanuginosum*			
40. *Isatis lusitanicia*	L		
41. *Kicksia spuria*			P
42. *Lagoecia cuminoides*			
43. *Lamium amplexicaule*			
44. *Legousia falcata*			
45. *Linum nodiflorum*			
46. *Linum pubescens*			
47. *Linum strictum*			
48. *Malcolmia chia*			
49. *Mandragora officinalis*	F		
50. *Melica angustifolia*			
51. *Mercurialis annua*	L		
52. *Minuartia hybrida*			
53. *Molucella spinosa*			
54. *Nigela arvensis*	S		
55. *Nonea obtusifolia*			
56. *Ochtodium aegyptiacum*			
57. *Onosma frutescens*			
58. *Oxalis pes-caprae*			
59. *Papaver carmeli*	S		
60. *Parietaria judaica*			
61. *Plantago cretica*	L		
62. *Plantago psyllium*	L		
63. *Pimpinella peregrina*			
64. *Podonosma syriaca*			
65. *Pterocephalus plumosus*			
66. *Reseda alba*			
67. *Ricotia lunaria*			
68. *Rosularia lineata*			
69. *Salvia hierosolymitana*	L		
70. *Salvia pinnata*	L		
71. *Salvia viridis*			
72. *Sanguisorbia minor*	L	P	
73. *Scabiosa prolifera*			
74. *Scaligeria napiformis*			
75. *Scutellaria subvelutina*			
76. *Scrophularia rubricaulis*			
77. *Sherardia arvensis*			

Table 14.2. *(cont.)*

78. *Silena aegyptiaca*
79. *Silena colorata*
80. *Scandix iberia*
81. *Sinapis arvensis*   L
82. *Stachys neurocalycina*
83. *Synelcosciadium carmeli*
84. *Theligonum cynocrambe*
85. *Thesium bergeri*
86. *Thlapsi arvense*
87. *Umbilicus intermedius*
88. *Valandia hispida*
89. *Valerina dioscoridis*
90. *Valerianella vesicaria*
91. *Verbascum tripolitanum*
92. *Verbascum sinuatum*
93. *Veronica cymbalaria*

   Total herbaceous species: 192

F – fruits; S – seeds; B – bulbs, corms, etc.; Fl – flowers; L – leaves; Sh – shoots; R – roots; C – capitulum; P – pasture for livestock; Br – browse, chiefly for goats; W – wood; ! – high value.

Source: Determination for human consumption according to Dafni 1983.

has been provided by findings at the Kasistra Caves near Lake Ioanina in Greece (Higgs et al. 1967). From this period Vernet (1973) reported findings of charcoal specimens of sclerophyll and phanerophyte "climax" species, such as Phyllirea and Quercus in southeastern France.

We can assume that those woody and herbaceous genotypes which developed the most efficient evolutionary strategies, with the help of vegetative and reproductive regeneration mechanisms to overcome the natural and human-induced stresses of fire, had the best chance to survive. Thus, all sclerophylls are obligatory root sprouters, whereas dwarf shrubs and perennial herbaceous plants are mostly facultative root sprouters and have dual vegetative and reproductive regeneration mechanisms. *Pinus halepensis,* the only indigenous conifer, like annual plants, relies on postfire seed germination, which is enhanced in many species (Naveh 1973).

It can be assumed that grazing pressure was sufficiently severe so as to act as an additional selection pressure through adaptive feedback. Mammalian as well as insect herbivores may have induced biochemical defense mechanisms in plants. Among these are tannins in oak species (Feeny 1975).

The etheric oils which are typical of many aromatic species may have increased their flammability. A good example of the coupling of survival mechanisms against fire, grazing, and drought in grasses is the development of hygroscopic awns and callous basal tips, enabling the burial of dissemulates several centimeters deep in the soil or in rock cracks, thereby achieving protection from both fire and grazing (Naveh 1973).

According to Perles (1977) the mastering of fire occurred about 100,000 years ago by Mousterian Neanderthaloids who produced lamps to light their caves and torches to carry fire. They could open dense forest and brush thicket to facilitate hunting and food collecting and to increase edible food by encouraging the lush regenerating trees, shrubs, invading grasses, bulbs, and tuberous plants.

That these people had reached a high intellectual level is inferred by their mortuary practices at Mt. Carmel and elsewhere. As reported by Solecki (1977) at the Shanidar cave in the Kurdish mountains, flowers which grew outside the cave were found in soil samples taken from around the burials of "Neanderthaloid IV." The plants included Achillea and Althaea, known for their medical value, the ornamentals Centaurea, Senecio, and Muscari, and *Ephedra altissima,* whose ramose branches were used for network or bedding. Such findings serve as another proof of the modifications of the natural vegetation by early peoples and their role in spreading herbaceous plants during the Pleistocene.

The Major Phase of Coevolution. Preagricultural broad-spectrum utilization of natural plant and animal resources and landscape modification by advanced upper and Epipaleolithic *Homo sapien sapiens* reached its peak in the late last pluvial, 10,000-15,000 years ago.

As described by Naveh (1984) for Mt Carmel, it can be surmised that this was achieved by the use of fire as a tool for the conversion of dense, climax forests, woodlands, and shrublands into open and richer seminatural woody and herbaceous vegetation. The mild, winter-rain climate favored a rich Mediterranean flora and fauna and the spread of Epipaleolithic food-collecting, hunting, and fishing populations into the ecotones of the mountains, foothills, coastal plains, and river valleys. The Carmel Natufians used carefully prepared, tiny sharp microliths to hunt game (especially gazelle), flint sickles to cut wild grasses, mortars, and pestles as pounding tools in the preparation of staple food from roasted cereals or acorns. They also collected fruits, bulbs, and acorns, constructed houses, and developed a complex and rich communal, cultural, and spiritual life (Bar Joseph 1984).

We should regard this rational, "protoagricultural" use of fire by the

Natufians as one of the most important features of broad-spectrum adaptation and intensive exploitation of coastal and upland resources.

In his paleo-ecological interpretations of faunal remains from Mt. Carmel, Tchernov (1984) described the landscape as "a kind of constant balance between open country and woodland." We can attribute this dynamic equilibrium to the intensively managed and utilized seminatural landscape. It created heterogeneous, probably fire-induced, mosaics of forests, woodlands, and shrublands, dominated by sclerophyll trees and shrubs with a rich understory of rapidly spreading, light-demanding herbaceous plants. These plants became dominant in the marshy, drier, and very rocky sites. Some served as progenitors of domesticated cereals, pulses, and vegetables, and a source for pasture plants and agricultural weeds.

The Final Phase of Coevolution. The transition from intensive food collection to food production and the domestication of plants and animals, called by Rindos (1984) "agricultural domestication," can be regarded as the culmination of the coevolution of early peoples and plants in the Mediterranean. In this process the Natufian and other Epipaleolithic cultures – by intensive environmental manipulation, including fire – probably served as an important link. The plants listed in Table 14.2 as beneficial for diverse human uses, and possibly additional plants as well, were abundant when the Sefunim wadi served as a major focus for the coevolutionary transition (Ronen 1984). There are good reasons to speculate that, in the transition from food collection by "passive cultivation" to food production by active cultivation and domestication, burning and the favorable seedbeds created thereby acted as a major trigger and multiplier effect.

Indirect archeological evidence for early neolithic land clearing in Israel is implied by great assemblages of stone axes in the Sefunim cave at Mt. Carmel (Ronen 1984). They could have been used for felling of oaks and other trees in the well-developed and dense forests. The ash seed-beds were used for cultivation of cereals and pulses. This system of slash-and-burn cultivation was repeated several thousand years later by the first neolithic farmers in Europe (Narr 1956).

It is also possible that cleared and burned forest fields served as "experimental" sites for many species and that those most suitable were further domesticated, while others became facultative weeds, adopting their present dual position as part of both seminatural and agricultural vegetation. Such newly opened niches also favored the evolution of obligatory weeds as an evolutionary "sideproduct" of cultivation and domestication.

Pons and Quezel (1985) showed that in southern France in the Rhone Valley early slash-and-burn agriculture is suggested by charcoal dated 7,350

B.C. There was a simultaneous decrease in the percentage of deciduous oak pollen, and higher percentages of Labiatae and Leguminosae, Plantago, Compositae and other species considered to be weeds of cereal cultivation. Cereal pollen appeared at the same time. Pons and Quezel (1985) interpreted earlier evidence of temporary clearance of *Q. pubescens* forest and a simultaneous increase of Plantago, Ericacae, and lightdemanding herbaceous species as a clearing of the preneolithic forest for grazing animals.

The rich findings of carbonized seeds at Al Kosh in southwest Iran point, according to Flannery (1969), to well-balanced diets of cultivated cereals and pulses mixed with food from wild grasses such as Avena, Aegilops, and Lolium, and the legumes, Medicago, and Lathyrus (Table 14.2). He suggests a closely integrated early neolithic economy for Israel and the Levant of cropping, herding, food collecting, and hunting. We can assume that the first major expansion of species accompanying people and their communities coincided with a retreat or even extinction of plants that could not withstand chronic disturbances. This transition occurred during the Epipaleolithic phase of intensive food collection and was concomitant with the creation of seminatural vegetation formations, part of "specialized domestication." The second, major wave of expansion occurred several thousand years later during "agricultural domestication" with the rise of weeds in cultivated fields.

Changes in the plant cover caused by human disturbances (termed "synanthropization"), of expansion of "hemerophilous" and decline of "hemerophobous" plants and its dynamics, have been reviewed by Kornas (1983) for Central Europe. Zohary (1974) provided an outline of the ecology and phytosociology of the synanthropic flora and vegetation in Israel and the Middle East. He distinguished between ruderal vegetation of human-created or influenced habitats, such as roadsides, dry refuse heaps, walls, and slopes, and segetal vegetation (including weeds) that grows in cultivated fields. He regarded humanity "from the very beginning" as an enemy of vegetation. He believed that already the pre-segetal – Paleolithic – impacts of overgathering and overhunting were wholly destructive and led to the extinction of numerous species, bringing humanity to the threshold of starvation and thereby initiating agriculture (Zohary 1983). Westhoff (1983), in the same volume, disagreed. So did Rindos (1984) who showed that the origins of agriculture are not to be deterministically explained as a response to climatic or demographic pressures. Rather, agriculture developed as an evolutionary process of reciprocal adaptation and coevolution which increased the fitness of all and was based on symbiotic, not antagonistic, relationships.

There is much to be learned about the use of fire for landscape management by comparisons with environments similar to the Mediterranean in North America and Australia. According studies by Heizer (1958) and Lewis (1973), the Native American tribes of the coast and foothills of central and southern California reached high levels of cultural complexity. They had evolved a unique material and spiritual symbiosis with the landscape, in which intentional use of fire for hunting and food collecting occupied an important place. Hallam (1979), in her study of aboriginal use of fire for management of vegetation, concluded that the long-term, fire-induced dependence between plant and human communities reached a balance in the nineteenth century. Her statement that "fire stick farming" was far from primitive and that its effect on the landscape may have been crucial is appropriate in describing advanced, late pluvial protoagricultural Mediterranean economies.

The Evolution and Degradation of the Agropastoral Mediterranean Landscape and Its Meta-stable Vegetation

The period spans the early Holocene and most of the historical times. It can be subdivided into two major phases:

The Final Formation and Peak of the Agricultural–Pastoral Mediterranean Landscape. The narrowing of the broad spectrum of neolithic agriculture into cereal field crops and the arrival of husbandry in the Early Holocene apparently caused the complete destruction of pristine vegetation in the lowlands. The destruction was followed by severe soil erosion, which, according to Dan and Yaalon (1971) can still be witnessed in the erosive exposure of ancient, calcified paleosols in the coastal plain of Israel.

The final formation of the Mediterranean agropastoral upland landscape was initiated by the domestication of fruit trees in the Bronze Age, around 5,000 B.C. (Zohary and Spiegel-Roy 1975). It was closely connected with the rise of protourban civilizations with their improved implements and artifacts. It was aided by the development of transportation and trade and led to more intensive and far-reaching ecological changes. The unique mutual adaptation of physical, biological, and cultural features of the coevolution of Paleolithic Mediterranean humanity and their seminatural landscapes was replaced by the unilateral human dominance which henceforth has governed the Mediterranean landscapes.

The process was culminated by the invention of iron tools several thousand years later, around the first millennia B.C. The tools made possible the uprooting of shrubs and trees on slopes and the clearing and terracing of upland fields. Wherever the slopes were too steep or rocky for agriculture, favorable microsites between rocky outcroppings were planted with such fruit trees as olives, figs, almonds, and pomegranates, and vines such as grapes. The natural woody vegetation was apparently left for soil protection along terrace walls and on steeper slopes between the terraces. Planted trees were protected from grazing animals by thorn or stone fences. Efficient, intensive, multiple, but rational use was made of rough terrain.

All other non-arable uplands served as pastures for goats and other live-stock as well as for "wildlife." Wild plants were collected for use as herbs, spices, medical plants, and a source for fuel, and for the construction of tools (includ-ing wooden ploughs). These "polyculture" patterns for multiple upland resource utilization lasted with varying intensities until recent times. They were exported from the Levant throughout the Mediterranean Basin by the Phoenicians and brought to the highest level of agrotechnical and hydro-technical sophistication during Roman times. They were combined with ir-rigation and water conservation, crop rotation, manuring, and stubble burn-ing for mineral fertilization as was documented in the Bible, the Talmud, and classical literature. Such multiple use can be regarded as one of the few instances in which agriculture improved the initial ecosystem factors of topo-graphy, soil parent material, and moisture regime on a long-term basis (Na-veh and Dan 1973) albeit, alas, at the expense of the natural flora and fauna.

That this system was not only ecologically but also economically viable and profitable can be judged from the fact that in the first century, according to Flavius Josephus, the rocky mountains of Galilee alone maintained a dense population of 2.5 million people, chiefly farmers, enjoying high incomes from the export of olive oil and wine.

The Phoenicians led the timber trade as early as 2,700 B.C., exporting cedar and other conifers from Lebanon and Israel to Egypt for the construc-tion of the temples and sarcophagus of Karnab, later to Mesopotamia and Babylon, and finally to Jerusalem for the construction of the temple by King Solomon. The extent of lumbering and deforestation can be judged by the fact that, according to the Bible, King Solomon forced a levy from the northern Israelite tribes of "four score thousand hewers in the mountains and 700,000 haulers."

It should be realized that, during this period, the Mediterranean herders continued the practice of intentional brush burning to increase herbaceous fodder on shrubland pastures. The demands of expanding and wealthy populations for timber, fuel, and charcoal lead to extensive forest clearing. The unfortunate combination of tree and wood cutting, fire, and grazing caused gradual landscape desiccation, especially in drier regions and on steeper and less fertile slopes.

We should be aware, however, of the dangers of such sweeping generalizations as the wholesale condemnation of fire, goat grazing, and wood cutting on Mediterranean uplands. The combination is alleged to have turned forest-covered mountain slopes into rock and scrub deserts. As described by Thirgood (1981), there were great differences between different countries and even between adjacent sites. Most shallow and rocky slopes which were neither terraced nor cultivated probably have not undergone any extreme change since postglacial and prehistorical times. As shown by Naveh and Dan (1973) their fertile and fine-structured brown rendzina and terra rossa soils have suffered much less from erosion than has been generally assumed. This relationship holds true only if the woody vegetation mantle has not been uprooted and the soil has not been disturbed. Due to great resilience and recuperative powers, acquired during their coevolution with continued pyric, ungulate, and human pressures, the hardy vegetation provides efficient soil protection as long as the woody plants can regenerate vegetatively from their extensive rootstocks; the herbaceous perennials from their underground bulbs, rhizomes, and other regenerative tissues; and the annuals can draw from sufficient seed reserves (Naveh 1975).

The Decline of the Agropastoral Landscape during Historical Times. During the decline of the Roman Empire from the downfall of the Byzantine Empire on, the cultivated uplands underwent dramatic changes in soil–vegetation systems. The changes were induced by historical changes in land use as described by Naveh and Dan (1973) and by Naveh (1986). As the chief controlling agent, humanity has changed all factors and variables of ecosystems in a series of degradation cycles that correspond roughly with the sequences of landscape and vegetation modification. Catastrophic soil erosion, flooding, and siltation leading to badlands and swamp formation occurred as the result of the neglect and abandonment of terrace walls.

General ecological and socioeconomic decline in Palestine started sometime after the Muslim conquest (640 A.D.) and lasted for about 1,300 years throughout the Arab, Crusader, Mameluk, and Turkish rules. Pastoral nomadism gradually replaced settled agriculture, and upland terraces were neglected. According to Taylor (1946), the depth of silt and gravel over Roman and Byzantine bridges indicates that between two and four billion cubic meters of soil were washed off the western side of the central Palestine hill country, which had been mostly terraced. Such landscape desiccation has its counterpart in other Mediterranean countries and can be proved by erosive changes since Roman times in river channels upstream and aggradation and sedimentation downstream (Vita Finci 1969).

Traveling in Palestine in about 680 A.D., Bishop Arndt described the Lake Kinnereth as fringed with woodlands. The thin, unbuttressed walls and wide roof-spans of the Byzantine churches and basilicas are archeological evidence of the ready availability of large and long timber. Later Crusader churches generally used woodless construction.

These anthropogenic functions, induced by changes in land use, are reflected in recent palynological findings in Israel (Bottema and Van Zeist 1981; Baruch 1987) and the western Mediterranean, as reviewed by Pons (1981) and by Pons and Quezel (1985). During periods of intensive agricultural activities and dense human population pressure (first in the Bronze period, and especially from the Hellenistic to the Byzantine period) the natural woody vegetation receded in the face of the extension of cultivated crops. Ecological deterioration further increased during periods of instability, warfare, and agricultural and population decay, such as the last period of the Ottoman Empire in the nineteenth century. Baruch (1983) showed that the composition of early postglacial forests and woodlands differed from that of the recent maquis and shrublands and that the abrupt increase of *Sarcopoterium spinosum* dwarf shrub formations in ancient times was connected with the abandonment of olive groves.

Beug (1967) showed that in the coastal region of Isteria, after the first Neolithic land clearing and cultivation (which started there only in the fifth millennium B.C.), evergreen scleropohylls extended inland into thinned stands of the more ancient sub-Mediterranean *Q. pubescens* forests. Pons (1981) concluded that the expansion of *Q. ilex* forests, generally considered as "the very type of Mediterranean climax," occurs like that of *Q. coccifera* "within a certain range of time which as a whole is contemporaneous with increased demographic pressure consistent with the establishment of settled agriculture. It can therefore be considered as the result of human intervention" (p. 36).

Pons and Quezel (1985) cited further palynological studies from many Mediterranean countries, showing the progressive decline of the deciduous *Q. pubescens* and other, more ancient forests in favor of *Q. ilex, Q. coccifera, Q. suber, Pinus halepensis,* and *P. nigra,* which dominate the so-called climax forest, woodland, and maquis formations, as a result of human disturbances during historical times.

The Neotechnological Impoverishment of the Open Mediterranean Landscape and Its Vegetation

This period started in Palestine after World War I and can be subdivided into pre- and post-World War II phases which will be discussed together.

The lowest point of agricultural and general socioeconomic decline was reached at the end of the Turkish rule. The population amounted to less than 300,000 people and Mediterranean scrub vegetation may have reached its greatest extent at that time. Since then, with growing population pressures, more and more of these shrublands have again been cleared for cultivation, exploited for fuel, charcoal, and limekilns. The last wave of large-scale forest destruction swept through Palestine during World War I when the remnants of the great Tabor oak forest in the Sharon Plains were destroyed to supply fuel for the railway and for the defense needs of the Turkish Army. Subsequently the area has been converted to citrus plantations and urban land (Eig 1933). Jewish colonization was inspired by the Zionist pioneering movement, striving not only to return to the Holy Land but also to reclaim and cultivate its neglected soils. This increased considerably during the British Mandatory rule from 1919 to 1947 leading to large-scale land reclamation, drainage of swamps and marshes, and to conversion of lowlands and plains into intensively cultivated, partly irrigated fields and plantations. In the uplands, traditional agropastoral land uses were continued. In the few Jewish hill settlements, however, terraces were reconstructed and attempts to modernize agriculture and develop a livestock economy were undertaken. The Mandatory Forest Service planted dense, chiefly monospecific Allepo pine forests on nontillable slopes. The planting was continued by the Jewish National Fund and greatly expanded after the foundation of the State of Israel. Simultaneously, gradually increasing urban-industrial development attracted more people to the coastal plains. At the same time, the Arabic population, benefiting from the improvement of health services and general conditions, also increased gradually due to both immigration and internal growth. This again increased pressures on the scarce land resources of the region.

Since World War II, and especially since the foundation of the State of Israel in 1948, the combined and synergetic processes of intensification of traditional and modern agricultural land uses and urban-industrial expansion have been growing at exponential rates. In the last 50 years the population has increased ten times, reaching more than 4 million. This has been accompanied not only by dramatic rises in agricultural and industrial production, but also in an increase in the standard of living with resulting growth in consumption of energy, motorized transport, demands for land for housing, road construction, raw materials, and also outdoor recreation for local and international tourism.

The major effect of acute human disturbance on the open landscape is the rapid loss and fragmentation of unspoiled natural ecosystems; their soil, plant, and animal resources; their production, protection, and regulatory functions. These have been replaced now either by heavily fertilized and sprayed agro-ecosystems or by built-up areas and urban-industrial wasteland. This transition is aggravated by the gradual functional, structural, and visual degradation of the remaining open landscape with concomitant biological impoverishment and ecological disruption by accelerated erosion and by soil, water, and air pollution from urban-industrial and agricultural sources. This process of neotechnological landscape despoilation has far-reaching and undesirable consequences for overall environmental quality and stability. It is typical for all Mediterranean countries and has been described by Henry (1977), Le Houreou (1981), Naveh and Lieberman (1984) and in a recent book on conservation of Mediterranean plants by Gomez Campo (1985). Israel, one of the smallest of the Mediterranean countries, has among the highest population densities and the highest densities of use of fertilizers, herbicides, and pesticides.

From the biological and ecological point of view, probably the greatest loss has been the drainage of the Hule Lake and swamps in the upper Galilee in the early 1950s. The aim of this pretentious reclamation project was to provide fertile, well-watered land for intensive agriculture and to supply peat from the lake's bottom. Not only were these goals never fully achieved, but also the economic benefits have lagged far behind expectations. The massive engineering project demanded costly regulation of the upper Jordan riverbed to prevent heavy flooding which resulted from draining the swamps and the lake. This change, in addition to intensive cotton cultivation, has caused rapid drying, even burning of the exposed peat and increased the rate of oxidation of organic matter. The process caused an alarming rise in nitrates in the Lake of Galilee, the major freshwater reservoir in Israel.

The drainage of this area meant the destruction of a unique habitat, one of the richest plant and wildlife habitats in the world, which bridged the diverse water-dependent faunas and floras of Europe, Africa, and Asia. From an area of 6,200 ha, a remnant of 40 ha was saved as the first nature reserve of Israel, but only after great efforts by a small, devoted group of biologists and nature lovers.

This project served as a driving force for the foundation of the Society for the Protection of Nature in Israel (SPNI) which has become the country's largest non-governmental organization, with 45,000 members. Its activities include the maintenance of 25 field schools; networks for observation, field studies, and computerized information on birds, wildlife, and plants; youth clubs for hikers; bird watchers; and the publication of one English and three Hebrew journals. The SPNI was awarded the Israel Prize in 1981. In 1963, with the help of an effective parliamentary lobby, the society initiated a special law for the protection of 95 percent of the wildlife, and many threatened plants, as well as designation of 30 National Parks and 145 sites as nature reserves, 129 of which are awaiting official proclamation. For the enforcement of this law and the administration of the reserves, the Nature Conservation Authority was created within the Ministry of Agriculture. These steps did not prevent, however, the loss of almost all wetland and marsh habitats as well as those of the shores and sand dunes.

As reported by Dafni and Agami (1976), over the past three decades some

Table 14.3. *List of plants now extinct in Israel*

Species	Year of last record	Ref.	Original habitat in Israel
Marsilea minuta L.	1941	HUJ[a]	Marshes
Suaeda hortensis Forrsk.	1928	HUJ	Coastal marshes
Silene physalodes Boiss.	Before 1849	Boissier (1849)	Mediterranean scrub
Silene papilosa Boiss.	1928	HUJ	Light soils
Nymphaea alba L.	1947	HUJ	Ponds, streams, and marshes
Ceratophyllum submersum L.	1947	HUJ	Ponds, streams, and marshes
Ranunculus trichophyllus Chaix	1949	HUJ	Marshes
Ranunculus saniculifolius Viv.	Before 1933	Post (1933)	Ponds
Acacia laeta R. Br.	1891	Post (1933)	Oases
Callitriche palustris L.	1954	HUJ	Ponds and marshes
Trifolium micranthus Viv.	1949	HUJ	Damp sands
Aphanes arvensis L.	1940	HUJ	Rock fissures
Lythrum borysthenicum (Schrank.) Litv.	1949	HUJ	Marshes
Hydrocotyle vulgaris L.	1940	HUJ	Marshes and streams
Scaligeria hermonis Post	1949	HUJ	Mediterranean dwarf shrub communities
Mosheiova galilaea Eig	1954	HUJ	Mediterranean dwarf shrub communities
Utricularia vulgaris L.	1951	HUJ	Ponds, marshes, and streams
Dipsacus laciniatus L.	1927	HUJ	Marshes
Najas minor All.	1946?	Eig et al. (1948)	Marshes
Valisneria spiralis L.	1941	HUJ	Marshes and ponds
Hydrocharis morsus-ranae L.	1952	HUJ	Marshes
Cyperus corymbosus Rhottb.	1956	HUJ	River banks
Cyperus latifolius Poir.	1927	HUJ	Ponds and river banks
Cyperus lanceus Thunb.	1942	HUJ	Marshes and river banks
Fuirena pubescens (Poir.) Kunth.	1926	HUJ	Marshes
Lemna trisulca L.	1926	HUJ	Ponds

[a] HUJ means according to the herbarium sheet deposited in the Hebrew University of Jerusalem.

Source: Reprinted from Dafni and Agami 1976, with permission.

26 species of higher plants, shown in Table 14.3, making up about 1 percent of the local flora, have become extinct. Twenty of these plants belong to wet habitats such as marshes, ponds, and river banks, and to the sandy-loam and poor sand and limestone "kurkar" substrates of the coastal plains. Losses of hydrophytes due to water exploitation and drainage schemes were predicted as early as 1929 by Eig (1929). Agami (1973) showed that certain hydrophytes growing along the Alexander and Yarkon rivers, together with the rich microflora and -fauna and the vertebrate species, have been extinguished by water pollution.

The vegetation of the coastal plains has also suffered from intensive cultivation and urban development. The plant communities of those habitats, described by Eig (1929), have been greatly altered in relative distribution. The community of *Desmostachia (Eragrostis) bipinnata–Centaurea procurens*, which dominated the sandy-loam Hamra soils, is almost extinct. Scrub and dwarf shrub communities, dominated by *Calycotome villosa, Cistus salvifolius*, and *C. incanus*, which invaded open patches and replaced richer herbaceous communities, are more widespread than in the past.

Altogether, according to the IUCN categories, 35 plant species are rare and threatened, 2 probably extinct, 15 endangered, 7 vulnerable, and 10 rare (Pollak 1984). Nine of the threatened species are endemic to the coastal plains.

No data are available on the extinction of segetal plant species in cultivated fields as a result of intensive herbicidal treatments which have eliminated most broadleaved weedy species, and encouraged more noxious, deep-rooted perennial grasses.

In the mountainous region, the creation of monotonous and highly flammable conifer plantations, which are now being gradually replaced by multispecies afforestation and the spread of scrub thickets, is resulting in a steady increase of devastating, hot wildfires and the accompanying costs of fire prevention, often unsuccessful. Here, there appear to have been no dramatic losses of species, but there are no reliable data. The chronic, cumulative effects of synergistic traditional and neotechnological disturbances are, however, most threatening. In addition to the loss of open landscapes and their fragmentation by urban-industrial developments, the floristic and structural diversity of the vegetation as well as faunistic species richness and abundance are constantly being reduced. The impoverishment is the result not only of very heavy, continuous grazing, browsing, wood cutting, and uprooting near Arabic villages and Bedouin settlements and of heavy, seasonal grazing by beef cattle and sheep around Jewish settlements, but also by complete cessation of human interference in some nature reserves and parks. In some of these, the heavy pressures of mass recreation are

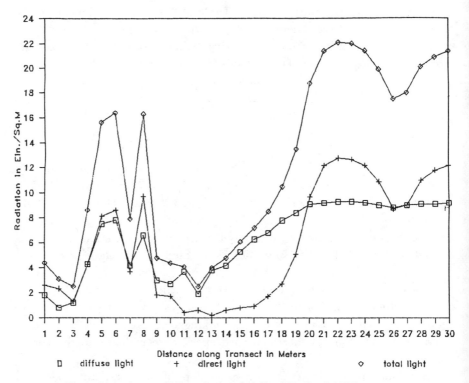

Figure 14.1. Average daily radiation, Oak Site (Woodcock 1986).

The initially vigorous vegetative regeneration of sclerophylls from stunted shoots and almost imperceptible rootstocks, observed after the decline of human and livestock pressures following the foundation of the State of Israel (Naveh 1955), was followed by the gradual encroachment of the shrub canopy and the almost total suppression of the herbaceous understory in undisturbed and protected maquis. It turned from a blessing more to a curse, when the denser brush thickets became stagnant, possibly senescent (Naveh 1971). Because of the accumulation of dry and dead branches and undecomposed litter, they, like the planted pine forests, become also more and more prone to hot and devastating wildfires. These impenetrable and monotonous, one-layered, tall shrub communities are dominated almost exclusively by *Quercus calliprinos*, with a few occasionally codominant shrubs and subordinate dwarf shrubs and very few shade-tolerant perennial grasses and geophytes which occur near open patches of rock outcrops and shrub edges. This transition in the margins meant a reduction in species richness of about 75 percent (to less than 30 species/0.1 ha) as well as significant reductions in other diversity parameters and in richness and abundance of birds, rodents, reptiles, and insects (Naveh and Whittaker 1979). That this reduction is related to the reduction in the amount of light reaching the lower plant strata is shown in Figure 14.1, which shows measurements along a transect across open, grassy patches alternating with closed patches of *Q. calliprinos* thickets (Woodcock 1986).

Similar tendencies toward lower structural and floristic diversity of herbaceous plants, combined with increased vulnerability to fire, can be observed in southern France (K. F. Schreiber and Z. Naveh, unpublished data). There, too, they are a result of the cessation of traditional silvo-pastoral practices of coppicing and goat grazing. Similar trends have been reported from the western Mediterranean, Adriatic *Q. ilex* forests (Horvat et al. 1974), and from the island of Lokrum, near Dubrovnic, which has been protected as a nature reserve since 1948 (Ilijanic and Hecimovic 1981).

As most endemics in the Mediterranean are small shrubs and herbs, they are among the first plant species to go extinct through brush reencroachment induced by conservation policies of total exclusion of human interference (Ruiz de la Torre 1985). One important group especially endangered due to its ornamental value is the flowering geophyte which includes many endemic and rare species. In most Mediterranean countries these are picked and sold and their bulbs exported in large amounts. In Israel, where they are better protected, this danger has been reduced. Even so, those with higher light demands may be smothered out by the cessation of burning, grazing, and cutting, as well as by afforestation (Naveh 1971).

Mt. Gilboa is an example. Located at the drier borders of the Mediterranean zone in Israel facing the Jordan Valley, it was mentioned in the Bible as a mountain, "with no dew nor rain." Because of its special biogeographical situation, it is distinguished by a species-rich mosaic of shrubs and dwarf shrubs, alternating with a dense herbaceous canopy. In 1976 and 1977 it had about 170 plant species/0.1 ha in representative sites combined with high faunistic diversity (Naveh and Whittaker 1979). The patchy shrub layer is dominated by a drought-resistant ecotype of *Pistacia lentiscus*, of great value in slope stabilization and landscape restoration (Shaviv 1978). Among the herbaceous plants is one of the most attractive geophytes, the endemic "Iris of the Gilboa" − *Iris hayneii* − which has been adopted as the emblem of the SPNI. Great parts of Mt. Gilboa's rocky slopes have been densely planted to *Pinus halepensis*, despite the fact that in these harsh climatic conditions, prospects for economic wood production are lower than for more favorable areas. Expensive fire protection measures have not prevented heavy tree losses by recent wildfires.

One of the last slopes with its vegetation intact could still be saved from "rehabilitation" by declaring it a nature reserve. But the reproduction of the scattered iris plants could be ensured only by introducing controlled, seasonal cattle grazing to reduce the competition of taller and more aggressive grasses, perennial herbs, and thistles, and also to reduce fire hazards.

One example of the threat of chronic, cumulative neotechnological impacts is the fate of the planted pine forests, covering about 50,000 ha, one-seventh of all non-arable uplands in Israel. The early rapid development of these hardy pioneer trees created the impression that foresters can fool nature and establish forests in the Mediterranean like those in central Europe. Their present low productivity is being threatened by the combined and probably synergistic effects of photochemical air pollutants and pest infestations. Recent field and laboratory studies (Naveh et al. 1981) revealed that widespread chlorotic mottling and decline is being caused in Israel, as in California, by atmospheric ozone concentrations above 0.05 ppm, followed in *P. halepensis* by severe infestations of *Matsucoccus josephi* scales. Most recently, ozone-stressed *P. canariensis* trees are also being attacked and killed by bark beetles in the coastal region, where ozone levels already exceed 0.1 ppm. Similar damage can be expected in all other rapidly developing Mediterranean countries. They have been observed by us also in Greece, in a forest above Thessaloniki, planted to *P. brutia,* where the sea breeze carries photochemical oxidants from urbanized, motorized coastal regions to forested slopes. Their damaging impact will doubtless increase everywhere.

We have not yet developed reliable quantitative parameters for the measurement of such threats and for exact predictions of their impact on organic life. But if the loss of all wetland and sandy habitats, the advanced degree of water pollution in rivers, and the decline of the pine trees are taken as signs of the neotechnological burden and resulting environmental degradation, then these threats have reached a critical level. If they proceed unhampered at the present speed and intensity, very soon only a few patches and islands of open landscapes and nature reserves with native Mediterranean vegetation will remain.

Discussion and Conclusions

From the foregoing description of the coevolution of Mediterranean landscapes and their vegetation from the Middle Pleistocene onwards and of the long history of chronic, agropastoral disturbances under which the present, seminatural vegetation evolved, the theory of the "natural development of Maquis and forest climax communities without human interference" in this region has become obsolete. As will be shown below, dynamic human-induced degeneration and regeneration processes render the thermodynamic ecosystem interpretations of Odum (1969) and by Margaleff (1968) as doubtful, as applied to the Mediterranean. Terms to account for this situation have been suggested such as "pseudoclimax," "paraclimax," and "disclimax." In these conditions, a dynamic balance (or, as shown below, a dynamic flow equilibrium) that may be attained at various levels of biotic (or anthropogenic) pressures is a more realistic concept. For such a situation, Vogl (1980) has coined the term "perturbation-dependent ecosystems."

Instead of the term "climax," Mediterranean ecologists could follow the example of Horvat et al. (1974) who used the term "potential, natural vegetation" for the Mediterranean vegetation, which would develop spontaneously if all human perturbations ceased. They distinguished between zonal (chiefly climatically conditioned), intrazonal (endemic), and extrazonal (edaphically and topographically conditioned) potential natural vegetation.

The closely interwoven environmental and cultural processes which shaped these landscapes and their vegetation for thousands of years have created complex and highly dynamic degradation and regeneration patterns which do not fit any preconceived, deterministic relay of floristic successional sequences. Contrary to the classical "facilitation model" (Connell and Slatyer 1977), after abandonment of cultivated uplands, most secondary successions are arrested at early grass or dwarf-shrub stages. The regeneration of the so-called climax sclerophylls is chiefly a process of vegetative resprouting from stunted or burned plants. It may occur also by direct invasion of abandoned orchards, vineyards, olive groves, or pine groves, and further is facilitated by birds and rodents and the shade of these trees. But it is evidently not preceded by "seral" stages of dwarf shrubs and shrubs (Debussche, Escarre, and Lepart 1982; Naveh, unpublished data). Therefore conservation strategies based on classical, deterministic succession-to-climax paradigms, still widely promoted in the Mediterranean (Tomaselli 1977; Di Castri et al. 1981), are not applicable.

In historical times human-driven degradation and regeneration cycles have lasted several hundred years, according to the duration of historical land-use periods. Now these functions have been replaced by exponentially accelerating degradation which endangers the future of the open Mediterranean landscape.

Throughout the long history of the agropastoral functions, the seminatural vegetation of open forests, shrublands, woodlands, and grasslands, and the agricultural vegetation of terrace patches and hand-cultivated rock polycultures have all become part of a closely interwoven mosaic. The transfer of fertility (through grazing) and of seeds (through grazing, wild herbivores, and insects) created ideal conditions for introgression and spontaneous hybridization of wild and cultivated plants and biotypes, and for the evolution of genotypes and ecotypes with high adaptation to this humanmodified habitat (Zohary 1969; Shaviv 1978; Nevo, Beiles, and Stone 1983; Nevo et al. 1986). As described elsewhere in more detail (Naveh 1975) selection pressures favored the survival of species and ecotypes, as well as plant communities, with the highest resilience to the combined effects of environmental rigor, defoliation by grazing, cutting, and burning, by maximizing their adaptive feedback responses to these stresses.

In the traditional Mediterranean pastoral systems great seasonal and annual fluctuations in productivity also acted as effective negative feedbacks in preventing overgrazing in a process similar to that regulating natural wildlife populations. The numbers of livestock which could be supported during periods of low food availability in early winter and in drought years were not sufficient to overgraze pastures during the spring flush of growth and seed setting, especially in the wetter years. At the same time, overcutting and overburning were prevented by burning and coppicing rotations to ensure sustained productivity and sufficient recovery.

These regular grazing, burning, and coppicing regimes apparently led to the establishment of a balance between trees, shrubs, herbs, grasses, and geophytes in those upland grasslands, woodlands, and shrublands, which were neither overgrazed nor overcoppiced or were completely rested for prolonged periods. The eminent geneticist Waddington (1975) coined the term "homeorhesis" from the Greek, meaning "preserving the flow," for such a dynamic flow equilibrium to denote the evolutionary stability of multifactorial systems or the preservation of the flow process of the evolutionary pathway of change through time. Homeorethic long-term meta-stability is not concerned with preserving the measures of some system components at a constant value as in homeostatic systems but acts to ensure that the system goes on changing in the same way that it has in the past.

Combined with the great macro- and microsite heterogeneity of the rocky and rough terrain, homeorethic flow equilibrium also ensured the great heterogeneity in temporal and spatial plant relationships and in patch dynamics of regeneration and degradation patterns. These, in turn, caused the great diversity of life forms, phenology, and regeneration niches.

This striking biological and ecological diversity contributed greatly to the aesthetic appeal of open Mediterranean landscapes and is the major asset for recreation and tourism (Naveh and Whittaker 1979; Di Castri 1981). With exponential neotechnological degradation, this homeorethic flow equilibrium is being disrupted by the combined and synergistic effects of intensified traditional and modern agropastoral pressures, neotechnological landscape

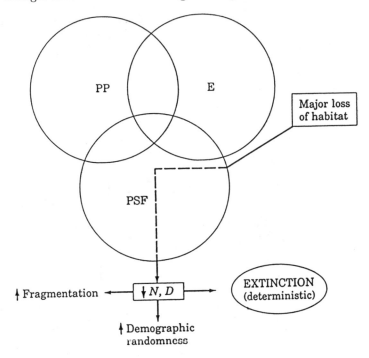

Figure 14.2. Consequences of a major loss of habitat. The population suffers reductions in population size and in distribution. One possible outcome is the immediate deterministic extinction of the population. Even if the population survives, it will be increasingly vulnerable to stochastic extinction ($\uparrow$ = increase; $\downarrow$ = decrease). (Reprinted from Gilpin and Soulé 1986, with permission.)

degradation, despoilation and pollution, urban-industrial sprawl, and uncontrolled mass recreation and tourism.

In concluding, we should regard these non-equilibrium and seminatural Mediterranean forests, shrublands, and grasslands as "perturbation-dependent systems" (Vogl 1980), driven by anthropogenic, agropastoral regeneration and degradation functions. These functions have induced a homeorethic flow equilibrium, ensuring evolutionary metastability and high structural, floristic, and genetic diversity which has become distorted. Our main challenge lies in the reestablishment of multifactorial homeorethic flow processes as based on active and dynamic conservation management.

As shown in the book on Mediterranean plant conservation (Gomez Campo 1985), earlier theories (Naveh 1971) rejecting the passive, climax-oriented protection approach have been recognized in the Mediterranean. The recommendations of Ruiz de la Torrez (1985) for constant human interference to conserve herbaceous species richness serve as general guidelines but should be integrated into comprehensive masterplans for

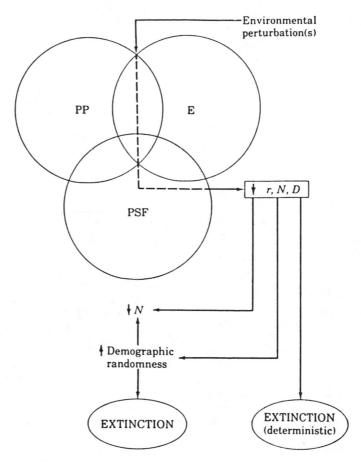

Figure 14.3. The effects of environmental perturbations on population growth rates and on the genetic effective population size. (Reprinted from Gilpin and Soulé 1986, with permission.)

multipurpose landscape ecological planning, management, and restoration for Mediterranean uplands (Naveh and Lieberman 1984).

In this paper we limit ourselves to the discussion of some of the major biological aspects of species richness conservation (Soulé 1986). Of special importance is the problem of minimum viable populations as affected by environmental perturbations and by major fragmentation or loss of habitat. For this purpose Gilpin and Soulé (1986) (Figure 14.2 and Figure 14.3) used the three fields of population phenotype (PP), environment (E), and population structure and fitness (PSF) to show that the fragmentation or loss of habitat can cause the immediate extinction of the population. It can also result in a reduction in population size (N) and distribution (D), depending on the intensity of fragmentation. The latter is stochastic extinction, induced, in general, by chronic disturbances and involving processes which are more subtle and more difficult to observe and prevent. They are also caused by environmental perturbations that may affect the population growth rate (r) and reduce the effective genetic population size (Ne). In both cases, the increase in demographic stochasticity will make the population increasingly vulnerable to stochastic extinction as is probably the case in the present distortion of agropastoral flow equilibrium.

In the same volume, Cody (1986) discussed the problems of diversity and rarity in Mediterranean climate regions. He showed that patterns of diversity are related to patterns of rarity and are largely affected by habitat, area, isolation, and fragmentation. By progressive habitat clearing and fragmentation, as is occurring now at such an alarming rate in the Mediterranean and in Israel, the first biota to become endangered and lost are the gamma (landscape) rarities, namely local endemics. According to Cody (1986) this happens with the richest Mediterranean biota to which those of Israel belong. The relationship probably also holds true for subspecies that are local edaphic and climatic ecotypes such as those of *Pistacia lentiscus* from Mt. Gilboa and many other subspecies which have not yet been recognized due to the lack of gene-ecological research in the Mediterranean. In California, climatic and edaphic diversity on ecotones between different biotic provinces are factors that promote speciation of higher plants. Therefore, the ecotones of the subhumid Mediterranean and semiarid Irano-Turanian regions in Israel, with their rich floras and faunas and their great genetic potentials of highly valuable plants for future economic uses, especially medical plants (Zohary 1974), deserve highest priority for conservation. Unfortunately, these are amongst the most heavily exploited and misused uplands.

The maintenance of both floristic and structural diversity in these communities requires the prevention of competitive reduction or exclusion and the establishment of a competitive equilibrium (Huston 1979; Pickett 1980). It apparently was achieved by a combination of the long evolutionary coexistence of many small herbaceous, chiefly annual, plants, in heterogeneous microsites and open, rocky grass patches, and the even longer evolutionary history of chronic disturbances by periodic defoliation stresses and climatic fluctuations, which reduced populations and biomass.

With these conditions any attempt to model the relationships of diversity and human disturbances should take into consideration both the evolutionary dimensions, as done by Naveh and Whittaker (1979), as well as the rate of competitive displacement and the frequency (or magnitude) of population reduction, as done by Huston (1979). By combining both models, it can be demonstrated that high diversity is associated with chronic, moderate levels of disturbances and environmental stress. We should be aware, however, of the serious limitations of such generalized prediction models which are based on total species diversity.

These relations were reviewed recently by Peet, Glenn-Levin, and Walker (1983). Studies by Naveh and Whittaker (1979) and Mann (1985) in Israel on this subject have shown that parameters of total plant species diversity not supplemented by structural partial diversity indices of different life-forms do not reflect the actual changes induced by such disturbances. Different lifeforms have different responses to trampling, browsing, and grazing. An abundance of not only taller shrubs, but also of the few shade-tolerant hemicryptophytes, such as *Piptatherum miliaceaum*, can adversely affect the smaller, heliophytic herbs and grasses. The many factors involved in environmental stress as well as the many modes, kinds, intensities, and frequencies of human and other disturbances can lead to differential reductions of populations and/or biomass. As shown in the case of trampling by park visitors and their cars on Mt. Carmel, responses may not fit always the expected bell-shaped curves of disturbance gradients (Mann 1985). It should be realized that, in the Mediterranean, the differences in selective grazing and browsing behavior on mixed shrublands and grasslands between different local, improved, or introduced breeds of cattle and sheep are sometimes so great that generalization on the impacts are almost meaningless.

The determination of management strategies of "optimum regimes of disturbances" aimed at the maintenance and enhancement of biological diversity, alone or in combination with other land use goals such as increase of economic productivity, recreation amenities, and scenic values, will require systematic long-term studies. They are presently almost completely lacking in the Mediterranean. If such studies are undertaken, the ensurance of regeneration niches, as emphasized by Grubb (1977), through controlled grazing, cutting, and burning, will be of primary importance. In nature reserves and other protected areas this could probably be achieved by the reintroduction of indigenous ungulate grazers and browsers to replace the domestic livestock.

Within management strategies, there is much scientific and practical value in the complete protection of well-selected, representative sites which could serve as references for the "potential natural vegetation," developing through time under these artificial conditions of non-interference. The main challenge lies in the continuation of rational, controlled interference in such a way that the conservation of biological and ecological diversity, integrity, and natural beauty be reconciled with the cultural and socioeconomic needs of this and future generations in the Mediterranean.

Acknowledgments

This study was partly supported by The Funds for Promotion of Research by the Technion, Israel Institute of Technology. The senior author is also grateful to the Rutgers State University of New Jersey who accomodated him during part of his Sabbatical leave, and especially to his host, Prof. S. T. A. Pickett, for his helpful comments.

References

Agami, M., 1973. The influence of water pollution on the vegetation of the Alexander and Yarkon Rivers. M. Sc. thesis, Department of Botany, Tel Aviv University (Hebrew).

Bar Joseph, O., 1984. Near East. In *Neue Forschungen zur Altsteinzeit*, 232–298.

Baruch, V., 1987. *The palynology of Late Holocene cores from Lake Kinnereth.* Hebrew University, Jerusalem, Department of Archeology (Hebrew).

Beug, H. J., 1967. Probleme der Vegetationsgeschichte in Sudeuropa. *Ber. Dtsch. Bot. Ges.* 80:682–689.

Bottema, S., and W. van Zeist, 1981. Palynological history of the Near East. In *Prehistoire du Levant*, 111–123. CNRS, Paris.

Clark, J. D., 1966. Acheulian occupation sites in the Middle East and Africa, a study in cultural variability. In J. D. Clark and F. C. Howell (Eds.), *Recent Studies in Paleoanthropology*, American Anthropologist, 68:394–412.

Cody, M. L., 1986. Diversity, rarity and conservation in Mediterranean climate regions. In M. E. Soule (Ed.), *Conservation Biology: The Science of Scarcity and Diversity*, pp. 122–152. Sinauer Associates Publishers, Sunderland, Massachusetts.

Connell, J. H., and R. O. Slatyer, 1977. Mechanisms of succession in natural communities and their role in community stability and organization. *The Amer. Natur.* 111:1119–1144.

Dafni, A., and M. Agami, 1976. Extinct plants of Israel. *Biol. Cons.* 10:49–52.

Dan, J., and D. H. Yaalon, 1971. On the origin and nature of the paleopedological formations in the central coastal fringes areas of Israel. In D. H. Yaalon (Ed.), *Paleopedology: Origin, Nature and Dating of Paleosols*, pp. 245–260. Israel Universities Press, Jerusalem.

Debussche, M., J. Escarre, and J. Lepart, 1982. Ornithochory and plant succession in Mediterranean abandonded orchards. *Vegetatio* 48:255–266.

Di Castri, F., 1981. Mediterranean-type shrublands of the world. In F. di Castri, F., W. Goodall, and R. L. Specht (Eds.), *Ecosystems of the World 11: Mediterranean-Type Shrublands*, pp. 1-52. Elsevier, New York.

Di Castri, F., W. Goodall, and R. Specht (Eds.), 1981. *Ecosystems of the World 11: Mediterranean-Type Shrublands*. Elsevier, New York.

Eig, A., 1929. On the vegetation of Palestine. *Bull. Inst. Agric. & Nat. Hist., Agric. Exp. Stn.* 7.

Eig, A., 1933. A historical–phytosociological essay on Palestinian forests of *Quercus aegilops L.* ssp. *ithaburensis* (Desc.) in past and present. *Beih. Bot, Cbl.* 51: 225–272.

Eig, A., 1939. The vegetation of the light soils belt of the coastal plain of Palestine. *Palest. J. Bot., Jer.*, Ser. I :255-308.

Escarre, Blanch J., 1979. Etude de successions post-culturales dans les Hautes Garrigues du Montpellierais. These doct. spce. Univ. Sci. Tech. du Languedoc, Montpellier.

Feeney, P., 1975. Biochemical co-evolution between plants and their insect herbivores. In L. D. Gilvert and P. H. Raven (Eds.), *Coevolution of Plants and Animals*, pp. 3–19. University of Texas Press, Austin.

Flannery, K. V., 1969. Origins and ecological effects of early domestication in Iran and the Near East. In P. J. Ucko and G. W. Dimbleby (Eds.), *The Domestication and Exploitation of Plants and Animals*, pp. 73–100. Aldine, Chicago.

Gilpin, M. E., and M. E. Soulé, 1986. Minimum viable populations. In M. E. Soule (Ed.), *Conservation Biology*, pp. 19–34. Sinauer Associates Publishers. Sanderland, Massachusetts.

Gomez-Campo, C., 1985. Conservation of plants in the Mediterranean: principles and problems. In C. Gommez-Campo (Ed.), *Conservation of Mediterranean Plants*, pp. 3–8. Junk, The Hague.

Grubb, P. J., 1977. The maintenance of species richness in plant communities and the importance of the regeneration niche. *Biol. Rev.* 52:107–145.

Hallam, S. J., 1979. *Fire and Hearth: A Study of Aboriginal Usage and European Usurpation in South-Western Australia.* Australia Institute of Aboriginal Studies, Canberra.

Heizer, D. F., 1958. *Prehistoric Central California: a problem in historical developmental classification.* Reports of ALUC Archeological Survey No. 41:19–26.

Henry, P. M., 1977. The Mediterranean: a threatened micro-cosmos. *Ambio* 6:300–307.

Higgs, E. S., C. Vita-Finci, D. R. Harris, and A. E. Fagg, 1967. The climate, environment and industries of Stone Age Greece. Part III. *Prehist. Soc.* 33:1–29.

Horowitz, A., 1979. *The Quaternary of Israel.* Academic Press, New York.

Horvat, I., V. Glavac, and H. Ellenberg, 1974. *Vegetation Suedosteuropas.* Gustav Fischer Verlag, Stuttgart.

Huston, M., 1979. A general hypothesis of species diversity. *Amer. Nat.* 113:81–101.

Ikeya, M., and A. N. Poulianos, 1979. ESR Age of the trace fire at Petralona. *Anthropos* 6:44–47.

Ilijanic, L. J., and S. Hecimovic, 1981. Zur Sukzession der Mediterranean Vegetation auf der Insel Lokrum by Dubrovnik. *Vegetatio* 46:75–81.

Jelinek, A. J., 1981. Middle Paleolithic of the Tabun Cave. In *Prehistoire du levant*, pp. 265–283. CNRS, Paris.

Jenny, H., 1961. Derivation of state factor equations of soils and ecosystems. *Soil Sci. Proc.* pp. 385–388.

Kaznelson, J., 1956. The variability of rainfall in Palestine and the statistical methods of its measurements. *Israel Meteorol. Serv.*, Ser. E4 (Hebrew).

Kornas, J., 1983. Man's impact on the vegetation in Central Europe. In W. Holzner, M. J. A. Werger, and I. Ikusima (Eds.), *Man's Impact on Vegetation*, pp. 277–286. Junk, The Hague.

Le Houerou, H. N., 1981. Impacts of man and his animals on Mediterranean vegetation. In F. di Castri, D. W. Goodall, and R. L. Specht (Eds.), *Ecosystems of the World 11: Mediterraean-Type Shrublands*, pp. 497–522. Elsevier, New York.

Leaky, R. E., and R. Lewin, 1979. *People of the Lake*. Avon Books, New York.

Lewis, H. T., 1973. *Pattern of Indian Burning in California: Ecology and Ethnohistory*. Ballena Press Anthropological Papers 1, Ramona, Calif.

Lowdermilk, W. C., 1944. *Palestine, Land of Promise*. Harper, New York.

Mann, A. L. E., 1985. Diversity of an upland Mediterranean ecosystem in the Carmel National Park and its applicability for conservation and management of recreation. Ph. Sc. thesis, Technion, Israel Institute of Technology.

Margaleff, R., 1968. *Perspectives in Ecological Theory*. University of Chicago Press, Chicago.

Mikesell, M. W., 1969. The deforestation of Mount Lebanon. *Geogr. Rev.* 59:1–18.

Narr, K. J., 1956. Early food-producing populations. In Thomas, W. L. (Ed.), *Man's Role in Changing the Face of the Earth*, pp. 134-151. University of Chicago Press, Chicago.

Naveh, Z., 1955. Some aspects of range improvement in a Mediterranean environment. *J. Range Mgt.* 8:265–271.

Naveh, Z., 1967. Mediterranean ecosystems and vegetation types in California and Israel. *Ecology* 48:445–459.

Naveh, Z., 1971. The conservation of ecological diversity of Mediterranean ecosystems through ecological management. In E. Duffy and A. S. Watt (Eds.), *The Scientific Management of Animal and Plant Communities for Conservation*, Symp. Brit. Ecol. Soc., 11, pp. 605–622. Blackwell Sci. Pub., Oxford.

Naveh, Z., 1973. *The ecology of fire in Israel*, pp. 131–170. Ann. Tall Timbers Fire Ecol. Conf., Tallahassee, Fla.

Naveh, Z., 1975. The evolutionary significance of fire in the Mediterranean region. *Vegetatio* 9:199–306.

Naveh, Z., 1982. The dependence of the productivity of a semi-arid Mediterranean hill pasture ecosystem on climatic fluctuations. *Agriculture and Environment* 7:47–61.

Naveh, Z., 1984. The vegetation of the Carmel and Nahal Sefunim and the evolution of the cultural landscape. In A. Ronen (Ed.), *The Sefunim Prehistoric Sites Mount Carmel Israel*, pp. 23–63. BAR International Series 230, Oxford.

Naveh, Z., 1986. Pasture and forest management in the Mediterranean uplands. In H. Finkel (Ed.), *Soil and Water Erosion in Semi-Arid Lands*, pp. 284–296. CRC Press, Inc. Boca Raton, Fla.

Naveh, Z., and J. Dan, 1973. The human degradation of Mediterranean landscapes in Israel. In F. di Castri and H. A. Mooney (Eds.), *Mediterranean-Type Ecosystems, Origin and Structure*, pp. 370–390. Springer-Verlag, New York.

Naveh, Z., and J. Kinski, 1975. *The effect of climate and management on species diversity of Tabor oak savanna pastures*, pp. 284–296. Proc. 6th Sci. Conf. Israel Soc. Ecology, June, Tel Aviv.

Naveh, Z., and R. H. Whittaker, 1979. Structural and floristic diversity of shrublands and woodlands in northern Israel and other Mediterranean areas. *Vegetatio* 41:171–190.

Naveh, Z., Steinberger E., and S. Chaim, 1981. Photochemical air pollutants – a new threat to Mediterranean conifer forests and upland ecosystems. *Environ. Conserv.* 7:301–309.

Naveh, Z., and A. S. Lieberman, 1984. *Landscape Ecology – Theory and Applications*.

Springer-Verlag, New York, Heidelberg, Berlin, Tokyo.

Nevo, E., A. Beiles, and D. Stone, 1983. Microgeographic edaphic differentiation in Hordein polymorphism. *Theor. Appl. Genet.* 64:123–132.

Nevo, E., A. Beiles, Olsvig-Whittaker, and Z. Naveh, 1986. Natural selection of allozyme polymorphisms: a microsite test revealing ecological genetic differentiation in wild barley. *Evolution* 40:13-20.

Odum, E. P., 1969. The strategy of ecosystem development. *Science* 164:262–270.

Peet, R. K., D. C. Glenn-Levin, and J. Walker, 1983. Prediction of man's impact on plant species diversity a challenge for vegetation science. In W. Holzner, M. J. A. Werger, and I. Ikusima (Eds.), *Man's Impact on Vegetation*, pp. 41–54. Junk, The Hague.

Perles, C., 1977. *Prehistoire du Feu*. Masson, Paris.

Pickett, S. T. A., 1980. Non-equilibrium coexistence of plants. *Bull. Torrey Bot. Club* 107:238–248.

Pignatti, S., 1978. Evolutionary trends in Mediterranean flora and vegetation. *Vegetatio* 37:175–185.

Pignatti, S., 1983. Human impact on the vegetation of the Mediterranean. In W. Holzner, M. J. A. Werger, and I. Ikusima (Eds.), *Man's Impact on Vegetation*, pp. 151–162. Junk, The Hague.

Pollak, G., 1984. The problems of threatened plant species on Hamra and Kurkar soil. Rotem, *Bull. Isr. Plant Inform Center* 13:56–69 (Hebrew).

Pons, A., 1981. The history of the Mediterranean shrublands. In F. di Castri, F. W. Goodall, and R. L. Specht (Eds.), *Ecosystems of the World, 11: Mediterranean-Type Shrublands*, pp. 131–138. Elsevier, New York.

Pons, A., and Quezel, 1985. The history of the flora and vegetation and past and present human disturbance in the Mediterranean. In C. Gommez-Campo (Ed.), *Conservation of Mediterranean Plants*, pp. 25-43. Junk, The Hague.

Reifenberg, A., 1955. *The Struggle between the Desert and the Sowns, Rise and Fall of the Levant.* Jewish Agency Publication Department, Jerusalem.

Rindos, D., 1984. *The Origin of Agriculture: An Evolutionary Perspective.* Academic Press, London.

Ronen, A., 1984. *The Sefunim Prehistoric Sites, Mount Carmel, Israel.* BAR International Series 230. Oxford.

Ruiz de la Torre, J. R., 1985. Conservation of plants within their native ecosystems. In C. Gommez-Campo (Ed.), *Plant Conservation in the Mediterranean*, pp. 197–219. Junk, The Hague.

Sauer, C. O., 1961. Sedentary and mobile bents in early societies. In S. L. Washburn (Ed.), *Social Life of Early Man*, pp. 256–66. Viking Fund. Publ. in Anthropology 31:.

Shaviv, I., 1978. Aut-ecological studies of *Pistacia lentiscus* in Israel. Ph. Sc. thesis, Technion, Israel Institute of Technology (Hebrew).

Solecki, R. S., 1977. The implications of the Shanidar Cave Neanderthal Flower burial. *Amer. New York Acad. Sciences* 293:114-124.

Soulé, M. E., 1986. *Conservation Biology: The Science of Scarcity and Diversity.* Sinauer Associates, Inc. Publishers, Sunderland, Mass.

Stebbins, G. L., 1982. *Darwin to DNA, Molecules to Humanity.* W. H. Freeman and Company, San Francisco.

Stekelis, M., 1960. The paleolithic deposits of Jisr Banat Yaqub. *Bull. Res. Conc.*

Israel, Sect. G. Geo-sciences 9:346–367.

Taylor, F., 1946. The destruction of the soil in Palestine. *Bull. Soil Conserv. Bd. Palest.* 2.

Tchernov, E., 1984. The fauna of Sefunim Cave, Mt. Carmel. In A. Ronen (Ed.), *The Sefunim Prehistoric Sites, Mt. Carmel*, pp. 401–422. B.A.R. International Series 230, Oxford.

Thirgood, J. V., 1981. *Man and the Mediterranean Forest*. Academic Press, London.

Tomaselli, R., 1977. Degradation of the Mediterranean maquis. In *Mediterranean Forests and Maquis: Ecology, Conservation and Management*, pp. 33–72. MAB Tech. Note 2. UNESCO, Paris.

Trabaud, L., 1981. Man and fire impacts on Mediterranean vegetation. In F. di Castri, F. W. Goodall, and R. L. Specht (Eds.), *Ecosystems of the World, 11: Mediterranean-Type Shrublands*, pp. 123–130. Elsevier, New York.

Vernet, J. L., 1973. Etude sur l'histoire de la végétation du sudest de la France au Quaternaire, d'après les charbons de bois principalement. *Paleobiol. Continent* 4:1–90.

Vita-Finci, C., 1969. *The Mediterranean Valleys: Geological Changes in Historical Times.* Cambridge University Press.

Vogl, R. J., 1980. The ecological factors that produce perturbation-dependent ecosystems. In J. Cairns, Jr. (Ed.), *The Recovery Process in Damaged Ecosystems*, pp. 63–94. Ann Arbor Science Publishers Inc., Ann Arbor, Michigan.

Waddington, C. H., 1975. *The Evolution of an Evolutionist*, pp. 252-266. Cornell University Press, Ithaca, N.Y.

Westhoff, V., 1983. Man's attitude towards vegetation. In W. Holzner, M. J. A. Werger, and I. Ikusima (Eds.), *Man's Impact on Vegetation*, pp. 7–24. Junk, The Hague.

Woodcock, J., 1986. Understory. Light and Vegetation Composition. M.Sc. thesis, Technion, Israel Institute of Technology, Haifa, Israel.

Zohary, D., 1969. The progenitors of wheat and barley in relation to domestication and agricultural dispersal in the Old World. In P. J. Uco and G. W. Dimpleby (Eds.), *The Domestication and Exploitation of Plants and Animals*, pp. 35–46. Aldine, Chicago.

Zohary, D., and P. Spiegel-Roy, 1975. Beginning of fruit growing in the Old World. *Science* 187:319–327.

Zohary, M., 1962. *Plant Life in Palestine*. Ronald Press, New York.

Zohary, M., 1974. *Geobotanical Foundations of the Middle East*. Gustav Fischer Verlag, Stuttgart.

Zohary, M., 1983. Man and vegetation in the Middle East. In W. Holzner, M. J. A. Werger, and I. Ikusima (Eds.), *Man's Impact on Vegetation*, pp. 287–296. Junk, The Hague.

15 *Bromus tectorum,* a Biotic Cause of Ecosystem Impoverishment in the Great Basin

W. D. BILLINGS

Editor's Note: Bromus tectorum is a desert annual, an exotic to North America. It offers us a classical case of biotic impoverishment: it is one of those small-bodied, rapidly reproducing, hardy plants that finds a variety of open niches around the world and changes the world. In this case, in the Great Basin of North America, its chance introduction is displacing an indigenous forest and a native shrubby ecosystem.

W. D. Billings has been a lifelong student of the vegetation of the earth, extending his insatiable curiosity and capacity for new knowledge with a continuing flow of equally intense and able students. Billings has been an especially avid student of deserts and tundra, both Arctic and montane. It is his lifelong interest in deserts that we have tapped here to draw out one of the best-documented and most important case histories of how one exotic has changed a landscape, reducing its potential for support of plants and animals, including people, for all of time.

Introduction

From the tropics to the boreal forest, the destruction of vegetation by clear-cutting or fire is a common occurrence. The resultant loss of floristic and faunistic diversity is, in the main, due to direct human interference and impact. Subtle invasions by pathogens or by most exotic animal and plant species more likely result in selective loss, one species at a time, as was the case with the loss of the American chestnut, *Castanea dentata* (Marsh.) Borkh., from the eastern deciduous forest due to attack by the Asiatic fungus *Endothia parasitica.* It is seldom that such alien invaders cause the destruction of most or all of the plant and animal species in an ecosystem.

If such an invader does change the actual or potential physical environment, there can be a rapid loss of the original biotic components of the community. An example of this is the loss of species characterizing the original grasslands of California by the invasion of annual plant species from the Mediterranean region (Jackson 1985; Mooney, Hamburg, and Drake 1986). Whereas the environmental change caused by the invaders in this instance is not clearly defined, the environmental cause of rapid biotic impoverishment in the sagebrush steppe ecosystem of the Great Basin in Utah and Nevada is more easily discerned. The original vegetation was

301

dominated by *Artemisia tridentata* Nutt. and other microphyllous shrubs with associated bunchgrasses and dicotyledonous herbs. The invader is the European annual grass *Bromus tectorum* L. and the resultant environmental change is fire (Billings 1948; Young and Evans 1978; West and Hassan 1985; Mack 1986). In Hawaii, a similar invasion by a fire-enhancing alien species, with resultant loss of native species, has been described by C. W. Smith (1985). The effects of such biological invasions on subsequent ecosystem properties has been reviewed by Vitousek (1986).

Original Vegetation of the Western Great Basin

The first Europeans to see the arid country just east of the Sierra Nevada were the trappers Jedediah Smith in 1827, Peter Skene Ogden in 1829–1830, and Joseph Walker in 1833. They led exploratory trapping parties based in the Rocky Mountains across the dry lands of the western Great Basin. Smith crossed the Sierra from the Spanish lands in California. Walker crossed from the east to California and later recrossed from the west. Ogden traveled south from the Columbia River to the lower Humboldt River and thence to Walker Lake on his way to the lower Colorado River. They made only casual observations on vegetation. The first scientific explorations were made by John C. Fremont and his expedition of U.S. Army topographic engineers. Fremont came down from the north through eastern Oregon into Nevada where in the winter of 1843–1844 he discovered Pyramid Lake. From there, in February 1844, he and Kit Carson crossed the snowy Sierra by way of Carson Pass. Fremont collected some plants and made casual descriptions of the vegetation of the western part of the basin, but the winter weather was scarcely conducive to doing more.

The first real descriptions of the plants of the dry regions in the rain-shadow of the Sierra are those of Lt. Beckwith, 3rd Artillery (1854), and his plant collector James A. Snyder. Beckwith commented frequently on the abundance of bunchgrasses of fine quality for his horses in the sagebrush vegetation along the 41st parallel of north-central and northwestern Nevada. Sereno Watson (1871), a member of King's survey of the 40th parallel, did more-intensive botanical collecting across northern Nevada. He described many new plant species from western Nevada, and he made useful observations of the vegetation.

The vegetational zonation of the western Great Basin has been described by Billings (1945), Billings (1951), Billings, Humphreys, and Darling (1954), and Holmgren (1972). The vertical zonation along an elevational gradient around the higher mountains and playas of the basin just east of the Sierra in western Nevada is diagrammed in Figure 15.1.

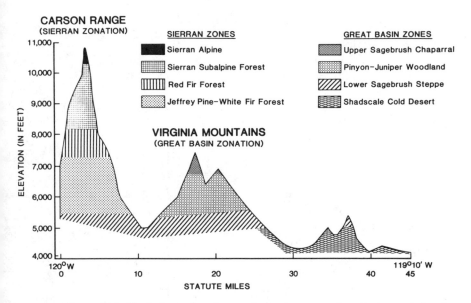

Figure 15.1. Vertical zonation of vegetation in the western Great Basin; vertical scale exaggerated. Note the sharp demarcation between Sierran vegetation in the Carson Range and Great Basin vegetation in the Virginia Mountains, separated only by a narrow valley.

The areal relationships of these vegetational zones was determined by the use of a map of about 30,000 miles² (78,000 km²) of western Nevada, compiled and drawn by Billings in 1954. Using a dot-grid overlay with 25 dots per inch², the areas of each of the principal ecosystems were estimated. The total number of dots used was 6,150, with each dot being the equivalent of 4.84 miles² (12.58km²). The lower sagebrush–grass steppe within the region mapped totaled 10,890 miles² (28,314 km²) or 36.6% of the area. If the open juniper–sagebrush savanna and the upper sagebrush community are included, the percentage of land dominated by Artemisia is about 40.74%. The *Atriplex confertifolia* cold desert ecosystem totals 10,251 miles² (26,653 km²) or 34.4% of the area. Pinyon–juniper woodland (*Pinus monophylla* and *Juniperus osteosperma*) makes up about 12.11% of the region. A representative part of the map in this research region is shown in Figure 15.2. Table 15.1 lists the areas of the main ecosystems and their percentages of the total area of the whole map.

Grazing Effects

The western Great Basin was not a part of the range of the bison. The rhizomatous C_4 sod grasses of the Great Plains on which the bison thrived do

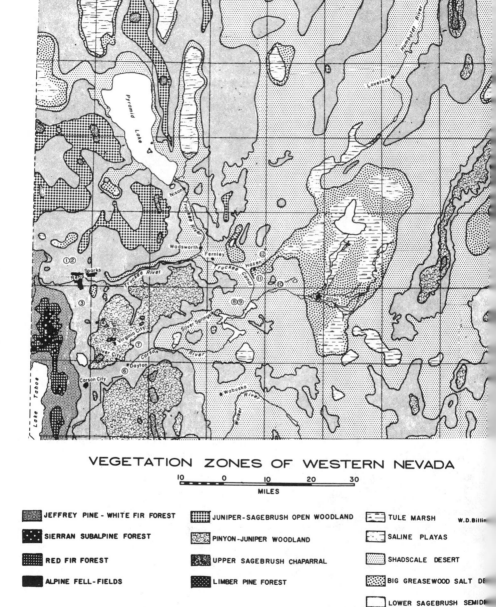

VEGETATION ZONES OF WESTERN NEVADA

10   0   10   20   30

MILES

JEFFREY PINE - WHITE FIR FOREST   JUNIPER-SAGEBRUSH OPEN WOODLAND   TULE MARSH   W.D.Billin

SIERRAN SUBALPINE FOREST   PINYON-JUNIPER WOODLAND   SALINE PLAYAS

RED FIR FOREST   UPPER SAGEBRUSH CHAPARRAL   SHADSCALE DESERT

ALPINE FELL-FIELDS   LIMBER PINE FOREST   BIG GREASEWOOD SALT DE

LOWER SAGEBRUSH SEMIDE

Figure 15.2. Portion of a map of the vegetation zones or biomes of western Nevada.

Table 15.1. *Areas and percentages of the principal ecosystems in western Nevada between latitudes 38° and 41°N and longitudes 117° and 120°W*

Ecosystem type	Area (miles²)	Area (km²)	% of total area
Alpine fell–fields	9.7	25.2	0.03
Cottonwood forest	101.6	264.2	0.34
Greasewood salt desert	1,403.6	3,649.4	4.72
Jeffrey pine–white fir forest	222.6	578.8	0.75
Juniper–sagebrush	701.8	1,824.7	2.36
Limber pine forest	135.5	352.3	0.46
Open water	411.4	1,069.6	1.38
Pinyon–juniper woodland	3,605.8	9,375.1	12.11
Red fir forest	96.8	251.7	0.33
Sagebrush, lower	10,890.0	28,314.0	36.59
Sagebrush, upper	532.4	1,384.2	1.79
Saline playas (bare)	1,069.6	2,781.0	3.59
Shadscale desert[a]	10,251.1	26,652.9	34.44
Sierran subalpine forest	19.4	50.4	0.07
Tule marsh	203.3	528.6	0.68
Willow meadow	111.3	289.4	0.37
Total	29,765.9	77,391.5	100.01

[a] Including dune vegetation and unstabilized dunes.

not grow on these summer-dry steppes of Nevada. Instead, perennial C_3 bunchgrasses of the genera Poa, Festuca, Agropyron, Oryzopsis, and Stipa dominated the grass stratum of the sagebrush formation. The principal native ungulate herbivores of this ecosystem were, and are, pronghorn antelope, mule deer, and desert bighorn sheep. Also, lagomorphs and many species of rodents are part of the herbivorous trophic level. The impact of these native animals on the sagebrush–grass community was apparently relatively light and the carrying capacity was seldom exceeded in "pristine" times with the possible exception of around springs and along streams.

During the 1840s and 1850s, the first overland wagon trains to California and Oregon with their accompanying herds of horses and cattle and bands of sheep introduced domestic livestock to the region. The grazing impacts appeared first along the California Trail, down the valley of the Humboldt, and from there across the Forty Mile Desert to the Carson and Truckee Rivers flowing eastward from the Sierra. From near his crossing of the lower Humboldt River Beckwith (1854) reported

June 10, 1854: Fine droves of cattle, which had been wintered near Great Salt Lake, passed today on their way to California, and one or two large flocks of sheep are but a few miles behind them. Latitude of camp, 40° 42′ 03″ N. . . .

June 9, 1854: The more experienced stock-drovers to California send their cattle back from the river to feed on the nutritious grass of the hills. (Beckwith 1854)

What were these "nutritious grasses"? The first good botanical evidence is provided by Watson (1871). He lists 68 species of Gramineae in 35 genera as occurring in the general region along the 40th parallel. Of these, 59 species in 33 genera occurred within the Great Basin. Some were restricted to the moister mountains of the eastern part of the basin. Watson estimated at least 9 of the taxa listed as having been introduced. These did not include *Bromus tectorum*, which had not yet arrived in the intermountain region. Watson in the 1860s listed about 10 species of bunchgrasses as important on the dry hills of northern and western Nevada. To bring Watson's synonymy up to date, using Cronquist, Holmgren, Holmgren, Reveal, and Holmgren (1977), these were:

> *Festuca idahoensis*
> *Poa sandbergii*
> *Poa canbyi*
> *Leucopoa kingii*
> *Agropyron spicatum*
> *Elymus cinereus*
> *Sitanion hystrix*
> *Oryzopsis hymenoides*
> *Stipa comata*
> *Stipa occidentalis*

Such scattered bunchgrasses did not carry fire well. Range fires in the original sagebrush–bunchgrass steppe apparently were rare or absent during the entire nineteenth century.

In the summer of 1902, P. B. Kennedy (1903) made one of the first, if not the first, range-condition surveys of the sagebrush–bunchgrass steppe in northern Nevada. His trip started at Beowawe in Eureka County on the Humboldt River. He traversed the Tuscarora Mountains about 55 miles to Stampede Creek and Indian Creek in Elko County. Robertson (1954), in 1952, retraced Kennedy's route comparing the 1902 range situation with that of 50 years later. Within that time, the following important changes had occurred in range condition on the foothills:

1   Desirable livestock browse shrubs decreased.
2   *Agropyron spicatum*, a prime forage bunchgrass, decreased from "abundant" to "generally absent" or "less than 5% density."
3   Annuals, notably cheatgrass (*Bromus tectorum*), not present in 1902, had "increased to an extreme degree."
4   Burn–scars were "absent or unimportant" in 1902. In 1952 much of the route was bordered or crossed by "burned-off-range" and covered by *Bromus tectorum* and "little rabbit-brush" (*Chrysothamnus viscidiflorus* subsp. *pumilus*).

5	*Artemisia tridentata* replaced "bluegrass meadows" at lower elevations.
6	"Stream channels had eroded deeper and wider."

According to Robertson (1954), these effects were the results of heavy grazing, the invasion of cheatgrass, and the occurrence of fires.

Most of the important bunchgrass taxa listed by Watson (1871) in the sagebrush steppe are still present here and there. However, with the possible exception of *Poa sandbergii*, all have decreased in density and biomass on most northern Nevada ranges in the 120 years since the start of Watson's explorations in 1867. Christensen and Johnson (1964) have reported a similar change in three valleys in central Utah where the original vegetation had abundant bunchgrasses (*Agropyron spicatum* and *Poa sandbergii*). Over-grazing has long since caused the replacement of these grasses by sagebrush and juniper. Young, Evans, and Major (1977) have provided good species lists of relatively undisturbed stands of sagebrush–grass communities as they now occur in the dry regions of the northwestern Great Basin of northeastern California (trans-Sierra and the Modoc Plateau). Their data also show the invasion of *Bromus tectorum* into all sagebrush–grass vegetation types especially at the lower elevations.

The Introduction of *Bromus tectorum* and the Coming of Fire

The seeds of the alien opportunist, *Bromus tectorum*, landed in the overgrazed and "open" sagebrush–bunchgrass steppe, now depleted of its perennial grasses. As Mack (1981, 1986) has documented, this invasion of a weedy annual grass from Europe and the trans-Caspian steppes occurred in the intermountain region during the last decade of the nineteenth century and the first decades of the twentieth. Bromus became the most abundant seed plant in the region and changed the nature of the sagebrush steppe ecosystem forever.

According to Mack (1981), the first collections of *Bromus tectorum* in the intermountain region were from Spence's Bridge, British Columbia, in 1889; Ritzville, Washington, in 1893; and Provo, Utah, in 1894. These are inland wheat-growing areas, which suggested that seeds of the species arrived as a contaminant in grain-seed supplies. By 1898 to 1904, collections of this Bromus were made throughout the dry regions of interior Washington, Oregon, and Utah. Within the next ten years to 1914, the weedy grass appeared here and there throughout eastern Washington and Oregon, southern Idaho, northern Nevada, and Utah. In another 15 years, it was abundant throughout the entire sagebrush steppe biome. As Aldo Leopold (1941) so aptly expressed it, ". . . the spread was often so rapid as to escape recording. One simply woke up one fine spring to find the range dominated by a new weed ... cheat grass (*Bromus tectorum*)."

The first Nevada collections of *Bromus tectorum* were from the northeastern part of the state in Elko County at Tuscarora and Skelton between 1905 and 1910. The first collection from western Nevada was by A. A. Heller from Reno in 1912. This collection (Heller #10488) is in the Herbarium of the University of Nevada, Reno. However, *Bromus tectorum* was present in Reno at least as early as 1906. Kennedy (February 1907) reported it, with *B. rubens* and other *Bromus* species as occupying "considerable areas along embankments, but always near the railroad or highways." There is no voucher specimen for this earlier presence.

Although not the only vector for the rapid distribution of cheatgrass, the railroads played an important role. An old resident of Verdi, Nevada, west of Reno, remembered that the first time he had seen it there was before World War I. This was in the year after some railroad stock cars had been swept out near that little town. The rapid spread of the grass beyond the railroads was aided by sheep, cattle, and horses as they were driven to rangelands. Automobile tires could also have been carriers of the seeds. Whatever the vectors, the climate was ideal for a winter annual that required moist soils during the cold season. Cheatgrass requires cold winter weather while vegetative in order to flower the following spring (Hulbert 1955; Billings, unpublished experiment).

Once cheatgrass became established on the range, the stage was set for wildfires which had been rare or non-existent in the original open bunchgrass–sagebrush vegetation of the nineteenth century. In 1902, in his 55-mile transect of Elko County, Kennedy (1903) found no burn scars and no *Bromus tectorum* in the sagebrush–bunchgrass vegetation. Fifty years later, Robertson (1954), retracing Kennedy's route, tallied 17 separate burned areas along the transect and cheatgrass everywhere along the way. I am not sure when the first cheatgrass-caused fires occurred in western and northern Nevada, but they were common by the 1930s. Pickford (1932) reported that, on burned-over areas in the Great Salt Lake district of Utah, *Bromus tectorum* had replaced sagebrush as a dominant and often covered burned sites in dense stands.

Bromus tectorum, an annual, dies and dries in late May or early June and is ready tinder for any spark, whether caused by lightning or humans, until autumn rains or snows come in October or November. Figure 15.3 shows such a fire in progress during the summer of 1941 in the Peavine Mountain foothills northwest of Reno. The area beyond the snow fence in the middleground was burned several years earlier and is now mainly covered with cheatgrass, as evinced by the light color of the dried plants. The

Figure 15.3. Typical sagebrush–grass fire carried by dry cheatgrass (*Bromus tectorum*) and sagebrush (Artemisia) on the lower slopes of Peavine Mt., northwest of Reno, summer 1941. Foreground is an older burn. Photography by W. D. Billings.

sagebrush community in the foreground is as yet unburned but *Bromus tectorum* is growing abundantly under and around the shrubs. It could burn at any time.

Without fire, cheatgrass invades overgrazed sagebrush range, where it forms an ephemeral annual stratum. Once the community is burned, the shrubs, particularly sagebrush, are killed. The seeds of *Bromus tectorum*, having been dropped into the dry soil between the shrubs, survive in this relatively cooler and often unburned microenvironment. If the next fall and winter are wet, the seeds germinate. The following spring, the burned area is a sward of green except for the dark, barren circles that mark the places where the shrubs burned and the fire was hottest.

As the years go by, the seeds of cheatgrass consolidate their gains across the burn. In the summers following moist winters, when this grass provides abundant tinder, fires become more likely and frequent (Billings 1948; Young and Evans 1978). The result is replacement of the sagebrush biome by great patches of annual grassland. These areas range in size from about one or two hectares to thousands of hectares. The rich floristic diversity of the original sagebrush communities is reduced not only by the loss of shrubby species but by that of native perennial and annual herbs as well. Some of this loss is due to fire (Billings 1948) and some to competition with the dense cover of the Bromus (Young, Evans, and Weaver 1976). As *Bromus tectorum* spreads upward in elevation on the mountain ranges of the Great Basin, fires are now destroying large areas of the pinyon-juniper biome (Koniak 1985) as well as the plant, bird, and animal species characteristic of this unique conifer woodland.

Vegetational Succession Following Fire

In the Sagebrush–Grass Steppe

After fire, revegetation by natural succession to a community resembling the original sagebrush–bunchgrass type is very slow, and for all practical purposes does not occur. As described earlier, *Bromus tectorum* becomes almost completely dominant. Even without repeated fires, a fire-prone annual grassland develops.

Within a few years, a few scattered shrubs begin to appear among the postfire annual grasses (Billings 1948). These shrubs originate almost entirely by sprouts from root systems that have survived the fire. Principal among these sprouting species is *Ephedra viridis*. Other shrubby taxa with similar tactics are *Prunus andersonii*, *Tetradymia canescens*, *T. glabrata,* and occasionally *Ribes velutinum*. In the Reno region, *Artemisia tridentata* and *Purshia tridentata* are killed by fire and do not sprout; they must re-invade from buried seeds or from seeds carried by wind, rodents, or birds. Purshia shows little or no sprouting in western Nevada although it has been reported by Blaisdell (1950) to sprout in the Snake River Plains. If Purshia is present in the pre-burn sagebrush community in the hills around Reno, it does reproduce to some extent from buried seeds following wildfires. *Tetradymia canescens* and *T. glabrata* reproduce both by sprouts and seeds. The strategy of *T. canescens* is to establish by sprouts quickly after the burn. Within two to three years, it produces abundant seeds from maturing sprouts when they reach about .3–.5 m tall. Where Tetradymia was present in the pre-burn vegetation, this allows quick dominance of those parts of the burn. And this was how this species became the dominant shrub in the first years following the fire on Peavine Mt. in 1941, shown in Figure 15.3.

In 1941, I put in fenced permanent plots near the head of "Ecology Canyon" in the eastern foothills of Peavine Mountain about 1 km west of old U.S. Highway 395 and 5 km northwest of the University of Nevada campus. This side ravine runs east to west with a south-facing and a north-facing

a

Figure 15.4. (a) The original vegetation of the sagebrush-grass plots at Ecology Canyon; summer 1941; (b) The same view 6 years after the wildfire of 1947. This photograph is from summer of 1953; (c) The same view 41 years following the fire. This photograph taken in May 1988. All 3 photographs by W. D. Billings.

slope. The vegetation at that time was an unburned, floristically simple community of Artemisia–Purshia–Ephedra with *Poa sandbergii* and *Bromus tectorum* among and between the shrubs. A set of small plots was put on each of the slope aspects within the fenced areas. Figure 15.4a shows the unburned sagebrush vegetation as it appeared on these slopes in 1941.

On July 15, 1947, a large wildfire of around 360 ha swept across this whole area of sagebrush shrubland. The vegetation within the fenced plots was destroyed by this fire. The next day almost no live plant material remained aboveground. Three months later, in an experimental attempt at controlling erosion, I planted seeds of the perennial grasses *Agropyron cristatum* (introduced), and *A. spicatum* (native) on both burned plots. Neither species had grown there pre-fire. By May, 1948, these grasses had germinated on the north-facing slope but failed to become established on the south-facing plot in spite of the latter having received more precipitation during the preceding winter. They were still present on the north-facing slope in 1953 in small numbers. By 1988, both species had established good populations on the

b

c

lower parts of the north-facing slope. But after 41 years, this site must be considered marginal for them.

The next repeat photograph was taken in July 1953 and is shown in Figure 15.4b. The photographic time interval was 12 years; the photograph shows the successional situation on north (left) and south-facing (right) slopes 6 years after the fire. Some shrubs, largely *Ephedra viridis* from sprouting and *Purshia tridentata* from buried seeds had, returned on the south-facing slope. The cover of *Bromus tectorum* on the south-facing slope returned quickly in the 6 elapsed years and had the same high albedo that characterized the pre-burn grass–sagebrush vegetation of 12 years earlier. The little arroyo between the slopes showed considerable erosion in the 6 years since the fire.

In the early summer of 1948, one year after the fire, I sampled the vegetation using a Latin square of fifty 0.1 m plots on each slope. The results are shown in Table 15.2. The slopes were still quite barren with only scattered annual plants on the south-facing slope and scarcely more on the north-facing one. Not surprisingly, *Bromus tectorum* was the most common species. Only one shrubby species (*Ephedra viridis*) had appeared, and it was scarcely visible.

The next vegetational sampling of these two slopes was during September 1953, six years after the fire. A presence list, combining both north- and south-facing plots, showed that 53 species of vascular plants had colonized the site in that time: 10 species of shrubs, 25 perennial species of herbaceous plants, including the two Agropyron species artificially seeded, and 19 species of annuals. Most of these were rare, however, and vegetational cover was low. Only the shrubby vegetation was sampled for density and coverage. This was done by using the random-pairs method of Cottam and Curtis (1956). The results of this sampling appear in Table 15.3.

In the short period of six growing seasons, a marked difference developed in the floristics and relative cover of the shrubs on the two slopes. On the south-facing slope, the number of shrubs per hectare was only 128 individuals with a total cover of only 28 m^2 per hectare. In contrast, there were 456 shrubs per hectare on the north-facing slope with a total coverage of 148 m^2 per hectare. *Ephedra viridis* was the principal shrubby species (from sprouts) on the south-facing slope, while *Ribes velutinum* and *Tetradymia canescens* (both from sprouts also) characterized the north-facing slope. About 1% of the north-facing slope had a cover of shrubs and there was even less (about 0.3%) on the south-facing slope.

In May, 1988, Jan Nachlinger and I repeated the vegetational sampling of 1948 and 1953 on both slopes using the same methods. These 1988 data appear in Tables 15.2 and 15.3 in comparison with the earlier data. The main changes in the herbaceous vegetation are the large increases in

Table 15.2. *Composition of herbaceous vegetation 1 year and 41 years following a complete fire in a sagebrush–grass community. Location: Ecology Canyon, northwest of Reno, Nevada. Fire date: 15 July 1947. Sampled by 50¹/₁₀-meter plots on each slope.*

Species	Frequency (%)		Density per m^2	
	1948	1988	1948	1988
South-facing Slope				
Annuals				
Bromus tectorum	44	96	12.8	98.8
Mentzelia albicaulis	2	2	0.2	1.2
Erodium cicutarium	2	82	0.2	71.4
Amsinckia tesselata	—	14	—	3.0
Perennial herbs				
Phlox longifolia	—	6	—	1.8
Crepis occidentalis	—	2	—	0.2
Poa sandbergii	—	2	—	0.2
Stipa thurberiana	—	2	—	0.2
North-facing Slope				
Annuals				
Bromus tectorum	34	78	5.0	94.6
Erodium cicutarium	—	4	—	2.0
Perennial Herbs				
Phlox longifolia	2	2	0.2	0.2
Crepis occidentalis	—	6	—	0.6
Poa sandbergii	12	56	2.4	23.4
Stipa thurberiana	—	2	—	0.2
Arabis sp.	—	8	—	1.0
Sitanion hystrix	—	8	—	0.8
Lygodesmia spinosa	—	14	—	2.4
Lupinus caudatus	—	2	—	0.2
Shrub sprouts or seedlings				
Ephedra viridis	2	4	0.8	0.4
Chrysothamnus nauseosus	—	2	—	0.2
Eriogonum microthecum	—	8	—	0.8
Purshia tridentata	—	2	—	0.2
Prunus andersonii	—	2	—	0.4
Tetradymia glabrata	—	2	—	0.2

the annual exotic species *Bromus tectorum* and *Erodium cicutarium*, especially the former, on the south-facing slope. These now dominate that site at the expense of the native flora. Bromus has also increased on the north-facing slope and may be partially responsible for the drastic decrease in the native perennial grass *Poa sandbergii* there in the 35 years since 1953.

As can be seen in Table 15.3, the shrubs have increased in the fire-free 41 years since 1947 but not to the extent of *Bromus tectorum* which now dominates

Table 15.3. *Shrubby vegetation on the Ecology Canyon plots as determined by the random-pairs method and cover frame in 1953 and 1988, 6 years and 41 years, respectively, after the fire of 1947*

Species	Number of points		Number of shrubs		Total cover in m²		Mean cover per shrub		% Relative density		Number of shrubs/ha.		% Total shrubby cover		Total cover in m²/ha.	
	1953	1988	1953	1988	1953	1988	1953	1988	1953	1988	1953	1988	1953	1988	1953	1988
South-facing slope (25 pairs, 15 meters apart)																
Ephedra viridis	22	10	32	16	5.9	7.32	0.18	0.46	64	32	82.1	388.5	53.8	63.1	14.9	178.7
Tetradymia glabrata	7	0	8	0	2.7	0	0.34	0	16	0	20.5	0	24.1	0	7.0	0
Gutierrezia sarothrae	5	7	5	13	1.7	0.48	0.34	0.04	10	26	12.8	315.6	15.7	4.1	5.3	12.6
Artemisia tridentata	3	2	3	3	0.3	0.9	0.1	0.3	6	6	7.7	72.8	2.8	7.7	0.3	21.8
Purshia tridentata	1	1	1	1	0.2	0.15	0.2	0.15	2	2	2.6	24.3	1.8	1.2	0.5	3.6
Prunus andersonii	1	0	1	0	0.2	0	0.2	0	2	0	2.6	0	1.8	0	0.5	0
Chrysothamnus nauseosus	0	10	0	17	0	2.75	0	0.16	0	34	0	412.8	0	23.7	0	66.0
Totals			50	50	11.0	11.6			100	100	128.3	1214.0	100	100	28.5	282.7
North-facing Slope (20 pairs, 15 meters apart)																
Ribes velutinum	9	3	14	3	6.2	1.9	0.44	0.63	35	7.5	159.8	178.6	47.7	6.7	70.3	112.5
Tetradymia canescens	9	3	15	5	3.5	0.65	0.23	0.13	38	12.5	173.5	297.6	26.9	2.3	39.9	38.7
Purshia tridentata	4	9	4	13	1.7	21.55	0.42	1.66	10	32.5	45.7	773.8	13.1	76.1	19.2	1284.5
Ephedra viridis	6	2	6	2	1.6	0.6	0.27	0.3	15	5.0	68.5	119.0	12.3	2.1	18.5	35.7
Prunus andersonii	1	2	1	2	0.02	0.11	0.02	0.055	2	5.0	9.1	119.0	0.2	0.4	0.2	6.5
Artemisia tridentata	0	2	0	2	0	0.8	0	0.4	0	5.0	0	119.0	0	2.8	0	47.6
Chrysothamnus nauseosus	0	7	0	9	0	2.35	0	0.26	0	22.5	0	535.7	0	8.3	0	139.3
Eriogonum microthecum	0	3	0	4	0	0.36	0	0.09	0	10.0	0	238.1	0	1.3	0	21.4
Totals			40	40	13.0	28.32			100	100	456.6	2381	100	100	148.1	1686.2

	South-facing slope		*North-facing slope*	
	1953	1988	1953	1988
Mean distance between shrubs (m) =	8.83	2.87	4.68	2.05
Mean cover per shrub (m) =	0.22	0.23	0.325	0.71
Total shrubby cover per hectare (m) =	28.5	282.7	148.1	1686.2
% shrubby cover per hectare =	0.3	2.8	1.5	16.9

Table 15.4. *Vegetational composition of an* unburned *sagebrush community on a southeast-facing slope near abandoned Nevada Central Mine site, Peavine Mt., c. 5 km SW of Ecology Canyon burned site. Plot size = 0.1 hectare with 50 4-m² subplots and 50-m herb coverage transect.*

Species	Frequency (%)	Absolute and relative cover
Annuals		
Bromus tectorum		323 cm = 51.9%
Collinsia parviflora		31 cm = 5.0%
Epilobium sp.		42 cm = 6.8%
Microsteris gracilis		2 cm = 0.3%
Blepharopappus scaber		113 cm = 18.2%
Plagiobothrys kingii		28 cm = 4.5%
Microseris linearifolia		7 cm = 1.1%
Perennial herbs		
Allium sp.		11 cm = 1.8%
Sitanion hystrix		44 cm = 7.1%
Perideridia bolanderi		11 cm = 1.8%
Phlox longifolia		5 cm = 0.8%
Poa sandbergii		5 cm = 0.8%
Shrubs		Density per ha.
Artemisia tridentata	88%	6,550
Purshia tridentata	2%	50
Chrysothamnus nauseosus	10%	300
Tetradymia glabrata	94%	6,600
Gutierrezia sarothrae	2%	50

the south-facing slope where shrubs constitute only 2.8% of the vegetational cover. However, the shrubby cover on the north-facing slope is now 17%, with *Purshia tridentata* (from seeds) leading the way in remarkable contrast to the situation on the south-facing slope. However, in a fire year of abundant annual grass, this could change overnight.

The near absence of postfire sagebrush on both slopes is remarkable. These low densities and lack of shrub cover after fire are strong reductions when compared to *unburned* sagebrush vegetation at the same elevation and rock type unaltered andesite about 5 km away, as shown in Table 15.4. At the unburned site, near abandoned Nevada Central Mine, the number of shrubs per hectare is 13,550, with *Artemisia tridentata* and *Tetradymia glabrata* sharing 97% of the shrub dominance about equally. Absolute herbaceous cover at the unburned site was less than 6%, with *Bromus tectorum*

a

b

Figure 15.5. (a) South-facing plot and slope at Ecology Canyon photographed in 1953, 6 years after the wildfire. Only a few scattered young shrubs in rather barren *Bromus tectorum* cover. (b) The same site in 1986, 39 years after fire. *Purshia tridentata* and *Ephedra viridis* are the principal scattered shrubs in a luxuriant cover of *Bromus*. There has been little recruitment of shrubs in the 33 years since 1953. Both photographs by W. D. Billings.

contributing over half. This vegetational cover is comparable in every way to that on the south-facing slope at Ecology Canyon before the fire of 1947.

At the time of the 1953 sampling of the Ecology Canyon plots, standard photographs were taken of each of the plots. In September 1986 I rephotographed the individual plots after a time lapse of 33 years and 39 years of postfire succession. For the south-facing plot, this set of repeat photography appears in Figures 15.5a and 15.5b. The present vegetation on the south-facing slope is, essentially, a sea of cheatgrass with widely scattered islands of *Ephedra viridis* and *Purshia tridentata*. Several of these shrubs can be seen in their youth in the 1953 photograph. *Chrysothamnus nauseosus* is also present, but sagebrush (*Artemisia tridentata*) is rare. The flammable tinder of *Bromus tectorum* is all too apparent.

During 1953, also, I made a repeat photograph of the canyon from exactly the same location as the pre-fire one taken in 1941. It shows the postfire damage comparatively on both slopes. In May 1988 I returned to that same spot and rephotographed it for the third time. The 1941, 1953, and 1988 photographs appear as Figures 15.4a, 15.4b, and 15.4c, respectively. They show original unburned vegetation, early recovery after fire, and strongly fire-modified vegetation still present even 41 years after burning.

In the Pinyon–Juniper Woodland

This ecosystem zone, dominated by *Pinus monophylla* and *Juniperus osteosperma*, is limited almost exclusively to the mountainsides of the Great Basin above the sagebrush biome and southeast of the Truckee and Humboldt Rivers (Figs. 15.1 and 15.2). The elevational limits range from ca. 1,600 to ca. 2,400 m. It is a bit more moist and snowy in the winter than the lower sagebrush steppe but less so than the upper sagebrush zone. In western Nevada, this woodland, with warmer nocturnal temperatures during the winter (Billings 1954), forms a thermal belt between the two sagebrush zones.

Since the spread of *Bromus tectorum* through western Nevada in the 1920s and 1930s, wildfires have occasionally moved upward from sagebrush into pinyon–juniper. These older fires were usually uncommon or patchy. However, in the last 25 years or so (Koniak 1985), burns into pinyon–juniper have become more frequent and extensive. In the Virginia Range and Pine Nut Mountains considerable areas of woodlands have been destroyed in the last two decades (Figure 15.6). As in the lower sagebrush zone, within a year or two after fire in pinyon–juniper, *Bromus tectorum* begins to dominate the herbaceous stratum. Where the pinyons have been killed, they eventually fall and decay leaving a more open site considerably different from that of the original closed woodland. Koniak found that the junipers and pinyons begin to reestablish 20 to 30 years after fire, but that tree cover was still "minimal" 60 years after burning.

Figure 15.6. Pinyon–juniper woodland destroyed by wildfire in the Virginia Mountains, Nevada. Light-colored, dry cheatgrass is already reestablishing. The pinyon trees are dead. Photograph by W. D. Billings, 1986. Elevation ca. 1,900 meters; Geiger Grade region.

Tausch and West (1988) studied a small mid-nineteenth century burn in pinyon–juniper (3 ha) in the mountains of southwestern Utah. There was a strong differential in the survival and establishment of juniper and pinyon. Thirty-eight percent of the existing *Juniperus osteosperma* trees were alive at the time of the fire but only 0.6 percent of the present trees of *Pinus monophylla*. Pinyon was destroyed in the fire but has come back more rapidly than juniper. But this was a small, light burn compared to those now occurring in western Nevada.

In the recent burns involving several hundred or thousands of hectares in pinyon–juniper that I have seen, it appears that reinvasion by the large seeds of pinyon and juniper would be difficult and slow over the long distances involved. The seeds are distributed by birds and mammals which are themselves integral parts of this woodland ecosystem and dependent on its physiognomy and food production. They are at danger in open country. Severely burned parts of the pinyon–juniper zone will be dominated by annual grassland with widely scattered shrubs for a long time to come.

Long-Term Implications of the Cheatgrass-Fire Problem

It is impossible to predict the intricate future of the cheatgrass-fire problem and its effects on Great Basin ecosystems. The following points are valid, however:

1   A number of native plant and animal species are at risk of being eliminated, locally and even regionally. Even where some remain, their populations are severely reduced. At the very least, this results in loss of genetic diversity.

2   More apparent is the threat to large, integrated, and operational ecosystems that could disappear once and for all. This is true for the sagebrush biome and has now become common in the pinyon–juniper zone at higher elevations. In the last few years, *Bromus tectorum* has migrated down into the sandy areas of the Carson Desert, where 40 years ago it was rare (Billings 1945). Young, Evans, and Swanson (1987) report that it has become abundant in Desert Queen Valley in the Hot Springs Mountains where it has outcompeted the important native plants *Oenothera deltoides* and *Oryzopsis hymenoides*.

3   Global CO_2 enrichment may strongly favor *Bromus tectorum*. According to recent work by Smith, Strain, and Sharkey (1987) this C^3 species consistently had the most positive response to high atmospheric carbon dioxide when compared with native desert grasses including *Oryzopsis hymenoides* and *Agropyron smithii*.

4   The cheatgrass-fire situation is one example demonstrating that not all global vegetational change is due to climatic change which can be modeled or predicted. Unpredictable events ("surprises") that can come quickly with the possibility of causing drastic and, often, irreversible change in ecosystems also must be considered.

5   It seems that very little can be done about such events after these weeds invade an ecosystem. In spite of billions of dollars spent on control of weedy plants such as *Halogeton glomeratus* on desert ranges, *Sorghum halapense* in corn, and *Abutilon theophrasti* in cotton, the foreign organism always seems to win or at least to stay ahead of the game. Indeed, *Bromus tectorum* seems to have won its conquest of the sagebrush ecosystem. The only viable alternative seems to be prevention of invasion. That means maintenance of the health of ecosystems by care and vigilance.

Acknowledgments

This work is the result of many years of discussions with colleagues and students. Particularly, I wish to acknowledge Dr. Joseph H. Robertson of the University of

Nevada, Reno, whose advice I have valued for so long. Some of the work reported here has been aided by NSF Grant BSR 85–04859 to Duke University for which I express appreciation. I thank my co-workers W. H. Schlesinger, E. H. DeLucia, Jan Nachlinger, and Shirley M. Billings for their help in the recent field work.

References

Beckwith, E. G., 1854. *Report of explorations for a route for the Pacific railroad of the line of the forty-first parallel of north latitude.* In Vol. II, House Rep. Ex. Doc. No. 91, 33rd Congress, 2nd session.

Billings, W. D., 1945. The plant associations of the Carson Desert region, western Nevada. *Butler Univ. Bot. Studies* 7:89–123.

Billings, W. D., 1948. Preliminary notes on fire succession in the sagebrush zone of western Nevada (abstract). *Bull. Ecol. Soc. Amer.* 29(2):30.

Billings, W. D., 1951. Vegetational zonation in the Great Basin of western North America. In *Compt. Rend. du Colloque sur Les Bases Ecologiques de la Régénération de la Végétation des Zones Arides*, pp. 101–122. Union Internat. Soc. Biol., Paris.

Billings, W. D., 1954. Temperature inversions in the pinyon–juniper zone of a Nevada mountain range. *Butler Univ. Bot. Studies* 11:112–118.

Billings, W. D., M. H. K. Humphreys, and J. B. Darling, 1954. *Environmental studies in the cold deserts and semi-deserts of the western Great Basin of North America.* Rept. Contract DA 44–109-qm–1261, Quartermaster Research and Development Command, U.S. Army.

Blaisdell, J. P., 1950. *Effects of controlled burning on bitterbrush on the upper Snake River Plains.* Intermountain Forest and Range Exp. Sta. Res. Paper 20, U.S. Forest Service, Ogden, Utah.

Christensen, E. M., and H. B. Johnson, 1964. Presettlement vegetation and vegetational change in three valleys in central Utah. *Brigham Young Univ. Sci. Bull., Biol.* Series 4:1–16.

Cottam, G., and J. T. Curtis, 1956. The use of distance measurements in phytosociological sampling. *Ecology* 37:451–460.

Cronquist, A., A. H. Holmgren, N. H. Holmgren, J. A. Reveal, and P. K. Holmgren, 1977. *Intermountain Flora: Vascular Plants of the Intermountain West, U.S.A.* Vol. 6. *The Monocotyledons.* New York Botanical Garden and Columbia University Press, New York.

Holmgren, N. H., 1972. Plant geography of the intermountain region. In Cronquist, A., A. H. Holmgren, N. H. Holmgren, and J. A. Reveal (Eds.), *Intermountain Flora: Vascular Plants of the Intermountain West, U.S.A.*, Vol. 1, pp. 77–161. New York Bot. Garden, and Hafner Publ. Co., Inc. New York.

Hulbert, L. C., 1955. Ecological studies of *Bromus tectorum* and other annual bromegrasses. *Ecological Monographs* 25:181–213.

Jackson, Louise E., 1985. Ecological origins of California's Mediterranean grasses. *J. Biogeography* 12:349–361.

Kennedy, P. B., 1903. Summer ranges of eastern Nevada sheep. *Nevada Agric. Exp. Sta. Bull.* 55.

Kennedy, P. B., 1907. Botanical features around Reno. *Muhlenbergiz* 3(2):17–32.

Koniak, S., 1985. Succession in pinyon–juniper woodlands following wildfire in the Great Basin. *Great Basin Naturalist* 45:556–566.

Leopold, A., 1941. Cheat takes over. *The Land* 1:310–313.

Mack, R. N., 1981. Invasion of *Bromus tectorum* L. into western North America: an ecological chronicle. *Agro-Ecosystems* 7:145–165.

Mack, R. N., 1986. Alien plant invasion into the intermountain west: a case history. In Mooney, H. A., and J. A. Drake (Eds.), *Ecology of Biological Invasions of North America and Hawaii, Ecological Studies 58*, pp. 191–213. Springer-Verlag, New York.

Mooney, H. A., S. P. Hamburg, and J. A. Drake, 1986. The invasions of plants and animals into California. In Mooney, H. A., and J. A. Drake (Eds.), *Ecology of Biological Invasions of North America and Hawaii. Ecological Studies 58*, pp. 250–272. Springer-Verlag, N. Y.

Pickford, G. D., 1932. The influence of continued heavy grazing and of promiscuous burning on spring–fall ranges in Utah. *Ecology* 13:159–171.

Robertson, J. H., 1954. Half–century changes on northern Nevada ranges. *J. Range Management* 7:117–121.

Smith, C. W., 1985. Impact of alien plants on Hawaii's native biota. In Stone, C. P., and J. M. Scott (Eds.), *Hawaii's Terrestrial Ecosystems: Preservation and Management*, pp. 180–250. Cooperative Park Studies Unit, University of Hawaii, Honolulu.

Smith, S. D., B. R. Strain, and T. D. Sharkey, 1987. Effects of CO_2 enrichment on four Great Basin grasses. *Functional Ecology* 1:139–143.

Tausch, R. J., and N. E. West, 1988. Differential establishment of pinyon and juniper following fire. *Amer. Midland Naturalist* 119 (1):174–184.

Vitousek, P. M., 1986. Biological invasions and ecosystem properties: Can species make a difference? In Mooney, H. A., and J. A. Drake (Eds.), *Ecology of Biological Invasions of North America and Hawaii. Ecological Studies 58*, pp. 163–175. Springer-Verlag, N. Y.

Watson, S., 1871. *Botany. U.S. Geological Exploration of the Fortieth Parallel*. Vol. 5. Washington, D.C.

West, N. E., and M. A. Hassan, 1985. Recovery of sagebrush-grass vegetation following wildfire. *J. Range Management* 38:131–134.

Young, J. A., and R. A. Evans, 1978. Population dynamics after wildfires in sagebrush grasslands. *J. Range Management* 31:283–289.

Young, J. A., R. A. Evans, and J. Major, 1972. Alien plants in the Great Basin. *J. Range Management* 25:194–201.

Young, J. A., R. A. Evans, and R. A. Weaver, 1976. Estimating potential downy brome competition after wildfires. *J. Range Management* 29:322–325.

Young, J. A., R. A. Evans, and S. Swanson, 1987. Snuff the candles in the desert. *Northern Nevada Native Plant Society Newsletter* 13(1):3–4.

16 Detecting Early Signs of Regional Air Pollution Injury to Coastal Sage Scrub

WALTER E. WESTMAN

Editor's Note: The challenge of proving the effects of air pollution on vegetation has been awkward and frustrating at best, the more awkward as venal interests have pressed ever more insistently for proof of specific causes and evidence that the damage is worth correction.

Walter Westman has addressed this challenge in the coastal region of southern California where the effects of one of the world's most insidious problems with air pollution have been accumulating for decades. He has used an extraordinary combination of techniques including field studies along well-defined gradients of pollution and chamber studies under controlled conditions. The field studies were supplemented with remotely sensed imagery.

The conclusions are classical, powerful, persuasive...and about as specific and definitive as they come: a trend toward impoverishment involves systematic reduction in the vigor of indigenous plants, an increase in the abundance of exotic annuals, an increase in the frequency of fire, and, on slopes, increased erosion including landslides. In parallel with the changes in the structure and successional patterns of the vegetation, Westman shows a series of biochemical changes in plants that include increases in the concentration of nitrogen in tissues after ozone exposure, an increase in the ash content with increasing pollution, and shifts in the chlorophyll content.

Here, in an apparently hardy, drought-resistant vegetation, the patterns of impoverishment become conspicuous when sought systematically and follow patterns similar to those found in other vegetations around the world. The most conspicuous changes are shifts in the composition of the communities, but these shifts are accompanied by measurable changes in the physiology of plants. The patterns of change are generalized patterns and not easily assignable to specific pollutants. The demands for detailed causes of specific changes, even in the biochemistry of plants, seem futile, at least at the moment. Direct measurements of pollutants in the environment, if made routinely, frequently, and reliably seem to offer the most sensitive measure of hazards. Westman shows in persuasive detail how failure to recognize biotic impoverishment as it occurs generates cumulative burdens on society.

323

...He sees that eagle float
For which the intricate Alps are a single nest.
                                            Stevens (1959)

Introduction

The coastal sage scrub is a drought-deciduous, soft-leaved shrubland of
the Mediterranean-climate region of California and northwestern Mexico
(Kirkpatrick and Hutchinson 1977; Westman 1983). Laboratory and field
studies have demonstrated that air pollution damages these native mesophyllous shrublands. Early signs of damage appear as subcellular alterations in
leaf biochemistry. The effect of more severe exposures extends to changes in
the structure of the vegetation (Figure 16.1) and under severe disturbance to
replacement of the shrubs by exotic annuals.

Experimental fumigation of the dominant species of the community with
ozone produces a series of changes in leaves (including increase in leaf
nitrogen, in chlorophyll a and b, and lignin) and a decline in carotenoids.
The same patterns appear when the species are exposed to ozone and sulfur
dioxide in combination. In addition, foliar sulfur increases under higher
sulfur dioxide exposures. In the Santa Monica Mountains in Los Angeles,
across a pollution gradient, these species exhibit the same trends in leaf
chemistry observed in plants exposed to combinations of pollutants in
chambers. A major mechanism for these changes may be premature senescence of leaves, and pollution-induced water stress, followed by leaf drop.
Dramatic increases in leaf drop were observed under fumigation. Increased
leaf loss was also observed in a coastal sage community downwind from a
point source of sulfur dioxide. In some sage species sulfur dioxide causes
stomates to remain open, aggravating water loss and leaf loss in these drought-
deciduous species. Visible leaf damage symptoms observed in fumigation
chambers also increased in intensity along the pollution gradient in the field.

Where dominant shrubs lose leaves or die out, the herbaceous understory
increases, particularly in the abundance of exotic annual grasses. One grass,
Bromus rubens, has evolved a pollution-tolerant strain downwind of industrial
pollution in less than 25 years. In the Riverside–San Bernardino basin,
which collects pollutants blown inland from Los Angeles, the richness of
native species has declined, and exotic annuals have increased. This pattern
can also be seen in the shifting patterns of herbaceous succession after fire in
the inland basin, a pattern initiated by grazing but possibly exacerbated by
the gradual exhaustion of root reserves in perennial shrubs and herbs
exposed to continual leaf loss due to air pollution. With the exhaustion of
root stores, resprouting after fire is weakened. Some species fail to resprout

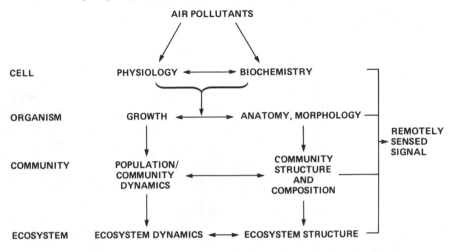

Figure 16.1. The sequence of changes in function (second column) and structure (third column) of plants at higher levels of organization due to gaseous pollutants. All structural features (third column) contribute to the reflected radiation signal from the remotely sensed scene.

altogether, changing the postfire floristic succession on a regional scale. Changes in leaf chemistry, anatomy, moisture content, canopy structure and species composition are all potentially measurable by airborne sensors. Efforts to detect changes caused by air pollution in coastal sage scrub by use of both the Thematic Mapper (LANDSAT) and a prototype sensor (the Airborne Imaging Spectrometer) have yielded insights into the conditions under which remote detection of vegetative stress could be feasible.

The Coastal Sage Community: Experiments with Air Pollution

Effects on Biochemistry

Among dominant shrubs of the highly variable coastal sage community are *Salvia mellifera, Rhus laurina, Encelia californica, Eriogonum cinereum,* and *Artemisia californica.* K. P. Preston, L. B. Weeks, and I exposed populations of these five species – along with four other shrub species and an exotic grass, *Bromus rubens* – to ozone and sulfur dioxide, alone and in combination. We conducted the experiment in open-topped forced-draft fumigation chambers at the Statewide Air Pollution Research Center facility in Riverside, California.[1]

Changes in the concentrations of nutrients in leaves of two of the species as exposure to pollutants increased appear in Figure 16.2, and correlations of nutrient changes with dose for five shrub species combined are shown in

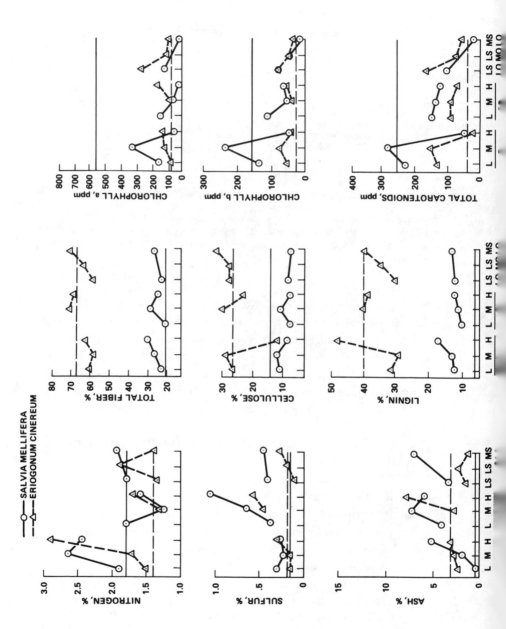

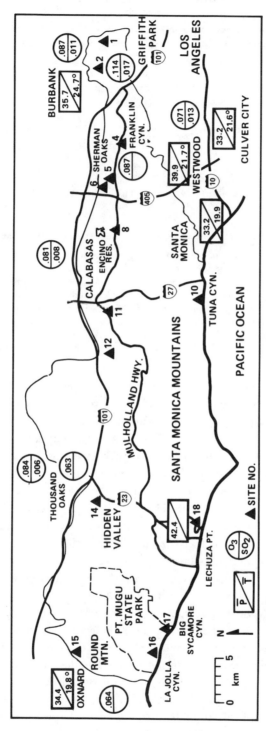

Figure 16.2. Changes in nutrient concentration of standing foliar crop in *Salvia mellifera* and *Eriogonum cinerum* at the end of 10 weeks of fumigation with pollutant treatments (see note 1 for concentrations). Control plants were growth in filtered-air chambers. In the case of *Salvia mellifera*, inadequate material was available from the control; leaves from *Salvia mellifera* growing in a clean-air area (Mt. Diablo, east of San Francisco) in December, 1985 are shown for control values. Horizontal lines show control levels.

Figure 16.3. Location of field study sites (triangles) in the Santa Monica Mountains, southwestern Los Angeles County. Circles show annual means of daily maximum hourly pollutant concentrations, ppm, for 1985 (California. Air Resources Board. 1986), except for the discontinued monitoring site at Mt. Lee in Griffith Park, where data are annual means during 1978–1982. Boxes show mean annual precipitation (cm) and temperature (°C) for U.S. Weather Bureau stations during 1950–1970. (Reprinted with permission from *Photogrammetric Engineering and Remote Sensing*, Copyright 1988 by the American Society for Photogrammetry and Remote Sensing; W. Westman and C. Price, "Detecting Air Pollution Stress in Southern California Vegetation Using LANDSAT Thematic Mapper Band Data," 54(9):1,305.)

Table 16.1. *Correlations* (r) *of foliar nutrient contents of five coastal sage species*

	$O_3{}^a$	$SO_2{}^b$	$O_3 + SO_2{}^c$	field gradient (W-E)^f
Total nitrogen	0.54^e	−0.09	0.29	0.18+
Total sulfur	−0.26	0.62^e	0.47^e	0.16
Chlorophyll *a*	0.11	−0.04	0.03	0.19+
Chlorophyll *b*	0.14	0.02	0.12	0.14
Chlorophyll *a/b*	−0.11	−0.03	−0.11	0.00
Total carotenoids	−0.22	−0.22	−0.40^d	−0.04
Total fiber	0.09	0.03	0.09	0.26^h
Cellulose	−0.12	0.05	−0.03	0.16
Lignin	0.25	−0.04	0.14	0.28^h
Ash	0.06	0.20	0.25	0.17

$^{a-c}$ Correlations of foliar nutrient contents with increasing pollutant dose for standing crop of foliage of five coastal sage species after 10 weeks of fumigation. ^{d} P < .05 ^{e} P < .01; n = 39. Of the 50 species–treatment combinations, eleven are missing due to insufficient sample material. ^{f} Correlations of foliar nutrient contents of four of the five coastal sage species from the Santa Monica Mountains with field site number, from east to west (see Fig. 16.3). Correlation signs have been reversed to show positive correlations with increasing pollution dose from west to east. + P < .10 ^{g} P < .05 ^{h} P < .01; n = 84. The fifth fumigated species, *Eriogonum cinereum*, is excluded here because it did not occur at the eastern end of the field gradient.

Table 16.1. Total nitrogen increased highly significantly with increasing ozone dose; other trends indicated an increase in chlorophyll *a* and *b*, a decline in the chlorophyll *a/b* ratio and total carotenoids, and an increase in lignin, ash, and total fiber, but these differences were not significant. Under sulfur dioxide treatment, total sulfur increased highly significantly. There was a non-significant decline in carotenoids and increase in ash. When ozone and sulfur dioxide were present together at low or moderate levels, the rise in sulfur and decline in carotenoids were both significant; there was also a tendency for nitrogen, chlorophyll *a* and *b*, and lignin to increase, and for the chlorophyll *a/b* ratio in leaves to decline. Of the other essential and trace elements, phosphorus, potassium, and lead increased under ozone doses (r = 0.30, 0.35, 0.30, respectively; n = 39; P < .05), and nickel increased significantly under sulfur treatment, alone or in combination with ozone (r = 0.41, 0.33, respectively; n = 39; P < .05).

The accumulation of sulfur in leaves under treatment with sulfur dioxide has been widely observed; young active leaves generally accumulate more sulfur than older leaves (Guderian 1977). The decline in the chlorophyll *a/b* ratio is also reported under both sulfur dioxide (Malhotra 1977) and ozone (Knudsen, Tibbetts, and Edwards 1977) treatments, although generally the absolute levels of chlorophyll also decline (Beckerson and Hofstra 1979; Malhotra and Kahn 1984). An increase in total nitrogen under ozone treatment is less widely reported. Tingey, Fites, and Wickliff (1973) report an increase in protein content of the N-fixing of *Glycine max* after a 24-hour exposure to ozone, but protein content in other species declined significantly under ozone treatment (Ting and Mukerji 1971; Constantinidou and Kozlowski 1979). Little is known of changes in total fiber, lignin, or other elements under such treatment.[2]

Field Trends

In April 1986, I sampled 14 sites of coastal sage scrub along an east–west pollution gradient in the Santa Monica Mountains of coastal Los Angeles County (Figure 16.3). The principal pollutant of concern in this region was ozone, which in 1985 reached 0.39 ppm (one hour maximum) at the eastern end of the gradient versus 0.18 ppm at the western end. Annual means of the daily maximum hourly values were 0.11 at the eastern end, versus 0.06 at the western end (Figure 16.3) (Cal. Air Res. Bd. 1986). Sulfur dioxide values are lower, with 0.02–0.04 ppm (highest hourly maxima) and 0.006–0.017 ppm annual averages of the daily maximum hourly values during 1985. Most pollutants tended to have higher concentrations on the northern side of the Santa Monica Mountains, facing the San Fernando Valley, than on the coastal side. Preliminary sampling indicated a more coastal distribution for sulfate than for nitrate in fog (Unger 1984). Suspended sulfates averaged 4–7 $\mu g/m^3$, and suspended nitrates averaged 10–14 $\mu g/m^3$ (annual geometric mean, 1985) over the eastern Santa Monica Mountains (Cal. Air Res. Bd. 1986). Nitrogen deposition has reached significant levels in the region. Ammonium and nitrate deposition on chaparral at inland chaparral sites in Santa Barbara and San Diego Counties have been estimated at 1.5–2.0 kg/ha/yr (Schlesinger, Gray, and Gilliam 1982; Ellis, Verfaillie, and Kummerow 1983); at the more polluted San Dimas Experimental Forest in eastern Los Angeles County, Riggan, Lockwood, and Lopez (1985) have reported nitrate deposition in precipitation at 8 kg/ha/yr, and throughfall in chaparral at 23 kg/ha/yr, a portion of which is referable to dry deposition.

Foliage of *Salvia mellifera*, *Artemisia californica*, *Rhus laurina*, and *Encelia californica* was collected from the study sites and analyzed for nutrients in the same way as for the fumigated samples. Correlations of the nutrient values with site number are shown in Table 16.1; site numbers increase from most-polluted (eastern) to least-polluted (western) sites. Correlations were weak, in part because of species-specific differences in nutrient content. Correlations were stronger when sampling was repeated, by leaf age and species, in 1987 (Westman and Malanson 1990). In the case of ash, peak levels occurred in the central portion of the gradient. Nevertheless, the trends were in the same direction as in the combined-pollutant treatments in the fumigation chamber: nitrogen, chlorophyll *a* and *b*, and sulfur rose toward

Table 16.2. *Loadings of foliar nutrients of four coastal sage species in the Santa Monica Mountains on the first two principal components (after varimax rotation)*

	Component 1	Component 2
Chlorophyll *a*	0.925	−0.117
Total nitrogen	0.876	−0.151
Total sulfur	0.856	−0.140
Chlorophyll *b*	0.792	−0.156
Total fiber	−0.263	0.940
Cellulose	−0.172	0.860
Lignin	−0.327	0.781
Ash	0.141	0.600
Total carotenoids	−0.312	0.411

the polluted end of the gradient, as did lignin and total fiber[3] (Table 16.2, Figure 16.4.).

The biochemical data currently are most consistent with the hypothesis that ozone, with or without additional pollutants such as sulfur dioxide, induces premature senescence which leads to accelerated leaf drop and water stress in the coastal sage dominants; secondary thickening of cell walls may also result from the pollution-induced water stress or accelerated aging.

Physiology

Although no physiological work has been conducted on the effects of ozone on coastal sage shrubs, some work on the effects of sulfur dioxide on stomatal conductance has been performed on *Salvia mellifera*. Winner (1981), working with leaf cuvettes in an environmental chamber, found that conductance and photosynthetic rates in Salvia increased within the first three hours of exposure to 0.1 or 0.2 ppm of sulfur dioxide, before declining. This relationship suggests that temporary peaks in sulfur dioxide could damage Salvia through indirect effects on increasing water loss through leaves.

Preston (1980, 1988) studied the growth of a *Salvia mellifera*-dominated sage-scrub community on coastal dunes downwind of a 25-year-old source of sulfur dioxide, an oil refinery/chemical complex, at Nipomo Mesa on the coast of California. He compared growth to a matched control site 40 km upwind. Mean maximum daytime ground-level concentrations occurred 1670 ± 250 m downwind and averaged 0.09 ± 0.08 ppm based on atmospheric modeling; under extremely unfavorable atmospheric conditions, which occur for about 0.7% of the year, maximum ground-level concentrations may reach 0.33 ppm. In 1985, maximum hourly concentrations of sulfur dioxide reached 0.35 ppm twice (Cal. Air Res. Bd. 1986).

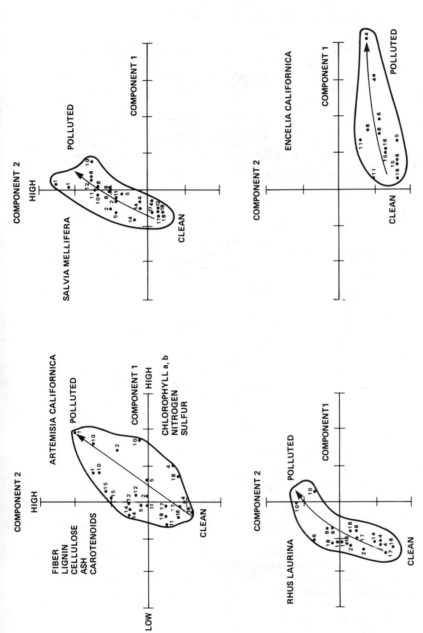

Figure 16.4. Factors scores for four sage species on the first two principal components of foliar nutrient concentration variation (see note 3). Labels on data points correspond to site numbers in Figure 16.3.

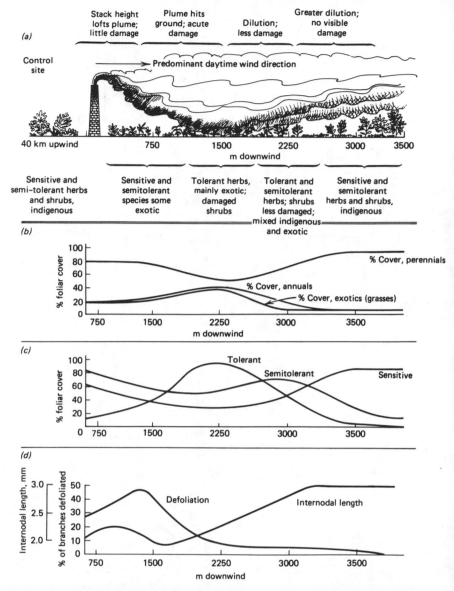

Figure 16.5. Community-level effects of chronic sulfur dioxide exposure to a coastal sage community on Nipomo Mesa, CA, dominated by *Salvia mellifera*. (a) Diagrammatic view of vegetation changes downwind of the refinery stack plume; (b) Changes in foliar cover at the site of perennials (both shrubs and herbs), annuals, and exotics (all grasses). The major exotic was a sulfur-dioxide-tolerant strain of annual bromegrass, *Bromus rubens*. All curves fit polynomial regression with $r^2 = 0.82$, $p = .01$; (c) Changes in cover of the twenty-one most widespread species, downwind. (d) Changes in branch defoliation and internodal length in *Salvia mellifera*. Curves in (c) and (d) fit by polynomial regression. (Data from Preston 1980, used with author's permission; figures a–c reproduced from Westman, 1985b, *Ecology, Impact Assessment, and Environmental Planning*, p. 285, with permission of John Wiley and Sons, Inc., copyright 1985.)

Preston found that stomatal conductance of Salvia on the polluted site was significantly (P < .05) greater than on the control site, and the mean transpiration rate on the polluted site was 38% higher. Salvia exhibited severe defoliation, with up to 45% more leafless branches compared to control sites. The pattern of defoliation corresponded to the pollution gradient (Figure 16.5d). By contrast, *Eriogonum parvifolium,* another mesophyllous shrub on the site, showed significantly higher stomatal resistance, and no adverse effects on foliar cover at locations adjacent to damaged Salvia plants (Preston 1980, 1988). The increases in leaf drop in the sulfur dioxide-sensitive Salvia may have been induced through accelerated water loss in this drought-deciduous species.

Morphology

Preston (1986) measured morphological changes in the sage shrubs under the fumigation described above. For all five shrub species there was a tendency to increase lateral branching, at least under low ozone and medium and high sulfur dioxide. Internodal lengths were reduced (except in *Rhus laurina*) under all treatments. Branch lengths and diameters were also reduced, except in Rhus and under low pollutant levels in Eriogonum.

Visual foliar damage increased in intensity during the fumigation (Westman et al. 1985). Forty percent of these symptoms, mostly characteristic of ozone damage, were also recognized in a survey of the same sage species at five sites across the pollution gradient in the Santa Monica Mountains. The intensity of the most common symptom on each species generally increased toward the polluted end of the gradient (Westman 1985a).

On the central California coast site of sulfur dioxide pollution, Preston (1980, 1988) observed a marked reduction in internodal length in *Salvia mellifera* relative to the control site (P < .01). Internodal length reached its nadir at the point of maximum ground-level pollution (Figure 16.5d). Salvia leaves on the control site were significantly thicker (P < .01) than on the polluted site. A similar correlation occurred in the fumigation chambers (Preston 1986).

Growth

Preston (1986) and Weeks (1987) reported extensively on the results of above- and belowground biomass changes under fumigation treatment in the sage species. All shrub species exhibited significant depressions in aboveground biomass production, and marked increases in leaf drop, even under the lowest ozone level (Preston 1986). Medium or high levels of sulfur dioxide were generally required to observe comparable effects. The most dramatic increases in leaf drop were seen in Rhus (8-, 60-, and 80-fold increases under low, medium, and high ozone relative to the control); the mean increases ($\pm$ S.E.) in leaf drop for the other four shrub species under low, medium, and high ozone were 3.1 $\pm$ 1.4, 3.6 $\pm$ 0.7, and 4.4 $\pm$ 0.6 fold, respectively; the effects of all but the low-ozone treatments were significantly different from the control (P < .05). Root mass was not significantly reduced by sulfur dioxide treatment except under high ozone levels, in three of the five species (Artemisia, Eriogonum, Rhus) (Weeks 1987).

The pattern of growth under stress from pollution favored shoot production, especially leaves, over root growth, but all growth was reduced and the new growth did not replace the losses. By the end of ten weeks, the shift generally resulted in significantly reduced shoot/root ratios (P < .05). This change was true of Eriogonum under high ozone, Salvia under medium and high ozone and under low and medium sulfur dioxide, Rhus under medium and high ozone and under medium sulfur dioxide, and Encelia under all ozone levels and under medium and high sulfur dioxide. Reductions in Artemisia were not significant (Preston 1986; Weeks 1987).

Total aboveground production, including leaf drop, was reduced relative to the control, though species differed in extent of sensitivity. Sensitivity to ozone, measured by reductions in total aboveground production, were, in decreasing order of sensitivity, Salvia = Encelia > Eriogonum > Rhus = Artemisia. For sulfur dioxide, the order was Salvia > Eriogonum = Encelia > Rhus > Artemisia (Preston 1986). For belowground production declines, sensitivity to ozone declined in the order Eriogonum > Artemisia = Encelia = Rhus > Salvia; to sulfur dioxide, Artemisia = Rhus > Encelia = Eriogonum = Salvia. Salvia root mass was significantly increased above control levels under low and medium sulfur dioxide; the root mass of Encelia was stimulated under low ozone (Weeks 1987). Since mean annual daily maximum hourly levels of ozone exceed the low-ozone fumigation treatment at the eastern end of the pollution gradient in the Santa Monica Mountains, it is reasonable to look for ozone-induced growth reductions in the field.

Structure and Composition of the Shrub Community

Some of the changes in community structure that occurred downwind of the sulfur dioxide source on Nipomo Mesa are shown in Figures 16.5b and c. As the canopy of perennial shrubs (mostly *Salvia mellifera*) thinned due to accelerated leaf loss, the herbaceous cover increased. In the upwind control site, annuals comprised only 3% of the cover, and there were no exotic species. By contrast, at the point of maximum pollution downwind, the cover of annuals reached 40%. The majority of the annual cover was contributed by *Bromus rubens,* an introduced grass from the Mediterranean.

Annuals are favored over perennials under chronic stress in part because of their ability to complete their life cycle quickly, and avoid stress during part of the year by seed dormancy (Westman 1985b, p. 290). Perennials, by contrast, are dependent on root reserves for regrowth in subsequent years. As seen in the fumigation trials, under chronic pollution stress root reserves can be depleted, ultimately reducing root mass and aboveground mass. In addition, by virtue of their short generation times, individuals with greater genetic resistance to the pollutant can increase more rapidly in a stressed population, relative to species that may take longer to reach sexual maturity. Further, the small size of the annual herbs permits a higher population density and number within the stressed region from which resistant strains can be selected.

Seedlings grown from brome seed collected at the Nipomo Mesa (refinery) site were exposed to fumigation with ozone and sulfur dioxide by the methods described earlier, along with seedlings grown from seeds of brome growing near Site 18 in the relatively clean air of the western Santa Monica Mountains (Figure 16.3). Plants from the clean-air population showed significantly greater growth reductions under all pollution treatments than did the refinery population (Westman et al. 1985; Preston 1986). Indeed, except under high-ozone treatment, the refinery population showed higher shoot and root mass under pollution exposure than in filtered air.

A partial explanation for these results lies in stomatal behavior. In both the clean-air and refinery populations, stomatal conductance decreased when the plants were exposed to ozone or sulfur dioxide (Westman et al. 1985; Preston 1986). In the refinery population, however, stomatal conductance was reduced by a substantially greater amount than in the clean-air population (0.3 vs. 4.1 fold reductions in conductance relative to filtered air under high sulfur dioxide in the clean-air and refinery populations, respectively; 5.8 vs. 9.5 fold reductions under medium ozone). A preexisting trait in the population, which imparts a mechanism for avoiding pollutant absorption, appears to have been selected for under the influence of 25 years of exposure to sulfur dioxide. How ozone achieves stomatal closure even better than sulfur dioxide in these populations is not known. Further, the mechanisms responsible for growth stimulation under pollutant exposure in the refinery population are unknown, although Preston (1986) suggests reduced water stress, sulfur fertilization, and/or hormonal stimulation as hypotheses to be explored. The relatively rapid evolution of pollution-resistant strains of grass under sulfur dioxide exposure has been reported before (Bell 1985).

In a survey of floristic variation in 67 coastal sage-scrub sites throughout its range, Westman (1979) noted a significant reduction in the percentage of foliar cover of native species in the Riverside–San Bernardino basin relative to other regions (75% vs. 98–125%) (Westman 1983). At the same time the cover of annuals increased (46% vs. 4–13%; Westman 1983), as did the cover of exotic species (36% vs. 3–12%). Westman had surveyed 43 habitat variables of climate, soil fertility, topography, and disturbance (fire, grazing, air pollution) at these sites. The mean annual concentration of oxidants was the variable most closely linked with the decline in native cover in the data set, using path analysis (Westman 1979). Semilog plots of species abundance (based on foliar cover) were used to compare 11 clean-air sites with 11 floristically comparable sites of high pollution load. Species richness was reduced and concentration of dominance was increased on the polluted-air sites (Westman 1979).

Westman later added 32 sites that were in comparably dry but less polluted areas to determine whether climatic or other factors could explain the observed patterns (Westman 1983). Although the Riverside basin is periodically grazed, the cover of exotic species there exceeded that on more heavily grazed island samples (36% vs. 19%) (Westman 1983); the same was true for annuals (46% vs. 20%). The shrub cover in the Riverside group (59%) was also lower than in drier sage groups to the southwest (Diegan type, 85%) (Westman 1983). The results of the expanded field survey are consistent with the hypothesis that pollution loads in the Riverside basin contribute to the decline in native shrub cover and to the increase in annuals, especially exotic grasses, in the region; patterns of diversity in relation to precipitation suggest that the Riverside basin could support a higher shrub cover. The Riverside basin does experience higher summer temperatures, however, so that increased evapotranspirative stress cannot be ruled out as a factor influencing the reduction in native perennial shrub cover.

The regional patterns of change in community structure in the Riverside basin are similar to those at the Nipomo Mesa site, where a point source of pollution was present. In both areas, the native cover of coastal sage shrubs declined and the percentage cover contributed by annual and exotic species increased.

Population and Community Dynamics

In addition to the compensatory response of short-lived herbs to the decline in shrub foliar cover under stress, as discussed above, pollution stress can directly affect the reproductive potential of dominant shrub species. The number of flowering stems as a percentage of control was reduced under all levels of sulfur dioxide treatment in fumigation chambers for *Salvia mellifera* and under medium and high levels of sulfur dioxide in *Artemisia californica* and

Encelia californica (Westman et al. 1985; Preston 1986). When biomass of floral parts was measured for *Salvia mellifera*, biomass was again significantly reduced (P < .05) under all sulfur dioxide treatments, and under medium and high levels of ozone. Preston (1980) observed a reduction in the number of flower whorls per flowering stem in *Salvia mellifera* at the Nipomo Mesa site relative to the control (*t*-test, P < .01).

Interaction with Fire

Fires occur repeatedly in these Mediterranean-type shrublands. Coastal sage scrub in the Santa Monica Mountains, for example, experienced a mean fire-return frequency of 20 years during 1930–1978 (Westman 1982). Using a simulation model based on life-history characteristics of the dominant sage-scrub species, derived from field data in the western Santa Monica Mountains, Malanson (1984) has shown that the composition of the sage-scrub canopy is critically influenced by fire interval. Community composition is also highly dependent on the ability of sage dominants to resprout continually from root crowns in the absence of fire (Malanson and Westman 1985). Pollution stress can affect both fire interval and the resprouting ability of sage shrubs, with and without fire.

The effect of fumigation treatments on sage shrubs was to reduce total aboveground production and to increase leaf production and leaf drop as a percentage of the total aboveground production (Preston 1986; Weeks 1987). The net effect of this shift at the ecosystem level would be to increase litter fall and reduce aboveground standing crop of shrubs. The increase in dead fuel could be expected to increase the frequency of fires at the site. According to the simulation model (Malanson 1984), a reduction in fire interval from 20 years to 10 years, over a 200-year period, would result in a decline in the foliar cover of all five dominants studied (*Salvia mellifera, S. leucophylla, Encelia californica, Eriogonum cinereum, Artemisia californica*), and an eventual loss of two of them. A dominant shrub species would be eliminated from the ecosystem after only one 10-year and two 20-year fire cycles but would persist through three fire cycles of intervals of 30 or 40 years (Westman and O'Leary 1986). The two species eventually eliminated from the system after 200 years of 10-year fire frequency are the two inherently weakest resprouters after fire: *Artemisia californica* and *Salvia mellifera*.

Pollution stress also affects resprouting directly. Under fumigation with high sulfur dioxide levels, the number of basal sprouts increased significantly (P < .05) in *Salvia mellifera, Artemisia californica*, and *Encelia californica; S. mellifera* responded similarly to high-ozone treatment (Westman et al. 1985; Preston 1986). This continual resprouting in the absence of fire would help to maintain the position of these species in the canopy in the short term (Malanson and Westman 1985). After fire, however, resprouting is dependent on root-starch reserves. High levels of ozone under fumigation treatment were capable of reducing root mass in some species, including *Artemisia californica,* an inherently weak resprouter after fire. The evidence suggests that a species like Artemisia would be particularly vulnerable under chronic ozone pollution, the indirect effects of which are to increase fire interval and reduce the capacity to resprout following fire.

The effect of chronic stress on resprouting of shrubs applies equally to perennial herbs dependent on root reserves for resprouting following defoliation. O'Leary and Westman (1988) compared the succession of the herb flora in the first five years after fire in four coastal sage sites in the western Santa Monica Mountains to that in four sites in the Riverside–San Bernardino basin. They found that sites subjected to intermittent grazing (all sites inland and one coastal site) had lost all perennial grass species except for a trace at the grazed coastal site. The cover of annuals, including especially the exotic grass, *Bromus rubens,* increased on these sites. Three of the four inland sites also exhibited a marked reduction in shrub resprouting, resulting in a net rise in herb cover during the early postfire years (Westman and O'Leary 1986).

While these results can be explained by the greater occurrence of inherently weakly reprouting shrubs inland and the existence of intermittent grazing pressure, chronic pollution stress could be acting to accentuate each of these. By the latter hypothesis, higher pollution (especially with ozone) inland weakens postfire resprouting of shrubs, enhancing herb growth. In the herb stratum, perennial grasses would be inhibited due to weakened root reserves and would be replaced by more resistant annual grasses, including the exotic annual *Bromus rubens.*

Soil Erosion and Nutrient Losses

To the extent that chronic pollution results in reduction in plant biomass, increased erosion of soil and nutrients can be expected. Although coastal sage once occupied both flat and sloping terrain in southern California, most of the coastal sage not already cleared for urbanization is on steep slopes susceptible both to surface erosion and mass movement. A reduction in foliar cover would be expected to result in reduced interception of rainfall by the canopy, increased surface runoff, and soil nutrient losses. At the same time, reductions in foliar cover would also reduce evapotranspiration. The latter could increase percolation of soil water to slip surfaces in underlying strata of the typically fractured bedrock of the region, adding to mudslide potential.

Increased fire frequency, due to accelerated leaf drop, would also lead to more circumstances in which winter storms erode bare soil, further accentuating surface erosion, mudslides, and nutrient losses. While the coastal sage has existed in a fire–flood cycle throughout the period of Mediterranean climate in the region, the implications of additional stress from chronic pollution are an acceleration of the fire–flood cycle, leading to impoverishment of the soil and of the plant communities dependent upon it. While studies of increased erosion in chaparral subject to biomass reduction have been conducted on the San Dimas Experimental Watershed in eastern Los Angeles County (Rice, Corbett, and Bailey 1969), no studies of erosion from coastal sage-scrub watersheds in clean and polluted sites have been published to date.

Detection of Air Pollution Injury by Remote Sensing

As in any epidemiological study, it is difficult to assign causal weights within a multivariate and interactive web of causation.

Nevertheless, mechanisms of potential injury have been demonstrated under fumigation-chamber conditions at pollutant levels occurring in the field; many of the same symptoms observed under fumigation treatment have been observed along pollution gradients both from point and regional pollution sources; regional field studies have highlighted ozone as an important predictor of community structure among multiple environmental and stress factors; and regional patterns of community structure and function, including succession, are consistent with the broad pattern of retrogression expected under chronic pollution stress. This pattern includes increased leaf drop, with associated changes in mean canopy chemistry, and a decline of native sage shrub cover and concomitant rise in annuals, including exotic grasses and pollution resistant species. In this final section, I review recent efforts to detect these changes remotely.

Efforts to detect pollution stress in vegetation by remote sensing have involved both the use of broad-banded optical sensors such as LANDSAT Thematic Mapper and narrow-banded optical sensors such as the Airborne Imaging Spectrometer (AIS). The latter is an experimental sensor, developed at the Jet Propulsion Laboratory, that is capable of sensing reflectance in the 900–2,400 nm region in relatively narrow wavebands (9.3 nm) with high ground resolution (8m × 8m pixels). Experimental work with laboratory and field-portable sensors has helped to differentiate the contributions of leaf moisture content, anatomy, pigment content, and leaf area index to reflectance of radiation from pollution-stressed plants (Westman and Price 1988a).

The potential to detect pollution-induced chemical differences in coastal sage scrub by analysis of reflectance spectra with narrow wavebands has been explored using laboratory, field-portable, and airborne (AIS) sensors. Detection of differences in leaf chemistry using laboratory spectrophotometers and dried ground-leaf materials of sage species has been demonstrated (Westman and Price 1987). The detection of such chemical differences in intact foliage of sage plants in the field or from aircraft has not been achieved to date (Price and Westman 1987). Some early efforts to detect chemical changes in forest canopies have recently been reported by Wessman et al. (1988). Much additional research with larger sample sizes will be needed before the potential for detection of leaf-chemical differences in vegetation canopies is fully assessed.

At the same time, progress is being made in understanding the potential for and limitations of detecting pollution-induced morphological changes in plant canopies from satellites. Westman and Price (1988b) obtained aircraft-based imagery simulating the characteristics of LANDSAT Thematic Mapper (TM) satellite images over the Santa Monica Mountains in 1985 (Westman and Price 1988b). Trends of change in spectral reflectance in coastal sage scrub along the pollution gradient in the mountains were examined to determine whether they were consistent with changes expected due to the increase in foliar damage symptoms along the gradient. Results indicated that the structural composition of coastal sage communities changed along the gradient from west to east (warmer, more polluted end; Figure 16.3). The coastal sage canopy becomes less continuous toward the east, and evergreen chaparral shrubs and native and exotic grasses and forbs occur in the gaps. These compositional changes are sufficient to obscure spectral effects from the relatively subtle foliar damage symptoms on the sage shrubs themselves (Westman and Price 1988b). LANDSAT TM imagery with a spatial resolution of about 30 m is more likely to be able to detect pollution-induced vegetation damage when major structural damage to a formerly closed-canopied vegetation is involved (dead trees and upper branches). Vogelmann and Rock (1986) have demonstrated such an application in the Camel's Hump area of Vermont, where dieback of red spruce has occurred.

In the Santa Monica Mountains, the use of the simulated LANDSAT imagery, along with field study, enabled an overview of structural and floristic variation in coastal sage scrub to be obtained. If pollution-induced changes to community structure, vigor, and composition were to occur in future years, quantitative analysis of LANDSAT images over time could prove useful and cost effective in monitoring such changes.

Acknowledgments

Unpublished data reported here were obtained with the support of the Division of Environmental Biology, National Science Foundation (DEB-7681712); the Land

Processes Branch, Earth Sciences Division, National Aeronautics and Space Administration (NASA) (677–21–35–08); and the Biospheric Research Section, Life Science Division, NASA (199–30–72–02). The manuscript was prepared while I held a National Research Council Research Associateship at NASA Ames Research Center. I thank Curtis Price for research assistance, and R. Thompson and G. Kats of the Statewide Air Pollution Research Center at Riverside for their cooperation during fumigation experiments.

Notes

1. In each chamber, we exposed five individuals of each species to low, medium, or high levels of ozone (0.1, 0.2, or 0.4 ppm), sulfur dioxide (0.05, 0.2, or 0.5 ppm), or low-low or low-medium combinations of the two pollutants. We replicated each chamber treatment twice, and exposed the plants for 40 hrs/wk for ten weeks. The two control chambers contained charcoal-filtered air. The plants were well watered, and fertilized with a complete Hoagland's solution except for phosphorus, which was kept in trace amounts so as not to suppress the growth of vascular-arbuscular mycorrhizae. The one-year-old seedlings were grown in one-gallon pots in native soil, which provided phosphorus at field levels (Westman et al. 1985; Preston 1986).

   The leaves present on the branches at the end of ten weeks were harvested, rinsed in deionized water, oven-dried, and analyzed for chemical content. A suite of essential elements were analyzed by optical emission spectrometry at the Laboratory of Biomedical and Environmental Sciences, UCLA (Alexander and McAnulty 1981); cellulose, lignin, and residual ash (together constituting total fiber) were analyzed by sequential acid digestion at the Agricultural Experiment Station laboratory at the University of Alaska, Palmer; total nitrogen was analyzed by the Kjeldahl method by the Plant and Soil Laboratory, Santa Clara; and chlorophyll *a* and *b*, and total carotenoids were analyzed from absorption values at 645, 662, and 470 nm at UCLA (Wellburn and Lichtenthaler 1982; Lichtenthaler and Wellburn 1983).

2. One hypothesis to explain the rise in nitrogen and chlorophyll contents of the leaves under ozone treatment is that, due to extensive ozone-induced leaf drop, the leaves remaining on the plant at the end of the experiment were mostly young, photosynthetically active, and active in synthesis of protein. The hypothesis is supported by data indicating large increases in leaf drop under higher doses of ozone during the fumigation experiment (see Growth section, pp. 333–334). Whether the enhanced leaf drop was caused by ozone-induced stomatal opening and subsequent moisture stress, or by premature senescence, is not known. It is known that the early-season, large leaves (dolichoblasts) in *Salvia mellifera* have a higher stomatal conductance in clean air than the later-season, small leaves on short axillary shoots (brachyblasts), which are generally the last to fall (Westman et al. 1985). Premature senescence and enhanced leaf drop have also been widely observed in other species under ozone stress (Guderian et al. 1985).

   The leaf-drop hypothesis is further supported by the observation that nitrogen and chlorophyll did not increase as much under sulfur dioxide treatment, and leaf drop under this pollutant was also less (see Growth section, p. 333), so that more old leaves would be included in the total sample.

   The secondary trend toward a rise in lignin and fiber content would not be expected if the leaves remaining on the plants were young and totally healthy. Instead, the rise in these compounds suggests that secondary thickening of cell walls has been hastened by the pollutant stress, perhaps as a speeding of the aging process, or as a response to water stress by increasing turgor pressure from cell walls. Fibers in the central vascular bundles of leaves of *Salvia mellifera* at the polluted end of the gradient showed thicker walls, with less lumenary space and more occlusions, compared to those from the cleaner area of the gradient (Westman, unpublished). The drop in chlorophyll *a/b* ratio in these leaves is also consistent with incipient damage to prematurely aging or water-stressed leaves.

3. To examine whether the nitrogen–chlorophyll–sulfur changes associated with accelerated leaf drop are at all independent of the lignin–fiber changes associated with accelerated maturation or water stress, the species nutrient values along the pollution gradient were subjected to principal components analysis, with orthogonal varimax rotation (Gamma = 1) (BMDP4M, Frane and Jennrich 1983). The first rotated axis accounted for 37% of the total variance in the data set, the second axis for 32%. Loadings of the nutrients on each component are shown in Table 16.2. The first component clearly expressed variation in the "leaf-drop" variables: chlorophyll *a*, *b*, nitrogen, sulfur; the second component expressed variation in cellulose, lignin, and ash (total fiber) – the secondary thickening variables – as well as total carotenoids. Three of the four species showed strong trends of increase in nitrogen, chlorophyll, and sulfur toward the polluted end of the field gradient. Pearson's correlation coefficient (r) between the site number and the factor score on the first component was -0.54 (P $<$ .01) for *Artemisia californica*, -0.42 (P $<$ .05) for *Salvia mellifera*, and -0.70 (P $<$ .01) for *Encelia californica*. Two of the species also showed a significant trend toward increase in cellulose and lignin towards the polluted end of the gradient. Correlations between site number and factor score on the second component were -0.39 (P $<$ .05) for Artemisia and -0.58 (P $<$ .01) for Salvia. Factor scores for the species on the two components are illustrated in Figure 16.4. Site 10, the easternmost coastal site, showed levels of the nutrients more characteristic of highly polluted sites, particularly for Artemisia and Salvia. Whether this is due to pollutant influences in the coastal fog (see, e.g., Waldman et al. 1982; Brewer et al. 1983), or some other factor, is not known.

Alternate hypotheses appear to explain the observed nutrient trends less fully. The increase in nitrogen and sulfur toward the east could be due to increased atmospheric deposition of these two elements as nitrate and sulfate. Atmospheric deposition was uniform in the fumigation trials, where the same increases were observed, however, suggesting that depositional patterns in the field might at most reinforce a preexisting trend. A second possibility is that "younger" leaves might occur at the eastern end due to climatically induced delays in onset of leaf growth. There is no consistent difference in annual rainfall across the gradient (Figure 16.3), nor in time of onset of rains (November), though temperatures are higher at the eastern end. If anything, the warmer temperatures would accelerate growth rates in the east, accentuating the secondary thickening trends, but not the tendency to have a larger proportion of young leaves on the branches. A third possibility is that increased water stress at the eastern end, due to higher evapotranspirative stress resulting from warmer temperatures, would lead to earlier leaf drop. While this hypothesis cannot be ruled out and may indeed accentuate trends later in the season, the samples were collected in early April, at the end of the five-month rainy season, when soil moisture stores are generally at very adequate levels. A fourth possibility is that natural variations in soil fertility explain the patterns. Soil samples at 10 cm depth from three pits at each site were analyzed for ammonium and nitrate, available phosphate (NaOAc extractant), Ca, Mg, pH, and water-holding capacity. Apart from high levels of nitrate, phosphate, and Ca at Site 5 and of Ca at Site 11, no significant variations in levels of these soil variables were observed.

Clearly more data on phenological processes, water stress, and atmospheric deposition patterns across the gradient would be desirable to winnow hypotheses more confidently.

References

Alexander, G. V., and L. T. McAnulty, 1981. Multielement analysis of plant-related tissues and fluids by optical emission spectrometry. *J. Plant Nutrition* 3:51–59.

Beckerson, D. W., and G. Hofstra, 1979. Effect of sulphur dioxide and ozone, singly or in combination, on leaf chlorophyll, RNA and protein in white bean. *Canadian J. Botany* 57:1940–1945.

Bell, J. N. B., 1985. SO_2 effects on the productivity of grass species. In W. E. Winner, H. A. Mooney, and R. A. Goldstein (Eds.), *Sulfur Dioxide and Vegetation. Physiology, Ecology, and Policy Issues*, pp. 209–226. Stanford University Press, Stanford, Calif.

Brewer, R. L., R. J. Gordon, L. S. Shepard, and E. C. Ellis, 1983. Chemistry of mist and fog from the Los Angeles urban area. *Atmos. Environ.* 17:2267–2270.

California Air Resources Board, 1986. *California Air Quality Data. Summary of 1985 Air Quality Data.* Vol. 17. Sacramento, Calif.

Constantinidou, H. A., and T. T. Kozlowski, 1979. Effects of sulfur dioxide and ozone on *Ulmus americana* seedlings, II. Carbohydrates, proteins, and lipids. *Can. J. Bot.* 57:176–184.

Ellis, B. A., J. R. Verfaillie, and J. Kummerow, 1983. Nutrient gain from wet and dry atmospheric deposition and rainfall acidity in southern California chaparral. *Oecologia* 60:118–121.

Frane, J., and R. Jennrich, 1983. Factor analysis. P4M. In W. J. Dixon (Ed.), *Computer Programs. BMDP.* University of California Press. Berkeley.

Guderian, R., 1977. *Air Pollution: Phytotoxicity of Acid Gases and Its Significance in Air Pollution Control.* Ecological Studies 22. Springer-Verlag, Berlin.

Guderian, R., D. T. Tingey, and R. Rabe, 1985. Effects of photochemical oxidants on plants. In R. Guderian (Ed.), *Air Pollution by Photochemical Oxidants. Formation, Transport, Control, and Effects on Plants*, pp. 129–296. Springer-Verlag, Berlin.

Kirkpatrick, J. B., and C. F. Hutchinson, 1977. The community composition of Californian coastal sage scrub. *Vegetatio* 35:21–33.

Knudson, L. L., T. W. Tibbitts, and G. E. Edwards, 1977. Measurement of ozone injury by determination of leaf chlorophyll concentration. *Plant Physiol.* 60:606–608.

Lichtenthaler, H. K., and A. R. Wellburn, 1983. Determination of total carotenoids and chlorophyll a and b of leaf extracts in different solvents. *Biochem. Soc. Trans.* 603:591–592.

Malanson. G. P., 1984. Linked Leslie matrices for the simulation of succession. *Ecol. Modelling* 21:13–20.

Malanson. G. P., and W. E. Westman, 1985. Postfire succession in Californian coastal sage scrub: the role of continual basal sprouting. *Amer. Midl. Nat.* 113:309–318.

Malhotra, S. S., 1977. Effects of aqueous sulphur dioxide on chlorophyll destruction in *Pinus contorta*. *New Phytol.* 78:101–109.

Malhotra, S. S., and A. A. Kahn, 1984. Biochemical and physiological impact of major pollutants. In M. Treshow (Ed.), *Air Pollution and Plant Life*. Wiley, Chichester.

O'Leary, J. F., and W. E. Westman, 1988. Regional disturbance effects on herb succession patterns in California coastal sage scrub. *J. Biogeogr.* 15:775–786.

Preston, K. P., 1980. Effects of sulfur dioxide pollution on coastal sage scrub. M. A. thesis, University of California, Los Angeles.

Preston, K. P., 1986. Ozone and sulfur dioxide effects on the growth of Californian coastal sage scrub species. Ph.D. dissertation, University of California, Los Angeles.

Preston, K. P., 1988. Effects of sulfur dioxide pollution on a Californian coastal sage scrub community. *Environ. Pollution* 51:179–195.

Price, C. V., and W. E. Westman, 1987. Toward detecting California shrubland canopy chemistry with AIS data. In G. Vane (Ed.), *Proc. 3rd Airborne Imaging Spectrometer Data Workshop*, pp. 91–99. Jet Propulsion Laboratory, Calif. Inst. Tech., and NASA. JPL Publ. 87–30, Pasadena, Calif.

Rice, R. M., E. S. Corbett, and R. G. Bailey, 1969. Soil slips related to vegetation, topography, and soil in southern California. *Water Resources Research* 5:647–659.

Riggan, P. J., R. N. Lockwood, and E. N. Lopez, 1985. Deposition and processing of airborne nitrogen pollutants in Mediterranean-type ecosystems of southern California. *Environ. Sci. Tech.* 19:781–789.

Schlesinger, W. H., J. T. Gray, and F. S. Gilliam, 1982. Atmospheric deposition processes and their importance as sources of nutrients in a chaparral ecosystem of southern California. *Water Resources Research* 18:623–629.

Stevens, W., 1959. Connoisseur of Chaos. In S. F. Morse (Ed.), *Poems by Wallace Stevens*, pp. 97–98. Vintage Books, New York.

Ting, I. P., and S. K. Mukerji, 1971. Leaf ontogeny as a factor in susceptibility to ozone: amino-acid and carbohydrate changes during expansion. *Amer. J. Bot.* 58:497–504.

Tingey, D. T., R. C. Fites, and C. Wickliff, 1973. Ozone alteration of nitrate reduction in soybean. *Physiol. Plant.* 29:33–38.

Unger, C. D., 1984. Calif. Air Resources Board internal memo, Jan. 18, 1984, cited in M. C. Shikiya, J. Broadbent, W. Nelson, and T. Taylor, *Acid Deposition in the South Coast Air Basin: An Assessment*. South Coast Air Quality Management District, El Monte, Calif.

Vogelmann, J. E., and B. N. Rock, 1986. Assessing forest decline in coniferous forests of Vermont using NS–001 Thematic Mapper Simulator data. *Int. J. Remote Sens.* 7:1303–1321.

Waldman, J. M., J. W. Munger, D. J. Jacob, R. C. Flagan, J. J. Morgan, and M. R. Hoffman, 1982. Chemical composition of acid fog. *Science* 218:677–680.

Weeks, L. B., 1987. Effects of ozone and sulfur dioxide on the belowground growth of

Californian coastal sage scrub. M. A. thesis, University of California, Los Angeles.

Wellburn, A. R., and H. K. Lichtenhaler, 1982. Program to calculate the amounts of chlorophyll a and b and total carotenoids from spectral values of plant extracts in different solvents. *Biochem. Microcomp. Users Gr. Newsletter* 7:22–25.

Wessman, C., J. Aber, D. L. Peterson, and J. Melillo, 1988. Remote sensing of canopy chemistry and nitrogen cycling in temperate forest ecosystems. *Nature* 335:154–156.

Westman, W. E., 1979. Oxidant effects on Californian coastal sage scrub. *Science* 205:1001–1003.

Westman, W. E., 1982. Coastal sage scrub succession. In *Proc. Intl. Symp. Dynamics and Management of Mediterranean-Type Ecosystems*, pp. 91–99. U.S. Forest Service, Pacific S.W. Forest Range Expt. Sta. Gen. Tech. Rep. PSW–58, Berkeley, Calif.

Westman, W. E., 1983. Xeric Mediterranean-type shrubland associations of Alta and Baja California and the community/continuum debate. *Vegetatio* 52:3–19.

Westman, W. E., 1985a. Air pollution injury to coastal sage in the Santa Monica Mountains, southern California. *Water, Air, and Soil Pollution* 26:19–41.

Westman, W. E., 1985b. *Ecology, Impact Assessment, and Environmental Planning.* Wiley-Interscience, New York.

Westman, W. E., and G. P. Malanson, 1990. Effects of climatic change on Mediterranean-type ecosystems in California and Baja California. In R. L. Peters and T. Lovejoy (Eds.), *Consequences of the Greenhouse Effect for Biological Diversity.* Yale University Press, New Haven.

Westman, W. E., and J. F. O'Leary, 1986. Measures of resilience: the response of coastal sage scrub to fire. *Vegetatio* 65:179–189.

Westman, W. E., K. P. Preston, and L. B. Weeks, 1985. Sulfur dioxide effects on the growth of native plants. In W. E. Winner, H. A. Mooney, and R. A. Goldstein (Eds.), *Sulfur Dioxide and Vegetation–Physiology, Ecology, and Policy Issues*, pp. 264–280. Stanford University Press, Stanford, Calif.

Westman, W. E., and C. V. Price, 1987. Remote detection of air pollution stress to vegetation: laboratory-level studies. In *Remote Sensing: Understanding the Earth as a System.* Vol. 1, pp. 451–456. Proc. Intl. Geoscience and Remote Sensing Symp., IEEE, New York.

Westman, W. E., and C. V. Price, 1988a. Spectral changes in conifers subjected to air pollution and water stress: experimental studies. *IEEE Trans. Geoscience and Remote Sensing* 26:11–21.

Westman, W. E., and C. V. Price, 1988b. Detecting air pollution stress in southern California vegetation using LANDSAT Thematic Mapper band data. *Photogr. Engr. Remote Sens.* 54:1305–1311.

Winner, W. E., 1981. The effect of SO_2 on photosynthesis and stomatal behavior of Mediterranean-climate shrubs. In N. S. Margaris and H. A. Mooney (Eds.), *Components of Productivity of Mediterranean-climate Regions: Basic and Applied Aspects*, pp. 91–103. Junk, The Hague.

17   Arctic Ecosystems: Patterns of Change in Response to Disturbance

L. C. BLISS

Editor's Note: The Arctic with its limited flora and fauna, its extremes of climate, its indigenous people, its ties to montane habitats of lower latitudes, and its uncertain history has always captured the interest of ecologists. The landscape, despite the vicissitudes of climate and the long months of darkness and frost, is a living landscape, a tightly integrated community, not open to easy invasion by exotics, its living systems strangely immune to disease. It is vulnerable, but disruption, when it comes, can be severe: "thermal karst erosion" is the phrase the specialists use to describe the destruction that occurs as the surface albedo drops and the sun melts the ground that is usually frozen. A trickle of water becomes an erosive force, transforming the tundra into a slurry of mud and eroding peat.

Efforts at stabilizing landscapes disturbed by human activities, building plant successions where none exists, have met with limited success. Massive efforts at introducing exotics have, fortunately, failed. The arctic ecosystems are closed corporations, not open to outsiders. Bliss shows that plant succession as recognized in lower-latitude communities is weakly developed, in some circumstances non-existent. But the communities are surprisingly resilient . . . to the point where the erosion starts. Once it starts, there is no cure in time of interest to this generation . . . or the next.

Bliss, who has devoted a career to the Arctic, has written comprehensively and sensitively about arctic ecosystems. He sees no mitigating circumstance in a rapid warming and no effective countermeasure.

Introduction

Extensive disturbance of the arctic tundra in North America by humans has been limited to the last 150 years. The most severe disturbances have been since World War II through exploration for petroleum. Responses, however, are slow in the Arctic, and there has been little time to appraise the effects of disturbance.

Theory in ecology also offers limited insights. Tundra ecosystems are usually considered "unstable" or "fragile" by comparison with temperate zone and tropical systems. Theory holds that low species richness allows greater oscillation of populations (MacArthur 1955), that systems with less

347

complex food webs and simpler avenues for energy flow are also less stable (Odum 1969), and that the ratio of gross production to biomass (*P/B*) is high in these less stable systems (Odum 1969). Strong seasonal climatic oscillations (Banfield 1975), slow growth rates for many species, and the role of ice-rich permafrost (Bliss 1970; Bliss et al. 1973) are additional factors that are thought to contribute to ecosystem instability in the Arctic. Dunbar (1970) added a further complication. He maintained that arctic systems are "immature" in an evolutionary sense due to the lack of maturity in soils rather than to low temperature alone. Tundra and taiga are youthful in that they have occupied their respective landscapes for only 2,000 to 10,000 years. As ecosystems, however, they have endured recent millennia with little change, while great changes occurred in the eastern deciduous forests of North America (Davis 1975), in deserts of the southwestern United States (Spaulding, Leopold, and Van Devender 1983), and elsewhere in normally more "stable" systems. Concepts of the stability of ecosystems are changing as we learn more about the Holocene, about recent Pleistocene shifts in dominant species, and as we consider the potential effects of rapid climatic change.

Stability and fragility have been used differently in referring to ecosystems. I shall use "stability" to describe the ability of an ecosystem to return to a steady state after disturbance and "fragility" to describe the ease with which it can be modified or destroyed by disturbance.

This chapter summarizes what we have learned over the past two decades about the stability of arctic ecosystems in response to short-term or acute disturbance, and it attempts to predict the consequences of global chronic disturbances.

Species Richness

Arctic ecosystems, both aquatic and terrestrial, contain few species compared to those of most temperate zone and tropical areas. Yet there is little evidence that these systems, in spite of limited species richness, are less stable than others. Fish species in northern Alaska, northern Yukon Territory, and the Mackenzie River Delta region number 20 to 22. In the Queen Elizabeth Islands and Greenland there are only 3 species and most lakes contain only arctic char. Richness of the crustacean fauna shows a similar pattern with 21 species in lakes at Cape Thompson (Hilliard and Tash 1966) and 9 species in ponds at Barrow (Stross, Miller, and Daley 1980). Lakes in the Queen Elizabeth Islands contain only 1 to 4 species (Stewart and MacDonald 1982; Stewart and Bernier 1983). Metabolism of these lacustrine ecosystems is slow but stable from year to year (Welch 1974;

Minns 1977; Hobbie 1980). Fish grow slowly but growth is limited more by low water temperature and nutrients than by invertebrate species richness or oscillations in their abundance.

Terrestrial ecosystems are also characterized by limited numbers of species. In most Low- and High-Arctic ecosystems there is one dominant species of lemming, and there may be one or two large herbivores. The populations of herbivores fluctuate greatly, but the number of species remains constant. Summary data for Barrow show oscillations from <1 to 155 animals/ha over seven years and <1 to 7 animals/ha on Devon Island over five years (Batzli 1981). When lemming populations are high at Barrow, the vegetation can be severely overgrazed resulting in the depression of primary production for that summer. Normally, grazing increases average primary production because the clipped material decomposes rapidly, releasing nutrients which are added to those released from animal urine and feces (Batzli 1981). The population density of microtines has a profound influence on certain predators. When lemming populations are low the numbers of fox, jaegers, and snowy owls are greatly reduced. Populations of caribou and musk-ox also fluctuate but their impact on plant cover and primary production is generally minor. These herbivores seldom harvest more than 1–3% of the available standing crop (live plus dead material). At these levels of herbivore utilization there is little impact on ecosystem stability. Although small- and large-mammal populations fluctuate year to year, their overall impact on ecosystem stability is limited.

There is a similar pattern in the number of vascular plant species which dominate most terrestrial ecosystems in both the Low and High Arctic with a significant northward reduction in their numbers and cover (Table 17.1). The most productive arctic ecosystems often have 2 to 4 species contributing 60 to 80% of the vascular plant production. This relationship is seldom true for the cryptogams, where species richness is much greater and productivity is broadly shared. The limited data available indicate that net primary production changes very little from year to year, although degree-days may vary 200–300% (Bliss 1977). If dominant plant species are removed by disease or other perturbation, the effect on herbivores could be devastating. *Carex stans* and *Salix arctica* comprise the bulk of food consumed by musk-ox (Hubert 1977). *Salix arctica* is also the major food source for arctic hare and ptarmigan. The distribution pattern for mammals in the High Arctic is closely correlated to that of the plant communities in which these species predominate. Collared lemming feed almost exclusively on *Salix arctica*, *Dryas integrifolia*, and *Saxifraga oppositifolia* (Fuller et al. 1977). At Barrow the brown lemming feed upon graminoids and mosses, again a diet of limited species (Batzli 1981). Caribou also graze selectively. Sedges and willows are

Table 17.1. *Species richness and plant cover for select locations from the Canadian Low Arctic (69°N) and the High Arctic (72–78°N). All data mean of 3, 50 × 50 m plots*

Location	Community	Number vascular species	Plant cover (%)		
			Vascular	Lichens	Mosses
Tuktoyaktuk 69°N					
Upland	low shrub–heath	29	92	13	38
Wetland	sedge meadow	20	67	0	7
Banks Island 72°N					
Upland	cushion plant–lichen	17	42	12	0
Wetland	sedge meadow	25	76	0	22
Melville Island 75°N					
Upland	cushion plant–lichen	16	20	52	5
Cornwallis Island 75°N					
Upland	cushion plant	13	2	0.5	0.1
	polar barren	5	1	0	0.1
Wetland	grass meadow	17	38	0	48
Devon Island 76°N					
Upland	cushion plant–lichen	17	57	25	11
	polar barren	5	0.6	1	0.1
Wetland	sedge–moss meadow	13	60	0	28
King Christian Island 78°N					
Upland	cryptogam–herb	11	11	63	13
Ellef Ringnes Island 78°N					
Upland	cryptogam–herb	10	9	3	3
	polar barren	4	2	0	0
Wetland	grass meadow	2	12	0	75

important forage plants in heath–tussock tundra and sedges are the major food plants in wet graminoid–moss tundra (White et al. 1981). The implications of these plant/animal links indicate that the elimination of one or more dominant species could result in profound changes in the structure and function of arctic ecosystems, especially those of the High Arctic. In this sense these systems are fragile. However, at the present time these systems remain stable.

Tundra Fires

Fires are common in the boreal forest and often in the forest-tundra transition. High Arctic ecosystems are not subject to fires because of their

Figure 17.1. Tundra fire (right side) resulting from clean-up of a well site (center photo). Note the grass seeded on mineral soils at the camp site; Mackenzie Delta region southwest of Tuktoyaktuk, NWT, Canada.

very low fuel load and the near absence of electrical storms in summer. Soviet scientists have long recognized that forest-tundra is often converted to shrub-tundra following fire, hence their reference to these landscapes as subarctic tundra. Tree seedlings of *Picea mariana* are eliminated unless the first three to six years following a fire are unusually warm and moist (Black and Bliss 1980).

Fires in the forest-tundra transition received little attention until the 1970s, when expanded activities in the north increased the frequency of wildfires. Because of discontinuities in plant cover, reduced fuel loads, and water-saturated peats in many areas (Wein and Bliss 1973a) (Figure 17.1), such fires generally cover less than 25 km². Fires result in the removal of litter and standing crop, darken and therefore warm soil surfaces, increase the depth of the active layer 30% to 50%, and release nutrients. Plant recovery following fire is rapid in low shrub and cottongrass. In tundra that supports dwarf-shrub heath rapid recovery from fire is due to the resprouting of shrubs and, in some sites, seedlings of *Eriophorum vaginatum*, *Carex bigelowii*, *Arctagrostis latifolia*, and *Calamagrostis canadensis* (Bliss and Wein 1972; Wein and Bliss 1973a; Racine 1981; Racine et al. 1983). Seed-bank size plays a critical role especially in tussock tundra (McGraw 1980). At sites in northwestern Canada and Alaska (Wein and Bliss 1973a) aboveground net production was 50–115% of controls in only one to two years after burning. Thirteen years after a fire at Elliott, Alaska, net aboveground production was 145% that of controls, although species composition was somewhat different (Fetcher et al. 1984).

The higher nutrient content of species within cottongrass-dwarf-shrub heath tundra results from the nutrient release following a burn, with resulting deeper thaw, warmer soils, and increased microbiological activity. Tundra and forest-tundra systems are "leaky." Loss of N and P were occurring six years after the Inuvik, Northwest Territory, fire (McLean et al. 1983). From these studies and observations, tundra ecosystems of the Low Arctic are not fragile in terms of fire. Rates of recovery of grasses, cottongrass, dwarf-heath shrubs, and taller (30–100 cm) birch and willow shrubs are rapid and there are seldom long-term impacts that result in habitat degradation unless the conversion of forest tundra to shrub tundra and the slow recovery of lichens following a burn of heath-lichen tundra are considered degradation.

Surface Disturbance

A major concern with regard to petroleum and other resource development in the Low Arctic is the melting of permafrost and the revegetation of abandoned sites, roads, and borrow pits. Because of its insulative properties, the peat layer is the most significant deterrent to permafrost melt and the development of thermokarst topography (karstlike topography resulting from melting of ground-ice and subsequent subsidence). There has been considerable research in Alaska (Johnson 1981) and in the Mackenzie River Delta region in Canada (Younkin 1976; Younkin and Martens 1985) to reduce the effects of surface disturbance and to speed recovery. Experiments in seeding with fertilizer have proven successful in providing a vegetation cover but not in preventing the melting of ice-rich permafrost where the peat layer is thin or has been removed. Disruption of the surface by summer roads (Figure 17.2), seismic activity, and the use of track vehicles (Klein 1970; Hernandez 1973) has been reduced by limiting off-road activity to winter and the use of temporary roads constructed in winter of snow and ice (Adam and Hermandez 1977; Bliss 1983). Word models have been developed to depict the relationship between removal of vegetation, permafrost melt, and revegetation that leads to a new thermal equilibrium (Figure 17.3).

There is less potential for thermokarst development in the High Arctic because permafrost temperatures are lower and ice content is generally less (Babb and Bliss 1974). Gully erosion can be a serious problem where there is

Figure 17.2. Use of track vehicles in summer to carry supplies to a gas blowout well site in 1970, Melville Island, NWT, Canada.

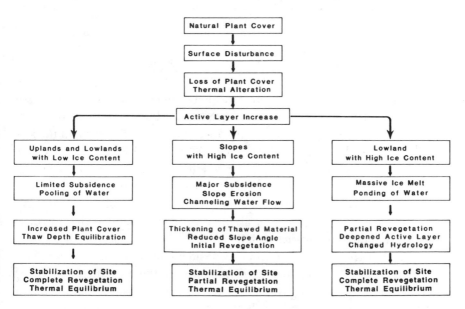

Fig 17.3. Word model of the relationships between vegetation removal, permafrost melt, reestablishment of vegetation, and the establishment of a new thermal equilibrium in upland sites. Based upon flow chart of Lawson (1986).

Figure 17.4. Gully erosion resulting from melting snow that was piled near camp the previous winter. Erosion of this kind is more common in the High Arctic where surface peats are non-existent except in graminoid–moss meadows; King Christian Island, NWT, Canada.

no surface peat layer. Snow piled up due to ploughing of airstrips and camps with resulting spring melt and erosion along minor ruts from vehicles can result in sizable gullies within one to three years (Figure 17.4). In the High Arctic terrain restoration is difficult because of the lack of gravel and the loss of soil volume with summer melt (French 1980). Establishing a plant cover is difficult due to slow rates of plant growth and the limited numbers of indigenous species that can be used in revegetation (Bliss 1978; Bliss and Grulke 1988). Of the species examined that show promise, all are graminoids. *Phippsia algida* produces abundant seedlings, and their growth is excellent in more nutrient-rich upland sites. *Alopecurus alpinus* produces little or no seed but growth from rhizomes is considerable in uplands. *Carex stans* is equally capable of rhizomatous development in wetlands. Experiments over ten years show that seeding with non-native species is unsuccessful (Younkin and Martens 1985; Bliss and Grulke 1988).

Other Surface Perturbations

Rehabilitation of the tundra after diesel fuel and crude oil spills is best accomplished by using absorbants and, in winter, by light burning. Studies

Figure 17.5. Gravel haul road (Dalton Highway) and adjacent Alyeska Pipeland and access gravel work pad just north of the Brooks Range, Alaska.

at Prudhoe Bay and near Inuvik, Northwest Territories, have shown that graminoids in wet sites are more tolerant of petroleum than the lichens, mosses, and vascular plants of upland sites (Wein and Bliss 1973b; Walker et al. 1978). These studies show that wet sedge-moss vegetation recovers to near normal in one to three years, and upland tussock-shrub tundra in five to ten years. *Picea mariana* trees often die one to three years after a spill from secondary effects. The seeding of native species with fertilizer has been quite successful (McKendrick and Mitchell 1978). Trampling saturated soils during a summer cleanup can do as much damage as the petroleum products themselves.

In the Arctic, gravel roads, provided they are thick enough, prevent permafrost melt and subsidence, but they produce side effects. Road dust from the Dalton Highway (Alyeska Pipeline Haul Road) is high in Ca, which, over time, may reduce or eliminate acidophylic species of moss. This could have implications for the insulation provided by mosses. The impact of dust on higher plants appears less problematic with the exception of the dwarf shrub *Cassiope tetragona* (Everett 1980). Crossroad drainage becomes a problem when culverts fill with gravel or with ice in winter. Water moving parallel to roads and increased flow from culverts can result in combined thermal and hydraulic erosion that can lead to thermokarst topography (Berg 1980).

A detailed mapping study of three areas within the Prudhoe Bay Oil Field from 1968 through 1983 has shown that the cumulative effects of roads and gravel pads for wells and camps has resulted in blocked drainages in this flat landscape (Walker et al. 1987). This has resulted in flooding 9% of the mapped area and 3% of the total area of the field (500 km^2). Thermokarst occupied 1% of the mapped area. These findings, while significant, are quite small compared with potential levels of flooding and thermokarst that might have occurred had not stringent regulations been developed prior to and during construction of the collecting system, roads, and well drilling. In spite of these problems it is generally accepted that the Prudhoe Bay Oil Field, its collecting system, the camps, and the pipeline corridors have been constructed and maintained in an environmentally acceptable manner (Figure 17.5), as presented by Alexander and Van Cleve (1983) in their review of the pipeline, the Alyeska Project, and petroleum exploration in the Mackenzie River Delta Region. Utilization of detailed ecological information during the development of industrial plans can help locate the least damaging routing of roads, pipelines, and the positioning of work camps, towns, and industrial facilities.

Acid Precipitation

Because polar regions are dominated by high-pressure systems with cold, dry, settling air masses, intrusion of low-pressure storm systems with potential loads of pollutants is limited. Should power stations that utilize high-sulfur oil or coal be built in the north, acid precipitation could result in limited areas. This would have major effects on the lichen component of many tundra plant communities and on the aquatic resources of lakes. Barren-ground and Peary caribou are dependent upon lichens for a major part of their winter diet. There is no indication that this will become a problem in the next several decades, but sites near power stations in arctic villages and sites of industrial development need to be monitored to assess the long-term impacts of stack emissions on lichens.

Plant Succession and Ruderal Species

In contrast with temperate and tropical regions, where plant succession has been studied intensively, few studies of succession have been conducted in the Arctic (Churchill and Hanson 1958). Nearly 30 years passed before this subject was examined again in detail (Arctic Alpine Research 1987, whole No. 4). The classical concept of directional replacement of species in succession seldom holds in the Arctic (Muller 1952; Churchill and Hanson 1958;

Svoboda and Henry 1987; Bliss 1988). Within these temperature-, water-, and nutrient-limited environments, few species are pioneers (*r*-selected). Shifts in the importance of species over time are more important than replacement of species through competition or facilitation. Succession appears to be directional but without replacement of species in many Low Arctic and polar semidesert environments; it is nondirectional in the most stressful polar deserts (Svoboda and Henry 1987). The classical model of directional replacement succession occurs on river gravels and older adjacent river terraces (Bliss and Cantlon 1957; Gill 1973) and on sand dunes (Peterson and Billings 1980) in the Low Arctic. Replacement or facilitation is an important phenomenon in the western islands of the Canadian Arctic Archipelago, where most species of vascular plants become established on moss and lichen mats rather than on bare soil (Sohlberg and Bliss 1984).

There are very few ruderal (*r*-selected) species in the Arctic; selective forces favor slow-growing, long-lived species. Since human-induced, surface disturbance is a recent phenomenon in the North American Arctic, there has been little time available for the selection of weedy species from the indigenous flora or from introductions. This is in contrast with the Soviet Arctic and subarctic where human manipulation of the land and the development of pastures has resulted in a larger number of weedy species (Dorogostaiskaya 1972).

In the Low Arctic *Epilobium angustifolium*, *E. latifolium*, *Equisetum arvense*, and *Senico congestus* are important colonizing forb species along with the graminoids *Arctagrostis latifolia*, *Arctophila fulva*, *Carex aquatilis*, *C. bigelowii*, *Eriophorum angustifolium*, *E. vaginatum*, *Juncus balticus*, *Luzula parviflora*, *Poa arctica*, and *P. glauca* and the shrubs *Betula grandulosa*, *Salix alaxensis*, *S. glauca*, and *S. planifolia* (Johnson 1981; Younkin and Martens 1985, 1987; Ebersole 1987; Kershaw and Kershaw 1987). All of these native species are long lived and with the exception of the *Epilobium* species, *Equisetum arvense*, *Senecio congestus*, and *Salix alaxensis*, all are species common to stable lowland or upland communities. Of the introduced grasses used in reseeding surface-disturbed soils, *Festura rubra* (arctared creeping red fescue) has been successful in maintaining populations in northern Alaska and the Mackenzie River Delta region. *Poa pratense* (Nugget Kentucky bluegrass) has maintained populations for 12 years on test plots in the Caribou Hills, east of the Mackenzie River, but appears less successful in northern Alaska (McKendrick 1987; Younkin and Martens 1987).

In the High Arctic there are no true colonizing species, but some species produce large amounts of viable seed and at times seedlings can be abundant. These include *Draba subcapitata*, *D. corymbosa*, *Saxifraga oppositifolia*, *Papaver radicatum*, and *Phippsia algida*. All of these species are long-lived and stress-tolerant, and they occur in rather diverse habitats from polar barrens with 1–2% total cover to mats of cryptogams with scattered vascular plants in the polar semideserts.

There is little indication that annuals or short-lived perennial ruderal species of more temperate regions will be able to invade arctic landscapes and assume the importance that European weeds have throughout much of the United States. The long photoperiod, short growing season, low temperature, and low soil nutrient and water content are strong barriers to the invasion and successful establishment of ruderal species. Should this occur, establishment of species will be most successful along airport runways, roads within villages and industrial sites such as the Prudhoe Bay Oil Field and comparable future sites in the Mackenzie Delta region.

Increase in Carbon Dixoide

Of the major perturbations affecting the Arctic, increased levels of CO_2, which would result in higher temperatures, have the potential for the most profound changes. Analyses of ice cores from Greenland indicate that atmospheric CO_2 concentration was as low as 180 to 200 ppm 18,000 to 15,000 years B.P. and that levels rose rapidly to 250–270 ppm at the end of the last ice age (10,000 years B.P.) (Neftel et al. 1982). There is weak evidence that CO_2 levels were 300–320 ppm near the start of the hypsithermal (8,000 years B.P.) and remained relatively constant until about 1950. In postglacial times the rate of change of CO_2 averaged 0.1 to 0.5 ppm/yr then abruptly increased to 1.5 ppm/yr at Mauna Loa from 1976 to 1982. The CO_2 concentration increased from 315 ppm in 1958 to 343 ppm in 1983. Reduced growth rates in fossil fuel consumption since 1980 may bring significant reduction in the recent rate of CO_2 increase (Gammon, Sundquist, and Fraser 1985).

Over the past 100 years near-surface air temperature has increased 0.5°C globally. Should CO_2 levels rise to 560 to 600 ppm it is estimated that the warming would be sufficient (Manabe and Stouffer 1979) to have profound influences on arctic ecosystems. In recent years there has been considerable laboratory and field research estimating effects on plant growth and carbon reserves.

The circumpolar Arctic covers about 5.6×10^6 km^2 of land or about 4% of the world's land (minus ice caps). The carbon stored in the Arctic is estimated to be 169×10^9 mT or about 11% of the world's carbon (Schlesinger 1979). The San Diego Workshop held in 1980 estimated the total carbon of the Arctic to be 59×10^9 mT or 3% of the world's carbon. Of this total carbon, only 11% is in the standing crop of the vegetation (Bliss et al. 1981). At Barrow, 98% of the organic carbon is in peat and dead organic matter. Net ecosystem production averages 69 $gC/m^2/yr$ (Chapin et al. 1980). On the Truelove Lowland on Devon Island, a comparable wet sedge-moss ecosystem has 96% of the carbon in peat and dead organic matter and a net ecosystem production of only 14 $gC/m^2/yr$ (Bliss 1977).

With the knowledge that increased concentrations of CO_2 will significantly raise mean temperatures in the Arctic, experiments have been performed on individual species and on small ecosystems. When individual species were exposed to short-term increases in CO_2 net photosynthesis increased by as much as 65% in *Eriophorum vaginatum* (Oechel and Strain 1985). Longer-term experiments on intact plants from tussock–dwarf-shrub heath tundra elicited different responses for different species. The evergreen species *Vaccinium vitis-idaea* and *Ledum palustre* showed a 10% decline in canopy photosynthesis while photosynthesis increased 208% in the deciduous shrubs *Vaccinium uliginosum* and *Betula nana*. Photosynthesis increased by 155% in *Eriophorum vaginatum* but declined 78% in *Carex bigelowii* when grown for 22 months at 675 ppm CO_2 (Oechel and Strain 1985).

In another set of experiments *Carex bigelowii*, *Betula nana*, and *Ledum palustre* were grown for three months at either 350 or 675 ppm CO_2 and at two levels of Hoagland's solution (1/60- and 1/8-strength). Biomass doubled in Carex and Betula and increased about 70% in Ledum with nutrient enrichment at both CO_2 levels. CO_2 enrichment alone did not increase leaf, root, or whole-plant growth. Higher nutrition during growth increased photosynthesis in Carex and Ledum, but decreased photosynthesis in Betula. Leaf photosynthesis increased during shoot growth with increased CO_2 concentration in Betula and Ledum. In Carex, photosynthesis decreased at high CO_2 levels and low nutrient levels, but not at high nutrient concentrations (Oberbauer et al. 1986). These data suggest that an enriched CO_2 environment, with or without nutrient limitations, would have little effect on net production of these species in a tussock–dwarf-shrub heath tundra landscape. These differential responses of species to CO_2 concentration and nutrient regime are similar to the growth responses of these same species when temperature, light, and nutrients were manipulated (Chapin and Shaver 1985).

Assuming a CO_2-induced rise in temperature, Billings and his students have studied CO_2 balance of soil cores representing the Barrow sedge-moss tundra. They found that, with a temperature rise of 4° C, the microcosms became a source rather than a sink for CO_2. They also found that lowering the water table 5 cm decreased net system carbon storage (Billings et al. 1982). They postulated that microbial respiration was higher at the higher temperature (8° vs. 4° C). Over time, this would result in a loss of peat and possible thermal erosion of tundra soils high in ice content. In a second set of

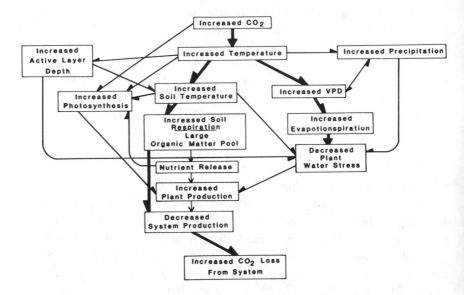

Figure 17.6. Word model of the hypothesized impact of increased atmospheric CO_2 and temperature upon a sedge–moss ecosystem in the Low and High Arctic. The presumed loss of carbon from the system is based upon the research of Billings et al. (1982, 1983, 1984).

experiments they compared net ecosystem CO_2 exchange at 400 vs. 800 ppm CO_2 at 8° C and with a high and low water table. While the results were not significantly different, there was a 48% increase in system carbon gain at the higher level of CO_2 (Billings et al. 1983). They concluded that this increased carbon gain would probably be offset by increased soil respiration resulting from higher temperatures and a lower water table. In a third set of experiments, ammonium nitrate was added to microcosms grown under "normal" and high CO_2 concentrations. They predicted and found that increased nitrogen enhanced leaf area and phytomass. The system gained 300 g CO_2/m^2 at a CO_2 concentration of 400 ppm vs. 412 g CO_2/m^2 at 800 ppm CO_2. In contrast, with no additional nitrogen, the controls were net losers of carbon (Billings et al. 1984).

Field greenhouse experiments in tussock–dwarf-shrub heath tundra at Toolik Lake, Alaska are providing similar results. Gross primary production decreased for the whole ecosystem when exposed to 510 and 680 ppm CO_2. Maximum photosynthetic rates were similar at all CO_2 concentrations, and canopy CO_2 conductance decreased with increasing CO_2 concentrations. This indicates an adjustment of the photosynthetic apparatus to yield comparable maximum rates of photosynthesis at different levels of CO_2 (Oechel and Strain 1985).

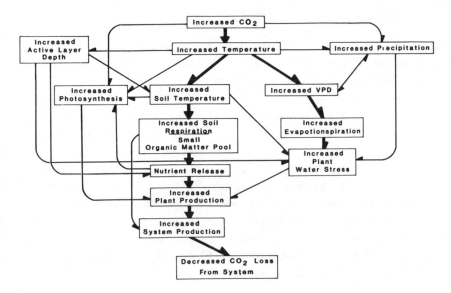

Figure 17.7. Word model of the hypothesized impact of increased atmospheric CO_2 and temperature upon cryptogam–herb and cushion plant ecosystems in the High Arctic. Low soil organic matter and significant temperature rise would result in carbon gain for these systems.

From these experiments it can be concluded that tundra ecosystems are not limited by CO_2 concentration. The impact of increased CO_2 levels will be indirect: higher temperature, greater depth of thaw, increased precipitation, decreased plant water stress, greater release of nutrients from the accelerated rate of peat decomposition, and the potential for thermokarst development with reduced insulation of peat in some ecosystems (Figure 17.6). Although plant production may increase, increased soil respiration from the large organic-matter pool overrides this. Thus system production decreases, and the entire system loses CO_2. In the High Arctic, the low level of organic matter in most ecosystems will result in increased ecosystem production and a decrease in CO_2 loss from the system as the levels of CO_2 and temperature rise (Figure 17.7).

These studies on select species and ecosystems in the Low Arctic tundra of Alaska are providing valuable information on the complex interactions of CO_2-induced changes in temperature, nutrients, and soil-water balance as they influence photosynthetic rates and plant growth. It is too early to predict the full implications of increased concentrations of CO_2 in the Arctic, but we can safely predict that the Arctic, and no doubt large parts of the Taiga, will become sources rather than sinks for CO_2 with a rise in both CO_2 and temperature.

Summary

Although arctic ecosystems have become subject to perturbations only recently, they show some of the same responses as those in more temperate regions. A limited flora and the lack of truly ruderal species result in less dramatic patterns of succession. The time for system recovery, measured in decades, seems little different from that of temperate grasslands and shrublands. If dominant species were lost because of initial low-species richness, many arctic terrestrial and aquatic systems would become vulnerable to changes in structure and function. Maintenance of permafrost is a key factor in the stability of these systems. There is potential for permafrost melt from rising temperature associated with increases in CO_2 levels. This, in addition to potential changes in species composition (loss of evergreen species) resulting from higher temperature, lower soil water levels, and increased decomposition of peat, is likely to be the most serious future environmental problem in the Arctic.

Acknowledgments

Research on which this paper is based has been funded by the Canadian Research Council, Environment Canada, Department of Indian and Northern Affairs, and the National Science Foundation. Logistic and camp support was provided by Polar Continental Shelf Project, Panarctic Oils, Ltd., and The Arctic Institute of North America. All of these agencies are gratefully acknowledged. Many graduate students contributed to the research and discussions on which this chapter is based.

References

Adam, K. M., and H. Hernandez, 1977. Snow and ice roads: ability to support traffic and effects on vegetation. *Arctic* 30:13–27.

Alexander, V., and K. Van Cleve, 1983. The Alaska pipeline: a success story. *Ann. Rev. Ecol. Syst.* 14:443–463.

Babb, T. A., and L. C. Bliss, 1974. Effects of physical disturbance on arctic vegetation in the Queen Elizabeth Islands. *Jour. Appl. Ecol.* 11:549–562.

Banfield, A. W. F., 1975. Are arctic ecosystems really fragile? In J. R. Luick, P. C. Lent, D. R. Klein, and R. G. White (Eds.), *Proceedings First International Reindeer and Caribou Symposium*, pp. 546–551. Biol. Papers Univ. Alaska, Special Rept. No. 1.

Batzli, G. O., 1981. Populations and energetics of small mammals in the tundra ecosystem. In L. C. Bliss, Q. W. Heal, and J. J. Moore (Eds.), *Tundra Ecosystems: A Comparative Analysis*, pp. 377–396. Cambridge University Press.

Berg, R. L., 1980. Road performance and associated investigations. In J. Brown and R. L. Berg (Eds.), *Environmental Engineering and Ecological Baseline Investigations along the Yukon River-Prudhoe Bay Haul Road*, pp. 53–100. U.S. Army Corps of Engineers. CRREL Rept. 80–19. Hanover, N.H.

Billings, W. D., J. O. Luken, D. A. Mortensen, and K. M. Peterson, 1982. Arctic tundra: a source or sink of atmospheric carbon dioxide in a changing environment? *Oecologia* 53:7–11.

Billings, W. D., J. O. Luken, D. A. Mortensen, and K. M. Peterson, 1983. Increasing atmospheric carbon dioxide: possible effects on arctic tundra. *Oecologia* 58:286–289.

Billings, W. D., K. M. Peterson, J. O. Luken, and D. A. Mortensen, 1984. Interaction of increasing atmospheric carbon dioxide and soil nitrogen on the carbon balance of tundra microcosome. *Oecologia* 65:26–29.

Black, R. A., and L. C. Bliss, 1980. Reproductive ecology of *Picea mariana* at treeline near Inuvik, Northwest Territories, Canada. *Ecol. Monogr.* 50:331–354.

Bliss, L. C., 1970. Oil and the ecology of the arctic. *Trans. Royal Soc. Can.* Series 4, 8:361–372.

Bliss, L. C., 1977. General summary, Truelove Lowland ecosystem. In L. C. Bliss (Ed.), *Truelove Lowland, Devon Island, Canada: A High Arctic Ecosystem*, pp. 657–675. University Alberta Press. Edmonton.

Bliss, L. C., 1978. Vegetation and revegetation within permafrost terrain. *Third Int. Conf. Permafrost* 2:31–50. National Research Council Canada, Ottawa.

Bliss, L. C., 1983. Modern human impact in the arctic. In W. Holzner, M. J. A. Werger and Ikuisima (Eds.), *Man's Impact on Vegetation*, pp. 213–225. Junk, Boston.

Bliss, L. C., 1988. Arctic tundra and polar desert biome. In M. G. Barbour and W. D. Billings (Eds.), *North American Terrestrial Vegetation*, pp. 1–32. Cambridge University Press.

Bliss, L. C., and J. E. Cantlon, 1957. Succession on river alluvium in northern Alaska. *Amer. Midl. Nat.* 58:452–469.

Bliss, L. C., G. M. Courtin, D. L. Pattie, R. R. Riewe, D. W. A. Whitfield, and P. Widden, 1973. Arctic tundra ecosystems. *Ann. Rev. Ecol. Syst.* 4:359–399.

Bliss, L. C., and N. E. Grulke, 1988. Revegetation in the High Arctic: its role in reclamation of surface disturbance. In P. Kershaw (Ed.), *Northern Environmental Disturbances*, pp. 43–55. Boreal Institute for Northern Studies, University Alberta, Edmonton.

Bliss, L. C., and R. W. Wein, 1972. Plant community responses to disturbances in the western Canadian Arctic. *Can. Jour. Bot.* 50:1097–1109.

Bliss, L. C., K. R. Everett, P. J. Webber, K. Van Cleve, and L. Viereck, 1981. Current areal extents and carbon contents of northern ecosystem types. In P. C. Miller (Ed.), *Carbon Balance in Northern Ecosystems and the Potential Effect of Carbon Dioxide Induced Climatic Change*, pp. 4–16. Report of Tundra CO_2 Workshop, March 1980, San Diego, Calif. U.S. Dept. Energy, Washington D.C.

Chapin, F. S., P. C. Miller, W. D. Billings, and P. I. Coyne, 1980. Carbon and nutrient budgets and their control in coastal tundra. In J. Brown, P. Miller, L. L. Tieszen, and F. L. Bunnell (Eds.), *An Arctic Ecosystem: The Coastal Tundra at Barrow, Alaska*, pp. 458–482. Dowden, Hutchinson, and Ross, Inc., Stroudsburg, Pa.

Chapin, F. S., and G. R. Shaver, 1985. Individualistic growth response of tundra plant species to environmental manipulation in the field. *Ecology* 66:564–576.

Churchill, E. D., and H. C. Hanson, 1958. The concept of climax in arctic and alpine vegetation. *Bot. Rev.* 24:127–191.

Davis, M., 1975. Pleistocene biogeography of temperate deciduous forests. *Geo-science and Man* 13:13–26.

Dorogostaiskaya, E. V., 1972. *Weeds of the Far North of the U.S.S.R.* Leningrad Sci. Pub. House, Leningrad.

Dunbar, M. J., 1970. The scientific importance of the circumpolar region and its flora and fauna. In W. A. Fuller and P. G. Kevan (Eds.), *Productivity and Conservation in Northern Circumpolar Lands,* pp. 71–77. IUCN New Ser. No. 16. Morges, Switzerland.

Ebersole, J. J., 1987. Short-term vegetation recovery at an Alaskan arctic coastal plain site. *Arct. Alp. Res.* 19:442–450.

Everett, K. R., 1980. Distribution and properties of road dust along the northern portion of the haul road. In J. Brown and R. L. Berg (Eds.), *Environmental Engineering and Ecological Baseline Investigations along the Yukon River-Prudhoe Bay Haul Road,* pp. 101–128. U.S. Army Corps of Engineers. CRREL Rept. 80–19. Hanover, N.H.

Fetcher, N., T. F. Beatly, B. Mullinax, and D. W. Winkler, 1984. Changes in arctic tussock tundra thirteen years after fire. *Ecology* 65:1332–1333.

French, H. M., 1980. Terrain, land use and waste drilling fluid disposal problems, arctic Canada. *Arctic* 33:794–806.

Fuller, W. A., A. M. Martell, R. F. C. Smith, and S. W. Speller, 1977. Biology and secondary production of *Dicrostonyx groenlandicus* on Treelove Lowland. In L. C. Bliss (Ed.), *Truelove Lowland, Devon Island, Canada: A High Arctic Ecosystem,* pp. 437–459. University Alberta Press, Edmonton.

Gammon, R. H., E. T. Sundquist, and P. J. Fraser, 1985. History of carbon dioxide in the atmosphere. In J. R. Trebalka (Ed.), *Atmospheric Carbon Dioxide and the Global Carbon Cycle,* pp. 25–62. DOE/ER–O239. U.S. Dept. Energy, Washington D.C.

Gill, D., 1973. Floristics of a plant succession sequence in the Mackenzie Delta, Northwest Territories. *Polarforschung* 43:55–65.

Hernandez, H., 1973. Natural plant recolonization of superficial disturbances, Tuktoyaktuk Peninsula region, N.W.T. *Can. Jour. Bot.* 51:2177–2196.

Hilliard, D. K., and J. C. Tash, 1966. Freshwater algae and zooplankton. In N. J. Wilimovsky, and J. N. Wolfe (Eds.), *Environment of the Cape Thompson Region, Alaska,* pp. 343–413. U.S. Atomic Energy Comm., U.S. Dept. Commerce, Springfield, Va.

Hobbie, J. E., 1980. Major findings. In J. E. Hobbie (Ed.), *Limnology of Tundra Ponds,* pp. 1–8. Dowden, Hutchinson, and Ross, Inc., Stroudsburg, Pa.

Hubert, B., 1977. Estimated productivity of muskox on Truelove Lowland, In L. C. Bliss (Ed.), *Truelove Lowland, Devon Island, Canada: A High Arctic Ecosystem,* pp. 467–491. University Alberta Press, Edmonton.

Johnson, L. A., 1981. *Revegetation and selected terrain disturbances along the Trans-Alaska pipeline.* U.S. Army Corps of Engineers. CRREL Rept. 81–12. Hanover, N.H.

Kershaw, G. P., and L. J. Kershaw, 1987. Successful plant colonizers on disturbances in tundra areas of northwestern Canada. *Arct. Alp. Res.* 19:451–460.

Klein, D. R., 1970. The impact of oil development in Alaska. In W. A. Fuller and P. G. Kevan (Eds.), *Productivity and Conservation in Northern Circumpolar Lands,* pp. 202–242. IUCN New Ser. No. 16. Morges, Switzerland.

Lawson, D. E., 1986. Response of permafrost terrain to disturbance: a synthesis of observations from northern Alaska, U.S.A. *Arct. Alp. Res.* 18:1–17.

MacArthur, R. H., 1955. Fluctuations of animal populations and a measure of community stability. *Ecology* 36:533–536.

MacLean, D. F., S. J. Woodley, M. G. Weber, and R. W. Wein, 1983. Fire and nutrient cycling. In R. W. Wein and D. A. MacLean (Eds.), *The Role of Fire in Northern Circumpolar Ecosystems*, pp. 111–132. Wiley, Toronto.

McGraw, J. B., 1980. Seed bank size and distribution of seeds in cottongrass tussock tundra, Eagle Creek, Alaska. *Can. J. Bot.* 58:1607–1611.

McKendrick, J. D., 1987. Plant succession on disturbed sites, North Slope, Alaska, U.S.A. *Arct. Alp. Res.* 19:554–565.

McKendrick, J. D., and W. M. Mitchell, 1978. Fertilizing and seeding oil-damaged arctic tundra to effect vegetation recovery Prudhoe Bay, Alaska. *Arctic* 31:296–304.

Manabe, S., R. T. Wetherald, 1975. The effects of doubling the CO_2 concentration on the climate of a general circulation model. *Jour. Atmos. Sci.* 32:3–15.

Minns, C.K., 1977. Limnology of some lakes on Truelove Lowland. In L. C. Bliss (Ed.), *Truelove Lowland, Devon Island, Canada: A High Arctic Ecosystem*, pp. 569–585. University of Alberta Press, Edmonton.

Muller, C. H., 1952. Plant succession in arctic heath and tundra in northern Scandinavia. *Bull. Torrey Bot. Club.* 79:296–309.

Neftel, A. F., F. Oeschger, H. Schwander, J. Stauffer, and R. Zumbrunn, 1982. Ice core measurements give atmospheric CO_2 content during the past 40,000 years. *Nature* 295:220–223.

Oberbauer, S. F., N. Sionit, S. J. Hastings, and W. C. Oechel, 1986. Effects of CO_2 enrichment and nutrition on growth, photosynthesis, and nutrient concentrations of Alaskan tundra plant species. *Can. J. Bot.* 64:2993–2998.

Odum, E. P., 1969. The strategy of ecosystem development. *Science* 164:262–270.

Oechel, W. C., and B. R. Strain, 1985. Native species responses to increased atmospheric carbon dioxide concentration. In B. R. Strain and J. C. Cure (Eds.), *Direct Effects of Increasing Carbon Dioxide on Vegetation*, pp. 117–154. DOE/ER–0238. U.S. Dept. Energy, Washington D.C.

Peterson, K. M., and W. D. Billings, 1980. Tundra vegetation patterns and succession in relation to microtopography near Atkasook, Alaska. *Arct. Alp. Res.* 12:473–482.

Racine, C. H., 1981. Tundra fire effects on soils and three plant communities along a hill-slope gradient in the Seward Peninsula, Alaska. *Arctic* 34:71–84.

Racine, C. H., W. A. Patterson, and J. G. Dennis, 1983. Permafrost thaw associated with tundra fires in northwest Alaska. In *Permafrost: Fourth International Conference, Proceedings*, pp. 1024–1029. Nat. Acad. Sciences, Washington D.C.

Schlesinger, W., 1979. The world carbon pool in soil organic matter: a source of atmospheric CO_2. In G. M. Woodwell (Ed.), *The Role of Terrestrial Vegetation in the Global Carbon Cycle: Methods for Appraising Changes*. Wiley, New York.

Sohlberg, E. H., and L. C. Bliss, 1984. Microscale pattern of vascular plant distribution in two high arctic plant communities. *Can. J. Bot.* 62:2033–2042.

Spaulding, W. G., E. B. Leopold, and T. R. Van Devender, 1983. The Late Wisconsin paleoecology of the North American southwest. In S. C. Porter (Ed.), *The Late Pleistocene Environments of the United States*, pp. 259–293. University of Minnesota Press, Minneapolis.

Stewart, D. B., and L. M. J. Bernier, 1983. *An aquatic survey of islands bordering Viscount Melville Sound, District of Franklin, Northwest Territories*. Background Rept. No. 2, Lands Directorate Env. Can. and Northern Env. Branch, Ottawa.

Stewart, D. B., and G. MacDonald, 1982. *An aquatic resource survey of Devon, Cornwallis, Somerset, and Northern Baffin islands, District of Franklin, Northwest Territories. 1980.* Env.

Studies No. 20. Indian Affairs and Northern Development, Ottawa.

Stross, R. G., M. C. Miller, and R. J. Daley, 1980. Zooplankton. In J. E. Hobbie (Ed.), *Limnology of Tundra Ponds*, pp. 251–296. Dowden, Hutchinson, and Ross, Inc., Stroudsburg, Pa.

Svoboda, J., and G. H. R. Henry, 1987. Succession in marginal arctic environments. *Arct. Alp. Res.* 19:373–384.

Walker, D. A., P. J. Webber, E. F. Binnian, K. R. Everett, N. D. Lederer, E. A. Nordstrand and M. D. Walker, 1987. Cumulative impacts of oil fields on northern Alaskan Landscapes. *Science* 238:757–761.

Walker, D. A., P. J. Webber, K. R. Everett, and J. Brown, 1978. Effects of crude and diesel oil spills on plant communities at Prudhoe Bay, Alaska and the derivation of oil spill sensitivity maps. *Arctic* 31:242–259.

Wein, R. W., and L. C. Bliss, 1973a. Changes in arctic *Eriophorum* tussock communities following fire. *Arct. Alp. Res.* 6:261–274.

Wein, R. W., and L. C. Bliss, 1973b. Experimental crude oil spills on arctic plant communities. *Jour. Appl. Ecol.* 10:671–682.

Welch, H. E., 1974. Metabolic rates of arctic lakes. *Limnol. Oceanogr.* 19:65–73.

White, R. G., F. L. Bunnell, E. Goare, T. Skogland, and B. Hubert, 1981. Ungulates on arctic ranges. In L. C. Bliss, O. W. Heal and J. J. Moore (Eds.), *Tundra Ecosystems: A Comparative Analysis*, pp. 397–483. Cambridge University Press.

Younkin, W. E. (Ed.), 1976. *Revegetation in the northern Mackenzie River Valley region.* Arctic Gas Biol. Ser. Vol. 38. Can. Arctic Gas Study Ltd., Calgary.

Younkin, W. E., and H. Martens, 1985. *Evaluation of selected reclamation studies in Northern Canada.* Rept. to Dept. Indian and Northern Affairs, Northern Environmental Protection Branch. Yellowknife, N. W. T., Canada. DSS File: 19SV.A7135-4-0027.

Younkin, W. E., and H. Martens, 1987. Long-term success of seeded species and their influence on native species invasion at abandoned rig site A-201 Caribou Hills, N.W.T., Canada. *Arct. Alp. Res.* 19:566–571.

Chronic Disturbance and Natural Ecosystems: Aquatic and Emergent Ecosystems

A. MARINE SYSTEMS

18 Changes in a Red Sea Coral Community Structure: A Long-Term Case History Study

Y. LOYA

Editor's Note: Occasionally a circumstance arises in nature that, treated imaginatively by a talented scholar, allows unusual insights into cause and effect. Yossi Loya, an Israeli ecologist, recognized such an opportunity in his studies of coral communities in the Gulf of Eilat and has used the chance to gather further insights into the patterns of diversity and dominance in natural communities under various types of stress. His observations not only reveal further details of the structure and function of these communities, but reconfirm the importance of long-continued studies of specific sites to determine changes under way in response to intensified human influence, details that would otherwise be lost as the biota moves inexorably through various stages of impoverishment in response to uncontrolled chronic disturbance.

Loya offers a case history study of a coral reef exposed in different places to oil pollution and climatic anomalies. While the circumstances seem specialized, they are increasingly common, and the observations Loya makes are emergent generalities, broadly applicable to natural communities under stress.

Introduction: The Reef at Eilat

One of the central questions of ecology deals with the mechanisms that generate and maintain the diversity of organisms. There have been many varied opinions and large numbers of publications on this subject. I review here briefly our studies of community structure of corals at Eilat, Red Sea, describe changes that have occurred in coral diversity due to human versus natural disturbances, and discuss mechanisms that promote and maintain high diversity of corals on the reef-flats of Eilat.

The Gulf of Eilat is the most eastern of the two northern horns of the Red Sea, which are separated by the Sinai Peninsula. The reefs of Eilat are of the fringing type. Scleractinian corals are the most important hermatypic (reef-building) organisms (Loya and Slobodkin 1971). Hermatypic corals play a key role in forming the structure of coral reefs and in providing substrate and shelter for a wide variety of organisms. Acute damage to corals may result in a collapse of the complex community of organisms that live in close association with the corals.

In 1969 the community structure of the coral reefs at Eilat was studied in

369

detail by means of line transects, each 10 m long (Loya 1972). Any coral species which overlapped the line was recorded, and its projected length on the line was measured to the nearest centimeter. The line transects were surveyed from the reef-flat to 30 m depth. Only the changes that occurred in the community structure of corals on the reef-flats will be dealt with here. The data provide estimates of the number of coral species, number of colonies, percentage of total living coverage, and diversity of corals.

The average number of species per transect obtained on reef-flats not affected by human activity at the northern Gulf of Eilat was 13.5 ± 3.8 to 15.7 ± 3.4 species per 10 m transect (Loya 1972, 1976a). This diversity is high for corals measured on reef-flats (within-habitat diversity) in view of the low total number of species known from Eilat (about 100) (Loya and Slobodkin 1971). By contrast, about 330 coral species are known from the Great Barrier Reef (GBR) (Veron 1986). However, within-habitat diversity on reef-flats is lower both on Australian inshore fringing reefs and on the GBR proper than in Eilat.

A similar method suggested by Loya (1972) was used to study coral diversity on GBR reef-flats. The only difference was the length of transect lines, 30 m, used in all GBR studies. On Lizard Island the average number of coral species per transect was 11.1 ± 4.8 (data computed from Pichon and Morrissey 1981); on Heron Island, 9.8 ± 4.1 (data computed from 12 transects; Loya, Pichon, Weizman-Best, unpublished data); and on an inshore reef at Magnetic Island, 4.8 ± 3.7 (data computed from 9 transects; Pichon, Loya, and Bull, unpublished data). Clearly, if GBR data are computed for a 10 m transect as in Eilat, the average number of species per transect will decrease. Since information on community structure and species diversity of GBR corals is limited, generalization on local patterns of diversity would be premature. I would like, however, to present two hypotheses developed from our long-term studies at Eilat to help interpret causes of the high coral diversity on the reef-flats of the northern Gulf of Eilat.

Changes in Coral Community Structure Due to Natural Catastrophes and Human Disturbance

The nature reserve of the Eilat coral reefs is 3 km south of the general port of Eilat, approximately 1 km south of two major oil terminals (Figure 18.1).

Oil tankers using the port of Eilat after 1970 caused two to three major oil spills monthly, during which the nature reserve was completely blackened by oil. Between 1971 and 1973, ninety-five such spills were reported to the Israeli Ministry of Transportation. This chronic oil pollution continued until 1978–1979. From that period until the present only sporadic and minor oil

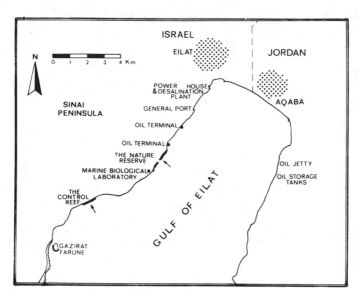

Figure 18.1. Map of the northern Gulf of Eilat showing study locations: the nature reserve and control reef (after Loya 1975).

spills have occurred, due to the drastic decrease in the number of tankers at Eilat, and the high fines inflicted by law on the shipping companies.

Since the wind direction along the Gulf of Eilat is predominantly from the north or northeast, oil spilled around the terminals is carried by surface currents toward the nature reserve. It does not, however, reach the control reef, which is further south. The "control reef" has been termed such as it was found to be free of oil pollution (Loya 1975) and served as a comparative site for studies on changes in the community structure of corals in the polluted nature reserve.

An unexpected and extremely low tide occurred at the northern part of the Gulf of Eilat between 15–20 September 1970 (Loya 1972). The water level fell approximately 20–25 cm below the reef-flat. As a result, the reef-flats were completely exposed to air and sun for three to four hours during the hottest time of the day. The air temperature ranged from a minimum of 34°C on 16 September to a maximum of 38.4°C on 18 September. The immediate consequence of the low tide was the death of approximately 80–85% of the hermatypic corals along the northern part of the Gulf (Loya 1975, 1976a). The high temperatures and desiccation were probably the direct cause of the sudden mortality. The community structure and species diversity of hermatypic corals had been studied in several reef locations along the northern Gulf of Eilat before the low tide (Loya 1972). Hence, the incident provided a unique opportunity to study recolonization in both a chronically polluted and a clean reef.

During the low tide the corals below the lowest water level were unharmed. Since the nature reserve and the control reefs were similar in community structure (Loya 1975), it was reasonable to assume that a similar stock of coral propagules existed in both. Theoretically, providing human activities had not had a harmful effect on the coral communities at the nature reserve, a similar rate of recolonization of corals could have been expected in both localities. Twenty-one transects (each 10 m long) were surveyed on the reef-flat of the nature reserve and 12 transects on the control reef. The exact locations of the transects at both sites were carefully marked by stainless steel nails, which enabled the same transects to be resurveyed in the following years.

Figure 18.2 summarizes changes in average number of species, colonies, living coverage, and diversity ($H\dot{n}$,[1] Shannon and Weaver 1948) of corals per transect, in both reefs, between 1969 and 1982. After testing for equality of variances, t-tests were run on the different averages obtained. No significant difference was found between the coral community structure of the nature reserve and that of the control reef in 1969 ($P > 0.05$) when all four statistics were compared. In 1973, 1976, and 1982, however, all these factors were significantly higher ($P < 0.05$) at the control reef compared to the nature reserve. A detailed account of changes in the community structure and species diversity of corals in 1969 and 1973 is given in Loya (1975, 1976a). Although both reefs suffered similar mass mortality of corals during the low tide (85% at the nature reserve and 81% at the control reef), a marked difference was observed in recovery three years later. The extent of recruitment was twenty-three times greater at the control reef. No significant difference was found in coral community regeneration (15% at the nature reserve and 19.2% at the control reef). While the number of species, number of colonies, living coverage and $H\dot{n}$ decreased drastically at the nature reserve three years after the low tide, the control reef exhibited rapid recruitment and recovery. The significantly higher coral cover at the control reef was mainly due to massive recruitment of the most abundant species (40% more colonies per transect in 1973 as compared to 1969), and in addition, to the complete regeneration of massive colonies that had suffered partial mortality during the low tide.

Interpretation of stability in ecological systems has long been a matter of controversy among researchers (Margalef 1969; Slobodkin and Sanders 1969; Woodwell and Smith 1969; MacArthur 1972; Boesch 1974; Colwell 1974; Orians 1974; Gray 1977; Connell and Sousa 1983; King and Pimm 1983; Pimm 1984; and others). I do not seek to contribute here to the theory of stability in ecological systems. However, if we accept, as a measure of

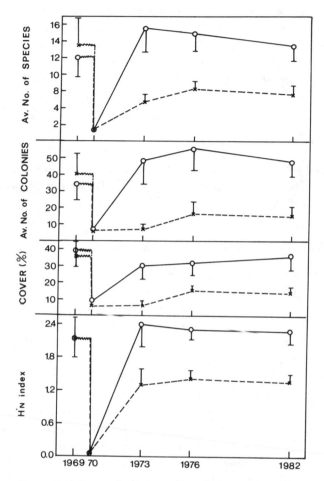

Figure 18.2. Changes in the average number of species, colonies, living coverage, and diversity of corals per transect in the reef-flats of the nature reserve and control reef between 1969 and 1982 (bars indicate standard deviations) (−x−, nature reserve; −o−, control reef).

community stability, the likelihood of return to a former configuration after external disturbance (as defined by Margalef 1969), there are marked differences between the nature reserve and the control reef. The nature reserve had not regained its former community structure and species diversity 12 years after the low tide, whereas the control reef showed remarkable resilience (as defined by Boesch 1974), and, only three years after a severe perturbation, had returned to its former configuration. A high correlation between the percentage contribution of the most common coral species to the total number of colonies and to the total living cover in the control reef before the low tide and three years later was obtained. Non-significant correlations were obtained when the same parameters were tested at the nature reserve (see Loya 1976a for details). It was concluded (Loya 1976a) that one of the differences between the human disturbance in this instance and natural catastrophes on coral reefs is the failure of the oil-polluted environment to return to its former configuration, whereas the reconstitution of reef areas denuded by natural disturbance was mainly a function of time. There are, unfortunately, few long-term quantitative coral reef community studies to test this view (for further discussion see Johannes 1972, 1975; Endean 1973; Loya 1976a; Bak and Engel 1979; Bak and Luckhurst 1980; Dollar and Grigg 1981; Pearson 1981; Bak and Criens 1983; Brown and Howard 1985).

Oil-Pollution Effects on Eilat Corals

Until 1975 there appeared no conclusive evidence that oil floating above the reef damages the corals (Johannes 1975). Until 1975 most of the studies of the effects of oil pollution on corals were either short-term incidental observations, or laboratory experiments that did not reflect the effects on corals in nature. Our long-term quantitative studies in situ and in the laboratory have established the vulnerability and sensitivity of hermatypic corals to crude-oil and oil components (Loya 1975, 1976a; Rinkevich and Loya 1977, 1979a; Loya and Rinkevich 1979, 1980).

As indicated earlier, clear differences were shown in coral recovery between the chronically polluted nature reserve and the clean control reef. I have suggested (Loya 1975) that chronic oil pollution could damage coral communities by (a) harming the reproductive system of corals, (b) decreasing the viability of coral larvae, and (c) changing some physical properties of the reef-flat, thus interfering with normal settlement of coral larvae. Obviously, any combination of these effects is also possible, and would inhibit coral recruitment in oil-polluted reefs.

The following is a summary of our studies on the effects of oil pollution on reef corals. Our major purpose was to test the general applicability of the hypotheses outlined above. The work confirmed the sensitivity of corals to oil pollution under the circumstances that prevailed in Eilat.

We chose the coral *Stylophora pistillata* for experimentation in the field and in the laboratory, since this is the most abundant coral in the Eilat reefs (Loya 1972), and its life history has been studied in detail (Loya 1976b, c, d; Rinkevich and Loya 1979b, c). Field experiments, observations, and histological studies on two populations of *S. pistillata* in a chronically oil-polluted reef near the oil terminals (Figure 18.1) and at the pollution-free control reef revealed detrimental effects on the polluted corals. The coral population at the polluted reef showed a higher mortality rate of colonies, a smaller number of breeding colonies, and decrease in the number of ovaria per polyp; a smaller number of planulae produced per coral head (fecundity was four times higher in the control reef), a decreased viability of planula-larvae with increased concentrations of oil, and lower success in settlement of larvae on artificial objects with increasing concentrations of oil (Rinkevich and Loya 1977).

Further studies on the effects of crude oil on the reproduction of *S. pistillata* in the laboratory, using large tanks with running sea-water, supported the field results (Rinkevich and Loya 1979c). Large and mature colonies of *S. pistillata* were cut into halves at the beginning of the reproductive period: to avoid expected variation between different colonies, one was placed in a periodically oil-polluted tank, the other in a clean tank. After two months, a significantly lower number of female gonads per polyp were recorded in 75 percent of the polluted halves, compared to the control halves. An additional effect of low concentrations of crude oil on *S. pistillata* is the immediate indication of mouth opening followed by abortion of premature larvae. Since premature extrusion of planulae occurs during an oil spill, their chances of survival or successful settlement are very low (Loya and Rinkevich 1979).

Our field and laboratory studies on the effects of oil pollution on corals may explain the lack of recolonization of corals in the chronically polluted nature reserve until 1979–1980.[2] However, although no major oil spills have occurred there since then, to date it has still not returned to its former community structure. It remains to be studied whether the failure of the coral community at the nature reserve to return to its former state is a result of the following: (a) a possible physical change of the reef-flat substrate (interfering with normal settlement of coral larvae), (b) algal domination of the area outcompeting corals for space and/or (c) increased tourist pressure. Rather than speculating on this issue, I prefer to address the wider question of the generation and maintenance of coral diversity.

Why Is Coral Diversity High on the Reef-Flats of the Northern Gulf of Eilat?

Hypothesis 1: Physical Disturbances

Unpredictable Midday Low Tides Act as Diversifying Forces by Preventing Monopolization of the Reef-Flat by Single or Few Competitively Superior Species. Because space for settlement and development is one of the most important limiting resources on coral reefs, overlap in the utilization of space may result in acute competition among coral populations (Lang 1973; Connell 1973, 1976, 1978; Grigg and Maragos 1974; Porter 1974; Loya 1976a; Maguire and Porter 1977) and other benthic organisms (Dayton 1971, 1975; Connell 1975;

Jackson and Buss 1975; Paine 1976; Sebens 1976, 1982; Jackson 1977; Buss and Jackson 1979; and others).

Resource monopolization by corals may take place through competitive interactions such as extracoelentric destruction, whereby the mesenterial digestive filaments of a dominant species extend onto the living tissues of an adjacent subdominant and destroy it (Lang 1973; Richardson, Dustan, and Lang 1979); rapid growth (Connell 1973); overtopping morphology (Porter 1974); or allelopathic effects (Sammarco et al. 1983). Abilities in these competitive mechanisms are species specific, and in areas of high densities on the reef have been shown to affect coral abundance and distribution patterns (Lang 1973; Grassle 1974; Grigg and Maragos 1974; Porter 1974; Connell 1976, 1978; Loya 1976a; Maguire and Porter 1977; Sheppard 1979, 1985; Porter, Battey, and Smith 1982).

Coral mass mortality on reefs may result from mechanical destruction during tropical storms, abnormally low or high seawater temperatures, floods of freshwater especially if accompanied by heavy siltation, exposure to air during midday air-temperature maxima, and Acanthaster predation (Glynn, Almodovar, and Gonzalez 1965; Glynn 1968, 1976, 1984; Stoddart 1969; Shinn 1972; Endean 1973; Grigg and Maragos 1974; Loya 1976a; Pearson 1981; Woodley et al. 1981; Brown and Howard 1985). The time required for recolonization and recovery of reefs after such disturbances varies from very short (two years, Shinn 1972) to prolonged periods of time (50 years or more, Grigg and Maragos 1974; Maguire and Porter 1977).

The role of disturbance on community structure and species diversity of natural communities has been documented and discussed by many investigators. (For selected bibliography and reviews, see Dayton 1971, 1975; Levin and Paine 1974; Connell 1978; Huston 1979; Paine and Levin 1981; Miller 1982; Thiery 1982; Connell and Sousa 1983; Sousa 1984; Pickett and White 1985, and others).

Grigg and Maragos (1974) proposed a model for coral community succession based on patterns of recolonization on submerged historic lava flows in Hawaii. By analyzing data sets from progressively older flows they found that diversity at first increased then gradually decreased as more and more species became established. They hypothesized that the decline in diversity in older flows was due to space limitation and competitive exclusion by dominant species, a process that took over 50 years. Glynn (1976) attributed the diversifying effect to recurrent and extreme tidal exposures of reef-flat corals off the Pacific coast of Panama. Tide-induced mortality of Pocilloporid corals, which are prime-space monopolists, resulted in increased coral species diversity.

I have suggested (Loya 1976a) that the unpredictably low tides at Eilat act

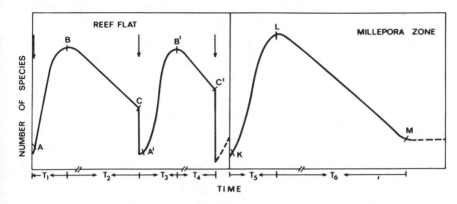

Figure 18.3. Hypothetical pattern of succession following catastrophic low tides (indicated by arrows) on the reef-flat and the undisturbed Millepora zone of the Eilat reefs. (From Loya 1976a, Copyright © 1976 *Ecology*. Reprinted with permission.)

as a diversifying force in a way similar to storm and swell damage in Hawaii (Grigg and Maragos 1974; Dollar 1982; Grigg 1983), and the Caribbean (Porter 1974; Glynn 1976). Connell's (1976) model of "the intermediate-disturbance hypothesis" best describes these examples in stating that the highest diversity of natural communities will be maintained in areas suffering disturbances intermediate on the scales of frequency and intensity.

Figure 18.3 (after Loya 1976a) presents hypothetical curves which describe the patterns of succession following disturbance on the reef-flat and the undisturbed Millepora zone (situated 0.5–2.0m below the reef-flat) at Eilat. The higher diversity recorded on the control reef three years after the low tide, compared to prior to devastation, may reflect a situation in which diversity continues to increase in time after a catastrophe (*AB* and *A'B'* in Figure 18.3) until space becomes a limiting factor and competitive interactions between species may cause a decline in diversity (*BC* and *B'C'*). The results obtained on the average number of species recorded on the reef-flat of the control reef between 1970 and 1982 support this pattern (Figure 18.2). The time interval required to reach "species equilibrium" (as defined by Wilson 1969) is quite short (approximately 5–7 years). The time interval for full recovery and for competitive interactions to take place (*T2* and *T4*) is expected to be much longer and more variable between different reefs depending on local conditions. Full recovery may be expected after 15–30 years or more (see Loya 1976a).

In contrast to the reef-flat community the Millepora zone is not exposed to air during the lowest water levels, although physical conditions are still rigorous in this zone (wave action, temperature fluctuations, etc.). Here, interspecific competition is not interrupted by catastrophic low tides and has a chance to become complete. Due to space monopolization by *M. dichotoma* (achieved by fast growth), this zone has high living coverage but low diversity.

In conclusion, the frequency of extremely low tides at the Gulf of Eilat seems to be such that the "species equilibrium" is never reached on the reef-flats, and interspecific competition is not carried out to completion. Monopolization of the reef-flats by competitively superior species is interrupted, providing an opportunity for more species to colonize vacant spaces. The high diversity recorded on reef-flats which are not perturbed by human activity probably reflects early successional stages.

Hypothesis 2: Coral Reproductive Strategies

Temporal Reproductive Isolation of Eilat Corals Generates High Diversity by Decreasing Interspecific Competition. Information on sexual (see Fadlallah 1983; Harrison et al. 1984; Richmond and Jokiel 1984; Shlesinger and Loya 1985; Babcock et al. 1986; Szmant 1986; for reviews and regional patterns) and asexual (see Highsmith 1982, for review) reproduction in corals has increased considerably in recent years. However, no study has considered coral reproductive patterns in relation to coral community structure and species diversity. In trying to explain the high within-habitat diversity of hermatypic corals on reef-flats in the northern Gulf of Eilat, my second hypothesis relates to the phenomenon of temporal reproductive isolation exhibited by the most abundant coral species at Eilat (Shlesinger and Loya 1985).

We have examined the reproductive patterns of 13 ecologically important coral species at Eilat (Figure 18.4). Although these species comprise only 13% of the total known species in Eilat, they are among the most abundant, contributing approximately 60–70% of the total living cover of coral communities on the reef-flats (Loya 1972). The major reproductive activities of these species (planular shedding or gamete spawning) occur in different seasons, different months, or different lunar phases within the same month (Figure 18.4). In contrast to the temporal reproductive isolation exhibited by Red Sea corals, many corals of the Great Barrier Reef of Australia are synchronous multispecific spawners (Harrison et al. 1984; Babcock et al. 1986). The mass spawning of 105 species takes place on only a few nights of the year, between the full and last quarter moon in late spring. Synchronous spawning was observed both within and between five reefs separated by as much as 500 km.

I have mentioned that space is a major limiting resource for settlement, growth, and development of reef corals. The major reproductive activity of most of the corals studied coincides with the seasonal disappearance of

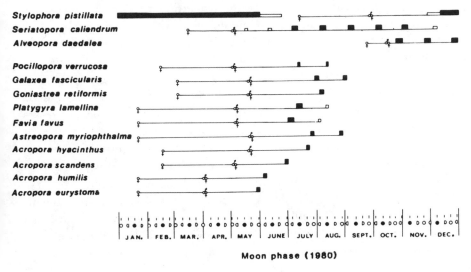

Figure 18.4. Reproductive pattern of thirteen scleractinian corals at Eilat in 1980. The first three species are brooders and the rest are broadcasting spawners. The results presented are in accordance with the lunar calendar, as follows: •, new moon; ◑ first quarter; ○, full moon; and ◐ last quarter. The period of gonadal development is represented by a solid line with indications of the onset of oogenesis (♀), and spermatogenesis (♂). Further development of both gonads is indicated by the line following the ♂ ♀ sign. Black bars represent massive spawning (90 to 100% of the population), and blank bars represent sporadic spawning (10 to 20% of the population). (Reprinted with modifications from Loya 1985, with permission. Copyright 1985 by the AAAS.)

benthic algae, a major competitor for space on the reef-flats of Eilat (i.e., mainly during June, July, and August) (Benayahu and Loya 1977a, b, 1981). Various species of algae progressively decline in abundance during the summer months, creating more space for coral settlement. During winter, algal cover on the reef-flats is very high and space for settlement is scarce. Thus, per unit of time, space availability for settlement on the reef-flats is more predictable during summer than in winter. It seems, therefore, that a better strategy for summer breeders among the corals is to concentrate their reproductive effort in one short period of time, in order to maximize reproductive success. By contrast, winter breeders like *S. pistillata* (the only species known so far to reproduce during winter) adopt an opposite strategy, spreading the risk of reproduction over a long period of time (December to May in the case of *S. pistillata*). During the winter, the availability of space in time is random due to occasional denudation of small areas by winter storms and, to a limited degree, by grazers. A long reproductive period seems an advantageous strategy.

On the reef-flats at Eilat, intraspecific synchronization of spawning and a discrete breeding period may be advantageous to each coral species, not only by reducing gametic wastage and preventing hybridization, but also by reducing interspecific competition among corals and between corals and algae on the reef-flats. Temporal reproductive isolation may act as a mechanism that generates high coral diversity there. By contrast, mass spawning exhibited by Great Barrier Reef corals probably increases interspecific competition among corals. However, whether this may be a cause for the relatively lower within-habitat diversity of corals on the reef-flats of the GBR compared to that in Eilat remains to be shown.

The two hypotheses presented are not mutually exclusive. The net result of high coral diversity on the reef-flats along the Gulf of Eilat which are not humanly perturbed may be a cumulative effect of both external abiotic factors such as disturbance through exposure to air during midday air-temperature maxima and biotic factors such as temporal reproductive isolation.

Notes

1. $H'n = -\Sigma\, Pi \ln Pi$; where $Pi = n_i/N$ and n_i = number individuals in the ith species and N = total number of individuals.
2. For reviews on the effects of oil pollution on coral reef communities, see Loya and Rinkevich (1980), Ray (1981), Knap et al. (1983), Fucik et al. (1984), and Bak (1987).

References

Babcock, R. C., G. D. Bull, P. L. Harrison, A. J. Heyward, J. K. Oliver, C. C. Wallace, and B. L. Willis, 1986. Synchronous spawnings of 105 scleractinian coral species on the Great Barrier Reef. *Mar. Biol.* 90:379–394.

Bak, R. P. M., 1987. Effects of chronic oil pollution on a Caribbean coral reef. *Mar. Pollut. Bull.* 10:534–539.

Bak, R. P. M., and M. S. Engel, 1979. Distribution, abundance and survival of juvenile hermatypic corals (Scleractinia) and the importance of life history strategies in the parent coral community. *Mar. Biol.* 54:341–352.

Bak, R. P. M., and B. E. Luckhurst, 1980. Constancy and change in coral reef habitats along depth gradients at Curaçao. *Oecologia* 47:145–155.

Bak, R. P. M., and S. R. Criens, 1983. Survival after fragmentation of colonies of *Madracis mirabilis, Acropora palmata* and *A. cervicornis* and the subsequent impact of coral disease. In E. D. Gomez et al. (Eds.), *Proc. 4th Inter. Coral Reef Symp.*, Manila 2:221–227. Univ. of the Philippines, Quezon City.

Benayahu, Y., and Y. Loya, 1977a. Seasonal occurrence of benthic algae communities and grazing regulation by sea urchins at the coral reefs of Eilat, Red Sea. In D. L. Taylor (Ed.), *Proc. Third Inter. Coral Reef Symp.: I. Biology*, pp. 383–389. University of Miami.

Benayahu, Y., and Y. Loya, 1977b. Space partitioning by stony corals, soft corals and algae in the northern Gulf of Eilat, Red Sea. *Helgolander wiss. Meeresunters,* 30:362–382.

Benayahu, Y., and Y. Loya, 1981. Competition for space among coral reef sessile organisms at Eilat, Red Sea. *Bull. Mar. Sci.* 31:514–522.

Boesch, D. F., 1974. Diversity, stability and response to human disturbance in estuarine ecosystems. In *Structure, Functioning and Management of Ecosystems,* pp.109–114. Proc. First Inter. congr. Ecol., Centre for Agricultural Publishing and Documentation, Wageningen, The Netherlands.

Brown, B. E., and L. S. Howard, 1985. Assessing the effects of "stress" on reef corals. *Adv. Mar. Biol.* 22:1–63.

Buss, L. W., and J. B. C. Jackson, 1979. Competitive networks: nontransitive competitive relationships in cryptic coral reef environments. *Amer. Natur.* 113: 223–234.

Colwell, R. K., 1974. Predictability, constancy, and contigency of periodic phenomena. *Ecology* 55:1148–1153.

Connell, J. H., 1973. Population ecology of reef-building corals. In O. A. Jones and R. Endean (Eds.), *Biology and Geology of Coral Reefs. Biology 1.* Vol. 2, pp. 205–245. Academic Press, New York.

Connell, J. H., 1975. Some mechanisms producing structure in natural communities: a model and evidence from field experiments. In M. L. Cody and J. Diamond (Eds.), *Ecology and Evolution of Communities,* pp. 460–490. Belknap, Cambridge, Mass.

Connell, J. H., 1976. Competitive interactions and the species diversity of corals. In G. O. Mackie (Ed.), *Coelenterate Ecology and Behavior,* pp. 51–58. Plenum, New York.

Connell, J. H., 1978. Diversity in tropical rain forests and coral reefs. *Science* 199:1302–1310.

Connell, J. H., and W. P. Sousa, 1983. On the evidence needed to judge ecological stability or persistence. *Amer. Natur.* 121:789–824.

Dayton, P. K., 1971. Competition, disturbance, and community organization: the provision and subsequent utilization of space in a rocky intertidal community. *Ecol. Monogr.* 41:351–389.

Dayton, P. K., 1975. Experimental evaluation of ecological dominance in a rocky intertidal community. *Ecol. Monogr.* 45:137–159.

Dollar, S. J., 1982. Wave stress and coral community structure in Hawaii. *Coral Reefs* 1:71–81.

Dollar, S. J., and R. W. Grigg, 1981. Impact of a kaolin clay spill on a coral reef in Hawaii. *Mar. Biol.* 65:269–276.

Endean, R., 1973. Destruction and recovery of coral reef communities. In O. A. Jones and R. Endean (Eds.), *Biology and Geology of Coral Reefs,* pp. 215–254. Academic Press, New York.

Fadlallah, Y. H., 1983. Sexual reproduction, development and larval biology in scleractinian corals. A review. *Coral Reefs* 2:129–150.

Fucik, K. W., Bright, T. J., and K. S. Goodman, 1984. Measurements of damage, recovery, and rehabilitation of coral reefs exposed to oil. In J. Cairns, Jr., and A. L. Buikems (Eds.), *Restoration of Habitats Impacted by Oil Spills,* pp. 115–133. Butterworth, London.

Glynn, P. W., 1968. Mass mortalities of echinoids and other reef flat organisms coincident with mid-day, low water exposures in Puerto Rico. *Mar. Biol.* 3:226–243.

Glynn, P. W., 1976. Some physical and biological determinants of coral community structure in the Eastern Pacific. *Ecol. Monogr.* 46:431–456.

Glynn, P. W., 1984. Widespread coral mortality and the 1982–83 El Niño warming event. *Environ. Conserv.* 11:133–146.

Glynn, P. W., L. R. Almodovar, and J. G. Gonzalez, 1965. Effects of Hurricane Edith on marine life in La Parguera, Puerto Rico. *Caribb. J. Sci.* 4:335–345.

Grassle, J. F., 1974. Variety in coral reef communities. In O. A. Jones and R. Endean (Eds.), *Biology and Geology of Coral Reefs*, Vol. 2., pp. 247–270. Academic Press, NewYork.

Gray, J. S., 1977. The stability of benthic ecosystems. *Helgol. Wiss. Meeresunters* 30:427–444.

Grigg, R. W., 1983. Community structure, succession and development of coral reefs in Hawaii. *Mar. Ecol. Prog. Ser.* 11:1–14.

Grigg, R. W., and J. E. Maragos, 1974. Recolonization of hermatypic corals on submerged lava flows in Hawaii. *Ecology* 5:387–395.

Harrison, P. L., R. C. Babcock, G. D. Bull, J. K. Oliver, C. C. Wallace, and B. L. Willis, 1984. Mass spawning in tropical reef corals. *Science* 223:1186–1189.

Highsmith, R. C., 1982. Reproduction by fragmentation in corals. *Mar. Ecol. Prog. Ser.* 7:207–226.

Huston, M., 1979. A general hypothesis of species diversity. *Amer. Natur.* 113: 81–101.

Jackson, J. B. C., 1977. Competition on hard marine substrata: the adaptive significance of solitary and colonial strategies. *Amer. Natur.* 111:743–767.

Jackson, J. B. C., and L. Buss, 1975. Allelopathy and spatial competition among coral reef invertebrates. *Proc. Nat. Acad. Sci.* 72:5160–5163.

Johannes, R. E., 1972. Coral reefs and pollution. In M. Ruivo (Ed.), *Marine Pollution and Sea Life*, pp. 364–371. Fishing News, London.

Johannes, R. E., 1975. Pollution and degradation of coral reef communities. In E. J. Ferguson and R. E. Johannes (Eds.), *Tropical Marine Pollution*, pp. 13–51. Elsevier, Amsterdam.

King, A. W., and S. L. Pimm, 1983. Complexity, diversity, and stability: a reconciliation of theoretical and empirical results. *Amer. Natur.* 122:229–239.

Knap, A. H., T. D. Sleeter, R. E. Dodge, S. C. Wyers, H. R. Frith, and S. R. Smith, 1983. The effects of oil spills and dispersant use on corals, a review and multidisciplinary approach. *Oil and Petrochemical Pollution* 1:157–169.

Lang, J. C., 1973. Interspecific aggression by scleractinian corals: 2. Why the race is not only to the swift. Coral Reef Project-Papers in Memory of Dr. T. F. Goreau. *Bull. Mar. Sci.* 23:260–279.

Levin, S. A., and R. T. Paine, 1974. Disturbance, patch formation, and community structure. *Proc. Nat. Acad. Sci.* 71:2744–2747.

Loya, Y., 1972. Community structure and species diversity of hermatypic corals at Eilat, Red Sea. *Mar. Biol.* 13:100–123.

Loya, Y., 1975. Possible effects of water pollution on the community structure of Red Sea corals. *Mar. Biol.* 29:177–185.

Loya, Y., 1976a. Recolonization of Red Sea corals affected by natural catastrophes and man-made perturbations. *Ecology* 57:278–289.

Loya, Y., 1976b. The Red Sea coral *Stylophora pistillata* is an r strategist. *Nature, Lond.* 259:478–480.

Loya, Y., 1976c. Settlement, mortality and recruitment of a Red Sea scleractinian coral population. In G. O. Mackie (Ed.), *Coelenterate Ecology and Behavior*, pp. 89–100. Plenum, New York.

Loya, Y., 1976d. Skeletal regeneration in a Red Sea scleractinian coral population. *Nature* 261:490–491.

Loya, Y., and B. Rinkevich, 1979. Abortion effect in corals induced by oil pollution. *Mar. Ecol. Prog. Ser.* 1:77–80.

Loya, Y., and B. Rinkevich, 1980. Effects of oil pollution on coral reef communities. *Mar. Ecol. Prog. Ser.* 3:167–180.

Loya, Y., and L. B. Slobodkin, 1971. The coral reefs of Eilat (Gulf of Eilat, Red Sea). In M. Yonge and D. R. Stoddart (Eds.), *Regional Variation of Indian Ocean Coral Reefs*, pp. 117–139. Symp. Zool. Soc. Lond. 28. Academic Press, New York.

MacArthur, R. H., 1972. *Geographical Ecology*. Harper and Row, New York.

Maguire, L. A., and J. W. Porter, 1977. A spatial model of growth and competition strategies in coral communties. *Ecol. Monogr.* 3:249–271.

Margalef, R., 1969. A practical proposal and model of interdependence. In G. M. Woodwell and H. H. Smith (Eds.), *Diversity and Stability in Ecological Systems*, pp. 25–37. Brookhaven symp. Biol. 22.

Miller, T. E., 1982. Community diversity and interactions between the size and frequency of disturbance. *Amer. Natur.* 120:533–536.

Orians, G. H., 1974. Diversity, stability and maturity in natural ecosytems. In W. H. van Dobben and R. H. Lowe-McConnell (Eds.), *Unifying Concepts in Ecology*, pp. 139–150. Junk, The Hague.

Paine, R. T., 1976. Controlled manipulations in the marine intertidal zone, and their contributions to ecological theory. In *The Changing Scene in the Natural Sciences*, pp. 245–270. Special Publication No. 12. Acad. Nat. Sci., Philadelphia.

Paine, R. T., and S. A. Levin, 1981. Intertidal landscapes: disturbance and the dynamics of pattern. *Ecol. Monogr.* 51:145–178.

Pearson, R. G., 1981. Recovery and recolonization of coral reefs. *Mar. Ecol. Prog. Ser.* 4:105–122.

Pichon, M., and J. Morrissey, 1981. Benthic zonation and community structure of south island reef, Lizard Island (Great Barrier Reef). *Bull. Mar. Sci.* 31:581–593.

Pickett, S. T. A., and P. S. White, 1985. *The Ecology of Natural Disturbance and Patch Dynamics*. Academic Press, New York.

Pimm, S. L., 1984. The complexity and stability of ecosystems. *Nature* 307:321–326.

Porter, J. W., 1974. Community structure of coral reefs on opposite sides of the isthmus of Panama. *Science* 186:543–545.

Porter, J. W., J. F. Battey, and G. J. Smith, 1982. Perturbation and change in coral reef communities. *Proc. Nat. Acad. Sci.* 79:1678–1681.

Ray, J. P., 1981. The effects of petroleum hydrocarbons on corals. Petroleum and the marine environment. *Petro. Mar.* 80:705–726.

Richardson, C. A., P. Dustan, and J. C. Lang, 1979. Maintenance of living space by sweeper tentacles of *Montastrea cavernosa*, a Caribbean reef coral. *Mar. Biol.* 55:181–186.

Richmond, R. H., and P. L. Jokiel, 1984. Lunar periodicity in larva release in the reef coral *Pocillopora damicornis* at Enewetak and Hawaii. *Bull. Mar. Sci.* 34:280–287.

Rinkevich, B., and Y. Loya, 1977. Harmful effects of chronic oil pollution on a Red Sea coral population. In D. L. Taylor (Ed.), *Proc. Third. Int. Coral Reef Symp: II. Geology*, pp. 585–591. Univ. of Miami, Miami.

Rinkevich, B., and Loya, Y, 1979a. Laboratory experiments on the effects of crude oil on the Red Sea coral *Stylophora pistillata*. *Mar. Pollut. Bull.* 10:328–330.

Rinkevich, B., and Y. Loya, 1979b. The reproduction of the Red Sea coral *Stylophora pistillata:* I. Gonads and planulae. *Mar. Ecol. Prog. Ser.* 1:133–144.

Rinkevich, B., and Y. Loya, 1979c. The reproduction of the Red Sea coral *Stylophora pistillata:* II. Synchronization in breeding and seasonality of planulae shedding. *Mar. Ecol. Prog. Ser.* 1:145–152.

Sammarco, P. W., J. C. Coll, S. La Barre, and B. Willis, 1983. Competitive strategies of soft corals (Coelenterata: Octocorallia): allelopathic effects on selected scleractinian corals. *Coral Reefs* 1:173–178.

Sebens, K. P., 1976. The ecology of sea anenomes in Caribbean Panama: utilization of space on a coral reef. In G. Mackie (Ed.), *Coelenterate Ecology and Behavior*, pp. 67–77. Plenum, Chicago.

Sebens, K. P., 1982. Competition for space: growth rate, reproductive output and escape in size. *Amer. Natur.* 120:189–197.

Shannon, C. E., and W. Weaver, 1948. *The Mathematical Theory of Communication*. Univ. of Illinois Press, Urbana, Illinois.

Sheppard, C. R. C., 1979. Interspecific aggression between reef corals with reference to their distribution. *Mar. Ecol. Prog. Ser.* 1:273–247.

Sheppard, C. R. C., 1985. Unoccupied substrate in the central Great Barrier Reef: role of coral interactions. *Mar. Ecol. Prog. Ser.* 25:259–268.

Shinn, E. A., 1972. *Coral reef recovery in Florida and the Persian Gulf*. Environmental Conservation Dept., Shell Oil Co., Houston, Texas.

Shlesinger, Y., and Y. Loya, 1985. Coral community reproductive patterns: Red Sea versus the Great Barrier Reef. *Science* 228:1333–1335.

Slobodkin, L. B., and H. L. Sanders, 1969. On the contribution of environmental predictability to species diversity. In G. M. Woodwell and H. H. Smith (Eds.), *Diversity and Stability in Ecological Systems*, pp. 82–95. Brookhaven Symp. Biol. No. 22. Brookhaven Nat. Lab., Upton, N.Y.

Sousa, W. P., 1984. The role of disturbance in natural communities. *Ann. Rev. Ecol. Syst.* 15:353–391.

Stoddart, D. R., 1969. Ecology and morphology of recent coral reefs. *Biol. Rev.* 44:433–498.

Szmant, A. M., 1986. Reproductive ecology of Caribbean coral reefs. *Coral Reefs* 5:43–53.

Thiery, R. G., 1982. Environmental instability and community diversity. *Biol. Rev.* 57:671–710.

Veron, J. E. N., 1986. *Corals of Australia and the Indo-Pacific*. Angus and Robertson Pub. London.

Wilson, E. O., 1969. The species equilibrium. In G. M. Woodwell and H. H. Smith (Eds.), *Diversity and Stability in Ecological Systems*, pp. 38–47. Brookhaven Symp. Biol. No. 22. Brookhaven Nat. Lab., Upton, N.Y.

Woodley, J. D., E. A. Chornesky, P. A. Clifford, J. B. C. Jackson, L. S. Kaufman, N. Knowlton, J. C. Lang, M. P. Pearson, J. W. Porter, M. C. Rooney, K. W. Rylaarsdam, V. J. Tunnicliffe, C. M. Wahle, J. L. Wulff, A. S. G. Curtis, M. D. Dallmeyer, B. P. Jupp, M. A. R. Koehl, J. Niegel, and E. M. Sides, 1981. Hurricane Allen's impact on Jamaican coral reefs. *Science* 213:749–755.

Woodwell, G. M., and H. H. Smith (Eds.), 1969. *Diversity and Stability in Ecological Systems*. Brookhaven Symp. Biol. No. 22. Brookhaven Nat. Lab., Upton, N.Y.

19   Are Deep-Sea Communities Resilient?

J. FREDERICK GRASSLE, NANCY J. MACIOLEK, AND JAMES A. BLAKE

Editor's Note: The bottom of the deep sea is dark and cold and a very old habitat by most terrestrial standards. Dr. Grassle and his colleagues have shown that the benthos contains an extraordinary diversity of life with different life histories and adaptations to habitat. A combined sample from 1,500 m to 2,500 m off New Jersey that covered a mere 21 m^2 yielded 798 species, a diversity that approaches the upper limits of what can be found on land anywhere. Another sampling off the East Coast of North America yielded nearly 600 species. Most deep-sea species are rare, and species once recognized as "cosmopolitan" are now seen as groups of species with restricted distributions. Experience in study of this extraordinary diversity remains minuscule in proportion to the area, and estimates of the total number of species in the oceans now exceed by many orders of magnitude the earlier estimate of 160,000. The experience is similar to that in tropical forests where access to the crowns of trees has recently revealed not only new populations of birds, but thousands of new insect populations. The knowledge has caused estimates of the total number of species on earth to soar to 10 million or more. Experience with the benthos may push this number higher still.

Chronic disturbance of either the benthos or the water column increases the abundance of a few species. In such sites one species may comprise more than 30 percent of the fauna and a few species will make up more than half of the total fauna. Factors that cause such a shift are many, including such minor or local changes as the entry of a fish carcass to the benthic region, or general disturbance such as a sudden change in temperature or contamination with sewage or other human wastes.

Not surprisingly, in view of the difficulty of working on the bottom of the oceanic abyss, two to three miles below the surface, the communities and their responses are imperfectly known. Patterns seem consistent with extensive experience on land where improved information reveals the extent to which species contain ecotypes specific to locales and where chronic disturbance reduces diversity both within and among species and favors groups of a few hardy species recognized as resistant to a wide variety of disturbances. The small glimpses we have of the benthos, one of the oldest and most extensive habitats on earth, offer still another view of evolution in process, including the responses to disturbance that seem, again not surprisingly, to be well established in all ecosystems.

Introduction

The prevalent view of the nature of deep-sea ecosystems has changed twice in the last two decades. The sea floor is not the impoverished desert that was envisioned by most biologists (e.g., Ekman 1953; Williams 1964) until publication of the first deep-sea studies using fine-mesh trawls that skimmed the animals from the surface layers of sediment (Hessler and Sanders 1967). Nor is it the uniform, aseasonal, "chemostatic" environment that was proposed to explain the rich diversity of deep-sea species (Sanders 1968). Although deep-sea environments are relatively uniform in temperature and seawater chemistry, the supply of food is seasonal and erratic and results in spatial patchiness. Large aggregates of organic matter from terrestrial, near-shore, and surface-dwelling plants and animals generate spatial and temporal heterogeneity. The activities of living animals on the bottom add to the mosaic of differing resources by altering the sediments or introducing biogenic structures. The relatively organic-rich surface layer of sediment that provides food for bottom-dwellers is resuspended by occasional intense current flows generated by events analogous to storms.

By using submersibles it has been possible to gain a close-up view of deep-sea life and to conduct in situ experiments. The information from the portholes and cameras of submarines has greatly altered our image of the deep sea but even these views are inadequate. Experiments on the sea floor, and more nearly complete analysis of a greater number of quantitative samples, in addition to improved first-hand observations have brought a revolution in thinking about the deep sea in the last decade. The ecological processes operating in the deep sea are more like those operating in other species-rich ecosystems than has been previously supposed. For example, the effects of small-scale disturbance are similar to the effects of gaps in rain-forest canopy produced by falling trees. Despite these similarities to dynamic processes operating in other environments, vast areas of sea floor are at one extreme of the known patterns of environmental change. In comparison to shallow water, most of the deep sea has modest levels of sediment deposition and resuspension and minimal changes in temperature and salinity. Biological activities outside the system supply organic materials that are a particularly important source of spatial and temporal heterogeneity. Deep-sea species have evolved a broad range of life histories and habitat specializations in response to differing aspects of this heterogeneity.

Species Diversity of Deep-Sea Benthos

Quantitative sampling on the continental slope off New Jersey indicates that deep-sea diversity has been underestimated (Grassle and Maciolek in preparation). A box corer was used to collect 233 samples, each with a surface area of 900 cm^2, from a 176 km transect along the depth contours between 1,500 m and 2,500 m depth. Thus, the combined surface area of

Table 19.1. *Number of species and number of families in each phylum from 233 0.09-m² samples taken between 1,500-m and 2,500-m depth on the continental slope off New Jersey*

	Number of species	Number of families
Cnidaria	19	10
Nemertea	22	1
Priapulida	2	1
Annelida	385	49
Echiurida	4	2
Sipuncula	15	3
Pogonophora	13	5
Mollusca	106	43
Arthropoda	185	40
Bryozoa	1	1
Brachiopoda	2	1
Echinodermata	39	13
Hemichordata	4	1
Chordata	1	1
Total	798	171

these samples is about 21 m². The number of species in these samples is 798 (Table 19.1). From 32° to 41° N latitude and several depths down to 3,000 m on the continental slope and rise off the eastern coast of the United States 554 samples (including the 233 samples from off New Jersey) contained nearly 1,600 species (Blake et al. 1987; Maciolek et al. 1987a, b). Since most deep-sea species are very rare, the sampling effort required to describe the limits of species distributions would be enormous. As more powerful techniques for distinguishing species are used, "cosmopolitan species" are being shown to be groups of related species with relatively restricted distributions. Since the surface area of the deep-sea floor below 1,000 m is on the order of 3×10^8 km², extrapolations from these data show an earlier estimate of 160,000 species in the oceans at all depths (Thorson 1971) to be orders of magnitude too low.

How Is Deep-Sea Diversity Maintained?

Spatial and temporal heterogeneity are maintained by biogenic structures, a patchy supply of food, and small-scale disturbance (Grassle and Morse-Porteous 1987). Burrows, mounds, shells, and other structures provide refuges and may enhance larval settlement or food supply by influencing the near-bottom flow regime. Irregularities in the surface of the bottom created by the activities of animals result in uneven distribution of organic material settling from the surface. Large organic aggregates such as pieces of wood, seaweed, grasses, and the bodies of surface dwellers such as salps or fish constitute a small-scale disturbance at the sites where they land and become patchy and ephemeral resources for recruiting populations.

Three broad-scale features of the deep sea have been cited as correlates of the high diversity: large surface area (Osman and Whitlatch 1978; Abele and Walters 1979), low food supply (Van Valen 1976), and relative constancy of the physical environment (Sanders 1968). The large surface area and the potential for wide dispersal of populations has allowed species to specialize on very rare ephemeral resources. The low food supply to large areas of the deep sea results in a low background concentration of organic matter in sediments. This low background enhances development of a mosaic of sharply contrasting food resources as material collects in response to currents and the uneven topography. The feeding activities of large epifaunal animals also add to this shifting pattern of disturbance on the spatial scale of individual organisms. The large-scale disruptions observed during storm events on continental shelves (Maciolek and Grassle 1987) homogenize and obliterate sediment structure. Such intense storm events occur at very few sites in the deep sea; therefore, the resource mosaic, produced by small patches of disturbance and organic input, survives long enough to provide the habitats for a diverse assemblage of species.

What Are the Consequences of Large-Scale Disturbances in Deep-Sea Ecosystems?

Some deep-sea areas are subjected to disruption of the entire community by large-scale disturbance, such as intense currents, mudslides, hydrothermal activity, upwelling, or low oxygen. Fewer species are found in regions subjected to these events. The reduction in species may be the result of widespread mortality or disruption of the habitat structures colonized by species in areas of greater sediment stability.

The best-studied region of intense currents is a lower continental rise site south of Halifax, Nova Scotia, with current velocities up to 73 cm/sec, suspended sediment concentrations up to 12 g/m^3, and ripple marks on the bottom (Hollister and McCave 1984). Meiofaunal diversity appears to be unaffected by these disturbances (Thistle 1983; Thistle and Sherman 1985). The polychaetes (the main macrofaunal group identified to species) have a relatively low diversity. The most common species contributes 34–39 percent of the individuals (Thistle, Yingst, and Fauchald 1985; Russell

1987). The most common species in less-disturbed deep-sea environments is 6–7 percent of the total number of macrofaunal individuals (Grassle and Morse-Porteous 1987; Grassle and Maciolek, in preparation).

In deep-sea trenches, mud slumps from the walls of the trench smother the deep-sea fauna. The occasional burial of the bottom fauna has been the explanation for low diversity in these environments (Jumars and Hessler 1976). Upwellings at upper continental slope depths off Walvis Bay on the West African coast result in increased surface productivity and reduced oxygen in sediments. The fauna is dominated by a filter-feeding epifaunal species and a few species relatively tolerant of low-oxygen conditions (Sanders 1969). Occasional periods of low oxygen in the overlying water have been used to explain the relatively low deep-sea diversity in Santa Catalina Basin off southern California (Jumars 1976).

Along the Mid-Ocean Ridges at depths of 2,000–4,000 m, fluids from hydrothermal vents result in increased microbial productivity. Dense populations of a considerably reduced number of species inhabit both hard-surface and soft-sediment environments in the vicinity of these vents (Grassle et al. 1985). The several reasons for the reduced diversity apply to a greater or lesser extent depending on proximity to the undiluted hydrothermal fluid. Fluctuating amounts of oxygen and toxic chemicals such as sulfide may prevent many deep-sea species from living at vents. The supply of hydrothermal fluid and hence the food supply fluctuates drastically so that species must be either highly mobile or continually colonizing to take advantage of the increased productivity.

In each of the instances of large-scale disturbance, the change in community structure is obvious from the disproportionate abundance of a few species. In relatively undisturbed parts of the deep sea the most common species generally forms less than 10 percent of the total fauna (Grassle and Maciolek, in preparation), whereas in highly disturbed areas there is usually a single species that comprises more than 30 percent of the fauna, and the top few species make up more than half the total number of individuals (Grassle and Morse-Porteous 1987). Deep-sea waste disposal and mining are likely to reduce diversity by increasing a few relatively tolerant species and reducing or eliminating many of the rare species. The relative susceptibilities of deep-sea species to human-made disturbances have yet to be investigated. Even though parts of the ocean are increasingly being used for waste disposal, effects of these activities on the highly diverse communities of the deep sea are not being studied. Small-scale recolonization experiments suggest that recovery will be slow in instances where the disturbance is large enough so that recolonization by planktonic dispersal stages predominates, rather than movements of adults through sediments (Grassle and Morse-

Porteous 1987). The most diverse deep-sea ecosystems are likely to be less resilient than most shallow-water ecosystems.

Are Deep-Sea Ecosystems Changing?

The longest series of quantitative estimates of population fluctuations are sets of three samples taken three times each year for two years at a number of stations on the slope off the eastern United States (Blake et al. 1987; Maciolek et al. 1987a, 1987b). A time series of qualitative samples from the Rockall Trough off the west coast of Scotland has been extremely valuable in determining growth and reproduction of a number of larger, common deep-sea species (Gage 1986; Tyler 1986). Some of the species can be aged by following cohorts of individuals in these samples. For example, by this method, the sea urchin *Echinus affinis* has been inferred to live up to 28 years. Direct experiments indicate the shortest time to maturity in sediment-dwelling species is one year in polychaetes and tunicates and two years in bivalves (Grassle and Morse-Porteous 1987). Some species of bivalves in sediments may live as long as a hundred years based on a single estimate using a radiometric technique to age the shells (Turekian et al. 1975). The resilience of deep-sea ecosystems cannot be predicted without studies of the population dynamics of a wide spectrum of deep-sea species.

Research Priorities

Organisms in, on, and immediately above deep-sea sediments are important in determining chemical transformations, flux, and burial of materials. These processes cannot be understood from bulk metabolic, biomass, or chemical measurements. Studies of the microhabitats of individual species, their feeding behavior, metabolism, and population dynamics are needed. Deep-sea ecosystems are the product of evolution, and although coevolution may be important, the unit that survives and replicates is the species. Single species or a small functional group of species may dominate a particular process. These species may be large or small, common or rare; and, without better descriptions of deep-sea systems, we will not know which they are.

Another reason for emphasizing studies at the species level is that there is a high variance associated with bulk measures that integrate processes operating at the species level. Oxygen uptake of sediments varies by a factor of two in adjacent measurements (Smith and Hinga 1983) and biomass may vary by an order of magnitude. By comparison, the abundances of the most common species in the deep sea show little variance between replicates or seasons (Blake et al. 1987; Maciolek et al. 1987a, 1987b) and can be a relatively sensitive measure of change when it occurs.

Severe pollution in coastal areas is resulting in increasing pressures to use the deep sea for waste disposal. Even shallow-water discharge of wastes can have consequences for the deep ocean. Radioactive wastes discharged at a single point into the Irish Sea have been traced in surface currents to the sites of deep-water formation in the Arctic Ocean. Currents containing traces of these wastes flow over deep-water communities of the western Atlantic (Livingston, Swift, and Ostland 1985; Aarkrog et al. 1987). Other studies have shown increased levels of organic pollutants in deep-sea sediments and bottom-dwelling organisms (e.g., Harvey and Steinhauer 1976; Farrington and Tripp 1977; Knap, Binkley, and Deuser 1986). In these circumstances it is prudent to describe quantitatively deep-sea communities over periods of years. Existing descriptions are inadequate for detecting change over intervals of decades.

Acknowledgments

This work was supported by Contract No. 14–12–0001–30064 from the U.S. Department of Interior, Minerals Management Service to Battelle Memorial Institute and National Science Foundation Grant No. OCE–8311201. The work was part of a study of potential impacts of oil- and gas-exploration activities off the eastern coast of the United States. We thank Diane Bennett, Susan Brown-Leger, Victoria Gibson, Judith Grassle, Rosemarie Petrecca, and Paul Snelgrove for useful comments on the manuscript.

References

Aarkrog, A., S. Boelskifte, H. Dahlgard, S. Duniec, L. Hallstadius, E. Holm, and J. N. Smith, 1987. Technetium-99 and Cesium-134 as long distance tracers in Arctic waters. *Estuarine, Coastal and Shelf Science* 24:637–647.

Abele, L. G., and K. Walters, 1979. Marine benthic diversity: a critique and alternative explanation. *Journal of Biogeography* 6:115–126.

Blake, J. A., B. Hecker, J. F. Grassle, B. Brown, M. Wade, P. D. Boehm, E. Baptiste, B. Hilbig, N. Maciolek, R. Petrecca, R. E. Ruff, V. Starczak, and L. Watling, 1987. *Study of biological processes on the U. S. South Atlantic slope and rise. Phase 2.* Final report prepared for U. S. Dept. of the Interior, Minerals Management Service, Washinton, D. C.

Ekman, S., 1953. *Zoogeography of the Sea*. Sidgwick and Jackson, London.

Farrington, J. W., and B. W. Tripp, 1977. Hydrocarbons in western North Atlantic surface sediments. *Geochimica et Cosmochimica Acta* 41:1627–1641.

Gage, J. D., 1986. The benthic fauna of the Rockall Trough: regional distribution and bathymetric zonation. *Proceedings of the Royal Society of Edinburgh* 88B:159–174.

Gage, J. D., and P. A. Tyler, 1985. Growth and recruitment of the deep-sea urchin

Echinus affinis. Marine Biology 90:41–53.

Grassle, J. F., L. S. Brown-Leger, L. Morse-Porteous, R. Petrecca, and I. Williams, 1985. Deep-sea fauna of sediments in the vicinity of hydrothermal vents. *Biological Society of Washington Bulletin* 6:443–452.

Grassle, J. F., and L. S. Morse-Porteous, 1987. Macrofaunal colonization of disturbed deep-sea environments and the structure of deep-sea benthic communities. *Deep-Sea Research* 34(12):1911–1950.

Harvey, G. R., and W. G. Steinhauer, 1976. Biogeochemistry of PCB and DDT in the North Atlantic. In J. Nriagu (Ed.), *Environmental Biogeochemistry*, Ann Arbor Science Publ., Ann Arbor, Mich.

Hessler, R. R., and H. L. Sanders, 1967. Faunal diversity in the deep sea. *Deep-Sea Research* 14:65–78.

Hollister, C. D., and I. N. McCave, 1984. Sedimentation under deep-sea storms. *Nature* 309:220–225.

Jumars, P. A., 1976. Deep-sea species diversity: does it have a characteristic scale? *Journal of Marine Research* 34:217–246.

Jumars, P. A., and R. R. Hessler, 1976. Hadal community structure: implications from the Aleutian Trench. *Journal of Marine Research* 34(4):547–560.

Knap, A. H., K. S. Binkley, and W. G. Deuser, 1986. Synthetic organic chemicals in the deep Sargasso Sea. *Nature* 319:572–574.

Livingston, H. H., J. H. Swift, and H. G.Ostlund, 1985. Artificial radionuclide tracer supply to the Denmark Strait overflow between 1972 and 1981. *Journal of Geophysical Research* 90(C4):6971–6982.

Maciolek, N. J., and J. F. Grassle, 1987. Variability of the benthic fauna, II. The seasonal variation, 1981–1982. In R. H. Backus (Ed.), *Georges Bank*, pp. 303–309. MIT Press, Cambridge, Mass.

Maciolek, N. J., J. F. Grassle, B. Hecker, P. D. Boehm, B. Brown, B. Dade, W. G. Steinhauer, E. Baptiste, R. E. Ruff, and R. Petrecca, 1987a. *Study of biological processes on the U.S. midAtlantic slope and rise*. Final report prepared for U. S. Dept. of the Interior, Minerals Management Service, Washington, D.C.

Maciolek, N. J., J. F. Grassle, B. Hecker, B. Brown, J. A. Blake, P. D. Boehm, R. Petrecca, S. Duffy, E. Baptiste, and R. E. Ruff, 1987b. *Study of biological processes on the U.S. North Atlantic slope and rise*. Final report prepared for U.S. Department of the Interior, Minerals Management Service, Washington, D.C.

Moody, J. A., B. Butman, and M. H. Bothner, 1987. Near-bottom suspended matter concentration on the Continental Shelf during storms: estimates based on *in situ* observations of light transmission and a particle size dependent transmissometer calibration. *Continental Shelf Research* 7:609–628.

Osman, R. W., and R. B. Whitlatch, 1978. Patterns of species diversity: fact or artifact? *Paleobiology* 4:41–54.

Russell, D. E., 1987. *Paedampharete acutiseries*, a new genus and species of Ampharetidae (Polychaeta) from the North Atlantic *HEBBLE* Area, exhibiting progenesis and broad intraspecific variation. *Bulletin of the Biological Society of Washington* 7:140–151.

Sanders, H. L., 1968. Marine benthic diversity: a comparative study. *American Naturalist* 102:243–282.

Sanders, H. L., 1969. Benthic marine diversity and the stabilitytime hypothesis. In *Diversity and Stability in Ecological Systems*, pp. 71–81, Brookhaven Symposia in Biology, No. 22.

Smith, K. L., and K. R. Hinga, 1983. Sediment community respiration in the deep sea. In G. T. Rowe (Ed.), *The Sea*, pp. 331–370. Wiley, New York.

Thistle, D., 1983. The stability-time hypothesis as a predictor of diversity in deep-sea soft-bottom communities: a test. *Deep-Sea Research* 30:267–277.

Thistle, D., and K. M. Sherman, 1985. The nematode fauna of a deep-sea site exposed to strong near-bottom currents. *Deep-Sea Research* 32(9):1077–1088.

Thistle, D., J. Y. Yingst, and K. Fauchald, 1985. A deep-sea benthic community exposed to strong near-bottom currents on the Scotian Rise (western Atlantic). *Marine Geology* 66:91–112.

Thorson, G., 1971. *Life in the Sea*. World University Library, McGraw-Hill Book Company, New York, Toronto.

Turekian, K. K., J. K. Cochran, D. P. Kharkar, R. M. Cerrato, J. M. Vaisnys, H. L. Sanders, J. F. Grassle, and J. A. Allen, 1975. Slow growth rate of a deep-sea clam determined by ^{228}Ra chronology. *Proc. Nat. Acad. Sci.* 72:2829–2832.

Tyler, P. A., 1986. Studies of a benthic time series: reproductive biology of benthic invertebrates in the Rockall Trough. *Proceedings of the Royal Society of Edinburgh* 88B:175–190.

Van Valen, L., 1976. Energy and evolution. *Evolutionary Theory* 1:179–229.

Williams, C. B., 1964. *Patterns in the Balance of Nature*. Academic Press, New York and London.

20   Species Dominance–Diversity Patterns in Oceanic Communities

JOHN A. McGOWAN

Editor's Note: The oceans cover two-thirds of the surface of the earth, support primary production variously estimated as one-third to more than one-half of the global total, have by far the largest fraction of the volume of an obviously finite biosphere, and support a diversity of living systems that is only now being revealed as new techniques of exploration are developed. The oceans are simultaneously accumulating disturbance from human activities, even before the extent and role of life in the oceans have been defined. Disturbance includes the removal of fish, such as the tuna from the pelagic food-webs of the Pacific, and the accumulation of wastes, now pervasive. An ocean free of human influences is of the past.

The wastes are a nagging problem whose effects remain obscure, at least in the open ocean. Some of the wastes are dumped deliberately as sewage and other offal from cities such as New York and Boston and Rio and Athens. Some are industrial wastes such as the radioactivity dumped into the Irish Sea from the British reprocessing plant at Sellafield and into the Bay of Biscay by the French. Some are carried by the great rivers of the world, collected from cities and industries along their shores, and mixed into the sediments and waters of coastal regions globally, gradually to enter the complex circulation of the abyssal seas. Others are carried much less conspicuously to the oceans in air to be scrubbed from the atmosphere in rain.

Whatever the source of the wastes, they accumulate in the oceans. We assume with a dream-borne optimism that they are somehow rendered innocuous, have no effect on the extraordinarily complex life of the oceans, and will not return to trouble us. The assumption does not stand scrutiny: when effects become obvious; when the radioactivity circulating around the shores of Europe becomes a clear hazard, as it is; when the fisheries are affected, as they are in many coastal zones; when pelagic communities show effects of the disturbance; it is too late to remove the toxins and very late to change the patterns of human behavior, fixed as they are by heavy investments in a leaky, wasteful, partially industrialized civilization.

John McGowan, one of a small group of distinguished scholars who over years have studied the planktonic communities of the open sea, addresses here the questions that such a scholar must address in trying to sort a way through the complexities of the physics, chemistry, and biology that produce recognizable communities in the pelagic seas. Are these communities likely to prove sensitive to the changes in the ocean brought about by human activities? They are, of course, and probably through patterns now well defined, but just how and when and where remain a puzzle, excitingly presented here by one who has had an extraordinary experience in the pursuit of insights into the life of the oceans.

395

Introduction

The rate of loss of terrestrial species appears to be increasing. This rate change is almost certainly due to human activities and is especially clear in large but still localized areas such as parts of Amazonia. But we can anticipate much larger-scale losses because of the predicted global climate changes brought about by human alteration of the mix of atmospheric gases by increasing those that are active in the process of radiative heating of the globe. It is predicted that this alteration of the atmosphere will change the climate at a rate exceeding that of past natural variations. The predicted warming is not, however, a uniform one but varies significantly geographically (Ramanathan 1988). Such changes should both alter the general large-scale circulation of the ocean (and atmosphere) and cause numerous, and perhaps intense, episodic, mesoscale perturbations as well. Such events will represent large and significant anomalies from the long-term mean environmental conditions and, therefore, potentially serious ecosystem disturbances. They may be of a kind and intensity well beyond the evolutionary "experience" of community members. Such events are suspected of having strong effects on species dominance, diversity patterns, and the normal functioning of community-ecosystems (Bolin et al. 1986).

In view of this prospect we may ask: What sort of observed climatic anomalies are important in affecting the dominance–diversity structure of ecosystems? And what are the consequences of the resulting structural rearrangements or species loss?

There is evidence that the exclusion of certain species, called "keystone" species, results in changes in overall diversity and a rearrangement of dominance structure (Paine 1980, and others). In addition to this empirical evidence there is speculation that the loss of any member of a natural community will have disruptive effects on the whole because of suspected close coupling between species structure and community function. Community function includes many processes, such as the flow of energy and materials through complicated webs, the cycling of essential plant nutrients such as nitrogen and phosphorus, the sequestering of pollutants, and the processing of atmospheric gasses such as O_2 and CO_2. Primary production, the efficiency with which carbon is transfered through the system and the fraction allocated to decomposers, may also depend on the species diversity of the community (Auclair 1983; Lamotte 1983; Rapp 1983).

We expect that in marine systems, at least, energy and materials flow systematically through regular pathways (Riley 1965; Steele 1974). These pathways are thought to have developed over a very long period of natural selection where competitive forces have tended to maximize the efficiency with which each entity or link (i.e., species) within the community food-web processes resources. Species are thought to achieve this efficiency by being selective specialists on certain fractions of the available spectrum of resources, thereby "allocating" resources and by so doing achieving a sort of dynamic species equilibrium. If this conceptual version of nature is substantially correct then it follows that the role of each link is important. The removal of one or more links can lead to a rearrangement of patterns of flow of energy and materials by a switching of pathways, a change in competitve relationships and that of predators and prey and, consequently, a loss of efficiency. All of this may occur over an unpredictable period of time and to an unpredictable degree. The entire functioning of the system as a pool or reservoir or productive organization would differ in this case since the turnover times and pathways through the machinery should change. The loss of many species might be very disruptive (Lovejoy 1986).

We do not have enough information either to support fully or to discount such a scenario, let alone to estimate the magnitude of changes from species impoverishment. But because of the perceived threat and because known feedback loops operate between climate and existing ecosystems, we take this and other such "plausible scenarios" seriously. There is enough theoretical and observational experience to consider them valid concepts, if not predictive tools.[1] The pelagic realm is a major fraction of the earth's surface. The organisms there should obey the same laws of growth, population genetics, Lotka–Volterra dynamics, and evolution as those elsewhere. Their biota, biogeography, life histories, productivity, and growth have been studied extensively as have their temporal and spatial variations in abundance (Reid et al. 1978). There are enough data and knowledge of the biology of pelagic species to provide us with the beginnings of an understanding of temporal and spatial patterns of pelagic community structure and to address the question of the consequences of loss of diversity.

Observations

The distribution and abundance of species of oceanic macroplankton have been carefully mapped in the North and South Pacific. On the basis of several thousand well-distributed data points, maps of many individual species patterns have been made (Brinton 1962; Beklemishev 1969; McGowan 1974; Reid et al. 1978). From these maps it may be seen that all species have populations covering broad spatial ranges and that there are patches or aggregations of varying intensity within these ranges (Figure 20.1). There are few basic spatial patterns and these tend to be repeated from taxon to taxon. There are copepod patterns similar to euphausiid patterns,

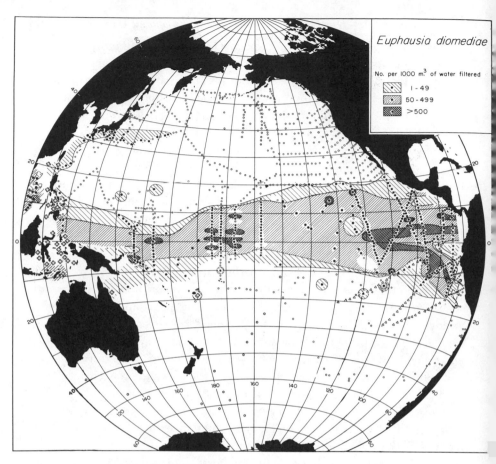

Figure 20.1. The distribution and abundance of *Euphausia diomediae*. This is an example of the species restricted to the equatorial circulation system but with a considerable heterogeneity of abundance within that system. It is typical of many other species of macrozooplankton in that most of them are limited to one or another of the major gyres or circulation systems, as shown in Figure 20.2. (Reprinted from Brinton 1962, with permission of Bulletin of Scripps Institution of Oceanography.)

which in turn are similar to those of chaetognaths, pteropods, and other groups (Figure 20.2). Phytoplankton, fish, squid, and even marine mammals tend to conform to this scheme. A simple visual inspection of a series of these maps shows that there is a basic agreement or concordance among species on the shape and size of ranges, range boundaries (Figure 20.3), and even on where to be abundant and where to be rare (Fager and McGowan 1963). These species assemblages not only cover a broad taxonomic spectrum but include all trophic levels as well. The assemblages are then, by definition, "communities" of organisms in which the species are found together in the same place at the same time more often than can be attributed to chance

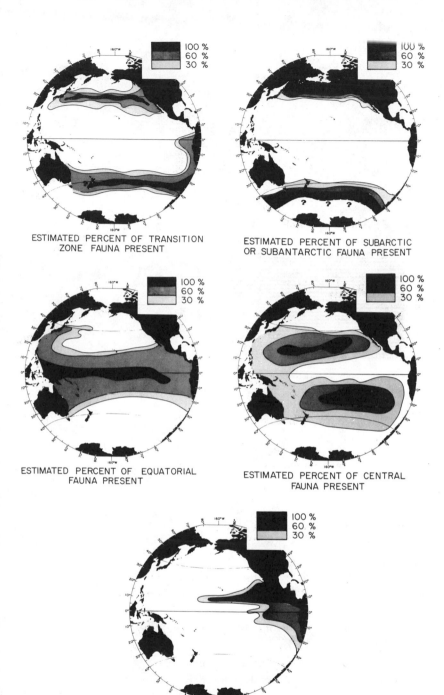

ESTIMATED PERCENT OF TRANSITION
ZONE FAUNA PRESENT

ESTIMATED PERCENT OF SUBARCTIC
OR SUBANTARCTIC FAUNA PRESENT

ESTIMATED PERCENT OF EQUATORIAL
FAUNA PRESENT

ESTIMATED PERCENT OF CENTRAL
FAUNA PRESENT

ESTIMATED PERCENT OF EASTERN
TROPICAL PACIFIC FAUNA PRESENT

Figure 20.2. Pelagic faunal provinces of the Pacific. These five areas and the
Antarctic each have separate and distinct species assemblages and climatologies.
(Reprinted from McGowan 1974, with permission from Oregon State University
Press.)

LATITUDE   NORTH   NEAR 155° W   MERIDIAN

Figure 20.3. Latitudinal ranges for seventy species of pelagic animals from nine taxa. Species ranges are large and there is substantial agreement on boundaries.

alone (Fager and McGowan 1963). These associations have been shown to persist over time by surveys taken decades apart. Therefore a time period representing many plankton generations shows the same large-scale species co-occurrence patterns (McGowan and Walker 1985).

The spatial patterns of these community assemblages make sense from the viewpoint of climatology and physical oceanography as well. Their boundaries coincide with those of the major circulation systems of the Pacific (Reid et al. 1978). There is continuity of water movement and a mechanism for the conservation of properties, including species populations, within systems. The circulation is basically wind-driven but is also influenced by thermohaline processes, the rotation of the earth, and the shape of the basin. All of these factors are very much a function of latitude and climatic zone. Each system is quite a different environment and seems to respond differently to large-scale climate-forcing processes (McGowan 1986). The different physical and climatic regimes are characterized by very different standing crops, annual productivities, and seasonalities as well as species assemblages. Paleontological evidence shows that these circulation systems have been in place for millions of years (McGowan 1974). Each is complete in the sense that all trophic levels are present, the life histories of the members are completed within the systems, and energy and elements are cycled and recycled within the systems in characteristic ways. The assemblages, therefore, have all the attributes associated with that higher level of organization called the community-ecosystem.

Repeated measurements within these oceanic areas, taken many years apart, show these features to be consistent, although each area has a different species diversity (Figure 20.4) and a different spectrum of physical variations.

Thus oceanic community-ecosystems resemble those of land in the first-order characteristics of the community level of biological organization. However, there are some very important differences that may strongly affect the maintenance of diversity and the stability of structure. It is these differences that may be most instructive to us in our attempt to understand which aspects of structure and function are likely to be important in buffering a system against perturbation or restoring it after disturbance. One major difference is that all of the bulk constituents and individuals within these oceanic communities are mobile and have three-dimensional spatial patterns. The spectrum of mobility ranges from that of simple, small-scale, molecular diffusion of some dissolved constituents (say phosphate ions) to the sustained high-speed swimming of a top carnivore like yellowfin tuna. Another difference is that all the important biota are widely dispersed compared to the land or the benthos, where sessile species may actually cover all the available space.

It seems unlikely that competition for sites or space is important to organization in the pelagic realm. Because of this, the role of "key" species or "dominants" may be qualitatively different in pelagic systems and, therefore, the consequences of loss or gain of species not the same as in sessile systems. A further difference lies in the fact that the ocean is constantly being stirred, and turbulent mixing on many scales and at many different energetic levels is of great importance. Such motion strongly affects the vertical replenishment of plant nutrients to the upper, lighted zone and affects productivity. Some scales of turbulence, however, may mix plants downward out of the light, inhibiting photosynthesis and redistributing patches of food for grazers. For these and many other reasons the degree of turbulent motion is important as both a stabilizing or a disturbing force. Regional systems differ with regard to the spectra of turbulent energy. Finally, oceanic systems differ from those of the land in that they are more remote from human influence.

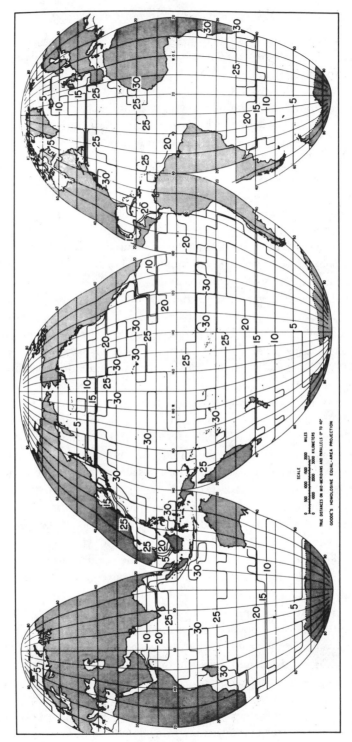

SCALE
MILES
0 500 1000 1500 2000
0 500 1000 1500 2000 2500 3000 KILOMETERS
TRUE DISTANCES ON MID-MERIDIANS AND PARALLELS 0° TO 40°

GOODE'S HOMOLOSINE EQUAL-AREA PROJECTION

Figure 20.4a. Euphausiid number of species per 5° square for the world oceans.

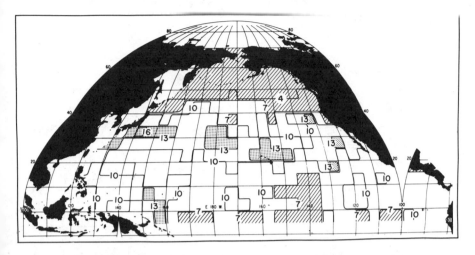

Figure 20.4b. Pteropod number of species per 5° square for the North Pacific. Both charts are based on all available literature records plus several thousand quantitative samples (Reid et al. 1978).

The Problems

Norton (1986), Slobodkin (1986), Fowler and MacMahon (1982), Terborgh and Winter (1980), and others have pointed out that the potential consequences of a species extinction may extend well beyond the species itself but "since so little is known of how species interact, it is usually not known which ones are essential for the continued functioning of a given system" (Norton 1986), or the degree to which such a removal affects the state of the system. In spite of this "deplorable lack" of scientific knowledge of ecosystems (Norton 1986), we can focus on areas where more information would be helpful by asking answerable questions of obvious relevance. Can we determine which species tend to be more susceptible to extinction? Are there criteria or characteristics that make some species more vulnerable than others (Terborgh 1974; Terborgh and Winter 1980; Slobodkin 1986)? Are there buffers against extinction? Are there redundancies or species whose loss will little affect the system because others take over their roles? Are there species whose loss will not matter? What kind and magnitude of environmental perturbations are important? What kind are not? Our knowledge of pelagic ecosystems can help us understand such questions.

Three regional studies of pelagic ecosystem structure and function have been carried out over a long enough period to allow appraisals of diversity, dominance structure, trophic structure, production, and standing crops through one or two severe disturbances. The regions are: the North Pacific Central Gyre, the South Pacific Central Gyre, and the California Current.

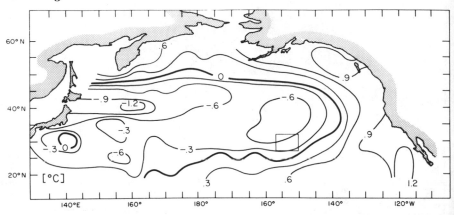

Figure 20.5. Changes in sea surface temperature (SST) over the North Pacific. Differences are winter values 1980–1985 minus those of 1968–1973. The rectangle indicates the region for our long-term study of ecosystem structure. (Reprinted from Venrick et al. 1987, *Science*, Vol. 238, 2 October, pp. 70–72, with permission. Copyright 1987 by AAAS.)

The latter is a large, very complex, ecotone with components from at least three other systems plus a few of its own endemics.

North Pacific Central Gyre

Although the gyre is an oligotrophic, high-diversity ecosystem, it is in many ways the most easily studied. It is simple because we have detected few, if any, changes in important aspects of structure since 1964 (when we began to study it as a system) and because of its great horizontal coherence. Since 1964 there have been several, natural, oceanographic perturbations, and the populations of top predators (tuna) have been reduced. The record shows episodic departures from the long-term mean of sea-surface temperature both in absolute terms and in standard deviations. For example between 1968 and 1969 there was an abrupt 2° C change in mean temperature of the upper 100 m of a very large area in the central Pacific Gyre ($>10^6$ km^2). The change was equal to or greater than the estimates of this area's negative temperature anomaly during the last glacial period (Climap 1976). In terms of heat exchange alone, this was an enormous perturbation. Also, beginning in the mid-1970s, there was a slower, systematic shift in climate of the region so that now there is a persistent negative temperature anomaly (about −0.6° C) throughout this entire area (Venrick et al. 1987). This latter shift was accompanied by a doubling of the phytoplankton biomass (Figure 20.5). Beginning in the mid-1960s, the catch per unit of effort of tuna, never very high, began to decline. By the 1970s a significant number of them had been removed from the system. There were then at least three events that could have affected system's state; the short, abrupt and the long, systematic changes in climate and the reduction of a top predator.

During this time we repeatedly measured the concentration and spatial structure of such components of the system as primary production, phytoplankton and zooplankton biomass, the abundance of small fish and their larvae, and, of course, physical-chemical attributes. In addition, species richness, dominance structure, and the persistence of dominance within important taxa were followed. The three-dimensional species spatial structure was studied for phytoplankton, several large taxa of zooplankton, and larval fish.

There were some changes during the perturbations. Primary production doubled during the cold-anomaly year of 1969. The zooplankton standing crop also almost doubled and then returned to normal. We could detect no species structure changes in either plants or animals however.

Both spatial and species structure in this domain are well defined and persistent. The abundance of copepod species varies in a regular way in the vertical and horizontal dimension. This aspect of structure did not change with time (Figures 20.6 and 20.7). Dominance within taxa (and between) is strong (Figure 20.8). Out of the 174 species of large, adult copepods present, only 17 accounted for more than 75 percent of the individuals. This same degree of species dominance was true of the phytoplankton, larval fish, and adult fish populations (Figure 20.9) (Loeb 1979; Venrick 1982; Barnett 1983) and persisted throughout both of the climatic perturbations. The high diversity of this system is due to the presence of many species whose mean abundance per species is less than 1 percent of the total number of species in their taxon present in the area. This is true at three distinctly different trophic levels. Not only is community complexity made up mainly of rare species but these species remain rare before, during, and after climatic perturbations (McGowan and Walker 1985). We have examined this persistence of dominance by comparing the rank order of copepod species abundance in samples separated in time from hours to about 10 years (Figure 20.10) and in space by about 600 m to over 800 km (Figure 20.11). On all of these space–time scales the abundant species stayed abundant, the common species stayed common, and the rare species stayed rare. During the approximately 10 years of our study there was no significant shift in dominance, no changes in species equilibrium, and even the small-scale three-dimensional spatial pattern remained the same. As our sampling effort approached the edge of this biogeographic province, some species did tend to drop out of the system earlier than others. However, we are unable to identify

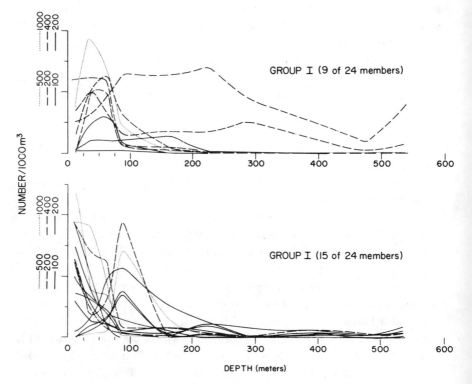

Figure 20.6. Copepod species abundance versus depth; the species have been grouped according to their degree of co-occurrence in the vertical plane (depth), from a series of repeated samples taken over a 10-day period. That is, there is three-dimensional co-occurrence. (Reprinted from McGowan and Walker 1979, with permission from *Ecological Monographs*.)

likely candidates for extinction on the basis of these observed gradients of species diversity. Some numerical dominants drop out as quickly as some rare species. There are no clear relationships to size, morphology, behavior, or habitat.

South Pacific Central Gyre

The South Pacific Central Gyre is very much an analog of the northern one. Its waters are warm and salty and its circulation is anticyclonic so, that as in the north, there is a net downwelling of water. As a consequence of this circulation it is an oligotrophic system where productivity is nutrient limited, again as in the north. Biomass patterns are also similar and species diversity is high (Reid et al. 1978).

Although we have fewer data from the South Pacific there are enough to ask if there are patterns of species structure similar to those of the North

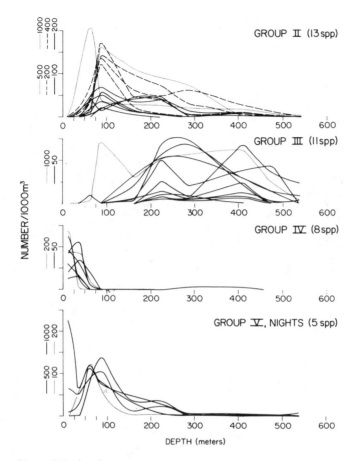

Figure 20.6. (*cont.*)

Gyre. The north and the south share most zooplankton and mesopelagic fish fauna; that is, there are amphitropical species patterns. The copepods in the south are dominated by only a few species although many are present (Figure 20.8). These stay dominant over time (many copepod generations) and the rare species stay rare, as in the north. Although diversity is high in the south there are fewer species present than in the north.

Using the criteria of persistence of species dominance structure, and the small overall range of variation in biomass and productivity, this ecosystem appears to be as stable as that of the north.

California Current

This eastern boundary current differs strongly from the two gyres in almost all attributes. It is wide open to advective transport of allochthonous waters

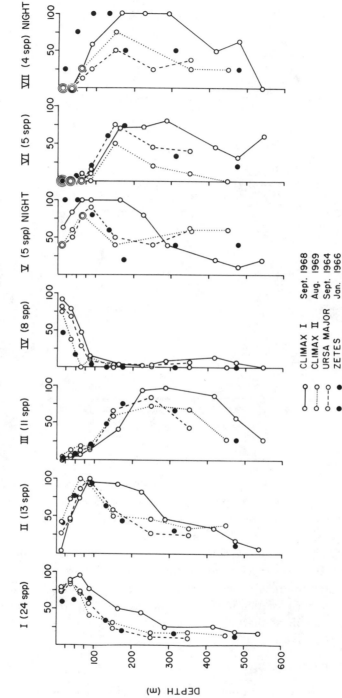

COHERENCE (Average % of Climax I group members present)

DEPTH (m)

CLIMAX I Sept. 1968
CLIMAX II Aug. 1969
URSA MAJOR Sept. 1964
ZETES   Jan. 1966

Figure 20.7. Vertical spatial species structure as in Figure 20.6, but from four different years. This demonstrates the long-term persistence of spatial structure. (Reprinted from McGowan and Walker 1979, with permission from *Ecological Monographs*.)

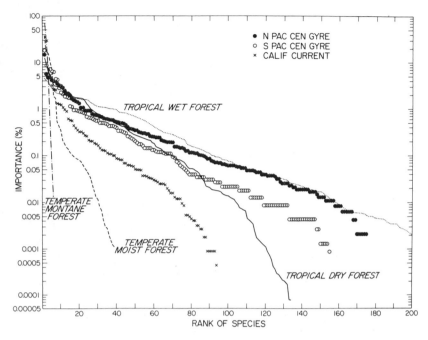

Figure 20.8. Copepod species abundance curves for the North and South Pacific Central Gyres and the California Current compared to those of forest tree species. The copepod data are the mean of seven individual cruise abundances. This is expressed as a percentage of the overall mean for all copepod species. The tree species curves are from Hubbell (1979). It is evident that there are strong similarities between the two types of systems, sessile and mobile, in this aspect of structure. (Reprinted from Hubbell, Vol. 203, 30 March 1979, pp. 1,299–1,309, with permission. Copyright 1979 by the AAAS.)

and populations from other contiguous systems with very different climates. It is highly diverse (Figure 20.8) but almost all the species present have much more extensive populations outside the area. There are strong north–south and inshore–offshore gradients in temperature, salinity, density, productivity, biomass, and species abundance. Diversity is highest in the central part of the region where tropical, subtropical, cool transitional, and subarctic species are found together in the same locale, and sometimes in the same sample (Figure 20.12). If "disturbance" is taken to be a significant and anomalous departure from the long-term mean conditions, then this domain also differs in the degree and frequency of both human and natural disturbance (Chelton, Bernal, and McGowan 1982). It has been intensively studied for over 30 years. During that time there have been two major El Niño events and several large coldwater episodes (Figure 20.13). Urban growth along the coast has been extensive, and the input of domestic and

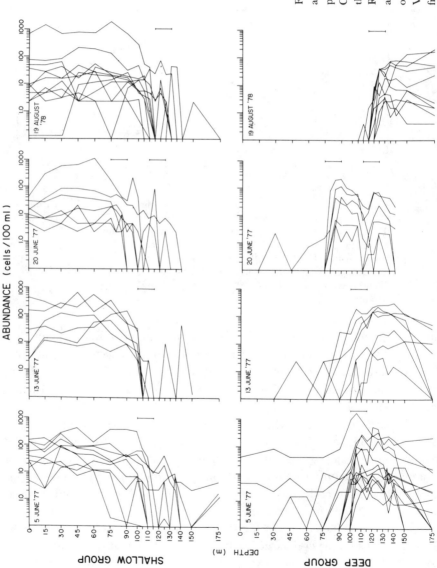

Figure 20.9. Spatial structure and relative abundances of phytoplankton species in the Central Gyre over time. Only the dominants are shown here. Relative mean aboundances for all 300 species span five orders of magnitude. (Reprinted from Venrick 1982, with permission from *Ecological Monographs*.)

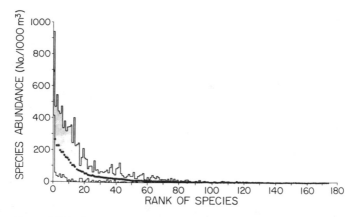

Figure 20.10. Copepod species dominance. Each dot is the overall mean abundance of a species from a 10-year set of data. The vertical bars are the ranges of seven individual cruise means. The rank correlation coefficients between these cruises are significant ($p < .001$ for all). (Reprinted from McGowan and Walker 1985, with permission from *Ecological Monographs*.)

industrial waste products through sewage outfalls, aerial fallout, and surface runoff has increased enormously, as has ship traffic and offshore oil production. In addition, the main predator of macrozooplankton, the Pacific sardine, has suffered a population decline from an estimated 4×10^6 tons to less than 5,000. Although this plankton feeder was eventually replaced by another species, the anchovy (MacCall 1979), there was a gap of about 14 years between the collapse of the sardine and the growth of the anchovy populations. Other planktivorous fish such as the jack mackerel or hake did not fill in this gap. The zooplankton existed for several years without substantial predation from populations that might be assumed to be some sort of keystone species. The system, however, did not restructure itself or collapse, nor were there species losses or gains in the prey assemblage. The dominance structure of zooplankton in the California Current as opposed to the two gyres (Figure 20.14) is normally highly variable, with large and frequent dominance shifts. There were no detectable systematic trends in dominance or diversity as a result of these events.

Both the 1958 and 1983 California El Niño episodes were very large anomalies from the long-term mean. Both lasted at least two years and both resulted in a diminution in plankton biomass by a factor of about 10×. There were extensive environmental changes of other kinds as well. A significant deepening of the thermocline, a lack of the normal seasonal upwelling, the concentration of phytoplankton into a "deep chlorophyll maximum" layer, and the invasion of many tropical and subtropical species normally quite

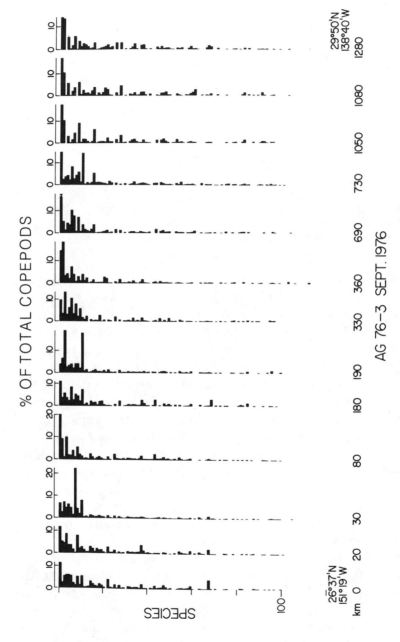

Figure 20.11. The dominance curves versus distance from our time-series study site. The species order is as in Figure 20.10. This shows that the dominance hierarchy is maintained over great horizontal distances as well as over time (Reprinted from McGowan and Walter 1985, with permission from Ecological Monographs).

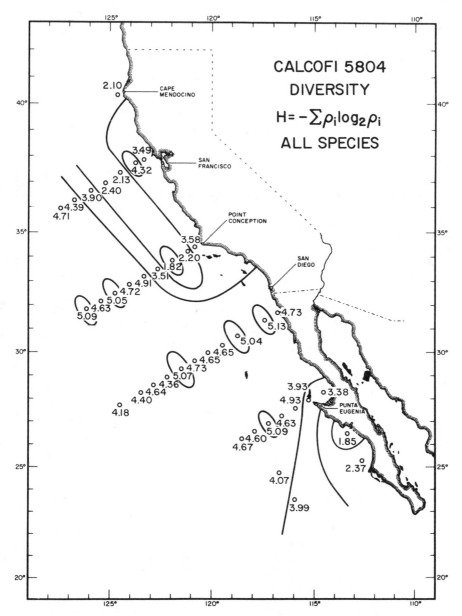

Figure 20.12. The spatial pattern of zooplankton diversity in the California Current as of April 1958. (Reprinted from McGowan and Miller 1980, with permission from CalCOFI Reports.)

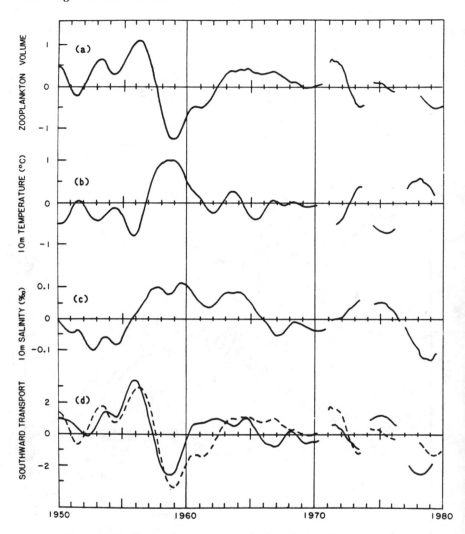

Figure 20.13. The low-frequency anomalies from the long-term means of environmental properties in the main body of the California Current. All in standardized units: (a) the abundance of macrozooplankton; (b) the temperature at the representative of the mixed layer depth of 10 m; (c) salinity at the representative depth of 10 m; (d) the southward transport of water or strength of the current, solid line; the broken line is the zooplankton anomaly from (a), repeated. There are over 50,000 data points in each anomaly curve (Chelton et al. 1982). The very large anomaly of the 1958–1959 El Niño can be clearly seen.

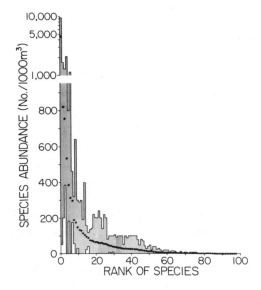

Figure 20.14. Dominance–diversity curve of copepods in the California Current. This curve was constructed in the same manner as that in Figure 20.10. There are a large number of non-significant rank correlations between times and places in this set.

rare in the area are all well documented (Wooster and Fluharty 1985). In spite of these large changes over a substantial time the system restored itself in both cases. The species list of zooplankton and pelagic fish, the relative population sizes, production, spatial patterns, and life histories seem to be no more or less variable now (1987) than they were during the early 1950s. There may have been subtle changes which persisted, especially very near shore or in bays, estuaries, and other restricted locales which we have not measured effectively with our time series. But there is no evidence for any large, general change in the community structure of the California Current system as a whole which stands out against its noisy background variability.

Discussion and Conclusions

Our concern is with the maintenance of natural communities. Are there patterns in the maintenance of diversity? How resilient are they? Are more-diverse communities more fragile? Can they suffer species loss and still function? Which species are most vulnerable? We wish to know what mechanisms stabilize these complex, dynamic organizations, and what buffers them against such unpredictable outside forces as climatic anomalies or episodic geologic upheavals or human activities.

Although it is not always explicitly stated, most ecologists seem to believe that the biotic structure of ecosystems is due to interspecific, functional relationships operating within the "normal" variation of the physical environment. These functional relationships are, primarily, Lotka–Volterra dynamics where stabilizing, density-dependent competition for resources and predator–prey interactions are the chief features of the mechanism of regulation and buffering (May 1976). In some versions of this body of theory, emigration and immigration between structurally different patches are included as part of the kinetics of diversity maintenance (Yodzis 1978; Paine and Levin 1981). Observations, experiments, and models have given strong support to these views. But most of the empirical validation has come from studies where space-limited, sessile organisms play an extremely important role. Forests, the marine littoral benthos, and coral reefs are the systems most studied. Work done in these environments shows that disturbances, many caused by human activity, can severely alter communities and bring about local species extinctions. The rate of these extinctions appears to be increasing. This increase in rate is the matter of great concern because the consequences of loss of diversity are by no means clear. Serious questions may be raised as to the degree to which present conceptual models can be used to predict what may happen to the functioning and dynamics of ecosystems suffering such losses. There are cogent reasons to fear that the consequences may be severe. Because of this widespread concern and because of our uncertainty, attempts have been made to point up critical areas of research.

They include resolving and sharpening our concepts of how communities are structured, what regulates the resilience of structure, and attempts to catalogue those characteristics that make a species a likely candidate for extinction (Holling 1973; Terborgh 1974; Norton 1986; Slobodkin 1986). At this point it seems to me that what are most needed are long-scale, critical empirical observations and the tracking of natural experiments, rather than more theory.

Our studies of mobile, pelagic community ecosystems can contribute to our conceptual basis and enhance our knowledge of the meaning of the patterns of diversity. Such work has led to the following observations:

1   All pelagic species populations are very large. While many, perhaps most species, are not abundant in terms of local concentrations per unit volume, they have huge ranges so that the total number of individuals in populations is great.

2   Most of the observed diversity (length of species list) is due to the presence of many rare or very rare species.

3   In both the North and South Pacific Central Gyres, dominance structure

persists over decades. This represents many generations of the small zooplankton. Absolute abundances of populations do not vary greatly. The rare species stay rare and the abundant stay abundant on all time–space sampling scales from hours to decades. This is strong evidence for long-term ecosystem structural stability.

4   Evidence for a general competitive equilibrium or resource allocation as a mechanism for structuring the community is weak. Evidence against it is strong.

5   There are large changes in dominance structure over relatively short time and space scales in the California Current. Absolute abundances within species populations may vary by a factor of 10 or more both within and between years.

6   There have been significant anomalies from the long-term mean climatic properties or disturbances in both the North and South Central Gyres. In the past 20 years there have been large natural disturbances such as El Niño and a vastly increased input of pollutants in the California Current. There has been a large-scale harvesting of many top predators high in the food web (i.e., commercial fish in the California Current. In spite of these events we have detected no loss of pelagic species nor persistent change in ecosystem structure anywhere.

7.   The North Central and South Central Gyre share species, as does the North Gyre and the California Current. The species list in the South Pacific is shorter than the North Pacific and the California list is much shorter than either. All three systems have persistent populations. The "missing" species do not appear to have an effect on system persistence or stability. There is no evidence that some species are more susceptible to these "extinctions" than others.

These results are in some ways reassuring. They can be interpreted to mean that pelagic systems are not fragile but rather robust. Although highly structured, structure is not strongly affected by either natural or human perturbations. Because there are many rare species, and because our two very stable and very similar systems do not have the same number of species, the concept of species redundancy gains credence. It is difficult to imagine that a species that makes up less than 0.01 percent of the total copepod or phytoplankton population plays an important role in food-web energetics or nitrogen cycling, nor can it be a very important competitor or predator or prey. On the basis of current theory of diversity maintenance and/or ecosystem stabilization it is difficult to see how these species play any role at all. Since there are many such rare species we might conclude that our pelagic systems could lose a substantial number of them with no ill effects. Yet these species are a regular and consistent feature of these systems. I believe it would be foolhardy to conclude they play no role at all, or that they are insignificant. We can only conclude that theory, as it now exists, cannot account for them, and from that we can conclude that the theory is flawed.

Or, perhaps the theory fails for mobile systems and remains adequate for the predominantly sessile ones for which it was designed. If that is the case, we have an important bifurcation in our comprehension of ecosystem biology (Dayton 1984). Although there are some strong structural similarities between sessile and mobile systems (Figure 20.8), it seems likely that the processes responsible for these patterns may be different. Maintenance of forest diversity and other sessile systems is often explained on the basis of disturbance, in that species which would otherwise outcompete their neighbors are prevented from doing so by the disturbance (Hubbell 1979; Paine 1980; Dayton 1984). This theory predicts that on some scale of patchiness (the disturbance scale) there should be shifts or reshuffles of the dominance hierarchy (Yodzis 1978). Our studies of the two gyre systems have failed to validate this prediction. Dominant species stay dominant and rare species stay rare on all of the time–space scales we have measured. On the other hand, in the California Current, disturbances, perturbations, exploitation, and other sorts of "damage" are frequent on virtually all scales. Such damage is quickly repaired by immigration, advection, stirring, and mixing, all of which are intense in this system. It appears that emigration and immigration brought about chiefly by the movement of water would play a far more important role than population interaction in diversity maintenance here. We cannot, at present, say how diversity is maintained in the two gyres.

Acknowledgments

The work reported here has received the long-term support of the State of California through the Marine Life Research Group of Scripps Institution of Oceanography. I am particularly indebted to Mrs. Patricia Walker, my collaborator on much of this work. I have benefited greatly from my association with Dr. Elizabeth Venrick and from many enjoyable discussions with Drs. Paul Dayton, Thomas Hayward, and the late E. W. Fager.

Note

1. More observations are needed on the species structure of natural communities, how persistent structure is through time and space, and whether any observed elimination or rearrangement of species is consistent with the stability and functioning of the systems. This is an aspect of the familiar question of the existence of multiple stable states (Holling 1973; Pimm 1980; Beddington 1984).

   By species structure, I mean: the number of species present in a system having a high degree of fidelity to it and spending a large proportion of their life in it; the mean and variance of the abundances of those species; the degree of dominance;

the persistence in time and space of this dominance and diversity; the three-dimensional spatial array of abundance, the degree of co-occurrence; and, finally, the overall spatial dimensions of such organized assemblages. The latter is necessary so that we may determine spatial coherence of structure, what the system boundaries look like, and the range of environmental variables over which they occur. Such information, acquired from a variety of habitats over time, would add substantially to our background knowledge and affect our evaluation of the role of diversity in the regulation of the function of complex systems. Followed through time we can observe directly the effect of great natural perturbations, such as El Niño, and other, less extreme events.

References

Auclair, D., 1983. "Natural" mixed forests and "artificial" monospecific forests. In H. A. Mooney and M. Gordon (Eds.), *Disturbance and Ecosystems, Components of Response*, pp. 49–82. Ecological Studies Vol. 44. Springer-Verlag, New York.

Barnett, M. A., 1983. Species structure and temporal stability of mesopelagic fish assemblages in the central gyres of the North and South Pacific Ocean. *Marine Biology* (Berlin) 74:245–256.

Beddington, J. R., 1984. The response of multispecies systems to perturbations. In R. M. May (Ed.), *Exploitation of Marine Communities*, pp. 209–225. Springer-Verlag, New York.

Beklemishev, C. W., 1969. *Ecology and Biogeography of the Open Ocean*, pp. 1–129. Publishing House Nauka, USSR (in Russian).

Bolin, B., B. R. Doos, J. Jager, R. A. Warrick (Eds.), 1986. *The Greenhouse Effect, Climate Change and Ecosystems*. Wiley, New York.

Brinton, E., 1962. The distribution of Pacific euphausiids. *Bulletin Scripps Institution Oceanography* 8(2):51–270.

Chelton, D. B., P. A. Bernal, and J. A. McGowan, 1982. Large-scale interannual physical and biological interaction in the California Current. *J. of Marine Research* 40(4):1095–1125.

Climap Project Members, 1976. The surface of the ice age earth. *Science* 191:1131–1137.

Dayton, P. K., 1984. Processes structuring some marine communities: are they general? In D. R. Strong, D. Simberloff, L. G. Abele, and A. B. Thistle (Eds.), *Ecological Communities*, pp. 181–197. Princeton University Press.

Fager, E. W., and J. A. McGowan, 1963. Zooplankton species groups in the North Pacific. *Science* 140(3566):453–460.

Fowler, C. W., and J. A. MacMahon, 1982. Selective extinction and speciation: their influence on the structure and functioning of communities and ecosystems. *The American Naturalist* 119(4):480–495.

Holling, C. S., 1973. Resilience and stability of ecological systems. *Annual Review of Ecology and Systematics* 4:1–24.

Hubbell, S. P., 1979. Tree dispersion, abundance, and diversity in a tropical dry forest. *Science* 203:1299–1309.

Lamotte, M., 1983. Research on the characteristics of energy flows within natural and man-altered ecosystems. In H. A. Mooney and M. Godron (Eds.), *Disturbance and*

Ecosystems, Components of Response, pp. 48–70. Ecological Studies Vol. 44. Springer-Verlag, New York.

Loeb, V. J., 1979. Larval fishes in the zooplankton community of the North Pacific central gyre. *Marine Biology* (Berlin) 53:173-191.

Lovejoy, T. E., 1986. Species leave the Ark one by one. In Bryan G. Norton (Ed.), *The Preservation of Species: The Value of Biological Diversity,* pp. 13–27. Princeton University Press.

MacCall, A. D., 1979. *Population estimates for the waning years of the Pacific Sardine fishery.* CalCOFI Reports Vol. 20, pp. 72–82. Scripps Institution Oceanography, La Jolla, Cal.

May, R. M. (Ed.), 1976. *Theoretical Ecology, Principles and Applications.* W. B. Saunders, Philadelphia.

McGowan, J. A., 1974. The nature of oceanic ecosystems. In C. B. Miller (Ed.), *The Biology of the Oceanic Pacific,* pp. 9–28. Oregon State University Press, Corvallis.

McGowan, J. A., 1986. The biogeography of pelagic ecosystems. In A. C. Pierrot-Bults, S. van der Spoel, B. J. Zahuranec, and R. K. Johnson (Eds.), *Pelagic Biogeography,* pp. 191–200. UNESCO Technical Papers in Marine Science 49, Paris.

McGowan, J. A., and C. B. Miller, 1980. *Larvel fish and zooplankton community structure.* CalCOFI Reports Vol. 21, pp. 29–36. Scripps Institution Oceanography, La Jolla, Cal.

McGowan, J. A., and P. W. Walker, 1979. Structure in the copepod community of the North Pacific central gyre. *Ecological Monographs* 49:195–226.

McGowan, J. A., and P. W. Walker, 1985. Dominance and diversity maintenance in an oceanic ecosystem. *Ecological Monographs* 55(1):103–118.

Norton, B. G., 1986. Epilogue. In B. G. Norton (Ed.), *The Preservation of Species: The Value of Biological Diversity,* pp. 268–283. Princeton University Press.

Paine, R. T., 1980. Food webs: linkage interaction strength and community infrastructure. *J. Animal Ecology* 49:667–685.

Paine, R. T., and S. A. Levin, 1981. Intertidal landscapes: disturbance and the dynamics of pattern. *Ecological Monographs* 51:145–178.

Pimm, S. L., 1980. Foodweb design and the effects of species deletion. *Oikos* 35:139.

Ramanathan, V., 1988. The greenhouse theory of climate change: a test by an inadvertent global experiment. *Science* 240:293–299.

Rapp, M., 1983. Some problems of disturbance on the nutrient cycling in ecosystems. In H.A. Mooney and M. Godron (Eds.), *Disturbance and Ecosystems, Components of Response.* Ecological Studies, Vol. 44, pp. 117–128. Springer-Verlag, New York.

Reid, J. L., E. Brinton, A. Fleminger, E. L. Venrick, and J. A. McGowan, 1978. Oceanic circulation and marine life. In H. Charnock and G. E. R. Deacon (Eds.), *Advances in Oceanography,* pp. 65–130. Plenum, New York.

Riley, G. A., 1965. A mathematical model of regional variations in plankton. *Limnology and Oceanography.* 10(Supp.):R202–R215.

Slobodkin, L. B., 1986. On the susceptibility of different species to extinction: elementary instructions for owners of a world. In B. G. Norton (Ed.), *The Preservation of Species: The Value of Biological Diversity,* pp. 226–242. Princeton University Press.

Steele, J. H., 1974. *The Structure of Marine Ecosystems.* Harvard University Press, Cambridge, Mass.

Terborgh, J., 1974. Preservation of natural diversity: the problem of extinction prone species. *Bioscience* 24:715–722.

Terborgh, J., and B. Winter, 1980. Some causes of extinction. In M. E. Soulé and B. A. Wilcox (Eds.), *Conservation Biology*, pp. 119–134. Sinauer Associates, Sunderland, Mass.

Venrick, E. L., 1982. Phytoplankton in an oligotrophic ocean: observations and questions. *Ecological Monographs* 52:129–154.

Venrick, E. L., J. A. McGowan, D. R. Cayan, and T. L. Hayward, 1987. Climate and chlorophyll *a*: long-term trends in the central North Pacific ocean. *Science* 238:70–72.

Wooster, W. S., and D. L. Fluharty, 1985. *El Niño North*. Washington Sea Grant Program. University of Washington, Seattle.

Yodzis, P., 1978. *Competition for space and the structure of ecological communities*. Lecture Notes in Biomathematics 25. Springer-Verlag, Berlin.

Chronic Disturbance and Natural
Ecosystems: Aquatic and Emergent
Ecosystems

B. FRESHWATER SYSTEMS

21 Natural and Anthropogenically Imposed Limitations to Biotic Richness in Fresh Waters

DAVID W. SCHINDLER

Editor's Note: Lakes and streams receive a disproportionate share of the disruption that follows the spread of human influences over the globe. The disruption reaches from the direct effects of dams and modifications of water courses to the disposal of sewage and the introduction of toxins including agricultural poisons. There is in addition the series of problems associated both with the depletion of the fish populations through harvest and with the introduction of exotics. And, more recently, we have recognized the seriousness of the problems associated with air pollution, including the acidification of rain and the cumulative effects on lakes. Now we see the further possibility that genetic engineers will be adding to the burdens already well known from the introduction of exotics by producing novel combinations of genes that may escape into nature to produce totally unforeseen effects.

In many ways, among all of science, the limnologists have led in defining the transitions under way in nature. The process of eutrophication was recognized first in aquatic systems and has since been recognized as a general phenomenon, the enrichment with nutrients mobilized by human activities, a first step in the continuum of change that is gradualy recognized as pollution, and, in a twist peculiar to nature, impoverishment.

The full array of effects and patterns laid forth so explicitly by Schindler is almost overwhelming. But the other message, only slightly less powerfully articulated, is that the changes are a continuum away from the status quo toward progressive impoverishment. That point always catches in the craw of my non-ecologist friends in science, who want to believe that human activities have improved the world in general and hold great potential for more improvements. They overlook the fact that a few generations are enough to select strains of a species for a particular site, and the flora and fauna of lakes and streams, even in the young landscape of the glaciated regions, is adjusted to its own particular circumstance of place and time. It works – and if it works, don't fix it.

Introduction

Freshwater ecosystems are especially suited to the investigation of factors controlling the distribution and abundance of species. Lakes and rivers occur in almost all latitudes and altitudes, a wide variety of geological settings and climates, and diverse shapes and sizes. In some cases, the biological

425

communities of lakes can be quite isolated, offering many of the advantages of islands. In other cases, series of aquatic systems are interconnected to varying degrees, ensuring a considerable degree of recolonization of damaged ecosystems. Representatives of several trophic levels in freshwater can be captured, and the chemical and physical environment characterized, with quite simple sampling apparatus. With relatively few exceptions, such as some groups of insects, the taxonomy of freshwater groups is well known, at least in comparison to other ecosystem types. As a result, it seems pertinent to begin this chapter by considering some of the natural factors that are known to control biotic richness in freshwaters, for these factors may provide some insights into general mechanisms controlling biotic richness in marine, wetland, and terrestrial ecosystems as well. Later, I shall give examples of how human activities have modified these natural patterns, and of how ignoring natural controls on biotic richness can lead to false interpretations. For an example of a more detailed treatment of natural controls on freshwater biotic richness, see Werner's (1986) treatment of fishes.

Why Be Concerned about Biotic Impoverishment of Freshwaters?

The diversity of species in natural aquatic communities varies tremendously, ranging from fewer than 100 species in polar lakes to many thousands of endemic species in large ancient lakes like Tanganyika and Baikal. Both types of ecosystems appear to function well, and productivity and biomass at all latitudes increase in proportion to nutrient supplies (Schindler 1978).

Good reasons for maintaining diversity have been documented in fairly simple communities. For example, less-diverse communities tend to be more easily displaced by exotic invaders (Moyle 1986), and to have the normal functioning of food chains, nutrient cycles, and ecosystem metabolism impaired by chemical stressors (Schindler et al. 1985; Schindler 1987). But does halving the number of species in a community where several thousand species are present cause the same danger as in a community where the same functions are carried out by a dozen or fewer species? At present, we simply do not know the answer to this question, and it seems prudent not to squander diversity needlessly until we are confident that it does no harm.

That being said, some of us would elect to preserve biological diversity even if it meant a considerable decline in our standard of living, for a world where all birds are starlings, all plants are genetically engineered cereals, all animals are domestic cattle, and all fish are cyprinids would be boring indeed.

The Natural Controls of Biotic Richness

In this chapter I use *biotic richness* to indicate the status quo for natural ecosystems, *enrichment* for increases in richness, and *impoverishment* for decreases. These are all general terms. Biotic richness can be expressed in a number of different ways, including number of species, evenness, diversity, biomass, yield, and production. I use *species richness* to refer to the number of species in a given ecosystem.

Physical Factors

Lake size, depth, and shoreline development have long been known to correlate with species richness in fresh waters (Brooks 1950; Barbour and Brown 1974; Tonn and Magnuson 1982; Eadie and Keast 1984) (Figure 21.1). Rawson (1956) also noted that there was an inverse correlation between mean depth and several measures of biotic richness. These factors must be taken into account when assessing the degree of biotic impoverishment caused by anthropogenic stresses. A global survey of lotic fishes reveals a strong correlation between basin size and species numbers (Figure 21.2). Natural catastrophes such as volcanic eruptions, destratification in unusual weather, depletion of oxygen under winter ice, and glaciation are other examples of natural phenomena that restrict species richness. For example, failure to consider the positive correlation between lake size and number of fish species would cause impoverishment due to acid rain to be overestimated, because acidification is most pronounced in small lakes, and larger lakes usually have richer fish faunas to start with (Figures 21.1 and 21.3) (Rago and Wiener 1986; Rahel 1986).

Geology and Hydrology

Geology exerts a major control on both species richness and, via its effects on water chemistry, susceptibility to impoverishment. For example, high-alkalinity lakes have more species of fishes than low-alkalinity lakes (Figure 21.3) (Rahel 1986). Low concentrations of calcium also limit the distribution of many species, including fishes (Brown 1982), Mollusca and Crustacea (Figure 21.4). Schindler (1971) noted that lakes with larger ratios of drainage basin to lake surface area had higher concentrations of most chemicals as well as higher indicators of biotic richness of several types, including phytoplankton production and standing crop and winter decomposition. Rawson (1961) deduced the general relationship between geology and productivity. He also noted that productivity was diminished in fast-flushing lakes. In general, the low weathering rates in hard-rock areas limit the natural inputs of phosphorus and nitrogen (Dillon and Kirchner 1975), the

428   D. W. SCHINDLER

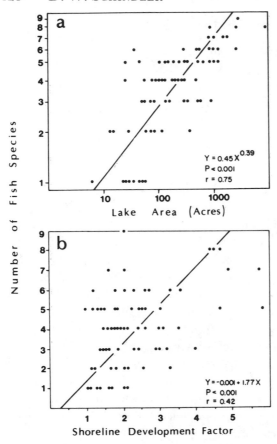

Figure 21.1. The relationship between the number of fish species per lake and (a) lake area and (b) the shoreline development factor. (Reprinted with modifications from Eadie and Keast 1984, with permission.)

elements that control standing crop and productivity of phytoplankton. Via plant productivity they also control the productivity and probably the biotic richness of higher trophic levels (Dillon and Rigler 1975).

The powerful controls that nutrients exert on the productivity and phytoplankton biomass in freshwater ecosystems have recently been elucidated (Vollenweider 1968, 1976). Models based on phosphorus input yield accurate predictions of chlorophyll concentration, phytoplankton biomass, and production for lakes of all sizes and latitudes, with water renewal constituting the only other factor of major importance (Dillon 1975; Vollenweider 1976; Schindler 1977, 1978; Schindler et al. 1978). The rate of lake acidification is also dependent on water renewal, via its effect on retention of sulfate and nitrate (Baker et al. 1986; Kelly et al. 1987).

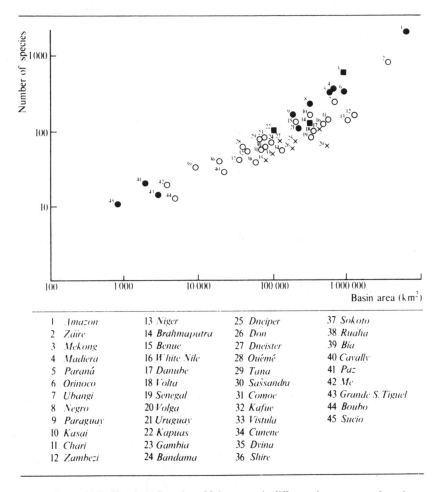

1	*Amazon*	13 *Niger*	25 *Dneiper*	37 *Sokoto*
2	*Zaïre*	14 *Brahmaputra*	26 *Don*	38 *Ruaha*
3	*Mekong*	15 *Benue*	27 *Dneister*	39 *Bia*
4	*Madiera*	16 *White Nile*	28 *Ouémé*	40 *Cavally*
5	*Paraná*	17 *Danube*	29 *Tana*	41 *Paz*
6	*Orinoco*	18 *Volta*	30 *Sassandra*	42 *Me*
7	*Ubangi*	19 *Senegal*	31 *Comoe*	43 *Grande S. Tiguel*
8	*Negro*	20 *Volga*	32 *Kafue*	44 *Boubo*
9	*Paraguay*	21 *Uruguay*	33 *Vistula*	45 *Sucio*
10	*Kasai*	22 *Kapuas*	34 *Cunene*	
11	*Chari*	23 *Gambia*	35 *Dvina*	
12	*Zambezi*	24 *Bandama*	36 *Shire*	

Figure 21.2. Number of species of fish present in different river systems plotted according to their basin areas: (●) South America; (○) Africa; (■) Europe; (×) Asia. (Reprinted from Welcomme 1979, with permission.)

Climate, Latitude, Altitude, and Basin Age

Water renewal is but one of many manifestations of climate. The expression of climatic effects depends upon lake size. For example, if two lakes are of equal area and have equal water inputs, a deep lake will have slower water renewal and thus greater nutrient retention than a shallow one. At the same latitude, shallow lakes tend to be warmer and in some cases more ephemeral than deep ones (Patalas and Salki 1984; Hecky 1986). Patalas (1970) also noted that productivity increased when lake waters were warmed by thermal effluents, although species numbers and biomass were not affected. Although

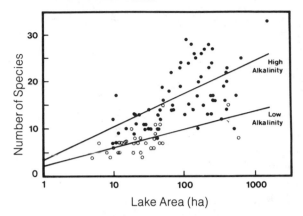

Figure 21.3. Relationship between the number of fish species and $\log_{10}$ (surface area) for high-alkalinity (●) and low-alkalinity (○) lakes in northern Wisconsin. The regression equation for the high-alkalinity lakes (> 10 mg/L as $CaCO_3$) is $Y = 2.67 + 7.15 \log_{10}$ (area) ($n = 67$, $r^2 = 0.35$), and for the low-alkalinity lakes (≤ 10 mg/L as $CaCO_3$) is $Y = 2.19 + 3.76 \log_{10}$ (area) ($n = 33$, $r^2 = 0.37$). (Reprinted from Rahel 1986, with permission.)

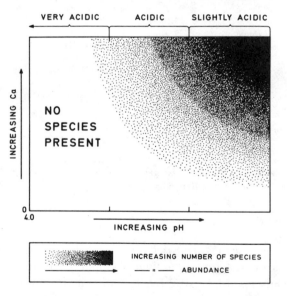

Figure 21.4. Schematical diagram showing the principle of reduced acid stress with increasing concentration of external calcium (lower pH values tolerated when calcium increases). Originally based on tolerance values for widespread species of snails, small mussels, and crustaceans studied in about 1,000 lakes in Norway. The same principle also holds true for certain other invertebrates and for fish. (Reprinted from Økland and Økland 1980 and 1986, with permission.)

warm, shallow lakes tend to have high zooplankton standing crops, deep lakes tend to have more species (Patalas 1975; Patalas 1984) (Figure 21.5). Low concentrations of oxygen under winter ice severely limit the diversity of fishes. Oxygen is affected by lake size, depth, trophic state, and the duration of winter ice and snow cover (Tonn and Magnuson 1982). The southern limits of many glacial relict species, which are cold stenotherms, is limited by water temperature, particularly in lakes without thermoclines.

In California, Strub et al. (1985) found that Pacific El Niño effects on productivity were evident in a shallow lake (Castle Lake, z_{max} = 34 m). In Lake Tahoe (z_{max} = 700 m) no El Niño effects were observed, and productivity was governed by the depth of spring mixing, which resupplied the euphotic zone with nutrients from the deep hypolimnion (Goldman and Jassby 1987).

The general decrease in species richness of ecosystems with increasing latitude or altitude is well known (MacArthur 1972; Kawecka and Szczesny 1984; Ward 1986). The effects of latitude and altitude on species richness are somewhat similar, probably because both are expressed via similar effects on glacial and geological history, climate, chemical weathering, water renewal, and difficulty for biological dispersal. High-latitude and high-altitude lakes and streams tend to have fewer species, particularly in upper trophic levels (Eadie and Keast 1984; Kawecka and Szczesny 1984; Ward 1986) (Figure 21.6, Tables 21.1 and 21.2), and to be less productive (Brylinsky and Mann 1973; Schindler 1978; Ward 1986).

Ecosystem age has a major effect on species richness, as exemplified by the great diversity of endemic species in Lake Baikal (Kozhov 1963), Lake Malawi, and Lake Tanganyika (Brooks 1950) (Figure 21.7). Interestingly, phytoplankton production and standing crop in Baikal and Tanganyika, ancient lakes of nearly identical size but 50° latitude apart, differ by only 2.5 percent (Hecky 1984, and personal communication), perhaps indicating that nutrients are more important than annual light regimes, temperature, or other factors which vary with latitude in controlling phytoplankton production and biomass. Schindler (1978) reaches similar conclusions for lakes from a variety of latitudes.

Biological Factors

Immigration is influenced not only by the dispersal powers of individual species, but also by the distance apart of aquatic ecosystems, and the order which a particular lake or stream occupies in a cascade of ecosystems. For example, Patalas (1981, and personal communication) found a large number of zooplankton species near the mouths of rivers entering Lake Winnipeg. Some originated from areas of Precambrian geology and entered via the Winnipeg

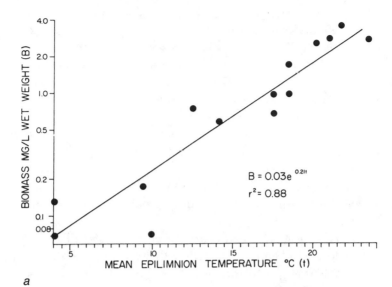

a

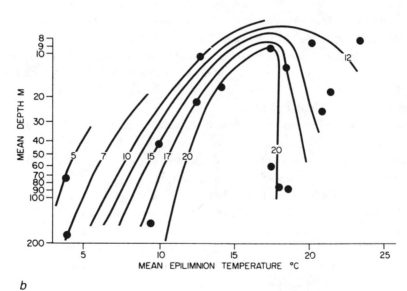

b

Figure 21.5. (a) The relationship between the abundance of planktonic crustaceans and the mean epilimnion temperature in midsummer in fourteen North America great lakes. (b) Crustacean plankton communities: the relationship between the number of species, the mean depth and the mean epilimnion temperature in midsummer in fourteen North American great lakes. (Reprinted from Patalas 1975, with permission.)

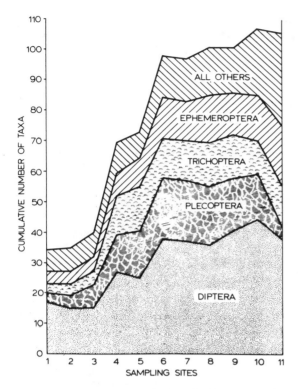

Figure 21.6. The contribution of major groups to the total number of macroinvertebrate taxa collected. Sampling sites, in the Rocky Mountains of Colorado, ranged from 1,500 m at Site 11 to 3,400 m at Site 1. (Reprinted from Ward 1986, with permission.)

River, whereas others came from the fertile Red River Valley via the Red River. Yet only about half of the species are found in pelagic regions of the lake. Tonn and Magnuson (1982) found that the diversity of fish faunas in lakes correlated with lake interconnectedness. In general, species diversity increases with increasing stream order or magnitude of discharge – that is, from upstream to downstream (Minshall and Peterson 1985). Phytoplankton species that have circumpolar distributions tend to produce similar assemblages in similar lakes regardless of their location or previous history, whereas many glacial relict species such as the opossum shrimp, *Mysis relicta;* the lake trout, *Salvelinus namaycush;* and the round whitefish, *Prosopuium cylindraceum* have expanded their distributions very little in the past 10,000 years, so that they are not even present in all habitats that would be suitable for them.

Biotic richness also varies within a single ecosystem, on several time scales.

Table 21.1. *Altitudinal distribution of* Trichoptera *in upper Dunajec*

Species	Presence at various altitudes (m)														
	1,680	1,600	1,500	1,400	1,300	1,200	1,100	1,000	900	800	700	600	500	400	300
Drusus monticola	+	+	+	+	+										
Rhyacophila philopotamoides	+	+		+	+										
R. glareosa	+	+	+	+	+		+	+							
Allogamus uncatus	+		+	+	+	+	+	+							
Acrophylax zerberus	+	+	+	+	+	+	+	+	+						
Drusus discolor	+	+		+	+		+	+	+	+					
Chaetopteryx polonica		+	+	+	+		+								
Lithax niger				+	+										
Apatania carpathica				+	+		+								
Psilopteryx psorosa psorosa				+	+	+	+	+							
Rhyacophila tristis				+				+	+	+	+				
Drusus carpathicus				+											
Melampophylax nepos				+		+	+	+							
Acrophylax vernalis				+			+	+	+						
Rhyacophila vulgaris				+			+	+	+						
Halesus rubricollis				+			+	+	+						
Rhyacophila polonica				+			+	+	+						
R. fasciata				+			+			+					
Allogamus starmachi						+	+								
Drusus annulatus							+	+							
Rhyacophila obliterata							+	+		+					
Drusus biguttatus							+	+	+	+					
Potamophylax cingulatus							+	+	+	+					
Allogamus auricollis							+	+	+	+	+				
Ecclisopteryx madida								+	+	+					
Glossosoma conformis								+	+	+					
Potamophylax latipennis									+	+	+				
Rhyacophila mocsaryi									+	+	+				
Ecclisopteryx dalecarlica									+	+	+				
Glossosoma intermedia									+	+	+	+			
Halesus interpunctatus									+	+					
Annitella obscurata									+	+	+				
Silo pallipes									+		+				
Sericostoma sp.									+	+	+	+			
Rhyacophila nubila									+	+	+	+		+	+
Polycentropus flavomaculatus									+	+	+	+		+	+
Hydropsyche pellucidula									+	+		+		+	+
Glossosoma boltoni										+	+	+			
Psychomyia pusilla										+	+	+		+	+
Hydropsyche bulbifera												+			
Chaetopteryx fusca												+			
Annitella thuringica												+			
Goera pilosa												+			
Lasiocephala basalis													+		
Agapetus delicatulus													+		
Brachycentrus subnubilus													+		
Cheumatopsyche lepida													+	+	
Hydroptila forcipata													+	+	+
Oligoplectrum maculatum													+	+	+

Source: Reprinted from Kawecka and Szczesny 1984, in *Ecology of European Rivers*, with permission from Blackwell Scientific Publications, Limited.

Table 21.2. *Altitudinal distribution of* Ephemeroptera *in upper Dunajec*

Species	Presence at various altitudes (m)														
	1,680	1,600	1,500	1,400	1,300	1,200	1,100	1,000	900	800	700	600	500	400	300
Rhithrogena loyolaea	+	+	+	+	+	+	+	+							
Baetis alpinus	+	+	+	+	+	+	+	+	+	+	+	+			
Ameletus inopinatus						+	+	+	+						
Rhithrogena iridina							+	+	+						
R. hybrida							+	+	+	+	+				
Ecdyonurus venosus							+	+	+	+	+	+	+	+	+
Baetis vernus								+	+	+	+	+	+	+	+
B. muticus								+	+	+	+	+	+	+	+
Rhithrogena ferruginea								+	+	+	+	+	+	+	+
Baetis melanonyx									+	+	+				
Ephemerella krieghoffi									+	+	+	+	+	+	+
Habroleptoides modesta										+	+	+	+	+	+
Baetis rhodani										+	+	+	+	+	+
Rhithrogena hercynia										+	+	+	+	+	+
Epeorus sylvicola										+	+	+	+	+	+
Baetis sinaicus										+	+	+	+	+	+
Caenis beskidensis										+	+	+	+	+	+
Ecdyonurus lateralis											+	+	+	+	+
Ephemerella major											+	+	+	+	+
Baetis scambus											+	+	+	+	+
B. lutheri											+	+	+	+	+
Siphlonurus lacustris												+	+	+	+
Ecdyonurus dispar												+	+	+	+
Centroptilum luteolum												+	+	+	+
Ephemera danica												+	+	+	+
Habrophlebia fusca												+	+	+	+
Baetis fuscatus												+	+	+	+
Ephemerella ignita												+	+	+	+
Oligoneuriella rhenana												+	+	+	+
Rhithrogena semicolorata												+	+	+	+
R. germanica												+	+	+	+
R. diaphana													+	+	+
Ecdyonurus insignis													+	+	+
E. torrentis													+	+	+
Heptagenia sulphurea													+	+	+
Habrophlebia lauta													+	+	+
Baetis vardarensis													+	+	+
Centroptilum pennulatum													+	+	+
Procloeon bifidum													+	+	+
Cloeon cognatum													+	+	+
Potamanthus luteus														+	+
Caenis horaria														+	+

Source: Reprinted from Kawecka and Szczesny 1984, in *Ecology of European Rivers*, with permission from Blackwell Scientific Publications, Limited.

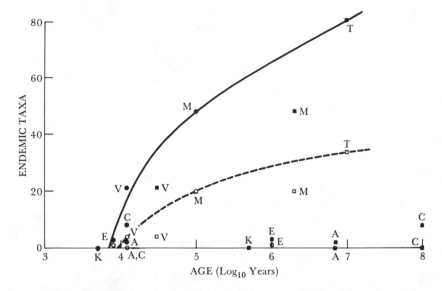

Figure 21.7. Relation of endemism of fish fauna to age of African lakes. The squares are for taxa against basin age while the circles are for taxa against age of the extant lake (i.e., time since last desiccation or major chemical transition). Open symbols (□, ○) represent endemic non-cichlid species; closed symbols (■, ●) represent sum of endemic non-cichlid species and endemic cichlid genera. Lake ages for Kivu (K), Victoria (V), Edward-George (E), Chad (C), and Albert (A) from Hecky (1978), Kendall (1969), Beadle (1974), and Livingstone (1975). The lake age for Malawi (M) and basin ages for Edward-George, Albert, and Kivu are estimated from sediment thicknesses determined by seismic-refraction studies and modern sedimentation rates with allowances for compaction (D. A. Livingstone, personal communication). Basin ages for Tanganyika (T), Malawi, Chad, and Victoria are from Beadle (1974). The lake age of Tanganyika is not known to be different from its basin age. Lines (drawn by eye) indicate accumulation of endemic non-cichlid species (- - -) and all endemic fish taxa (———) with lake age. (Reprinted from Hecky 1984, p. 436. Copyright 1984 by AAAS. Reprinted here with permission of the publisher.)

For example, chrysophyceans and cryptophyceans which are adapted to low light and heterotrophic metabolism dominate all oligotrophic northern lakes in winter (Schindler and Holmgren 1971; Holmgren 1983), whereas succession during the ice-free season is dictated by the abundance of nutrients such as nitrogen, phosphorus, and silica (Pearsall 1930; Schelske and Stoermer 1971; Schindler 1977).

Several other natural biological factors are also known to affect the species richness of fishes or plankton in North American waters. These include the abundance and diversity of prey, and the height of rooted macrophytes (Tonn and Magnuson 1982; Eadie and Keast 1984; Carpenter et al. 1985).

Obviously, the above are but a few examples of natural controls on the biotic richness of freshwater systems. The subject deserves treatment in depth, as done for fishes by Werner (1986), but my sole purpose here is to illustrate that there are natural factors that must be accounted for when considering the degree of human effect on biotic richness. Obviously, ignoring natural controls on biotic richness can easily lead to false interpretations of the effects of human activities.

Natural Catastrophes

Periodic extirpations or perhaps even extinctions can be caused by volcanic eruptions, meteoritic impacts, or other infrequent natural occurrences. The worst of these appear to have caused a degree of species impoverishment comparable to that imposed by modern humanity.

The best-documented freshwater examples are from studies of lakes near recent volcanic eruptions. Unusually high acidities can destroy biota for long periods (Bortelson et al. 1977; Sigurdson 1977). Photosynthesis by phyto-plankton in Spirit Lake, near Mt. St. Helens, was depressed for over two years (Ward et al. 1983). Microbial decomposition of organic matter, reduction of nitrate, and chemosynthesis either remained stable or increased (Dahm et al. 1981; Baross et al. 1982; Staley et al. 1982). The rates of recovery of ecosystems from natural events that occur too infrequently to have caused adaptation may give us some idea of how resilient aquatic ecosystems are likely to be when faced with humanity's unusual stresses.

Human Effects on Biotic Richness

The Effects of Acid Rain on Biotic Richness

The acid rain problem has prompted recent investigations of its effects on most freshwater taxa and trophic levels. It therefore provides an excellent example of how human activities can impoverish natural ecosystems, for information on effects is more complete than for most other aquatic problems.

There is a general tendency for the number of species of all aquatic taxa to decrease as acidity increases (Figure 21.8), regardless of whether the acidity is natural or anthropogenically introduced. As a result, setting a threshold pH below which freshwaters are considered to be damaged, as is usually done, is an inadequate approach to the problem, for any increase in acidity (decrease in pH) below pH values of 6.5 to 7 is likely to eliminate some species from the biological community. For example, when chemical models were used to deduce the change in pH of lakes in the northwestern United States caused by acid rain, many lakes of the Adirondacks, Poconos–

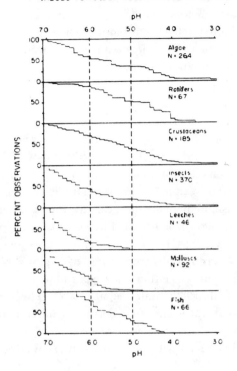

Figure 21.8. Minimum pH values reported for field observations of aquatic taxa, showing the percentage reduction from pH 7.0 to pH 3.0 The range of pH from 6.0 to 5.0 is shown within the dotted lines. N is the number of species included in each panel. (Redrawn from Eilers et al. 1984, by Mills and Schindler 1986; reprinted with permission.)

Catskills, and New England were predicted to have losses of large numbers of species from biotic communities due to acid rain (Schindler et al., 1989). Below I treat other effects of acidification on biotic richness.

One early hypothesis was that acidification caused decreases in phytoplankton biomass and productivity of lakes (Grahn et al. 1974). Several recent investigations have concluded that acidification of lakes does not directly cause decreases in primary production (Almer et al. 1978; Dillon et al. 1979; Schindler et al. 1985; Schindler 1988a). Production and biomass appear to be a function of phosphorus input (Dillon et al. 1979). There is, however, evidence that acidification reduces the export of phosphorus from terrestrial watersheds, perhaps exerting an indirect control on production

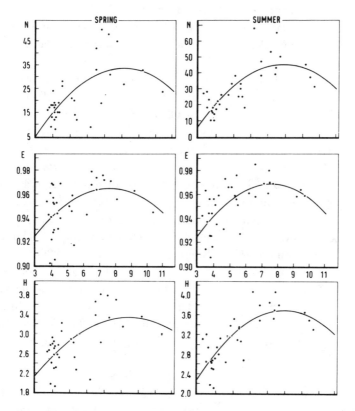

Figure 21.9. The relations between different diversity indices of phytoplankton assemblages in the "open" water zone and the pH of poorly buffered waters. N: number of species; E: evenness; H: Shannon–Weaver index. (Reprinted from Geelen and Leuven 1986, with permission.)

and biomass in lakes (Broberg and Persson 1984; Persson and Broberg 1985).

Acidification has pronounced effects on phytoplankton species. Earliest effects, at pH values of 6 to 7, include simple species replacements (see, e.g., Nygaard 1956; Battarbee et al. 1986). At lower pH values, both species numbers and diversity begin to decrease (Figure 21.9) (Schindler et al. 1985; Findlay and Kasian 1986; Geelen and Leuven 1986).

The numerous diatom taxa which dominate the littoral zones of circumneutral softwater lakes (Stockner and Armstrong 1971) are replaced by massive blooms of a few species of filamentous green or bluegreen species at pH values below 5.8 (Müller 1980; Schindler et al. 1985). In particular, Zygnemales dominate the littoral zones of acid lakes in both Europe and

North America (Turner et al. 1987). These probably cause modification of habitat for other species. For example, Schindler et al. (1985) and Mills et al. (1987) observed that lake trout avoided their preferred spawning grounds once they had become covered by mats of *Mougeotia*.

Surveys have also shown that the number of species, the diversity, and the biomass of zooplankton decrease as acidity increases (Sprules 1975; Confer et al. 1983). Only two species of limnetic Cladocera are commonly found at pH values below 5. Several species of Copepoda are also intolerant of acidic pH values (CARP 1985). A few acidophilic taxa, such as the crustaceans *Holopedium gibberum* and *Diaptomus minutus*, and the rotifer *Keratella taurocephala* often tend to make up almost the entire biomass of zooplankton at low pH.

Zoobenthos include many organisms which are very sensitive to acidification. Crustaceans of the genera Mysis, Hyalella, Gammarus, Lepidurus, and Pontoporeia disappear at pH values of 5.8 to 6.0 (Økland and Økland 1980, 1986; Nero and Schindler 1983; Stephenson and Mackie 1986; Grapentine 1987). Crayfish of the genus Orconectes are only slightly less sensitive (Berrill et al. 1985; Schindler et al. 1985; France 1987). A decline in species of mollusks in lakes acidified by acid deposition has been observed in several countries (reviewed by Økland and Økland 1980, 1986). In Canada, the genus Amnicola has disappeared from acidified lakes (Rooke and Mackie 1984).

Some groups of benthic insects are also acid-sensitive. Several species of Ephemeroptera and Plecoptera have been eliminated from acidified streams in Ontario (Hall and Ide 1987) and Scandinavia (Engblom and Lingdell 1984). The overall emergence of Chironomidae in Lake 223 increased in proportion to phytoplankton production, despite a pH decrease from 6.5 to 5.0 (Schindler et al. 1985). On the other hand, decreasing the pH from 6.5 to 5.0 caused the number of species to be halved, from approximately 70 species to about 35 (I. Davies, personal communication). Other Insecta appear to be highly resistant to acidification. In some cases, elimination of predatory fishes has allowed insects to become the top predators in acidified lakes (Henrikson et al. 1980; Nilssen et al. 1980).

The decline in fish in acidified lakes is reviewed by Eilers et al. (1984), Magnuson et al. (1984), and Mills and Schindler (1986). Several species of minnows are among the most sensitive taxa. *Notropis, Pimephales, Phoxinus,* and *Umbra* species are about as sensitive as mollusks and crustaceans. Juveniles of most species are more sensitive than adults, with recruitment failures often preceding increased adult mortalities by several years. Phoxinus is the only genus of minnow in Scandinavia, so that it plays a key role in the food chain of softwater lakes. Its high sensitivity to acidification may be one reason why so many sport fisheries in acidified regions of Norway and Sweden have collapsed in a few decades. In North America, with its more diverse cyprinid fauna, some species replacements occur during the course of acidification. This redundancy may make North American food webs somewhat more difficult to damage than those of Scandinavia. The impoverishment of food webs can cause starvation of predatory fishes (Schindler et al. 1985). This clearly increases their vulnerability to acidification (Kwain et al. 1984; Cunningham and Shuter 1986).

The extirpation of populations of larger fish by acidification is very well documented for some areas. The following is a brief summary, largely based on the review by Baker and Schofield (1985).

In the La Cloche Mountains of Ontario, Harvey and colleagues estimate that 388 fish populations were lost from 50 of the lakes investigated which had pH values <6 (Harvey and Lee 1982). Fourteen of the 31 lakes with pH <5 had no fish. In some lakes, several species disappeared during the 15 years spanned by the investigation. Similarly, near Wawa, Ontario, Somers and Harvey (1984) estimated that 83 fish populations had been lost from 16 of the 34 lakes surveyed. On a broader scale, Marmorek et al. (1988) estimated that acid rain had extirpated 25,700 fish populations from 137,415 lakes in Ontario.

In Nova Scotia, Watt et al. (1983) documented the decline of Atlantic salmon catches between 1935 and 1980 in 10 rivers with pH < 5. Catches had reached zero by 1980. In contrast, salmon catches were stable in 12 rivers with pH > 5 (Figure 21.10).

In Norway, the decline of Atlantic salmon in acidic rivers is similar to that in Nova Scotia. In addition, a survey of 5,000 lakes in an area of 33,000 km^2 in southern Norway revealed that fish populations had been severely damaged. In 40 percent of this area, fish populations are extinct, or nearly so.

In Sweden, the results from the 100 lakes reported so far reveal heavy losses of minnows, roach, char, and trout. The overall problem is probably about as great as Norway's.

Some of the observed biotic impoverishment is due to secondary effects of acid rain. For example, in some cases aluminum released from terrestrial soils causes greater fish mortalities than expected from hydrogen ion alone (Baker and Schofield 1982). Starvation, due to impoverishment of the food chain, already has been mentioned. Parasitism was implicated as one factor causing the decline of *Orconectes virilis* in Lake 223 (France and Graham 1985), although its importance relative to several other factors is unknown (Schindler et al. 1985). Nilsson et al. (1984) discuss the effect of acidification on community structure via alterations of competition and predation.

The above studies represent only a small proportion of acidified lakes. Of

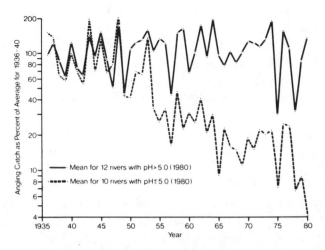

Figure 21.10. Atlantic salmon angling data normalized to facilitate the comparison between high- and low-pH rivers. Each river's catch was expressed as a percentage of the mean catch in 1936–1940 so as to give all rivers equal weighting, and the two groups were then averaged by year. (Reprinted from Watt et al. 1983, with permission.)

the 700,000 lakes in eastern, temperate regions of Canada, 50 percent have alkalinities less than 50 μeq/L, and 22 percent have pH values less than 6 (Kelso et al. 1986). Any further reduction in pH, when present values are so low, is certain to cause biotic impoverishment. For example, Schindler et al. (1989) estimate that in lakes of the northeastern United States, over 50 percent of the species in some groups have been eliminated by acidification.

The natural controls on biotic richness reviewed earlier have been shown to be important in interpreting the effects of acid rain on lakes. Because smaller lakes are usually more vulnerable to acidification, failure to consider the positive correlation between lake size and species richness may lead to overestimates of acid rain damage (Rago and Wiener 1986; Rahel 1986) (Figure 21.3). Mollusks and crustaceans are more severely affected by acidification at low concentrations of calcium (Økland and Økland 1980, 1986). Acidification also mobilizes a number of toxic trace metals, so that synergistic effects on biota are to be expected (Kahl and Norton 1983; NAS 1985; Stokes, this volume).

Tragically, reversing acidification does not appear to result in the rapid recovery of biotic richness, regardless of whether it is done by reducing acid inputs (Schindler 1986) or liming (Raddum and Fjellheim 1984).

Eutrophication and Biotic Richness in Lakes

Eutrophication can have a multitude of effects on the richness of biological communities, some positive and some negative. The effect in a particular ecosystem appears to depend on lake size, depth, thermal stratification, water renewal (therefore indirectly upon climate), the ratio of incoming nutrients, and the species present.

Phosphorus is the nutrient primarily associated with eutrophication (Vollenweider 1968, 1976; Schindler 1974; Schindler et al. 1978). In theory, primary and secondary productivity, and biomass at all trophic levels in lakes, should increase in proportion to added phosphorus (Dillon and Rigler 1975). Unfortunately, secondary factors usually keep these theoretical possibilities from being realized, and species impoverishment seems frequently to accompany eutrophication, despite increases in production and standing crop of algae.

For example, in oligotrophic lakes, a replacement of natural species (typically chrysophyceans, cryptophyceans, and diatoms) with green and bluegreen species, and a reduction in species diversity, accompanied all whole-lake eutrophication experiments, due to increased pH or inadequate supplies of nitrogen. This phenomenon has also been observed in most culturally eutrophied lakes (Smith 1983). There is some tendency for this problem to correct itself over time, because the N:P and C:P ratios are adjusted by a number of biogeochemical mechanisms (Schindler 1977, 1985; Schindler et al. 1987).

Higher production by primary producers in eutrophied lakes often causes impoverishment of species by secondary factors. For example, a change in producer species often eliminates edible algal species, replacing them with less edible ones. The bluegreen algae which accompany fertilization with low N:P ratios cannot be easily grazed or digested by all zooplankton (Porter 1973). In addition, elevated or depressed pH may result from high rates of nitrogen uptake in lakes fertilized with both nitrogen and phosphorus, depending on whether uptake of nitrate or ammonium predominates (Schindler et al. 1973, 1985b). Either high or low pH will eliminate many species of crustacean zooplankton (O'Brien and DeNoyelles 1972; CARP 1985; Malley et al. 1989).

Oxygen depletion may occur in the hypolimnion of shallow, thermally stratified eutrophic lakes, eliminating cold-water species of animals (Hasler 1947; Jonasson 1969). Anoxia also may occur in the epilimnion, or under ice, in hypereutrophic lakes, with devastating results for fishes and other species with oxic metabolism (Schindler and Comita 1972; Barica 1975, 1981). Oxygen depletion at the sediment–water interface causes oligotrophic species of chironomids to be replaced by eutrophic forms. The number of species is also typically reduced once hypolimnetic anoxia develops (Brundin 1949; Ahrén and Grimas 1965; Cook and Johnson 1974; Saether 1975).

Excessive eutrophication is thought to be at least partly responsible for the declines of some fish species largely in the mid-twentieth century (Beeton 1969; Larkin and Northcote 1969; Christie 1974), although the roles of overfishing and invasions by exotic species cannot be discounted. The massive diurnal oxygen "sag" caused by inputs of sewage is believed to have eliminated the salmon fishery from the Thames River and estuary by the mid-nineteenth century (Gameson and Wheeler 1977).

Reservoir Formation

The scale of human-made impoundments is enormous. Over 12,000 structures more than 15 m high impound roughly 4,000 km^3 of water, altering flows and promoting interbasin transfers of biotas. Impoundment rivers or lake outlets can cause either increases or decreases in various measures of biotic richness, depending on the particular location and configuration of the ecosystems and impoundment structures. A comprehensive review of impoundment studies is far beyond the scope of this chapter, and I shall give only a few examples to illustrate the breadth of effects possible.

A common response to impoundment is a temporary increase in the production of fish and other organisms, the "reservoir paradigm" (Ellis 1936; Baranov 1961; Hecky et al. 1984). This probably results from the release of nutrients by flooded soils, which can sometimes cause excessive eutrophication (Foundation for Research Development 1985). Exotic species often invade impounded systems, particularly where interbasin transfers of water are made. Examples are many, including fishes, other animals, and rooted plants (Davies and Walker 1986). Biotic invasions will be treated in more detail later.

In some cases, increased inputs of fine clays cause reservoirs to become turbid, so that phytoplankton production becomes light, rather than nutrient, limited. Melting of permafrost-stabilized banks caused such problems in Southern Indian Lake of northern Manitoba (Hecky and Guildford 1984). Organic staining can cause similar effects when peatlands are flooded (Baranov 1961). The flooding of peatlands can also cause increased concentrations of mercury to appear in fishes, with possible adverse consequences for mammalian predators, including humans (Bodaly et al. 1984a, b).

In general, when outflows from thermally stratified reservoirs are drawn from cold hypolimnions, a decline in both species numbers and biomass occurs for several kilometers downstream (Stanford and Ward 1986).

When impoundment causes the temperature of reservoirs to cool, biotic richness is reduced and dominant species may change. For example, Patalas and Salki (1984) found that diversion of the Churchill River from Southern Indian Lake caused the northern part of the lake to become cooler. Zooplankton biomass decreased, and dominance of zooplankton communities shifted from warm-water to cold-water species. Similarly, Wiens and Rosenberg (1984) noted that *Hexagenia limbata,* a warm-water species of mayfly near the northern edge of its range, declined dramatically in northern parts of the lake.

Damming for hydroelectric power, irrigation or other uses has severely restricted the migration of fishes in many rivers (e.g., Salo and Stober 1977; Decamps et al. 1984). Neu (1982) has shown that widespread hydroelectric development on rivers which drain to estuaries and coastal shelves can cause major disruptions in temperature, salinity, and circulation during biologically important seasons of the year for marine organisms. The implications for biological impoverishment are massive, yet scarcely investigated, considering the large scale of present impoundments, particularly in Canada and the Soviet Union.

Species Introductions and Removals

Introductions of exotic species (biological pollutants) appear to have the most serious consequences for biotic richness of any anthropogenic activities. A general treatment of the problem would require several volumes, for much work has been done since Elton (1958) elucidated the widespread nature of the problem. Ironically, many introductions are done with the intention of increasing some aspect of biotic richness. Aquatic examples are numerous: introductions of carp and water hyacinth to North America (Sculthorpe 1967; Moyle 1986); duckweed (*Elodea canadensis*) to Europe (Rorslett et al. 1986); sea lamprey, rainbow smelt, and alewife to the St. Lawrence Great Lakes (Christie 1974; Moyle 1986); European milfoil to the Chesapeake Bay (Bayley et al. 1978); nile perch to Lake Victoria (Barel et al. 1985); Tanganyika sardine to lakes Kariba and Kivu (Dumont 1986); the peacock bass to Lake Gatun (Zaret and Paine 1973); and several mollusk species to the San Francisco estuary (Nichols et al. 1986) (Figure 21.11) have all displaced natural species or altered community structure. In North America, introductions have been so widespread that it has been impossible to deduce what the natural ranges were for many species. Balon and Bruton (1986) and Moyle (1986) review problems due to fish introductions, which include habitat changes, introductions of parasites and diseases, competition, predation on and hybridization with natural species, and overcrowding. Remarkably, 24 families of fishes have been successfully introduced into

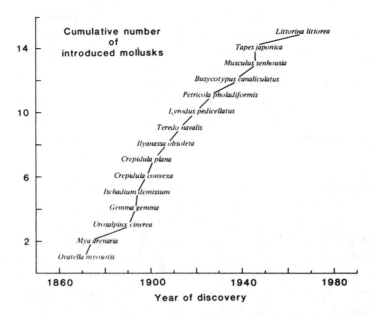

Figure 21.11. Cumulative number of introduced mollusks by date of discovery. The period of most rapid increase, the 1890s, coincides with the period of maximum oyster importation. (Reprinted from Nichols et al. 1986, data from J. T. Carlton, with permission.)

North America. Magnuson (1976) argued that the isolation and relatively young age of most glacial lakes has left them with fragile, undersaturated species assemblages which are easily modified by introduction of exotics or deletions due to overfishing. For example, the introduction of exotics has doubled the number of fish species in Lake Wingra, Wisconsin, and in Clear Lake, California.

Moyle (1986) made similar arguments in comparing the success of introduced fish species in the eastern and western United States. He pointed out that introduced species were much more successful (5 to 9 per ecosystem) in western North America, where the number of natural species is low, than in eastern North America, where fish species are much more numerous (20 to over 100 species per system). In the latter case, exotic species did not usually replace native species, even when they survived. In western states, exotics constitute 30 to 60 percent of the total number of species, while in the East, 5 to 20 percent is normal.

Moyle also hypothesized that the success of the lamprey and alewife in the Great Lakes was because prey species in the lakes were unaccustomed to their style of predation, and because predators on these two species were absent. He speculates that the subsequent success of pelagic salmon species is due to their resistance to lamprey attacks, and familiarity with the current prey species.

The best examples of removal of organisms from aquatic ecosystems are for fish, because of their obvious interest to humans. Christie (1974) and Magnuson (1976) believe that both overfishing and lamprey introduction eliminated lake trout and burbot from the more oligotrophic St. Lawrence Great Lakes. Both authors review other fisheries changes, their causes and consequences. Friedrich and Müller (1984) record the elimination of eight species from the Rhine, and the introduction of numerous exotic species. Similar situations have occurred in most other large European rivers, including the Danube, the Elbe, and the Main (Friedrich and Müller 1984). Theoretically, the removal of species, particularly from assemblages of low diversity, should cause open niches which can be occupied by new invaders. For example, elimination of the fathead minnow, *Pimephales promelas*, by the artificial acidification of Lake 223 allowed an explosive invasion of brook stickleback (Schindler 1986).

Pesticides

Pesticide applications to terrestrial watersheds often affect non-target aquatic organisms. For example, DDT sprayed to control spruce budworm in New Brunswick caused complete losses of insects in major streams (Laws 1981). Very high losses of salmon were also recorded. Although insects reappeared within a few weeks after spraying, the species composition was drastically altered for five or six years. The replacement species were not suitable as food for young salmon. Due to biomagnification, predatory bird species receive enough DDT, dieldrin, and PCBs to depress reproduction (Laws 1981).

Atrazine, the most widely used herbicide in North American agriculture, is known to suppress phytoplankton production and species diversity at concentrations often found in waters downstream from sprayed croplands (deNoyelles et al. 1982). Similar effects of terbutryn and simazine on periphyton community structure were recorded by Goldsborough and Robinson (1986). Pesticides caused community-wide reductions of species in experimentally polluted streams (Eaton et al. 1986).

Some pesticides are deliberately applied to freshwaters, to control unwanted pests. In all cases, impoverishment of non-target organisms occurs. For example, Sebastien et al. (1989) studied the effects of methoxychlor, commonly used to control blackflies, on non-target species in the Souris River, Manitoba. Short-term reductions in species richness and total numbers of benthic organisms were recorded, but buffered by recolonization from upstream.

Trace Metals

Many trace metals have had their mobility in the environment increased severalfold by human activities (Lantzy and Mackenzie 1979). Metals such as cadmium, zinc, mercury, and copper have enormous potential for impoverishing freshwater ecosystems, at concentrations which are scarcely detectable by even the most recent methods (Wood 1974). Several species of zooplankton suffer reproductive failures at cadmium concentrations less than 1 µg/L (Marshall and Mellinger 1980). This concentration is approached or exceeded in lakes near smelters (Franzin and McFarlane 1981; Lawrence and Holoka 1987) and will be approached within a few decades in Lake Michigan, if present rates of increase in cadmium continue (Muhlbaier and Tisue 1981). Toxicity thresholds for effects of trace metals on phytoplankton are very low (Gächter 1979; Campbell and Stokes 1985). Increased metal contamination of lake sediments in the twentieth century has been observed wherever studies have been done in the Northern Hemisphere (for example, Goldberg et al. 1981; Kahl and Norton 1983; National Academy of Sciences 1985). This increase has been shown to be correlated with increased concentrations of metals in fish (Johnson 1987).

There is some evidence for synergistic effects of metals. In an extensive controlled study of the combined effects of five metals, all at the legal concentration for Swiss rivers, decreased production and species richness in phytoplankton, zooplankton, and bottom fauna were recorded. Phytoplankton biomass recovered somewhat, due to a switch to metal-tolerant species (Gächter 1979).

Many metals are also known to increase in concentration and/or toxicity as lakes acidify. Bioaccumulation tends to increase toxicity to upper trophic levels, particularly for mercury (National Academy of Sciences 1985). Many organisms also develop increased resistance to metals (Klaverkamp et al. 1984), presumably reducing the impoverishment of species. The resistance has been attributed to the increased production of metal-binding protein(s), known as metallotheionine. The increase in this protein may be a useful indicator of impending impoverishment due to further increases in toxic trace metals. It seems likely that once this mechanism's limitations are exceeded, impoverishment would proceed swiftly.

Climate Change

As discussed above, there is a general correlation between average temperature and several indices of biological richness. For example, fisheries are generally much more productive at warmer temperature (Schlesinger and Regier 1983). Because a considerable warming is expected in the next century due to increasing concentrations of greenhouse gasses, higher production at several trophic levels might be expected.

On the other hand, the temperature tolerances of many stenothermic northern species may be exceeded, causing them to be extirpated over wide areas. Examples include lake trout and whitefish, as well as many invertebrates, such as Mysis, Lepidurus, and Pontoporeia. Given the vulnerability of open niches in simple northern ecosystems to invaders, ensuring that desirable species replace those eliminated may be an important undertaking.

Multiply Stressed Systems

Usually, it is possible to detect biotic impoverishment much more easily than to deduce what causes it, because few aquatic ecosystems are affected by single stresses. In order to deduce which environmental insults are responsible, it is often necessary to perform whole-ecosystem experiments of the type practiced at ELA and Hubbard Brook. But even such "dissections" of causes may not be a reliable guide to necessary controls, for some stresses may be synergistic or antagonistic in effect, as discussed above for trace metals. Below, I give two examples of important, multiply-stressed freshwater ecosystems. Estuaries are similarly affected (see Nichols et al. 1986). Bormann (this volume) and chapters in Hutchinson and Meema (1987) document multiple stresses on forest ecosystems.

The St. Lawrence Great Lakes. Eutrophication, toxic metals, introduction of pesticides and other toxic organic compounds, overfishing, and introduction of exotic species are among the documented problems that have modified biotic richness in the Great Lakes. A chronicle of Great Lake woes is updated annually by the International Joint Commission, in its annual report. See also Christie (1974).

The Rhine River. As in the Great Lakes, physical, chemical, and biological alterations have taken place. Of 11 species of fishes originally present in the lower Rhine, only the eel *Anguilla anguilla* is still common. The number of species in other freshwater groups was reduced by 40 percent between 1918 and 1955, with some sensitive groups such as Ephemeroptera, Plecoptera, and Trichoptera reduced much more (Table 21.3). Wolff (1978) gives an excellent review. The recent chemical spills resulting from an industrial fire in Switzerland are reported to have had devastating consequences for the Rhine, but detailed biological results are still unreported.

Genetic Engineering. The engineering of superorganisms, whether they be giant trout, "super cows," or hyperproductive corn, could constitute a serious future threat to biotic diversity. There is public demand for such superorganisms to replace natural organisms, and the financial returns from such genetic meddling are expected to be enormous (Doyle 1985). Given our

Table 21.3. *Composition of the benthic and littoral fauna of the Rhine before 1918 (after Lauterborn 1916–1918) and in 1955 (after Knopp 1957)*

	Upper Rhine		Middle Rhine		Lower Rhine	
	1918	1955	1918	1955	1918[a]	1955
Spongillidae	5	2	1	2	1	2
Vermes	7	10	5	11	2	15
Crustacea	3	3	3	4	1	2
Plecoptera	12	0	12	0	1	0
Ephemeroptera	9	1	3	1	5	0
Neuroptera	0	0	0	0	1	0
Odonata	1	2	0	0	0	0
Rhynchota	1	0	1	0	1	0
Diptera	5	3	3	2	1	3
Trichoptera	9	3	11	1	5	2
Coleoptera	2	1	2	0	0	0
Bryozoa	3	1	2	1	1	3
Mollusca	20	14	18	12	17	8
Total	77	40	61	34	36	35

[a] According to Lauterborn (1916–1918) the Lower Rhine has been investigated insufficiently.

Source: Reprinted from Wolff 1978, in *The Breakdown and Restoration of Ecosystems*, with permission from Plenum Publishing Corp.

dismal record in introducing exotic, but non-engineered species into new habitats, the introduction of organisms which have limited gene pools designed for single, specific purposes has fearsome implications. They may not only eliminate natural species under normal conditions, but once established they may be more susceptible than natural species to rare epidemics or unusual weather conditions (Doyle 1985). We simply do not know the answers to these possibilities. Research and public education on this problem should be begun now, for widespread use of such organisms will be proposed in the very near future.

Global Biotic Impoverishment in Fresh Waters

Recently, much concern has been expressed about the loss of diversity caused by clearing of tropical forests (reviewed by Fearnside, this volume). I share this concern, but believe that there are two problems with freshwater impoverishment about which we should be equally concerned. In contrast to the high visibility of tropical forest destruction, which can be clearly seen either from the ground or from satellite photos, aquatic impoverishment is invisible, and undetectable except by intensive ecological studies.

One area of concern is for tropical freshwaters. Many human populations rely heavily on these for food. For example, it has been estimated that 70 percent of the protein used by humans in Malawi is derived from fisheries (R. E. Hecky, personal communication). The yield from natural fish populations in the Sahel is similar in magnitude to that of cattle in the region (Durand 1983). In contrast, aquaculture currently produces less than 1 percent of the fisheries yield in Africa. Protein supplied by wild terrestrial animals is no longer important, and much of the pressure for tropical forest clearing results from demands for agricultural land. The integrity of natural tropical fisheries and the development of aquaculture should thus be of great concern to humans (see Carmouze et al. 1983). Oil exploration should also be of concern in this regard, but information is almost lacking (R. E. Hecky, personal communication).

In contrast to agriculture, where at least the rudiments of management are known, almost nothing is known about the management of tropical freshwater fisheries. Indeed, I have been unable to find any information on the extent to which the vast riverine fishery of South America has been exploited, let alone on how sensitive it might be to harvesting or other human interference.

A second area of immediate concern is the gradual acidification of north temperate softwater lakes. As mentioned above, over 700,000 lakes are estimated to be susceptible to damaging levels of acid deposition in eastern Canada alone (Kelso et al. 1986), and I believe that number is an underestimate. When softwater areas of the United States and Eurasia are added, probably between 1 and 2 million lakes are so poorly buffered that they are susceptible to biotic impoverishment from acidification in the next 50 years. Although data are few, thousands of kilometers of softwater streams and rivers are equally vulnerable.

Although the number of endangered species in north temperate lakes is certainly lower than in either lakes or terrestrial ecosystems of the tropics, the naturally low biotic richness of northern ecosystems may render their functioning more susceptible to disturbance than tropical ones, because these systems have fewer redundant species (Magnuson 1976; and as discussed above). Many of the key fish and invertebrate species in softwater north temperate lakes also have very poor dispersal powers, and their reinvasion of habitats from which they are eliminated is unlikely, unless they are deliberately restocked by humans. Examples include the genera Salvelinus and Coregonus among fishes and Mysis, Pontoporeia, Lepidurus, Hyalella, and Amnicola among invertebrates. Several of these species developed during the Pleistocene – that is, they are recent adaptations to cold-freshwater environments, and are often the sole species occupying their particular ecological niches. These species are all known to be sensitive to acidification. Many would also be eliminated by slightly increasing temperatures, as is predicted from human-induced climate change (discussed by Schindler et al. in press).

In brief, the *number* of species extirpated is not the only important measure of biotic impoverishment. The elimination of a few key species from northern lakes could have as large an effect on ecosystem integrity, function, and fisheries production as the elimination of many species in an analogous tropical ecosystem. Remarkably, this link between the functioning of ecosystem processes and community composition has seldom been addressed (Schindler 1988b).

What Must Be Done

In summary, our concerns for biotic impoverishment in freshwaters should include ecosystems at all latitudes, regardless of whether the natural community contains a dozen species or many thousands. While more species may be extirpated at tropical latitudes, it may be easier to disrupt the function of critical food chains at high latitudes, where little redundancy is present in biological communities. We must begin to address the question of how much diversity is necessary to maintain food-chain integrity and ecosystem function, for in this day of "cost–benefit" analyses, arguments based purely on esthetics are usually not considered.

Our greatest handicap in being able to estimate the extent and rate of biological impoverishment is the lack of reasonably complete biological inventories for any extensive region. As a result, we are unable to tell whether a species is absent from a habitat because it has been eliminated by human activity, or because it was not there in the first place. Sound taxonomy and zoogeography must therefore be ranked as among the most important of sciences in the years ahead. Indeed, the situation is little improved from when S. A. Forbes addressed this issue over a century ago (Forbes 1883). Indeed, the situation in North America seems to be worsening for many groups.

Wetlands

If our knowledge of freshwater communities is inadequate for freshwaters, it is even worse in wetlands. The extent and diversity of wetlands have been reduced by drainage, agriculture, and air pollution (Gorham et al. 1984; Lee et al. 1987). For example, Rosenberg et al. (1988) studied the species of chironomids in a small bog in northwestern Ontario. Of 84 species recorded, 23 were new North American or Canadian records, and 10 were previously undescribed!

Acknowledgments

R. E. Hecky, G. D. Koshinsky, D. Rosenberg, and K. Patalas provided many fruitful discussions and key references for this summary. Work on the manuscript was supported by the Canadian Department of Fisheries and Oceans.

References

Ahren, T., and U. Grimas, 1965. The composition of the bottom fauna in two basins of Lake Mälaren. *Rep. Inst. Freshwater Res. Drottningholm* 46:49–57.

Almer, B., W. Dickson, D. Ekström, and E. Hornström, 1978. Sulfur pollution and the aquatic ecosystem. In J. O. Nriagu (Ed.), *Sulfur in the Environment: Part II, Ecological Impacts*, pp. 271–311. Wiley, New York.

Baker, J. P., and C. Schofield, 1982. Aluminum toxicity to fish in acidic waters. *Water, Air, Soil Pollut.* 18:289–309.

Baker, J. P., and C. L. Schofield, 1985. Acidification impacts on fish populations: a review. In D. D. Adams, and W. P. Page (Eds.), *Acid Deposition: Environmental, Economic and Policy Issues*, pp. 183–221. Plenum, New York.

Baker, L. A., P. L. Brezonik, and C. D. Pollman, 1986. Model of internal alkalinity generation: sulfate retention component. *Water, Air, Soil Pollut.* 30:89–94.

Balon, E. K., and M. N. Bruton, 1986. Introduction of alien species or why scientific advice is not needed. *Env. Biol. Fishes* 16:225-230.

Baranov, I. V., 1961. *The Storage Lakes of the U.S.S.R. and Their Importance for Fishery*, pp. 139–183. Israel Proj. Sci. Transl., Jerusalem, 1966.

Barbour C. D., and J. H. Brown, 1974. Fish species diversity in lakes. *Am. Nat.* 108:473–489.

Barel, C. D. N., P. Dorite, P. H. Greenwood, G. Fryer, N. Hughes, P. P. N. Jackson, K. Kawanabe, R. H. Lowe-McConnell, M. Nagoshi, A. J. Ribbink, E. Trewavas, F. Witte, and K. Yamaska, 1985. Destruction of fisheries in Africa's lakes. *Nature* 315:19–20.

Barica, J., 1975. Collapses of algal blooms in prairie pothole lakes: their mechanisms and ecological impact. *Verh. int. Ver. Limnol.* 19:606–615.

Barica, J., 1981. Hypereutrophy – the ultimate stage of eutrophication. *Wat. Qual. Bull.* 6:95–98.

Baross, J. A., C. N. Dahm, A. K. Ward, M. D. Lilley, and J. R. Sedell, 1982. Initial microbiological response in lakes to the Mount St. Helens eruption. *Nature* 296:49–52.

Battarbee, R. W., J. P. Smol, and J. Meriläinen, 1986. Diatoms as indicators of pH: an historical review. In J. P. Smol, R. W. Battarbee, R. B. Davis, and J. Meriläinen (Eds.), *Diatoms and Lake Acidity*, pp. 5–14. Junk, Dordrecht, The Netherlands.

Bayley, S. E., V. L. Stotts, P. F. Springer, and J. Steenis, 1978. Changes in submerged macrophyte populations at the head of Chesapeake Bay, 1958–1975. *Estuaries* 1:73–84.

Beeton, A. M., 1969. Changes in the environment and biota of the Great Lakes. In *Eutrophication: Causes, Consequences, Correctives*, pp. 150–187. National Academy of Sciences, Washington, D.C.

Berrill, M., L. Hollett, A. Margosian, and J. Hudson, 1985. Variation in tolerance to low environmental pH by the crayfish *Orconectes rusticus*, *O. propinquis* and *Cambarus robustus*. *Can. J. Zool.* 63:2586–2589.

Bodaly, R. A., R. E. Hecky, and R. J. P. Fudge, 1984a. Increases in fish mercury levels in lakes flooded by the Churchill River diversion in northern Manitoba. *Can. J. Fish. Aquat. Sci.* 41:682–691.

Bodaly, R. A., T. W. D. Johnson, R. J. P. Fudge, and J. W. Clayton, 1984b. Collapse of the lake whitefish (*Coregonus clupeaformis*) fishery in Southern Indian Lake, Manitoba, following lake impoundment and river diversion. *Can. J. Fish. Aquat. Sci.* 41:692–700.

Bortelson, C. G., R. T. Wilson, and B. L. Foxworthy, 1977. *Water quality effects on Baker Lake of recent volcanic activity at Mount Baker*, Washington. Geol. Survey Prof. Paper 1022–B.

Broberg, O., and G. Persson, 1984. External budgets for phosphorus, nitrogen and dissolved organic carbon for the acidified Lake Gärdsjön. *Arch. Hydrobiol.* 99:160–175.

Brooks, J. L., 1950. Speciation in ancient lakes. *Quart. Rev. Biol.* 25:131–176.

Brown, D. J. A., 1982. The effect of pH and calcium on fish and fisheries. *Water, Air, Soil Pollut.* 18:343–351.

Brundin, L., 1949. Chironomiden und andere Bodentiere der sudschwedischen Urge birgsseen. *Rep. Inst. Freshw. Res. Drottningholm* 30:1–914.

Brylinsky, M., and K. H. Mann, 1973. An analysis of factors governing productivity in lakes and reservoirs. *Limnol. Oceanogr.* 18:1–14.

Campbell, P. G. C., and P. M. Stokes, 1985. Acidification and toxicity of metals to aquatic biota. *Can. J. Fish. Aquat. Sci.* 42:2034–2049.

Carmouze, J. P., J. R. Durand, and C. Leveque, 1983. *Lake Chad: ecology and productivity of a shallow tropical ecosystem*. Monogr. Biol. 53. Junk, The Hague.

CARP (Critical Assessment Review Papers), 1985. *The atmospheric deposition phenomenon and its effects*. EPA–600/8–83–0168. Washington, D.C.

Carpenter, S. R., J. F. Kitchell, and J. R. Hodgson, 1985. Cascading trophic interactions and lake productivity. *Bioscience* 35:634–639.

Christie, W. J., 1974. Changes in fish species composition of the Great Lakes. *J. Fish. Res. Board Can.* 31:827–854.

Confer, J. L., T. Kaaret, and G. E. Likens, 1983. Zooplankton diversity and biomass in recently acidified lakes. *Can. J. Fish. Aquat. Sci.* 40:36–42.

Cook, D. G., and M. G. Johnson, 1974. Benthic macroinvertebrates of the St. Lawrence Great Lakes. *J. Fish. Res. Board Can.* 31:763–782.

Cunningham, G. L., and B. J. Shuter, 1986. Interaction of low pH and starvation on body weight and composition of young-of-year smallmouth bass (*Micropterus dolomieui*). *Can. J. Fish. Aquat. Sci.* 43:869–876.

Dahm, C. N., J. A. Baross, A. K. Ward, M. D. Lilley, R. C. Wissmar, and A. H. Devol, 1981. *North Coldwater Lake and vicinity: limnology, chemistry, and microbiology*. Final Rep., U.S. Army Corps of Engineers, Portland, OR.

Davies, B. R., and K. F. Walker (Eds.), 1986. *The Ecology of River Systems*. Junk, The Hague.

Decamps, H., J. Capblanq, and J. N. Tourenq, 1984. Lot. In B. A. Whitton (Ed.), *Ecology of European Rivers*, pp. 207–235. Blackwell, Oxford.

deNoyelles, F., W. D. Kettle, and D. E. Sinn, 1982. The responses of plankton communities in experimental ponds to atrazine, the most heavily used pesticide in the United States. *Ecology* 63:1285–1293.

Dillon, P. J., 1975. The phosphorus budget of Cameron Lake, Ontario: the importance of flushing rate to the degree of eutrophy of lakes. *Limnol. Oceanogr.* 20:28–39.

Dillon, P. J., and W. B. Kirchner, 1975. The effects of ecology and land use on the export of phosphorus from watersheds. *Wat. Res.* 9:135–148.

Dillon, P. J., and F. H. Rigler, 1975. A simple method for predicting the capacity of a lake for development based on lake trophic status. *J. Fish. Res. Board Can.* 32:1519–1531.

Dillon, P. J., N. D. Yan, W. H. Scheider, and N. Conroy, 1979. Acidic lakes in Ontario, Canada: characterization, extent and responses to base and nutrient addition. *Ergebn. Limnol.* 13:317–336.

Doyle, J., 1985. *Altered Harvest: Agriculture, Genetics and the Fate of the World's Food Supply.* Penguin Books, New York.

Dumont, H. J., 1986. The Tanganyika sardine in Lake Kivu: another ecodisaster for Africa? *Environ. Conserv.* 13:143–148.

Durand, J. R., 1983. The exploitation of fish stocks in the Lake Chad region. In Carmouze, J. P., J. R. Durand, and C. Leveque (Eds.), *Lake Chad: Ecology and Productivity of a Shallow Tropical Ecosystem*, pp. 425–481. Monogr. Biol. 53, Junk, The Hague.

Eadie, J., McA., and A. Keast, 1984. Resource heterogeneity and fish species diversity in lakes. *Can. J. Zool.* 62:1689–1695.

Eaton, J. A. J., R. Hermanutz, R. Kiefer, L. Mueller, R. Anderson, R. Erickson, B. Nordling, J. Rogers, and H. Pritchard, 1986. Biological effects of continuous and intermittent dosing of outdoor experimental streams with chloropyrifos. In R. C. Bahner, and D. J. Hansen (Eds.), *Aquatic Toxicology and Hazard Assessment: Eighth Symposium*, pp. 85–118. ASTM STP 891. American Society for Testing and Materials, Philadelphia.

Eilers, J. M., G. L. Lien, and R. G. Berg, 1984. Aquatic organisms in acidic environments: a literature review. *Wisc. Dep. Nat. Resour. Tech. Bull.* 150. Madison, Wisc.

Ellis, M. M., 1936. Some fishery problems in impounded waters. *Trans. Amer. Fish. Soc.* 66:63–75.

Elton, C. S., 1958. *The Ecology of Invasions by Plants and Animals.* Methuen, London.

Engblom E., and P. E. Lingdell, 1984. The mapping of short-term acidification with the help of biological indicators. *Rep. Inst. Freshwater Res. Drottningholm* 61: 60–68.

Findlay, D. L., and S. E. M. Kasian, 1986. Phytoplankton community responses to acidification of Lake 223, Experimental Lakes Area, northwestern Ontario. *Water, Air, Soil Pollut.* 30:719–726.

Forbes, S. A., 1883. The first food of the common whitefish. *Bull. Illinois State Lab. Nat. Hist.* 1:95–109.

Foundation for Research Development, 1985. *The limnology of Hartbeespoort Dam.* South African National Scientific Programmes Report No. 110, Council for Scientific and Industrial Research, Pretoria.

France, R. L., 1987. Reproductive impairment of the crayfish *Orconectes virilis* in response to acidification of Lake 223. *Can. J. Fish. Aquat. Sci.* 44 (Suppl. 1):97–106.

France, R. L., and L. Graham, 1985. Increased microsporidian parasitism of the crayfish *Orconectes virilis* in an experimentally acidified lake. *Water, Air, Soil Pollut.* 26:129–136.

456   D. W. SCHINDLER

Franzin, W. G., and G. A. McFarlane, 1981. Elevated Zn, Cd and Pb concentrations in waters of ice-covered lakes near a base metal smelter during snow melt, April 1977. *Environ. Pollut.* Series B (2):11–19.

Friedrich, G., and D. Müller, 1984. Rhine. In B. A. Whitton (Ed.), *Ecology of European Rivers*, pp. 265–316. Blackwell, Oxford.

Gächter, R., 1979. MELIMEX, an experimental heavy metal pollution study: goals, experimental design and major findings. *Schweiz. Z. Hydrol.* 41:169–176.

Gameson, A. L. H., and A. Wheeler, 1977. Restoration and recovery of the Thames Estuary. In J. Cairns, Jr., K. L. Dickson, and E. E. Herricks (Eds.), *Recovery and Restoration of Damaged Ecosystems*, pp. 72–101. University of Virginia Press, Charlottesville.

Geelen, J. F. M., and R. J. E. W. Leuven, 1986. Impact of acidification on phytoplankton and zooplankton communities. *Experimentia* 42:486–494.

Goldberg, E. D., V. F. Hodge, J. J. Griffin, and M. Koide, 1981. The impact of fossil fuel combustion on the sediments of Lake Michigan. *Environ. Sci. Technol.* 15:446–471.

Goldman, C. R., and A. Jassby, 1990. Spring mixing depth and annual productivity fluctuations in Lake Tahoe, a deep subalpine lake. In M. M. Tilzer and C. Serruya (Eds.), *Large Lakes: Ecological Structures and Functions*. Springer-Verlag, Berlin.

Goldsborough, L. G., and G. G. C. Robinson, 1986. Change in periphytic algal community structure as a consequence of short herbicide exposures. *Hydrobiologia* 139:177–192.

Gorham, E., S. E. Bayley, and D. W. Schindler, 1984. Ecological effects of acid deposition upon peatlands: a neglected field in "acid-rain" research. *Can. J. Fish. Aquat. Sci.* 41:1256–1268.

Grahn, O., H. Hultberg, and L. Landner, 1974. Oligotrophication, a self-accelerating process in lakes subjected to excessive supply of acid substances. *Ambio.* 3:93–94.

Grapentine, L. C., 1987. Consequences of environmental acidification to the freshwater amphipod *Hyalella azteca*. M. Sc. thesis, University of Manitoba, Winnipeg.

Hall, R. J., and F. P. Ide, 1987. Evidence of acidification effects on stream insect communities in central Ontario between 1937 and 1985. *Can. J. Fish. Aquat. Sci.* 44(9):1652–1657.

Harvey, H. H., and C. Lee, 1982. Historical fisheries changes related to surface water pH changes in Canada. In T. A. Haines (Ed.), *Acid Rain/Fisheries*, pp. 45–55. Amer. Fish. Soc., Bethesda, Md.

Hasler, A. D., 1947. Eutrophication of lakes by domestic drainage. *Ecology* 28:383–395.

Hecky, R. E., 1984. African lakes and their trophic efficiencies: a temporal perspective. In D. G. Meyers, and J. R. Strickler (Eds.), *Trophic Interactions within Aquatic Ecosystems*, pp. 405–448. American Association for the Advancement of Science, Washington, D.C.

Hecky, R. E., 1986. Book review. *Limnol. Oceanogr.* 31:907.

Hecky, R. E., and S. J. Guildford, 1984. Primary productivity of Southern Indian Lake before, during, and after impoundment and Churchill River diversion. *Can. J. Fish. Aquat. Sci.* 41:591–604.

Hecky, R. E., R. W. Newbury, R. A. Bodaly, K. Patalas, and D. M. Rosenberg, 1984.

Environmental impact prediction and assessment: the Southern Indian Lake experience. *Can. J. Fish. Aquat. Sci.* 41:720–732.

Henrikson, L., H. G. Oscarson, and J. A. E. Stenson, 1980. Does the change of predator system contribute to the biotic development in acidified lakes? In D. Drablos and A. Tollan (Eds.), *Ecological Impact of Acid Precipitation*, p. 316. SNSF Project, Oslo, Norway.

Holmgren, S., 1983. Phytoplankton biomass and algal composition in natural, fertilized and polluted subarctic lakes. Ph.D. dissertation, University of Uppsala, Sweden.

Hutchinson, T. C., and K. Meema (Eds.), 1987. *Effects of Atmospheric Pollutants on Forests, Wetlands and Agricultural Ecosystems*. Springer-Verlag, New York.

Johnson, M. G., 1987. Trace element loadings to sediments of fourteen Ontario lakes and correlations with concentrations in fish. *Can. J. Fish. Aquat. Sci.* 41:3–13.

Jonasson, P., 1969. Bottom fauna and eutrophication. In *Eutrophication: Causes, Consequences, Corrections*, pp. 274–305. National Academy of Sciences, Washington, D.C.

Kahl, J. S., and S. A. Norton, 1983. *Metal Input and Mobilization in Two Acid-Stressed Lakes in Maine*. Land and Water Resources Center, University of Maine, Orono.

Kawecka, B., and B. Szczesny, 1984. Dunajec. In B. A. Whitton (Ed.), *Ecology of European Rivers*, pp. 499–526. Blackwell, Oxford.

Kelly, C. A., J. W. M. Rudd, R. H. Hesslein, D. W. Schindler, P. J. Dillon, C. T. Driscoll, S. A. Gherini, and R. E. Hecky, 1987. Prediction of biological acid neutralization in lakes. *Biogeochemistry* 3:129–140.

Kelso, J. R. M., C. K. Minns, J. E. Gray, and M. L. Jones, 1986. Acidification of surface waters in eastern Canada and its relationship to aquatic biota. *Can. Spec. Publ. Fish. Aquat. Sci.* 87. Dep. Fisheries and Oceans, Ottawa.

Klaverkamp, J. F., W. A. MacDonald, D. A. Duncan, and R. Wagemann, 1984. Metallothionein and acclimation to heavy metals in fish: a review. In V. W. Cairns, P. V. Hodson, and J. O. Nriagu (Eds.), *Contaminant Effects on Fisheries*, pp. 99–113. Wiley, New York, Adv. Environ. Sci. Technol. 16 (784C).

Kozhov, M., 1963. *Lake Baikal and Its Life*. Junk, The Hague.

Kwain, W., R. W. McCauley, and J. A. MacLean, 1984. Susceptibility of starved, juvenile smallmouth bass, *Micropterus dolomieui* (Lacépède) to low pH. *J. Fish. Biol.* 25:501–504.

Lantzy, R. J., and F. T. MacKenzie, 1979. Atmospheric trace metals: global cycles and assessment of man's impact. *Geochim. Cosmochim. Acta* 43:511–525.

Larkin, P. A., and T. G. Northcote, 1969. Fish as indices of eutrophication. In *Eutrophication: Causes, Consequences, Correctives*, pp. 256–273. National Academy of Sciences, Washington, D.C.

Lawrence, S. G., and M. H. Holoka, 1987. Effects of low concentrations of cadmium on the crustacean zooplankton community of an artificially acidified lake. *Can. J. Fish. Aquat. Sci.* 44 (Suppl. 1):163–172.

Laws, E. A., 1981. *Aquatic Pollution*. Wiley, New York.

Lee, J. A., M. C. Press, S. Woodin, and P. Ferguson, 1987. Responses to acidic deposition in ombrotrophic mires. In T. C. Hutchinson and K. Meema (Eds.), *Effects of Atmospheric Pollutants on Forests, Wetlands and Agricultural Ecosystems*, pp. 549–560. Springer-Verlag, New York.

MacArthur, R. H., 1972. *Geographical Ecology*. Harper and Row, New York.

458 D. W. Schindler

Magnuson, J. J., 1976. Managing with exotics – a game of chance. *Trans. Amer. Fish. Soc.* 105:1–9.

Magnuson, J. J., J. P. Baker, and E. J. Rahel, 1984. A critical assessment of effects of acidification on fisheries in North America. *Phil. Trans. R. Soc. Lond.* B305:501–516.

Malley, D. F., P. S. S. Chang, D. L. Findlay, and G. A. Linsey, 1988. Extreme perturbation of the zooplankton community of a small Precambrian Shield lake by the addition of nutrients. *Verh. Internat. Verein. Limnol.* 23:1821–1824.

Marmorek, D. R., M. L. Jones, C. K. Minns, and F. C. Elder, 1988. Assessing the potential extent of damage to inland fisheries in eastern Canada due to acidic deposition: I. Development and evaluation of a simple "site" model. *Can. J. Fish. Aquat. Sci.* (in press).

Marshall. J. S., and D. L. Mellinger, 1980. Dynamics of cadmium-stressed plankton communities. *Can. J. Fish. Aquat. Sci.* 37:403-414.

Mills, K. H., S. M. Chalanchuk, L. C. Mohr, and I. J. Davies, 1987. Responses of fish populations in Lake 223 to 8 years of experimental acidification. *Can. J. Fish. Aquat. Sci.* 44 (Suppl. 1):114–125.

Mills, K. H., and D. W. Schindler, 1986. Biological indicators of lake acidification. *Water, Air, Soil Pollut.* 30:779–789.

Minshall, G. W., and R. C. Peterson, Jr., 1985. Towards a theory of macroinvertebrate community structure in stream ecosystems. *Arch. Hydrobiol.* 104:49–76.

Moyle, P. B., 1986. Fish introductions into North America: pattern and ecological impact. In H. A. Mooney and J. A. Drake (Eds.), *Ecology of Biological Invasions of North America and Hawaii*, pp. 27–43. Springer-Verlag, New York.

Muhlbaier, J., and G. T. Tisue, 1981. Cadmium in the southern basin of Lake Michigan. *Water, Air, Soil Pollut.* 14:3–11.

Müller, P., 1980. Effects of artificial acidification on the growth of epilithiphyton. *Can. J. Fish. Aquat. Sci.* 37:355–363.

National Academy of Sciences (U.S.A.), 1985. *Acid Deposition: Effects on Geochemical Cycling and Biological Availability of Trace Elements*. National Academy Press, Washington, D.C.

Nero, R. W., and D. W. Schindler, 1983. The decline of *Mysis relicta* during the acidification of Lake 223. *Can. J. Fish. Aquat. Sci.* 40:1905–1911.

Neu, H. J. A., 1982. Man-made storage of water resources – a liability to the ocean environment? Part I. *Marine Poll. Bull.* 13:7–12.

Nichols, F. H., J. E. Cloern, S. N. Luona, and D. H. Peterson, 1986. The modification of an estuary. *Science* 231:567–572.

Nilsson, J. P., T. Østdahl, and W. T. W. Potts, 1984. Species replacements in acidified lakes: physiology, predation or competition? *Rep. Inst. Freshw. Res. Drottningholm* 61:148–153.

Nygaard, G., 1956. Ancient and recent flora of diatoms and Chrysophyceae in Lake Gribso. Studies of humic acid Lake Gribso. *Fol. Limnol. Scand.* 8:32–94.

O'Brien, W. J., and F. DeNoyelles, Jr., 1972. Photosynthetically elevated pH as a factor in zooplankton mortality in nutrient enriched ponds. *Ecology* 53:605–614.

Økland, J., and K. A. Økland, 1980. pH level and food organisms for fish: Studies of 1000 lakes in Norway. In D. Drabløs and A. Tollan (Eds.), *Ecological Impact of Acid Precipitation*, pp. 326–327. SNSF Project, Oslo, Norway.

Økland, J., and K. A. Økland, 1986. The effects of acid deposition on benthic animals in lakes and streams. *Experimentia* 42:471–486.

Patalas, K., 1970. Primary and secondary production in a lake heated by a thermal power plant. In *The Environmental Challenges of the 70s*, pp. 267–271. 16th Annual Technical Meeting, Mt. Prospect, Ill.

Patalas, K., 1975. The crustacean plankton communities of fourteen North American great lakes. *Verh. Internat. Verein. Limnol.* 19:504–511.

Patalas, K., 1981. Spatial structure of the crustacean plankton community in Lake Winnipeg, Canada. *Verh. Internat. Verein. Limnol.* 21:305–311.

Patalas, K., 1984. The geographical distribution of *Mesocyclops edax* (S. A. Forbes) in lakes of Canada. In G. Schriever, H. K. Schminke, and C.-T. Shih (Eds.), *Syllogeus 58*, pp. 400–408. National Museum of Natural Sciences, Ottawa, Canada.

Patalas, K., and A. Salki, 1984. Effects of impoundment and diversion on the crustacean plankton of Southern Indian Lake. *Can. J. Fish. Aquat. Sci.* 41:613–637.

Pearsall, W. H., 1930. Phytoplankton in the English lakes: I. The proportions in the waters of some dissolved substances of biological importance. *J. Ecol.* 18:306–320.

Persson, G., and O. Broberg, 1985. Nutrient concentration in the acidified Lake Gärdsjön: the role of transport and retention of phosphorus, nitrogen and DOC in watershed and lake. *Ecol. Bull.* 37:158–175.

Porter, K., 1973. Selective grazing and differential digestion of algae and zooplankton. *Nature* (Lond.) 244:179–180.

Raddum, G. G., and A. Fjellheim, 1984. Acidification and early warning organisms in freshwater in western Norway. *Verh. Internat. Verein. Limnol.* 22:1973–1980.

Rago, P. J., and J. G. Wiener, 1986. Does pH affect fish species richness when lake area is considered? *Trans. Amer. Fish. Soc.* 115:438–447.

Rahel, F. J., 1986. Biogeographic influences on fish species composition of northern Wisconsin lakes with applications for lake acidification. *Can. J. Fish. Aquat. Sci.* 43:124–134.

Rawson, D. S., 1956. Algal indicators of trophic lake types. *Limnol. Oceanogr.* 1:18–25.

Rawson, D. S., 1961. A critical analysis of the limnological variables used in assessing the productivity of northern Saskatchewan lakes. *Verh. Internat. Verein. Limnol.* 14:160–166.

Rooke, J. B., and G. L. Mackie, 1984. Mollusca of six low-alkalinity lakes in Ontario, Canada. *Can. J. Fish. Aquat. Sci.* 41:777–782.

Rorslett, B., D. Berge, and S. W. Johansen, 1986. Lake enrichment by submerged macrophytes: a Norwegian whole-lake experience with *Elodea canadensis*. *Aquat. Bot.* 26:325–340.

Rosenberg, D. M., A. P. Wiens, and B. Bilyj, 1988. Chironomidae (Diptera) of peatlands in northwestern Ontario. *Holarctic Ecology* 11:19–31.

Saether, O. A., 1975. Nearctic chironomids as indicators of lake typology. *Verh. Internat. Verein. Limnol.* 19:3127–3133.

Salo, E. O., and O. J. Stober, 1977. Man's impact on the Columbia River stocks of salmon. In W. van Winkle (Ed.), *Assessing the Effects of Power Plant-Induced Mortality on Fish Populations*, pp. 36–45. Pergamon Press, New York.

Schelske, C., and D. F. Stoermer, 1971. Eutrophication, silica depletion and predicted changes in algal quality in Lake Michigan. *Science* 173:423–424.

Schindler, D. W., 1971. A hypothesis to explain differences and similarities among lakes in the Experimental Lakes Area, northwestern Ontario. *J. Fish. Res. Board Can.* 28:245–301.

460   D. W. Schindler

Schindler, D. W., 1974. Review of hydrobiological studies, Vols. 2 and 3. *Limnol. Oceanogr.* 18:819–820.

Schindler, D. W., 1977. Evolution of phosphorus limitation in lakes: natural mechanisms compensate for deficiencies of nitrogen and carbon in eutrophied lakes. *Science* 195:260–262.

Schindler, D. W., 1978. Factors regulating phytoplankton production and standing crop in the world's freshwaters. *Limnol. Oceanogr.* 23:478–486.

Schindler, D. W., 1985. The coupling of elemental cycles by organisms: evidence from whole lake chemical perturbations. In W. Stumm (Ed.), *Chemical Processes in Lakes*, pp. 225–250. Wiley, New York.

Schindler, D. W., 1986. Recovery of Canadian lakes from acidification. In H. Barth (Ed.), *Reversibility of Acidification*, pp. 2–13. Elsevier Applied Science, New York.

Schindler, D. W., 1987. Detecting ecosystem responses to anthropogenic stress. *Can. J. Fish. Aquat. Sci.* 44 (Suppl. 1):6–25.

Schindler, D. W., 1988a. Effects of acid rain on freshwater ecosystems. *Science* 239:149–157.

Schindler, D. W., 1988b. Experimental studies of chemical stressors on whole lake ecosystems. Edgardo Baldi Memorial Lecture. *Verh. Internat. Verein. Limnol.* 23:11–41.

Schindler, D. W., 1990. Experimental perturbations of whole lakes as tests of ecosystem structure and function. *Oikos* 57(1):25–41.

Schindler, D. W., and S. K. Holmgren, 1971. Primary production and phytoplankton in the Experimental Lakes Area (ELA) northwestern Ontario and other low-carbonate waters and a liquid scintillation method for determining ^{14}C activity in photosynthesis. *J. Fish. Res. Board Can.* 28:189–201.

Schindler, D. W., and G. W. Comita, 1972. The dependence of primary production upon physical and chemical factors in a small senescing lake, including the effects of complete winter oxygen depletion. *Arch. Hydrobiol.* 69:413–451.

Schindler, D. W., H. Kling, R. V. Schmidt, J. Prokopowich, V. E. Frost, R. A. Reid, and M. Capel, 1973. Eutrophication of Lake 227 by addition of phosphate and nitrate: Part 2. The second, third and fourth years of enrichment, 1970, 1971, and 1972. *J. Fish. Res. Board Can.* 30:1415–1440.

Schindler, D. W., E. J. Fee, and T. Ruszczynski, 1978. Phosphorus input and its consequences for phytoplankton standing crop and production in the Experimental Lakes Area and in similar lakes. *J. Fish. Res. Board Can.* 35:190–196.

Schindler, D. W., K. H. Mills, D. F. Malley, D. L. Findlay, J. A. Shearer, I. J. Davies, M. A. Turner, G. A. Linsey, and D. R. Cruikshank, 1985. Long-term ecosystem stress: the effects of years of acidification on a small lake. *Science* 228:1395–1401.

Schindler, D. W., R. H. Hesslein, and M. A. Turner, 1987. Exchange of nutrients between sediments and water after 15 years of experimental eutrophication. *Can. J. Fish. Aquat. Sci.* 44 (Suppl. 1):26–33.

Schindler, D. W., S. E. M. Kasian, and R. H. Hesslein, 1989. Biological impoverishment in lakes of the midwestern and northeastern U.S.A. from acid rain. *Environ. Sci. Technol.* 25:573–579.

Schindler, D. W., K. Beaty, E. J. Fee, D. Cruikshank, E. R. DeBruyn, D. L. Findlay, G. Linsey, J. A. Shearer, M. P. Stainton, and M. A. Turner, in press. Effects of climatic warning on lakes of the central boreax forest. *Science*.

Schlesinger, D. A., and H. A. Regier, 1983. Relationship between environmental temperature and yields of subarctic and temperate zone fish species. *Can. J. Fish. Aquat. Sci.* 40:1829–1837.

Sculthorpe, C. D., 1967. *The Biology of Aquatic Vascular Plants.* St. Martin's Press, New York.

Sebastien, R. J., R. A. Brust, and D. M. Rosenberg, 1989. Impact of methoxychlor on selected non-target organisms of the Souris River, Manitoba. *Can. J. Fish. Aquat. Sci.* 46:1047–1061.

Sigurdson, H., 1977. Chemistry of the crater lake during the 1971–72 Soufriere eruption. *J. Volcanol. Geothermal Res.* 2:165–186.

Smith, V. H., 1983. How nitrogen to phosphorus ratios favor dominance by blue-green algae in lake phytoplankton. *Science* 221:669–671.

Somers, K. M., and H. H. Harvey, 1984. Alteration of fish communities in lakes stressed by acid deposition and heavy metals near Wawa, Ontario. *Can. J. Fish. Aquat. Sci.* 41:20–29.

Sprules, W. G., 1975. Midsummer crustacean zooplankton communities in acid-stressed lakes. *J. Fish. Res. Board Can.* 30:389–395.

Staley, J. T., L. G. Lehmicke, F. E. Palmer, R. W. Peet, and R. C. Wissmar, 1982. Impact of Mount St. Helens eruption on bacteriology of lakes in the blast zone. *Appl. Environ. Microbiol.* 43:664–670.

Stanford, J. A., and J. V. Ward, 1986. Fish of the Colorado system. In B. R. Davies and K. F. Walker (Eds.), *The Ecology of River Systems*, pp. 385–402. Junk, The Hague.

Stephenson, M., and G. L. Mackie, 1986. Lake acidification as a limiting factor in the distribution of the freshwater amphipod *Hyalella azteca. Can. J. Fish. Aquat. Sci.* 43:288–292.

Stockner, J. G., and F. A. J. Armstrong, 1971. Periphyton of the Experimental Lakes, northwestern Ontario. *J. Fish. Res. Board Can.* 28:171–187.

Strub, P. T., T. Powell, and C. R. Goldman, 1985. Climatic forcing: effects of El Niño on a small, temperate lake. *Science* 227:55–57.

Tonn, W. M., and J. J. Magnuson, 1982. Patterns in the species composition and richness of fish assemblages in northern Wisconsin lakes. *Ecology* 63:1149–1166.

Turner, M. A., M. B. Jackson, D. L. Findlay, R. W. Graham, E. R. DeBruyn, and E. M. Vandermeer, 1987. Early responses of periphyton to experimental lake acidification. *Can. J. Fish. Aquat. Sci.* 44 (Suppl. 1):135–149.

Vollenweider, R. A., 1968. *Scientific fundamentals of eutrophication of lakes and flowing waters, with particular reference to nitrogen and phosphorus as factors in eutrophication.* Tech. Rep. Organization for Economic Cooperation and Development. Paris, DAS/DSI/68,27.

Vollenweider, R. A., 1976. Advances in defining the critical loading levels for phosphorus in lake eutrophication. *Mem. Ist. Ital. Idrobiol.* 33:53–83.

Ward, A. K., J. A. Baross, C. N. Dahm, M. D. Lilley, and J. R. Sedell, 1983. Qualitative and quantitative observations on aquatic algal communities and recolonization within the blast zone of Mount St. Helens, 1980 and 1981. *J. Phycol.* 19:238–247.

Ward, J. V., 1986. Altitudinal zonation in a Rocky Mountain stream. *Arch. Hydrobiol. Suppl.* 74:133–199.

Watt, W. D., C. D. Scott, and W. J. White, 1983. Evidence of acidification of some

462   D. W. Schindler

Nova Scotian rivers and its affect on Atlantic salmon, *Salmo salar. Can. J. Fish. Aquat. Sci.* 40:462–473.

Welcomme, R. L., 1979. *Fisheries Ecology of Floodplain Rivers.* Longman, New York.

Werner, E. E., 1986. Species interactions in freshwater fish communities. In J. Diamond, and T. J. Case (Eds.), *Community Ecology*, pp. 344–358. Harper and Row, New York.

Wiens, A. P., and D. M. Rosenberg, 1984. Effect of impoundment and river diversion on profundal macrobenthos of Southern Indian Lake, Manitoba. *Can. J. Fish. Aquat. Sci.* 41:638–648.

Wolff, W. J., 1978. The degradation of ecosystems in the Rhine. In M. W. Holdgate, and M. J. Woodman (Eds.), *The Breakdown and Restoration of Ecosystems*, pp. 169–191. Plenum, New York.

Wood, J. M., 1974. Biological cycles for toxic elements in the environment. *Science* 183:1049–1052.

Zaret, T. M., and R. T. Paine, 1973. Species introductions in a tropical lake. *Science* 182:449–455.

22 Human Impacts on the South Florida Wetlands: The Everglades and Big Cypress Swamp

WILLIAM A. NIERING

Editor's Note: The Everglades of southern Florida are a subtropical wetland, unique in North America but taken here as an example of wetlands globally. They are as unusual and rich as the Anavilhanas of the Rio Negro, the Pantanal of the southwestern Amazon Basin, and the moist prairies of North America. They have suffered a succession of disruptions, including hunting, logging, fire, abrupt and fundamental changes in the water regime, and the encroachment of farms with their toxins aimed at "pests." William Niering, an indefatigable student of ecology and a fountain of knowledge, points to the richness of the region by observing that it supports more than 1,000 species of higher plants, 300 species of birds, 60 species of reptiles and amphibians, and 25 species of mammals. Its role in maintaining fisheries of the southern coasts is certain, yet poorly known.

The Everglades are vulnerable and are being encroached upon rapidly. The patterns of change are familiar; the causes, textbook cases. But the effects are diffuse, erratic, difficult to codify, open to interpretation and argument. They become clear when species are threatened, habitats lost, water flows disrupted, whole populations eliminated. At that point they appear to be isolated disasters, such as a fish kill, caused by some quirk of environment and of no general significance. Niering has summarized these changes on the basis of years of experience. He treats the scholarly and the political as inseparable, which they are. The story is a powerful argument for the role of government in establishing the limits of the spread of human influences, the fallacy of the assumption that there is any force that will moderate avarice apart from communal action through government to preserve those aspects of environment that are dear or essential or of special scientific or scholarly interest.

Introduction

The Everglades and Big Cypress Swamp in south Florida (Figure 22.1) comprise a unique set of wetland ecosystems. Over the last half-century, they have been subjected to a multiplicity of environmental impacts that have greatly modified their ecology. Although no species is thought to have been lost in the Everglades (Kushlan 1989; W. B. Robertson, personal communication), these southern Florida wetlands have more than 30 species that are endangered and threatened. Here, floristic and faunistic elements of the Caribbean mingle with those of North America resulting in a blend of

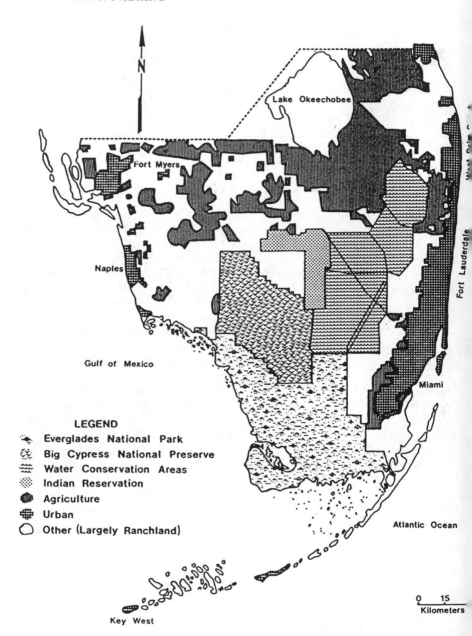

Figure 22.1.   Land use in south Florida (from Veri et al. 1975, Okavango Delta Symposium).(Niering)

species which makes it one of the most distinctive wetland complexes in the world (George 1972; Hofstetter 1983; Niering 1985; Mitsch and Gosselink 1986). In 1976 the Everglades were designated a Biosphere Preserve of UNESCO's Man and the Biosphere Program. In 1978 most of Everglades National Park became part of a National Wilderness Preserve, and in 1979 the park was designated a World Heritage Site (Hendrix and Morehead 1983). The purpose of this chapter is to highlight certain of the human impacts that have modified these wetlands and to consider prospects for future restoration.

The Ecological Setting

The Everglades originally covered more than 10,000 km^2 (Davis 1943), extending southward from Lake Okeechobee as a curved strip 65 km wide and 167 km long (Figure 22.1). Everglades National Park, comprising 5,668 km^2, covers most of the southern part of the Glades (Robertson 1959; Stark and Werner 1976). It is a vast graminoid-dominated wetland. The upper reaches are covered by sawgrass (*Cladium jamaicensis*) marshes which are replaced to the south by wet prairie and finally by a fringing belt of mangrove, primarily red mangrove (*Rhizophora mangle*), along the Gulf Coast (Davis 1943, 1967; Hofstetter 1983). Within the Glades are scattered islands of bay and willow and hardwood hammocks dominated by subtropical trees. The 2.8 cm/km southward slope favors the slow movement of water through this "sea of grass" during the rainy season. Historically, the flow included the overflow from Lake Okeechobee, but since 1,600 km^2 directly south of the lake were drained and converted to agricultural use, this no longer occurs.

To the west of the park, comprising 3,120 km^2 lies the Big Cypress Swamp, dominated by three distinctive cypress communities that form a continuum with the dwarf cypress on the harsher wet sites. The cypress domes in wetter depressions and mostly flooded strands are characterized by impressive cypress (*Taxodium distichum*) towering over 30 m in height and reaching 1–2 m in diameter. Most of the stands have been lumbered, however. Today the Corkscrew Swamp Sanctuary, owned by the National Audubon Society, is one of the last remnants of these magnificent forests. Mixed hardwood swamps and postlumbered wetlands are part of the Big Cypress pattern as well. Within this region, the Big Cypress National Preserve, comprising 2,023 km^2, has been set aside to help protect regional hydrology as well as the unique Fakahatchee Strand.

The pattern of vegetation is diverse, the flora comprising over 1000 seed plants. The fauna is spectacular (Robertson 1959; George 1972). Over 300 bird species, many of limited distribution in the United States, have been recorded. Some of those of special interest are the snail (Everglade) kite (*Rostrhamus sociabilis*), bald eagle (*Haliaeetus leucocephalus*), reddish egret (*Dichromanassa rufescens*), roseate spoonbill (*Ajaia ajaja*), and mangrove cuckoo (*Coccyzus minor*). There are 60 known species of reptiles and amphibians, including three listed federally as threatened or endangered. They are the American alligator (*Alligator mississippiensis*), the American crocodile (*Crocodylus acutus*), and the green sea turtle (*Chelonia mydas*). There are 25 native mammals, of which the West Indian manatee (*Trichechus manatus*) and the Florida panther (*Felis concolor coryi*) are two noteworthy endangered species.

Limestone underlies the wetlands. They are covered by peat and marl deposits of varying depth. The climate is subtropical with a rainy summer and dry winter season. Lightning-caused fires have been an integral part of their evolution. Periodic freezes have affected large areas of the mangrove community which reaches its northern limits in Florida. Severe hurricanes occasionally sweep across the south Florida wetlands and can drastically modify the region for decades (Robertson and Muller 1961; Craighead 1964).

Environmental Impacts and Biotic Response

One of the first major impacts on the biota was commercial hunting of the spectacular wading birds. In the 1870s it was estimated that 2.5 million wading birds nested in south Florida. They included snowy egrets (*Egretta thula*), great egrets (*Casmerodius albus*), great blue herons (*Ardea herodias*), wood storks (*Mycteria americana*), white ibis (*Eudocimus albus*), Louisiana herons (*Egretta tricolor*), and little blue herons (*Egretta caerulea*) (Hendrix and Morehead 1983). In the 1880s and 1890s commercial hunting caused a severe decline in the wading-bird population, whose feathers were used by the millinery industry. Plume hunting declined following the passage of the Lacey Act and populations began to recover. Since the 1930s, however, there has been a steady decline in numbers due to habitat loss and hydrologic disruptions.

Flooding has long been a problem in the Everglades. An extensive canal and drainage scheme was begun in the 1920s. In the 1960s a more sophisticated water-management system was constructed by the U.S. Army Corps of Engineers. It included 1,500 miles of levees and canals and three Conservation Areas which could impound and release water when and where it was deemed necessary, which further interrupted the natural flow originating from Lake Okeechobee. Water management for flood control, agricultural use, wildlife, recreation, and maintenance of Everglades National Park was now under human control – the South Florida Water

Management District. In the years that followed, both excessively dry and wet seasons occurred. A severe natural drought in 1971, accentuated by an inadequate natural water flow into Everglades National Park, resulted in severe wildlife losses (Ward 1972). During a very wet season in the 1980s the Everglades were so severely flooded that the deer herd was threatened with drowning.

Drainage has also taken its toll; about three-fourths of the historic Glades have been lost, primarily to agriculture. Although most of the cypress swamps have been cut over, plant collectors still seek out unusual plants, especially the rare epiphytes, which are very profitable. The introduction of exotic plants which subsequently have become naturalized is further contributing to biotic impoverishment. Some of these impacts will be examined in greater detail.

Hydrologic Changes

Research over the past few decades has documented that certain wetland animal populations are integrally adapted to a fluctuating hydrology which has been seriously disrupted. In 1960 the wood stork population was around 6,000. By 1972 it had declined to 1,800 (Kushlan et al. 1975). During this period their nesting was successful only in 1967. It was not until 1974 that conditions were again favorable and 1,000 pairs of birds produced 1,900 young (Ogden et al. 1978). It has been documented that wood storks initiate and successfully complete breeding only when the Everglades are in a drying cycle and the wetland pools concentrate small fish. During feeding the birds grope blindly, using a touch reflex (tactolocation) that is faster than the eye (Kahl 1964). Several species of sunfish with four other fish species make up 84 percent of their diet (Ogden et al. 1976). From 1967 to 1982 in south Florida the stork population decreased 75 percent (Kushlan and Frohring 1986). Excessively high seasonal water levels, mostly human-induced, accounted for the storks' repeated failures to reproduce. With proper water-level manipulation, however, the storks can be induced to breed.

In contrast to the wood stork, the endangered snail kite is favored by continuously flooded conditions. In some areas, as a result of human-induced water-level changes, the population has increased (Kushlan and Bass 1983b). As a specialized feeder on the apple snail (*Pomacea paludosa*), however, its future is insecure. Shooting and encroachment by exotic plants pose additional threats to its survival. Although it may appear incongruous that two birds with opposite requirements can coexist, over an area as large as the original Everglades there was probably adequate temporal and geographical heterogeneity that some years would have favored kites, and others, storks.

The fish populations of the Everglades are also keyed to seasonal water changes (Kushlan and Lodge 1974). Over a 27-month period during which the water level was stable rather than fluctuating, there was a striking shift from small-sized omnivorous fish to larger-sized carnivorous fish which are poorly adapted to oscillating water conditions (Kushlan 1976). Although there was a decrease in fish density, it was noted that biomass, average size, species richness, and diversity increased. Such changes may also affect certain predator–prey relationships.

Although the alligator, which has been protected for the last decade, has made a dramatic comeback, it is still threatened, especially in the Shark River Slough, where nest flooding is the most critical factor to reproductive success. Between 1975 and 1980, when water levels remained continuously high over the summer, mean annual egg loss was 40.5 percent (Kushlan and Jacobsen 1990). Nesting is keyed to water-level fluctuations during the rainy season. Under natural conditions the height for egg placement is correlated with maximum water levels. Although flooding associated with tropical storms can occasionally cause mortality, in 1982 the opening of the floodgates from one of the conservation areas resulted in a 98 percent loss of the eggs laid that year. Alligator-maintained pools can further serve as refuges for fish during dry seasons, contribute to overall habitat diversity, and maintain species richness in the Glades (Kushlan 1974).

Historically, the waters in Everglades National Park have contributed to commercial and recreational fisheries (Hendrix and Morehead 1983). This resource has declined, however, and most experts agree it is correlated with changes in upland watershed management (Davis 1979). Research is under way to understand how adjacent ecosystems, especially the wetlands, are coupled with estuarine waters. Odum (1970) documented the importance of mangroves in contributing to fisheries productivity, but this community suffered widespread destruction in many areas. Filling and other alterations resulting in the loss or modification of other wetland types have probably been contributory. It should be noted that fish populations are critical to wading birds and other wildlife.

Changing Fire Regimes

Drainage and droughts due to human water manipulation have drastically changed the character of the fire regime in both the Everglades and Big Cypress Swamp wetlands (Wade and Hofstetter 1980). Traditionally, the Everglades burned when the soils were moist or actually flooded. With more severe droughts which lower the water table, fire intensity has increased and dried out the peat soils, which then burn. Egler (1952) contends that "the herbaceous Everglades and the surrounding pinelands were born in fire; that they can survive only with fires; and that they are dying today because of fires."

At issue is how the changing fire regime affects the various plant communities and associated wildlife. The decline of sawgrass in the wet prairies has been attributed to the burning of the deep peat soils where it normally grows most vigorously (Craighead 1971). Forthman (1973) attributed the decline in some stands to litter accumulation, although burning stimulated recovery. Others believe that altered hydroperiod, nutritional deficiencies, and insect damage are involved (Hofstetter and Parsons 1975; Hofstetter 1976). Although sawgrass and an associated graminoid, maiden cane (*Panicum hemitomon*), have overlapping hydrologic tolerances, the latter can stand deeper water and become better established on exposed sites. Severe burns and altered hydrologic cycles can shift the dominance of such species.

The cypress and mixed-hardwood swamps are also fire related. All dwarf cypress stands have been burned. Due to drainage the intensity of these burnings has increased in recent decades. Cypress domes can be completely burned out, favoring the invasion of exotic woody species. Even wetter strands with an old cypress occasionally show fire scars and, in the absence of fire, hardwood trees tend to replace the cypress. Postlumbered cypress and mixed hardwood swamps are especially vulnerable to wild fires, particularly if drainage accompanied the lumbering operation. Such fires can favor the development of dense shrubby cover and further arrest the return of the original swamp forest species (Marois and Ewel 1983).

Uncontrolled wildfires can have a detrimental influence on most wildlife including birds, raccoons, opossums, rodents, snakes, turtles, and frogs (Robertson 1953). Bird mortality is usually limited to those nesting near the ground (Robertson and Kushlan 1974), but frog populations can be set back five years by severe sawgrass fires (Ligas 1960). Turtles are often the most common victims (Werner 1978). Practically all reported wildlife mortality occurs during wildfires. Most of the intense fires are related to lowered water tables and they are usually the most destructive. It appears that the wildlife was better attuned to natural fire regimes.

Role of Exotic Species

In the south Florida wetlands, exotic plants pose a very serious threat to the indigenous vegetation. Three aggressive exotics – Australian pine (*Casuarina* spp.), cajeput or punk tree (*Melaleuca quinquenervia*), and Brazilian pepper (*Schinus terebinthifolius*) – are capable of colonizing disturbed sites faster than native species and once established can shade out the natives (Hendrix and Morehead 1983). Eradication is very difficult. *Casuarina* spp. are invading some of the marl prairies. All three species are susceptible to fire but only one, *C. equisetifolia,* does not sprout after fire, so periodic fires can serve to arrest this species.

Melaleuca is a common invader of the prairie marshes. It is moving rapidly both eastward and westward into the wetlands from the coastal ridges. Single trees become established and soon reproduce to become dense monocultures that shade out the typical wet-prairie flora. It readily invades disturbed sites as well (Alexander and Allen 1973; Myers 1975; Austin 1976) and can become established in undisturbed communities (Woodall 1978). Disturbed cypress forests, even strands, have been taken over by this aggressive Australian introduction which, since its seed dispersal is favored by fire, literally thrives on fire. By the year 2,000 it is estimated that Melaleuca will cover vast acreages of the Everglades south of Lake Okeechobee and north of Everglades National Park.

Brazilian pepper, a large shrub or small tree introduced from Brazil, is an aggressive shade-tolerant invader of abandoned land. It fruits in winter and the fruit is carried by birds into cypress swamps, even to the least-flooded sections of the mangrove region. When mangroves are killed by periodic freezes, Schinus can colonize many square miles (Olmsted and Yates 1984). Since the seedlings cannot tolerate flooding, wetland drainage further favors spreading.

Exotic fishes pose another potential threat. Although the Everglades continue to support a vigorous native fish population despite the exotics (Kushlan 1986), it may be only a matter of time until the extensive flooding permits a dramatic increase of those already present or until a particularly successful exotic arrives.

Threats to Endangered Species

The south Florida wetlands harbor a large number of endangered, threatened, and rare species. The wood stork, snail kite, and alligator have been mentioned. There are many others. The Cape Sable seaside sparrow (*Ammospiza maritima mirabilis*) is now found throughout its original range and numbers over 6,600 birds. Over 98 percent of its habitat is open muhly grass (*Muhlenbergia filipes*) marl habitats with a one- to six-month hydroperiod (Kushlan and Bass 1983a). Current threats to this habitat include the invasion of exotic plants and the absence of fire (Kushlan et al. 1982). Among endangered reptiles are the crocodile and the green sea turtle. The crocodile, now fewer than 500 in number, is associated with both fresh- and saltwater habitats. The young crocodile needs some exposure to saline water to survive and is therefore affected by water-level manipulation. Current studies indicate the population to be relatively stable although the range has decreased somewhat due to habitat loss. Protection of the North Largo site as part of the Crocodile Lake Wildlife Refuge is urgently needed (Kushlan 1988). Further problems include: the endangered green sea turtle, which is highly dependent upon the aquatic beds of turtle grass (*Thalassia testudinum*) in the shallow coastal waters; the West Indian manatee (*Trichechus manatus*), easily injured by boat propellers and harassed by swimmers; and the endangered Florida panther, which is dependent on sizable tracts of undisturbed wetlands.

Lumbering and plant collectors are encroaching on certain endangered, threatened, and rare plants, especially epiphytic orchids and the bromeliads found in swamp forests and hammocks. Several dozen of these unusual plants, restricted to the Fakahatchee Strand and other localized sites, are in grave danger from unscrupulous collectors in spite of being protected by law. A few examples will serve to represent this mostly subtropical group of plant species which reach their northern limit in southern Florida (Ward 1978).

The epiphytic leafless orchid (*Campylocentrum pachyrrhizum*), the range of which extends into Venezuela, through Trinidad and the Antilles, occurs in the Fakahatchee Strand. In the absence of leaves it carries on photosynthesis in the roots. The threatened powdery catopsis (*Catopsis beteroniana*), a tank bromeliad, is a recently discovered, insectivorous epiphyte found in tropical hammocks and occasionally in mangrove swamps. The white powder which covers the inner and outer portions of the overlapping linear leaves acts as a lubricant that causes the insects attracted to the white surface to slide into the water-filled leaf axils and drown. The white powder reflects ultraviolet light and is highly visible to flying insects. It also prevents insects from escaping. The air plant (*Tillandsia pruinosa*), also threatened, was unknown in Florida until 1956. It looks like a furry, many-legged tarantula and is found only in limited areas of the Fakahatchee. In the 1960s the plants were sold as novelties along the Tamiami Trail. Fortunately, they have escaped exploitation in the dense, trackless Fakahatchee wilderness.

Several epiphytic ferns are also endangered. The tropical bird's nest spleenwort (*Asplenium serratum*), with vase-shaped rosettes of leaves which resembles a bird's nest, is widespread in the West Indies and Central and South America. Although it is rare in south Florida it has great horticultural appeal and is a target for both amateur and commercial collectors. It is found in the protected Matheson Hammock and, if control of collection cannot be established in the Collier County cypress swamps, this may be the last surviving station in the United States. The auricled spleenwort (*Asplenium auritum*) has fronds that curl up in dry weather like the more common resurrection fern. It has disappeared from lumbered areas and is only found in the Fakahatchee and Deep Lake cypress strands.

These rare and endangered plants at the northern limit of their range are in an ecologically precarious environment. The added human impact could easily lead to extinction.

Future Prospects

Although the wetlands have been seriously modified by a multiplicity of impacts, there is currently a political climate favorable to restoration. In response to citizen action, Governor Robert Graham took positive action in the early 1980s. In 1983 several members of the South Florida Water Management District were replaced by others more environmentally inclined and in accord with the governor's goals. The water district is working on a model to restore the natural flow of water into parts of the Everglades which is already under way in Everglades National Park. In an effort to duplicate natural flow and to assess soil development and wildlife habitat restoration (Schneider and Hartwell 1984) an attempt is being made to acquire a 247 km experimental tract contiguous to a water conservation area which will receive water from the Miami Canal. Restoration of the Kissimmee watershed which feeds Lake Okeechobee was started in 1984. It had been shortened by canals to half its original length in 1964 which was causing eutrophication of Lake Okeechobee. In 1976 state legislation was enacted to restore it to its original state. Another positive move toward protecting endangered, threatened, or rare species in the Fakahatchee and other south Florida wetlands has been the passage of the Florida Preservation of Native Flora Law (1978).

The wetlands are currently surrounded by over two million people. Development pressure continues and water demands for other purposes than maintaining the unique biota are increasing. At issue are the realistic prospects for restoring or rehabilitating this wetland complex. It is being addressed as restoration efforts are initiated. Prevention of water intrusion into the Biscayne aquifer, which provides water for the coastal population, agriculture, and the remaining natural ecosystems, will demand careful monitoring in simulating natural hydrological cycles in the remaining relatively natural wetland communities. Some already have been irreversibly changed. Flooded water-conservation areas are wetter and support a more hydrophytic plant community than the typical sawgrass emergent marshes. Water quality has been altered by agricultural runoff and substrate changes. Exposed bedrock is mineralizing the waters. Research has documented the critical role of water-level changes in the life histories of many of the species. With proper manipulation of water, populations can be restored.

The replacement of the native biota by exotic species, especially Melaleuca and Schinus, is a very real threat. Every effort must be made to understand life histories and possible weak points of such exotics in order to arrest their spread. The preservation of the mosaic of wetland ecosystems versus individual wetland species, especially those endangered, poses another problem. In some cases the ecological requirements of both may be similar; in others this may not be true. This issue and others were eloquently addressed by Kushlan in 1979. It will be a challenge, but, with dedication and the application of the best ecological expertise available, major portions of the south Florida wetlands can yet be preserved.

References

Alexander, T. R., and G. C. Allen, 1973. *Recent and long-term changes and patterns in south Florida.* Final report, Part 1. Mimeo. Rep. (EVER–N–51) U.S. Dept. Interior, Nat. Park Svc. No. PB 231939.

Austin, D. F., 1976. Vegetation of southeastern Florida: I. Pine Jog. *Fla. Sci.* 39(4): 230–235.

Craighead, F. C., Sr., 1964. Land, mangroves and hurricanes. *The Fairchild Tropical Garden Bull.* 19(4):1–28.

Craighead, F. C., Sr., 1971. *The Trees of South Florida:* Vol. 1. *The Natural Environments and Their Succession.* University of Miami Press, Coral Gables, Fla.

Davis, G. E., 1979. *Changes in the Everglades National Park red drum and spotted sea trout fisheries 1958–1978: fishing pressure, environmental stress or natural cycle?*, pp. 81–87. Colloquium Gulf State Marine Fisheries Comm.

Davis, J. H., Jr., 1943. The natural features of southern Florida, especially the Everglades. *Fla. Geol. Surv. Bull.* 25.

Davis, J. H., Jr., 1967. *General map of natural vegetation of Florida.* University of Florida, Ag. Expt. Sta. Circular S–178.

Egler, F. E., 1952. Southeast saline Everglades vegetation, Florida, and its management. *Vegetatio* 3(4–5):213–265.

Forthman, C. A., 1973. The effects of prescribed burning on sawgrass, *Cladium jamaicensis* Crantz, in south Florida. M.S. thesis. University of Miami, Coral Gables, Fla.

George, J. C., 1972. *Everglades Wild Guide.* Nat. Hist. Series. Office of Pub., Nat. Park Svc., U.S.D.I.

Hendrix, G., and J. Morehead, 1983. Everglades National Park: an imperiled wetland. *Ambio* 12(3–4):153–157.

Hofstetter, R. H., 1976. *Current status of vegetation and possible indications of vegetation trends in the Everglades.* Final report. Mimeo. Dept. of Biology, University of Miami, Coral Gables, Fla.

Hofstetter, R. H., 1983. Wetlands in the United Sates. In A. J. P. Gore (Ed.), *Mires: Swamp, Bog, Fen and Moor. B. Regional Studies*, pp. 201–244. Elsevier.

Hofstetter, R. H., and F. Parsons, 1975. *Effects of fire in the ecosystem: an ecological study of the effects of fire on the wet prairie, sawgrass glades, and pineland communities of south Florida.* Final report, part 2. Mimeo. Rep. U.S. Dept. Interior, Nat. Park Svc. (EVER–N–48) No. PB 264463.

Kahl, M. P., 1964. Food ecology of the wood stork (*Mycteria americana*) in Florida. *Ecol. Monogr.* 34:97–117.

Kushlan, J. A., 1974. Observations on the role of the American alligator (*Alligator mississippiensis*) in the southern Florida wetlands. *Copeia* 4:993–996.

Kushlan, J. A., 1976. Environmental stability and fish community diversity. *Ecology* 57:821–825.

Kushlan, J. A., 1979. Design and management of continental wildlife reserves: lessons from the Everglades. *Biological Conservation* 15:281–290.

Kushlan, J. A., 1986. Exotic fishes of the Everglades: a reconsideration of proven impact. *Environmental Conservation* 13:67–69.

Kushlan, J. A., 1988. Conservation and management of the American crocodile. *Environmental Management* 12:777–790.

Kushlan, J. A., 1989. Wetlands and wildlife, the Everglades perspective, pp. 773–790. In R. R. Scharitz and J. W. Gibbons (Eds.), *Freshwater Wetlands and Wildlife*. DOE Sym. Series 61, Oak Ridge, Tenn.

Kushlan, J. A., and T. E. Lodge, 1974. Ecological and distributional notes on freshwater fish of southern Florida. *Science* 37:110–128.

Kushlan, J. A., J. C. Ogden, and A. L. Higer, 1975. *Relation of water level and fish availability to wood stork reproduction in the southern Everglades, Florida*. U.S. Dept. Interior Geol. Surv., U.S. Nat. Park Svc.

Kushlan, J. A., O. L. Bass, Jr., L. L. Loope, W. B. Robertson, Jr., P. C. Rosendahl, and D. L. Taylor, 1982. *Cape Sable Sparrow Management Plan*. Report M–660. Nat. Park Svc., South Florida Res. Center.

Kushlan, J. A., and O. L. Bass, Jr., 1983a. Habitat use and the distribution of the Cape Sable sparrow. Reprinted from *The Seaside Sparrow: Its Biology and Management*, pp. 139–146. North Carolina Biol. Survey, N.C. State Museum.

Kushlan, J. A., and O. L. Bass, Jr., 1983b. The snail kite in the southern Everglades. *Florida Field Naturalist* 11:108–111.

Kushlan, J. A., and P. C. Frohring, 1986. The history of the southern Florida wood stork population. *Wilson Bull.* 98(3):368–386.

Kushlan, J. A., and T. Jacobsen, 1990. Environmental variability in the reproductive success of Everglades alligator. *J. Herp.* 24:176–184.

Ligas, F. J., 1960. *Recommended program for CA3*. Florida Game and Freshwater Fish Comm.

Marois, K., and K. C. Ewel, 1983. Natural and management-related variation in cypress domes. *Forest Sci.* 29(3):627–640.

Mitsch, W. J., and J. G. Gosselink, 1986. *Wetlands*. Van Nostrand Reinhold Co., New York.

Myers, R. L., 1975. The relationship of site conditions to the invading capability of *Melaleuca quinquenervia* in southwest Florida. M.S. thesis. University of Florida, Gainesville.

Niering, W. A., 1985. *Wetlands*. (The Audubon Society Nature Guides) Chanticleer, New York.

Odum, W. E., 1970. Pathways of energy flow in a south Florida estuary. Ph.D. Diss. University of Miami.

Ogden, J. C., J. A. Kushlan, and J. T. Tilmant, 1976. Prey selectivity by the wood stork. *Condor* 78:324–330.

Ogden, J. C., J. A. Kushlan, and J. T. Tilmant, 1978. *The food habits and nesting success of wood storks in Everglades National Park 1974.* Natural Resources Report No. 16. U.S. Dept. Interior, Nat. Park Svc.

Olmsted, I., and S. Yates, 1984. Florida's pepper problem. *Garden* 8:20–23.

Robertson, W. B., Jr., 1953. *A survey of fire effects in Everglades National Park.* Mimeo Report. U.S. Dept. Interior, Nat. Park Svc.

Robertson, W. B., Jr., 1959. *Everglades – The Park Story.* University of Miami Press, Coral Gables, Fla.

Robertson, W. B., Jr., and J. A. Kushlan, 1974. The southern Florida avifauna. In P. J. Gleason (comp.), *Environments of South Florida: Present and Past*, pp. 414–452. Mem. 2. Miami Geol. Soc., Miami.

Robertson, W. B., Jr., and H. B. Muller, 1961. Wild winds and wildlife. *Audubon Mag.* November–December.

Schneider, W. J., and J. H. Hartwell, 1984. Troubled waters of the Everglades. *Nat. Hist.* 93(11):47–57.

Stark, J. E., and H. Werner, 1976. *Natural history and management of Everglades National Park. Proc. of symposium on the Okavango Delta and its future utilisation.* National Museum and Botswana Society, Gaborone, Botswana.

Wade, D., J. Ewel, and R. H. Hofstetter, 1980. *Fire in south Florida ecosystems.* U.S. Dept. Ag., Forest Svc. General Technical Report SE–17. Southeast For. Expt. Sta., Ashville, N.C.

Ward, D. B., 1978. *Plants: Vol. 5. Rare and Endangered Biota of Florida.* University Presses of Florida, Gainesville.

Ward, R., 1972. The imperiled Everglades. *Nat. Geog.* 141(1):1-27.

Werner, H. W., 1978. *The effect of fire type along a relative humidity gradient in a rockland pine forest.* Mimeo. Rep. U.S. Dept. Interior, Everglades Nat. Park, Homestead, Fla.

Woodall, S., 1978. *Melaleuca* in Florida. Mimeo. Prog. Rep. U.S. Dept. Ag., Forest Svc. Resour. Lab., Lehigh Acres, Fla.

23 The Impoverishment of Aquatic Communities by Smelter Activities near Sudbury, Canada

N. D. YAN AND P. M. WELBOURN

Editor's Note: The landscape around Sudbury, Ontario, has been devastated over several decades by the gaseous emissions of smelters. The extent of the devastation is difficult to define, but forests have been destroyed by air pollution and prevented from recovering over an area of more than a hundred square miles. The cause is oxides of sulphur and heavy metals emitted over decades from a series of smelting operations. Lakes and streams have been affected as well.

Yan and Welbourn address the problem of defining the patterns of changes in plant and animal communities of lakes and ponds affected by air-borne pollutants 13 km from the smelter. Surprisingly enough, the effects, although cumulative, are reversible, at least in part. They are faithful to patterns reported elsewhere: the small-bodied, rapid reproducers are more resistant; the large-bodied are commonly more vulnerable. Food webs are abridged, fish populations lost, and certain populations explode in response to removal of competitors. So the effects present an interesting mixture of direct effects of toxins, including aluminum washed off the acidified land, and indirect effects due to changes in predator or consumer pressure.

The transitions are all in the direction of steepening the dominance/diversity curves by concentrating production in one or a few species. The impoverishment leads to increased vulnerability to further disturbance. The example is unusual and compelling.

These extraordinary circumstances offer powerful insights into the patterns of nature, which are much closer to universal than we might have expected. Yan and Welbourn, distinguished ecologists, offer us a rich, new insight into whither the effects of pollution.

Introduction

Acidification and trace metal contamination of surface waters are common environmental problems, often occurring in combination, associated with the mining and smelting of metal-rich ores (Nriagu 1984). Receiving waters may be acidified either by the emission of acidic substances, principally SO_2, from smelters and their deposition on lakes and their drainage basins, or by the influx of waters acidified by seepage through mine tailings or waste rock. Similarly, the sources of metals may be emissions into the atmosphere and subsequent deposition, leaching from tailings or slag piles, or export from contaminated watersheds. This export may be increased by strong acid

477

deposition which accelerates the rate of weathering of minerals in the watershed.

If the only pathway for acid influx is atmospheric transport and deposition, the severity and geographic extent of watershed acidification depend on the rates of emission of S to the atmosphere, the atmospheric conditions at the time of release (which affect rates of S transport and deposition), and the acid-neutralizing capacity of the water bodies. The S content of the ore, the production of the smelter, and the processing and emission-abatement procedures it employs determine rates of SO_2 emissions. Rates of supply of acid-neutralizing capacity to receiving waters are determined both by the hydrologic and geological setting of the water body and by the activities of its microflora (Kelly et al. 1982). In general, effects of acidification are seen at considerable distances from large point sources. Conroy et al. (1976), for example, reported a zone containing lakes of depressed pH (<5.5) extending 130 km northeast of the smelter complex in Sudbury, Canada.

In contrast to the acid precursors, metals are usually emitted in particulate form. Because the deposition velocities of particulates greatly exceed those of gasses, the contaminated zone generally extends tens rather than hundreds of kilometers from the emission source (Conroy et al. 1976). The effect of metal release is, of course, related to the degree of contamination of the receiving waters, but the relationship is not simple. Variations in the fate and transport (Jackson et al. 1980) and in the toxicity and bioaccumulative potential (Kaiser 1980; Krantzberg 1987) of the metals are determined in part by inherent elemental properties. Changes in physical (e.g., temperature, particle resuspension) or chemical (e.g., pH, redox potential) attributes of the receiving waters also influence metal behavior. Furthermore, effects cannot be assessed without consideration of the composition of biotic assemblages, because metal sensitivity varies widely among taxa (Williams et al. 1985).

The biological impacts of the acidification and/or metal contamination of water bodies near smelters range from changes in the relative abundance of species to extinction of populations or even entire trophic levels in particular lakes (see, for example, Harvey and Lee 1982). Three kinds of study indicate that these changes are in fact a result of smelter emissions. Firstly, controlled toxicological studies indicate that the concentrations of metals and hydrogen ions, alone – let alone in combination – that are encountered in lakes near smelters are in the range of lethality for chronic exposure (e.g., Table 23.1). Secondly, field surveys generally indicate that the severity of effects decreases with distance from the smelters (Keller and Pitblado 1984). Finally, changes in industrial activities which reduce acid and metal emissions have resulted

Table 23.1. *Summary of average[a] pH, trace metal, and total phosphorus levels of Clearwater Lake (mean of 1973–1979) near Sudbury and of fifteen non-impacted Canadian Shield Lakes in Muskoka and Haliburton districts (M–H) about 200 km from Sudbury (from Yan and Miller 1984). Units for metals are µg/L. Chronic lethality thresholds (16% reproductive impairment in µg/L, from Biesinger and Christensen 1972) for* Daphnia magna *are also listed.*

	Clearwater	M–H	Lethal level
pH	4.27	> 6.0	
Cd[b]	0.70	< 0.02	0.17
Cu	86.4	< 2	22
Ni	267	< 2	30
Al	394	42	320
Mn	300	33	4100
Fe	91	98	4380
Total P	4.9	8.2	

[a] Average of weekly to biweekly, whole lake, morphometrically weighted composite, unfiltered samples.
[b] Midsummer, epilimnetic sample from 1985 (from Yan et al., in press).

in rapid improvements in water quality, the degree of improvement being inversely related to the distance from the smelter complex (Keller and Pitblado 1986).

The specific objectives of this chapter are

1   to review the evidence for the impoverishment of freshwater biota caused by the atmospheric emission of acids and metals by smelters near Sudbury, Ontario, Canada,

2   to describe structural changes in communities in affected lakes and suggest resulting changes in functional attributes, and

3   to examine the resilience of impoverished communities to an additional stress.

In Canada, environmental impacts of smelters in Flin Flon, Manitoba (Franzin 1984); Wawa, Ontario (Gorham and Gordon 1963; Somers and Harvey 1984); and Noranda, Quebec (BEST 1979), have been described, but the effects that are most extensively documented are those attributable to the mining, smelting, and ancillary lumbering operations that have occurred over the last century near Sudbury, Ontario. Because of the extensive data available for Sudbury lakes (see, for example, Nriagu 1984), we have chosen to focus on studies of Clearwater Lake and other small lakes near Sudbury. Clearwater Lake is 13 km from the major Sudbury smelter; the water-quality degradation of the lake is particularly severe for lakes affected solely by atmospheric transport of pollutants.

Paleolimnological studies indicate that lakes in the Sudbury area had much lower acidity and metal levels prior to the operation of local smelters (Dillon and Smith 1984; Dixit and Evans 1986), but we have no preimpact descriptions of the biota of the lakes. Effects must, therefore, be inferred from comparisons with unaffected lakes that are in the same biogeographic region and have similar morphometry, ionic strength, and nutrient status. Fifteen lakes in the Haliburton and Muskoka districts of south-central Ontario, 200 km southeast of Sudbury, are used for this purpose. Dillon et al. (1986a) have described the morphometry, water chemistry, and plankton communities of these reference lakes.

Historical Background of the Sudbury Problem

Copper and nickel have been extracted from the rich sulphide ores of the Sudbury Igneous Complex (Faggart et al. 1985) almost continuously since the deposits were first discovered in 1883. Prior to 1930, the metals were extracted in open roasting beds. Huge tracts of forest were destroyed by logging to fuel the beds and by the massive ground-level sulphur-dioxide fumigations that they produced (Hutchinson 1979). The first tall stacks were constructed in the 1920s and 1930s to disperse emissions and reduce the severity of ground-level fumigations, but total SO_2 emissions continued to increase through the 1950s. Major impacts on terrestrial and aquatic ecosystems were reported at the time (see, for example, Linzon 1958; Gorham and Gordon 1960; Johnson and Owen 1966). Emissions of SO_2 peaked in the 1960s at over 2 million metric tons/yr. Emissions have declined steadily since 1970; they are currently 0.5–0.7 million metric tons/yr (Dillon et al. 1986b).

While 1,000 metric tons of Ni and 2,000 metric tons of Cu were also discharged annually into the atmosphere in the mid-1960s, (Conroy et al. 1976), average levels declined to 500 and 670 metric tons/yr, respectively, between 1973 and 1981 (Keller and Pitblado 1986).

The effects of the historical and current SO_2 and metal emissions on terrestrial ecosystems in the Sudbury area are discussed by Hutchinson (1979). As an example of the severe impairment of water quality of lakes close to Sudbury, the metal levels and pH of Clearwater Lake are compared with values from the reference lakes in Table 23.1. Sulphuric acid, much of which originates as SO_2 directly absorbed by the lake and its watershed (Dillon et al. 1982), is the acid source. Elevated levels of Cu, Ni, and, in part, Zn, are attributable to very high levels of atmospheric deposition (Table

Table 23.2. *A comparison of bulk deposition rates of metals[a] from the atmosphere at Clearwater Lake and in Muskoka–Haliburton (M–H). Values are in $mg/m^2/yr$ measured from June 1977 to May 1978 (Jeffries 1984)*

Metal	Clearwater	M–H
Cu	87.4	2.1
Ni	81.6	<1.5
Zn	66.7	15.7
Al	40.6	65.4
Fe	215	101

[a] Bulk collectors seriously underestimate total input of acids because they do not efficiently collect SO_2 (Dillon et al. 1982).

23.2), but elevated levels of Al are attributable to enhanced rates of weathering of watershed materials by the input of strong acid. A comparison of ambient metal levels in the lake with chronically lethal thresholds for *Daphnia magna* (Table 23.1) indicates the toxic nature of the waters of the lake.

Evidence for Biotic Impoverishment

We define impoverishment as a "significant" decrease in any expression of the richness or standing stock of an assemblage of aquatic biota, declines in expressions of richness taking precedence. Impoverishment would, therefore, result from a decrease in species richness, whether standing stock decreased or otherwise. A decrease in standing stock without an increase in richness would also be considered impoverishment.

Declines in species richness are given precedence over decreases in standing stock both because reduction in richness more closely approximates the conventional meaning of the term "species impoverishment," and also for pragmatic reasons. Richness data exhibit less temporal variability than biomass data. To illustrate the latter point we manipulated 1977 crustacean zooplankton biomass and richness data for seven of the non-acidic reference lakes. Means of all possible combinations of subsets of the data of sizes one to six were compared with the mean of all 23 samples collected over the ice-free season (the "best" mean in Figure 23.1). For any subsample size, subset means for biomass deviated from the best mean by approximately three times more than did subsample means of richness (Figure 23.1). Therefore, confidence limits for estimates of zooplankton richness are narrower than

AVERAGE DEVIATION (%) OF SUBSET FROM BEST MEAN

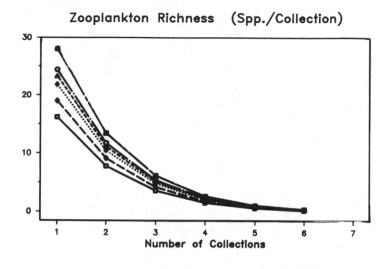

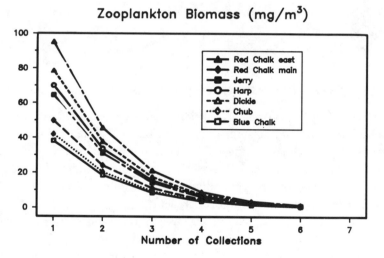

Figure 23.1. Relationship between average subset size (number of collections) and average deviation of subset mean from the best mean which included all data (n = 23) for the ice-free season of 1977 for each lake. The upper figure was previously mistakenly identified (Yan 1986, Figure 1) as the biomass figure.

those for estimates of biomass, for data sets of similar size, and small data sets can be used to detect changes in richness.

The species, or in the case of phytoplankton, generic, richness of several assemblages of pelagic organisms in Clearwater Lake is compared with that in the reference lakes in Table 23.3. The low richness in Clearwater Lake is

Table 23.3. *A comparison of values of species richness and biomass at various trophic levels in Clearwater (Cr) and Muskoka–Haliburton (MH) lakes.*

Biotic assemblage	Richness			Biomass		
	Cr	MH	Source	Cr	MH	Source
Phytoplankton (genera/collection)	8.9	19.0	(a)	122	178	(f)
Macrophytes (species/lake)	8.0	19.0	(b)	326	67	(f)
Planktonic rotifers	4.4	8.9	(c)	3.1	0.4	(f)
Crustacean zooplankton						
Herbivores	2.5	7.3	(d)	8.1	42.5	(d,g)
Predators	1.2	3.7	(d)	0.47	14.9	(d,g)
Fish	0	7.9	(e)	(0)	93	(h)

Note: Richness is given as species/collection, and biomass as mg/m^3 dw except where otherwise indicated. Wet to dry weight ratios of 5:1 were used to calculate phytoplankton and fish biomass. The MH data are means of seven to fifteen lakes, except for the macrophyte and fish biomass data, where values for only two lakes were available

Source: (a) Yan 1979
 (b) Yan et al. 1985a
 (c) Yan and Geiling 1985, and unpublished data
 (d) Ministry of the Environment 1982; Hitchin and Yan 1983
 (e) Yan et al. 1985b
 (f) Yan and Miller 1984
 (g) Yan 1986
 (h) Harvey and Lee 1981; Sprules et al. 1983

evident, especially at the higher trophic levels. By any definition, the complete absence of fish from the lake certainly represents impoverishment! There are several possible explanations for the smaller proportional declines in richness at the bottom of the food chain. In the pelagic waters, organisms of lower trophic levels are short-lived; hence, they have had many more generations to adapt to the contaminated environment than have the long-lived top predators. Their larger initial population sizes, and, possibly, larger gene pools also increase the possibility for the occurrence of tolerant varieties. Because species at the bottom of the food web also have more rapid dispersal mechanisms among lakes without direct water connections (Lansbury 1955; Maguire 1963), tolerant forms should rapidly recolonize lakes vacated by sensitive varieties.

Because richness responds to the number, not the identity, of taxa, declines in richness at the bottom of the food web might also be retarded by recolonization from "shadow" habitats. Littoral species might move into pelagic habitats vacated by plankton. For example, populations of *Chydorus sphaericus*, normally a littoral cladoceran, exploded in Sudbury-area lakes when the biomass of more typically planktonic species crashed after lake water pH was experimentally elevated (Yan and Dillon 1984). It is less clear that richness at the top of the food web could be augmented from such shadow habitats. However, large predatory insects were not included in the work in the Sudbury lakes. These typically littoral organisms could at least partially occupy the vacated top predator niche (Henrikson and Oscarson 1978; Bendell and McNicol 1987). Most fishermen would, of course, insist such occupation was far from satisfactory. A final explanation is suggested by the recent work of Borgmann (1985), who noted the less-than-perfect efficiency of particle-size conversion in lakes, and proposed that if toxicants reduced the standing stock of prey whose abundance controlled that of their predators, such reductions in standing stock would be magnified at higher levels of the food chain (i.e., in larger particles). It is not clear if such effects would lower richness, however.

While richness was depressed in Clearwater Lake at all trophic levels, standing stocks of primary producers and planktonic rotifers did not show a decrease in the comparison (Table 23.3). The elevated rotifer biomass is almost certainly the result of a reduction in the abundance of crustacean competitors (Hurlbert and Mulla 1981; Neill 1984; Yan and Geiling 1985). Phosphorus is the element that normally controls phytoplankton yield in Canadian Shield Lakes (Schindler 1977). As the levels of phosphorus in Clearwater Lake were not unusually low for an oligotrophic system (Table 23.1), the lack of reduction of algal biomass is not surprising. However, the greatly elevated macrophyte biomass is unexpected. High plant cover has similarly been observed in a large number of other acid- and metal-contaminated lakes in the Sudbury area (Hitchin et al. 1984); hence, the Clearwater Lake observation does not appear to be an anomaly. As yet we cannot explain this observation.

Unfortunately, extensive data on bacteria and benthic invertebrate communities do not exist for Clearwater Lake. Based on their size, life history patterns, and the considerations discussed above, we anticipate that bacterial species richness (if it could be measured) would not be as depressed as was richness at higher levels of the food web. Some, albeit minimal, evidence also indicates that open-water bacterial standing stocks and respiration rates are not reduced in Clearwater Lake. Scheider et al. (1975) noted that bacterial densities were as high in Clearwater Lake as in Harp Lake, one of the non-stressed reference lakes. Rates of oxygen consumption in hypolimnetic waters of the lake are within the range observed for Shield Lakes (0.013 mg $O_2/cm^2/d$, Yan and Miller 1984) suggesting that respiration rates of hypolimnetic microflora are not depressed. Because many large benthic invertebrates are acid-sensitive (Okland and Okland 1986), we assume this fauna is depauperate in the lake. However, one extremely hardy crayfish species, *Cambarus bartoni*, persists in the lake (Berrill et al. 1985).

Changes in Structure and Function Related to Impoverishment

Decrease in Mean Size of Biota

The rate of food uptake and growth are intimately linked to organism size in pelagic communities, both because of the familiar dependence of metabolic rate on body size, and because of the relationship between organism size and food-web position (Dickie et al. 1987). Changes in the size structure of communities may, therefore, have profound implications for energy flow in aquatic ecosystems.

In reviewing a number of studies on the effects of metals and acidification on the composition of pelagic communities a pattern emerges regarding changes in organism size. In general, there is a tendency for small-bodied organisms to replace larger ones. For example, three large zooplankters (*Holopedium gibberum, Daphnia galeata mendotae*, and *D. pulex*) are the dominant herbivorous Cladocera in north temperate lakes (Yan et al. 1988). *H. gibberum* is particularly sensitive to metals (Lawrence and Holoka 1987) while the two *Daphnia* species are very acid-sensitive (Price and Swift 1985). The dominant zooplankters in acid- and metal-contaminated lakes near Sudbury are smaller, more tolerant Crustacea, typically *Diaptomus minutus* and *Bosmina longirostris* (Dillon et al. 1984). The increased importance of rotifers (Table 23.3), the smallest metazoans, in the pelagic zone is also consistent with the trend towards reduced size, as is the loss of fish and such large pelagic predators as *Mysis relicta* (Nero and Schindler 1983).

Shortening of Food Chains

The apparent selective loss of organisms at the higher trophic levels, culminating in the complete absence of fish in an extreme situation such as in Clearwater Lake, probably results in a shortening of the food chain. The extensive loss of predatory zooplankton from the lake (Table 23.3) is another structural change that should shorten food chains in the lake. While the long- or short-term consequences of such changes provide fascinating material for speculation, such questions have not been directly examined. Unfortunately, recent models of trophic-level interaction developed in non-stressed lakes are probably not applicable to the pelagic zone of such contaminated lakes. Hence, their ability to guide speculative research may be limited. For example, elimination of fish has certainly not resulted in increases in the biomass of large zooplankton in Clearwater Lake (Table 23.3) as such models would predict (McQueen et al. 1986).

The obvious explanation for the failure of such models when applied to smelter-stressed lakes is that the normal predatory controls of zooplankton standing stock do not exist. This is perhaps not surprising given the poor water quality of such lakes (e.g., Table 23.1). What may be less evident is that reduced grazer biomass may lower algal richness in an insidious example of positive feedback. McCauley and Briand (1979) demonstrated that lowering grazer densities may result in increased exploitive competition between algal species which culminates in the elimination of some, generally inedible, algal taxa. Hence, low phytoplankton richness may have both a direct cause, related to metals and acidity exceeding toxic thresholds, and an indirect cause, related to food-chain alteration.

Abnormally High Biomass of a Few Species

The impoverishment of pelagic communities in acid- and metal-contaminated lakes is often accompanied by major alterations in the shape of dominance–diversity curves (Odum 1971, p. 236). A kind of asymmetry is often observed in which one or a few species have exceptionally high biomass. One is reminded of the monoculture in agriculture or sylviculture, the hazards of which do not require elaboration here. A common response in the phytoplankton, for example, is an increase in biomass of dinoflagellates (usually one or two species of Peridinium). This has been observed both in surveys of acidic lakes (Dickson et al. 1975; Yan 1979; Crisman et al. 1980; Stokes and Yung 1985), and in acidification experiments (Yan and Stokes 1978; Schindler et al. 1985). Similarly, while *Bosmina longirostris* and *Cyclops vernalis* are relatively unimportant contributors to average zooplankton biomass in non-acidic lakes, they comprise virtually all (97.2%) of the total biomass on average in Clearwater Lake (Figure 23.2). *B. longirostris* alone accounted for 87% of the biomass on average prior to 1980, and it remains the dominant zooplankter to this day (Yan, unpublished data). A further example is the almost exclusive dominance of the rotifer assemblage of Clearwater Lake by *Keratella taurocephala* (Yan and Geiling 1985).

The pattern is not limited to the pelagic zone. For example, the metaphytic clouds of green algae which begin to proliferate as lakes acidify are dominated (up to 90% of the biomass) by one or two species of the algae Zygnema, Zygogonium, and Mougeotia (Stokes and Howell 1987; Turner

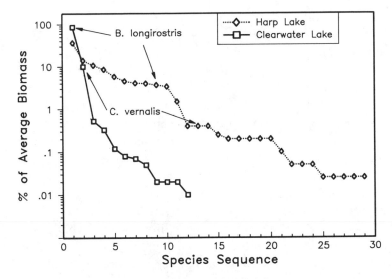

Figure 23.2. A dominance–diversity curve for crustacean zooplankton observed in Clearwater Lake between 1973 and 1979 and in Harp Lake, a non-acidic reference lake, between 1976 and 1979. Data are ice-free season means taken from Ministry of the Environment (1982) and Hitchin and Yan (1983).

et al 1987). The elevated macrophyte biomass in Clearwater Lake is attributable almost entirely to the presence in the lake of dense monospecific beds of the pipewort, *Eriocaulon septangulare* (Wile et al. 1984).

In most cases we cannot explain the unusually high biomass developed by specific taxa. The organisms certainly must be able to tolerate elevated acid and metal levels, but preference for such conditions is not a prerequisite for the establishment of dense populations. In fact as all of the above-mentioned organisms occur in both contaminated and reference lakes in Ontario, no such preference is indicated. The most obvious alternative explanation for the unusually large standing stocks of these taxa is a substantial reduction in the magnitude of biological controlling factors, either competitive or predatory. In the case of the explosion of Keratella, at least, there is strong support for this suggestion from the experimental literature. Hurlbert and Mulla (1981) noted that an almost universal response to a decline in the biomass of large crustacean zooplankton in numerous experimental studies was a large increase in the biomass of rotifers, principally Keratella. Loss of grazers has been suggested (Hendrey 1976) as an explanation for the increased standing stock of filamentous algae. Recent studies (Howell and France, unpublished data) support this factor as contributing to the phenomenon.

Increased Temporal Variability in Standing Stock

Marmorek (1982) included data from Clearwater Lake in his consideration of the effects of acidification on temporal variability in plankton biomass. Summarizing these results, Stokes (1984) indicated that the coefficient of variation of zooplankton biomass (calculated from changes over the ice-free season) varied from 80 to 130% in eight data sets with pH <5.0. Coefficients of variation were about half these values in non-acidic lakes. Marmorek proposed that the higher temporal variability in biomass in the acidic lakes was attributable to their depauperate faunas. He suggested there were "holes" in the temporal organization of the communities in the acidic lakes (i.e., time periods of exceptionally low biomass) that would not have existed in the presence of a complete fauna. Clearly, temporal variance is not calculable after the complete collapse of a trophic level, but should Marmorek's hypothesis be verified, it would imply that such a collapse would be preceded by a period of increasing temporal variability. If Marmorek is correct, then the extent of depression in richness required to initiate an increase in the coefficient of variation should increase as one descends the food web. This is because the "holes" should be more readily filled by tolerant members of lower as compared with higher trophic levels, because of the larger number of taxa, shorter generation times, and, perhaps, greater degree of resource overlap among members near the base of the food chain.

The Sensitivity of Impoverished Systems to Additional Stress

Because of the potential for populations of tolerant taxa to expand when acid-sensitive competitors are eliminated, changes in community standing stocks or production are not usually among the first signs of biological damage accompanying acidification. Schindler et al. (1985), for example, noted that when the fathead minnow, Pimephales, disappeared during the experimental acidification of Lake 223 in northwestern Ontario, populations of the pearl dace, Semotilus, increased substantially. Similarly, *Daphnia catawba* population size increased after the disappearance of the more acid-sensitive *Daphnia galeata mendotae*. Such redundancy must have limits. The greater the magnitude of species impoverishment, the greater is the chance that the loss of one additional species will irreversibly alter ecosystem structure and function. An example from a nutrient-manipulation experiment conducted in a Sudbury-area lake illustrates this possibility.

Yan and Lafrance (1984) added phosphorus and nitrogen to Mountaintop

Table 23.4. *A summary of ice-free season-average levels of total phosphorus (TP, mg/m³), phytoplankton biomass (PB, mg/m³ wet weight), zooplankton biomass (ZB, mg/m³ dry weight), and proportional composition of Rotifera, Cladocera, and Copepoda in Mountaintop and Labelle Lakes.*

| | | | | | % of Total biomass | | |
Lake	Year	TP	PB	ZB	Rotif	Clad	Copep
Mountaintop	1976	58	700	160	9	39	52
	1977	66	2,000	95	49	2	49
	1978	82	6,900	4	46	2	52
Labelle	1977	64	1,600	36	13	3	84
	1978	68	2,400	79	8	4	88

Source: Yan and Lafrance 1984.

Lake, a small, acidic (pH 4.6) lake north of Sudbury, and to Labelle Lake, a much less acidic (pH 6) reference lake with abundant fish. Before the experiment, the biota of Mountaintop Lake was impoverished much like Clearwater Lake. There were no fish and each zooplankton collection contained an average of only 3.6 species of planktonic Crustacea. In Labelle Lake, additions of fertilizer produced a small increase in plankton biomass, but in Mountaintop Lake biomass fluctuated widely (Table 23.4). In 1976, there were virtually no planktivores in the lake and zooplankton biomass reached such high levels that phytoplankton biomass became almost immeasurably low for two months despite high TP levels. However, in the second year of treatment, populations of the zooplanktivorous phantom midge, Chaoborus, exploded. The biomass of zooplankton crashed in response to this, despite continued fertilization (Table 23.4). In summary, the reduction in water quality, the probable cause of low zooplankton richness and the absence of fish, reduced the resilience of the whole community to the stress of fertilization. This was manifest in wide fluctuations in biomass, culminating in the virtual elimination of zooplankton, a very bizarre response to nutrient enrichment.

Conclusions

The key concerns for managers of lakes affected by smelters are the extent and severity of the problem, its implications for both ecosystem function and multipurpose water-use planning, and, critically, the degree of reversibility of biological damage should acid and metal influx decrease. The problem is clearly severe in acidic, metal-contaminated lakes in the Sudbury area.

Species have been lost from all trophic levels in a large number of lakes (Dillon et al. 1979; Keller and Pitblado 1984), but the upper trophic levels, the fish, have been hardest hit. There have been shifts in size structure which have implications for energy flow throughout the food chain; unusual taxa are frequently dominant; the resilience to additional stresses is reduced.

There is, however, recent cause for cautious optimism on the reversibility issue. Both synoptic surveys and long-term monitoring programs indicate that acid and metal levels in lakes in the area have declined over the last decade in response to reductions in local emissions (Dillon et al. 1986b; Hutchinson and Havas 1986; Keller and Pitblado 1986). The pH of Swan Lake, for example, increased from 4.0 in 1977 to 5.1 in 1984, and MacIsaac et al. (1986) cautiously attributed the substantial decline in importance of the previously dominant acidophilic rotifer, *Keratella taurocephala*, to the increase in pH. Similarly, Gunn and Keller (1984) attributed the appearance of lake trout recruits in Whitepine Lake, after a decade of absence, to improvements in water quality. While no other published evidence of spontaneous recovery of aquatic biota is available, sensitive species of Daphnia are appearing in some formerly acidic lakes (W. Keller, Ontario Ministry of the Environment, personal communication). It is delightfully clear that the devastated terrestrial environs of Sudbury can be improved by intensive management (Lautenbach 1987). Recently Gunn et al. (1987) successfully replanted trout in formerly acid lakes (with metal levels that were relatively low for the area). The same possibility for "recovery" may exist for the more severely impoverished lakes of the region.

References

Anonymous, 1982. *Sudbury Environmental Study.* Supplementary Volume to SES 009/82, Ontario Ministry of the Environment Rep. Dorset, Ontario.

Bendell, B. E., and D. K. McNicol, 1987. Fish predation, lake acidity and the composition of aquatic insect assemblages. *Hydrobiol.* 150:193–202.

Berrill, M., L. Hollett, A. Margosian, and J. Hudson, 1985. Variation in tolerance to low environmental pH by the crayfish *Orconectes rusticus, O. propinquus,* and *Cambarus robustus. Can. J. Zool.* 63:2586–2589.

BEST, 1979. *Projet "Region Noranda."* Bureau d'etude sur les substances toxiques, Gouvernement du Quebec. Quebec City.

Biesinger, K. E., and G. M. Christensen, 1972. Effects of various metals on survival, growth, reproduction, and metabolism of *Daphnia magna. J. Fish. Res. Bd. Canada* 29:1691–1700.

Borgmann, U., 1985. Predicting the effect of toxic substances on pelagic ecosystems. *Sci. Tot. Environ.* 44:111–121.

Conroy, N., K., Hawley, W. Keller, and C. Lafrance, 1976. Influences of the atmosphere on lakes in the Sudbury area. *Internat. Assoc. Great Lakes Res.* 2(Supp. 1):146–165.

Crisman, T. L., R. L. Schulze, P. L. Brezonik, and S. A. Bloom, 1980. Acid precipitation: the biotic response in Florida lakes. In D. Drablos and A. Tollan (Eds.), *Ecological Impact of Acid Precipitation, Proc. of Internat. Symp.*, pp. 296–297. Oslo.

Dickie, L. M., S. R. Kerr, and P. R. Boudreau, 1987. Size-dependent processes underlying regularities in ecosystem structure. *Ecol. Monogr.* 57:233–250.

Dickson, W., E. Hornstrom, C. Ekstrom, and D. Almer, 1975. Rodinsjoar Soder Om Dalaben. *Inform. fran. Drottningholm.* 7. Drottningholm, Sweden.

Dillon, P. J., and P. J. Smith, 1984. Trace metal and nutrient accumulation in the sediments of lakes near Sudbury, Ontario. In J. Nriagu (Ed.), *Environmental Impacts of Smelters*, pp. 375–416. Wiley, New York.

Dillon, P. J., N. D. Yan, W. A. Scheider, and N. Conroy, 1979. Acidic lakes in Ontario, Canada: characterization, extent and response to base and nutrient additions. *Arch. Hydrobiol. Beih. Ergebn. Limnol.* 13:317–336.

Dillon, P. J., D. S. Jeffries, and W. A. Scheider, 1982. The use of calibrated lakes and watersheds for estimating atmospheric deposition near a large point source. *Water, Air, Soil Pollut.* 18:241–258.

Dillon, P. J., N. D. Yan, and H. H. Harvey, 1984. Acidic deposition: effects on aquatic ecosystems. *CRC Critical Rev. Environ. Control.* 13:167–194.

Dillon, P. J., K. H. Nicholls, W. A. Scheider, N. D. Yan, and D. S. Jeffries, 1986a. *Lakeshore Capacity Study: Trophic Status*, Ont., Min. Municip. Aff. Rep. Toronto.

Dillon, P. J., R. A. Reid, and R. Girard, 1986b. Changes in the chemistry of lakes near Sudbury, Ontario, following reductions of SO_2 emissions. *Water, Air, Soil Pollut.* 31:59–65.

Dixit, S. S., and R. D. Evans, 1986. Spatial variability in sedimentary algal microfossils and its bearing on diatom-inferred pH reconstructions. *Can. J. Fish. Aquat. Sci.* 43:1836–1845.

Faggart, B. E., Jr., A. R. Basu, and M. Tatsumoto, 1985. Origin of the Sudbury Complex by meteoritic impact: neodymium isotopic evidence. *Science* 230:436–439.

Franzin, W. G., 1984. Aquatic contamination in the vicinity of the base metal smelter at Flin Flon, Manitoba, Canada – a case study. In J. Nriagu (Ed.), *Environmental Impacts of Smelters*, pp. 523-550. Wiley, New York.

Gorham, E., and A. G. Gordon, 1960. The influence of smelter fumes upon the chemical composition of lakes near Sudbury, Ontario, and upon the surrounding vegetation. *Can. J. Bot.* 38:477–487.

Gorham, E., and A. G. Gordon, 1963. Ecological aspects of air pollution from an iron-sintering plant at Wawa, Ontario. *Can. J. Bot.* 41:1063–1078.

Gunn, J. M., and W. Keller, 1984. Spawning site water chemistry and lake trout (*Salvelinus namaycush*) sac fry survival during spring snowmelt. *Can. J. Fish. Aquat. Sci.* 41:319–329.

Gunn, J. M., M. J. McMurtry, J. N. Bowlby, J. M. Casselman, and V. A. Liimatainen, 1987. Survival and growth of stocked lake trout in relation to body size, stocking season, lake acidity, and biomass of competitors. *Trans. Amer. Fish. Soc.* 116:618–627.

Harvey, H. H., and C. Lee, 1981. *Fish populations in the calibrated watersheds of Muskoka–Haliburton.* Rep. to the Ontario Ministry of the Environment, University of Toronto.

Harvey, H. H., and C. Lee, 1982. Historical fisheries changes related to surface water pH changes in Canada. In T. A. Haines and R. E Johnson (Eds.), *Acid Rain/ Fisheries*, pp. 45–55. Amer. Fish. Soc. Pub. Bethesda, Md.

Hendrey, G. R., 1976. *Effects of pH on the growth of periphytic algae in artificial stream channels*. Sur. Nedbrs Virkning pa Skog og Fisk. Project IR 25/76. Oslo.

Henrikson, L., and H. G. Oscarson, 1978. Fish predation limiting abundance and distribution of *Glaenocorisa p.propinqua*. *Oikos*. 31:102–105.

Hitchin, G. G., and N. D. Yan, 1983. *Crustacean zooplankton communities of the Muskoka–Haliburton study lakes: methods and 1976–1979 data*. Ont. Min. Environ. Data Rep. DR 83/9. Dorset, Ontario.

Hitchin, G. G., I. Wilc, G. E. Miller, and N. D. Yan, 1984. *Macrophyte data from 46 southern Ontario soft-water lakes of varying pH*. Ont. Min. Environ. Data Rep. DR 84/2. Dorset, Ontario.

Hurlbert, S. H., and M. S. Mulla, 1981. Impacts of mosquitofish (*Gambusia affinis*) predation of plankton communities. *Hydrobiol*. 83:125–151.

Hutchinson, T. C., 1979. Copper contamination of ecosystems caused by smelter activities. In J. Nriagu (Ed.), *Copper in the Environment*, pp 451–502. Wiley, New York.

Hutchinson, T. C., and M. Havas, 1986. Recovery of previously acidified lakes near Coniston, Canada following reductions in atmospheric sulphur and metal emissions. *Water, Air, Soil Pollut*. 28:319–333.

Jackson, T. A., G. Kipphut, R. H. Hesslein, and D. W. Schindler, 1980. Experimental study of trace metal chemistry in soft-water lakes at different pH levels. *Can. J. Fish. Aquat. Sci.* 37:387–402.

Jeffries, D. S., 1984. Atmospheric deposition in the Sudbury area. In J. Nriagu (Ed.), *Environmental Impacts of Smelters*, pp. 117–154. Wiley, New York.

Johnson, M. G., and G. E. Owen, 1966. Biological survey of streams and lakes in the Sudbury area: 1965. *Ont. Water Res. Comm. Rep.* Ont. Min. Environ., Toronto.

Kaiser, K. L. E., 1980. Correlation and prediction of metal toxicity to aquatic biota. *Can. J. Fish. Aquat. Sci.* 37:211–218.

Keller, W., and R. J. Pitblado, 1984. Crustacean plankton in northeastern Ontario lakes subjected to acidic deposition. *Water, Air, Soil Pollut*. 23:271–291.

Keller, W., and J. R. Pitblado, 1986. Water quality changes in Sudbury area lakes: a comparison of synoptic surveys in 1974–1976 and 1981–1983. *Water, Air, Soil Pollut*. 29:285–296.

Kelly, C. A., J. W. M. Rudd, R. B. Cook, and D. W. Schindler, 1982. The potential importance of bacterial processes in regulating rate of lake acidification. *Limnol. Oceanogr.* 27:868–882.

Krantzberg, G. B., 1987. A study of the role of biotic and abiotic factors in modifying metal accumulation by *Chironomus*. Ph.D. dissertation, University of Toronto.

Lansbury, I., 1955. Some notes on invertebrates other than insecta found attached to water-bugs (Hemiptera, Heteroptera). *Entomolog*. 88:139–140.

Lautenbach, W. E., 1987. The greening of Sudbury. *J. Soil. Wat. Conserv.* 42:228–231.

Lawrence, S. G., and M. H. Holoka, 1987. Effects of low concentrations of cadmium on the crustacean zooplankton community of an artificially acidified lake. *Can. J. Fish. Aquat. Sci.* 44 (Supp. 1):163–172.

Linzon, S. N., 1958. *The influence of smelter fumes on the growth of white pine in the Sudbury region*. Ont. Dept. Lands Forest. and Ont. Dept. Mines Rep. Toronto.

MacIsaac, H. J., W. Keller, T. C. Hutchinson, and N. D. Yan, 1986. Natural changes in the planktonic Rotifera of a small acid lake near Sudbury, Ontario, following water quality improvements. *Water, Air, Soil Pollut.* 31:791–797.

Maguire, B., Jr., 1963. The passive dispersal of small aquatic organisms and their colonization of isolated bodies of water. *Ecol. Monogr.* 33:161–185.

Marmorek, D., 1982. The effect of lake acidification on zooplankton community structure and phytoplankton–zooplankton interactions: an experimental approach. M. Sc. thesis, University of British Columbia, Vancouver.

McCauley, E., and F. Briand, 1979. Zooplankton grazing and phytoplankton species richness: field tests of the predation hypothesis. *Limnol. Oceanogr.* 24:243–252.

McQueen, D. J., J. R. Post, and E. L. Mills, 1986. Trophic relationships in freshwater pelagic ecosystems. *Can. J. Fish. Aquat. Sci.* 43:1571–1581.

Neill, W. E., 1984. Regulation of rotifer densities by crustacean zooplankton in an oligotrophic montane lake in British Columbia. *Oecologia* (Berlin) 61:175–181.

Nero, R. W., and D. W. Schindler, 1983. Decline of *Mysis relicta* during the acidification of Lake 223. *Can. J. Fish. Aquat. Sci.* 40:1905–1911.

Nriagu, J., 1984. *Environmental Impacts of Smelters.* Wiley, New York.

Odum, E. P., 1971. *Fundamentals of Ecology*, 3rd ed. W. B. Saunders Co., Philadelphia.

Okland, J., and K. A. Okland, 1986. The effects of acid deposition on benthic animals in lakes and streams. *Experientia* 42:471–486.

Price, E. E., and M. C. Swift, 1985. Inter- and intra-specific variability in the response of zooplankton to acid stress. *Can. J. Fish. Aquat. Sci.* 42:1749–1754.

Scheider, W. A., J. Adamski, and M. Paylor, 1975. *Reclamation of acidified lakes near Sudbury, Ontario.* Ont. Min. Environ. Rep, Toronto.

Schindler, D. W., 1977. Evolution of phosphorus limitation in lakes. *Science*, 195:260–262.

Schindler, D. W., K. H. Mills, D. F. Malley, D. L. Findlay, J. A. Shearer, I. J. Davies, M. A. Turner, G. A. Linsey, and D. R. Cruikshank, 1985. Long-term ecosystem stress: the effects of years of experimental acidification of a small lake. *Science.* 228:1395–1401.

Somers, K. M., and H. H. Harvey, 1984. Alteration of fish communities in lakes stressed by acid deposition and heavy metals near Wawa, Ontario. *Can. J. Fish. Aquat. Sci.* 41:20–29.

Sprules, W. G., J. M. Casselman, and B. J. Shuter, 1983. Size distribution of pelagic particles in lakes. *Can. J. Fish. Aquat. Sci.* 40:1761–1769.

Stokes, P. M., 1984. Clearwater Lake: study of an acidified lake ecosystem. In P. J. Sheehan, D. R. Miller, G. C. Butler, and P. H. Bourdeau (Eds.), *Effects of Pollutants at the Ecosystem Level*, pp. 229–253. Wiley, New York.

Stokes, P. M., and E. T. Howell, 1987. *The usefulness of periphyton to detect lake chronic or episodic acidification and/or recovery in the context of a long-term monitoring program.* Report to U.S. Environmental Protection Agency, contract 7B0860NASA. University of Toronto.
to U.S. Environmental Protection Agency, contract 7B0860NASA.

Stokes, P. M., and Y. K. Yung, 1985. Phytoplankton in selected LaCloche (Ontario) lakes, pH 4.2–7.0, with special reference to algae as indicators of chemical characteristics. In J. P. Smol, R. W. Battarbee. R. B. Davis, and J. Merilainen (Eds.), *Diatoms and Lake Acidity*, pp. 57–72. Junk, The Hague.

Turner, M. A., M. B. Jackson, D. L. Findley, R. W. Graham, E. R. DeBruyn, and E. M. Vandermeir, 1987. Early responses of periphyton to experimental lake acidification. *Can. J. Fish. Aquat. Sci.* 44:135–149.

Wile, I., G. E. Miller, G. G. Hitchin, and N. D. Yan, 1984. Species composition and biomass of the macrophyte vegetation of one acidified and two acid-sensitive lakes in Ontario. *Canadian Field Natur.* 99:308–312.

Williams, K. A., D. W. J. Green, and D. Pascoe, 1985. Studies on the acute toxicity of pollutants to freshwater macroinvertebrates 1. Cadmium. *Arch. Hydrobiol.* 102:461–471.

Yan, N. D., 1979. Phytoplankton community of an acidified, heavy metal-contaminated lake near Sudbury, Ontario: 1973–1977. *Water, Air, Soil Pollut.* 11:43–55.

Yan, N. D., 1986. Empirical prediction of crustacean zooplankton biomass in nutrient-poor Canadian Shield lakes. *Can. J. Fish. Aquat. Sci.* 43:788–796.

Yan, N. D., and P. Stokes, 1978. Phytoplankton of an acidic lake and its responses to experimental alterations of pH. *Environ. Conserv.* 5:93–100.

Yan, N. D., and P. J. Dillon, 1984. Experimental neutralization of lakes near Sudbury, Ontario. In J. Nriagu (Ed.), *Environmental Impacts of Smelters,* pp. 417–456. Wiley, New York.

Yan, N. D., and G. E. Miller, 1984. Effects of deposition of acids and metals on chemistry and biology of lakes near Sudbury, Ontario. In J. Nriagu (Ed.), *Environmental Impacts of Smelters,* pp. 243–282. Wiley, New York.

Yan, N. D., and C. Lafrance, 1984. Responses of acidic and neutralized lakes near Sudbury, Ontario, to nutrient enrichment. In J. Nriagu (Ed.), *Environmental Impacts of Smelters,* pp. 457–521. Wiley, New York.

Yan, N. D., and W. Geiling, 1985. Elevated planktonic rotifer biomass in acidified, metal contaminated lakes near Sudbury, Ontario. *Hydrobiol.* 120:199–205.

Yan, N. D., G. E. Miller, I. Wile, and G. G. Hitchin, 1985a. Richness of aquatic macrophyte floras of softwater lakes of differing pH and trace metal content in Ontario, Canada. *Aquatic Bot.* 23:27–40.

Yan, N. D., R. W. Nero, W. Keller, and D. C. Lasenby, 1985b. Are *Chaoborus* larvae more abundant in acidified than in non-acidified lakes in central Canada. *Holartic Ecol.* 8:93–99.

Yan, N. D., W. Keller, J. R. Pitblado, and G. L. Mackie, 1988. *Daphnia–Holopedium* relationships in Canadian Shield lakes ranging in acidity. *Verh. Internat. Verein. Limnol.* 23:252–257.

Yan, N.D., G. L. Mackie, and P. J. Dillon, in press. Cadmium concentrations of crustacean zooplankton of acidified and nonacidified Canadian Shield lakes. *Environ Sci. Tech.* 24.

24   Biotic Impoverishment: Effects of Anthropogenic Stress

JOHN CAIRNS, JR., AND JAMES R. PRATT

Editor's Note: Tests of theory in ecology are often difficult, sometimes impossible. John Cairns has brought a lifetime of experience to bear on the practical questions of pollution using simple aquatic systems to shed light on hypotheses in ecology that are otherwise difficult to examine. He recognizes two types of impoverishment, losses of diversity in a landscape as human effects spread, and the in situ transitions that accumulate under chronic disturbance, usually, but not always, reducing the diversity of a community and making it more vulnerable both to invasion and other disruption. The insights are refreshing, if complex and disturbing. For us they confirm the patterns now familiar: chronic disturbance in aquatic systems favors the hardy cosmopolitan species that reproduce rapidly and usually do not form the basis of complex food webs. The patterns are systematic and predictable and increasingly common. One of the greatest dangers is that the disturbances will become so close to universal that sources of species for reintroduction will be lost, despite the general hardiness of the protists with which he works.

Introduction

Anthropogenic stress commonly leads to changes in ecosystems that are regressive and best described as "impoverishment." Most of these disturbances are chronic. Catastrophic disturbances, such as nuclear war or rapid global climatic change, will cause immediate and severe effects that we can only poorly estimate. For other disturbances, such as acid rain and various toxins, experience is abundant and data are available. In both instances there is debate over causes, details of effects, and the magnitude and importance of the "risks" to the human enterprise.

The relationship between cause and effect is clearest locally. Janzen (1988) points out that

when the Spaniards arrived, there were 550,000 km² of dry forest on the Pacific side of lowland tropical Mesoamerica. Equal to about five Guatemalas or one France in area, this dry forest occupied as much or more of the Mesoamerican lowlands as did rain forests. Today, less than 2% of this dry forest exists as undisturbed wild-

495

lands, and only 0.08% of it lies within national parks or other kinds of conserved areas.

The transition is one of countless examples of the human impact on terrestrial ecosystems and constitutes a serious and probably irreversible loss of unique plant and animal communities. Their replacement by impoverished grazing lands, agriculture, and scrub constitutes one type of biotic impoverishment that is all too common. Our emphasis here, however, is on more subtle but equally important transitions.

Not only have terrestrial systems suffered, but there has been comparable damage to freshwater and marine systems. A recent world conference on large lakes (Schmidtke 1988) introduced evidence of anthropogenic stress to lakes throughout a range of climatic zones, political systems, and cultures in various stages of technological development. Worldwide, rivers have been dammed, diverted to other drainage basins, and used to carry away wastes. The ocean is a repository for wastes that cannot be disposed of on land and is the recipient of most of the wastes placed in rivers. Small pieces of plastic are ubiquitous in the oceans and are ingested by fish and other organisms. All these physical and chemical disruptions produce biotic effects, although they have not been well defined.

One of the most important responses to both chronic and acute disturbance is by "opportunistic species." In most communities, a variety of species might be considered functionally redundant because several of them appear to contribute nearly identical functions to the larger system. In our work with protozoan communities, we have observed that, for short-lived taxa with high turnover rates (Schoener 1984), predicting specific community composition is nearly impossible. A large number of species, the resting stages of which are in the sediments, are capable of increasing their populations suddenly in response to changed conditions. Although the exact environmental requirements of these "opportunistic species" are not well known, the species appear to be ubiquitous, and an increase in their abundance alone may indicate disturbance.

When a community or ecosystem becomes impoverished, redundant taxa are frequently unavailable for recruitment into the community. In this discussion, we present examples of laboratory experiments with aquatic systems that illustrate community-level effects of disturbance. In most of these, we controlled community complexity by manipulating the colonization of artificial substrates. Artificial substrates colonized by aquatic microbes provide complex communities for study that can be maintained and manipulated in the laboratory. They offer opportunities for experimental approaches to control the structure of communities and a new view of the process of impoverishment.

Is Biotic Impoverishment Detectable for Organisms with a Cosmopolitan Distribution?

There are groups of organisms such as the protists (protozoa, diatoms and other algae) that appear to have a cosmopolitan distribution, occurring wherever suitable ecological conditions are found. Although evidence for such distribution is not conclusive, it is noteworthy that protists are routinely identified in all parts of the world by means of such standard volumes as Kahl's (1935) monograph on ciliates or Pascher's (1913–1927) treatise on flagellates or Walton's (1915) volume on euglenids.

A few years ago, Dr. Shen Yun-fen of the Institute of Hydrobiology in Wuhan, People's Republic of China, visited Virginia Tech to learn new techniques involving protists and artificial substrates. As the same species are found near both Wuhan and Blacksburg, Virginia, there was no difficulty over species. Although the possibility exists that large numbers of physiological species are hiding behind morphological facades, airborne transport and wide distribution of morphological "species" of protists are generally accepted and widely documented. Even if a variety of physiological species does exist behind the facade of each morphological species, it does not change the major premise of this discussion.

Reflecting on the possibility of determining the loss of protist species with cosmopolitan distribution, one of the authors (Cairns) remembered his major professor, D. H. Wenrich, recounting collecting *Stokesia vernalis* Wenrich. This is a particularly striking organism even for a protist and not likely to be confused with other genera. However, even Wenrich, who named the organism, had not observed it regularly and the authors have seen it only infrequently in spite of extensive field studies during which the probability of encountering a rare species was markedly enhanced. Failure to find such an infrequently seen species for many years, even on a worldwide basis, might not cause comment. At what point, then, should it be determined that a species has disappeared? Because there is no global (or national) biological inventory, such as that proposed for the United States, and there is no central data-gathering repository for observations on species occurrence, it is unlikely that such a disappearance would ever be noted.

Although most of the attention focused on biotic impoverishment and loss of global species diversity has been on endemic species, the loss of species with a cosmopolitan distribution could have greater impact. Infrequent sighting of certain species does not mean that they do not periodically occur in large numbers but possibly are not recorded due to the small numbers of observers. The number of people studying protists is small, and many work only with laboratory cultures or specialize on one or two species. Those noticing the loss of a species not customarily used in the laboratory is likely to be small.

Presumably, transient species such as those that appear at a particular locus for brief periods only have a cosmopolitan distribution and a transport system that moves them around the world with regularity. The current drastic global biotic impoverishment of tropical rain forests is clearly altering global climate and presumably affecting the transport system for a number of species. A group of organisms that once had a cosmopolitan distribution may well be threatened before scientists are aware of the threat.

Estimating the Environmental Impact of Biotechnology

Even when biotic impoverishment does not result in global extinction of species, local reduction in abundance may induce invading organisms to thrive in ecosystems in disequilibrium. Ecosystems with a balanced biological community should be better able to exclude invaders such as genetically engineered microorganisms than those in disequilibrium. Although the consequences of the release and establishment of genetically engineered microorganisms are not clear, biotic impoverishment may provide greater opportunity for organisms to persist in ecosystems in which they otherwise might not be able to do so.

There are major differences between the introduction of chemicals into the environment and the introduction of organisms (e.g., Dean-Ross 1986): (a) organisms can reproduce and grow or may lie dormant for long periods of time and then become active, and (b) organisms may displace one or more naturally occurring species and alter community and ecosystem function. We have found, in experiments in our own laboratory, that successful colonization by species invading a natural community is likely to occur in communities that are species-poor.

To examine the potential for invasion of existing communities, we introduced concentrated suspensions of *Euglena* sp. to achieve approximately 10^5 cells/ml in experimental systems containing either immature (1-day old, 30 species) or mature (21-day old, 50 species) communities. We counted the number of Euglena invading the communities and surviving in the surrounding medium over a 14-day period. In experimental systems containing mature communities, little colonization occurred and the invading species became "extinct" almost immediately (Figure 24.1). Invading Euglena were more successful in experimental systems with immature communities. While the numbers of Euglena in the medium decreased rapidly, the numbers of individuals in the substrate-associated community remained comparatively high for several days before being lost from the experimental systems. Al-

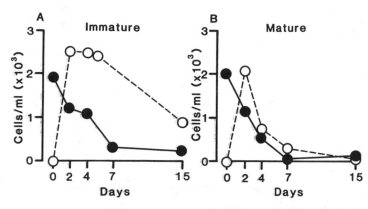

Figure 24.1. Results of invasion of natural communities by *Euglena*. Open circles are numbers of *Euglena* cells invading communities. Solid circles are numbers of Euglena cells remaining in surrounding medium. Immature communities were 1 day old (thirty species), and mature communities were 21 days old (fifty species) at the start of experiments. (Reprinted from Cairns and Pratt 1986, with permission. Copyright ASTM.)

though the end result in both systems was the extinction of the invading species, the trajectory by which it occurred differed considerably. This suggests that simpler communities are less capable of excluding invaders and forebodes the potential for some invaders to successfully colonize species-poor communities. This is a phenomenon well known in agriculture and generally considered a successional problem restricted to managed eco-systems. However, mature systems can be adversely affected and simplified by toxic materials. It would be useful to examine the potential for species invasion in a community simplified by toxic stress which might be important in assessing the impact of genetically engineered microorganisms on an agricultural ecosystem from which they invade aquatic systems in turn stressed by human activities.

A major criterion for determining the establishment of the products of biotechnology in a natural community is the ecotoxicological stress to which the community has been exposed. This factor, more than anything else, requires the coupling of ecotoxicology with the assessment of environmental damage caused by products of biotechnology such as new or modified organisms. There are, however, important differences. First, only a few disseminules (seeds, cysts, spores, living trophic stages) need be transported to a new location for successful establishment of the altered species. Additionally, instead of following a typical chemical dispersion gradient, novel organisms may follow a stepping-stone process, leaping, so to speak, from one suitable habitat to another even though the sites may be widely separated geographically. Even a very small habitat in a vast area of unsuitable habitat could store and disperse these new organisms. As a consequence, sampling patterns and strategies must be markedly altered to account for this difference. A final, but nevertheless important, difference is the fact that many such organisms will have resting stages in their life cycles, and it will be important to be able to predict with considerable accuracy those conditions that will reactivate the organisms. This pattern of dispersal is not greatly different from the accumulation of a chemical in a particular compartment and subsequent release by altered conditions.

Ecosystem Toxicants, Ecosystem Assimilative Capacity, and Biotic Impoverishment

During the early stages of the Industrial Revolution, waste discharges were small and sufficiently innocuous that rivers and streams were able to cleanse themselves before reaching the next downstream user of water. Short rivers intensely used, such as the Thames, were exceptions (Gameson and Wheeler 1977). The observation that natural ecosystems, like humans, can accommodate a certain loading of otherwise harmful material was favorably recognized as assimilative capacity. Regulatory measures are frequently designed to determine the amount of a particular substance below which no adverse biological effects occur. For some contaminants, such as radioactive materials, such a threshold may not exist (Woodwell 1975). However, it is possible that, for most chemicals in all but the most fragile ecosystems, a series of thresholds or breakpoints exists (May 1977). For example, in single-species acute-toxicity tests, lethality will occur at one concentration and tissue damage may be observed without lethality at a lower one. At a still lower concentration, there may be interference with enzyme or respiratory function. Behavior may be altered at a still lower one. There is evidence, described by May, that ecosystems may respond in a similar fashion.

The two problems with this approach are (a) the threshold(s) are not the same for every chemical, and (b) thresholds may exist below present capacity for recognizing them. Odum et al. (1979) hypothesized that stress may increase the variability of natural systems and make the determination of a threshold more difficult. If this hypothesis is correct, an increase in variability itself is a useful threshold.

Maugh (1978) gave a one-page summary of the overall problem of potentially toxic materials. At that time, the American Chemical Society's (ACS) computer registry contained 4,039,907 distinct entities, and the number had been increasing at the rate of about 6,000 per week. Of these, the ACS has given the Environmental Protection Agency (EPA) a preliminary list of approximately 33,000 chemicals thought to be in common use. The EPA believes that there may be as many as 50,000 chemicals in daily use, not including pesticides, pharmaceuticals, or food additives. The Food and Drug Administration estimated approximately 4,000 active ingredients in drugs and 2,000 more used as excipients (inert ingredients), as well as 2,500 additives for nutritive purposes and 3,000 more to promote product life. Taken all together, Maugh estimated about 63,000 chemicals in common use. Although the computer registry of chemicals has changed in various ways, most notably by increasing in size, the estimates of chemicals thought to be in common use remains roughly the same. The difficulty of obtaining a precise number has not diminished.

The conservative estimate of 20,000 chemicals in extensive common use is impressive, particularly in terms of the transformation products likely to result when they are released into the environment. It would be comforting if they were dispersed uniformly, thereby diminishing their concentration and their potential toxicity. However, they are more likely to be partitioned into specific environmental compartments. The biota may concentrate them further.

If estimates of the potential harm such chemicals may cause in ecosystems are in error, either because we misjudged the environmental concentration of the original substance, its transformation products, or the ecological effects of these concentrations, biotic impoverishment is likely to result. It is not necessary to kill a species outright but merely to interfere with some vital process in order to eliminate it.

Most estimates of hazards are based on laboratory toxicity tests with single species. One of the assumptions of this approach is that it is possible to select the most sensitive species and, by protecting this species, all other species will be protected. There is a less explicit assumption that all interactions and ecosystem processes will be protected if the surrogate (test) species are protected. Assumptions are rarely explicitly stated and validation of estimates of safety or harm are either non-existent or carried out less rigorously than normal scientific peer review would require (Cairns 1986). Few toxicity experiments are carried out at levels of biological organization higher than single species, although a case could be made for doing so (Cairns 1983) entirely on the basis of management needs. Several years ago, we demonstrated that trace levels of toxic materials could reduce species richness in microbial communities, and that this reduction was more severe in communities with fewer species (Cairns et al. 1980). Using systems differing only in richness of the species source, with the same stress (0.56 mg Cu/1), after seven days, species numbers in experimental systems with immature species sources (about 30 species) were reduced by over 80

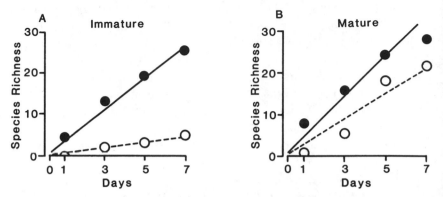

Figure 24.2. Effect of 0.56 mg/l copper on protozoan colonization in laboratory microecosystems established with mature (20-day-old) and immature (1-day-old) microbial communities: (a) comparison of colonization from mature communities in control systems (solid circles) and from mature communities in toxicant dosed systems (open circles); (b) comparison of colonization from immature communities in control systems (solid circles) and from immature communities in toxicant-dosed systems (open circles).

percent, while species loss in systems with mature communities was only about 30 percent (Figure 24.2). We interpreted this as a difference in community maturity tightly linked to the colonization process.

Human activities do not always result in the loss of species. In some circumstances, disturbance may lead to increases in species number. Odum et al. (1979) hypothesized a subsidy-stress gradient and suggested that low levels of disturbance often act as "subsidies" to ecosystems. This relationship is easily understood as an addition of biologically useful materials such as inorganic nutrients or carbon. Our own research has shown, however, that when the stress level is low, more general stresses can lead to a non-linear response. We have seen this in microcosm experiments testing toxic materials ranging from simple toxicants, such as chlorine, to complex industrial effluents. When we continuously supplied low levels of atrazine (3–300 µg/l) to replicate microcosms, we found that species numbers (Figure 24.3) and biomass (Figure 24.4) were enhanced at low doses (10–30 µg/l) but severely reduced at higher doses. It is difficult to understand how a general herbicide (photophosphorylation inhibitor) such as atrazine is a subsidy to the system.

Results of these experiments suggest that, rather than a subsidy, the stress response resulting in enhanced species numbers and biomass is probably a result of the loss in populations of certain critical species, thereby allowing other taxa to proliferate. In an experimental system containing several

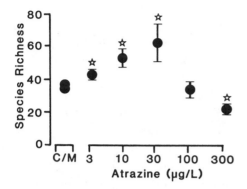

Figure 24.3. Number of protozoan species colonizing artificial substrates in laboratory microcosms dosed with atrazine: C = control, M = carrier solvent (methanol) control; stars mark treatments significantly different from controls (p = 0.05, Dunnett's test). Some error bars were too small to be plotted on this scale.

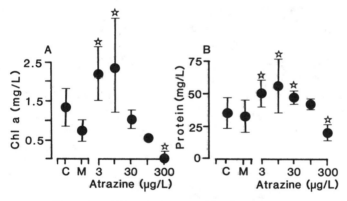

Figure 24.4. Effect of atrazine on (a) chlorophyll biomass and (b) protein biomass development on artificial substrates in laboratory microcosms. Stars mark treatments significantly different from controls (p = 0.05, Dunnett's test).

hundred species, it is difficult to pinpoint keystone taxa that might exert these controlling effects. The critical point is that enhancement of species numbers or biomass should not necessarily by interpreted as "good" since the response may, in fact, be the removal of certain critical members of the ecosystem and should be viewed as an early warning that more severe, chronic effects are likely if the stress is increased. Further, biomass enhancement cannot always be explained as nutrient enhancement but may be a response to differences in resource allocation, not absolute resource abundance. If this non-linear response to stress is common, "enhancement" may be a first sign of stress and the final observation of impoverishment as a very severe stress response (Meier 1972).

Single-species tests are essential for determining growth, reproductive success, preference, and avoidance reactions, as well as many other useful attributes of species (National Research Council 1981). Whether they can be used to predict effects of toxicants on nutrient spiraling or energy transport in ecological systems is another matter. Multiple lines of evidence are required for prudent management decisions about the hazard of potentially toxic materials. Until we are able to predict more accurately and reliably the effects of individual chemicals and mixtures on different levels of biological organization, it would be prudent to be less dependent upon single-species toxicity testing. If the assumptions upon which environmental protection decisions are made are flawed, species impoverishment will result.

Summary

Simple communities are not capable of the same responses to stress as more complex communities. This may be a result of fewer redundant species in the species pool capable of exploiting changing conditions or of biological differences in the taxa found in early successional or immature communities as compared to those taxa found in later successional (more mature) stages. The result of these differences, the underlying biology of which is poorly known, is the inability of communities to disperse propagules to new habitat, to respond to toxic chemicals, or, in the case of simple communities, to exclude invaders. Continual erosion of biological diversity may result in the loss of key species that regulate numbers of other taxa and allocation of resources to biomass.

References

Cairns, J., Jr., 1983. The case for simultaneous testing at different levels of biological organization. In W. E. Bishop, R. D. Cardwell, and B. B. Heidolph (Eds.), *Aquatic Toxicology and Hazard Assessment: Sixth Symposium*, pp. 111–127. Special Technical Publication 802. American Society for Testing and Materials, Philadelphia.

Cairns, J., Jr., 1986. What is meant by validation of predictions based on laboratory toxicity tests? *Hydrobiologia* 137:271–278.

Cairns, J., Jr., K. M. Hart, and M. S. Henebry, 1980. The effects of a sublethal dose of copper sulfate on the colonization rate of freshwater protozoan communities. *Am. Midl. Nat.* 104:93–101.

Cairns, J., Jr., and J. R. Pratt, 1986. Factors affecting the acceptance and rejection of genetically altered microorganisms by established natural aquatic communities. In T. M. Poston and R. Purdy (Eds.), *Aquatic Toxicology and Environmental Fate: Ninth Symposium*, pp. 207–221. ASTM STP 921, American Society for Testing and Materials, Philadelphia.

Dean-Ross, D., 1986. Release of genetically engineered organisms: hazard assessment. *ASM News* 52(11):572–575.

Gameson, A. L. H., and A. Wheeler, 1977. Restoration and recovery of the Thames estuary. In J. Cairns, Jr., K. L. Dickson, and E. E. Herricks (Eds.), *Recovery and Restoration of Damaged Ecosystems*, pp. 72–101. University Press of Virginia, Charlottesville.

Janzen, D. H., 1988. Guanacaste National Park: tropical, ecological, and cultural restoration. In J. Cairns, Jr. (Ed.), *Rehabilitation of Damaged Ecosystems*, pp. 143–192. CRC Press, Boca Raton, Fla.

Kahl, A., 1935. Wimpertiere oder Ciliata (infusoria). In F. Dahl (Ed.), *Die Tierwelt Deutschlands. Urtiere oder Protozoa*. I. G. Fischer, Jena, East Germany.

Maugh, T. H., II., 1978. Chemicals: how many are there? *Science* 199:162.

May, R. M., 1977. Thresholds and breakpoints in ecosystems with a multiplicity of stable states. *Nature* 269:471–477.

Meier, R. L., 1972. Communications stress. *Ann. Rev. Ecol. Syst.* 3:289–314.

National Research Council, 1981. *Testing for Effects of Chemicals on Ecosystems*. National Academy Press, Washington, D.C.

Odum, E. P., J. T. Fin, and E. H. Franz, 1979. Perturbation theory and the subsidy-stress gradient. *BioScience* 29:349–352.

Pascher, A., 1913–1927. *Flagellates in Die Susswasser-flora Deutschlands, Osterreichs und der Schweiz*. I. G. Fischer, Jena, East Germany.

Schmidtke, N. W., 1988. *Toxic Contaminants in Large Lakes*, 4 volumes. Lewis Publishers, Inc., Chelsea, Mich.

Schoener, T. R., 1984. Rates of species turnover decrease from lower to high organisms – a review of the data. *Oikos* 41:372–378.

Walton, L. B., 1915. A review of the described species of the order Euglenoidina, Bloch, class Flagellata (protozoa) with particular reference to those found in city water supplies and in other localities of Ohio. *Ohio State Univ. Bull.* 1(4):343–450.

Woodwell, G. M., 1975. The threshold problem in ecosystems. In S. A. Levin (Ed.), *Ecosystem Analysis and Prediction*, pp. 9–21. Society of Industrial and Applied Mathematics, Philadelphia.

Part V

Conclusion: Steps toward a World That Runs Itself

---

25   Steps toward Sustainability

JAMES GUSTAVE SPETH

My assignment has been to listen, reflect on what I have heard, and offer some final comments from the perspective of someone who, for good or ill, has been in our nation's capital working on environmental policy, both domestic and international, for almost twenty years.

The research represented in this volume certainly shows the limitations of the "one-pollutant/one-effect" approach to environmental regulation. That's not the way natural systems work. It is not consistent with the goal "design with nature." When we look at natural systems, we see multiple stresses – chemical and physical, natural and humanly generated. The benefit of these critiques of one-pollutant/one-effect is that they force us to focus beyond individual pollutants to the underlying processes that generate pollution.

The widespread global effects of pollutants on natural biological systems are demonstrated clearly. In regulatory circles there has been a tendency to think of pollution principally in terms of health effects. That has certainly been the dominant thrust of EPA initiatives in recent years. As a useful corrective, this work calls attention forcefully to the long-term, cumulative effects of pollutants on the *biota*.

Similarly, this work focuses attention on the chronic, insidious changes caused by multiple stresses on biological systems. We tend to think more of dramatic "physical" changes – deforestation, desertification, extinction, and so on. Now we must be aware of more subtle biological erosion and impoverishment. An analogy to human health may be useful. We have concerns with both sickness and death. Environmental policymakers tend to be motivated by "death" – the clearing of a forest, the channelization of a stream, the extinction of a species. The approach here is to look more at "sickness and ill-health" – the gradual weakening and depletion of natural systems. Such weakening can lead to death but is important long before it does.

Of course it is also useful to play the devil's advocate, to ask what is so bad about biological impoverishment? People do care about public health. That's the basis of the EPA's focus on it. But why should they care about "the

509

biota" and biological impoverishment? I think we know the answer to this question, but we need to articulate it more vigorously.

To stand back and ask how societies can move from scientific concerns to constructive action to address these problems, we need three things: First, a positive vision of a possible society that is both economically prosperous and environmentally rich; we should at least be able to identify the great transitions needed to reach this society. Put otherwise, we need attractive ends. Second, we need to find specific, workable policies to achieve this future. That is, we need realistic means. And third, we need the collective social and political will to move to this future. Many would say that this is the dimension that is most lacking – that the needed political strength is not there.

To address the first of these challenges it is necessary to identify several essential macrotransitions. We are confronted by multifaceted problems that cut across sectors and regions. In response, we should consider broad transitions that have multiple benefits. Are these transitions under way? How can we speed them along?

Transition One is the shift away from the era of fossil fuels; from the extraction, transport, and particularly combustion of the various fossil fuels responsible for so much of environmental damage toward an era of energy efficiency and renewable energy.

Transition Two is the move from an era of heavily polluting, capital- and materials-intensive, high-throughput technologies to an era of new technologies, soft and hard, that do not place heavy demands on natural systems because they are extremely efficient in the use of new materials, rely on inputs that have low environmental costs, and recover and recycle materials, and are hence more "closed."

Transition Three is the transition to a future in which societies manage renewable natural resources for their income and cease depleting the planet's capital. Economic development projects of all types must be pursued with this objective – sustainability – in mind, and renewable resources managed for long-term, environmentally sound production.

Transition Four is the transition to a stable world population. Through appropriate policies promoting economic advancement, education, improving the status of women, infant care, and family-planning services, global population growth should be halted before it doubles again.

Transition Five is the transition to honest prices – to economics that does not subsidize the consumption of, and thus waste, natural resources; that recognizes the economic and other values of natural ecosystems and their services to society; and that accounts the depreciation of natural assets just as rigorously as capital assets. The transition in economic analysis is almost certainly necessary to the others.

Turning to the issue of political will for change, I would like to offer a few comments on political motivation, at least in the United States. In our society and in many others, the political will to act decisively exists when many people and some leaders care deeply about the costs of inaction. When values that people hold dear and cherish – whether economic or spiritual – are threatened by current conditions or tendencies, open political systems usually respond. It is helpful, but by no means necessary, that the policymakers have enough information on which to base sound policy, although heroic measures have often been taken in the face of great uncertainties and even of great ignorance – one reason governments make so many mistakes.

In the context of the United States, we must communicate, to both the public and political leaders, credible information showing that the current destruction and impoverishment of the natural environment pose a grave threat both to the long-term economic and even security interests of the United States and to the beauty, richness, and diversity of the natural world.

We must forcefully present to the public and to policy leaders the fact that society now has a choice – a clear fork in the road. There are diverging paths ahead. Our success in this choice, and steering it in the right direction, will depend on how credibly we present the case that an attractive future exists and can be realized through reasonable measures. What is accepted as "reasonable" will depend in part on the evidence that current trends are indeed threatening.

Unfortunately, our success in mobilizing public support and achieving the needed transitions will also depend on developments that are outside our immediate concerns, though closely related to them. In the face of grinding poverty or economic upheaval, governments everywhere will pay insufficient heed to the environment. Our success is linked closely to addressing the problems of the world's poor, to promoting sustained and sustainable economic growth, and to achieving a wider sharing of economic benefits, among and within nations. Our cause depends in many ways on achieving greater economic equity.

Now that East–West tensions are dying down, it is crucial to improve relations on the North–South axis. None of the global environmental problems we face can be solved without a new era of heightened cooperation and agreement between industrial and developing countries in policy areas as diverse as international trade and debt, development and assistance, energy, technology transfer, and population. Once reached, these agreements will come to be seen as nothing less than a global compact between North and South for environmental protection and economic progress.

Since these great world problems are linked and interrelated in many ways, it is easy to see why discouragement sets in in some quarters. But it is far more useful to think optimistically, or at least existentially. The fact that these problems are linked means that we, as people and as institutions, are linked, at least potentially, to literally thousands of other organizations and initiatives large and small. We have only just begun to realize the possibilities for building coalitions that can generate political action. We are well advised to remember that politicians ride the waves; people *make* waves.

26   A Reaction from a Multitude

DONELLA H. MEADOWS

Introduction

"I am large. I contain multitudes," said Walt Whitman to explain why he sometimes contradicted himself. Every human being contains multitudes. I have never been more aware of the multitudes within me than at this conference of field ecologists describing their work.

I am not a field ecologist. Most of the research reported here is new to me. It strikes me at many levels, revealing both the multitudinousness of my own responses, and the inherent complexity of the planetary ecosystems, which can touch a person in so many ways.

I was trained in biophysics, which, although it is a very different science, allows me to understand and to admire field work, not only for its difficulty (to a lab scientist like me, studies in the Arctic, or under the ocean, or in a peat bog look difficult), but also for its inherent elegance.

I am a systems analyst, and I am fascinated with the feedback systems that have been described here. They are full of synergisms, exponentials, non-linearities; they are *beautiful* systems. They make me want to run to my computer and start modeling. My systems experience also makes me sensitive to the vital role of information in changing system behavior, a bias that you will find permeating my comments here.

I am a journalist, a syndicated columnist, and I have been wondering how best to communicate in 800 words or less the important stories that were told which the public needs to know about.

Something in my nature also makes me an activist. When I hear about a problem, I want to solve it. Throughout the conference, as one environmental atrocity after another was described, I asked myself, "What can we *do* about that?" That is the primary question I would like to address in this paper.

But first I want to mention another person in the multitude I have discovered in myself. I am someone who loves this planet and all its mysterious, inexplicable, weird, and lovely forms of life. The conference took me on an unexpected emotional roller coaster. The ups were joy and wonder

513

in the glorious intricacies of well-functioning ecosystems. The downs were anger and grief as the senseless impoverishment or destruction of those systems were recounted. I was surprised at how keenly I felt that grief. I didn't know how much I cared.

The conference was not only concerned with interesting science, detailed systems studies, work worth writing about in a newspaper, and work that calls for action. It was also documenting the desecration of my – your – our – temple. The list of assaults is astonishing: oil spills, radiation, introduction of foreign species, acidification, eutrophication, deforestation, mining, heavy metals, hazardous organic chemicals, overgrazing, fire, air pollution, and, finally, disruption of whole biogeochemical cycles and global climate change. The effects on the biosphere seem to be irreversible – in Sudbury the red maple sprouts die off, in Winnipeg the lake trout have stopped reproducing, the palmetto did not naturally come back to Bermuda, the rain forest can't regenerate itself in Brazil, the cheatgrass has taken over the intermountain West.

Though I knew there were problems, I did not know how pervasive they are. Though I knew I cared, I did not know how very much. The fact that I didn't know about the damage and that I wasn't in touch with my caring are suggestive to me. If other people also don't know and aren't in touch, that may indicate some answers to the question I asked above: What can we do?

I am going to assume that the "we" in that question refers to people like us, those who are knowledgeable about what is happening to the planet. If the destruction of ecosystems continues, if the geochemical cycles are deranged, if the beautiful and stabilizing diversities of nature are destroyed, we may justifiably point blaming fingers at people who are greedy or shortsighted or ignorant. If I were talking with them, I could come up with plenty of advice for them. But fingers could also be pointed at the scientists who knew and didn't speak out, or who didn't persist long and hard enough to penetrate people's barriers and make them listen.

I know how hard it is to put forth information that tells people that their present, comfortable way of doing things is not working. I know how much incomprehension and resistance can be generated by simple messages of the type "if we don't change our direction, we will end up where we are heading." I know how much competing information, much of it disinformation, has to be overcome. But if we don't operate from an absolute determination to make our information known and reckoned with, we will be as responsible for the environmental disasters of the planet as anyone else. It will be little comfort to say "I told you so."

With that sobering introduction, what can we do?

With my systems bias, I can see three generic things to do: acquire more relevant and powerful information about what is happening to the world's ecosystems; communicate more effectively the information we already have; and make sure that information is used to generate both political will and intelligent policies to stop environmental destruction.

More Information

Research in ecology is vitally important, and it has hardly begun. Some of the most important questions are still far from answered, either for specific ecosystems or for the planet as a whole. Are there indeed thresholds below which ecological assaults are tolerable, above which they are not? If there are thresholds, where are they, and, most important, what are the signs of their approach? How resilient, really, are ecosystems? At what point does destruction become irreversible? Is irreversibility an off–on state, or a continuum of increasing time to repair damage? To what extent are the small cogwheels of specific ecosystems tied to the great flywheels of geochemical cycles? Aside from the disequilibria in atmospheric carbon dioxide and ozone, and the possibility of setting off nuclear weapons, are there other already-visible potential global ecological catastrophes?

To answer these vital questions at any rate commensurate with the rate at which we are losing ecosystems, there have to be more research ecologists, better funded. There are plenty of people who can make that happen, but I want to raise the question of what ecologists themselves can do to increase their ranks and productivity.

I would guess that, being typical scientists, most ecologists could do much better at showing young people why they should become ecologists – the heart and soul reasons as well as the mind reasons. Most scientists don't easily talk about the thrill of their work, the love and dedication that propels it, the excitement and fascination. The more enthusiasm is allowed to show, the better.

Ecologists and scientists could do better at telling governments and foundations about the importance of their work as scientists. We were taught to be too modest, too careful. That training is fine for scientific presentations, but it has to be shed at fund-raising time. Most competitors for funds and political attention do not bind themselves to high standards of truthfulness or modesty. As Eville Gorham pointed out, Reaganomics and Star Wars and their successors have far less valid theoretical foundations or global importance than the work of this conference. Their proponents have commanded power and resources because they do not play by scientific rules in political arenas. That's a lesson most ecologists have yet to learn.

I would also guess that, as with most scientific fields, there are effective networks and organizations in the ecological field to pass around results, but that those associations aren't used as deliberately as they might be to work together to get attention. I know how effective the joint message of ecologists can be, because I heard at this conference many voices raised together, from many parts of the world, reporting on many different ecosystems. They made a compelling impression. Ecologists are much more powerful together than they are separately, and I suspect they have not fully exploited that joint power.

More Awareness: How to Tell the World What Ecologists Know

I discovered how badly trained I was to communicate to the public when I worked with an activist group dedicated to ending hunger. I was one of their information sources, since I knew the statistics, the theory, and most of the experts in the field.

"How many hungry people are there and where are they?" they would ask me. I would respond with a long disquisition about the various definitions of hunger, the problems with the world data base, the confounding of hunger with poverty and poor health care. Their eyes would glaze over, and when I was finished, they would politely re-ask the question. They simply wanted to know where to begin and roughly how big a job it would be to end hunger. When you want to *do something*, you don't need all the details and caveats of science.

After many discussions, the hunger group, for strategic purposes, chose Africa as a major focus. For publicity purposes they reduced the mind-boggling big numbers in the statistics (somewhere between 13 and 17 million people die each year of hunger-related causes) to numbers that could be understood by ordinary people. EACH MINUTE 21 PEOPLE DIE OF HUNGER, they proclaimed, AND 18 OF THEM ARE CHILDREN. That statement is far from scientific, but it is reasonably accurate, and it is *compelling*. It catches attention and initiates action.

I learned a lot from the hunger people about turning the sort of scientific information I normally traffic in, which is interesting only to other scientists, into information that makes a difference to policymakers and the public. ONE SPECIES OF LIFE BECOMES EXTINCT EVERY DAY is an unscientific statement, but one that makes people take notice. We need more such statements. If scientists can't bring themselves to make them, at least they should not criticize people who can.

We forget how unbelievably primitive is the information base upon which most policy is made. Several good examples have been given here. "We're still catching fish; so everything must be fine." "I've been in Saudi Arabia and seen healthy coral; the oil tankers can't be doing any harm." "It's just normal insect damage that's killing the trees." The public needs to understand the most basic principles – a renewable resource must be managed not from its stock level but from its rate of renewal; a single sample does not constitute a trend; a sudden visible stress may appear only because of the presence of long-term invisible stress.

I remember Paul Ehrlich telling me, when he was making many public appearances talking about the simple dynamics of exponential population growth, "I get so tired of saying the same thing over and over and over." Nevertheless, that is what must be done. Society forms itself around the things that are said over and over. Our society says things such as: economic growth is necessary and good; if someone profits from an activity, it ought to be done; nature only has value when it is exploited; we can't afford the luxury of cleaning up pollution; new technologies will come along and solve all our problems. Someone has got to start saying some different and more truthful things about how the planet operates. Who will do it, if not ourselves, as scientists and ecologists?

Every one of us should communicate more often, more simply, more to the point. We don't need to sacrifice scientific accuracy to do that. We don't need to pretend that we know what we don't know – in fact one of the greatest contributions we could make is to point out how much of what is taken as known in the policy world is in fact wildly uncertain. We do need to give up our compulsion toward precision and complexity. We do need to understand what information is most needed to make a decision, and to deliver only that information, leaving out irrelevant details, no matter how fascinating we think they are.

Along that line, I would like to make an appeal for the development of *indicators*, simple numbers that could appear on the nightly news along with the GNP and the Dow-Jones average. We need indicators that give people an idea of whether their environment is getting better or worse. I have just come from a conference of resource analysts who began discussing how to create such an indicator. We quickly bogged down in complexity – how can we have one number when there are dozens of incommensurate resources? What can we do about inadequate data? How can we even measure such complicated things?

The economists apparently did not have such qualms when they invented the GNP, which is an aggregate measure of hundreds of distinct economic activities, which had never before been measured, and which required an incredible effort in data gathering. Nonetheless, within 50 years virtually all countries in the world have learned to calculate some semblance of a GNP statistic, and, more important, all countries have come to rank themselves and set their goals by that statistic, not because it's a worthy index of human welfare, but because it's the only index they've got.

Probably the single most effective thing the ecological community could do would be to agree upon and support an ecological indicator, for single nations and for the world as a whole. It could be the Audubon Christmas bird count, the density of lichens, the concentration of carbon dioxide in the atmosphere, the area of standing tropical forests, the number of miles of unpolluted beach per person, the amount of silt in the Mississippi River, or some weighted average of all these. *Something,* however imperfect, is better than nothing.

Environmentalists have gotten a reputation for being unnecessarily gloomy, and for liking birds and bunnies more than people. To some extent we deserve that reputation. Some of us deliver dire warnings with undisguised relish. Many of us unconsciously communicate disrespect for and resentment of the human race. If we want to be effective, we must stop that.

The reaction to David Wingate's description at the conference of the reestablishment of the native Bermuda ecosystems proved that some good news mixed in with the bad can be tremendously invigorating. It can communicate all the basic lessons about how ecosystems work, while simultaneously giving people positive ideas of how to act and what to do. People are more responsive to new ideas when they are challenged by example, rather than loaded with guilt. People aiming toward a positive vision have a better idea of where to go than people fleeing from a possible disaster. Good examples of ecological stewardship can be found and they are just as important to communicate as the bad examples.

I learned another valuable lesson from the hunger group when they told me, "we assume that every person we talk to is the key to ending hunger." That made me realize that I had been assuming that nearly every person I talked to (except the few I had classified as good guys) was the cause of environmental destruction. It was a terribly negative attitude, which, though I never said it out loud, came through clearly.

Now, after some practice, I find it natural to see everyone as a steward of the planet, as a partner in the protection and restoration of ecosystems. Of course some people may not be. But at least now I give them a chance. Even when I am talking to documented bad guys, gross polluters, I try to remember Gandhi's admonition to distinguish a bad act from a bad person. Absolutely anyone can be enrolled in the preservation of the planet, and everyone has something special to contribute to that effort. If we can keep that in mind when we talk to people, we will suddenly find them much more responsive.

It may be too much to ask scientists to take on public relations activities, to develop indicators, to collect good-news stories, to develop benevolent attitudes toward the human race, when above all we need scientists to be scientists. A closer partnership between scientists and expert communicators is called for. The scientific community could help in that partnership, not only by seeking it out, but by ceasing to hold "popularizers" in disdain. Popularization is exactly what is needed – popularization in a positive vein, which can bring forth positive action.

More Political Will: How Do You Awaken Caring?

All the information in the world, delivered with punch and clarity, will have no effect if it reaches people who do not care.

Yossi Loya bemoaned the fact that the Israelis don't seem interested in their coral reefs. He wishes that they were like the Australians, to whom the Great Barrier Reef is as much a symbol of national pride as the pyramids are to the Egyptians.

Fred Grassle showed a cartoon with one matron saying to another, "I don't know why I don't care about the bottom of the ocean, but I just don't."

The Hungarians, who have only one large lake – Lake Balaton, entwined in Hungarian history, song, and poetry – have recently committed hundreds of millions of dollars to save it from eutrophication. Residents of Oslo would probably exile anyone who tried to build a housing development in their Nordmarka, the vast area of trails and parks around their city. Yet in other parts of the world lakes eutrophy and cities expand into greenbelts and no one seems to care.

We all know that caring is the heart of the issue. But how do we create caring? Or where it already exists but is dormant, how do we awaken it?

Some clues can come from examining where our own caring came from.

Mine came from my mother. She took me to the (few remaining) prairies and forest preserves in suburban Chicago, where I grew up. She taught me the names of the trees and birds and helped me make a herbarium of wildflowers. I came to be at home in those wild places. The creatures in them seemed like my friends. The first experience of real pain I remember was coming upon a bulldozer ripping through my favorite wild strawberry patch to clear a lot for a new house. That happened when I was very young, and I still carry an irrational hatred for bulldozers.

I conclude that people have to know nature – preferably through direct experience – in order to love and protect nature. We ought to get kids, especially city kids, out into natural areas as much as possible, in every part of the world.

There are undoubtedly other keys to caring to be found in one's own experience. I believe that a deep identity with nature is inherent in the human species. One has only to watch a child react to a flower or an animal to get that impression. But caring can get covered over with concepts and rationalizations and social and economic pressures, and it must be uncovered, reawakened.

We are sometimes advised to capture people's interest by speaking of matters about which they have been conditioned to care – economic matters. We are asked to explain why, in economic terms, biota should be preserved. I think we can easily meet that challenge. Nearly every straight economic analysis *that takes into account the whole system with all externalities* shows the enormous value of the biota. We should speak that economic language, do those calculations, and play that game – we can win it.

But at the same time, we should make it abundantly clear that it's only a game. Economics must be demoted from the ultimate arbiter and accountant of modern society to what it really is – one discipline, one incomplete way of seeing things that is based too much on narrowly defined rationality and too little on morality. We should never let economics trivialize the moral enormity of the loss of a species or the destruction of a natural community. We should never fail in economic discussions to reiterate – without the slightest apology – that nature has its own worth far beyond the feeble calculus of human purposes. Under the spell of economics, society keeps forgetting what is really important. We have to keep remembering.

What I'm trying to say throughout this disquisition is: we must stay in touch with our own caring, keep it alive, and share it in order to waken it in others, as it was wakened in me. Nothing is more unacceptable or more difficult in our culture of materialism and rationality than to share one's deep moral commitments. But nothing is more effective.

Eville Gorham, who has a knack for bursting out with impassioned one-liners, said we should make "no discharge" an ideal toward which we strive, though we may never attain it – like truth. That comment said a lot, not only about "no discharge," but about truth.

Though we may never find complete truth, the closer we come to it the more clearly we will see that we all love and worship this incredible planet we find ourselves inhabiting. We love and care for all species on it, including other human beings. Closer yet to truth, we don't know who or what we are without our connections with all other manifestations of life. We are essentially inseparable from the earth, from its creatures, and from each other. We are they and they are us, and when any one person, species, or ecosystem is impoverished, we are all impoverished. We have multitudes within us and we are interconnected with multitudes.

At the moment I write these words they are a complete reality to me. Five minutes from now I will surely forget that reality, accept the conceptual separations that make up my usual consciousness, and act in my usual self-serving way – I will return to my unawakened state. This cycle has happened to me many times before.

Moments of truth are fleeting. They are of value only if we seize them as opportunities to make commitments that we will abide by, even when we have lost sight of the truth. I guess that's what caring is – a set of commitments we follow just because we have made them. We made them at a time when we knew their rightness, and we maintain some sense of their rightness even when we are half asleep, when we are tempted by expedience or short-term gain or selfishness.

To awaken the caring in others, all we can do is keep it awake in ourselves. We can remember that it's there even when we are preoccupied. We can express it as best we can, every opportunity we get. We can strive to design the mundane details of our lives to be consistent with our caring. We can forgive ourselves and others when we and they forget, and then we can remember, and care again.

Name Index

Subject Index

(Page numbers in italics indicate material in figures or in tables)

Amazon, *see* Brazil, rain forests of Brazilian Amazonia
anchovy, to replace sardine as macrozooplankton predator, 411
annuals vs. perennials under chronic stress, 335
aquaculture, 451
aquatic systems, chronic disturbance in, 495
Arctic ecosystems: increased carbon dioxide levels and, 358–61; instability of, 347–8; limited richness of, 348–50; succession in, 356–8
Arctic landscapes: erosion in, 347, *356;* gully erosion in, *353;* limited success of efforts to stabilize disturbed, 347; restoration problems in, 353; surface disturbances in, 351, *352, 353–6;* thermokarst topography development and, 351
arctic tundra: disturbance of, 347; fires in, 350–1; increase in atmospheric carbon dioxide and, 358–61; rehabilitation following diesel and fuel oil spills, 353–5; weedy species in, 357
atmosphere: biotic responses to changes in, 114; biotic responses and pathways of interactions and, 114–21; carbon in, 4; fluctuation of carbon dioxide in, 3; observed changes in, 112–14; possible future changes in, *113;* trace gasses in, 4; warming of, 4; *see also* climatic change, greenhouse gasses
atrazine, *503*
Australian plant communities, edaphic range with respect to total nitrogen and total phosphorus, *180*
automobile exhausts, 51

bamboo, 211
beaver, 69
Bermuda: evergreen forest of, 135; fauna of, 135–6, 137, 139–40; feral animals in, 133, 135; government park system in, 137; history of, 133, 135–7; human population of, 136; introduced animal species in, 133, 135, 136; introduced plant species in, 137; reforestation effort in, 137; *see also* Nonsuch Island (Burmuda)
Bermuda cedar (*Juniperus bermudiana*), 133–4, 135, *138;* reintroduction and reestablishment of, 142–3; scale insects and, 136–7, 139, *142, 143*
Big Cypress National Reserve (Florida), 465
Big Cypress Swamp (Florida), 463
biological control, 142–3
biological inventories, lack of needed, 452
biomass, interpretation of increased, 503
biotechnology, environmental impact of, 498–500
biotic impoverishment, 9, 22, 500–4; changes in structure and function in lake, 485–8; change in vegetation characteristic of progressive, 14; in Clearwater Lake (Ontario, Canada), 482–5; of continental and island forests, 206; from deforestation, 239; patterns of, 21–3; of peatlands, 78–87; personal and national impoverishment and, 211; principles of, 10; stages of, 177; theory of chronic, 202; as a threat to economic and political security, 111
biotic regulation of output, 28
biotic richness: human effects on, 437–43; natural controls of, 427–37
birds: in Bermuda, 133–7, 141, 143–4, 145–6, 147–8; of New Zealand, 154, 155–6, 161, *163, 164, 165;* role in facilitating invasion of alien species, 206

bison, 303
bogs, 65; domed, 73; lumbering of forested, 81; nature of, 69; *see also* peat
Brazil: encouragement of tree felling for crops in, 226; industry and forest destruction in, 228, 247; inflation and deforestation in, 226; Legal Amazon region of, *214;* legalizing land claims established by deforestation in, 228; migration of human population to Amazon area of, 222; *Nossa Natureza* (Our Nature) program in, 227; population pressures in, 221, 222; real estate speculation and deforestation in, 224; sources of forest loss in, 229; tax credits for wood processing industries in, 249; tax holidays for wood processing firms in, 247; uneconomic conversion of forest for cattle ranching in, 249, 250–3; *see also* rain forests of Brazilian Amazonia
Bromus tectorum, 6; CO_2 enrichment favoring, 320; as a fire-enhancing invader, 302; fires and, 308–10, 320–1; invasion of sagebrush–grass vegetation by, 307; migration into new areas by, 320; vectors of, 308
Brookhaven irradiated Forest Experiment, 11; abundance of most abundant species along the gradient of exposure in, *20;* chronic vs. acute exposures to ionizing radiation and, 13–14; diversity of plants along gradient of ionizing radiation and, *18;* effects of chronic exposure to ionizing radiation and, 14–21; effect of irradiation on early successional communities in, 20–1; irradiation of forests and, 12–13; patterns of disturbance and impoverishment and, 21, 23
browsing, 294
bunch grass, 305; fire and, 306

cadmium, 448
Cahow conservation project (Bermuda), 134, 145–6
California; *see* coastal sage scrub community (California)
California Current: low-frequency anomalies in main body of, *414*
Canada, predicted spread of hemlock in, 104–5; *see also* Clearwater Lake (Sudbury, Ontario, Canada)
carbon: accumulation and release rates in peatlands, 82–3; respiration of soil, 125
carbon dioxide: annual fluctuations in the atmosphere, 3; combustion of fossil fuels and, 4; forests and, 3; peatlands and, 85–6
Caribbean Conservation Corporation, 149
caribou, 91
Castle Harbour Island National Park (Bermuda), 133, 137
cattle ranching: uneconomic conversion of forest for, 249, 250–3; *see also* grazing; pasture
cattle and sheep, impacts of, 294
cemeteries in Israel, sacred oak groves in, 262
cesium-137 in a northern food chain, *86*
charcoal, large scale destruction of Brazilian forest and making of, 228
cheat grass; *see Bromus tectorum*
chemicals: introduction into environment, 498; number of, 500–1; products from release of, 501; *see also names of specific chemicals or types of chemicals*
Chernobyl accident, 85
chlorinated organic compounds: accumulation in peats, 84–5; immobilization by peats, 77

524

lakes (cont.)
cies in, 428; eutrophication and biotic richness
of, 433–44; number of fish species and size of,
428; nutrient manipulation experiments and,
488–9; periods of exceptionally low biomass in
acidic, 488; pH and diatom replacement by
filamentous algal blooms, 439; pH and number of taxa in, 438, 439; phosphorus and,
438–9, 479; phytoplankton in, 482, 486, 487,
489; recovery of impoverished, 490, smelter-
stressed, 477, 478–9, 485–8, 489–90; zooplankton in, 432, 481–90
lake waters, acidification of, 119–20
LANDSAT, 212, 213, 220; detection of vegetative stress and, 325, 339–40; inability to identify deforested areas under old second growth,
218
landscape: changes in New England, 25; restoring an impoverished, 133
land use in south Florida, 464
lead in lichens, 51
lichens, 45, 46, 48, 49, 50–5, 356, 357; ionizing
radiation and, 21
livestock replacement by indigenous grazers and
browsers in protected areas, 294
logging in U.S. National forests, 239
long-term data, 369, 370–80; need for, 40
lumbering of forested bogs, 81

Man and the Biosphere Program (UNESCO),
465
marsh habitats, artificial creation of (Bermuda),
146, 147
Mediterranean Basin: conservation strategies in,
287, 289; decline of agropastoral
landscape during historical times,
280–1; ecological characteristics of, 260–3;
ecological planning, management, and restoration of uplands of, 290–1; evolution and degradation of the landscape and its meta-stable
vegetation, 278–81; fire in, 266, 268, 275–6,
277, 286, 288; human population pressures in,
281; human role in biotic impoverishment of,
259; neotechnological impoverishment in,
281–8; resilience and recuperative power of
vegetation in, 280; see also Israel
mercury, 448; flooding of peatlands and, 444
metals, particulate emissions from smelters of,
478
methane, 4
Metrosideros: rain forests dominated by, 200,
201–2; successional ecotypes of, 205
microorganisms, introduction of genetically engineered, 498
migration of human populations to Amazon, 222
mining: in the deep sea, 389; of metal-rich ores,
477; open-cut (Australia), 191
Minnesota, peatland protection in, 91–2
mismanagement of vulnerable flora and fauna,
151, 282, 285, 290–1
moss, vascular plants on mats of, 357
Mt. Gilboa (Israel), 287

Nagasaki, 17
National Crop Loss Assessment Network
(NCLAN), 37
natural communities: acidification and change in
structure of, 441; ecosystem processes and
composition of, 452; mechanism for structuring, 417; responses to chronic disturbances of,
10

natural resources, management of renewable,
509
natural systems: gradual weakening and depletion of, 509; technologies that do not place
heavy demands on, 510; time scale for change
in, 123–6; see also ecosystems
nature reserves, 151, 158, 170, 283, 465
Nevada: changes in sagebush-bunchgrass steppe
in northern, 306; ecosystems in western, 305;
ungulate herbivores of steppes of, 305; vegetation zones of western, 304; see also Great Basin
of North America; Ecology Canyon (Nevada);
sagebush-steppe ecosystem
New Zealand: birds of, 154, 155–6, 161, 163,
164, 165; conservation in, 168–70; damage to
indigenous ecosystems in, 156–60; estimated
indigenous forest in, 153; European period in,
157–61, 163–4; features of indigenous vertebrates in, 156; forest clearing in, 156, 157,
158, 160; insects in, 160, 161; introduced animals in, 157; islands off of, 158; lowland forests of, 164–8; national parks, sanctuaries, and
reserves in, 158, 170; Polynesian era in, 156–
7; prehuman period in, 152, 154–6; status of
native and introduced species in, 155; wetland
reduction in, 167
nickel, 477, 480, 481
nitrate concentrations in cloud water, 35
nitrogen cycle, 121, 122–3
nitrogen deposition, 117
nitrogen loss: in disturbed forests, 125; fire and,
187
nitrogen oxides, 50, 114, 120
Nonsuch Island (Bermuda), 136; before restoration, 133; deliberate reintroductions and habitat restoration on, 141–5; elements of restoration of, 133–4; elimination and exclusion of
exotic species on, 140–1; forest restoration in,
139; living museum project and, 134, 137,
139–40, 141–5
North American Cloud Water Project, 32–4
nutrient manipulation experiment, 487, 488–9

ocean depths, vertical spatial species structure at
various, 408
oceans: community ecosystems in, 401; disturbance from human activities in, 395; dominants or key species in ecosystems of, 401; Eu-
phausid species per 5° square in, 402;
microbes' role in, 122; mining in, 389; nitrogen in, 122; stirring and mixing in, 401; surface flora of, 125; wastes dumped into, 395,
409, 411; see also Pacific ocean; deep sea entries
oil spills, see petroleum spills
open-top chamber experiments, 38, 39–40
opportunistic species, 496
organisms: chronic biospheric disturbances and
large slowly reproducing vs. small rapidly reproducing, 6, 476; competing with interest of
people, 10; insignificant,82
organisms with cosmopolitan distribution, impoverishment and, 497–8
ozone, 34, 36–8, 50, 112, 114, 288; pollution experiments with, 324–5, 328–9; rise in chlorophyll and nitrogen in leaves under treatment
with, 341n2

Pacific Ocean: pelagic ecosystems in, 403–15; pelagic faunal provinces of the, 399; pteropod
number of species per 5° square in North, 403;
see also deep sea communities; oceans

528